AMERICAN GIRL'S HANDY BOOK

Making the Most of Outdoor Fun

LINA BEARD & ADELIA B. BEARD

THE DERRYDALE PRESS
Lanham and New York

THE DERRYDALE PRESS

Published in the United States of America
by The Derrydale Press
A Member of the Rowman & Littlefield Publishing Group
4720 Boston Way, Lanham, Maryland 20706

Distributed by NATIONAL BOOK NETWORK, INC.

Original copyright 1887, 1898 by Charles Scribner's Sons
First Derrydale Printing 2002

Library of Congress Control Number: 2002101660
ISBN 1-58667-089-1 (pbk. : alk. paper)

⊖™ The paper used in this publication meets the minimum requirements of
American National Standard for Information Sciences—Permanence of
Paper for Printed Library Materials, ANSI/NISO Z39.48–1992.
Manufactured in the United States of America.

PREFACE.

"I DO wish some one would write a book like that for girls," is the remark we have frequently heard when a new book of sports for boys has made its appearance ; but it was not until the publication of the " American Boy's Handy Book " that it occurred to us to write a book for the American boy's neglected sisters, which should be equally original and practical.

In the " Girl's Handy Book," which it has been our endeavor to make peculiarly American, we have sought to introduce original and novel ideas, and by their aid to open new avenues of enterprise and enjoyment.

One of our objects is to impress upon the minds of the girls the fact that they all possess talent and ability to achieve more than they suppose possible, and we would encourage a belief in the truth of the remark said to have been made by a famous Frenchman : " When you Americans undertake anything you never stop to ascertain if it be possible, you simply *do it.*"

We desire also to help awaken the inventive faculty, usually uncultivated in girls, and, by giving detailed methods of new work and amusements, to put them on the road which they can travel and explore alone.

We know well the feeling of hopelessness which accompanies vague directions, and, to make our explanations plain and lucid, we have ourselves, with very few exceptions, made all of the articles, played the games, and solved the problems described.

The materials employed in the construction of the various articles are within easy reach of all, and the outlay, in most cases, little or nothing.

We scarcely deem it necessary to point out the fact that in supplying healthy, sensible work and amusement for leisure hours, employment is given whose whole tendency is to refine the tastes and ambitions of our American girls.

A few of our chapters are taken from articles which were written by us for, and published by, the *Youth's Companion, St. Nicholas, Harper's Young People, Golden Days*, and *Wide Awake.*

CONTENTS.

Contents.   vii

AUTUMN.

CHAPTER XVII.

Halloween Parties, 189 ; Melted Lead, 190 ; Nutshell Boats, 192 ; "Three Luggies," 193 ; Roasting Nuts, 193 ; Kaling, 194 ; The Magic Mirror, 194 ; Three Tin Cups, 195 ; The Ring Cake, 195 ; Bobbing for Apples, 196 ; The Ghostly Fire, 197 ; The Fairy's Gifts, 198.

CHAPTER XVIII.

Fresh Autumn Wild Flowers, 202 ; Buckeye Portière, 204 ; Panel of Fall Decorations, 205 ; Louis Quinze Screen, 206 ; A Panel of Field Corn, 209 ; Ornamental Gourds, 210 ; Gourd-Dippers and Bowls, 211 ; Vases, 212 ; Small Decorations, 214 ; Brackets, 214.

CHAPTER XIX.

"Little Brown Squirrel," 218 ; Rules for Nutting-Parties, 221.

CHAPTER XX.

CHAPTER XXI.

CHAPTER XXII.

Materials for Water-Color Painting, 238 ; Flowers, 239 ; Landscapes, 241 ; Painting from Notes, 244.

WINTER.

CHAPTER XXIX.

The American Girl's Handy Book.

CHAPTER I.

FIRST OF APRIL.

 HIS is the children's own day, and no assumption of dignity on the part of their elders can deter them from exercising the privileges granted to them by acknowledged custom and precedent.

"April fool! April fool!" cries my little nephew, as he dances with delight to see his aunt walk out of the room with a piece of white paper dangling from a hooked pin, attached to her dress.

"April fool! April fool!" shout the children in the street, thus announcing the success of some practical joke.

"April fool!" laughs everyone at the table, when some unfortunate bites into a brown, wholesome-looking cruller, only to find it a delusion and a snare, the coat of a cruller, but the inside of cotton.

"April fool! April fool!" is what even the little sparrows seem to chirp, as with a " s-w-h-e-r-r " they sweep down from the tree and, frightening away the kitten, take forcible possession of her bone. What does all this mean ? Why is the first day of April called " All-Fools-Day," and when or where did the custom of the day originate ? Who can tell ? No one seems to know. Even the derivation of the word April does not appear to have been definitely settled, and this saucy month, with her mischievous tricks and pranks, her surprises and mysteries, fools and puzzles our wisest men.

Through many centuries the observance of All-Fools-Day has descended to us. In many climes and many countries this day is chosen as the proper time for playing tricks on the unsuspecting.

" Festum Fatuorum," or " Fools' Holiday," is what it was called in England at the time of the arrival of the early Christians in that country.

Easily caught like the mackerel, which are plentiful on the French coast in April and are said to be deficient in understanding, the April fool in France derives his name from that fish, and is called " Poisson d'Avril " or " April Fish," and again, " Silly Mackerel." From the cuckoo, a bird that does not know enough to build its own nest, the appellation of " gowk " is taken, and is given to the foolish one in Scotland who allows himself to be duped on this day.

In India at the festival called Huli Festival held on the last day of March, the natives make merry at the expense of their friends, just as we do, and their fool is called " Huli Fool."

So in the East and in the West, in the North and in the South, in the oldest nation as well as the youngest, is this ridiculous custom observed, and, as if to make it still more ridiculous, no one apparently knows why.

Now, girls, since this holiday has descended to us from so far back that its origin appears lost in the dim twilight of past ages, there surely must be some reason for its existence, and that reason may be, that "a little nonsense now and then is relished by the wisest men," and is therefore wholesome as an occasional diet. So why not help to perpetuate it ; not with rude, practical jokes, but with comical surprises, and absurd, but unembarrassing, situations. Much harmless fun can be derived from the privileges of this day, devoted as it is to nonsense, and we introduce the April Fool Party as an excellent means of concentrating the fun, and furnishing plenty of merriment to the young folks who are bent on having a good time.

First of April Party.

I remember, when quite a little girl, I was granted the privilege of celebrating my birthday, which came on the 1st of April, with a candy-pull, and a few days previous to the event I started joyfully off to invite my friends. The invitations were laughingly given and accepted, and it did not occur to me that I would be suspected of playing a joke, although the party was to be on April-Fools-Day. It seems, however, that my good intentions were doubted, and the children were undecided whether to come or not. I had begun to suspect that a joke was to be played on me by their all remaining away, before they finally arrived in a body, having taken the precaution of coming in that way, so that if the party were a hoax they would all be fooled together.

I relate this incident that warning may be taken from my experience, and that it may be understood how important it is to make the guests invited to your First of April party realize that the invitations are given in good faith, and that your friends are expected to be on hand at the appointed time.

It is well, in giving a party of this kind, to have the whole programme laid out beforehand, so that everything may go smoothly and nothing be forgotten.

The few methods of April fooling given here need not constitute the whole entertainment; the list may be added to by the young hostess, who will, no doubt, have many ideas of her own to carry out. We will head our list with the

Mirror Tableau.

This novel tableau is made ready in the following manner :

In a door-way, or bay-window draped with full curtains, place a large mirror. Instead of having the curtains suspended from the usual pole, it is best to stretch a wire across the space and slip the curtain-rings upon that, as they will slide more readily on the wire ; and when it is time to draw back the drapery it should be done quickly. A table placed before the curtains will serve as a barricade, keeping the too curious from taking a peep at the hidden mysteries before they are ready to be revealed.

At the time selected, remove the table, and request all those desiring to see the tableau to arrange themselves in front of the curtain, and to remain perfectly quiet, as any movement will disturb those taking part.

If the front rows of the audience can be induced to kneel or sit upon the floor, those in the rear can obtain a better view, and it will, at the same time, make the group more effective. When perfect quiet is obtained, give the signal to your assistant, who must stand opposite to you at the side of the curtain, and with her help quickly draw aside the draperies, thus disclosing the tableau of a group of young people, motionless, gazing into the mirror with eager and expectant eyes. For an instant the audience will be held spell-bound, scarcely realizing that they themselves are forming the pretty tableau.

" We are April Fools," written with soap on the mirror near the top, as shown in the illustration, tells what character the actors are assuming, and gives a name to the tableau.

The Mirror Tableau.

During the interval which should be allowed to intervene before introducing the next thing on the programme, the guests will find amusement in the many harmless practical jokes which are awaiting the unwary in all manner of places.

For instance, some boy will print APRIL FOOL in large white letters on his own back, by simply resting for a moment in a convenient chair upon whose snowy tidy the dreaded words have previously been printed backwards with white chalk. On the dark woolly surface of the coat, the white letters will be perfectly transferred, and the boy, little knowing what he has done, or the cause of the merriment, will join in the general laughter his appearance creates.

A treacherous divan can be provided by removing the top of a low, flat packing-box, and putting in its place brown wrapping-paper, tacking it down around the edges of the box. With a piece of drapery thrown over it, entirely concealing the box, and sofa pillows placed upon it, leaning against the wall, the divan looks exceedingly comfortable and inviting. But woe unto the person who mistakes appearances for reality, for to attempt to sit upon this seeming substantial couch is but to break through and sit upon the floor instead.

The box used for the divan should not be more than twelve inches high, so that the fall will be only funny, not dangerous.

The next diversion may be a

Noah's Ark Peep-show.

Make the peep-show of a box about two and a half feet long and one foot and a half high. Remove the top and both of the end-pieces (Fig. 1). Cut from pasteboard a slide to exactly fit the box, and place it in the middle, thus cutting off the view from either end, as shown in Fig. 1. Make a curtain in two pieces, and tack them around the upper edge of the

Fig 1

Noah's Ark Peep-show.

box, letting them meet at each end. Stout pieces of twine, stretched across the openings at the ends of the box, will serve to attach the drapery at these points.

Almost any kind of material will answer for this purpose, provided it is not too thin and is of some bright hue, for the peep-show should be made to look as gay as possible. Place the box upon a high stand, and so arrange it that a strong light will shine down into it, making the interior, from end to end, perfectly light.

From a list, previously prepared, of the animals supposed to be on exhibition, read the first two, and invite two persons, a girl and a boy, for instance, to look into the peep-show. We will suppose that the first animals on the list are the raven and the dove. Inform your would-be audience that you have two of Noah's special pets to show them ; that from the girls' point of view will be seen a raven, and from the boys', a dove.

When taking their places at the box, one at each end, the two spectators must part the curtain, and, putting their faces between, hold the drapery together under their chins. This is to keep the remainder of the company from obtaining a glimpse into the wonderful show before their turns arrive.

When all is ready, and the two wondering faces are hidden between the folds of the peep-show curtains, with the words, "Behold the pretty dove, and the mischievous raven," remove the slide, and expose to the astonished gaze of each spectator a companion's familiar face at the opposite end of the box. Of course, upon retiring from the show, its secret must be kept, otherwise the joke will be spoiled for those whose turns are yet to come.

Before the next two take their station at the box, replace the slide and pretend to rearrange the show, to divert the suspicion that the box is empty.

The Supper

can be made the means of perpetrating many practical jokes. The shams must be so intermingled with the real delicacies that one can never be sure what the consequences may be of partaking too rashly of even the most tempting-looking morsel.

Small blocks of wood covered with batter and browned in the oven are excellent imitations of cakes. Dainty confectionery, in crimped papers, can be made of small radishes covered with icing of different colors. Button-moulds coated with chocolate will readily be mistaken for candy.

If a small pasteboard pill-box is first filled with flour, and the top then covered with tissue-paper pasted down around the edges, it will look, when iced, like a delicate little cake, and will cause much merriment when anyone bites into it; for the moment the paper cover is broken the flour will fly in every direction. The fertile brain of girls, on mischief bent, will suggest many more frauds of this kind, and enough surprises may be prepared to make the supper as merry as anything else on the evening's programme.

Before leaving this subject, once more let the caution be given to keep the jokes entirely harmless. It is only poor fun that can be obtained at the expense of injuring others, or by running the slightest risk of hurting them in any way.

The spirit of mischief must be kept within bounds even on All-Fools-Day.

Gathering Wild Flowers.

CHAPTER II.

WILD FLOWERS AND THEIR PRESERVATION.

ONG before the first green leaves make their appearance, while the snows of winter still linger in the shaded nooks, and the branches are still bare, though blushing with the full, flowing sap that tinges their tips pink, yellow, and red—when the air is filled with a sweet freshness and delicate fragrance—it is charming in our rambles to find scattered here and there upon the hill-side, down among the roots of the great trees, or under the hedges delicate little wild flowers waving on their fragile stalks with the faintest passing breeze. They are so exquisitely beautiful with their tender hues and graceful shapes, that a longing comes to possess them.

And why not keep them fresh at home? Plants live in the earth and require light, air, and moisture. All of these requirements can be and are fulfilled in thousands of homes where plants are kept, all over the world. But these are *wild flowers.* True, and they may need something to be found only in the wild woods. What, then, is it? Let us see. Earth, light, and air abound everywhere. Still, upon inspection we discover that the soil around our timid wild flowers is somewhat different from that to be found in our door-yards. But what is simpler than to take the earth up with the plant?

Be careful in

Transplanting Wild Flowers

to dig well all around and under the roots, so that the earth surrounding and clinging to the plant may be taken up at the same time (Fig. 2). After covering the root and soil adhering to it with a layer of clay, mud, or damp earth (Fig. 3) set the root in a large leaf, and tie it up with string or a wisp of grass (Fig 4), in order to make sure the soil

does not fall off the plant. Thus se-cured the specimens will keep nicely until you reach home; then plant them in a shady place and keep the ground moist. Beautiful little woodland gardens are made in this way, where within a few steps of the door a glimpse may be had of the fair forest flowers.

Sweet-scented white violets, delicate little anemones, odd yellow violets, and quaint jack-in-the-pulpits, with many others, not forgetting the graceful ferns, are now growing in the shaded corner of the writer's lawn, transplanted there from their home in the woods, where she found them one lovely spring morning, when out with a party of friends on a hunt for wild flowers.

The day was perfect, filled with sunshine and the song of birds. All nature appeared glad and joyous, and the trees seemed veiled in the softest greens and pinks of budding leaves.

It was a happy party that went wandering into the forest, straying here and there, and finding new treasures at nearly every step, stopping to gather a few of the violets that gave a purple tinge to the ground for yards around, then rambling on to the spot that was covered with the fragile anemone, each girl laden with the flowers she loved best. Some had taken them up roots and all, while others preferred the

Cut Wild Flowers.

For these it is best to use a tin box of convenient size and form shutting closely. The flowers must be fresh and not at all damp ; in such a box they can be kept for days bright and unfading. They may also safely be sent to friends at a distance, though it is better, when

Sending Flowers by Mail,

if you wish to send a quantity, to pack them in a strong pasteboard or wooden box. First lay down a piece of oiled paper of the proper size ; spread a thin layer of damp paper on this ; next a layer of flowers, then one of thin wet paper ; and so on until the box is full. Over the last layer place a dry paper, and cover this with oiled paper or tin-foil ; put the lid on the box and tie it down securely.

By this method a larger number of flowers can be sent in a given space than when simply inclosed in a tin box.

The writer has often sent daisies from New York to Cincinnati where they arrived as fresh as when first gathered.

For the benefit of those who wish directions for sending flowers by mail, we give the following on authority of the *American Agriculturist.*

"The law passed some years since by Congress, allowing packages of plants to be sent by mail, if not over four pounds in weight, was a capital arrangement for those who lived at a distance from railroad and express offices, but it is so hampered with the various constructions given by the Post Office Department, that it is difficult to know what is required by the officials. The law now is, we believe, as follows : A package, weighing four pounds or less, can be sent at the rate of two cents per four ounces, but the writing of the words "roots" or "plants" makes a letter of it, and is charged letter postage. Nothing should be written except the address, and the package must not be sealed, or contain any writing, and it must be so fastened that the postmaster can examine the contents if he wishes. The plants may, however, be numbered, and their names sent by letter."

Now let us think of some way in which these lovely blossoms can be preserved.

In Germany they excel in making decorations for rooms, dinner-tables, etc., of

Preserved Flowers.

Bright-colored flowers are best adapted to this method. White flowers are apt to turn yellow. Jack-in-the-pulpits, clover, roses, and daisies came out beautifully when the writer dried them, and why should not many other kinds do just as well? Try and see.

Procure three or four quarts of fine sand ; white scouring-sand is the best; wash it perfectly clean. This can be tested by pouring the water off until it looks quite clear ; then dry the sand, by placing it in a clean tin in the oven. When it is dry—fully dry and cool—pour enough in a box to enable the flowers to stand by themselves, their stems embedded in the sand, which should be a mass of fine particles of uniform size.

If the flowers are cut so that they all measure nearly the same length from the tip of the blossom to the end of the stem, they can more readily be covered with sand.

Fig. 5

Preserved Flowers.

The flowers must be fresh and entirely free from moisture. Place them stem downward in the sandy layer, and very gently

2

and slowly pour in the sand a little at a time, until each leaf and petal is firmly held in place (Fig. 5); then fill the box with sand nearly two inches above the level of the flowers.

It is very essential that every particle of the flower rest in the sand, and that in filling up, the smallest petal has not been bent or crumpled.

Take care not to shake the box lest the flowers inside be injured. Set it in a warm, dry place, and let it stand at least two weeks.

This manner of preserving flowers retains the color, while the shape of the leaves and petals remains unaltered. The flowers will keep for years.

There are other ways also of preserving flowers.

Pressed Flowers and Leaves.

Although these are perfectly flat, they seldom fade and are very pretty and useful. Have ready a large book or a quantity of old newspapers and several weights. Use the newspapers for leaves and ferns—blotting-paper is best for the flowers. Both the flowers and leaves should be fresh and without moisture. Place them as nearly in their natural positions as possible in the book or papers, and press, allowing several thicknesses of paper between each layer. Remove the specimens to dry papers each day until perfectly dry.

Some flowers must be immersed—all but the flower head— in boiling water for a few minutes, before pressing, to prevent them from turning black. Orchids are of this nature.

If possible, it is well to obtain all parts of a plant, the roots as well as the seeds, for a more interesting collection can thus be made than from the flower and leaf alone.

It is advisable to be provided with a blank book or, what is still better, pieces of stiff white paper of uniform size on which to mount the flowers or leaves when dried ; also with a small bottle of mucilage and a brush for fastening them, and some narrow strips of court-plaster or gummed paper for the stems and thicker parts of the plants. The sooner they can be mounted the better. Place them carefully on the paper, writing beneath the locality and date of finding. Flowers and leaves thus prepared make beautiful herbariums. Should you desire

Leaves and Ferns for Decoration,

first press them nicely; then give them a coat of wax, by ironing them on both sides with a hot iron over which a piece of beeswax has first been rubbed. Cover the specimens completely with wax, as this renders them quite pliable, and they are no longer brittle nor easily broken. Sprays of small leaves can be pressed entire.

To heighten the effect, use dry colors, rubbing them in, and selecting those corresponding with the color of the leaves when first gathered.

The colors must be put on before the coating of wax. Ferns should be gathered when nearly full grown, and, after they are pressed, painted light green with oil-colors ; in that case the beeswax is not used. The oil in the paint, like the wax, makes the specimens more substantial, and they look quite fresh and fair.

Sometimes the late autumn frosts will bleach the ferns perfectly white ; then are they even more delicate than before Nature changed their color. We have seen the

Color of Flowers Changed,

and it is a very pretty experiment, very simple, too. Immerse the flowers in ammonia, and you will be surprised to see white lilies change to a delicate yellow, pink roses turn a lovely light green, while dark-red sweet-peas assume blue and rich purple tints ; and the change is so rapid it is almost like magic. Another interesting experiment is making

Natural Wax Flowers

by dipping the fresh buds and blossoms in paraffine just sufficiently hot to liquefy it ; first the stems of the flowers ; when these have cooled and hardened, then the flowers or sprays, holding them by the stalks and moving them gently. When they are completely covered the flowers are removed and lightly shaken, in order to throw off the superfluous wax. The flowers are then suspended until perfectly dry, when they are found hermetically sealed in a film of paraffine, while they still keep their beautiful coloring and natural forms, and for a while even their perfume. Now let us find what can be done

To Freshen Cut Flowers.

When the heat has made them wilt, clip the stems and set the flowers in cold water ; in a few hours they will regain their freshness and beauty.

Some flowers, however, must be differently treated, such as heliotrope and mignonette ; these keep if placed *upon* damp moss or cotton and set in a cold place at night.

Rosebuds will retain their freshness for hours when not placed in water, if the ends of the stems are snipped off, and immediately tipped with melted sealing-wax ; this excludes the air, and so keeps the flowers from drooping.

If roses are wilted before they can be placed in water, cut off the ends of the stalks and immerse in very hot water for a minute or two, and they will regain their pristine freshness.

Another way to keep flowers fresh is to put a pinch of nitrate of soda into the glass each time you change the water.

Nitrate of potash or saltpetre in a powder has nearly the same effect, or a drop of hartshorn.

If plants are chilled by frost, shower them with cold water, and leave in a cool room ; or set the pot in cold water and keep in a moderately cool place. Now one word about

Crystallized Flowers,

that sparkle and look so beautiful. They must first be dried in sand, then crystallized in the same way as dried grasses—the rougher the surface the better will it crystallize. Dissolve as much alum in boiling water as it will hold ; when this is determined, pour it off and boil the solution down to one-half.

Suspend the flowers by a net-work of string tied across the top of a pail into which they must hang ; then pour into the pail the boiling alum water, which must completely cover the flowers, and leave it undisturbed twelve hours, or all night.

The flowers should not touch each other or the sides of the bucket. Be careful in removing them the next morning, as the crystals are easily broken off.

Flowers or sprays of grass may be beautifully frosted by dipping them in a solution of gum-arabic and sprinkling them with powdered isinglass.

Flowers are not only very beautiful, but many of them possess a fragrance so sweet that we would fain learn how to keep the

Perfume of Flowers.

Rose-leaves are the most simply prepared. Take a covered jar, fill it with sweet-scented rose-leaves, and scatter through them some salt. Keep the jar closed tight, and when the petals have dried the "scent of the roses will cling to them still," so that every time the jar is opened a delicious fragrance will fill the air. Or you can cover the rose-leaves with melted lard, and leave them for a day or two in some place at a temperature of about 140° F.; then cool it and knead the lard in alcohol. Pour off the alcohol in fancy glass bottles and use as handkerchief perfume.

For varieties we find this method:

"The delicate odor of pinks and other flowers may be obtained as follows : Get a glass funnel, with the narrow end drawn to a point ; in this place lumps of ice with salt, by which a very low temperature is produced. The funnel should be supported on an ordinary retort-stand and placed near the flowering plants, when water and the ethereal odor of the blossom will be deposited on the exterior of the glass funnel, and will trickle down to the point, from which it drops at intervals into a glass vessel below. The scent thus obtained is very perfect, but is apt to become sour in a few days unless some pure alcohol is added. By this process many odors may be procured for comparison and study. To obtain the odor in perfection the blossom must be in its prime."

Dry some sweet clover, and the fragrance will be sweet and pleasant. Fill a fancy bag of some thin sheer material with the clover, and you will find that you have imprisoned the fresh breath of summer. Old-time lavender can be prepared in the same way.

Our thoughts so far have been for the flowers in their season. But did it ever occur to you that it is possible to have

Spring Flowers in Winter?

If you search in the woods during December you may find, tucked away in sheltered spots, little woodland plants which, when taken up and carefully transplanted in a flower-pot and set in a sunny window, will soon begin to grow, sending up tender stems, and in about three weeks will blossom. The little fairy-like flowers seem even more beautiful coming in the cold wintry weather.

Fruit-tree twigs and sprays from flowering shrubs will blossom when the ground is white with snow, if cut from trees about the first of February, placed in well-heated water in a warm room, and the water changed every day for some that is almost but not quite hot.

The twigs being kept warm will blossom in a few weeks.

It is quite a pretty idea to take up and plant in a little flower-pot

The Four-leaved Clover.

Very frequently you may find a tuft bearing only the mystic number, and should it happen to have a five- or six-leaved clover in with the others, they will add to the luck.

If you possess one of these charmed plants, it is said "good luck" will always be near at hand.

Besides the foregoing directions for the preservation of flowers, plants, etc., there are numerous other methods, which, although not experimentally verified by the writer, are no doubt as worthy of a place here as any of the former.

The following recipes have been culled from various old papers, books, etc.

Some Old-fashioned Methods of Preserving Flowers.

The first of these ways is more properly intended for botanical collections, and is often resorted to by collectors of rare blossoms.   It consists in placing

Flowers in Alcohol,

and possesses the great advantage of preserving the flowers for years, and keeping their most delicate fibres uninjured.   They make invaluable specimens to sketch from, and though their beauty may be somewhat impaired by loss of color, their outlines remain perfect.

Place the flowers in a wide-mouthed bottle, fill it to the top with alcohol, cork it tightly, and cover the cork with plaster-of-Paris or melted beeswax, thus hermetically sealing it.   Do not use sealing-wax, as experience has taught us that the fumes of the alcohol soften the wax, and not only spoil the neat appearance of the bottle, but allow the spirits to evaporate.

Another way is to

Bottle Flowers.

Carefully seal the ends of the stems with sealing-wax, place them in an empty bottle—both flowers and bottle must be perfectly dry—cork the bottle, and hermetically seal it with either sealing-wax or beeswax.

The next method has greater possibilities of beauty, and consequently the reader will be more interested in learning

How to Preserve a Vaseful of Flowers for a Year.

Take home your basket of wild flowers, " nodding violets," cowslips, bright-eyed anemones, and all the lovely offerings of the woods, and before arranging them in the vase, carefully seal the stem of each flower.   Place a glass shade over the vase ; be careful that flowers, vase, and shade are perfectly dry; then fill up the groove in the wood, in which the shade stands, with melted wax. By covering the wax with chenille it can be perfectly hidden.

Flowers kept in this way will last for a twelvemonth.

The flowers preserved in an empty bottle may be taken out, the wax cut from the stems, and, if arranged in a bouquet, will last as long as perfectly fresh flowers.

Those in the alcohol lose their color after being immersed for a time, and will not last when removed from the alcohol.

In following any of these directions be careful not to tie the flowers. No string must be used. The flower stems must be loose and separate from each other.

A florist of much experience in preserving bouquets for an indefinite period gives this recipe for

Keeping Bouquets Fresh a Long Time.

When you receive a bouquet sprinkle it lightly with fresh water, then put it into a vessel containing some soapsuds ; this will take the place of the roots and keep the flowers bright as new. Take the bouquet out of the suds every morning, and lay it sideways, the stems entering first, in clean water ; keep it there a minute or two, then take it out, and sprinkle the flowers lightly by the hand with water ; replace it in the soapsuds, and it will bloom as fresh as when first gathered.

The soapsuds need changing every three or four days. By observing these rules a bouquet can be kept bright and beautiful for at least a month, and will last longer in a very passable state. From another source we learn how

To Keep Flowers or Fruit a whole Year perfectly Fresh.

Mix one pound of nitre with two pounds of sal ammoniac and three pounds of clean common sand ; then in dry weather take fruit of any sort which is not fully ripe, allowing the stalks to remain, and put them one by one into an open glass until it is quite full ; cover the glass with oiled cloth, closely tied down. Put the glass three or four inches down in the earth in a dry cellar, and surround it on all sides to the depth of three or four inches with the above mixture. The fruit will thus be preserved quite fresh all the year round.

In giving the following recipe for the manufacture of rose-water, it may be as well to state that the original verse is given, not for its merit as such, but simply because it is the form in which the recipe reached the writer.

Rose-water.

" When the bushes of roses are full,
    As most of them are about June,
'Tis high time to gather, or pull
    The leaves of the flowers. As soon
As you've picked all you need for the time,
    To each *quart of water* unite
A *peck of the leaves*, which, if prime—
    And they will be, if pulled off aright—
May be *placed in a still* near at hand,
    On a *very slow fire.* When done,
Bottle off, and permit it to *stand*
    For three days ere you cork down each one."

CHAPTER III.

THE WALKING CLUB.

 SOUND of girlish voices is suddenly heard in the quiet village streets, as our Walking Club, issuing from the house of one of its members, starts off on the first tramp of the season. The gay chatter and bubbling laughter blend with the twittering and chirping of the birds fluttering among the budding trees, and all these merry sounds seem in perfect harmony with the youthful gladness of the bright morning.

There is a subtle power and exhilaration in the spring sunshine that stimulates the blood, and sends it tingling through our veins, as with light-springing steps we quickly leave the village behind us and penetrate into the outlying country, stopping now and then to secure a branch of the downy pussy-willow or brilliant red blossoms of the maple, and again to admire a distant view where the trees seem enveloped in a hazy mist of delicate color; on we go, exploring sequestered spots or entering deep into the woods in search of early wild flowers.

Although possibly timid as individuals, as a club we are brave enough; for a party of fourteen or sixteen girls, including

The Walking Club.

our merry little chaperon, may go, with impunity, where it would not be so pleasant for one to venture alone.

Once a week all through that delightful spring the club might have been seen, now upon a road leading in this direction, now in that. And, often as we stepped aside to allow a carriage to pass, its occupants would lean forward smiling, and waving their hands in greeting; for the moment, perhaps, feeling in sympathy with the vigorous young life that preferred this mode of loco-motion to being carried about on the downiest cushions of the easiest of carriages. A ride which accorded with the unconventional mood of our club was not despised however, for, urged on by the girls, our little matron would make bold to accost some countryman driving a vehicle sufficiently large, and persuade him, in the terms of the country, to "give us a lift." Jolting about in a springless wagon or hay-cart was not in the least enervating, and we experienced no indolent wish to continue our journey on wheels when forced by diverging roads to leave our equipage. It was not until the ever-increasing heat of the sun, and our own languid disinclination to much exertion, warned us that the mildness of spring had passed, that we concluded to disband for the summer. In the fall we again fell into rank, and came home from our walks laden with the gorgeous trophies of autumn, as we had once carried in triumph the tasselled branches and dainty flowers of spring.

We continued our tramps into the early winter, when the frosty crispness of the air made it very bracing, and the brisk exercise of walking brought the healthy color to cheek and lip of the young pedestrians.

Such a club as this, which at the same time promotes health, good spirits, and sociability, is one that most girls will enjoy and derive benefit from.

A closer acquaintance with Nature, which these walks afford, is not the least of their benefits, and to her true lover, Nature has many delightful surprises and secrets to reveal; and as has been said, even for for those who cannot read her deeper meanings she has a language which calls attention to hei more outward forms of beauty, and which one may study until gradually, with slowly opening eyes, is seen more and more of the exquisite perfection of her work, that long ago might have been seen had one but chosen to look.

As a society, the Walking Club is one of the most informal.

No officers are needed, although a secretary may sometimes be found useful when any word is to be sent to absent members.

The membership of the club should be large enough to insure the attendance of at least twelve or fourteen on each walk; for in this case, as I have said, safety lies in numbers. At a place of meeting previously appointed, the members should assemble, and, before starting on their walk, the route to be taken should be decided by vote; a decision on this point will be more quickly arrived at if a chairman be appointed to keep order.

The first walk should not be too long. Three miles is a good walk to start with; a mile and a half out and the same home again. Gradually the distance can be lengthened, and the club be able to take a ten-mile walk without feeling fatigue.

To Make the Exercise of Walking Healthful, and therefore
the more Enjoyable, these Rules should
be Observed.

1st. *Carry the body erect on the
hips, the shoulders thrown back,
the chest raised, and the head
square on the shoulders.*

2d. *Breathe through the nose
while walking rapidly, otherwise the mouth will become dry
and the breath short.*

3d. *Wear loosely fitting clothes
that will permit a free motion
of the limbs, and shoes with
broad, moderately thick soles
and low, broad heels. In all
cases a girl's skirts should be
supported from the shoulders,
and in walking any distance it
is absolutely necessary for comfort that there should be no
weight upon the hips.*

CHAPTER IV.

EASTER.

VERYWHERE the children are playing with eggs ; eggs colored in every hue—mottled, striped, and gilded ; real eggs and imitation ones ; sugar, glass, and wooden eggs ; for this is Easter-tide, and not only in America, but in many far-away countries, where the habits and customs are very different from ours, does Easter bring to the children the highly prized, gayly-colored eggs.

How nice it would be if we could take a peep into these foreign countries, and discover what else Easter brings the little ones besides the pretty eggs, and also how the people of such widely differing nations keep this happy festival common to all.

If we could look into England now, we should find that the ceremonies there begin on Palm Sunday (the last Sunday before Easter), and on that day many people go a-palming, only they do not, of course, find palm, but gather instead branches of willow, which they stick into their hats and button-holes. On Good-Friday we might see, on almost every breakfast-table, those hot spicy cakes with a cross stamped on the face, known to many of us as well as to our English cousins, as "hot cross buns." We should feel very much at home looking into the churches on Easter Sunday, for we should find them beautifully

3

decorated with flowers, and hear the Easter anthems chanted as we might in our own country. I do not think we can see in America, though, the ceremony which, on Easter Monday, is performed by the charity school-children in England. Were we among the spectators who, with shouts and merry laughter, crowd around to watch this performance, we should see the children take their places, with their backs against the outside of the church, and then join hands until a circle is formed around the building, thus completing what is called "clipping the church."

It would be great fun to see the Easter celebration in Russia, which includes many peculiar customs, and where the children receive presents as we do at Christmas, besides more eggs than any of us ever thought of possessing; some of the eggs being beautifully made of glass or porcelain, and filled with sugar-plums or small presents. How amusing it would be to watch the people, following a custom always observed on Easter Monday in this queer land, as they go about kissing relations, friends, and acquaintances, wherever they happen to meet them.

If we were really in this great, cold, furry country, we might go with the children to make their Easter visits, and, on entering a house, hear the greeting, "Jesus Christ is risen," and the answer, "Yes, he is risen;" then after kissing the inmates and exchanging eggs with them, go to visit elsewhere.

All this would seem very strange to American eyes; and it would be a strange sight too, if we could look into the cities of Spain and see the people in the streets shooting at stuffed figures of Judas Iscariot.

A passing glance at Ireland on Easter morning would show us the people making haste to be out at sunrise to see the sun dance in a pool or pail of clear water.

It would be worth while to give more than a passing glance into Germany at this season, for in this country, where the children's happiness is so much thought of and so well provided for, Easter Monday is looked upon as a grand holiday, and all the young people appear in their gala costumes ready for any fun or frolic that may be going on. It is a pretty sight when the little peasant-girls, in their quaint gowns and odd little caps, dance on the green with the boys, whose costumes are equally as picturesque ; and it is also entertaining to watch them as they play various games with their many-colored eggs.

In Germany, too, we should find that the children believe as sincerely in the Easter hare as they do in Santa Claus in our country ; and the saying, that "the hares lay the Easter eggs," is never doubted by the little ones.

After visiting in imagination all these foreign countries to see their Easter celebrations, it may prove interesting to turn our eyes toward home, for, since our country is so large—as large almost as all Europe put together—perhaps some of our little citizens who have never been in Washington do not know how, in the capital of the United States, the children hold high carnival on Easter Monday, nor how the grounds of the White House and also of the Capitol are given up to them on this day that they may frolic on the lawns ·and roll their eggs down the hills. It would be as novel a sight to some of us as any found abroad, to see several thousand children rolling and tossing their eggs, while shells of every hue cover the grass in all directions.

The following newspaper item, cut from the *Evening Star*, Washington, D. C., April 27, 1886, shows how these rights of the little Americans are recognized and respected, and how unmolested they enjoy the privileges of Easter Monday.

"THE EASTER EGG-ROLLING.

"CHILDREN SHAKE HANDS WITH THE PRESIDENT.

" The crowd in the White House grounds greatly increased yesterday afternoon, so that the grounds were literally packed with children. The crowd was the largest and best appearing that has collected there in many years. The President and Colonel Lamont watched the children for some time from the library window.

At the President's reception at half-past one o'clock hundreds of children gave up their sport temporarily and thronged the East Room to shake hands with the President."

Easter Egg Games.

In the game they play at Washington, on the hills sloping from the White House, the child whose egg reaches the foot of the hill in an unbroken condition takes the one worsted in the journey down. Another game for two is played by knocking the eggs together ; each child holds an egg firmly in his hand so that only the small end is visible, and then the two eggs are struck against each other until one is cracked, when the victorious player adds it to his stock, or devours it on the spot. I would not like to state the number of eggs eaten on these occasions, but there is a boy (*not a girl*) who once consumed fourteen and lived to tell the tale.

Sometimes the egg which breaks another is called " the cock of one," and when it has broken two it is " cock of two," and so on. When an egg which is cock of one or more is broken, the number of trophies won by the victim is added to the score of the conquering egg and it becomes " cock of three " or more. Here is a game which comes from Germany, and although in that country it is played exclusively by boys, there is no reason why the girls should not participate in it as well. Two baskets are necessary for this game, one large and shallow filled with soft shavings, the other shallow also, but smaller, and filled with eggs. The plan of the game is that one player is to run a given distance, while another safely throws the eggs from one basket to the other, she who completes her task first being the winner. When the baskets are prepared, and the distance the eggs are to be thrown decided upon, the two contestants draw lots to determine who shall run and who shall throw. This settled, the player who throws takes the basket of eggs, and one after another quickly tosses them the length of the course and into the basket of shavings, which is placed on the ground at the end of the course opposite the thrower. In Germany this basket is held by an assistant, but anyone occupying that position might receive some severe blows from the hard eggs thrown by unpractised hands, and it answers the purpose just as well to place the basket on the ground. Meantime the other player runs the distance (decided beforehand) to an appointed goal, marks it as a proof of having touched it, and should she succeed in returning before all the eggs are thrown, the victory and prize are her reward ; otherwise they belong to the thrower.

The game finished, a prize is presented to the successful contestant. Should any of the eggs pitched by the thrower fail to light in the basket, they must be gathered up and thrown again before the runner returns, as the eggs must all be in the basket before the thrower wins the game.

" Bunching eggs " comes from Ireland, and is played in very much the same manner as the game played with a slate and pencil, and known to all children as " tit, tat, toe, three in a row." A pan or large dish filled with sand or sawdust is set upon a table, around which the children stand, each supplied with eggs ; the eggs of each player must be all of one color, and unlike those of any other player. The object of the game is for each player to so place her eggs, standing them upright in the sand, or sawdust, as to bring five in a row touching each other.

In turn each player puts down an egg, sometimes filling out a row for herself, at others cutting off the line of an opponent ; and the one who first succeeds in obtaining the desired row sings out—

> " The raven, chough, and crow,
> Say five in a row."

Another pretty game from Ireland called " Touch " is played in the following manner :

Six eggs of the different colors—green, red, black, blue, white, and gold are placed in a row in the sand used for the other game. One of the players is blindfolded and given a light wand or stick, with which she must touch one of the eggs, while at the same time she recites these lines :

> Peggy, Patrick, Mike, and Meg,
> See me touch my Easter egg ;
> Green, and red, and black, and blue,
> Count for six, five, four, and two.
> If I touch an egg of white,
> A forfeit then will be your right ;
> If I touch an egg of gold,
> It is mine to have and hold.

As is told in the rhyme, the eggs each have a different value. Green counts six ; red, five ; black, four ; and blue, two ; and the gold egg is worth more than all put together, for when a player touches that, she wins the game and a forfeit of an egg from each of the other players. The white egg is worth less than nothing, since it not only has no value but whoever touches it with the wand must pay a forfeit.

Each player is in turn blindfolded and makes her trial, keeping account of the value of the eggs she has touched. When the sum of twenty has been reached by anyone the game is ended, without the aid of the gold egg. The position of the eggs are changed after each trial, that the person about to touch them may not know where it is best to place her wand.

Easter Egg Dolls.

In some of the large confectionery stores in New York City may be found at Easter-tide quaint little Easter offerings, looking at first sight exactly like dolls' heads surmounted by pretty little head-dresses. As dolls are not peculiarly appropriate gifts for Easter, one naturally examines them closer, to ascertain if there is anything about them significant of the day, and in so doing quickly discovers that the heads are not made of wax or china, as was at first supposed, but are simply egg-shells from which the eggs have been blown, leaving the shell perfect. Little faces are painted upon these shells, and the cunning caps or bonnets are made of tissue paper.

Now it is our purpose to teach the children who do not live in New York and have never seen these pretty toys, and also those who, having seen, cannot afford to purchase them, just how to make some of these little men and women, and how to fashion a variety of head-dresses not to be found in the stores.

To begin with, select several nice large eggs, those of a pinkish yellow are preferable, being something of a flesh-tint. These eggs should be blown, or the shells emptied of their contents; to blow them make a small hole in each end of the shell, and, taking it gently between the thumb and forefinger, put one hole to the lips; then blow, not too hard, but steadily, until the egg has all run out of the other end.

The face must be painted next, and to those who know nothing of drawing this will seem no easy task, until by carefully observing the following direction they will find that it is

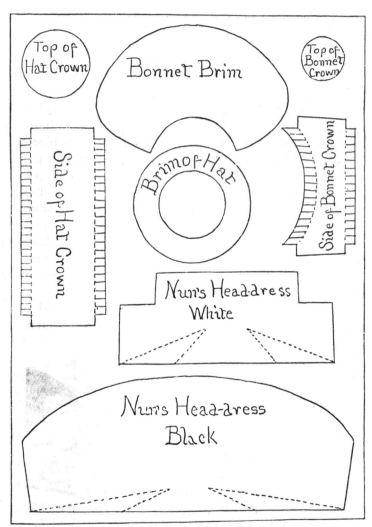

Top of Hat Crown

Bonnet Brim

Top of Bonnet Crown

Side of Hat Crown

Brim of Hat

Side of Bonnet Crown

Nun's Head-dress
White

Nun's Head-dress
Black

Patterns for Head-dresses.

in the power of anyone to produce as pretty a face as could be wished for.

Among picture-cards, or in almost any juvenile book, may be found many pretty faces of a suitable size which can be transferred to the egg in this way. Lay a piece of tracing-paper over the head selected, and with a soft lead-pencil trace carefully all the lines indicating the features; then place the paper on the shell so that the pencil-marks are next to it, and with a hard pencil, or ivory knitting-needle, go over the lines again, thus transferring the soft pencil-marks to the shell.

The Nun.

Touch up and strengthen the features with a fine paint-brush and india-ink. Anyone understanding painting may color the face in natural tints, but it looks very nicely done merely in outline.

The simplest arrangement for holding the little head erect is a small pasteboard box turned upside down, and having a hole cut in the bottom just large enough to admit the small end of the shell; this will support the head nicely, and also form the shoulders.

Make the hair of raw cotton blackened with ink, and fasten it on the head with mucilage. When all of the foregoing directions have been carried out it is time to attend to the head-dresses, and we will begin with the quaint and old-fashioned poke-bonnet. Cut this bonnet from ordi-

The Old-fashioned Girl.

nary brown wrapping-paper after the pattern shown in diagram; sew together the ends of the " side of crown," then sew the curved side (which is cut in slits as shown in pattern, and folded back as indicated by dotted line) to the smallest part of brim ; fold in the strips marked on the straight "side of crown" and fasten on the " top of crown" with mucilage. The trimming for the bonnet consists of a fold and bow of colored tissue paper.

Make the man's hat of shiny black paper by the pattern in

The Dude.

diagram, and fasten together in the same manner as the bonnet, rolling the sides of the brim when finished. Black and white tissue-paper folded to fit the head, as shown by the dotted lines in the pattern, forms the head-dress of the nun.

By copying the head-dresses of different nations, an odd and curious assembly of these Easter-egg dolls can be formed ; but that must be worked out at some future time, for we have yet to tell how to construct some Easter toys that cannot be found in any store. The

Humpty Dumpty

who " sat on a wall," and the " Humpty Dumpty" who " had a great fall," must have been like the one I am about to describe, made of an egg ; for it is pretty certain that if he should fall, " all the king's horses and all the king's men couldn't put" this " Humpty Dumpty together again " any more than they could the other.

The diagram shows the frame of this little fellow and how it is joined together. A large egg should be chosen ; and when the contents have been blown from the shell, four holes must be pricked in it for the arms and legs to pass through, as shown in the diagram. These limbs are made of rather fine bonnet-

Diagram of Humpty Dumpty.

wire, the piece used for the arms being about eight inches long. The hand is made by bending up one end of the wire as in diagram, and with softened beeswax covering the loop thus formed. When one hand has been finished off in this way, the other end of the wire, still straight, should be passed through one of the holes near the small end of the shell and out through the one opposite, then bent up into a hand and arm in the same manner as described.

The wire for the legs and feet must be ten inches long. The diagram shows how it is bent to form the feet. On this frame, wax can easily be modelled to look like a foot ; a coating of red paint will add to the appearance, as red boots look well with the costume to be worn. The wire for the legs should be bent in a curve in the middle (see diagram) before it is passed through the shell. Again, as with the hands, one foot must be finished and the legs fastened on before the other foot can be made.

Humpty Dumpty.

The figure of Humpty Dumpty being thus prepared, his face must be painted ; water-colors are the best for this purpose. The jollier the expression of his face, the funnier the little man will look.

Patterns for trousers, jacket, and hat are shown in the diagrams. The trousers should be cut from white cotton cloth two and a half inches long and six inches wide. A slit an inch and a half long, cut in the middle, separates the legs of the trousers, which must, of course, be sewed up. Dotted lines at top and bottom show where a gathering thread should be run, the bottom gathers forming ruffles around the ankles. White should also be used for the jacket, cutting it three and a half inches long and five inches wide. The shape of the jacket may be seen in the diagram, dotted lines showing where the sleeves are to be gathered around the wrist. Collar and pockets of red— the patterns of which are given—finish the little garment. A white hat four inches around the brim and two inches high is decorated with a band of red, which should be sewed on the edge and turned up.

When dressing Humpty Dumpty, fasten his garments on to his body here and there with glue, which will hold them securely in place. The hat also should be glued to his head, as it is difficult otherwise to keep it on.

Miss Rolly-poly.

Little Miss Rolly-poly, who decidedly refuses to lie down, always regaining an upright posture, no matter in what position she is placed, is made in the following manner: After the contents have been blown from the shell, the hole of the small end is enlarged gradually until it is about a half-inch in diameter; the shell is then placed in an upright position (a box with a hole cut in it just large enough to hold the egg firmly makes a good

Miss Rolly-poly.

stand) and melted sealing-wax is poured in; on top of this melted lead is poured, all the while care being taken to keep the shell perfectly steady, that the weight may fall exactly in the centre and make a perfect balance. A small quantity of lead is sufficient for the purpose, as the shell is so very light.

Miss Rolly-poly requires no limbs ; when her babyish face is painted she is ready for her costume. The dress is simply· made of a strip of colored cloth, and is two inches long and seven inches wide. The white apron is fastened to the dress· as

Diagram of Miss Rolly-poly.

shown in the diagram. Sleeves are made of pieces of the dress material about one inch long and one and a half inch wide. They are rolled up and fastened with needle and thread, then sewed on to the dress in the position shown in the diagram. Pockets are made for the apron, and the ends of the sleeves tucked in them, which makes it appear as though the hands were hidden in the pockets. The cap, made of the same ma- terial, or of a color harmonizing with the dress, is four inches round the brim and one inch high ; it is sewed together at the two ends, and gathered into a pompon on top, as is shown by the dotted lines in the diagram. A little glue should also be used to fasten this dolly's dress and cap on.

Mandolin.

A pretty little toy mandolin is made of the lengthwise half of an egg-shell. To separate the shell in this way it is necessary to pierce holes with a needle along the line where the division is to be made, which will cause it to break evenly ; or the egg may be boiled hard and then cut in half with a very sharp knife. Fig. 6 is cut from stiff paper, and the strings drawn with pen and ink ; then the shell is fastened to it on the opposite side by pasting a narrow strip of white tissue paper over the edges of the shell and frame, joining them together. The top of the handle is bent down a little and a narrow ribbon tied to it. To make the mandolin still more complete, paint the handle mahogany color, with a fine needle stitch

The Mandolin.

on strings of yellow silk, and paint the egg-shell into pumpkin-like divisions of yellow and mahogany.

The Owl.

To turn a hen's egg into an owl has not before, I imagine, been thought possible ; yet it is easy enough, and requires but a very

Wing.   Diagram of Owl.

short time to accomplish the transformation, when one knows just how to go to work.   No incubator is needed to hatch this

Owl Complete.

bird, as only the shell is used, the contents having been disposed of in the manner before described. We commence the formation of the little owl by making two holes near the large end of the shell in the position shown in diagram.

By looking at the next diagram the manner of making the feet and legs may be seen.   A short piece of wire is bent in the shape given, and is wrapped on to a longer wire with strong thread, thus forming three toes, which are quite enough for a bird that will never walk.   One foot made, the wire is passed through the shell, having first been bent into a curve, as in the description of Humpty Dumpty. When the last foot has been fastened on, the wire should be pushed back into the shell, allowing but little of the legs to show. The wings are cut by the pattern given, and are painted to resemble feathers as much as possible. Brown is the best color to use. By the diagram may be seen how the head and body are painted.

Maple-wax Easter Eggs.

Empty the egg-shell of its contents and open a place at the small end the size of a silver dime. Stand it in an upright position with the largest opening on top, and leave it while you prepare the maple-wax, or candy. Mix enough water with some maple sugar to dissolve it, and set on the fire to cook; when it will harden in cold water it is done. Carefully fill the egg-shell with the hot maple-wax, and keeping it in an upright position, set it on the ice to cool. When the wax is perfectly cold and hard, paste an artificial daisy over the opening in the shell. Maple-wax is the nicest kind of candy, and done up in this way will remain firm and hard for a long while ; and therefore these maple-wax eggs make excellent Easter gifts to send away to one's friend at a distance. The best way to pack them is to wrap them in cotton and then put them in a tin baking-powder box, filling up the interstices with cotton to keep them from knocking about.

The box, of course, must be wrapped in paper and tied securely with a string. Packed like this, they may travel safely all over the United States. The writer sent several the distance of over seven hundred miles, and they arrived at their destination in as perfect condition as when they left her hands.

Bonbon Box.

Select a box two or three inches high—a round one is best —which has a lid that covers the entire box. Cut some straw

4

or hay in pieces long enough to reach from the top to the edge, and glue it on the sides of the lid, covering them completely. Prepare as many halves of egg-shells as will cover the top, allowing a space one inch wide around the edge. Glue the shells down, and fill up the spaces between with straw. Near the edge, on the opposite sides, glue a loop of narrow white ribbon; these loops are to lift it with. Then glue straw on all the uncovered parts of the lid, making it a little thicker and higher at the edges. When the box is finished it resembles a nest of eggs, and makes an appropriate and acceptable Easter gift.

Easter Cards.

It is a very pretty custom, that of sending Easter cards, altogether too pretty to be allowed to lapse into disuse, as many

customs which are merely the expression of sentiment are apt to do in this busy, practical country of ours. One experiences a great deal of pleasure in selecting from the stock of beautiful cards found in the stores just before Easter those that seem suitable for one's friends, but more pleasure will be derived from home-made Easter cards, both to the sender and recipient; for it is true that into everything we make we put a part of ourselves, and into many a home-made article is woven loving thoughts which make the gift priceless, although the materials of which it is composed may have cost little or nothing.

Several years ago the writer was visiting a friend in the country twenty miles from the nearest town where Easter cards

could be purchased, but when Easter approached we sent off
our cards, just the same, and I am sure our friends were as
pleased with them, and more pleased, than if they had been of
the most expensive kind. This is how we made them :

It was an early spring, and the woods were filled with wild-
flowers, anemones and violets mostly ; these we gathered, and
arranging them in small bunches, stuck the stems through little
slits cut in cards or pieces of heavy paper, as they are some-

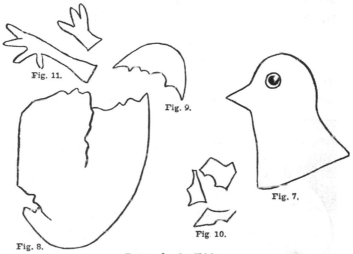

Fig. 11.

Fig. 9.

Fig. 7.

Fig 10.

Fig. 8.

Pattern for the Chicken.

times fastened in books when pressed. Underneath the bouquet
we wrote the name of the person for whom it was intended,
with some friendly message appropriate to the season, and
signed our own names ; then we carefully folded each in writing paper, taking pains not to crumple the flowers, and enclosing them in envelopes, sent them to their destination through
the mail. Any kind of flowers can be used for these Easter
cards, and instead of putting the stems through slits in the

card, they may be tied to them with narrow ribbon. A card to be sent only a short distance should be put in a box just deep enough to leave room for the flowers, and fastened in some way to keep it from moving about; in this way it will reach its destination sweet and fresh.

To those who can paint their Easter cards we have no suggestions to offer, for they have an unlimited supply of designs at their command, and with their power of decoration, may turn almost anything into an Easter card, from a piece of satin ribbon, upon which they sketchily paint a spray of flowers, to an elaborate picture. A few suggestions are here given which our younger readers may like to carry out, as the cards we describe are easily made, and adapted to amuse the children.

"Stepping through the White House" the first card is called, and it represents a little chicken breaking through its shell. The pattern of the chicken is given in the diagrams. Fig. 7, the head and neck, is cut from yellow flannel; Figs. 8, 9, and 10, the main part and fragments of shell, are of white paper, and Fig. 11, the feet, of black paper. These are pasted to a tinted card, as shown in illustration. The eye and bill are made black with ink or paint.

The Little Quakeress.

Little Quakeress.

Half an egg-shell, with the face and hair painted on it, forms the head. The cap is made of white tissue paper cut in four strips ; one, for the crown, is six and a half inches long, and a little over one and a half wide ; another, for the brim, is four and a half inches long and one inch wide ;

while the strings are each three and a half inches long, and one and a half wide. The crown is plaited in the centre, the brim folded lengthwise through the middle, and sewed to the crown. The strings are fastened on either side of the cap, and crossed in front ; then the cap is pasted on the head, the surplus paper folded back, and the whole glued on a card. The ends of the strings are also fastened to the card, forming a Quaker kerchief.

Lawn-Tennis with Our Own Net.

CHAPTER V.

HOW TO MAKE A LAWN-TENNIS NET.

 ET us see ; it was that old medical gentleman, Galen the Greek, who first wrote upon tennis, speaking of the sport as healthy exercise, was it not ? Well, girls, it really does not matter much to us whether he was the first to write it up and the Greeks the first to play it, or whether the game originated in France in the fifteenth century, as some claim. What *we* want to know is, can we all learn to play tennis ? Does it cost much ? What kind of gowns and shoes must we wear ? And is it an enjoyable game ?

There is no doubt, we think, of its being a right royal pastime, as it has been called both the " king of games " and the " game of kings ; " the latter because it was enjoyed by princes and nobles—so much enjoyed, that in both England and France edicts were published forbidding the common people to play it.

Girls, do you wonder if they always had the choice of courts, and so never took part in the fun of spinning the racket in the air while the adversary called out " rough " or " smooth ; " or whether they played as we do, taking their defeats pleasantly and wearing their honors gracefully, while always doing their very best ?

They must have played well, for it is said that Louis XI., Henry II., and Charles IX., were experts, and that Henry VIII. of England was extremely fond of the sport.

We can easily learn to play this most popular and exhilarating of games. But we must be suitably clothed in order to thoroughly enjoy it and receive all the benefit the recreation brings to both mind and body.

Flannel seems to be the best material for a tennis suit—it is so soft and yielding, and so well adapted for a defence against either cold or heat. Then, make your tennis gown of flannel ; the skirt in plaits, without drapery ; the postilion basque of Jersey cloth, soft and elastic, matching the skirt in color.

An Old Game.

Sew the skirt of your gown on a sleeveless waist, made of lining or muslin. The Jersey will fit nicely over this, and you can play better and feel far more comfortable than when the weight is allowed to drag on the hips. For it is nonsense to attempt to take part in any athletic game unless you can have perfect freedom of action ; in short, you should be so dressed as to be utterly unconscious of your clothing.

Either crochet a Tam O' Shanter hat or make one of the dress material, as these are not so apt to fall off while running as a straw hat. " Last, but not least," come the shoes. Of course, rubber-soled shoes are the best. But if these are not to be had, remove the heels from an old pair of ordinary shoes, and they will do very well ; heels roughen and cut the courts.

The actual cost of a lawn-tennis set need only be the price of the rackets and balls, and rope and cord necessary when you learn

How to Make a Lawn-Tennis Net,

which is not difficult.

First procure two pieces of cotton rope, three-sixteenths of an inch in size, each thirty-four feet long, costing about twenty-five cents apiece. Then one and a half pound of hammock

Stake.   Peg.

twine or macrimé cord, No. 24, which will not cost more than fifty cents. Next, two lengths of cotton rope for guy-ropes, each five feet, price, both included, ten cents ; making the total amount $1.10 for a strong, firm, tennis net which will prove serviceable and last many a season.

Runner.

The other materials necessary are all home-made. These consist

Runner and Guy-rope.

of two stakes, each five feet long (Fig. 12). Any kind of a strong pole, when sharpened at one end and a notch cut

The Fid.

at the other, will answer the purpose. Four pegs, each one foot long (Fig. 13). These may be easily made of old broomsticks. Four runners (Fig. 14), each five inches long, one and a quarter wide, and about half an inch thick, with holes bored near each end large enough to allow the guy-rope (Fig. 15) to pass through. A fid or mesh-stick of any kind of wood (Fig. 16), about a foot or ten inches long, with circumference measuring three inches. A hammock-needle (Fig. 17), nine or ten inches long and one wide, which may be bought for ten cents, or whittled out of a piece of ash or hickory by some kind brother. Tassels are not necessary, though it is much better to have them, as they make the top line of the net more distinct and add to its appearance. Make about forty bright-colored tassels of worsted, or bits of flannel

Fig 17

Fig 19

Fig 20

Fig 18

Hammock-needle.

Needle Threaded.

cut in very narrow strips, three inches long, allowing ten or twelve strips to each tassel. Commence your tennis net by first threading the needle ; take it in the left hand, and use the thumb to hold the end of the cord in place while looping it over the tongue (see Fig. 18); pass the cord down under the needle to the opposite side, and catch it over the tongue. Repeat this until the needle is full.

Next, take a piece of rope thirty-four feet long, and make a long loop in one end, tying the knot so that it can readily be untied again. Throw the loop over some convenient hook or door-knob (Fig. 19) with the knot at the knob or hook. Tie the cord on the needle to the loop, place the fid or mesh-stick under the cord close to the loop (Fig. 20), with the thumb on the cord to hold it in place (Fig. 25), while you pass the needle around the mesh-stick, and, with its point toward you, pass it through the loop from the top, bringing it over the mesh-stick. This will make the first half of the knot (Fig. 21). Pull this tight, holding it in place with the thumb while you throw the cord over your hand, which forms the loop as seen in Fig. 22. Then pass the needle from under

Knots.

through the loop, pulling it tight to fasten the knot. Hold it in place with the thumb, and repeat these movements for the next knot. Fig. 23 shows a number of these knots finished. A in Fig. 23 is a knot before it is drawn tight; B in Figs. 21, 22, 23 is the string that runs to the needle, C is the rope, and D is the mesh-stick. About two hundred and sixty-four of these knots or meshes will make the net the regular length, thirty-three feet.

In knitting across, the meshes will accumulate on the fid; shove them off to the left, a few at a time, to make space for others. When the desired number of meshes are finished to form the first row, shove them all off the fid, as shown in Fig. 24.

Begin the next row by again placing the fid under the cord (Fig. 24). Take up the first mesh, drawing it close to the mesh-stick, hold it in place with the thumb while throwing the cord over your hand, pass the needle on the left-hand side of the mesh from under through the loop (Fig. 25); pull this tight, and you will have tied the common knitting-knot. Repeat this with all the loops until the row is finished.

When it becomes necessary to thread or fill the needle, tie the ends of the cord with the knot shown in Fig. 26, which, when properly tightened, cannot slip. Wrap each end of the cord from the knot securely to the main cord with strong thread, to give the net a neat appearance.

Continue netting until the net is three feet wide. Then untie the rope, and spread the net by sliding the knots apart, and fasten the second rope to the bottom of the net by tying the rope securely to the first mesh with the cord on the needle ; then carry the rope and cord to the next mesh, hold the rope, cord, and mesh firmly in place, and throw the cord over your hand, passing the needle down through the mesh under the rope and

cord out through the loop (Fig. 27). Pull this tight, and continue in like manner, knitting each successive mesh to the rope until the net is all fastened on. Turn back the end of the rope and wrap it down neatly with strong string

Fig. 26.

(Fig. 28). In the same way secure the other end, and also the ends of the first or top rope.

Fig. 25.

This completes the lawn-tennis net proper. The bright tassels can now be tied at intervals along the top of the net, and four pieces of twine fastened on each end of the net at equal distances apart. These are for tying the net to the poles (Fig. 29).

To erect the lawn-tennis net, plant the two poles firmly in the ground a little over thirty-three feet apart, tie the net to the poles, then drive in the pegs, two to each pole, about five feet from the pole (Fig. 30); slide a runner on each end of the

Fig. 27.

Fig. 28.

two guy-ropes by first threading the rope through one of the holes in the runner, then pass the rope over the side down through the other hole and fasten it with a knot (Fig. 15). Next tie around the notch in the top of the poles the guy-ropes, with runners attached, and slip each loop made by the runner over each peg (Fig. 31), allowing the rope to fall in the groove A near the top of the peg; tighten the rope by pushing up the runners. The stakes are thus held in position by ropes running out to the pegs in the ground (Fig. 30).

Now we understand how to make and erect a lawn-tennis net; but what shall we do about the court? Of course, that must be all ready before we can set up the net. We must now learn how to lay out a

Lawn-Tennis Court.

The best ground for this is turf, though it may be of asphalt, or earth mixed with fine gravel; sometimes wood is used.

The diagram on page 64 (Fig. 32) shows the construction of a lawn-tennis court for two, three, or four-handed games.

Lay out the court with a hundred-foot measuring-tape, by marking the lines with whitewash, chalk, paint, or plaster-of-Paris.

First the side line, seventy-eight feet,

Fig. 30.—The Home-Made Net.

AB. This gives you one side of your court. Then the base line, thirty-six feet, AC, which, with their parallel lines CD and DB, form the boundaries of a court for four-handed games. Now lay off the side lines of the single court, EG and FH, which are parallel to the others and four and a half feet inside of them. Divide the court across the centre by the net, fastened to the poles O and P. The lines EF and GH are called base lines. Twenty-one feet from the net, mark the service lines, MN and TV. Then make the central longitudinal line, IJ, and the court is complete.

Now everything is prepared for the game. Hold your racket firmly, and try to keep the ball flying over the net, back and forth, as often as possible.

For the guidance of those who have had no opportunity of learning to play lawn-tennis the following rules are given, as adopted by the United States National Lawn-Tennis Association.

First, however, we would say that it is not necessary always to have an umpire or a referee, as spoken of in the

Rules for Lawn-Tennis.

THE GAME.

1. The choice of sides, and the right to serve in the first game, shall be decided by toss; provided that, if the winner of the toss choose the right to serve, the other player shall have choice of sides, and *vice versa*. If one player choose the court, the other may elect not to serve.

2. The players shall stand on opposite sides of the net; the player who first delivers the ball shall be called the *server*, and the other the *striker-out*.

Fig. 32

LAWN-TENNIS COURT.

3. At the end of the first game the striker-out shall become server, and the server shall become striker-out ; and so on, alternately, in all the subsequent games of the set, or series of sets.

4. The server shall serve with one foot on the base line, and with the other foot behind that line, but not necessarily upon the ground. He shall deliver the service from the right to the left courts alternately, beginning from the right.

5. The ball served must drop between the service line, half-court line, and side line of the court, diagonally opposite to that from which it was served.

6. It is a *fault* if the server fail to strike the ball, or if the ball served drop in the net, or beyond the service line, or out of court, or in the wrong court ; or if the server do not stand as directed by law 4.

7. A ball falling on a line is regarded as falling in the court bounded by that line.

8. A fault cannot be taken.

9. After a fault the server shall serve again from the same court from which he served that fault, unless it was a fault because he served from the wrong court.

10. A fault cannot be claimed after the next service is delivered.

11. The server shall not serve till the striker-out is ready. If the latter attempt to return the service he shall be deemed ready.

12. A service or fault, delivered when the striker-out is not ready counts for nothing.

13. The service shall not be *volleyed*, i.e., taken, before it has touched the ground.

14. A ball is in play on leaving the server's racket, except as provided for in law 6.

15. It is a good return, although the ball touch the net ; but

5

a service, otherwise good, which touches the net, shall count for nothing.

16. The server wins a stroke if the striker-out volley the service, or if he fail to return the service or the ball in play ; or if he return the service or the ball in play so that it drops outside of his opponent's court ; or if he otherwise lose a stroke, as provided by law 18.

17. The striker-out wins a stroke if the server serve two consecutive faults ; or if he fail to return the ball in play ; or if he return the ball in play so that it drops outside of his opponent's court ; or if he otherwise lose a stroke as provided by law 18.

18. Either player loses a stroke if he return the service or the ball in play so that it touches a post of the net ; or if the ball touch him or anything that he wears or carries, except his racket in the act of striking ; or if he touch the ball with his racket more than once ; or if he touch the net or any of its supports while the ball is in play ; or if he volley the ball before it has passed the net.

19. In case any player is obstructed by any accident, the ball shall be considered a *let.*

20. On either player winning his first stroke, the score is called 15 for that player ; on either player winning his second stroke, the score is called 30 for that player ; on either player winning his third stroke, the score is called 40 for that player ; and the fourth stroke won by either player is scored game for that player, except as below : If both players have won three strokes, the score is called *deuce ;* and the next stroke won by either player is scored *advantage* for that player. If the same player wins the next stroke, he wins the game ; if he loses the next stroke the score returns to deuce ; and so on, until one player wins the two strokes immediately following the score of deuce, when game is scored for that player.

21. The player who first wins six games wins the set; except as follows: If both players win five games, the score is called *games all;* and the next game won by either player is scored *advantage game* for that player. If the same player wins the next game, he wins the set; if he loses the next game, the score returns to games all; and so on, until either player wins the two games immediately following the score of games all, when he wins the set. But individual clubs, at their own tournaments, may modify this rule at their discretion.

22. The players shall change sides at the end of every set; but the umpire, on appeal from either player, before the toss for choice, may direct the players to change sides at the end of every game of each set, if, in his opinion, either side have a distinct advantage, owing to the sun, wind, or any other accidental cause; but if the appeal be made after the toss for choice, the umpire can only direct the players to change sides at the end of every game of the odd or deciding set.

23. When a series of sets is played, the player who served in the last game of one set shall be striker-out in the first game of the next.

24. The referee shall call the game after an interval of five minutes between sets, if either player so order.

25. The above laws shall apply to the three-handed and four-handed games, except as below:

26. In the three-handed game, the single player shall serve in every alternate game.

27. In the four-handed game, the pair who have the right to serve in the first game shall decide which partner shall do so; and the opposing pair shall decide in like manner for the second game. The partner of the player who served in the first game shall serve in the third, and the partner of the player who served in the second game shall serve in the fourth; and the same order shall be maintained in all the subsequent games of the set.

28. At the beginning of the next set, either partner of the pair which struck out in the last game of the last set may serve, and the same privilege is given to their opponents in the second game of the new set.

29. The players shall take the service alternately throughout the game ; a player cannot receive a service delivered to his partner ; and the order of service and striking out once established shall not be altered, nor shall the striker-out change courts to receive the service, till the end of the set.

30. It is a fault if the ball served does not drop between the service line, half-court line, and service side line of the court, diagonally opposite to that from which it was served.

31. In matches, the decision of the umpire shall be final. Should there be two umpires, they shall divide the court between them, and the decision of each shall be final in his share of the court.

ODDS.

A *bisque* is one point which can be taken by the receiver of the odds at any time in the set except as follows :

(*a*) A bisque cannot be taken after a service is delivered.

(*b*) The server may not take a bisque after a fault, but the srriker-out may do so.

One or more bisques may be given to increase or diminish other odds.

Half fifteen is one stroke given at the beginning of the second, fourth, and every subsequent alternate game of a set.

Fifteen is one stroke given at the beginning of every game of a set.

Half thirty is one stroke given at the beginning of the first game, two strokes given at the beginning of the second game ; and so on, alternately, in all the subsequent games of the set.

Thirty is two strokes given at the beginning of every game of a set.

Half forty is two strokes given at the beginning of the first game, three strokes given at the beginning of the second game ; and so on, alternately, in all the subsequent games of the set.

Forty is three strokes given at the beginning of every game of a set.

Half court : The players may agree into which half court, right or left, the giver of the odds shall play; and the latter loses a stroke if the ball returned by him drop outside any of the lines which bound that half court.

THE BALLS.

The balls shall measure not less than $2\frac{15}{32}$ inches, nor more than $2\frac{1}{2}$ inches in diameter ; and shall weigh not less than $1\frac{15}{16}$ oz., nor more than 2 oz.

The May-Pole Dance.

CHAPTER VI.

MAY-DAY.

Ho! the merrie first of Maie
Bryngs the daunce and blossoms gaie,
To make of lyfe a holiday.

N the merry heart of youth the old song
still finds an echo, and this day, with
its relics of pagan customs, celebrating, in the advent of spring, nature's
renewed fertility, is a festival full of
fun for the children.

Some of the ceremonies of May-
day, handed down from generation to
generation, were brought to America
in old colonial days by the English,
but owing, perhaps, to the stern puri-
tanical training of most of the early
settlers, the customs did not thrive here as in the mother country, and many of them have died out altogether.

May-day is one of the many holidays still celebrated, that
originated among the pagans ages ago, and it is said that the
practice of choosing a May-queen and crowning her with flowers
is a remnant of the ceremonies in honor of Flora, the goddess
of flowers, which were held in Rome the last four days of April
and the first of May.

There was, at one time, a very pretty custom observed in

Merrie England of fastening bunches of flowering shrubs and branches of sycamore and hawthorn upon the doors of those neighbors whose good lives and kindly habits were thus recognized by their friends.

The maids and matrons of England formerly had a way of their own of observing the day. On the first of May they would all go trooping out with the earliest rays of the morning sun, to bathe their faces in the magic dew, which glistened upon the grass once a year only, and was supposed to render the features moistened with it beautiful for the next twelve months.

When the writer was a wee little girl there lived next door to her home two old maiden ladies, who always kept a bottle of May-dew among their treasures. Although the ladies in question had long since passed that period when maidens are supposed to be lovely, superstitious persons might have found confirmation of a belief in the power of the dew, when they looked upon the sweet and kindly faces of these old maids. Faith in the fabled efficacy of May-dew will probably lose its last adherents when the two old ladies, very aged now, leave this world ; but other pretty customs, from which all the superstitious elements seem to have departed, should not be allowed to die out, and we intend this chapter on May-day sports as a reminder that May-day is a holiday and should be fittingly celebrated by the older girls as well as the little children, who, in these times, seem to be the only ones to remember the day.

May-day Sports.

A May-day custom, and a very pretty one, still survives among the children in our New England States. It is that of hanging upon the door-knobs of friends and neighbors pretty spring-offerings in the shape of small baskets filled with flowers, wild ones, if they can be obtained ; if not, the window-gardens at home are heavily taxed to supply the deficiency. When the dusky twilight approaches, it is time for the merry bands of young folks to start out on this lovely errand of going from house to house, leaving behind them the evidence of their flying visit in these sweetest of May-offerings. Silently approaching a door, they hang a May-basket upon the knob and, with a loud rap, or ring of the bell, scamper off, and flee as though for life.

These little Mayers are sometimes pursued, but few are ever caught, for the recipients of the baskets know that to capture a child, carry

Fig. 33.   The Straw Basket.

her into the house and treat her to sweetmeats, usually dear to the youthful palate, will not compensate the little prisoner for being held captive and thereby missing the fun going on among the other children.

How to Make May-baskets.

The dainty little baskets which are used by the Mayers are generally of home manufacture. They are made of almost any material, and in a variety of shapes. Some, constructed of cardboard, are covered with crimped tissue-paper, or with gilt, silver, or colored paper. They are never large unless flowers are plentiful, and even in that case a small basket is prettier.

Our first illustration represents a May-basket made of straws. Fig. 33 shows the frame of this basket, for which three straws seven inches long are required; these are sewed together, two and one-half inches from the bottom, forming a tripod. For the sides eighteen straws are necessary, six on each side, of graduating lengths; the three top straws being five inches long and the lowest ones three and one-half inches. These are sewed to the frame, log-cabin fashion, one upon another.

The bottom of the basket is made of a three-cornered piece of card-board cut to fit; three straws, two and one-half inches long, hold the base of the frame in position. A handle formed of three ribbons finishes off this May-basket very prettily; a ribbon is tied to each corner of the basket; the other ends meeting form a bow, as shown in the illustration.

Birch-bark Baskets

are quite appropriate for wild flowers, and one in the shape of a canoe can be made from a strip of bark six and one-half inches long and four inches wide. Fig. 34 gives the pattern of this basket. The dotted lines show where the ends are to be sewed together; a ribbon sewed to each end of the canoe serves for a handle.

Card-board Baskets,

cut after the pattern Fig. 35, can be covered with gilt, silver, or crimped tissue-paper as desired; paper lace or fringe is sometimes placed around the edges of baskets of this kind, as a border to rest the flowers upon. The card-board basket shown in illustration is joined together by buttonhole stitching of col-ored-silk floss ; slits are cut in two sides and a ribbon slipped

Fig 34.

The Birch-bark Basket.

through, the ends of which are tied in bow-knots to hold them in place.

May-day Combat.

This game, although suggested by the ceremonies which, ac-cording to Waldron, usher in the month of May in the Isle of

Man, is entirely new and bids fair to become popular, as it combines the elements of beauty, sentiment and mirth.

A number of young people separate into two parties, each having its queen ; one the Queen of May, the other Queen of Winter. The May-queen and her attendants should be decked with flowers, Winter and her retinue being without decoration. Equipped with the appropriate implements of warfare between the two seasons, namely, a wreath of flowers for spring and a ball of raw cotton, or wool, representing snow, for winter, the contending forces draw up in opposing lines, the space between being about twelve feet. Each line is headed by its respective queen, who holds her missile in her hand.

The Card-board Basket.

Fig. 35.

The game is commenced by the two queens simultaneously tossing the wreath and ball to someone in the opposite line, whose name is called as the missile is thrown. Should the person to whom it is thrown fail to catch it, she is made prisoner and must do battle on the other side, being released only when she succeeds in catching the missile belonging to her own party.

When the wreath and ball are caught, they are instantly tossed back to the opposite rank, and so the game goes on. Hostilities must cease when prisoners are being taken or released, to be recommenced when both sides announce themselves ready.

If either queen is captured she is ransomed by the return of all the prisoners taken on her side ; should she have no prisoners to release, the game is ended.

If the May-queen and her forces are defeated, they must strip off their floral decorations and give them to the victors, who, decked in these trophies, become the representatives of Spring, and the Queen of Winter is made Queen of May and is crowned by her vanquished and dethroned opponent. The former May-queen and her retinue, after offering their congratulations, must serve as attendants on the triumphant queen and do her bidding.

When the May-queen proves victorious the programme is reversed, and Winter and her party become the subjects of May.

The May-pole.

An old writer, speaking of the May-games held in England, says, " Their cheefest jewell is their Maie-poole," and to leave the May-pole out of our list of May-sports would indeed deprive the day of one of its most important and prettiest features. The appropriate place for the May-pole is, of course, out of doors ; yet the climate in most of our Northern States is so changeable and uncertain it may be found necessary for comfort to hold the festivities in the house, and in that case the following directions for erecting the pole in a room of moderate dimensions will be found useful.

How to Erect a May-pole in the House.

A May-pole from ten to twelve feet high is as tall as the ceilings of most rooms will admit.

The pole should be round, smooth, and about five inches in diameter at the base, growing gradually smaller toward the top.

For its support a wooden box is necessary, the average size being three feet long, two feet wide, and one foot high. Re-

move the top of the box, and directly in the centre of it cut a hole large enough to admit the pole. Take two sticks, two inches wide, and long enough to fit lengthwise in the box, and two shorter ones fitting the

Fig. 36.

box crosswise, and nail them securely in the position shown in Fig. 36, driving the nails from the outside of the box. Slip the pole through the hole which has been cut in the top, and then stand it in an upright position between the four sticks in the centre of the box (Fig. 37). Be sure that the pole stands perfectly straight; then, before nailing down the top, fill the box with sand, bricks, or stones, packing them tightly around the pole; this will give sufficient weight to prevent its tipping. Nail the top on, and cover the box with moss or green cloth, and bank it up with flowers.

How to Dress a May-pole.

In olden times the May-poles were painted in alternate stripes of yellow and black, but a white pole is prettier and shows the decorations to better advantage. Tack the ends of eight or ten variously colored ribbons, one and one-half inch wide, around the pole near the top. For a pole ten feet high the ribbons should be four yards long. Around where the ribbons are fastened on, suspend a wreath of flowers, as shown in Fig. 38. Decorate the extreme tip of the pole with gaily colored streamers, or small flags.

May-pole Dance.

An even number of persons are required for this dance; half the number take the end of a ribbon in the right hand and half in the left; they then stand facing alternately right and left. When the dance commences, each dancer facing the right passes under the ribbon held by the one opposite facing the left; she then allows the next person going to the left to pass under her ribbon, and so, tripping in and out, under and over, the ribbons are woven around the pole.

After continuing for a while, according to the above directions, the dancers separate into two equal divisions, and each party, independent of the other, plaits a strip which hangs loosely from the pole.

Fig. 37.

In performing this variation the two parties stand on either side of the pole, and all those facing the right pass on in that direction, going in and out as at first, until the last person going to the right has passed the last person going to the left in her division; then, transferring the ribbons to their other hands, they all turn and reverse the order. Thus they continue, going back and forth until the plait is about a foot in length, when another change is made by the two parties joining forces again ; this time, all those facing the left proceed in that direction, passing under the ribbons of all the others who are going to the right, thus forming two circles, one within the other. After going twice around the pole in this order, the dancers composing the inner circle take the outside and the others pass beneath their ribbons, again circling the pole twice ; then, after going through the first figure once more the dance may be ended, or the whole order may be reversed, and the ribbons, in that way, be unplaited again.

Fig. 38.

An appropriate song, with words set to a dancing air, should be sung by those taking part in the May-pole dance.

SUMMER

CHAPTER VII.

MIDSUMMER EVE.

N the minds of most of us, midsummer is associated with dry, dusty roads, parched vegetation, the shrill cry of the locust,* the shriller notes of the mosquitoes, and the hum of myriads of other insects; but, girls, midsummer does not come at this time : astronomy fixes the date at June 21st, the longest day of the year, when the leaves are still glossy green with the fresh sap circulating through their veins, giving them that healthy, juicy look so refreshing to the eye, and the heat of the sun has not yet dried to a white powder the firm country roads over which we delight to wander.

Ages ago the Pagans used to celebrate the day with rejoicing, because old Sol's bright face had broken loose from the clouds of winter, and the rain and mists of spring. They symbolized the revolution of the season by rolling great wooden wheels down the hill-sides; sometimes attaching straw to the outer circle and setting fire to it at night, making a miniature midnight sun as it dashed down the steep incline.

The people also believed that ill-luck rolled away from them with the fiery wheel, and to this day you will see Fortune or

---

* *Cicada*, commonly known among children as the locust.

"Ye vertue of a rare Cole that is to be found at Midsummer Eve under ye root of plantane and of mugwort Ye effects whereof are wonderful Whosoever weareth or beareth ye same about with them shall be freed from ye plague lightning and all ills"

Midsummer-eve Party.

Misfortune represented as travelling, like an acrobat at a circus, upon a wheel.

All the elves, brownies, and fays were supposed to be on hand at midsummer night, and it is this old superstition that Shakespeare has so beautifully illustrated in his " Midsummer Night's Dream."

It was on midsummer eve that the supposed invisible seeds of the fern could be gathered which rendered the fortunate possessor invisible whenever he chose to carry them about with him. Among other strange and some quite pretty superstitions, there is a tradition that a coal, found attached to the roots of the mugwort or plantain on midsummer eve, will keep away misfortune and insure good luck to the finder.

The girls of to-day who, although advanced enough to discard the superstitious element, can appreciate the poetic ideas symbolized by these ancient rites, may take hints for the entertainment of themselves and friends from the old belief in the mysteries and charms of midsummer eve.

Games can be invented, and pretty keepsakes and souvenirs exchanged upon this night, that will translate ancient paganism into modern good feeling and fellowship.

The New Fern-leaf Game.

Some one who has charge of the games shows to the assembled girls and boys a fern-leaf, and explains to them the legend connected with it, and the power of the seed to render the possessor invisible. Next she blindfolds them all; then, choosing one from among them, she removes the bandage from the player's eyes without allowing the others to know who has been selected to be the bearer of the magic fern. After giving the fern-leaf into the keeping of the chosen one, she places the latter in the centre of a ring formed by the rest of the players, who take hold of hands and circle round ; then, still holding hands, they forward to the centre and return ; letting go hands, they forward again, this time the fern-bearer joins in the ranks. Once more the ring is formed and they circle round, singing these lines :

Round goes the wheel,	To the one who finds
Round goes the year,	The seeds of the fern,
For woe or for weal,	Misfortune and evil
Midsummer is here.	To good luck will turn.

At the word " turn," each player seizes another and cries out, " fern, fern ! " at the same time removing the handkerchief from the eyes.

To the one who really has captured the magic fern a pretty card or silk badge, bearing a pictured fern and some appropriate motto, is given, as a token that the entire company wish all possible good luck to the possessor.

The Plantain Test.

To test fortune in this way, fill a large pan or bowl with clean dry sand ; provide as many plantain-plants as there are players, and to the roots of all but one tie, with a narrow ribbon, a bonbon which contains within its wrapper a verse indicating that the wrong plant has been chosen. To the one reserved from the rest attach a small piece of coal, or charcoal, wrapped in a bonbon paper which also encloses a verse describing the magic powers of the coal. Place all of the plants in the sand, making them look as though growing there. All this should be prepared before the party assembles, that no one may know to which plant the coal is fastened.

When the appointed time arrives, explain to the company that to the root of one of the plants in the bowl is fastened a coal which, according to old superstition, will secure to the finder perfect health for life. Then let each person in turn pull from the sand one of the plants. The one who finds the coal should be heartily congratulated, as she is supposed to have gained the good will of fortune and to be exempt from all the ills that flesh is heir to. The plantain is not difficult to secure, as it grows in almost every grass-plot, much to the annoyance of those who take pride in their lawns. Should the name be unfamiliar to some of our readers, the accompanying illustration will help them recognize the weed.

A pretty charm for the watch-chain can be made of the coal which is to bring the finder such good luck,* by having it cut to a proper size and shape, and a gold or silver band put around it. This will make it a souvenir, carrying out the old idea that the magic coal should be worn upon the person to bring the coveted good fortune.

Magic Plantain.

Rhymes to be enclosed in the paper with the magic coal:

Where my roots are intertwined
Lo, the magic coal you find.
Buried deep beneath the sand,
Waiting for your favored hand,

* Cannel coal is the best to use, for it is hard, will take a high polish like jet, and can be carved with a pen-knife.

I have held it free from harm ;
Take, and wear the mystic charm.
From the lightning's deadly stroke,
From the fire it may invoke,
From all illness, pain, and strife,
May it guard thee safe through life.

Rhymes to be enclosed in bonbons tied to the roots of plantains which do not bring good luck :

Though ye seek, ye seek in vain
Fortune's favor thus to gain,
For I bring to you no coal
To write your name on Fortune's roll.

———

Pity 'tis you thought it best
To pick out me from all the rest,
For no root of mine comes near
The coal that brings good fortune here.

———

Chance capricious, captures choice ;
Fickle Fortune favors few ;
When deaf to love, or reason's voice,
What makes you think she'll favor you ?

———

I am no messenger of fate,
You find this out, alas ! too late ;
I bring no magic coal with me,
From pains and ills to set you free.

Any bright girl can scribble off little jingles of this sort that
will do very well for the plantain test, or appropriate quotations
may be selected for the purpose.

Fortune's Wheel.

Just where Fortune will fail each member of the company
present is discovered in the following game :

The entire party forms into a circle, standing about two feet apart; then a wheel or hoop is started around the inside of the ring, and kept going by each one giving it a gentle push with the hand, sending it to the person next in the circle. As the wheel goes around the players sing these lines, pronouncing a word as each player touches the wheel, as if counting out.

> Fortune's wheel we speed along
> The while we sing our mystic song.
> Bring happiness, fame, power, and wealth,
> True love, long life, good friends, and health,
> Success in music, poetry, art,
> And with it all a merry heart.

When the wheel drops at the feet of anyone as a gift of Fortune is being sung, or if they fail to strike it as it passes, or, striking, they send it into the centre of the ring instead of to their next neighbor, it denotes that Fortune will withhold that special gift from them, and they must leave the circle, for good luck has deserted them.

The game continues until only one player remains, and this person, who has succeeded in keeping the wheel moving, is Fortune's favorite, and will possess all the gifts the mythical Goddess can bestow.

Starfish Portière.

CHAPTER VIII.

SEA-SIDE COTTAGE DECORATION.

 IMPLY to enter a house is enough to start some people to planning how it can, might, or should be decorated. The love of beauty seems to be inherent in the feminine character, and it is the nature of most girls to make their surroundings as beautiful as circumstances will permit. Those who have taste and ability for decoration can see no barren or homely room without being seized with the desire to banish its uncomeliness, and substitute grace and beauty in its stead.

The ordinary cottage at the sea-shore is a boon to such natures, for it is peculiarly well adapted to amateur decoration. Its cciled walls offer plain, even, flat tinted surfaces for any kind of ornamentation, and the absence of plaster makes it possible to drive nails wherever it is desirable to have them.

During a summer spent in one of these cottages on the coast of Maine, its many possibilities in the way of decoration were revealed, and personal experience has demonstrated that even the plainest of these temporary abiding-places is capable of being greatly beautified in a short time, and with materials usually close at hand, being obtainable from the fishermen and from the sea itself.

The windows first claim our attention in any house and our little cottage is no exception to the rule. With, or without, the regulation shades, windows should always be draped; the formality of their straight lines and angles can be subdued in no other way.

Fig. 39

Diagram of Ring.

Light, airy curtains are suitable for summer, and the prettiest, most graceful window-drapery imaginable can be made of ordinary fish-net. An oar for a pole; rings made of rope (Fig. 39); the looping formed of a rope tied in a sailor's knot; and a wooden hoop, such as is used to attach the sail to the mast on a sail-boat (Fig. 40) are all that are necessary for the completion of this nautical curtain. Small rings screwed into the oar, with corresponding hooks in the window-frame just above the window, will hold the oar securely in place. The looping should hang from a hook fastened in the wall near the window. The illustration given here will aid the imagination in picturing the effect of a window treated in this simple manner. Another pretty curtain may

Fig. 40

Looping for Curtains.

be made of unbleached cotton, with bands of blue at top and bottom covered with the ever- decorative fish-net.

Gray linen curtains, with strips of the net set in as insertion at top and bottom, will also be found extremely pretty and serviceable; or they may be composed of strips

of linen and net, of equal width, running the length of the
curtain. Made up in either way the effect is excellent.

Sea-side Cottage Window.

From window-drapery we will turn to that suitable for the
door-ways. Portières, in a room where the prevailing tints are

gray and light wood-color, should not present too violent a contrast to those subdued tones. A curtain of wood-brown, neither

Fig. 41

Diagram of Tying Knot.

Fig. 42

Fastening End of Rope.

too dark nor too light, will give the needed strength and decision, without destroying the harmonious coloring. One can be quickly and easily made of brown canton flannel and decorated with dried starfish, as shown in the illustration of the starfish portière. The starfish are soft enough to admit of being sewed to the curtain, and they should be placed with the underside out, as that is much prettier than the back, showing as it does two shades of color. A heavy rope with a knot at each end, stretched taut across the door-way and held in place with two hooks, will answer for a pole, and the drapery can be hung from it with iron rings. If the rope is very heavy the

Fig. 43

Diagram of Book-shelves.

ends will have to be parted into strands before the knots can be tied. Figs. 41 and 42 show the manner of tying the knot and fastening the end of a moderately heavy rope.

Book-shelves made of half of a flat-bottomed row-boat is not only an appropriate piece of furniture for a cottage by the sea, but also a very useful one. The fact of its shape allowing it to

Row-boat Book-shelves.

occupy a corner makes it a welcome addition to the furnishing, since there are so few things adapted to fill that angle.   Fig. 43

shows half of boat with cleats nailed on to hold the shelves, which must be made to fit the boat.   The shelves, when resting on the cleats, are secure enough, and need not be fastened in any other way.   If the book-shelves, when finished, are painted black, unvarnished, they will have the appearance of being ebonized.

The evidence of a womanly presence in the shape of a dainty

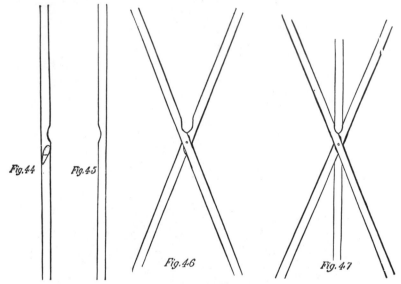

Diagram of Crab-net Work-basket.

work-basket always gives a home-like look to a room, and when this useful trifle happens to be prettily designed it contributes not a little to the decorations.   The standing work-basket represented here is manufactured of a crab-net, with the handle removed, fastened to a tripod stand.

The tripod may be made of bamboo, or any kind of straight sticks about the length of a walking-cane.   Upon one of the sticks two notches must be cut ; one exactly in the centre, and the other at one side just below (see Fig. 44). The second stick needs but one notch, which should match the upper one on the first stick (Fig. 45). The third stick has no notches.

To fasten them together, Fig. 45 must be laid across Fig. 44 as in Fig. 46, and the two fastened together with screws. The third stick must then be placed across the others, fitting in the two upper notches ; this must be secured with two screws, one passing through each of the other sticks (Fig. 47).

The stand when finished should be painted black, and the crab-net, which has previously been gilded, fastened in place by tying it on to each stick with a cord and tassel made of rope and gilded. Notches cut in the sticks, about three inches from the top, will afford a resting-place for the cord and keep it from slipping.

The hat-rack, which our drawing represents, makes an excellent and convenient hall-decoration. The materials used in its construction are a small mirror,

Crab-net Work-basket.

which can be procured at any country store ; four boards, whose length and breadth depend upon the size of the mirror ; two oars, with one-third of each handle sawed off ; one dozen large-sized nails, or small spikes, and a piece of rope about twelve feet long. The frame is made by nailing the boards together as shown in illustration, placing the end-boards on top.

7

The opening left in the centre should be one inch smaller than the mirror. When eight of the spikes have been driven into the frame at regular distances the mirror must be fastened on the back with strips of leather or sail-cloth, as shown in diagram (Fig. 48). The diagram also shows how the oars are held in place and the rope attached. The knot

Fig. 48.

Diagram of Hat-rack.

Hat-rack.

in which the rope is tied is called a true-lover's knot, and can readily be fashioned by studying the diagram. Small nails driven through the rope where it crosses the back of the oar will keep the loops from slipping out of place. The remaining four spikes are to suspend the hat-rack from, and must be driven into the wall so that two will hold the top loop, and the others the extreme upper corners of the side loops.

The frame and oars may be painted black and the spikes and ropes gilded, or the whole will look well painted yellow or brown.

A handsome screen can be made in the following manner : Procure a nice, firm clothes-horse, saw off the legs close to the bottom cross-piece, then cover the whole neatly, on both sides, with dark green cambric. Next tack smoothly on one side of each fold light-brown wrapping-paper, which comes quite wide, and may be bought by the yard. For the border use dark-green canton flannel cut in strips eight inches wide. Tack this around each fold of the screen with gimp-tacks, and paste the inside edges smoothly over the paper.

The decorations of the screen shown in the illustration are composed entirely of products of the sea.

Two panels are shown. One is decorated with sea-weed, dried starfish, and shells. Sea-weed and shells also are used on the other, but a group of horseshoe crabs take the place of the starfish.

Sea-weed of various kinds suitable for this use can be found along the coast, and they may be gathered and dried in this way. Loosen the sea-weed from whatever it is attached to, and while still in the water slip a piece of stiff paper beneath it and lift it out. Quite a number can be carried on the same paper, but they should be taken home as soon as possible and placed in a tub of fresh water. The tub will give the larger kinds room to spread out, when a smaller vessel would cramp and rumple them. On sheets of paper, of the kind used for the screen, carefully lift each sea-weed out of the water, and with a small camel-hair brush straighten the parts that are too much folded, and separate those that lie too closely together. Should a plant be very much crumpled when taken out, quickly replace it in the water and try again.

Marine Screen.

When they have all been satisfactorily spread on the paper and have become partially dry, they must be pressed by laying the paper which holds the sea-weed on a piece of blotting-paper or folded newspaper, and over it a piece of linen or fine cotton cloth; then over that another piece of blotting-, or news-paper; then again the paper with sea-weed, and so on; when all are finished the entire heap should be placed between two boards with a moderately heavy weight on top. When the sea-weed is quite dry—which it will be in three or four days—it will be found that some varieties will cling closely to the paper on which they have been spread, while others can readily be removed. Do not try to separate the first-mentioned kind from the paper, but with sharp scissors neatly trim off the edges around the weed; the paper underneath being the same as that of the screen on which it is to be pasted, it will not show. The other sea-weed can be taken from the paper and fastened to the screen with mucilage.

Horseshoe Crab Bag.

Before commencing the decoration some idea of the design, or the effect to be produced, should be decided upon ; then with deft fingers the articles used can be glued in place. When the glue is dry the whole must be given a coat of white varnish. This will help to hold things in place, and will also keep the seaweed from chipping off.

Vase.

An odd little bag for holding fancy work is made of two large horseshoe crab shells, with a satin bag fastened between them and tied at the top with a bow of ribbon. The main part of the bag can be of cambric the color of the satin, cut to fit the shells, the puff showing at the sides being of the satin.

A pretty little vase can be made of the shells of three sea-urchins, of graduating sizes, placed one upon another, the smallest on top. The small hole in the bottom of the largest one should be filled up with damp plaster-of-Paris which will h a r d e n very quickly. The other two shells must have the small holes enlarged to the size of the one at the top ; they can then be joined together with the plaster, and the vase be used for flowers or vines.

Candlestick.

A sea-urchin and good-sized starfish make the prettiest kind of a candlestick, and the addition of a brass-headed tack on every point but one of the starfish gives it a nice finish and furnishes feet for it to stand on ; the point left without a foot forms the handle by which it may be carried. The tacks should be stuck into the fish first, and then the sea-urchin fastened on with plaster-of-Paris. Not more than ten minutes are consumed in making a candlestick of this kind, and it will be found to be quite as useful as it is pretty and unique.

The walls of the cottage can be decorated in many ways with the beautiful ornaments the sea furnishes. Over one of the doors in the cottage alluded to at the beginning of this chapter there was an ornamentation that looked exactly like wood-carving, but was only a group of starfish arranged and tacked on the wall in a decorative form. The fish being nearly the exact color of the background, the deception was almost perfect.

If the walls of a room are divided off into panels, and each panel decorated in the manner described for the screen, the effect will be most exquisite.

On entering such a room one might almost imagine oneself to be a mermaid, and this a lovely chamber beneath the sea.

So much can be done by one's own hands it depends greatly, if not entirely, upon the taste or time one is willing to devote to it what this sea-side habitation shall be ; whether the little cottage shall be in harmony with its surroundings, seemingly a part of the place, or whether it shall be only a cheap frame-structure, looking as though it belonged in a country town and had been carried to the coast in a capricious gale of wind, with decorations, if it has any, inappropriate and unsuited to the sea-shore.

How to Dry Starfish.

Collect the most perfect specimens of all sizes, wash them in fresh water, and then spread on a board in a dry place (not in the sun) and leave them undisturbed for a few days, or until thoroughly dried.

How to Polish Shells.

Wash your shells in clean, fresh water; procure a small quantity of muriatic acid and have in readiness two-thirds as much water as acid. Place the shells in a basin, pour the water upon them, then the acid ; let them remain a few minutes, then take them out and wash again in clear water. Rub each shell with a soft woollen cloth. A fine enamelled surface can be given by rubbing them with a little oil and finely powdered pumice-stone, and then with a chamois-skin.

To bleach fresh-water shells to a snowy whiteness, wash them perfectly clean and then put them in a jar containing a solution of chloride of lime, place the vessel in the sun, and, when the shells are sufficiently bleached, remove and wash them in clear water. Polish them in the manner before described.

CHAPTER IX.

A GIRL'S FOURTH OF JULY.

ECORATIONS are seen here, there, and everywhere. How beautifully the flags and streamers look as they wave in the breeze. All the houses and streets are gay with bunting. We listen with a thrill of patriotic excitement to the national airs played by bands of music as the different parades pass our doors.

The spirit of independence fills the very air we breathe. Whiz! zip! bang! go the firearms. The noise is enchanting and the smell of powder delightful.

This is our grand national holiday, the glorious Fourth, when all the United States grows enthusiastic, and in various appropriate ways manifests its patriotism.

The celebration, commencing in the early morn and lasting until late in the evening, gives ample time for fireworks, games, and illuminations. And the girls can take active part in, and enjoy these martial festivities, help to decorate the house and grounds, and in the evening do their part toward the illumination. Then there are the beautiful daylight fireworks to

The Fourth of July Party.

be sent off, and games to be played ; all adding to the enjoyment and making up their celebration of Independence Day.
Although

Interior Decoration

for the Fourth of July has not been considered as necessary as the decoration for the outside of the house, still it is appropriate and used to some extent, especially when the house is thrown open to guests. Then, with a little thought and care the home may be decked and adorned in the most attractive manner.

If you chance to be the happy possessor of the portrait of some revolutionary ancestor, let this form the centre of your decorations.

Bring forward any relics of the colonial times and make them hold a prominent place, for all such things are historical and of great interest, though of course they are not essential. Strips of bunting, cheese-cloth, or tissue-paper, in red and white and blue are necessary, and must do their part in adding to the gayety of the scene. These can be arranged in festoons, and made into wreaths, stars etc., to be used as ornaments on the wall.

There is nothing, perhaps, more appropriate for decoration than flags, though it requires some ingenuity to decorate with our American flag on account of the blue being in one corner. However we will try. Take two flags without staffs and baste them together as in Fig. 49, bringing the blues side by side ; pleat up the top of each to the centre and you will have Fig. 50 with the stripes at the bottom running from end to end.

Now take two more flags reversed, the stripes being at the top the stars at the base, and pleat them in the centre, it gives the same idea in another form. For this style of adornment use the flags which may be had at any dry-goods store ; they come by the bolt, cost but a few cents each, and are much softer and fold better than the more expensive glazed ones. Other modes of draping the stars-and-stripes will suggest themselves : place

Fig. 49

the " colors " in different positions until some good design is found, and you will enjoy it all the more for having made the combination yourself.

Fig. 50

Tiny flags fastened to the chandeliers, and pinned in groups on the curtains give to the room quite a holiday appearance. This is for the daylight.   In the evening we will have

In-door Illumination,

which can be made very brilliant by simply using a number of lighted candles.

Should you desire to have it more elaborate, the words Liberty and Independence can be printed on the windows by cutting the letters forming the words from thick paper and gumming them to the window-panes, so when the room is lighted they will show plainly from the outside.

You may also make of tissue-paper a Liberty-bell, Goddess of Liberty, American Eagle, and flags. Gum these on the edges and fasten them to the windows; place a bright light behind them and the tints of the paper will shine out in all their brilliancy. The Goddess of Liberty's face, the feathers on the eagle, and the lettering on the bell must all be drawn with a paint-brush and ink or black paint.

In making any or all of these, it will be of great assistance if you secure a picture of the object to copy from.

Having provided for the inside of the house it now behooves us to turn our attention to

Out-of-door Decoration

consisting principally of flags raised on poles, hung from windows, and disposed in numerous and various ways.

The many devices representative of our country may be used with good effect. Thus, a large United States shield can be made of colored paper or inexpensive cloth tacked on a piece of card-board, cut in the desired shape, and the shield suspended from the window flat against the house, as a picture is hung on the wall. Other emblems can be manufactured in the same way.

Small trees or tall bushes covered all over from top to bottom with flags and streamers look beautiful, and all the gayer, when the wind blows, causing them to wave and flutter.

Fasten the flags and streamers on the tree with string.

Some girls think that the

Illumination in the Open Air.

is best of all, for then they can give their fancy free play, and create all sorts of odd and novel designs.

The bright-colored Chinese lanterns are very decorative. Suppose we begin with these. Fasten securely here and there,

Fig. 51

on the lawn, large paper Japanese umbrellas in upright positions. This is accomplished by binding the handles of the umbrellas

Fig. 52

securely to poles which have been sharpened at one end, and planting the pointed end of the poles firmly in the ground.

From every other rib of the umbrella suspend a lighted

Chinese lantern by a wire long enough to prevent any danger of setting the little canopy on fire. The effect produced is both novel and pretty.

A popular method of arranging the lanterns is stringing them on wires, stretched from house to house, or from tree to tree, so forming, as it were, a fringe of lights.

Again, they may be placed at intervals on the ground, fastened to trees or hung on the piazza, some in groups of twos or threes, others singly, these being of many odd shapes and sizes. Piazzas are very good sites for the display of colored umbrellas, which may hang, inverted, from the ceiling, with a tiny lighted Chinese lantern suspended from each rib. Let me repeat, be careful not to have the wires so short that the light is in dangerous proximity to the umbrella.

Another pleasing illumination is to make a large flag of colored-paper with strong pieces of tape pasted along both top and bottom, the ends of the tape extending beyond the flag. Tie the tape to two trees, poles, or pillars of the porch, and place a light back of the flag, to bring out the colors clearly and distinctly.

Illuminated tents are made by placing poles in the fashion of Fig. 51, and using large flags, low-priced colored cloth or strong paper as a covering, Fig. 52. The corners are tied down to pegs in the ground, and, when two or three candles are set in the tent, the effect is very pleasing.

All young people delight in the noise and excitement of

Fireworks,

and here are some pyrotechnics which any girl can easily make. They are daylight fireworks, and most of them may be sent off from a balcony or window, and all with no danger of fire or burns.

One of the simplest to try is the

Parachute.

Cut a piece of tissue-paper five inches square, twist each corner and tie with a piece of thread eight inches long, Fig. 53 ;

Fig. 53   *Fig. 54*

Parachutes.

wrap a small pebble in a piece of paper and tie the four pieces of thread securely to the pebble, Fig. 54. This makes a light airy little parachute, which, when sent out from the window, will, with a favorable wind, sail up and off over the house-tops. Make a number of parachutes in different colors and send them off one after another in succession. Next we will have what we call

Thunderbolts

fashioned of bright-colored tissue-paper. Cut the paper in pieces four inches wide and eight inches long. Then cut each piece into strips reaching about one-third of the length of the piece of paper (Fig. 55), pinch the uncut end of the paper together and twist it

Fig. 55   *Fig. 56*

Thunderbolts.

tightly so that it will not become undone (Fig. 56). Open the window and throw these out a few at a time. They will turn heavy end down and dart off with the fringed end fluttering. Now and then they will waver a moment in one spot, and then dart off in another direction ; so they go whirling, zigzagging and bowing as if they were alive.

Something different from these are the comical little

Whirls,

made by cutting circular pieces of writing- or common wrapping-paper into simple spiral forms (Fig. 57). The centre of the spirals are weighted by small pieces of wood, or other not too heavy substance gummed on the paper.

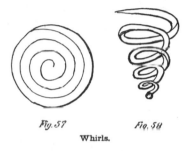

Fig. 57   *Fig. 58*

Whirls.

When a number of these are freed in mid-air the weight will draw the spirals out, and present a curious sight, as with serpentine motion they all come wriggling and twisting toward the ground (Fig. 58). In these paper fire-works, we know of nothing prettier than the

Winged Fancies,

consisting of birds and butterflies.

The birds may be cut out of wrapping-paper, measuring seven and a half inches long and ten inches from tip to tip of the wings (Fig 59), a burnt match stuck in and out of the neck, will give the bird sufficient weight. When tossed from a height these paper swallows fly and skim through the air in the most delightful birdlike fashion.

Both birds and butterflies are folded through the centre lengthwise, then unfolded and straightened out, this helps to give them form and they fly better.

8

The patterns here given are possibly not as graceful in shape as could be made, but the writer drew the patterns from the

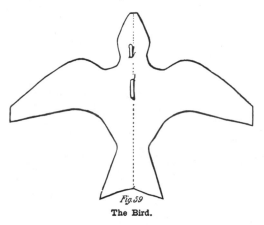

Fig. 59
The Bird.

best fliers among an experimental lot of winged fancies, having found them better than others that could boast of more beauty.

Butterflies are made of bright colored tissue-paper cut from the pattern (Fig 60), and have short pieces of broom-straws as weights. These also should be lightly thrown from a height, when they will flutter and fly downward, sometimes settling on a tree or bush as if seeking the sweets of flowers, and appearing very bright and pretty as they float hither and thither on the air.

A ring of the ever-twirling

Pin-wheels

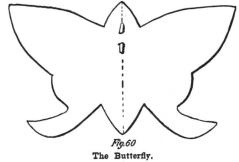

Fig. 60
The Butterfly.

is gay and attractive, just the thing for the lawn on the Fourth of July. To manufacture one, select a nice firm barrel-hoop, and nail it securely on one end of a clothes-pole or broom-stick (Fig. 61), sharpen the other end of the pole

to a point ; if the hoop seems inclined to split when nailing,
first bore holes with a gimlet or burn them
with a red-hot nail or wire for the nails to
pass through.

Cover the barrel-hoop several inches
deep with straw, lay the straw on and tie
it down with string.

Prepare a number of pin-wheels by
cutting squares of red and white and blue
paper, fold them twice diagonally through
the centre and cut the folds up within a
short distance of the middle. Turn over
every other point to meet the centre,
pierce the four points and the centre with
a pin, then fasten the pin firmly to the
end of a stick. The pin must be left long
enough to allow the paper to turn easily.

Stick the straw wreath full of pin-
wheels, then plant the pole securely in the
ground and you will have a ring of Fourth
of July pin-wheels which will look pretty
all day long.

Be sure to place the wreath facing
the breeze, so the pin-wheels may be kept in constant motion. Reserve the

Fig 61

Pin-wheel.

Bombs

until the last. They are simple in construction, but quite startling when they go off.

Fasten together two very stiff flat pieces of steel (Fig. 62),
those sold for the back of dress-skirts work well, and use
a strong string many yards long to tie them with. Bring
up the four ends of the steels and tie them with a slip knot

(Fig. 63), in order that it may easily fly open. Place the cage thus formed in the centre of a square piece of tissue-paper.

Now cut strips of different colored tissue-paper, four inches long, and twist each piece at one end.

Put these in the centre of the cage and bring up the four corners of the square of paper, allowing the string to come out of the top. Twist the corners together and close up the small openings by folding over the edges of the paper. This

Fig. 62

Fig. 63

makes a bomb somewhat resembling a common torpedo enlarged to many times its original size.

Pass the string through a screw-eye which has been screwed in the end of a flag-pole or broomstick, and place the pole out of the window. Then drop the end of the string down to the lawn below. Fasten one end of the pole in the window by binding it firmly to a strong, heavy chair, or secure it in any other way most convenient so there will not be the slightest danger of its falling.

Everything being ready, descend to the lawn, and pull the string so the bomb will rise slowly up to the pole.

When it is within a short distance of the screw-eye, give the twine a sudden sharp jerk which will cause the bomb to come in contact with the pole with sufficient force to untie the slip-knot, the elastic-metal ribs will fly back causing the bomb to burst and fill the air with bright shreds, flying, gliding, and darting everywhere in the most eccentric manner, making the air brilliant with floating colors.

Let your Fourth of July

Lawn Party

partake of the patriotic traditions, and as far as possible help to celebrate our Nation's birthday in an appropriate manner.

Paper fire-works may form part of the entertainment, it being optional with the hostess whether they come before or after the games, or are interspersed between them.

The party opens with the signing of the

Declaration of Independence.

To each guest is given a brown-paper bag, and when all have assembled on the lawn, the hostess steps forward facing the company, and asks all to kindly keep quiet and listen for a few moments while she reads or repeats their Declaration of Independence, she then reads :

We girls are, and of right should be, free and independent of all boys' sports, having resources and amusements befitting the celebration of the Fourth of July, independent of all those belonging exclusively to boys.

Then follows the signing of the same, by each in turn writing her name beneath the declaration. This accomplished, the hostess gives the signal and each guest fills her bag with air, by holding it close to her mouth, gathering it tightly around, and blowing into it, then grasping it firmly in the right hand, being careful not to let any air escape.

At another signal, all simultaneously bring their hands forcibly and quickly together, striking the paper bags with the left hand, which bursts the bags and causes a report almost equal to that of pistols.

All the bags exploding at one time, gives a salute worthy of the name and creates much merriment.

The salute may be varied by bursting the bags in quick succession, so that it will sound something like a volley of musketry.

This introduction is followed by games to be played on the lawn.

For the new game of

Toss,

make nine disks of card-board, painted or covered with paper, red and white and blue, three of each color.

Place in the centre of the lawn a fancy waste-basket, and let each player in turn stand at a distance of six feet from the basket. It is better to have the station marked by a stone or stick, at the place designated.

If played by sides, two stations, one on either side of the basket will be necessary.

The object of the game is to throw the disks into the basket, and they are valued according to color ; red counts one, white two, and blue three.

If played by sides, each side should play five rounds, ninety being the highest possible tally for any one player.

This is an easy and pleasant game, and may be played with or without sides. The hostess keeps account, and at the end of the game gives a knot of red, white, and blue ribbons as a prize to the one having the highest score.

We hardly recognize our old friends in the new and gigantic

Fourth of July Jackstraws.

These are all in holiday attire, and so much larger than any we have seen that they are even more attractive, and afford greater amusement than those which we have hitherto enjoyed.

It does not take long to make them. Cover a number of light slender sticks, three or four feet long, with paper or cloth, some red, some white, and others blue. The colors count respectively, red one, white two, and blue three. Provide another longer stick with a hook in one end to be used in taking the jackstraws from the pile.

Stand the sticks up so as to meet at the top, and spread out like a tent at the bottom. Each player then takes the hook in turn and tries to remove a jackstraw, without shaking or throwing down any of the others. The one scoring the highest, wins the game and is entitled to the prize.

Progressive games seem to be very popular, and deservedly so, as they possess an interest peculiarly their own.

Here is a new and novel one, called

Fig. 64.

Progressive Mining.

It is played with flower-pots filled with sand or loose earth, called mines. A small flag on a slender staff is placed upright in the centre of each flower-pot (Fig. 64). The staff should be stuck down in the sand only just far enough to keep it steady in its position. Each player in turn removes a little sand from the mine with a stick called a wand, taking

great care not to upset the flag ; for the one causing the flag
to fall loses the game. The number
of mines needed will depend upon
the number of persons playing, as
one flower-pot is required for every
two players.

Each one taking part in the game,
is provided with a wand. Slender
bamboo canes make excellent wands,
and may be decorated with red, white
and blue ribbons, tied on the handles.
Should the canes be difficult to procure, then any kind of light slender
stick will serve the purpose.

The hostess should prepare blank
envelopes, each containing a ribbon
badge, or score sheet, of different
colors, two of each ; these are all
numbered, the figures being painted
or pasted on the ribbons to designate
the place to be taken, thus two reds
are marked 1, meaning that they are
to occupy the first or prize mine. The
blues are marked 2, showing that
they take the second mine, and so on.
The last or lowest place is called the
booby mine. Each badge should
have a small pocket attached (Fig.
65), for holding stamps ; these are cut
in any desired form from gold and

Fig. 65

silver paper, which has previously
been covered with mucilage on the under side, like a common
postage-stamp.

The hostess passes around the envelopes, each guest takes one, and upon opening it discovers where and with whom she is to play.

The preliminaries being settled, and all having taken their places, the hostess starts the game by ringing a little bell.

When one of the players at the prize mine upsets the flag, the other calls out *prize*, and if the flags have not already fallen in the other mines, the couples play as quickly as possible until all the flags are down.

The winner at the prize mine fastens a gold stamp on her ribbon badge, while the loser at the booby mine, ornaments hers with silver seal.

The game is now rearranged, the winner at the prize mine remains at her station, and the loser goes down to the booby mine, while all those winning at the other mines move up, each one respectively to the next higher mine, for it is only at the prize mine where the loser moves her place and the victor remains stationary.

When these details are settled, the flag-staffs are again planted in the flower-pots and the signal given for a new game.

The player with the largest number of gold stamps on her score-sheet, receives the victor's prize, and the one having the most silver stamps is entitled to the booby prize.

The prizes are given when the game is ended. They should consist of some pretty little article made by the hostess herself, and, if practicable, appropriate to the day, such as a delicate satin sachet in the form of a Liberty bell, with the lettering painted on it.

A pretty pin-cushion, with a cover made of a miniature silken flag, or a dainty pen-wiper in the shape of Liberty's cap. Other more expensive gifts are not in good taste.

The booby prize should be something grotesque or comical.

As the mothers and sisters of 1776 took a full share in the

hardships and trials of the Revolution, and actively assisted in gaining our independence, it is eminently fit and proper that American girls should show their appreciation of such bravery and heroism by assisting in the annual celebration of our famous Independence Day.

Fourth of July seems heretofore to have been considered altogether too exclusively a boy's holiday, and it is with a hope of stimulating a renewed activity, and awakening in the heart of every girl in the United States a sense of proprietary interest in the day, that we suggest new methods of celebrating our national holiday.

CHAPTER X.

PRINTING FROM NATURE'S TYPES.

AST summer we made some lovely impressions of flowers, leaves, and sprays ; then we tried landscapes and all sorts of beautiful designs. It is really delightful and fascinating work. You are led on and on, always with a fancy to try something else to see how it will come out, and seldom, if ever, is it a disappointment or failure, a new interest being felt with every fresh print made. Moreover, you are sure of having your picture original and the only one of its kind, for as no two flowers or leaves are precisely alike, so no print can be an exact copy of another. And then it takes only a few moments for the work which could not be accomplished in thrice the time should a drawing be made of the same design.

Let me tell you how to make an " Impression Album" a book of printed flowers and leaves. You who have houseplants will find it a delightful winter recreation, a novel pleasure, and you can enjoy the pretty work even more during your summer vacation, with wild flowers at your command.

The " prints " are taken from the natural flowers or leaves themselves. Girls who have no knowledge at all of drawing or of printing can with little trouble make these Impression Al-

Making Prints.

bums, and students of botany will find the work supplies valuable memoranda of leaves and plants, as the print preserves details of the form, fibre and veining of foliage and petal such as no drawing or photograph can. The printing can be made wholly accurate, giving all the minutiæ of construction. The tools required to make these print-pictures

Pink Oxalis.

Smilax.

are simple, and consist of a piece of glass, a palette-knife or table-knife and some printers' ink which comes in small tin boxes and can be procured at any stationery store, and a pad made of a ball of cotton tied in a piece of soft silk or satin.

The printers' pad used by the writer for spreading the ink, was manufactured of the satin lining taken from a gentleman's old hat, and answered the purpose admirably, being a good size, measuring nearly four inches in diameter. The album

Evergreen Moss.

itself may be a common blank-book, with every other leaf cut out, in order to make room for the prints, which are on pieces

of blank unruled paper of uniform size, and small enough to fit
in the album and leave a margin all around the piece inserted,
so that the book when opened may be neat and attractive.
Having all your tools at hand, select the leaves you wish to
print. These must be free from dust or dew and perfectly fresh.

First, with your knife, place a small quantity of printers' ink
on the piece of glass and smooth it as evenly as possible over
the surface. Then press the printers' pad down lightly, lifting,
and again pressing, until the
ink is evenly distributed on the
pad ; next, select a leaf and
place it face, or right side, downward on a piece of folded newspaper; press the inked pad down
on the under side of the leaf,
which is now, of course, lying
upward, repeating the operation
until the leaf is sufficiently covered with ink. Carefully place
the leaf, inked side down, on
the centre of the piece of paper
you have previously cut for the
album ; over this lay a piece of
common yellow wrapping-paper,

Skeleton Geranium Leaves.

or any paper that is not too thick or stiff, and rub the finger
gently all over the covered leaf. Remove the outside paper
and very *carefully* take up the leaf. You will find an exact
impress of the natural green leaf showing every one of the delicate fibres.

The picture is now ready to be pasted in the album, with a
thin, delicate paste, touching only the corners. It is a good
plan to write under each leaf the name of the plant or tree from
which it was taken, with the date, and such facts as you would

like to recall. Very valuable botanical collections can thus be
made. Flowers are more difficult to print than leaves, owing
to less "relief" in the films;
still they make charming pictures when successfully
treated, sometimes

A Winter Landscape.
Printed from Nature's Type.

having the appearance of photographs of flowers with all the
lights and shadows.

When printing flowers, proceed in the same manner as with the leaves. Sweet peas, roses, daisies, wild carrot, clover, and verbenas, all make beautiful impressions which look like photographs. Grasses of various kinds also print well.

In making a spray, it is best to have a definite idea of the form you desire it to take. If possible secure as a copy a natural spray of the kind you wish to print. Then first print all the leaves in the positions they are to occupy, and connect them by drawing in the branch with pen and India-ink.

Maple Leaves.
Printed from Nature's Type.

The Winter Landscape is printed from dried twigs, grasses, and little leafless plants, so arranged as to resemble trees and shrubbery.

Only have a little confidence and you can make etchings from nature. Should you not understand drawing or composition, do not be discouraged; obtain a picture to copy, and then hunt up little plants and soft twigs as nearly as possible corresponding in shape and character to the trees in the copy; in this way you can produce very creditable landscapes.

Botanical impressions may be used for "fancy work" by being printed on satin, and the decorated satin made up as though it were painted or embroidered ; patches for silk quilts have been prettily decorated by this process. The printings also make beautiful patterns for outline work, much truer to nature than those made in any other manner and afford infinite variety for "borders" and "corners." Even satin dresses can be beautifully ornamented with impressions of leaves instead of the "hand painting" so long in use. You can, of course, see that should several colors of printers' ink be used, beautiful combinations and pleasing variety would be obtained, and that probably some unique and novel decorations would be secured.

Letter-paper ornamented with a delicate design printed from nature's types is very dainty and pretty, and in many other forms can these simple and beautiful decorations be used.

Then bring leaves and blossoms from the woods or dooryard, and half an hour may be delightfully spent in printing "impressions" which will teach a lesson in botany, while the great variety of leaf forms, difference in texture, fibre, veining and finish cannot fail to attract your attention and call forth your admiration.

Corn Roast.

CHAPTER XI.

PICNICS, BURGOOS AND CORN-ROASTS.

RACES of foreign ancestors are apparent occasionally in most of us, true Americans though we be. It is perhaps a spice of gypsy blood in our veins that sets our pulses throbbing with pleasant excitement when, seated in an old hay-wagon, we go bumping and thumping down the road prepared for a delightful holiday.

With camp-kettle swinging beneath, and coffee-pot stowed safely away within the wagon, do we not feel able to provide as savory dishes for our picnic dinner as any concocted by the gypsies themselves? Surely no coffee is ever so delicious as that cooked over the camp-fire, albeit it tastes somewhat smoky when prepared by hands inexperienced in the art of out-door cooking ; but if the fish we broil is a little burned, and the baked potatoes rather hard in the middle, who cares? Hearty, healthy appetites, which the early morning drive through the fresh, exhilarating air has developed, laugh at such trifles and dinner is voted a success in spite of sundry mistakes and mishaps in its preparation.

There are *picnics* and *picnics*. When one drives out in a fine carriage to meet a fine company, and partake of a fine lunch prepared by fine servants, is one kind.

When one goes with a large party, on a boat, and takes a lunch of sandwiches, cake, pickles, hard-boiled eggs, etc., which is spread on the grass at the landing and eaten as quickly as possible, is another kind ; but the picnic most enjoyed by young people who are not afraid of a little work, which is only play to them, is the one where the raw materials for the dinner are taken and the cooking, or most of it, is done, gypsy fashion, by the picnickers themselves.

A pleasant innovation in the ordinary routine of a picnic is

A Burgoo.

Thirty or forty years ago the men of Kentucky, in celebration of a holiday, would get up what they called a burgoo. In character it was very much like the clam-bake of to-day, but instead of chowder, or baked clams, the company prepared and partook of a soup or stew made of almost everything edible. Early in the morning the party would meet at the appointed place and decide what each should contribute toward the making of this most delectable stew.

Those who were fond of hunting would go forth in search of birds, squirrels, rabbits, and game of all kinds, with which the woods were filled. Some caught fish, and others provided fowl, pork, vegetables, and condiments.

As the ingredients were brought in, those who had charge of the cooking prepared and dropped them into an immense pot which, half full of water, was suspended over a roaring fire.

When everything of which the stew was composed was

cooked to shreds, the burgoo was pronounced done, and was served in tin cups, and eaten with shell spoons, made by splitting a stick and wedging a mussel-shell in the opening.

That this was a most appetizing feast I know from an old gentleman who has frequently attended the burgoos and partaken of the stew. Of course at a picnic composed of girls and boys, it would not do to depend upon the game which might be shot and the fish which might be caught, for the dinner, but the burgoo should be adapted to the ways and means of the party, and each member should provide something for the stew. The following recipe will make enough for fifteen or twenty persons.

Burgoo Stew.

Two pounds of salt pork, the same of lean beef; two good-sized chickens, or fowls of any kind ; two quarts of oysters, the same of clams ; twelve potatoes, four turnips, one onion, two quarts of tomatoes, and any other vegetables which may be obtainable. Make a bouquet of parsley, celery, and a very little bay-leaf, thyme and hyssop, tied together with thread.

Fig. 66

Put the beef, fowl, pork, oysters, clams and a handful of salt in a large iron kettle, three-quarters full of water ; skim it before it begins to boil hard, and add the other ingredients ; keep the kettle covered and boil until the bones fall from the meat. Serve hot with crackers. Wild game and fish may also be added to the recipe. When a burgoo is decided upon, it is best to prepare a light lunch to be eaten about eleven o'clock, and have the heartier meal at four or five in the afternoon, as it requires some time for the stew to cook.

Our illustration shows four ways of suspending the kettle over the fire. While the girls are preparing the ingredients for the stew, the boys will build a fire in some such fashion as is shown upon page 135, and put the kettle on. The best way to boil coffee is to make or build a kind of little stove of stones and mud, and set the coffee-pot on top, as shown in Fig. 66 ; this will prevent the smoky taste it is apt to have when placed directly on the fire.

A Corn-roast.

During the season when green corn is plentiful, there is no better way of having a real jolly time than by getting up a corn-roast. It is not as elaborate an affair as the burgoo. Some green corn, a long pole sharpened at one end, for each member of the party and a large fire built in some open space where there will be no danger of causing conflagration makes us ready for the corn-roast.

Several summers ago a gay party of friends from New York and vicinity took possession of and occupied for a few months a little cottage at a place on the coast of Maine called Ocean Point.

Toward the end of August, when all places of interest had been explored, when the stock of shells, star-fish, and such like treasures had grown beyond the accommodation of an ordinary trunk, and the minds of the sojourners were beginning to be filled with thoughts of a speedy return home, green corn, for the first time that summer, made its appearance. This was hailed with delight, and a farewell lark, in the form of a corn-

THEN THE BOYS WILL BUILD THE FIRE IN SOME SUCH FASHION AND PUT THE KETTLE ON roast, was promptly proposed and almost as promptly carried into execution.

The place selected on which to build the fire was a large rock jutting out into a little cove called "Grimes Cove." Here the party met about three o'clock in the afternoon, each member bringing only such dishes as were considered necessary for his or her own use. It is needless to say that the supply was not very plentiful, many limiting themselves to a cup and spoon ; still as the supper was to consist merely of roasted corn, bread and coffee, these answered every purpose.

Not only was the corn roasted on the ends of the long poles, but bread was toasted, and in true American fashion it was eaten piping hot. One of the gentlemen, much to the amusement of the rest of the party, produced a piece of breakfast bacon, which he fastened on to the end of his pole and toasted over the glowing embers, declaring that it was better cooked in that way than in any other.

Fig. 67

Yes, corn-roasts are great fun, and they can be held almost any place where a large fire can be safely built. It is best to allow the fire to burn down until it is a glowing pile of coals ; then sticking the sharp end of a pole into an ear of corn (Fig. 67), and standing as far from the fire as the length of the pole will permit, it can be held close to the hot embers until thoroughly cooked ; then with butter and salt this roasted corn is excellent eating.

Enough corn should be provided to allow several ears to

each member of the party, as mishaps are liable to occur, and the tempting ear of corn may be devoured by the flames, instead of the person for whom it was intended.

The poles, about six feet in length, should be as light as possible, for if too heavy they will tire the hands and arms of those holding them.

White Clover Design.

CHAPTER XII.

BOTANY AS APPLIED TO ART.

 HERE is a book of most lovely designs open to everyone whose eyes are open to see.

Grasses, leaves, blossoms, and even buds and seed-vessels supply material for beautiful patterns.

We need not look far for suggestions. Truly "that is best which lieth nearest, shape from that thy work of art."

At your very doorway the wonders of botany may be studied. Carefully inspect the tree blossoms in the early spring ; the maple, willow, birch, any in fact which happen to be convenient, and you will find suggestions of rare designs.

Clover, plantain, pepper-grass, dandelions, vines and twigs, offer ideas which can be adapted to ornamental art.

A love of nature will quicken and stimulate the faculties ; take the flowers and plants for instructors, and they will teach and guide you.

Though there cannot be found an exact duplicate of any blossom or leaf, still these may be conventionalized by arranging them in all sorts of symmetrical designs.

There is no mystery about the matter, for all the designs

are conceived upon the most simple of geometric laws. We are now following in the steps of the old masters, and an unlimited field of new combinations opens before us.

When making designs for this chapter, the writer did not select the objects she thought would be most decorative, but anything which chanced to fall in the way ; and what she has done you can do, provided, of course, that you have ordinary skill with the pencil.

The Peony Leaf.

Suppose you do not know how to draw at all ! Even then you can design. Take the first thing you see, which in this

Fig. 68.   Fig. 69.

case happens to be a peony leaf (Fig. 68). That is, assuming that you are seated by the side of the writer.

Now watch ! We will pull it apart thus (Fig. 69). Next with a pair of scissors, a knife, or fingers snip off the stems, and group the leaves in any way we chose. We will try this combination (Fig. 70). If you do not understand drawing, we must fasten the leaves down upon a piece of paper as they are arranged, and trace around them, following their edges

with a pencil until the outline is complete (Fig. 70). By simply repeating this figure at regular intervals we have a very
pretty border design and
one that is truly original,
for the writer had no more
idea than you, what was
to be the result of this experiment. In order to
make the pattern exact,
draw lines as in Fig. 71,
for a guide ; then draw
the figure according to the
foundation lines (Fig. 72).
When finished, erase the
lines and the design stands
a conventionalized peony
leaf, Fig. 73. By making
a tracing of the first pattern, you can repeat it any
number of times. It requires no great or peculiar genius to
design well, and it is a mistaken, old-fashioned idea to suppose

Fig. 70.

because you never have done any original work in art that you
never can. Do not slavishly follow other people, but believe

Fig. 74

Bunch of Turnips

that there is implanted in you the same elements that belong to those whose designs you admire, then commence and design for yourself. That you may have a start in your new art, we will try something else, a vegetable this time, for here comes the green-grocery man with a basket full of as quaint decorations as are ever painted with bamboo-handled brush by the Japanese.

A Bunch of Turnips.

Take the first bunch of vegetables on the top of the basket. What are they? turnips? Well that requires a little skill as a draughtsman, but we will sketch this one and you can copy it (Fig. 74). Now repeat it (Fig. 75), or place the bunches

Fig. 75.

in a row and you will have another border design. After a few experiments you will see that anything will make a decoration even the humble kitchen vegetables.

Decorative Lines.

Figs. 76 and 77 are simply graceful curves, such as anyone can make with a pen or pencil, and may be used in many

Fig. 78.   Fig. 76.   Fig. 77.

ways : cross them and they form Fig. 78, use this as half the design, duplicating it for the other half and it gives Fig. 79.

Fig. 79,

We now have graceful and beautiful foundation lines on which any vine or flower may be placed as ornamentation. We will

Fig 80

select the rose, allowing the lines to form the stems and using as ornament the bud, flower and seed-vessels, remembering that one side must be an exact duplicate of the other (see Fig. 80).

With these curves invent new designs by placing them together in different ways, and choose for decoration anything which may strike your fancy.

Plant Cross-section Designs.

Have you ever noticed how curiously some leaves are curled before opening ? Watch them as they commence to expand and grow, and you will be delighted with the great variety and unique designs formed by the folding and rolling of these leaf-buds.

Cut a bud square across in the centre with a sharp knife, and this will show the nicety of arrangment of the young

Fig.81   *Fig.82*   *Fig.83*   *Fig.84*

leaves. The leaf-bud of the sage (Fig. 81), rosemary (Fig. 82), apricot (Fig. 83), and still another variety of pattern (Fig. 84), are all singular natural designs.

The petals of flower-buds are also folded in many ways, affording odd designs ; if cut in like manner as the leaves, the cross-sections will be as beautiful. Fig. 85, the lilac bud, and the oleander (Fig. 86), give some idea of these odd designs.

Fig. 85   Fig. 86

Submit all kinds of buds to the test by cutting them in halves, and carefully examining the two parts, observe how nicely and

Fig. 87

orderly the leaves are folded together. In this way you will find many natural ornamental patterns.

Nor must we neglect the seed-vessels; when these in their

turn are cut open, they present excellent designs. Fig. 87 is a
cross-section of the seed-vessel of the harebell.   Other seeds
will furnish queer forms and figures to be obtained in no other
way.

Flower Sprays.

The common white clover with its trefoil leaf is very pretty,
and if a few sprays are placed together in a graceful manner it
is surprising how readily they
lend themselves to decoration.
Experiment with these, gather
a few blossoms and leaves,
group them on the centre of a
piece of paper, and make an
outline of the group ; then
trace it off in order to repeat
the copy at equal intervals
from the central figure (see illustration, page 138); this
makes a very simple and yet
beautiful design for embroidery, needle-work, or wall-paper
pattern.   In the same manner try grasses and different kinds
of flowers.

Fig.88

Conventional designs can also be formed by simply inclosing
a natural spray in a geometrical figure.   Fig. 88 is a circle, but
a square, triangle, diamond, oval, or any geometrical figure
may take the place of the circle.

Changing the Color

of a natural object gives still another style of ornamental art.
A spray of flowers and leaves in one color on a background of
different tint is an example.   The spray may be brown on a

yellow background, or a dull blue on white background, either way it will be conventionalized. So you see that by merely making natural objects all in one tint, you can have a great variety of designs suitable for china, embroidery, wall paper, and many other decorations. It is instructive to examine the panels, screens, or painted china of the Japanese. There is a freedom and crispness about their ornamental art, which is very attractive.

Fig. 89

The method the Japanese frequently employ is to diminish the size of the fruit or flowers while increasing the size of the leaves, and vice-versa; in this way they invent designs without losing the character of the object they copy, and it is really a very simple, yet effective method.

Suppose you try and see what you can make with it. The next time you have an opportunity, notice how the Oriental artists carry out this idea in their decorations, and it will help you in making your designs.

Fig. 91

Burs.

The tenacious little burs found clinging to your dress after a country walk, when grouped together are not without beauty. Fig. 89 is formed of four of these burs placed at right angles making an ornament, and when the ornament is repeated at regular intervals as in Fig. 90, it forms a border design.

Fig. 90.

Seeds with downy or feathery tails are well adapted for decorations ; three grouped together (Fig. 91), is a design of itself,

which may also be re-duplicated (Fig. 92). The horse-chest-
nut or buckeye is decorative, and makes an odd design (Fig.
93).   Also the seed-vessel of the
Velvet-leaf or Abutilon avicennæ
(Figs. 94 and 95).

The Water-Lily.

In the illustration of the water-
lily, the writer has conventionalized
it by curving the stem around the
flower and duplicating the same, always making the stem meet the next
lily, then inclosing the flowers in two straight lines, so forming

Fig. 92.

Fig. 93.

a water-lily border.   Now, girls, you can realize how very simple it is to apply botany to art, and make for
yourselves new and original designs.

The knowledge of plants is not only interesting but useful in connection with art,
in selecting and determining appropriate designs for wood-carving, hammered brass, or
any kind of ornamentation or decoration.   The cross-section of

Fig. 94.

Fig. 95.

some trees will furnish very good designs and the differently formed roots of plants and flowers will aid you in ornamental art.

So we find that Nature offers us exquisite designs, in many

Fig. 96.

shapes and forms, and we have only to stretch out our hand and take what we want.

"Beauty doth truly inhabit everywhere," for "it is mind alone that is beautiful, and in perceiving beauty, we only contemplate the shadow of our own affections."

A Door-Step Party. 1884

Quiet Games for Hot Weather

CHAPTER XIII.

DOOR-STEP PARTY AND QUIET GAMES FOR HOT WEATHER.

IN the State of Kentucky, in one of whose towns the writer's early childhood was spent, the summers are long, and frequently very hot spells occur when even in the early morning hours there is no refreshing coolness in the air. As the sun rises higher and higher in the heavens, its rays grow fiercer and fiercer, until by afternoon, the heat is so intense that few persons care to venture out of doors, unless compelled by business or necessity to do so. At dusk, however, after the heat of the day is spent, and the air, although not cool, is a degree or two less hot, the population of the town makes itself visible. Ladies and children clad in the thinnest of white and light colored muslin gowns, emerge from the houses to sit upon piazza and door-step, and there welcome the husband, father, and brothers of the family upon their return from business; that business which is never neglected no matter what the thermometer may register. After tea the door-steps are once more taken possession of, and to enter the house again until ready to retire for the night, is not to be thought of. Friends and neighbors making social calls are received and entertained informally upon the door-steps, and sometimes when the party becomes too large for the steps to accommodate, chairs are placed upon the pavement immediately in front of the door, and no one feels, while occupying one of these seats, that the position is at all public or conspicuous.

Hatless and bonnetless as all of the ladies and children are, the warmth of the evenings making all head coverings and extra wraps unnecessary and uncomfortable, the streets present a gay and fête-like appearance seldom seen in our eastern towns.

At least this is as it was when, as one of the band of merry children, I played " Oats-peas-beans " and " Come Philanders," upon the sidewalk, and I do not think these customs have changed much since then.

Later, when I and my young friends had outgrown the " ring-around-arosy " games, we used to gather upon the door-step, and there chatter away about the day's doings, or whatever interested us at the time. When tired of talking, we would amuse ourselves by playing quiet games or telling stories. Sometimes the thoughtful mother of our young hostess would add to our enjoyment by serving some light refreshment, such as ice-cream or fruit. The greatest treat, and the one most appreciated, was when we were invited to partake of a great crisp frozen water-melon, whose blood-red core, sweet as sugar and cold as ice, quickly melted away between the rosy lips of the little guests. We were not always thus favored, however ; the refreshments were ever a pleasant surprise, but the pleasure of our evening was not marred by their absence.

The remembrance of what very pleasant times we used to have at these impromptu little parties, urges me to devote some pages of this book to the description of a door-step party, that by acting upon the suggestion, others may enjoy them even as did that group of little Kentucky girls.

Now is just the time for a door-step party ; now when the beauty of the evening lures us from the lighted parlor to the shadowy piazza whose coolness is so attractive after the long, hot summer day. Here soft breezes fan our cheeks, and here, perhaps, the moonlight filtering through vine and trellis, is carpeting the floor with lacy shadows, and with its soft mysterious light is casting a glamour over all familiar things.

It is a modest little fête, this door-step party, a simple way of entertaining one's friends of a summer evening when the heat will not permit of the exertion of active games. The delightful out-door surroundings give it a novel charm and make it entirely different from the frolics usually indulged in during the winter season.

Because the entertainment is not noisy it need not be the less enjoyable, and a party of bright, merry girls will derive plenty of amusement and fun from the quiet games of a door-step party. The following will give an idea of what games are suitable for an occasion of this kind.

Five Minutes' Conversation

is not exactly a game, although there are rules which must be obeyed in order to make it interesting.

A programme with small pencil attached, like the one shown in Fig. 97, should be given to each guest upon her arrival. The engagements for five minutes' conversation are made by putting your name down on your friend's card opposite the time chosen for your conversation with her,

Five minutes only are allowed for one conversation.

Two or more consecutive engagements with one person are not allowable. When engagements are made and programmes filled, the hostess, or anyone willing to be time-keeper, must ring a bell giving notice that the conversation is to begin.

At the end of five minutes the bell is to be rung again, when all talking must instantly cease, the exchange of positions be quickly made, and a new conversation be commenced.

Fig. 97

The time-keeper should be strictly attentive to her duties, for the bell must be rung regularly at the end of every five minutes.

The hour allotted to this new mode of conversation will pass very quickly, and cannot become in the least tiresome, as the time spent in talking to any one person is so very short.

Blind-man's Singing-school.

One of the party must be blindfolded to take the part of teacher. The class composed of the rest of the players should sit in a line facing her.

The teacher informs her scholars that they will begin the lesson by singing the scales. Then the head girl, or the one at the top of the line, sings ah! and the next, ah! a little higher or lower, and so it goes down the line ; each one in turn uttering ah! in any key or note she please ; in a high shrill voice, or the deepest tone a girlish throat is capable of. The teacher should listen attentively, and when she thinks she recognizes a voice she must command the class to stop while she makes some criticism on the manner in which the note is sung, at the same time calling the singer by name.

When one of the players is named correctly, she must be blindfolded and become teacher, while the former teacher takes her place in the class.

A general exchange of seats is made before the singing lesson recommences, that the voices may not be guessed by the direction from which they come. To give variety to this game the second teacher may direct the class to sing a song, selecting some well-known nursery rhyme ; then, beginning at the top of the line as before, each player must sing the word which comes to her to supply. It is the privilege of each teacher to direct the class to sing whatever she may choose, either song or exercise.

A Game of Noted Men,

is played in this way : The hostess begins the game by saying, I know a celebrated poet ; the first part of his name is very black, and the last is an elevation. Whoever gives the right name, which is Coleridge (coal, ridge), in her turn describes the name of some noted person. She may choose Shakespeare and say, I give the name of a noted author and poet ; the first part is something people are apt to do when they are cold, the last is a weapon of warfare.

There are quite a number of names which will do nicely for this game ; a few of them are—

Wordsworth—words, worth.
Cornwall—corn, wall.
Howitt—how, it.
Milman—mill, man.

Shelley—shell, lea.
Washington—washing, ton.
Fillmore—fill, more.
Longfellow—long, fellow.

When giving a name to be guessed, the profession of the man, whether poet, author, statesman, or soldier, must be given, but nothing else should be told about him.

What will You Take to the Picnic?

can be played very nicely while the party are enjoying some light refreshments.

The hostess alone should be in the secret, and these directions are addressed only to her.

Commence the game by announcing that you propose to give a picnic, that it depends upon what your guests will bring for lunch whether they will be allowed to attend, and that each one must furnish two articles of food. Then ask the person nearest you, What will you take to the picnic? If the name of neither of the articles she mentions commences with the initial letter of her Christian name or surname tell her she cannot go, and put the question to the next person, asking each in turn, What will you take to the picnic?

For example, we will suppose that the name of one of the party is Susan Davis, and she says she will take crackers and lemons, she cannot go, as neither of her names commence with

C or L ; but if she proproses to take salmon and doughnuts, she will be doubly welcome, since S and D are both her initials. Should she say sugar and cream, she could go for one of her names commences with S.

Continue to put the question to each player until all, or nearly all, have discovered why their proposed contribution to the lunch secures them a welcome, or debars them from attending the picnic.

Assumed Characters.

In this game some well-known novelist is selected—Dickens, for instance—and each player chooses one of his characters to personate, telling no one her choice. Then one of the players relates the life as though it were her own, and portrays with voice and gesture the character she has assumed. Of course no names must be mentioned.

The person who first guesses what character is being personated has the privilege of deciding who shall be the next to tell her story.

The game of Assumed Characters will prove to be very entertaining if each player does her part and makes her narrative as amusing and interesting as possible.

Shadow Verbs.

A white sheet is fastened tightly across a French window, or doorway opening upon the piazza, and a large lamp set behind it.

The company separates into two parties ; one enters the house, while the other remains seated upon the piazza facing the suspended sheet.

The outside party chooses a verb which the others are to guess and perform. When their decision is made they call the leader of the inside party and say, " The verb we have chosen rhymes with rake," or whatever it may rhyme with. The leader then joins her followers and consults with them what the first guess shall be. It is best to take the verbs which rhyme with the noun given in alphabetical order. Bake would come first for rake, and if it is decided that they shall act this, several of the party step before the lamp, which casts their shadows on the sheet and, without speaking, go through the motions of making and baking bread. If the guess is right (that is if to bake was the verb chosen) the spectators clap their hands; if wrong, they cry, No, no.

When they hear the no, no, the actors retire and arrange what to do next. Make, quake, take, wake are all acted in turn, until the clap of approval announces that they have been successful in guessing the verb. Then the actors take the seats vacated by the spectators, who in their turn enter the house to become shadows and act the verbs chosen by the other party, and the game goes on as before. A little ingenuity on the part of the players in producing funny and absurd shadows makes the whole thing very laughable and causes great amusement.

There are an unlimited number of games that may be played, but the object of this chapter is not so much to describe the games as it is to illustrate those that are appropriate to the quiet and delightful entertainment known as a doorstep party.

CHAPTER XIV.

HOW TO MAKE A HAMMOCK.

NDERNEATH the spreading branches of the cool, shady tree swings our hammock. Through the intertwining boughs the golden sunlight is sifted in bright little dashes on the leafy foliage below. Lying ensconced in its lacy meshes idly listening to the hum of the busy bumble-bees at work among the red clover, or gazing up through the leafy canopy to the blue heavens where now and then fleecy white clouds float softly past, or watching a flight of birds skim o'er the distant horizon, who would not be lulled by the harmony of the summer day! A delightful languor steals over us and we unconsciously drift into the land of dreams where perfect rest is found. We awaken refreshed, to again gently swing back and forth and vaguely wonder who could have first thought of this most delightful invention. It is said that we owe the luxury to the Athenian, General Alcibiades, who, in 415 B.C. first made the swinging bed. The word hammock is taken from hamacas or hamac, an Indian word which Columbus relates as being used by the Indians to signify a hanging bed composed of netting. What these uncivilized red men made with their rude implements, we ought to be able with our modern facilities to accomplish very easily and quickly.

Home-made Comforts.

It is not difficult to make a hammock ; anyone can soon knit
one that is strong and comfortable, and it should not cost more

Fig.98

Fig.99

Mesh-sticks.

than fifty cents.   The materials required will be one hammock-
needle about nine inches long (this can be whittled out of hickory or ash, or purchased for ten cents) ; two
iron rings two and one-half inches in diameter, which will cost about five cents each ;
two mesh-sticks or fids, one twenty inches
long and eight inches wide bevelled on both

Fig. 100.—Hammock Needle.   Fig. 101.—The Loop.   Fig. 102.—Small Fid and Loop.

edges (Fig. 98) : the other nine inches long and two and one-
half inches wide, bevelled on the long edge (Fig. 99) ; these
you can easily make yourself from any kind of wood.

II

One pound of Macremé cord number twenty-four, or hammock twine of the same number, which can be had for less than

thirty cents; colored cord comes five cents extra.

Wind the cord in balls, as it is then more convenient to handle, and begin making your hammock. First, thread the needle by taking it in the left hand and using the thumb to hold the end of the cord in place, while looping it over the tongue (Fig. 100); pass the cord down under the needle to the opposite side and catch it over the tongue; repeat this until the needle is full.

Next, make a loop of a piece of cord two yards long and fasten this to any suitable place

(Fig. 101)—a door-knob will do very well; then tie the cord on your needle three inches from the end to this loop. Place the small fid under the cord, the bevelled edge close to the loop (Fig. 102). With your thumb on the cord to hold it in place while you pass the needle around the fid, and with its point toward you, pass it through the loop from the top, bringing it over the fid, so forming the first half of the knot (Fig. 103). Pull this taut, holding it in place with your thumb while throwing the cord over your hand, which forms the loop as in (Fig. 104). Then pass the needle from under through the loops, drawing it tight to fasten the knot. Hold it in place with your thumb, and repeat the operation for the next knot. Fig. 105 shows a number of these knots finished. A is a loosened knot, making plain its construction. B, in Figs. 103, 104, and 105, is the cord running to the needle, and D is the fid.

Fig. 106.—Meshes.

When thirty meshes are finished shove them off the fid (Fig. 106), as this number will make the hammock sufficiently wide.

Commence the next row by again placing the fid under the cord, and take up the first mesh, drawing it close to the fid; hold it in place with your thumb while

Fig. 107.—Commencing the Second Row.

throwing the cord over your hand; pass the needle on the left hand-side of the mesh from under through the loop thrown over your hand (Fig. 107); pull this tight and you will have tied the common knitting-knot; proceed in like manner with all the loops in rotation until the row is finished. When it is

necessary to thread or fill your needle, tie the ends of the cord with the fisherman's knot shown in Fig. 108, which

Fig. 108.—Fisherman's Knot.

cannot slip when properly tightened. Wrap each end of the cord from the knot securely to the main cord with strong thread to give a neat appearance to the hammock.

Continue knitting until thirty rows are finished.

Then use the large fid, knitting one row on the short side first, next one on the long side. This accomplished, knit the meshes to the ring by passing the needle through it from the top, knitting them to the ring in rotation as if they were on the mesh-stick or fid (Fig. 109). When finished tie the string securely to the ring, and one end of your hammock is finished.

Cut the loop on which the first row was knitted, and draw it through the knots. Tie the end of the cord on your needle to the same piece used in fastening

Fig. 109.
On the Ring.

Fig. 110.

the end of the first needleful to the loop (Fig. 110), and knit the long meshes to the other ring as described. This completed, the hammock is finished.

To swing it, secure two pieces of strong rope and fasten them firmly to the iron rings, the length of the rope depending upon the space between the two points from which you wish it to hang. These should be if possible twelve or fifteen feet apart and at least ten feet high, to give your hammock sufficient room to swing freely.

This suspended bed will furnish a welcome retreat when the weather is too warm to admit of games, walks, or other amusements. Then, with some favorite book, or if even reading is too much of an exertion, simply to lie indolently in the hammock is a comfort, so restful and quiet that the time quickly passes, and we are made better and brighter for our short, passive repose.

Very decorative nets, and useful ones of many kinds, including fish-nets and minnow-seines, are made with the same stitch as that used in the hammock. The size of the mesh is regulated by the circumference of the fid, and the twine used is fine or coarse, according to the style of net desired.

Barrel Hammock.

When in the Catskills last summer the writer saw for the first time a hammock made of a barrel. It was painted red and looked very cheery and inviting hanging under the green boughs ; the two colors, being complementary, harmonized beautifully.

This hammock was made of a piece of strong rope twenty feet long threaded in and out of barrel staves, and was substantial and durable. The construction of such a hammock is very simple. Remove the top and bottom hoops and nails from a firm, clean barrel. Then before taking off the remaining hoops draw a pencil-line around both ends of the barrel, being careful to have the marking three inches from and parallel to the edges ; this is for a guide when making the two holes in each end of all the staves. Bore the holes with a five-eighth of an inch augur or a red-hot poker, using the pencil-line as a centre ; leave an equal margin on both sides of the staves, and at the same time enough space in the centre to preclude all danger of breakage.

Fasten the staves together by threading the rope through the hole from the outside of the first stave, then across the inside of the stave down through the other hole (see illustration). Continue threading until one side is finished, then in like manner thread the other side. Knock off the remaining hoops and the staves will appear as shown at bottom of illustration. Tie the two ends of the rope together and fasten loops of rope on both ends ; these should be of sufficient length to conveniently swing the hammock. When threading the staves let the rope be loose enough to leave a space of an inch or so between each stave when the barrel is spread out in the form of a hammock.

In this way you can have a serviceable hammock, the cost of which will be about twenty-five cents and a little labor.

Grandmamma's Dolls.

CHAPTER XV.

CORN-HUSK AND FLOWER DOLLS.

O such beautiful dolls as delight the hearts of the children of to-day, ever peeped forth from the Christmas-stockings of our grandmothers or great-grandmothers when they were little girls. In those times there were not, as there are now, thousands of people doing nothing but making toys for the entertainment and pleasure of the little ones, and the motherly little hearts were fain to content themselves with lavishing unlimited affection and care upon a rag, wooden, or corn-husk baby, made and dressed at home. Since then almost every child tired of, and surfeited with handsome and expensive toys, has been glad at times to get grandma to make for her a real old-fashioned dollie which might be hugged in rapturous moments of affection without fear of dislocating some of its numerous joints, or putting out of order its speaking or crying apparatus;

and might in times of forgetfulness be dropped on the floor
and suffer no injury thereby.   Such a doll is just the kind to
adopt for the summer.   The fine French doll with
its delicate wax or china face, silky hair, and
dainty toilets, is more suited to the elegances of
the parlor than to the wear and tear of out-door
life, and everyone knows that summer holidays
spent in the country are far too precious to be
wasted taking care of anyone's complexion, let
alone a doll's ; so it is best to leave the city doll
in her city home, safe out of harm's way, and
manufacture, from materials to be found in the
country, one more suited to
country surroundings.

Corn - husks, corn - cobs,
and ordinary garden flowers
can be made into dolls which,
although not quite so pretty
nor so shapely as those produced from more costly material, yet possess a charm
of their own which the children are not slow
to perceive.

Fig. III
Head Commenced.

Little Indian girls, to whom store babies
are unknown, make the most complete and
durable corn-husk dolls, and the following
directions tell just how to construct them :

Provide yourself with the husks of several large ears of corn, and from among
them select the soft white ones which grow
closest to the ear.   Place the stiff ends of

Fig. 112
The Corn Husk.

two husks together, fold a long, soft husk in a lengthwise strip,
and wind it around the ends so placed as in Fig. 111.   Select

the softest and widest husk you can find, fold it across the centre and place a piece of strong thread through it (as in Fig. 112), draw it in, tie it securely (Fig. 113), place it entirely over the husks you have w o u n d, then bring it down smoothly and tie with thread underneath (Fig. 114); this will form the head and neck. To make the arms,

Fig. 115
Head and Arms.

divide the husks below t h e n e c k in two equal parts, fold toge t h e r t w o ui m o r e husks and i n s e r t them in the division (Fig. 115). Hold the arms in place with one hand, while with the other you fold alternately over each shoulder several layers of husks, allowing them to extend down the

Fig. 113
Corn-husk Tied.

Fig. 114
Head Finished.

front and back. When the little form seems plump enough, use your best husks for the topmost layers and wrap the waist with strong thread, tying it securely (Fig. 116). Next divide the husks below the waist and make the legs by neatly wrapping each portion with thread, trimming them off evenly at the feet. Finally, twist the arms once or twice, tie, and trim them off at the hands. The features can be drawn on the face with pen and ink, or may be formed of small thorns from the rose-bush. Fig. 117 shows the doll complete, minus its costume, which may be of almost any style or material, from the pretty robe of a civilized lady to the more

Fig.116
Head, Arms, and Body.

Fig.117
Finished Doll.

scanty garments of its originator, the Indian. The doll is represented in full Indian costume in Fig. 118. The war-paint and tomahawk are not necessary here, as he is smoking a pipe of peace. His apparel is composed of one garment, which is cut from a broad, soft corn-husk, after the pattern given in Fig. 119. A narrow strip of husk tied about his waist forms the belt.

His head-dress is made of small chicken feathers stuck at

regular intervals into a strip of husk. The corn-silk hair is placed on his head, and on top of that one end of the head-dress is fastened with a thorn.

A small twig is used for the stem of his pipe, and two rose-bush thorns form the bowl. Instead of using a thorn for his

Fig. 118
A Real Indian Doll.

Fig. 119
The Indian's Dress.

mouth, a round hole is punched in the face and the stem of the pipe inserted.

Mary Jane.

Here is another way of making a doll which is very easy and simple. First find a young ear of corn, one on which the silk has not turned brown ; then with a crab-apple for a head and a leaf of the corn to dress her with, you have your material.

12

Cut off squarely that end of the ear where the husks are puckered, to join the stalk, and carefully take the silk from the other
end, disturbing as little as possible the closely wrapped husks.

Roll part of the leaf (as indicated in Fig. 120) for the arms,
then with a small twig fasten the head to the arms ; stick the

Material and Parts of Doll.   Mary Jane.

other end of the twig into the small end of the corn-cob, and
the doll is ready for dressing. Her bonnet is made of the leaf
just where it joins the stalk (Fig. 121), and is fastened to her
head with a thorn. Before adjusting the bonnet, however, the
silk must be placed on the head to form the hair.

Make the scarf of part of the leaf (Fig. 122), fold it around the shoulders, and secure it with thorns.

The features also are made of thorns.

When her toilet is complete, you can but acknowledge that this rosy-cheeked little maid, peeping from beneath her poke-bonnet, is very cunning indeed.

Flower Dolls.

The flower lady with the baby is made of a yellow gourd flower; the small gourd attached, which has just begun to

form, serves for her head; a green gourd leaf is used for her shawl, and her bonnet is made of a smaller leaf folded to fit her head. The baby is a white gourd bud, with a cap made of a leaf. A small twig stuck through part of the lady's shawl, through the baby, and into the lady doll, holds the child in place and makes it appear as though clasped in the mother's arms.

The features of both dolls are scratched on with a pin and then inked. To make the lady stand erect, a small twig is stuck into the heart of the flower, and the other end into the top of a small paste-board-box lid.

The other flower doll is made of the common garden flowers. The underskirt is a petunia ; a Canterbury-bell forms the over-skirt and waist; small twigs, or broom-straws stuck through buds of the phlox, are the arms, and the head is a daisy with the petals cut off to look like a bonnet. The features are made with pen and ink on the yellow centre. A reversed daisy forms the parasol.

If the flowers named are not at hand, those of a similar shape will answer just as well.

Gaily dressed little ladies can be made of the brilliantly tinted hollyhocks, and many other flowers can also be trans-formed into these pretty though perishable dolls.

CHAPTER XVI.

HOW TO MAKE A FAN.

" That graceful toy whose
moving play
With gentle gales relieves
the sultry day."

FAN is only a pretty trifle,
yet it has been made rather
an important one. To man-
age a fan gracefully was some
time ago considered very essential by fair dames of society, and in the dainty hand
of many a famous beauty it
has played a conspicuous
part. Queen Elizabeth regarded it with so much favor that
she was called the " Patron of Fans," and she made a rule that
no present save a fan should be accepted by English queens
from their subjects.

Although held in such high esteem, it is only since the in-
flux of any and every thing Japanese that we have had fans in
such profusion, and have discovered how effective they are
when used for decorative purposes.

A brilliantly tinted fan is of equal value in giving just the
right touch of color to a costume or the decorations of a room,
and this chapter will show how the girls can make the fans

themselves, and have for use or for the adornment of their rooms those of various shapes, sizes, and colors. The first fan represented here is made in the form of a butterfly. The principal articles necessary for its manufacture are a strip of smooth, brown wrapping-paper, stiff enough to keep its folds, and two sticks for handles. The ribbon which, in the illustration, ties the handles together looks pretty, but is not indispensable; an elastic band, or one made of narrow ribbon, slipped over the sticks will do as well.

Butterfly Fan.

The paper must be twenty-eight inches long and five and one-half inches wide. In order to fold it evenly it should be ruled across with lines one-half inch apart, as shown in diagram of butterfly (page 179). When the paper is prepared the pattern can be copied from the diagram, which is half of the butterfly. By counting the lines and using them as guides for obtaining the proportions, an exact reproduction of

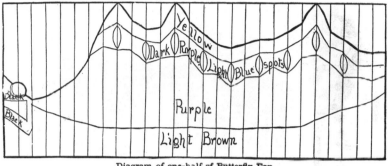

Diagram of one-half of Butterfly Fan.

this pattern can be made. The outlines being drawn, the paper must be plaited, one fold on top of another, until twenty-seven plaits have been laid. Smoothing out the paper again, the butterfly should be painted with water-colors in flat, even tints.

The lower part of diagram is the body of the insect and is of a light-brown color, also the space just below the head, which is surrounded by a strip of black.

The head and eyes are black, the eyes having a half-circle of white to separate them from the head. The main part of the wings

Fig. 123.   Fig. 125.
Folded Fans.

Fig 124.
Handle.

are a brownish purple, next to which comes a border of very dark purple with light-blue spots. The outer border is light yellow. When the paint is quite dry the extra paper at the top of the butterfly is to be cut away. Again the fan must be

plaited in the folds already formed, and the plaits fastened together at one end with a strong needle and thread, as shown in diagram (Fig. 123). Fig. 124 shows the shape of the handles, two of which are required; they should be about nine inches long, one-third of an inch wide,

The Mikado Fan.

and one-eighth of an inch thick. A handle must be glued to the last fold at each end of the fan (see Fig. 125). The fan should be kept closed until the glue is dry, when it may be opened and used at pleasure.

Our next sketch is that of the Mikado fan, and represents a Japanese lady who, with her fan held aloft, is making a bowing salutation.

This fan is made of the same paper as that used for the butterfly, and is cut the same width ; there are, however, twenty-nine plaits instead of twenty-seven, as in the other. The diagram gives the pattern in two parts, and the colors it is to be painted ; the face and hands should be of a flesh-tint and the features done with black in outline. The directions for putting together the butterfly apply as well to the Mikado fan.

Pattern of Mikado Fan.

The third illustration shows a fan made in the shape of a daisy. Diagram on page 183 shows a section of the pattern.

White paper should be used, and it must be laid in thirty-four plaits, which will give the flower fifteen whole and two half petals, the half petals being at each end.

The tinted part of pattern indicates where it is painted yellow to form the centre of the daisy.

For a plain round fan no pattern is needed. It is made simply of a strip of paper, of the width used for the other fans, and has about thirty plaits. When fans of this kind are made of colored paper in solid tints they are very pretty. Pieces of bright, figured wall-paper left from papering a room can be utilized, and quite effective fans be made of them to use for decoration.

Daisy Fan.

Another style of fan is represented in our last illustration. It is made of twenty slats of cardboard cut after pattern Fig. 126. These slats are joined together at the top and centre with narrow ribbon passed through the slits cut for it, as shown in Fig. 127. Over the ribbon where it passes through the top slits, on the wrong side of the fan, square pieces of paper are pasted, which hold the ribbon down securely at these points. The paper is pasted only at each end of the ribbon in the middle row. It is best to leave one end of this ribbon loose until the fan is joined at the bottom ; then opening the fan, and drawing the ribbon until it fits the fan smoothly, it can be cut the right length and the loose end fastened down. A ribbon is also used to hold the slats together at the bottom ; a bow at each side keeps them in place (see Fig. 128). When a large fan for decoration is desired, the slats should be about eighteen inches long, two and a half inches wide at the top, and one and a half inch wide at the bottom. The fan may be larger still, in which case it can be used as a screen to set before an empty fire-place. For this purpose the slats have to be two feet long, four inches wide at the top, and two and a half inches wide at the bottom.

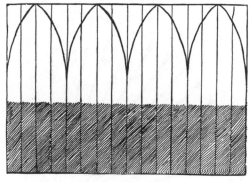

Pattern for Daisy Fan.

The proportions of the slats for a small hand-fan are eight and a half inches long, one and a half inch wide at the top, and one inch wide at the bottom. The large fans should be made of heavier cardboard or pasteboard than that used for smaller ones.

Construction of Cardboard Fan.

Colored cardboard, which can be bought at almost any stationer's, is the best to use, but the slats of ordinary white cardboard may be covered with colored paper if more convenient.

These fans may be varied to suit the taste of the girls who make them.   Instead of a solid color, one can be made with

alternate slats of red and white, blue and yellow, or any other colors that harmonize. Another may show all the tints of the rainbow, and for use on the Fourth of July one might display the red, white, and blue.

Some will look especially handsome if prettily painted. A dark-red fan with a branch of dogwood-blossoms painted across it makes a charming wall decoration, as does also one of light blue with pine-branch and cone painted in brown or black.

Cardboard Fan.

A gilt fan lightens up a dusky corner beautifully; it can be curved around to fit the place, and catching and reflecting the light at all angles, as it does, it is quite effective.

CHAPTER XVII.

ALL-HALLOW-EVE.

R A D I A N T and beautiful October, whose changing color heralds the approach of winter, gives us our first autumn holiday, if Halloween can now be called a holiday. Before the Christian era, in the days of the ancient Celts and their priests, the Druids, the eve of the first of November was the time for one of the three principal festivals of the year. The first of May was celebrated for the sowing; the solstice on the twenty-first of June for the ripening, and the eve of the first of November for the harvesting. At each of these festivals great fires were built on the hill-tops in honor of the sun, which the people worshipped. When Christianity took the place of the heathen religion, the Church, instead of forbidding the celebration of these days, gave them different meanings, and in this way the ancient harvest-festival of the Celts became All-Hallow-Eve, or the eve of All-Saints-Day, the first day of November having been dedicated to all of the saints.

For a long while most of the old customs of these holidays were retained; then, although new ceremonies were gradually introduced, Hallow-Eve remained the night of the year for wild, mysterious, and superstitious rites. Fairies and all supernatural beings were believed to be abroad at this time, and to exercise more than their usual power over earthly mortals. Because the fairy folk were believed to be so near us on Hallow-

Kaling.

een, it was considered the best evening of the season for the practice of magic, and the customs observed on this night became mostly those of divination, by the aid of which it was thought the future might be read.

Before proceeding further with this subject we desire our readers to appreciate and fully understand that we are far from wishing to inculcate any superstitious belief in the power of charms to forecast future events; that we regard all fortune-telling as nonsense, pure and simple, and only insert it here, as we would any other game, for the sake of the amusement it affords. Although, to make our descriptions more intelligible, we announce the results of charms as facts, we would not have it understood that they are to be taken as such.

Nowadays, so practical has the world become, no fairy, witch, or geni could we conjure up, were we to practice all the charms and spells ever known to soothsayer or seer. Our busy, common-sense age allows no fairies to interfere with its concerns, and these creatures, who existed only in the belief of the people, must needs vanish, to return no more, when that belief is gone.

A few fortune-telling games are all that now remain of the weird ceremonies that once constituted the rites of Halloween, and the spirit of this old heathen holiday is once more changed, for it is now considered only an occasion for fun and frolic.

It was the custom for quite a number of years of some friends of the writer to give a Halloween party on each recurring Halloween ; and merrier, jollier parties than those were, it would not be easy to devise. The home which opened wide its hospitable doors to the favored few on this night is a country-house, large and spacious; there is a basement under the whole lower floor, which is divided into kitchen, laundry, and various store-rooms intersected with passages, and this basement, deserted by the servants, was given up to the use of the Halloween revellers. The rooms and passage-ways were decorated

with and lighted by Chinese lanterns, which produced a subdued glow in their immediate vicinity, but left mysterious
shadows in nooks and corners.

Putting aside conventionality and dignity as we laid aside
our wraps, ready for any fun or mischief that might be on
hand, we proceeded down-stairs and into the kitchen, where
a large pot of candy was found bubbling over the fire. This
candy, poured into plates half-full of nuts, was eaten at intervals during the evening, and served to keep up the spirits of
those who were inclined to be cast down by the less pleasing
of Fortune's decrees. With plenty of room and no fear of
breaking or destroying anything, which is apt to put a check
upon frolics in the parlor, the company could give full vent to
their high spirits. Now in this room, now in that, again flitting
through the dim passages and around dark corners, each person
seemed to be everywhere at once, and although the party was
limited to about twenty-five, there appeared to be at least twice
that number present. Bursts of merry laughter and little
screams of pretended terror would announce, now and then, that
some charm was being gone through with and someone's fortune being told. All sorts of games were played, and the variety of our entertainment made the evening pass very quickly.
All too soon the hands of the kitchen clock warned the guests
that to reach home at a seasonable hour they must put an end
to their Halloween festivities. A number of the following
methods of telling fortunes were tried at these parties, one
might say with success, for we certainly succeeded in accomplishing our main object, which was, to have a good time. By

Melted Lead

we used to ascertain what the occupation of one's future husband would be. The fortune is told in this way : Each girl, in

turn, holds a door-key in one hand, while with the other hand she pours the melted lead, from an iron spoon or ladle, through the handle of the key into a pan of cold water.

In the fanciful shapes the lead assumes can be traced resemblances to all sorts of things. Sometimes it is a sword or gun, which indicates that a soldier will win the fair prize; again, traces of a ship may be seen: then the favored one is to be a sailor; a plough suggests a farmer; a book, a professor, or perhaps a minister; and when the lead forms only drops, it seems to mean that the gentle inquirer will not marry, or if she does, her husband will be of no profession.

Nutshell Boats

foretell in a general way what their owner's future life will be. They should be prepared beforehand in this manner : Split an

Fig.129

English walnut directly in half, remove the kernel, and clear away any of the partitions which may remain in the shell; then place a short piece of heavy cotton string in the shell and pour around it melted beeswax. Mould the wax into a cone shape around the string, as shown in Fig. 129, allowing the end to come out at the top. Fig. 130 shows what it is like when finished.

Fig.130

The tapers first being lighted, several of these little craft are launched at the same time, by their respective owners, upon the sea of life, or, in other words, in a tub of water.

When a light burns steadily until the wax is all melted, and the frail bark safely rides the waves (which are occasioned by stirring the water with a stick, or shaking the tub from side to side), a happy life is predicted, and a long one.

When two boats come in contact, it means that their owners will meet and have mutual interests some time during their lives.

If one boat crosses another's path, it denotes that their owners will do the same.

If two boats come together and continue to sail about side by side, their owners will in some way pass much of their lives together.

When a boat clings closely to the sides of the tub, refusing to sail out into the centre, it shows that its owner will be a stay-at-home.

Touching often at the side of the tub is indicative of short voyages ; and extended travel is predicted when a boat seldom touches the tub.

It depends a good deal upon the fancy and imagination of those testing their fate how the antics of the little fleet are interpreted, and the meanings given to the movements of the boats create no end of fun.

"Three Luggies." *

" In order, on the clean hearth-stane,
   The luggies three are ranged,
And ev'ry time great care is ta'en
   To see them duly changed."

The three bowls, or dishes, one containing clear water, one milky, and the other nothing at all, are placed in a row on the hearth-stone or table, and the girl wishing to try her fortune is blindfolded and led up to where the dishes stand. She is then told to put her left hand into one of the bowls. If she dips her fingers in the clear water, she will marry a bachelor ; if in the milky water, a widower ; and if into the empty bowl, it is a sure sign that she will live in single blessedness all her days.

This ceremony must be gone through with three times, and the hand be dipped twice in the same bowl, in order to make the prediction of any value.

Roasting Nuts

is the charm by which the friendship of anyone may be tested. The applicant for knowledge on this point names two nuts, one for her friend and the other for herself, and then places them side by side upon the grate, or a shovel held over the fire. If they burn quietly, it is prophetic of a long and happy friend-

* Dishes.

ship kept up by both parties ; but if in roasting they burst with a loud report and fly apart, they are decidedly uncongenial, and should not seek much intercourse. The movements of the nuts while heating are closely watched, for the tempers of the persons for whom they are named is said to be thus revealed.

Kaling

is a mode of telling one's fortune not as well known, perhaps, as the foregoing methods. The ceremony is carried out in the following manner : Two girls are blindfolded and started off on the path to the kitchen-garden and cabbage-patch, where each pulls up the first stalk she finds. They then return at once to the house, where the bandages are removed and the mysterious stalks examined.

According to the state of the stalk, so will be the gatherer's fate. If it is straight or crooked, large or small, so will the future husband be ; if it has a pleasant taste, or the reverse, the character of the person will correspond, and the quantity of earth clinging to the roots denotes whether their riches will be little or great.

When there are no cabbages at hand, almost any other garden vegetable will answer ; and if there be objections to going out-of-doors, vegetables of various kinds, such as turnips, beets, and parsnips, may be placed on a table, and the persons blindfolded can choose from them. No doubt the charm will work as well with the plants upon a table as when they are pulled from a kitchen-garden.

The Magic Mirror,

which is simply a hand-glass on ordinary occasions, and gains its mysterious power only on Halloween, divulges, under certain conditions, the delightful secret of how many bits of good-fortune will fall to one's share during the ensuing year. The conditions are that the person wishing to know how bright her prospects are shall go to an open window or door from which the moon is visible, and, standing with her face in-doors, hold her mirror so that the moon will be reflected in it. The number of moons she sees there betokens the number of times something pleasant will happen to her before the advent of another Halloween.

Three Tin Cups

partially filled with water are balanced on the small ends of three funnels, which are placed in a row on the floor, about two feet apart. Over these cups, one after another, each member of the party must leap in turn. Whoever succeeds in leaping over all three cups without knocking any of them off will make an early marriage. The person who knocks over one will marry when not so young. The marriage of the one who tips over two cups will be deferred until late in life, and she who leaps none of them safely will not be married at all.

To guard against wet feet very little water should be put in the cups—only enough to make the players careful about tipping them over.

The Ring Cake

is always an object of interest at Halloween parties. The cake itself is made like the ordinary kind, but before it is baked a plain gold ring is hidden in the dough, not to be taken out until the cake is cut and it falls to the share of the fortunate person in whose slice it happens to be found. The ring is sometimes put in a flour-cake, which is simply flour packed into a cake-mould so firmly that when it is turned out it retains the shape of the mould and can be sliced off with a knife. Each member of the party cuts her or his own section of flour, and whoever secures the ring, it is confidently stated, will be the first of the group to marry.

Some Halloween games apparently have no particular meaning attached to them, but seem to be devised for the purpose of creating as much fun as possible.

Bobbing for Apples

is, perhaps, familiar to most of our readers, but we give a description of it here for the benefit of the few who may not know the game so well.

In a large tub full of fresh, cold water several apples are placed, and it is the object of the participators to take them out of the water with their teeth.

As the rosy-cheeked, tempting fruit bobs about within easy reach, it looks simple enough to secure a prize ; but the apples are so round and slippery, so aggravatingly illusive, that, unless you thrust your head and neck beneath the cold water, regardless of consequences, and drive an apple to the bottom, the feat cannot be accomplished. The girls can seldom be induced to try their luck in this game, but usually content themselves with looking on, immensely enjoying the frantic endeavors of the boys to succeed at any cost.

The Apple and Candle Game

is another favorite sport for Halloween, and is played as follows : From the ceiling is suspended a stout cord, the lower end of which is securely tied to the centre of a stick about a foot and a half long. On one end of the stick is fastened an apple, on the other a lighted candle. The string is set in motion, swinging back and forth like a pendulum, and the contestants for the prize stand ready, each in turn, to make a grab for the apple, which must be caught in the teeth before it can be won. Frequently the candle is caught instead of the apple, which mishap sends the spectators off into shouts of merriment ; but although funny, it is at the same time a little dangerous to catch a lighted candle in one's teeth, and we would suggest that a bag made of cheese-cloth, or like thin material, be filled with flour and tied to the stick in place of the candle. When the person essaying to snatch the fruit is struck in the face with the bag, and is covered with flour instead of the glory anticipated, as much mirth will result as can possibly arise when the old and dangerous practice of using a candle is clung to.

The Ghostly Fire

should not be lit unless all of the party have strong nerves, for the light it produces is rather unearthly, and may affect some members unpleasantly. We, at our Halloween parties, never omitted this rite, however, its very weirdness proving its strongest attraction. Salt and alcohol were put in a dish, with a few raisins, and set on fire. As soon as the flame leaped up we clasped hands and gayly danced around the table, upon which burned our mystic fire. The laughing eyes and lips looked in strange contrast to the pale faces of their owners, from which the greenish light had taken every vestige of color. The dance was not prolonged, for it was our duty, before the fire was spent, to snatch from the flames the raisins we had put in the dish. This can be done, if one is careful, without as much as scorching the fingers, and I never knew of anyone burning themselves while making the attempt.

Trying for a Raisin

is a very laughable performance. The raisin, which must be a good-sized one, is strung on and pushed exactly to the middle of a soft cotton string about one yard long. Two aspirants for the prize then take each an end of the string, which they put in their mouths and commence to chew, taking it up as fast as they can—the raisin falling to the share of the person who succeeds in reaching it first.

A Lighted Candle

is again used in a game which is exceedingly amusing. The candle is placed upon a table in full view of everyone ; then one of the players is blindfolded, turned around several times, and set free to seek for the candle and blow out the light, if possible.

To see girls, with their hands clasped behind them, going crazily about the room, blowing at anything and everything, is very ludicrous. They seldom find the candle, and even when the table is reached it is difficult to blow in such a direction as to extinguish the flame.

The Fairy's Gifts

are suggested as a new and original ending of a Halloween frolic.

The Fairy Godmother, in Mother Hubbard costume, carries a large basket under her cloak or shawl. She enters the room and announces that she has a certain number of gifts which she proposes to distribute among the company. After cautioning all that the contents must be kept secret, she passes to each person a folded paper. On one is written "*Wealth,*" on another "*Honor,*" on the third "*Fame,*" etc., and some of the papers are left blank.

Those whose papers contain the names of gifts are then blindfolded, preparatory to receiving their behests.

The first is led up and made to kneel before the Fairy Godmother, to whom she repeats these words :

> Most gracious Fairy, the gift you give
> I shall treasure and keep as long as I live.

Then the paper containing the name of the gift is handed the Fairy, who reads it aloud very solemnly : " *Wealth* "—and, turning to her basket, she takes from it a new dust-pan, to which is attached a ribbon-loop, at the same time reciting these lines :

Your choice is bad when you intrust
Your happiness where moth and rust,
In time, turn all your wealth to dust.

From a paper-bag the Fairy pours a small amount of dust over the kneeling girl, and hangs the dust-pan around her neck.

The next person who has drawn a prize is then brought forward and the performance is repeated, only altering the Fairy's speech. For *"Honor,"* she will say:

Your honor crowds shall loud declare,
But in your heart, no crowd is there,
You'll find, like *Falstaff,* " honor's air."

The present here is a pair of bellows, from which the Fairy blows a blast on the bowed head before her as she utters the word *air.* The bellows, like the dust-pan, are hung by a ribbon around the recipient's neck.

For *"Fame,"* the Fairy gives a wreath of roses, and says, as she adjusts the crown:

When Fame doth weave a laurel-wreath,
He weaves this subtle charm beneath;
" For every evil thought that's born
The laurel grows a prickly thorn ;
But where pure thought and love reposes,
The laurel-wreath's a wreath of roses."

Buckeye Portière.

CHAPTER XVIII.

NATURE'S FALL DECORATIONS, AND HOW TO USE THEM.

HESE beautiful decorations are free to all who care to possess them. Every autumn comes to us laden with ornaments which no skilled workman can rival. The graceful golden-rod, so rich in color, sways and bends over the low stone walls, and in the fields wild flowers of all kinds grow in great profusion. White, spreading wild carrot, yellow and white daisies, light and dark purple asters, and sumach, with its varied hues, give color to the landscape on our bright fall days. There are also the queer-shaped pods and feathery, silky seeds peculiar to some wild plants; among others the poor "vagabond thistle," which has donned its robe of glistening white, although some of its tribe still wear their faded purple gowns. The latter may be gathered for thistle-puffs, and all the objects mentioned can be used in home decorations.

We cannot pass by unnoticed the brown milk-weed pods, for within the shells, full well we know, are hidden the silvery, downy seeds which make such pretty milk-weed balls. Here, too, we notice the rich coloring of bark as well as foliage, the bright scarlet berries contrasting with the brown, yellow, and green leaves. The vine, once a fresh green, is now changed to deep crimson ; even the tiny leaves of the wild strawberry and some grasses have touches of red on their edges.

How the rich coloring of autumn differs from the delicate tints of spring, when the promise was made in bud and leaf, which is now realized in the bountiful harvests !

Having such a wealth to glean from, we scarcely know what to take first ; but for decorations to last only a few hours it would be difficult to imagine anything more brilliantly appropriate than

Fresh Autumn Wild Flowers

and small branches of brilliant fall leaves. At the time of this writing wild flowers are very popular ; one of our daily papers records a wedding which recently took place, where the display of wild flowers was beautiful in the extreme. Curtains of wood-ferns were caught back with golden-rod, and a bower of holly and oak was fringed with clusters of scarlet bitter-sweet berries. Daisies were also used in abundance, while the beauty of the little church was enhanced by the masses of white blossoms and oak-branches.

This idea can be used advantageously in decorating the house for evening parties and receptions, or afternoon teas and coffees. Have the flowers and foliage in masses, the effect is much better ; and if you gather very large, hardy ferns with their roots attached they will make exceedingly graceful decorations, and placed in water or wet sand they will remain fresh for days.

When golden-rod is gathered in its prime it will keep nearly all winter without fading. Do not put it in water ; all that is necessary is to keep it dry. The rich brown cat-tails should be treated in the same manner ; these must be gathered at their best, before they are too ripe. Bitter-sweet berries will last for months and retain a bright red. The old-fashioned honesty, with its white, satiny pods, keeps perfectly for any length of time. The wild rose-bush in the fall is decked with seed-coverings, which closely resemble scarlet berries; these will last for many weeks. The wild clematis, with its festoons of hazy fluff, will keep for a long time, and always looks well when thrown over and on the top corner of a portière and allowed to hang naturally down a little on one side, or arranged in a similar manner over the tops of windows, doors, pictures, or wherever it will look graceful. It should hang out of harm's way, as it is brittle and easily broken when dry.

For entertainments, the more elaborate and bountiful the decorations of fresh wild flowers the more beautiful will the house appear; but for every-day life during the cold weather, when we have only the dried fall plants, we may almost make up for the lack of fresh flowers by using judgment and taste in arranging the dried ones. Though wild flowers

A Young Decorator.

are beautiful, you must use taste in their arrangement and not mingle them together promiscuously, but make a judicious selection, for where a light bunch of golden-rod would be the very thing needed to give color to a particular spot, should the dark cat-tails be placed there the effect might be lost. There are places where some high, stiff decoration would look best, and others where the soft, swaying clematis seems to belong. As with everything else, so with our decorations, we must seek to have harmony.

Who has not admired the dark-brown, glossy buckeyes and horse-chestnuts, and wondered what use could be made of them? Children love to gather them and come home with their pockets and baskets full, only to play with them for awhile, and then the pretty dark balls, each marked with a spot of light cream-color, are thrown away or lost.

Now, the next time the buckeyes are collected save every one and make a

Buckeye Portière.

The writer assures you that you will find it much easier to do this than she did to make a picture of the curtain, for it is difficult with a pen-and-ink drawing to give an idea of the richness of color in the handsome hangings these horse-chestnuts make when properly fashioned into a portière for hall or doorway. Two full bushels of buckeyes will be needed to make a curtain two yards and a half long and one yard and a quarter wide.

Take a very large, long needle and a strong, waxed thread a little longer than you desire to have your curtain, make a large knot in the end of the thread, and commence to string your buckeyes in the same way as stringing beads or buttons. Continue until the thread in the needle is exhausted, then tie the thread in a large knot close to the last buckeye, leaving a length of three inches of thread. Make your other strands in the same way.   When all are finished, fasten as many small screw-eyes in a straight line on a curtain-pole, or a rustic pole if desired, as there are strands of buckeyes, and tie securely to each screw-eye one string of buckeyes.   When all are fastened

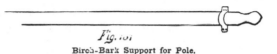

Fig. 131

Birch-Bark Support for Pole.

on, your portière is finished and ready to be hung.   This is easily accomplished if the pole used is a regular curtain-pole, as they always come with brackets ; but should your pole be rustic, it must be supported by bands of strong birch-bark, or leather, as in Fig. 131.   Our illustration shows over the portière a

Panel of Fall Decorations.

These also look handsome over windows and doors, and you are at liberty to use ornaments of all styles, for the panels are placed where there is no danger of anything coming in contact with them to break off the decorations or mar their beauty. Any kind of board will do for the panel, rough or smooth, as you like.   Paint the board a pure white, then decide on your ornaments, which may be a chestnut-branch with bursting burs attached, sprays of common wayside velvet-leaf with clusters of pods clinging to them, a piece of black-berry vine with its twigs, thorns, and dried berries, or branches of buckeyes with some of the nuts falling from their horned shells.

Select according to your fancy, and gild the decorations chosen, then tack them on the panel.   It is best to place the ornaments on the board while the paint is soft and wet, for then it will help to fasten the decoration more securely ; if the paint be put on thick where the ornaments are to be placed, they will lie partially embedded in the paint, and when it dries they will appear as if carved from the wood.*

A white and gold panel made in this way is very pretty and inexpensive.

The fall decorations also enable us to make a very effective

Louis Quinze Screen.

For this it is necessary to have two small wooden hoops, such as children roll along the streets; fasten these together with a

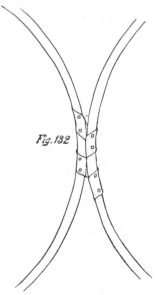

Fig. 132

Hinge for Louis Quinze Screen.

strong piece of white tape, two or three inches wide, cut the end of the tape bias, tack this on the side of one of the hoops, bring it around between and over the other hoop, and tack it again, repeat the operation and the hinge will be finished (Fig. 132). If you look at the hinge on a wooden clothes-horse you will understand how to make one. Fig. 133 shows the hoops fastened together. Now cut two pieces of coarse, strong cotton cloth, a little larger around than the hoops, and place one of the pieces smoothly over one of the hoops ; tack it down, driving the tacks in far apart, and so that they can be easily extracted ; if the cloth wrinkles, keep changing it until the surface is perfectly even ; when this is accomplished carefully tack the covering securely down, keeping it smooth and

---

* For this work the staple-tacks used for tacking down matting will be found very convenient.

without wrinkles. In like manner tack the remaining piece of cloth on the other hoop. Next get four broomsticks and cut a notch on each one, at exactly the same distance from the top, for the hoops to fit in. Then measure where you wish the hoops to be placed and cut another notch on each stick a certain distance from the bottom ; all the sticks must be of the same length and have the notches cut in the same places, so each one may be a duplicate of the others. Mark the hoops where the sticks are to fit, and then fasten them firmly on with small screws. Make

Fig. 133

Hoops Fastened Together for Louis Quinze Screen.

the screen strong, so that there will not be any danger of its coming apart. Give each cloth a sizing of common flour-paste on both sides, then scrape off all the paste with a knife ; in this way the cloth will be starched and prepared to receive the paint. When the screen is thoroughly dry, sew a branch across one of the disks and some waxed fall leaves in the places where they would naturally lie on the branch ; when these are securely attached, decorate the other disk with something different ; acorns can be used if cut in halves ; but never place any ornaments on the screen which will not lie flat, for if they stand out they will be broken off or injured by persons passing and brushing against them. Now give the screen a coat of white paint all over, including the branch and leaves, but do not paint the hinge. Set the screen away until it is perfectly dry, then gild the branches and leaves, connecting the latter with the twigs by painting a line of

Louis Quinze Screen.

gold between the two. Gild a ring around each pole near the top and another near the bottom, and cover the edges of the hoops where the cloth has been fastened on by tacking white gimp around each one, using fancy brass-headed tacks and placing them at equal distances apart; this completes the ornamental screen.

Should you desire it, the screen can be painted black or any other color, and the decorations bronzed instead of gilded. The bronzes come in different shades, and the color of real bronze can be easily copied.

As an ornament for the dining-room

A Panel of Field-Corn

is very decorative and easy to make. When the corn ripens, select some nice, firm, golden ears, with husks and without; then break off pieces of corn-stalk and group them together, as in the illustration; cover a board of

14

requisite size with a piece of old black velvet ; if you have no velvet, paint the board black, and after tying the corn firmly together, tack it securely on the board, and the dark background will bring out the many yellow tints of the decoration beautifully ; fasten two screw-eyes in the back of the board, by which to attach the wire, and the panel will be ready to hang on the wall.

The corn can also be fastened to a rough board of the desired size and the panel and decoration bronzed, using green bronze for the background and portions of the group, while all the edges and prominent points should be of copper-colored bronze.

Early in November the many varieties of gourds ripen, and their odd and fantastic forms seem like nature's suggestions of the unique in ornamentation. So suggestive are they that it needs but little originality to make them into many useful and beautiful articles. As a decoration for looping over the poles of portières, and for holding back draperies, these

Ornamental Gourds

are convenient. They must first be allowed to become perfectly dry ; then they can be made into tasselled festoons. Take six mock-oranges, which imitate so closely our real oranges in color, size, and form, and cut a hole about the size of a silver dime in the top and bottom of each one ; then shake out the seeds. To make the openings in the gourds, first bore a small hole with the point of a large needle, then twist the needle around and around until it will easily pass through. Next, carefully enlarge the opening with a sharp penknife until it is of the stated size. Make a rope two yards and a half long of Persian colored wools or worsted ; on the end fasten a slender tassel, six or seven inches long, made of the same worsted ; now string one of the bright orange-gourds on the rope down against the tassel, which should be large enough to prevent the gourd from slipping off ; make another similar tassel, and attach it to the rope about twelve inches from the first one, and thread another gourd on the rope, bringing it down against the second tassel ; proceed in like manner with the remaining gourds, making a tassel for each one, and you will have a decoration unlike any to be found elsewhere.

We are all more or less familiar with the

Gourd-Dippers

so common in the South, where, in olden times, scarcely a spring bubbled in a rustic nook that was not supplied with its drinking-gourd. These dippers are made by sawing an opening in the large part of the gourd, scraping out the contents, and making the inside as smooth as possible with sand-paper. They need no ornamentation.

The kind of gourds resembling flattened globes can be made into graceful and unique

Bowls.

The gourds must be sawed into two parts, with the inside of each sand-papered, and flowers painted, with oil-colors, on the outside. After they have thoroughly dried, give a coat of white varnish to both the inside and outside. A pretty

Bonbon-Box

can be fashioned of one of these gourds. Saw off the top, which will serve as a lid, and fasten it to the bowl with narrow ribbons tied through holes at the back of each ; line both lid and box with satin by gluing it along the edges with stiff glue put on sparingly, and cover the raw edge of the satin with chenille ; this is also put on with a little glue. Do not allow the chenille to interfere with the closing of the box, but place it along the inside edge of the box and lid.

Another form is the

● Bottle-Gourd.

Ornament this with ivy-leaves painted as if twined around bowl and neck, and when the paint is dry varnish the gourd all over ; if you wish it for use as well as decoration, saw off the top about two or three inches deep, shake out the seeds, then fit a cork in the piece cut off, and so glue it in that the cork may extend an inch downward to fit in the bottle.

The large egg-shaped gourds look well as

Vases.

Select a deep-colored gourd, saw off the top and scrape out the inside ; then varnish the vase and mount it on feet of

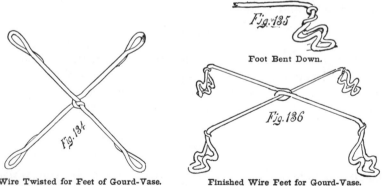

Fig. 135

Foot Bent Down.

Fig. 134

Fig. 136

Wire Twisted for Feet of Gourd-Vase.   Finished Wire Feet for Gourd-Vase.

twisted wire, made according to Fig. 134 ; bend down the feet, as in Fig. 135, when the wire will be formed into Fig. 136. To fasten this on the vase, first bore holes in the bottom of the gourd, then sew the feet firmly on, passing the needle through

Ornamental and Useful Gourds.

the holes previously made and bending the wire a little to fit to the gourd. Gild the wire feet, and your vase is finished. Another way is to save the top sawed off, fasten an ornament of twisted wire on the top of it, and then, after making the vase as the one just described, add bands of gilded cardboard made to fit the gourd, fastening them to the vase with glue. Handles can also be fashioned of cardboard and sewed to the upper band before it is glued to the vase, as in the illustration.

There are many other ways of utilizing gourds, but we will leave it to your ingenuity to think up new and pretty conceits.

Pine-cones, large and small, acorns, and balls from the sweet-gum tree, can be used as

Small Decorations.

Never try to fasten them by the natural stems, for these will soon break off, but place in each one a small screw-eye, and when tied in groups they form ornaments for waste-baskets and fancy baskets of all kinds. We have seen chandeliers with gilded cones hanging from the different points, and being the identical color of the chandelier, they seemed of the same metal, and added novelty and grace to its appearance.

There are some varieties of the tree-fungi which make dark, rich-colored

Brackets.

Use heavy cardboard or thin board as a covering for the back ; have this fit the fungus perfectly, and fasten it securely in position with very stiff glue or nails. Paint the back the same color as the fungus, and on either side of the upper edge place screw-eyes by which to fasten up the bracket.

Many of the curiously formed galls and oak-apples to be found on different trees can also be employed as ornaments.

Nothing can be finer than our brilliant autumn season, which is said to be more beautiful in this than in other countries, with its crisp mornings and bright sunny afternoons.

When the weather is too lovely to remain in-doors, and all nature invites us out, then is the time to gather our fall decorations.

The Little Brown Squirrel.

CHAPTER XIX.

NUTTING-PARTIES.

FF they go with bright, laughing eyes and glowing cheeks, each one carrying a light little basket or fancy bag slung carelessly on her arm. The girls are full of life and spirits as they walk briskly along toward the woods in the delightful fall weather, talking and laughing in a happy, thoughtless fashion, now telling where the best nuts are to be found, the shortest route to take, or where the prettiest walks lead, and again lingering or stopping to admire the many wonderful beauties of autumn. Leaving the road they enter the woods, where the dry leaves rustle pleasantly beneath their feet, and in some places the gold and brown leaves through which they walk lie ankle-deep.

All this is fully enjoyed by the party as they proceed on their way discussing the best place for lunch, which consideration is quite important, as it is necessary, if possible, to be near a clear, cool spring ; otherwise the water must be transported.

Arriving at the selected spot about noon, all bring. forward their baskets and bags to contribute the contents to their "nutting-dinner." Soon the white cloth is laid and the tempting feast spread, when the hungry but merry maidens gather around to relish their repast in the forest, where, all about, are seen sure signs of coming winter.

The airy dining-hall is carpeted with the softest moss, and the gorgeous coloring of the surrounding foliage is far more beautiful than the most costly tapestry, while the sky forming the roof is of the serenest blue.

Now and then the sound of falling nuts is heard as they drop from the trees. This is music in the ears of the girls, and they hurry through their lunch, collect the empty baskets, and are soon busy gathering the glossy brown chestnuts, which are thrashed down from the branches by some of the party, who use long poles for the purpose. Down comes the shower of nuts and burs, and away the party scamper to patiently wait until it is over, as the prickly burs are things to be avoided. Some wise girls have brought tweezers to use in pulling open these thorny coverings. Others have their hands well protected by heavy gloves which cannot easily be penetrated with the bristling spikes.

It does not take long to fill their bags, and the one who first succeeds in the feat receives the title of "Little Brown Squirrel." Then all the others, for the rest of the day, obey her wishes. Nor is this difficult, for their Little Brown Squirrel is blithe and gay, generous and kind, and does all in her power to render her subjects happy.

As they turn their faces homeward the girls plan for another nutting-party to come off soon, for they wish to make the most of the glorious Indian summer, which belongs, we claim, exclusively to our country, and which may last a week or only a few days.

The chestnuts are brought home, where in the evening some are eaten raw, others have the shells slit and are then roasted or boiled, making a sort of chestnut festival, as in the North of Italy, only of course on a very much smaller scale, for there the peasants gather chestnuts all day long and have a merry-making

when the sun goes down. This harvest lasts over three weeks and is a
very important one to the dark-eyed
Italians, who dry the nuts and grind
them to flour, which is used for bread
and cakes during the barren season.
The harvest in the Apennines is quite
an event, as the trees are plentiful,
the fruit is good, and the people gladly celebrate the season.

Our thin, white-shelled shag-bark
hickory-nut is peculiarly American,
and many a nutting-party have found
its delicate and agreeable flavor very
welcome when, gathered around a
large rock, they crack a few to sample their fruit before returning home.

Blossom and Fruit of the Chestnut-Tree.

These nuts are only cooked by covering the kernels with hot
candy, and thus prepared, they make a delicious sweetmeat.

When cracking hickory-nuts, hold each nut firmly by the

flat sides, bringing uppermost one of the narrow sides; strike this and the nut will open so that the halves fall out, or may be easily extracted, and occasionally the kernels will come out whole. We have seen quaint little figures, with the heads made of hickory-nuts, the pointed end forming the nose, and the eyes and mouth marked with ink, giving a comical expression to the peaked face.

The neat little three-cornered beech-nut is easy and pleasant to gather, making a desirable change for the " nutters " after going for other kinds, and the trees with their beautiful foliage render the scene very attractive. But not more so than do the lofty and stately walnut-trees with their rich, brown fruit encased in such rough shells, whose outside covering is so juicy that, unless we are very cautious, it will stain our hands its own dark color. The black-walnut tree (J. nigra) is indigenous to the United States, and we are informed that a celebrated specimen is still standing at Roslyn, L. I., where the seed was planted in 1713. The tree measures twenty-five feet in circumference at three feet from the ground.

Butter-nuts, so significant during our civil war, also belong to America; the meat, though quite oily, is sweet and agreeable.

Butter-nuts will repay anyone for gathering them, though, like the walnut, the outer husk is apt to stain the fingers; but this may be avoided by wearing gloves while handling the fruit. The cross-sections of the shells, when properly polished, make pretty ornaments.

Although we are all fond of the round little hazel-nut, they do not seem to be as plentiful as could be wished, and it is seldom we have the pleasure of going hazel-nutting, yet when the opportunity occurs, it is rare sport and an event to be talked of afterward.

Nuts are to be found in all portions of the country, and the varieties depend upon the section in which you live.

Rules for Nutting-Parties.

1. In selecting the members of a nutting-party be careful to choose only those on whom you can safely depend for cheerfulness, kindly feeling, and a willingness on their part to do all in their power to assist, should occasion arise, in letting down the bars of a fence, going for water, or anything which might happen to require their services.

2. Decide by majority any case of controversy in regard to destination, the best place and way of crossing a brook, which route to take, or in fact any question concerning the comfort and pleasure of the party, until the "Little Brown Squirrel" wins her title. Then she rules absolutely and settles all questions according to her best judgment, giving council and friendly advice to those who ask it. All

Pea-Nut Vine and Fruit.

differences being referred to her, the decision is considered final, and the party must obey when their Little Brown Squirrel directs.

3. The one who gathers the greatest quantity of nuts in a given time wins, and receives the above much-desired title. The standard of measure being previously decided upon by the party, the time may be either long or short, as desired.

4. The badge given to the successful competitor may consist of fall leaves or nuts tied with a brown ribbon. This she keeps in remembrance of the delightful day spent nutting in the woods when she was a Little Brown Squirrel.

Select, if possible, a day in Indian summer for your nutting-party, and it is well to wear a gown that will not easily tear, catch the dust, or spot—not that these accidents are always to be met with on such excursions, but they might happen, and we must be on the safe side, so that no thought or anxiety need be given to the clothing.

If your party contemplates a series of nutting-picnics, propose that they shall go for different varieties each time. This will add novelty and zest to the excursions; and should the distance in some cases be too great for a walk, secure a vehicle with a good reliable driver, and the ride will be particularly enjoyed. This mode of travelling procures another change in the programme, which should be as varied as you can make it. Let the plates for your dinner be of wood or paper, to avoid the necessity of carrying them home. A table-cloth made of large sheets of white paper is a good substitute for damask, and after doing service the paper may be thrown away, leaving your baskets entirely empty to be filled with nuts.

There grows a nut, highly prized, that is never gathered by nutting-parties. Nor could they see it if they examined every tree throughout the country. Yet it flourishes in this climate, and may be seen any day at the fruit-stores and corner-stands. The shells of these furnish odd fancies for little trifles made by girlish fingers. Cut in the shape of slippers and glued to a card, they seem suitable for a wood-nymph, and the card is used as a birthday or *menu* card. Strung together with needle and thread, and dressed in costume with black thread for hair, they make quite a good-looking Japanese.

Glued on a twig and marked with ink in representation of the birds, they look not unlike owls perched on a limb. When divided in halves the shells are transformed into tiny boats with tissue-paper sails. This nut boasts of four names: gouber, pindar, ground-nut, and the familiar name of pea-nut.

CHAPTER XX.

HOW TO MAKE A TELEPHONE.

 ELLO! Hello! What is it you say? You can really make a telephone? What fun! How far will it work? You think it can be heard a long distance? Very good. Could we manage to construct such a one? How, pray tell us?

The answer which came back over the line we give in a more concise form, as follows:

The best way to make a simple telephone is to procure two round, medium-sized tin baking-powder boxes, and remove the bottoms with a pair of pinchers; then soak two pieces of Whatman's drawing-paper, or any other strong paper, in a basin of water for a few moments, and when thoroughly wet take them out and place one smoothly over the end of each box. Fasten these down by winding a waxed cotton twine securely over the paper and box, and tying it tightly (Fig. 137). This done, allow the drums to become wholly dry, when they should be firm, even, and without wrinkles. Next cut away that portion of the paper which stands out, frill-like, beyond the string, and paste a narrow strip of paper around over the twine (Fig. 138). Wax a piece of string of the desired length, and with a large needle or pin carefully punch a hole in the centre of each drum; thread one end of the waxed string through one of the holes and make a large knot in the end, then cautiously pull the string until the knot rests on the inside surface of the paper.

Connect the other box to the string in like manner, so that the twine will have a box fastened on each end.

The telephone is now ready for use ; and if the distance is short, the line may be stretched taut from point to point. But should the space be great, supports will be needed and loops must be made of the twine and fastened at intervals on trees, corners of the houses, or any available points, with the connecting cord passed through these loops (Fig. 139), which act as supports. Keep the course of the waxed string as straight as possible, and, as far as practicable, avoid sharp angles. This style of telephone we know, from personal experience, works perfectly at the distance of

Fig. 139

fifty yards, and doubtless it will do as well when the line is stretched much farther. Be particular, in selecting the tin

15

baking-powder boxes, to have them round and even ; if they are old and battered the experiment may not prove satisfactory.

Listening.

We find the telephone very useful and convenient, besides affording any amount of amusement and fun ; with its aid we converse with acquaintances, even though they be at a distance. The friendly little instrument carries the voice all along the slender line to the very ears of our best friend, and we can chat away as freely and almost as easily as if side by side. What a comfort to be able, when seated in your own room, to listen to the voice of some companion, living perhaps blocks away, and it is such a pleasure, too, to have questions answered immediately, which is impossible in communications made by letter. Nor is this a pleasure to be enjoyed at rare intervals, for as long as the telephone lasts it can be used at any time for a short or long talk, as one may feel inclined. The consultations, the plans, the sport, and merriment to be had with the telephone can scarcely be appreciated by one who is not the happy possessor of such an instrument.

When the weather will not permit of a walk or a visit, the telephone brings us, if not face to face, at least within speaking distance of those to whom we desire to talk.

There are many other easy methods of making telephones. They can be manufactured as described without waxing the

string, or the boxes may be used unaltered, in which case the
tin bottoms serve as drums, and the holes for the string are
made in the centre of each by driving a small tack through.
With these instruments the voice cannot be sent a great distance, but when only a short line is needed they succeed very
well.

More complicated telephones are made with the drums of
bladder and the line of soft, flexible wire. Though good and
serviceable, they are more
difficult to make and require
more time and labor.

The two beef-bladders
used for such a telephone
must first be blown up, tied,
and left about thirty hours,
or until they are stretched,
but not dried. When in
proper condition, cut off the
necks and portion of the
ends, then soak them in
warm water, and they will
become very pliable and
light in color. Having previously prepared two square
pieces of board by very carefully cutting out a perfect
circle in the centre of each,
about as large as a medium-
sized pie-pan or a tea-plate,
place the bladders smoothly
but not tightly over the

Speaking.

openings, allowing the outside of the bladder to come on the
bottom, and fasten it all around the circle, a little distance

from the edge, with tacks so driven in that they may be easily removed.

Try the drums with your finger; if they stretch evenly they are correct, if they wrinkle, change them until they stretch perfectly smooth. Then tack a piece of firm tape securely around the edge of the circle, and cut off the bladder reaching beyond the tape. Next fasten four feet of soft, flexible wire to a large-sized gutta-percha button by threading it through the two opposite holes in the centre of the button; pass the other end of the wire through the middle of the bladder, bringing the button flat against its surface.

After attaching a weight of about seven pounds to the end of the wire, place the drum in the sun until perfectly dry. Proceed with the other in the same manner, and when both are well dried, fasten one on each end of the line and attach the drum-wires to the principal wire by loops; then stretch it firm and tight. This telephone will also need loops for supports, which should be of wire. When the instrument is carefully and properly made it will carry the voice three or four miles or more, giving every word and tone distinctly and clearly.

CHAPTER XXI.

HOW TO DRAW.*

OULD you like to learn to draw, to sketch from nature ? Don't you think that it would be delightful to be able to take out your pencils and paper and copy some scene you want to remember, or produce a likeness of any bird or animal which strikes your fancy ?

Many will say, " I'd like it very well, but I *can't draw.*"

You can write, can hold a pencil, and trace lines upon the paper; and if you can do this, you can draw a little. A girl who can learn anything can learn to draw if she will give the same attention to it that she gives to other things.

Fig. 140

Now we are not going to talk about copying pictures which someone else has already drawn, for there is not much satisfaction in making imitations of other people's work ; it is much more gratifying to make the original drawings ourselves ; but to do this we need some direction.

---

* The material for this chapter is from an article written by Professor Frank Beard for Harper's Young People. By permission of Harper & Brothers.

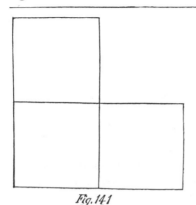

Fig. 141

The reason it is easier to copy a picture than to draw the real object is because the lines to be copied are all laid out on the flat surface of the picture ; but to draw the object we must find out where to trace the lines for ourselves.

For instance, suppose we are to draw a flower-pot and plant. If we have the picture before us, we can readily see where all the lines are placed upon the paper, but in viewing a real plant and pot we are apt to become confused in trying to discover the directions and proportions of the lines.

Fig. 142

Therefore we must learn *to see things as they appear*, not as they really are. This may seem strange to you, because one is apt to think that a thing must appear as it is ; but let us look into the matter.

We will take a square box (Fig. 140). Now, we know that all the sides are the same size, that the top is as large as the side, and that one side is as large as another ; but if you try to draw it so, you will find it impossible, because, although you know that the top and sides are the same size as the front, they do not look so, and you draw things as they look, not as they really are.

What would our cube look like if we tried to make the sides K and H just like the side I ? Why, like Fig. 141. Don't you see that would be no box at all ?

Take another example. We all know that a man's leg is longer than his arm, but it doesn't always appear so. Measure the arms and legs of Fig. 142, and you will see by actual measurement the arms are longer than the legs, and yet it looks right, because the legs are projected toward you ; in other words, the legs are *fore shortened.*

Fig. 143

The great secret of drawing from nature is to train the eye to see a real object just like a picture.

Now let us return to our flower-pot again. We will suppose we are drawing from a real flower-pot and plant. We determine how large we will make our sketch, and begin operations by drawing a vertical line (a straight upright line). Along this line we will mark out the proportions of the plant and pot, as in Fig. 143.

We may easily discover that the plant is longer than the pot. This can be done by holding the pencil upright before the eye at arm's length, as in Fig. 144, so that it will cover the pot, and measuring by the thumb the height of the pot, then raising the arm so as to cover the plant, and comparing the measurement of the pot with the plant. The lines drawn from the eye Fig. 144) show how the pencil makes the measurement on the object.

After settling the question of the height of the flower-pot and plant, we will mark the measurements on the line. And

Fig. 144

now we will draw in the pot, leaving the straight line through its centre.

On observing the plant we will see that it is not exactly straight, and here again the straight line will be of assistance.

By holding up our pencil, which represents the straight line, we will discover that the main stem of the plant leans considerably to the left. Guided by the line, we can get the curve of the stem about right. Now we sketch the stem. Along the straight line we again measure the distance from the top of each leaf and flower to the pot, as in Fig. 145. We can see several leaves, each reaching a certain height. Observing the same plan of measurement, we find that the top of the lowest leaf is about the same height from the pot as the height of the pot itself, and again from the top of the lowest leaf to the top of the plant measures the same distance.

By drawing another vertical line just touching the right side of the pot, we find that it touches the ex- treme edge of the leaf. Thus we find the exact situation of the leaf. By the same method we find the right places for the other leaves and flowers, and after we know just where they belong, we draw them in, and find that we have produced a very creditable outline from nature.

We need not confine ourselves to one or two guiding lines in sketching an object; in fact, we may use as many straight lines as will help us to get the correct proportions; not only vertical and horizontal lines, but slanting lines will also assist us in most cases.

The sketch of a dog (Fig. 146) will give an idea of the way to employ all lines necessary in sketching from nature.

Fig. 145

A few words will be all that is necessary to explain this illustration.

There lies the dog on the floor, and we seat ourselves at a little distance from it with pencil and paper. We will start off with a horizontal line (A); then we can form some idea as to whether the little dog lies along a straight line, or in case the bottom line slants, how much it slants. Then draw the vertical line (B E). Now suppose we hold our pencil upright, in such a position as to touch the back of the knee-joint of the foreleg, we will find that it passes through the middle of the dog's back, as represented by the line (B E); so we have found the places for these parts.

Another horizontal line (C D) drawn above the first will touch just over the right eye, pass through the middle of the left ear, through the middle of the neck, cut off the foreleg, and run along the top of the two hind legs, passing through the knee of the left one. This will show us that the top of the right eye, the ear, and the top of both hindlegs are on a line. It will also help us to get the proportions above and below the line ; then by drawing a line from D to the point F on the horizontal line A, we find that the lower edges of the left hind and fore legs are on the same line, which, if extended a little farther down, will touch the edge of the dog's mouth. With these lines to guide us we cannot go far astray in our proportions.

One of the chief difficulties in following this method of drawing from nature is to hold our measuring-stick exactly vertical or horizontal. This difficulty can be overcome by providing yourself with a T-square (Fig. *Fig.147* 147) and attaching to it, at the point P, a string with a weight tied on the other end so that it will hang plumb. By using this we can be sure whether we hold it straight or not, for in case we tip it too much on one side or the other the string will swerve from the middle of the upright stick. Of course, whenever we hold the T-square perfectly straight, the string will fall straight down the middle of the upright, and the top of the T will then give us a true horizontal line. A little thought and practice will lead you to thoroughly understand this method, and when you really understand it you will have an unerring guide to assist you. Of course, as the eye and hand become more trained, with practice and observation, the work will become easier, and you will not need the T-square.

In beginning the practice of drawing from nature, we had better confine our first efforts to things that will stand still, for without a practised hand it will be almost impossible to sketch a restless subject ; but if we attempt to do so, we should follow the methods before taught as nearly as possible.

Now, suppose we step out of doors in search of something to sketch. The first moving object our eyes rest upon is a goose, and we decide to use him as a model.

But he is so restless, will not keep still an instant. First we have a front view, then a side view, and again he turns his back upon us. If we really must have his picture, the only way is to catch him and tie him up.

Yet even now he is a difficult subject, twisting and turning, and bobbing his head about. Determined on sketching him, however, we observe the position in which he remains the longest time, or assumes oftenest, and begin our work.

We first note the general proportions. Is his body as thick as it is long ? Is his neck as long as his body ? Are his legs nearest the head or tail ? Is the head' as long as the neck ? What part reaches the highest, or what part the lowest ? We hastily but carefully consider these questions and determine in our own mind the answers, for we must get an idea of the proportions before we begin our sketch.

Now we draw a horizontal line along our paper, and then hold up our pencil horizontally, so that it will answer for a straight line drawn across the body of the real goose (Fig. 148). This will represent the horizontal line on the paper. Noticing then the directions the outlines of the goose

Fig. 148

take from the horizontal line (represented by the pencil), we sketch them in on the paper, remembering that one of the most important things is to get the right directions of the lines.

Observe that in Fig. 149 the line G is directed to too high a point, and makes the body too thick and out of proportion.

Fig. 149　　　　　　　*Fig. 150*

In sketching it is best to make all lines straight instead of curves, for in this way we are more likely to get the right directions. Our first rough sketch of the goose ought to have something of the appearance of Fig. 150, and as we work it up more carefully it will become as nicely rounded as we could desire.

One of the most common faults a beginner is apt to commit is to try to do too much, either by choosing too great a subject, such as a large landscape, or by putting too many little things into the composition. Take care of the large things, and the little things will take care of themselves.

If our subject be a clump of trees at some distance, we should not attempt to draw in separate leaves, but endeavor to get the true shape of the tree, simply indicating the leaves by a few lines. Neither must we attempt, in our first sketches, to put in all the shadows we see ; the strong principal ones are all that are necessary. A background of hills and trees should be merely suggested by a few lines, because the light striking upon them gives a very light appearance.

Draw as simply as possible. Ten pictures are spoiled by putting in too much work, where one is spoiled by too little.

Don't be discouraged. Every effort will show improvement, if you really put your mind and heart in your work. As for

Materials,

a sheet of drawing paper, a No. 2 lead-pencil, and a piece of soft rubber are all you really need to commence with. Later it will be well to have a drawing-pad and several more pencils.

CHAPTER XXII.

HOW TO PAINT IN WATER-COLORS.

HERE is a certain charm in water-color painting—a charm distinctly its own—which lies, as Penley says, " in the beauty and truthfulness of its aerial tones." Without this quality a water-color, as a water-color, is a failure.

This transparency of effect does not depend alone upon the manner of painting or the colors employed, but much rests with the paper we use. In the days when our mothers and grandmothers were taught painting at school, the finest, smoothest cardboard was thought necessary ; but we have since learned that the flat, smooth paper tends decidedly toward producing a flat, smooth effect in the picture painted upon it, while the rough, uneven surface of the paper now in use helps to produce depth and atmosphere. Therefore it is always best to have *rough* paper to paint upon. We give below the

Materials for Water-Color Painting.

1. A block of rough drawing or water-color paper.

It is better to buy it in blocks than by the sheet, as it is much more easily handled, and is always ready for use.

2. Brushes. The best brushes are made of sable, and although costing more to begin with, it is really more econom-

ical to purchase them than to choose the less expensive camel's-hair; for the sable are by far the most satisfactory, and will last much longer. Three or four brushes are sufficient. As Devoe & Co. number them, they should range between No. 3, which is small enough for ordinary painting, and No. 19, for clouds, backgrounds, etc.

3. Colors. A tin sketching-box of moist colors, which also contains a palette, is very useful, but the colors can be bought separately in tubes or pans.

Water-color painting seems by its qualities to be especially adapted to flowers and landscapes, and as this is to be a chapter, not a book, on water-colors, we will confine ourselves to the principal points to be observed in these two departments, and will commence with the

Flowers.

Few oil-paintings, however well executed, give the delicate, exquisite texture of a flower as nearly as water-colors. The semitransparency of a rose-petal, the juicy, translucent green of the young leaf, it is difficult to truthfully represent in other than these colors, whose essential quality is transparency. To preserve this transparency of color, everything about the painting must be kept exceedingly neat. The brushes must be thoroughly washed before using them for a different tint from that already upon them, and plenty of water, changed frequently, is necessary.

Having arranged your materials conveniently upon a table, place your paper so that it will lie at an angle slanting toward you, not perfectly flat upon the table; this can be done by putting books under the edge farthest from you, thus raising it up. Stand the flowers you wish to copy in such a position that the light will fall upon them only from one direction and pro-

16

duce decided shadows; the effect will then be much better than when the light is more diffused.

Always arrange your model exactly as you want to paint it, and leave nothing to your idea of how it ought to look. If you do not intend to have any background other than the white paper, place something white behind your flowers. If you want a colored background, arrange the color you have chosen behind the flowers, and paint it as you see it. Commence your work by sketching lightly, as correctly and rapidly as you can, the outline of your flower. Try

Painting in Water-Colors.

something simple at first; say a bunch of heart's-ease or pansies, and when drawing them try to get the character of both flower and leaf. Observe how the stem curves where it is attached to the flower, and at what angles the stems of the flowers and the leaves join the main stalk. Given character, an outline drawing painted in flat tints will closely resemble nature; without it, the most beautifully finished painting will not look like the flower it is intended to represent.

When your outline is drawn in, dip your largest brush in clear water, and go over the whole surface of your paper;

then place a piece of blotting-paper over the paper to soak up the water, leaving it simply damp, not wet.

If you are using tube colors, have ready on a porcelain palette, or ordinary dinner-plate, these colors : crimson lake, cobalt blue, indigo, Prussian blue, and gamboge. Put in your lightest tints first, leaving the white paper for the highest light ; then paint in your darker tints and shadows, and get the effect.

If your flower is what we call the johnny-jump-up, the lowest petal will be yellow. Paint this in with a light wash of gamboge, leaving, as we have said, the white paper for touches of high light. The two upper petals will probably be a deep claret-color ; this is made by mixing crimson lake and cobalt blue, the crimson lake predominating. The two central petals may be a bluish lavender, and this color is made by mixing a little crimson lake with cobalt blue. Use plenty of water ; but do not let it run, and keep the colors of the petals distinct.

Paint the stems and leaves, where they are a rich green, with a mixture of gamboge and Prussian blue, and where they appear gray as the light touches them, a pale wash of indigo will give the desired effect.

Keep your shadows broad and distinct, and your tints as flat as you can. Leave out details altogether in your first paintings, and add them afterward only when you can do so without spoiling the effect.

When a tinted background is desired, put it in quickly in a flat tint, before commencing the flowers. It is best not to bring the tint quite up to the outline, as a narrow edge of white left around the flower gives a pleasant, sketchy look to the painting.

Landscapes.

In your first studies from nature keep to simple subjects, and treat them simply, without any attempt at elaboration.

Choose, for instance, a picturesque corner of an old fence, with perhaps a bit of field and sky for the background. Sketch in the principal features in the foreground in outline, and indicate the horizon, if it comes in the picture.

Penley says, in his "System of Water-Color Painting," "White paper is too opaque to paint upon without some wash of color being first passed over it," and he recommends a thin wash of *yellow ochre* and *brown madder*, which should be put all over the surface of the paper except on the high lights in the foreground, which are best left crisp and white.

Notwithstanding what Penley says in this matter, it must be borne in mind that some artists do not believe in successive washes, but claim that the color desired should be put upon the white paper at once.

If the yellow tint is used, let it become quite dry and then wash it over with a large brush and *clean* water ; then, as in the flower painting, soak up the water with blotting-paper ; the blotting-paper must also be quite clean. While the paper is damp, not wet, begin with a blue tint—a light wash of cobalt will give it—and put in the sky *in a flat tint ;* bring the same color down all over your sketch except in the high lights. The blue tint gives atmosphere and distance. Let your paper again become quite dry, and then wash it over as before, in clear water.

The process of laying on color and lightly washing over it afterward should be repeated several times, "and the result will be a transparent aerial tone."

Keep your extreme distance bluish, your middle distance warmer in tone, but not too strong, and the principal objects in your foreground strong.

Leave out small objects, and with light and shade seek to obtain the effect.

Keep your colors pure or your sketch will be dull.

Contrast has much to do in producing strength and character.

Phillips says that, " in aiming at opposition of color, we must select that which gives force to the foreground, and consequently communicates the appearance of air in the distance. Thus, if the general tone of the light be warm and yellow, we should have blues and purples in the foreground ; if the lights be cool, reds and yellows in the foreground give atmosphere to distance, as neither of these colors in a positive state is found in the middle or remote distance."

The three principal contrasts are blue opposed to orange, red to green, and yellow to purple ; and " a good first lesson in sketching in color will be to put in your shadows with color opposite to the object in light ; and by carrying out this principle of opposition throughout the scale you will obtain an endless variety of contrasts." It is the general rule in most painting to have cool shadows to warm lights, and warm shadows to cool lights. We all know that a *green* picture is very disagreeable, and although a green field *is* green, it must not be made intensely so. An untrained eye will not see how nature tones down the vivid color with shadows, and softens it with the atmosphere ; but when the eye has learned to look at nature in the right way this difficulty will be overcome. Howard says, " green must be sparingly used, even in landscapes, whose greatest charm consists of vegetation."

Foliage in some form will present itself in almost every landscape, and it is therefore necessary to have a few general principles to guide you in this important feature. In sketching trees be sure to get the character of their trunks, limbs, branches, and general form ; also the texture of the bark, rough or smooth. You will see that the foliage appears in layers, one above another. Sketch in the outlines of the principal layers, where they are tipped with light ; then go over the whole tree with a local color, and afterward separate the light from shadow. Each mass is edged with light, while its base is in shadow, as a rule. Omit *details*, and keep to your *masses* of light and shade. If your tree is in the foreground, leave the white paper for crisp touches of high light. The tone of your fence will probably be gray, but do not take it for granted that it is *all* gray ; look for other colors, and you will find brown, blue, green, and sometimes red. Put these in as you see them, letting the edges melt into each other, as they will do when the paper is damp ; but have each color pure, and do not try to mix them.

Painting from Notes

is not as difficult as one might imagine. With a little practice it is easily learned. The following directions will tell how to paint a sunset on the meadows, from notes made at sunset on the meadows on Long Island.

Take a piece of Whatman's rough drawing-paper, or a kind that is termed egg-shell cartoon, the size decided upon for your picture. Have ready a large dish of clean water, brushes, and paints. Draw a pencil-line along the centre of your paper for your horizon, Fig. 151 ; then directly on the line paint a streak of vermilion. Put the color on quite damp, and make it about half an inch broad, extending one-fourth of an inch on either side of the horizon-line, Fig. 152. Next, quickly paint a yellow streak above and below the red one, making each streak of the same size and parallel, and leaving a little white paper between the different colors, Fig. 153. With a clean brush dipped in clean water carefully moisten the paper between the streaks, and allow the edges of the colors to mingle, Fig. 154. Before this has time to dry, paint a blue streak above and below, about half an inch from the yellow, Fig. 155 ; then with the clean brush dampen the white paper between, being careful not to get it too wet ; there should be just enough moisture to en-able the colors to flow and mingle at the edges, Fig. 156. This may be aided by holding the paper first one side up and then the other, until the edges are evenly blended. Now, before the horizon is quite dry, while it is still damp enough to cause

How to Paint a Sunset in Water-Colors.

the paint to spread, fill a brush with Payne's gray, which should be rather dark and not too wet, touch the point of your brush here and there along the horizon, now a little above and now a little below, and you will find that the paint will spread and make

Fig. 159

excellent trees for the distance, Fig. 157.

When your work is dry enough to paint over without spreading the color, mix some green and black, and green and brown; paint in the meadow, using the color made of green and black for the extreme and middle distance, the color made of green and brown for the foreground, leaving spaces for streams and ponds, and your sunset upon the meadow is finished. A pretty little sketch it is, too, Fig. 158.

A different composition can be made by proceeding as directed as far as Fig. 156,

Fig. 160
Leaf from an Artist's Note-Book.

and then, instead of putting in trees on the horizon, hills running to points in the water can be painted in a flat tint with the Payne's gray, and a vessel with masts painted in the foreground, as in Fig. 159. This also makes a pretty and effective little sketch.

Fig. 160 shows sunset notes taken while aboard a ferryboat in the winter of 1886–87. From these you can see just how the notes are made ; but you must make *your own notes*, because what is perfectly intelligible to the writer of the sunset memoranda is an enigma to another person. For example, in Fig. 160, " Rose-tinted sky " may mean almost any shade of red, or blue and red mixed, but " Rose-tinted sky " no doubt brings before the mind's eye of the writer of the notes the exact color of the sky at the time the notes were made.

A Study in Oil.

CHAPTER XXIII.

HOW TO PAINT IN OIL-COLORS.

HE difference between oil- and water-color painting lies in the fact that, although especially well adapted to the portrayal of some subjects, water-color has its limitations, while with oil-colors any subject, from the simplest study in still-life to the grandest conception of a great artist, can be represented, and no limit has yet been reached in its possibilities.

But there are first steps to be taken in all things, and the greatest artist who ever lived had to make a beginning and learn the preliminaries of painting before he could produce a picture. To these steps, then, we will turn our attention, and the first will be the necessary

Materials.

The following list of colors, with their combinations, will be found sufficient for most purposes.

YELLOWS.	REDS.	BLUES.	GREENS.
Yellow Ochre,	Vermilion,	Permanent Blue,	Terre Verte,
Naples Yellow,	Light Red,	Cobalt,	Emerald Green,
Light Cadmium,	Indian Red,	Antwerp Blue.	Light Zinnober
Orange Cadmium.	Venetian Red,		Green.

Burnt Sienna,   Rose Madder.

Silver White,   Raw Umber,   Vandyke Brown, Ivory Black.

Winsor & Newton's colors are acknowledged by most artists to be the best, but the writer personally prefers German white, as in her opinion it is not so stiff, and mixes better with other colors than the Winsor & Newton.

The Easel

may be simply a pine one, which can be purchased from any dealer at the cost of about one dollar. More elaborate easels are, of course, more expensive; but as the merits of a picture do not depend upon the easel which holds it, a common pine one will do.

The Palette

should be light in weight and not too small; oiled and not varnished. A very light-colored wood is not desirable; one of walnut or cedar, about eighteen inches long, is the best to use, and will cost from thirty to sixty cents.

Brushes,

both of sable and bristles, are used, but we would advise a beginner to work with bristle brushes only, for the first attempt should be to obtain a broad style of painting, without the finished details which the sable brushes are used for.

About four different sizes of flat bristle brushes are needed to commence with; there should be two of each size, the largest one inch wide, and the smallest not more than a quarter of an inch in width.

The Palette-Knife

is used for taking up color on the palette, for cleaning the palette, and sometimes for scraping a picture after its first painting.

It should be flexible, but not too limber. The cost will be from twenty-five cents upward.

Oil-Cups

are fastened on to the palette, and are used for oil and turpentine. The double ones range in price from eight cents to twenty. The single ones, without cover, can be bought for five cents.

A Paint-Box

for holding colors, palette, and brushes will cost from one dollar and twenty-five cents up. It is convenient to have one, and necessary when going out sketching, but for painting at home any kind of tin box will answer for the paints. The palette can be hung up, and the brushes put in a vase or jar, handles downward, which will keep them nicely.

Mediums.

Boiled linseed-oil or poppy-oil, siccatif Courtray, and turpentine.

Canvas.

In selecting canvas choose that of a warm-gray or creamy tone, for it is difficult to give warmth to a picture painted on a cold-gray canvas. The German sketching-canvas is quite cheap, and does very well to commence on. It is best to buy it on the stretcher, as a girl's fingers are seldom strong enough to stretch the canvas as tight as it should be. A very good sketching-canvas, 18 × 24, can be bought in New York City for twenty-five cents.

Several clean pieces of old white cotton-cloth are necessary for wiping brushes, cleaning knife and palette, etc.

The Light

in the studio, or room in which you paint, should come from one direction only, and fall from above. This can be managed by covering the lower sash of the window with dark muslin, or anything that will shut out the light. A shawl will answer for a temporary curtain.

Most artists prefer that while painting the light should come from behind over the left shoulder.

Our advice to beginners in all the departments of art is the same : commence with simple subjects.

Your first study should be from still-life (which means any inanimate object used for artistic study), and let the object selected be of a shape that requires but little drawing ; for your aim now is to learn to handle your colors, and it is not desirable to have your mind distracted by complicated drawing. A vase placed on a piece of drapery, which is also brought up to form the background, is a good subject ; the drapery should be of one color, and of a tone that will contrast agreeably with the vase and give it prominence.

Arrange whatever object you have decided to paint so that it will show decided masses of light and shade ; place your easel at a sufficient distance from it to obtain the general effect of shape and color without seeing too much detail ; arrange your canvas on the easel so that you will neither have to look up nor down upon it, but straight before you ; then sketch in the object you are about to copy in outline. Observe the edges of the heaviest shadows, and draw them also in outline. Charcoal is better than a pencil for sketching on canvas, as it can be easily rubbed off with a clean cloth if the drawing is incorrect. When the sketch is finished, dust off the charcoal lightly and go over the lines again with a camel's-hair brush and India ink.

Setting the Palette

is a term used for arranging the colors in a convenient manner upon the palette. The colors should always occupy the same position, so that, the places once learned, you will never be at a loss to find the color you want. Fig. 161 shows a con-

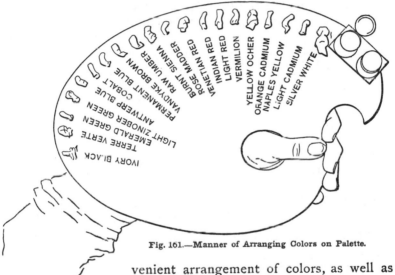

Fig. 161.—Manner of Arranging Colors on Palette.

venient arrangement of colors, as well as the position of the oil-cans.

Fill one of your oil-cans one-third full of turpentine, to which add enough siccatif Courtray to turn it the color of strong coffee. Dip one of your good-sized brushes in this mixture and scrape it off on the edge of the can, that the brush may not be too wet; then take up some burnt sienna on the brush and put it on your palette about an inch or so below the terre verte, add some terre verte, and mix the two with your brush. Lay in all the shadows of the vase, or whatever object you are about to paint, in a flat, even tone with the color thus formed, keeping it thin with the turpentine and siccatif.

Mix a tint as near the required color as you can, and go over the whole background without regard to light or shade ; cover all the background ; do not leave any white or bare canvas showing.

The general effect being thus obtained, it is easier to see what colors are needed for further painting.

Select a medium tint between the high lights and half-tones, and paint in the lights of the vase in a flat, even tint ; then go over the shadows again with a medium tone, still keeping them in one flat, even mass. Should you lose the outline at any time, dip a rag in turpentine and wash off the paint that covers it.

Having progressed this far, the painting should be left to dry.

The turpentine and siccatif Courtray have such drying properties that by the next day you may work again on the study.

Begin the second painting by putting in the half-tints. These unite the decided light and shade, and should be dragged over their edges, but not blended with them. Once more go over the shadows, strengthening them and putting in the reflected lights.

Add more color in the lights where it is needed, and put in the high lights with clear, crisp touches. Work on your background in this second painting. Indicate the shadows, but do not make them strong, except the one which will probably be cast by the object ; that can be strengthened, as it helps to set the object out from the background and gives the idea of space. Do not make the background strong ; keep it toned down, that it may not become too prominent. Drag the background a little over the edges of the vase, or whatever it may be you are painting, and then paint over it again with the colors of the vase. Do this while working around the edges of the vase, or object, to prevent its looking flat, as if it were pasted on.

These directions are to be applied to painting any subject ; but after you have learned how to manage the colors and wish to really paint a picture, the medium must be changed from turpentine and siccatif Courtray to oil, either linseed or poppy, using the turpentine only for the first effect of shadow.

When oil is used it will require two or three days for the picture to dry. Many advise the use of but little oil, and there are artists who dissapprove of any medium at all.

Before commencing the second painting, a coating of poppy-oil should be put all over the canvas with a large, flat camel's-hair brush. Every bit should be covered without touching the brush twice to the same spot. This softens the first coat of paint sufficiently to allow of its blending with the next. If a raw potato be cut in half and rubbed over the painting before the oil is put on, it will prevent the oil from crawling, or separating into drops on the canvas.

Do not use the same brushes for dark and light tints, but keep them separate. Mix your tints on your palette, the dark tint below the dark colors, and the light tint below the light colors.

In putting away your work after painting, be sure that the tops are screwed on to all your color-tubes, and arrange them neatly in their box. Clean your palette with the palette-knife, and then wipe it off with a rag. Dip your brushes, one by one, in turpentine and wipe them on a rag ; this removes most of the paint and makes them easier to wash. Warm, not hot, water should be used for washing the brushes. The best way is to hold several brushes in the right hand, their sticks being in an upright position, dip them in the water, rub them on a piece of common soap, and then scrub them round and round on the palm of the left hand ; rinse them in clear water, and wipe dry with a clean rag.

17

Our limited space will not allow of our going more fully into the details of painting ; but we hope that these directions will give some idea of how to make a beginning as a painter in oil-colors, and after you have made a start you will find two good professors at your elbow to help you along and encourage you —Prof. Judgment and Prof. Experience.

CHAPTER XXIV.

HOW TO MODEL IN CLAY AND WAX.

N eminent artist once remarked within the writer's hearing that, should he bring into his studio the first dozen boys he happened to meet on the street, taking them as they came, he would probably be able to teach at least half of them to model within six months, whereas there might not be one of them who could be taught to paint at all. Possibly none of these boys would ever become great sculptors, but they could learn to model moderately well. If that is the case with boys, who are apt to be so awkward and clumsy, how quickly could a girl's deft fingers learn to mould and form the plastic clay or wax into life-like forms. In some of the institutions for the blind, deaf and dumb, modelling is taught with great success. Quickly the sensitive fingers of the young inmates run over the object to be copied, and skilfully they reproduce in their clay the form conveyed to them by touch alone. It is pleasant to think that these silent little workers have this new pleasure added to their somewhat limited stock; but at the same time the fact puts to shame some of us who, having all our faculties, the use of all our senses, and not infrequently artistic ability in addition, do so little with the talents intrusted to our care.

Let us to work then, girls, and see if we cannot accomplish at least as much as our unfortunate sisters, who have neither sight nor hearing to guide them.

Modelling in Clay.

The great difficulty we encounter in learning to draw—which is representing things as they appear, not as they really are—will not trouble us in this other department of art, for in modelling it must be our aim to do precisely the reverse, and reproduce an object exactly *as it is*, not as it appears.

Modelling, besides its own worth, is of value as an aid to drawing, for it teaches form, and the shadows on an object can be drawn more intelligently and correctly when it is known just what formations produce them.

A great deal can be done in modelling without the aid of a teacher. So, not waiting to look up a professor, suppose we commence by ourselves and see what we can do. It is very fascinating work, and if a few failures are the result of our first attempt, we need not be discouraged, for what others can do, we also can accomplish.

The writer has lately been initiated into the mysteries of this art, and since, as they say, the person just graduated from a primary department is best fitted to teach in that department, perhaps the hints given here may be better suited to the understanding of beginners than if they were written by a great sculptor, who might forget that everyone does not know, as well as he does himself, the preliminary steps necessary even in accomplishing the grandest results.

Instead of entering into the later and more artistically finished processes we will confine ourselves to the prelude or introduction to modelling ; and then, girls, with the object before you, your only guide and instructor, you must work out the rest for yourselves.

The first thing to do is to provide your

Materials,

and here is a list of all you will need :

1. Clay, such as is used by potters, perfectly free from grit.

2. Modelling-tools. These can be bought at any artists material store, and the simplest ones might be made at home

Fig. 162

Modelling Tools

of hard wood. Only a few tools are necessary for a beginner ; Fig. 162 shows those most useful. The fingers and thumbs are the best of all tools, and a great deal can be done with them, though for fine, delicate modelling tools must be used.

3. Modelling-stand. A regular modelling-stand with rotary platform will cost from eight to twelve dollars and the expense may be an objection ; but the writer has found that an ordinary high office-stool with revolving seat makes a good substitute. If the stool is not high enough it can be raised by placing on the seat a drawing- or pastry-board, and on top of that a square wooden box about one foot high and broad enough to allow sufficient room for a good-sized head and bust.

4. Basin of water and towel for washing and drying the hands.

How to Manage Clay.

Clay costs, near New York, from one to three cents per pound, and about fifty pounds will be required. If possible buy it moist, but if dry, put it into an earthenware jar, or anything that will hold water, and cover with clear water. Let it remain until thoroughly moistened; then with a stick stir the clay around as, when a small girl, you did the mud while making mud-pies, until it is free from lumps and is perfectly smooth ; clear away from the sides of the jar and pile it up in the centre.

When it is dry enough not to be muddy and is still pliable, it is in a fit condition to work with. It is necessary to keep your hands perfectly clean and conveniences for washing them should be handy. Do not use muddy water or a dusty towel.

Fig. 163

Use any tools that will produce the result desired with the greatest ease ; a little experience will soon determine what they are, but as a rule the largest are best.

When leaving unfinished work cover it with a damp cloth to keep it moist. If you are working on a head, and the features have been commenced, stick a small wooden tool in the head just above the forehead to hold the cloth away from the face, for it is liable to soften the nose and push it out of shape if it rests upon it.

A frame made of laths (Fig. 163) covered with oil-cloth or rubber (an old gossamer water-proof will be just the thing), placed over the modelling, will keep it better than the cloth, as

Fig. 164

it excludes the air and prevents its drying (Fig. 164). When using the frame, sprinkle your work by dipping a clean whisk-broom into water and shaking it over the clay. Remember, the clay must always be kept moist and pliable and never allowed to dry. If it does become dry and hard there is nothing to do but to put it back into the jar, and go through the process of damping it again.

Keep your tools clean, and do not allow the metal ones to become rusty, as they will if carelessly left on the modelling-stand when not in use. To avoid trouble of this kind it is best to put your tools in a box where they will be perfectly dry. Unless you wish to go through one of the writer's first experiences, when she was obliged to let her tools lie in a pan of kerosene oil for two days, and then clean them with knife-brick.

How to Preserve Modelled Clay.

If terra-cotta clay is used, it can be baked in a kiln, which will, while hardening, turn it a fine buff terra-cotta color, and make the object, if well modelled, ornamental enough for almost any use.

From the other clay, plaster casts can be taken, and the article reproduced in plaster as many times as desired.

Hints for Modelling a Head.

Always work from a model, and it is best to try copying plaster casts before attempting to model from life.

Place on the centre of your stand a wooden or tin box (a

Fig. 165   Fig. 166   Fig. 167

How to Model a Head.

cigar-box will do) to form the base ; cover this with clay in the form of Fig. 165, and stick a support in the middle, as shown in diagram. The support may be a piece of kindling-wood eight inches long and about one inch thick.

Build up the clay around this stick, as in Fig. 166, and with your hands mould the clay, piecing it out here, and cutting off there, until it bears some resemblance to a head, as in Fig. 167.

Still using your hands, get the general proportions of the head, and then commence the features. Begin with the profile, using tools when necessary, and try for character without detail ; then turn the head a little and work from that point of view ; always look at your model from the same point of view as you do your work. Turn the head in the opposite direction and model the other side, keeping the face evenly balanced. Continue turning your work little by little, until each outline it presents is as near as you can get like the corresponding outline of your model, and then work up the detail.

In modelling any object the same process, of viewing the model from all points, must be gone through with.

Do not strive to obtain a likeness at first, but be careful to have all of your outlines correct, and the likeness will come of itself.

How to Model in Wax.

Modelling-wax prepared at home is much better than any that can be purchased. The following recipe is a very good one :

Modelling-wax.

1 pound pure yellow beeswax.
½ pound corn-starch.
4 ounces Venice turpentine.
1½ ounce Venetian red powder.
½ ounce sweet-oil.
Put the wax on the stove in a saucepan and let it melt ; *take*

off and pour in the turpentine. Never attempt to add this while the wax is near the fire, as it is extremely dangerous. It is a good idea, when buying the ingredients, to have the oil and turpentine put in the same bottle (which should have a wide neck), then they can be poured into the wax at the same time. Warm the bottle of oil and turpentine in hot water to soften before mixing with the wax. Keep stirring all the time. Pour in the corn-starch and Venetian red. When the corn-starch is dissolved the wax is ready for use.

Bas-relief Figure in Wax.

Modelling-wax is much more expensive than clay; it is used principally for small objects and those that require fine workmanship. It is quite useful for sketchy work, as it may be carried about almost like a sketch-book, and being so much cleaner than clay, it can be used even in the parlor without damage to table or carpet. With the wax on a small board one can sit at a table and work very comfortably. The tools for clay modelling may also be used for wax ; probably the smallest will be most useful.

As cold weather advances, we like to pass the evenings in some agreeable occupation, that may be carried on without disturbing the family group around the fireside. For such occasions, modelling in wax will make a pleasant pastime. Sitting quietly, taking part in the general conversation, or listening while someone reads aloud, one may model the wax into many pretty forms to be preserved afterward in plaster, or, obtaining a profile view, a likeness

Bas-relief Head in Wax.

of one of the group may be done in bas-relief. If a slate is used to work on, it will make a good foundation, and the head can first be drawn on it in outline and the wax built over it, using the drawing as a guide. The slate is smooth and firm, and it is a good idea to use it as a foundation for all wax bas-relief, especially when plaster casts are to be taken from the modelling, for in that case the panel forming the background must be perfectly even.

Making Plaster Casts.

CHAPTER XXV.

HOW TO MAKE PLASTER CASTS.

T is not at all difficult ; anyone can succeed in it who will take the pains to follow carefully the directions given here for making plaster casts. Without the knowledge of drawing or modelling you can in this way reproduce almost any article in a very short time.

Casting in plaster is really so simple a process that even a child can soon learn to manage it nicely.

You will need a board, about a foot and a half square, upon which to work, fifteen or twenty pounds of clay, five pounds of plaster-of-Paris, a cup of warm melted lard, and several small wooden pegs ; these can be made of wooden tooth-picks or matches broken in two.

Select an object with few angles and a smooth surface to experiment on ; a firm round apple will do. Rub the lard all over the apple until every particle is greased ; then lay it in the centre of your board. Take some clay and pack it around it just as high as the middle of the apple, forming a square, as in Fig. 168. Smooth the clay off on the edges and stick pegs in diagonal opposite corners (Fig. 168) ; then with more clay build a wall close around the apple and its case, making the sides one inch higher than the top of the apple (Fig. 169). Put a cupful of clear water into a pan or dish, and stir in enough plaster of Paris to make it like batter ; pour the plaster over the apple, filling the clay box to the top. This makes a half mould of

Fig. 168

Fig. 169

Fig. 170

clay and a half mould of plaster.

When the plaster is hard, which will be in a very short time, pull away your clay wall, and take out the apple and half plaster mould together, lifting the apple from its half clay mould.

Remove the clay from your board and set the plaster mould containing the apple in the centre. Rub lard over the apple and upper edge of the mould, build around it the clay wall, as you did the first time ; roll a small piece of clay into a slender conical shape and stand it upright on top of the apple, as in Fig. 169. This will make a hole through which to pour the plaster when filling the completed mould, and it must stand high enough to reach above the top of the clay wall.

Pour the plaster over the apple as at first, and let it set or harden. Take away the wall of clay once more, and carefully separate the two parts of the mould with the blade of a table-knife ; remove the apple, and all is ready for the final cast which is to produce your plaster fruit (Fig. 170).

Thoroughly grease the inside of your mould, fit the two parts together, and wrap and tie them with string to hold them in place.

Pour in the plaster, through the hole left in one-half of the mould, until it is quite full ; then gently shake it to send the plaster into all small crevices.

Let your mould stand without moving again until sufficient time has elapsed for the plaster to harden ; then gently separate the two parts and you will find a perfect cast of the apple.

The ridge made by the joining of the mould you must scrape off with a sharp knife, or rub with sand-paper.

In taking casts of almost any object not too complicated, this same method must be employed. The only difficulty lies in deciding just where to place the dividing-line, which must be exactly at the broadest part of your model, otherwise you will break your mould in taking the object out.

In casting a hand the clay must be built up around each finger to precisely its widest part ; therefore it is a good plan, before commencing, to mark on the hand, with a fine paint-brush and ink, the line that is to be observed.

When making casts of long objects, or those that are larger at one end than the other, such as vases, always lay them on one side, as a much better mould can be obtained in that way.

I have read that if milk-and-water is used for mixing the plaster, or, after the cast has hardened, if a little oil, in which wax has been dissolved, be applied to the surface, it will take a high polish ; and if left for a while in a smoky room it will acquire the look of old ivory.

The same writer also states, without giving the proportions, that liquid gum-arabic and sufficient alum in solution, mixed and put into the slip or soft plaster, will make the cast so hard that it can be set as a panel in a cabinet.

The dead white of plaster-casts is frequently objected to when they are wanted for ornaments ; but that difficulty is easily overcome by mixing dry colors with the plaster before wetting it.

Fig. 171

Fig. 172

A small quantity of yellow ochre will make the plaster creamy or ivory-like ; brown will give a wood color, and red a terra-cotta.

Plaster-casts can also be bronzed with gold, red, or green bronze, which makes quite handsome ornaments of them.   A plaster panel in bass-relief, bronzed with gold bronze and mounted on black or dark-colored velvet, is an exceedingly rich wall decoration.

To mount a panel of this kind you must first secure a smooth, flat piece of board, not more than half an inch thick, and just large enough to allow about four inches of the background to show all around the panel when it is mounted.   Cover the board with velvet or velveteen, bringing it smoothly over the edges, and tacking it down at the back.   Fasten on it a small brass hook.   Fig. 171 is the best kind to use, which is tacked to the board with small, brass tacks.

Make a ring or loop for hanging the panel in this way :

Take a piece of wire about three inches long, form a small loop in the middle, and give the wire several twists ; then bend the ends out on each side.

Scrape a narrow place in the top edge of the panel, just long enough to admit the wire, and about half an inch deep ; then place the wire in this little ditch and fill up the hole to the top with soft plaster. When this hardens the ring will be quite secure. Fig. 172.

CHAPTER XXVI.

CHINA PAINTING.

ERTAINLY you can paint on china ; have
confidence, and do not hesitate because you
may never have studied art, but select the
china you wish to decorate and we will go
to work.   First, take what is needed for
present use from the following

List of Materials.

PALETTE.

A common square, white china tile is the best palette for
mineral colors ; but in case you have no tile, an old white plate
will answer the purpose.

BRUSHES.

These are of camel's-hair, Figs. 173 and 174, are broad and
flat, and are used in placing the color on the china when the surface is to be tinted.   Fig. 175 is for blending the color after it is
on the china ; it is called a blender, and is useful where borders
and surfaces are to be tinted.   Figs. 176 and 178 are for general use.   Fig. 177, with its long, slender point, is for gilding,
another similar brush is needed for India-ink.   Mark the two
brushes in some way to distinguish them one from the other,
and never use either for any paint except that for which it is

intended. Fig. 179 is a stipple for blending the colors when painting a face, a fish, the sky of a landscape, or wherever delicate, fine blending is needed.

To clean the brushes after using : dip them in turpentine and wipe off the paint on a cotton cloth, repeating the operation until the brushes are perfectly clean ; then dip them in fat oil, and bring them out smooth to a fine point. Do not allow the brushes to become bent over, if the box is not long enough

Fig.173   Fig.174   Fig.175   Fig.176   Fig.177 Fig.178 Fig.179

Brushes for China Painting (about one-half actual size).

for them to lie out straight, remove the quills from the wooden handles and they can easily be replaced when needed. Should the brushes seem a little stiff at the next painting, immerse them in turpentine ; this will make them soft and pliable.

To save the expensive gold paint, the gilder should be kept exclusively for gilding, and need not be cleaned, as it will not be injured if the hairs are carefully straightened out and the brush put away with the gold.

KNIVES.

Fig. 180 is a horn palette-knife for mixing Lacroix white, the yellows, and all such colors as are injured by contact with

18

metal. It is the only knife used with the mat paints for Royal Worcester decoration. Fig. 181 is a steel palette-knife for general use. Fig. 182 is a steel scraper for removing paint from the china when necessary. Always clean the knives after mixing one color, before using them for another.

Fig. 180   Fig. 181 Fig. 182
Horn Palette- Steel Palette- Steel
knife.   knife.   Scraper.
(Reduced sizes.)

PAD.

This is made of a ball of cotton tied in a piece of soft lining-silk, fine linen, or cotton-cloth (Fig. 183) and is used for tinting.

THE PAINTS

are Lacroix's colors; they come in tubes and should be squeezed out on the palette and used as in oil painting, with a little turpentine and fat oil when desired. To moisten the colors while painting dip your brush, carefully, without shaking or moving it around, into the turpentine or oil, and then in the color. Allow the paint to lie on the palette as it comes from the tube, except when two colors are mixed, or when using the stipple for blending one tint with another, or when tinting, then the paint must be mixed and rubbed down with oil and turpentine. Keep the colors in a *cool* place, and when returning them to the box, after you have finished painting, do not lay them back on the same side. Always remember to

Fig. 183.
Printer's Pad.

turn them over so that the color will not separate from the oil. If you are careful and follow these hints, your colors will keep in a good condition. We would advise you to purchase the paints as they are needed, thereby avoiding all unnecessary expenditure.

OILS.

Fat oil is for general use in painting. Clove oil is used in its place when two or more tints are to be blended together, as in painting a face, etc. Capavia oil is always mixed with the colors for grounding.

TURPENTINE

is in constant demand in china painting. It is used with all the different oils, paints, bronzes, and gilt, and should be poured in a small cup or any little vessel, and kept convenient while painting.

TAR PASTE

comes in bottles, and is used to take the color off of tinted backgrounds, in order to leave a clean surface of the china in which to paint the design in different colors. The paste should be rubbed down smooth on the tile with the palette-knife ; if it is too hard, a little tar oil may be added. A small brush is best to use for the paste in covering the design you wish to wash out ; but be very careful to keep within the outlines, for this mixture will take off the color wherever it touches. When the tint is light the paste may be wiped off in a few moments ; but when it is dark, the paste must be allowed to remain on for perhaps hours before the paint will be sufficiently softened to remove.

Use small balls of raw cotton-batting in wiping off the paste, and take a fresh piece for every stroke. If any of the tar paste is left on the tile after using, scrape it off with your palette-knife, and return it to the bottle.

MAT GOLD

is for gilding, and can be either burnished or highly polished. It comes on a little square of glass inclosed in a box. This gold can also be used as solid ornamentation or for delicate tracery, and is sometimes used over colors, greens excepted, but is then never so bright as when on the plain white china.

The gold is prepared for painting on a tile kept expressly for the purpose, and which must not be used for any other paint. Place some of the gold on the palette with your palette-knife, and mix a little turpentine with it by dipping your palette-knife in the turpentine and rubbing down the gold with the turpentine on the knife. If more is needed, again dip your knife in the liquid, and do so as often as it is necessary ; but you must use the utmost care not to have the gold too thin ; gild with it as stiff as it can be smoothly applied.

Should any gold remain on the palette after the gilding is finished, mix in a little turpentine and scrape it all up with your palette-knife, then replace the gold on the square of glass.

Silver is used the same as gold.

The bronzes are for handles and conventional flowers or figures ; they are rich and pleasing in effect.

PURE GOLD

cannot be employed for gilding plain white china. It also comes on a little square of glass and is used for gilding over colors. It can be applied over any mineral paint or relief, and may be polished or burnished as desired.

This gold is mixed with turpentine, for use in the same manner as mat gold.

RELIEF.

The best is mat relief, which comes in a powder, and is used for both tube and mat colors. It is prepared by mixing with a very little fat oil and turpentine, and should be applied stiff enough to make a raised line. It is useful where a small raised surface is desired, as on the edge of a leaf or the petals of flowers. A fish-net is much more effective if the gilt be put on over the relief. Should the relief dry and become too stiff while using, soften it from time to time with a little turpentine, always using the horn knife for mixing, as the steel knife should never be used with the relief, and the relief must always be fired before the gilt is applied.

Enamel white can be mixed with delicate tints, turpentine, and a very little fat oil for raised flowers ; or the white alone may be used for pearls, imitation of lace, or embroidery, but its use is limited and it will not stand two firings, so should always be the last paint applied.

MAT COLORS

are for Royal Worcester decorations. They come in powders, and when mixed with a little oil and turpentine are used in the same way as the Lacroix tube paints.

BOX FOR MATERIALS.

Select a light wooden box, or one of strong pasteboard ; have the box of a convenient size to contain all your painting materials.

PIECES OF SOFT, OLD MUSLIN,

torn in different sizes, and plenty of them, are very essential for cleaning brushes and rubbing paint off the tile or china ; the demand for clean pieces will be constant while painting.

CHINA.

Have this of the very finest French ware, without spots or other imperfections of the surface, and never attempt to decorate china after it has been used, for it seldom proves satisfactory.

A Monochrome Painting.

For this we will need a tile, a pad, a broad flat brush (Fig. 173), some turpentine, capavia, two tubes of paint—one copper-water green, the other brown green—a palette-knife, and some pieces of cotton cloth. Now be sure your china is perfectly clean and dry, then mix your copper-water green for

Tinting.

Place enough color on your palette to cover the entire surface to be tinted; dip your palette-knife in the capavia oil and tap it off the knife on the tile ; in the same way place turpentine on the tile with the oil, and use your palette-knife to *thoroughly* mix the paint, oil, and turpentine. If the mixture seems too stiff add a little more oil and turpentine, but be careful not to have the paint too thin so that it will run ; test its consistency with a brush on a clean place on the tile.

As a rule, the proportions for tinting should be five drops of paint to three of capavia, mixed with a little turpentine.

The paint being prepared, take the flat brush and begin to paint ; rapidly cover the entire surface with color. Then go over the tinting with a pad, touching lightly and gently, not letting the pad rest a moment on the paint, nor touching it twice in the same place in succession. Continue going over and over it until the grounding is even and of a uniform tint. Then set the china away to dry, in a safe place, where it will be free from dust. Always make a fresh pad every time you tint, and a separate one for each color used, as a pad cannot do service more than once.

All tinted grounds and borders are made in this way, the capavia oil and turpentine being mixed with any of the grounding colors you may wish to use. Tinting is very easily and quickly done ; but should anything happen to spot or mar the evenness of the grounding, the paint must all be washed off with turpentine, and the china tinted over again.

When your green-tinted china is perfectly dry, gather some maple leaves and with the brown-green paint try a

New Method of Decorating China.

The leaves must be free from dust and moisture and perfectly fresh. Place a small quantity of paint on the palette, do not mix the paint with oil or turpentine, but rub it down well on the tile as it comes from the tube ; make the paint perfectly smooth, now press a small clean pad down lightly, lifting and again pressing until the paint is smoothly distributed on the pad ; next select a leaf and place it face or right side downward on a piece of folded newspaper, then press the pad down on the under side of the leaf, which is now lying upward, repeating the operation until the leaf is sufficiently covered with paint. This done, carefully place the leaf painted side downward on the china, over it lay a piece of common wrapping paper, and rub your finger gently all over the covered leaf. Then remove the outside paper and very carefully take up the leaf, when an exact impress of the natural leaf will be printed on the china. Repeat the operation with another leaf either larger or smaller, and still another, using as many as you wish ; connect the leaves to a central branch by making the stems and branch in the same color with a small paint-brush. To do this paint a long line for the branch and other smaller ones for the stems of the leaves. Set the china away to dry, and it will be ready for firing. Very pretty effects may be secured by using two shades of one color for the tinting and designs. First tint the china, and when it is perfectly dry, ornament it with the same paint in the manner described, making the ground of a lighter tint than the decorations. The colors of fall leaves can be used on white china, or you may make the combinations and designs of whatever is most pleasing.

It is well to have some idea of what your decoration is to be like before commencing with the leaves. If you desire a spray, try to place the leaves as they are on the natural spray, or as represented in some picture taken for a guide. The prints also look well used in a conventional style. As any kind of leaves or grasses that will print can be employed, your decorations will always be original and true to nature.

Flowers are more difficult to print, yet when the impressions are successful they are very beautiful.

You will find this new idea an interesting method of ornamenting china, while the decorations may be made in much less time than is usually required. The style is suitable for dinner-sets, vases, tiles, plaques, and lamps, and it requires no knowledge of drawing or painting to decorate china in this simple yet effective manner.

Tracing.

Lay a piece of tracing-paper over the design to be copied and trace the outlines very carefully with a hard lead-pencil. Then have your china perfectly clean and dry, and give it a wash all over with a clean cotton cloth wet with clear turpentine. Place a piece of red transfer-paper on the china, and having determined exactly where you wish the design, lay the tracing-paper over the transfer-paper on the space for decoration. Use

bits of gummed paper on the corners of the transfer- and tracing-paper to hold them in place, and carefully go over the lines
with a lead-pencil, remove the papers, and the design will be
clearly outlined on the ware. Now rub a little India-ink on a
common individual butter-plate of white china, and using a fine
brush, very carefully paint over the red marks with the India-
ink, making your lines as distinct and delicate as possible.
When this is finished, again wash the china with turpentine to
remove any of the red coloring which may be apparent on its
surface. Thus prepared the design can be painted, or the china
may first be tinted and allowed to dry, when the outlines will
be plainly visible through the tinting, and the color can be removed from the design with tar paste. Use the scraper to take
the grounding off of minute spaces. For those skilled in drawing it will not be necessary to trace the design, as it can readily
be sketched on the china with a lead-pencil after the ware has
first received a coat of turpentine, and when tinted the decoration can be drawn on after the grounding has thoroughly dried,
and the color may be removed as before.

Mottled Grounds.

Prepare the paint as for tinting, only make it more moist,
and dab it lightly over the china by means of a piece of cotton
cloth on the end of your finger ; this will give the china a mottled appearance which in some cases is preferred to the plain
grounding.

Snow Landscape.

We will take for example Fig. 184.

After tracing the design, paint a streak across the sky, just
back and a little above the trees, with carnation No. 1 mixed
with clove oil and turpentine, then another narrow streak above

it of a lighter shade, and another still lighter of the same color, allowing each tint to meet. Next mix light sky-blue with clove oil and turpentine, and paint as deep a tint as it will make across the sky at the top of the plate, graduating it down to the

Fig. 184

red ; use the stipple immediately while the paint is wet to blend the colors and tints ; this finished, make the reflections on the ice, beginning with carnation No. 1 for the ice nearest the castle, and ending near the bottom of the plate with the deepest shade of light sky-blue, using the colors mixed for the sky. Paint the foliage in the background with neutral gray and sky-blue mixed with turpentine and fat oil for the darker tones, and turquoise-blue with neutral gray, turpentine and fat oil for the lighter parts, also for shading the darker portions of the snow. Then take brown No. 4 as it comes from the tube, with a little turpentine when necessary, for the shading of the trees in the foreground, the outlining of the castle, and the tufts of grass and edges of the ice in places where the copy requires it.

Leave the white china for the high lights and the white snow on the roof of the castle, on the trees, and here and there on the ground.

Paint the castle with neutral gray and yellow ochre mixed with turpentine and fat oil, and its windows with brown No. 4, using the color as it comes from the tube. Now allow the plate to dry and then have it fired, after which mix carnation No. 1 with clove oil and turpentine, and touch up the sky and reflections on the ice, using the stipple if necessary; then mix light sky-blue with clove oil and turpentine and paint the sky where that color is required and the light shadows on the snow; then take yellow ochre for portions of the trees, places in the foreground, and touching up the castle; mix this color with fat-oil and turpentine.

Again strengthen the trees and other places, where the painting requires it, with brown No. 4, unmixed, except with a little turpentine when necessary; for the last touches mix relief-white with fat oil and clean turpentine, using the horn-palette knife always when mixing the white; this is to be laid on, in little raised places, where the snow is whitest on the ground and where the snow has lodged in the trees.

Now inclose the snow scene with a gilt band, using the stipple to make an uneven edge of gilt on the surrounding white rim; the gold next to the picture must be perfectly smooth and even; put this on with your fine long-haired brush;

then make a similar band on the edge of the plate and it will
be finished and ready for its last firing.

Almost any snow landscape with a sunset sky may be
painted in this way.

Often you can find Christmas cards which will furnish very
good copies.

Fig.185

How to Paint a Head on China.

Select a pretty copy from some photograph, as in Fig.
185; very carefully trace the head on a plate and go over the
lines with Indian ink; next give the plate another wash with

turpentine, to remove all remains of the color from the transfer-paper ; then mix thoroughly two parts of carnation No. 2 with one part of ivory-yellow, adding a little turpentine and clove oil; give the face and neck a wash with this color and touch up the cheeks with carnation No. 1 mixed with clove oil and turpentine ; now lay on the shadows with neutral gray, five parts, mixed with deep chrome-green, one part, using clove oil and turpentine in mixing the colors ; last, the deepest shadows with brown No. 4, two parts, to one of ivory-black, mixed together with clove oil and turpentine, and immediately before any of the paint dries use the stipple to blend the colors, making the face round out and have the blending soft and true to nature ; set your copy before you and try to have the shadows on the face you paint correspond exactly with those in the copy.

Now leave the face and neck, and place some brown No. 4 on the tile ; do not mix it with anything ; use it as it comes from the tube, dipping your brush in turpentine when it becomes necessary to thin the paint a little ; with this paint the shading of the hair and follow with your brush, as nearly as possible, the sway of the masses. That finished, paint the eyes, eyebrows, and nostrils with brown No. 4 and ivory-black mixed together as they come from the tubes, using when necessary a little turpentine ; then mix a little carnation No. 1 with fat oil for the lips. Next turn your attention to the drapery ; shade the white material with gray No. 1, unmixed, and gray No. 2 for the deeper shadows, mixed with fat oil and turpentine.

For the handkerchief on the head mix emerald-green with fat-oil and turpentine ; put it on in a light tint, so that the handkerchief can be shaded, when dry, with the same color.

When the plate is dry, it is ready to be fired. After it has been fired touch up the shading on the face and neck with two parts of carnation No. 2 mixed with one of brown No. 4, using clove oil and turpentine while mixing; and for the deepest shadows mix two parts of brown and one of ivory-black together with clove oil and turpentine. This must be put on carefully, so that the shadows will not be too dark. Use the stipple to blend the shadows ; then give the hair a wash of yellow ochre all over, and touch up the handkerchief on the head with emerald green, the same you used before.

For the background of the head mix light coffee, turpentine, and capavia oil ; make it an even tint with the blender (Fig. 175); the brush must be clean and dry, and used in the same manner as the pad in tinting, then, for the outer border, mix celestial-blue with capavia and turpentine, and with your large flat brush paint the border and blend it to an even tint with your pad. When this is finished wipe off the paint around the edge as evenly as possible, so that the bare china may be left to receive a band of gold. Roll up a piece of white cotton cloth into a small point and with this remove the paint around the inner edge of the blue border, making an even narrow white band ; this is also to be gilded.

On a clean tile mix the mat gold with turpentine, and using the slender, fine, long-haired brush, carefully cover the white bands of china with gold ; when this is finished the plate is ready for the second and last firing. If a fairer complexion be desired, make the flesh-tints of the same colors, only lighter in tint ; try the paint on the edge of the tile until the tint is correct. Always try your colors this way when painting any design. For blue eyes use sky-blue shaded with black ; the high light of the eye may be left the white of the china. If you wish the hair very light, take ivory-yellow and shade with sepia and black.

Once more we say, be *very* careful in tracing not to get the head or features out of drawing, as so much depends upon the correct outlines. Before sending china to be fired, paint in small figures the date on which it was decorated and add your name or initials.

How to Paint a Carp, Sea-weed, and Fish-net on China.

Having traced in your design very carefully, mix one part of neutral gray with two parts of sky-blue, some clove oil, and turpentine ; with this paint the upper edge of the back of the fish dark, graduating to white along near the centre of the fish ; stipple this so that it will look even, soft, and rounding, keeping it dark on the edge and tinting down to the white china ; paint the tail and dorsal fins a flat tint of gray No. 2 mixed with fat oil and turpentine ; then mix carnation No. 2 with fat oil and turpentine for a flat tint on gills, mouth, and ventral fin ; shade the mouth with the same color and paint the anal and pectoral fins a flat tint of carnation No. 2 mixed
with sepia ; when dry
shade with the same
color, and also shade
the gills and fins
painted carnation
with carnation, and

Fig. 186.

the dorsal fins and tail shade with ivory-black mixed with fat oil and turpentine ; try the paint with your brush until you get rather a gray tint instead of black, and use thin for the shading , now paint the rows of spots along the back of the fish ivory-black, making the dots smaller as they approach the tail ; and with your eraser take the paint off of the eye, leaving a clean white spot of china ; paint a fine circle around this in ivory-black ; then paint a portion of the eye black, leaving the white china for the high lights ; in painting the scales and lower part of the fish use gray No. 1 as it comes from the tube, mark an outline of gray along the lower edge of the fish and stipple it off in the white, remembering this gray must occupy only a narrow line along the lower edge of the fish.

Commence to mark the scales in gray No. 1 by making a
line of them with a fine-pointed brush downward across the
body of the fish (Fig. 186) and this will be a guide to build out
from (Fig. 187); after the painting has thoroughly dried begin
again by marking, on the head and around the eye, the tiny
scales in gray No. 2, with a little fat oil and turpentine, and paint
a line along the upper edge of the head and back with brown
No. 4, and another lighter line of the same color along the back
just below and adjoining the first one; paint the eye and
markings on the head brown and strengthen the tail and dorsal fins with gray No. 2; touch up around the gills with sky
blue, also with yellow ochre where the copy requires it. Then

Fig. 187

turn your attention
to the sea-weeds;
mark the thread-like
branches of these in
different colors, using
carnation, brown No.
4, gray No. 2, and
brown-green; paint
each weed in one color, place the sea-weeds on one side or
corner of the plate, making them branch out this way and that,
as in nature. Now clean off your palette and mix some mat
relief for the fish-net, which is to be placed over and across a
portion of the plate; with a lead-pencil mark the netting on
the plate, but do not touch the fish; then with a very fine
brush follow the markings with the relief, when it is necessary
to paint across the fish, your eye and the copy must be your
guides, as it would take the paint off the fish to attempt any
marking on it. The relief on the fish cannot be altered, so be
careful to have it correct the first time. Should the line of relief be too broad in other places, remove it with your scraper
and make another trial. When the plate is perfectly dry it

must be fired, after which put in a background of warm gray mixed with capavia and turpentine ; bring this to an even tint with the blender, and if any paint blends over on the fish wipe it off while the color is damp ; also remove the paint from the netting and set the china away to allow the color to thoroughly dry ; next paint broad sweeps across the plate, but not over the fish, with gray No. 2 mixed with fat oil and turpentine, to represent the different tints of the water, and again remove the paint from the net ; now touch up the sea-weed and the fish where they need strengthening, then give the fish a very light wash of gray No. 1.

Here and there along the upper edges of the water colored gray No. 2 make a very fine line with enamel or relief-white mixed with a little fat oil and turpentine ; gild the fish-net, us-ing either pure gold or mat gold, cover the relief carefully with the gold, and put it on thick but in fine lines ; this accomplished, finish by gilding the edges of the plate with mat gold, and when dry send it to be fired. To avoid mistakes when sending china to be fired, state whether you wish the gold burnished, dull, or polished.

Foliage on China Made With a Sponge.

Prepare the paint with fat oil and turpentine, rub it down smooth, then with a small sponge apply the colors, using differ-ent shades as the first dry, and touching up afterward with a brush ; in this way you can also paint backgrounds which can-not be made with the brush.

Mixing Colors.

The best way to paint with safety when you are in doubt what colors will mix, is to test them yourself. For this pur-

19

pose take a French china plate and make experiments with different colors on the plate ; at the same time write down a memorandum of the paints used and of those mixed, have the plate fired ; then paste your memorandum on the back. Use this for reference, and with experience will come the full knowledge of the use of all the paints.

Royal Worcester Ware

is very delicate and dainty and something quite novel for amateurs in the way of china decorations.

Very beautiful pieces of this ware may be seen now in all the leading china establishments in New York City, and so choice is it that even some of the largest jewelry stores have rare Royal Worcester vases among their most valuable articles on exhibition.

We know of no book that teaches this art of decoration, and although we have seen some amateur work which only an expert could distinguish from the genuine article itself, we think our exposition of the method is the first of its kind printed in this country ; and girls, if you would know the secret, so that you also may be able to paint and gild in this beautiful fashion, you have only to listen while the writer tells how to decorate a Royal Worcester vase as she did ; then you will have a practicable and detailed method which we know to be good, having tried it.

Select a vase of the finest French china, and be sure that it is perfectly clean, dry, and free from dust. Then with a clean white cotton cloth give the vase a wash all over with clear turpentine, and having chosen your design, make a tracing of it on the vase, and it will be ready for grounding. Mix enough mat lemon-yellow to cover the entire surface of the vase. First place a little of the powder on the tile, then dip your palette-knife in the capavia oil and tap it off on the tile ; in the same way drop turpentine on the tile with the oil. Use a horn palette-knife and *thoroughly* mix the paint, oil, and turpentine ; if the mixture seems too stiff, add a little more oil and turpentine, but be careful not to have the paint too thin, so that it will run ; try the paint with a·brush on a clean place on the tile to see if it is of the right consistency and shade ; do not let the color be too intense ; it should be of a delicate tint, and if it is too dark add a very little more oil. Take a broad, flat brush and begin to paint at the top of the vase, passing around with short strokes rapidly over its whole surface ; go over the tinting with a pad, touching lightly and gently ; then set the vase away to dry in a dry place free from dust. The Indian-ink outlines will be plainly visible through the paint, and when the grounding or tinting has *thoroughly* hardened, to remove the color from the design, mix a little of the tar paste upon a clean tile by working it with your palette-knife until it is smooth.

Fig. 188.—Royal Worcester Vase.

Use a small brush and go over the design with this mixture, covering every part except the stems and fine grasses ; be very careful not to go outside of the lines. When the design is all painted with the paste, begin at that first covered and wipe off the tar paste with small

pieces of cotton batting rolled into little balls, using a fresh wad
for each stroke ; clean it all off carefully and the vase will present vacant white china spots where the flowers, leaves, and bird
are soon to appear. For a guide we will take Fig. 188. Now
mix a little mat pink with fat oil and turpentine in the same way
you prepared the grounding yellow, only this time fat oil takes
the place of capavia ; use the horn palette-knife as before ; the
steel knife should never be used with the Royal Worcester
colors, as the metal is apt to rub in with the paint, dulling and
spoiling the colors. Paint all the flowers a flat tint of light
pink. Always try the color first on the tile until you have the
desired shade. By the time all the flowers have received their
tint of color, those first painted will be dry enough for shading.
Observe attentively the copy, and notice where the different
flowers are shaded ; then shade yours with the same color, following as nearly as possible the copy before you.

For painting the leaves, mix separately with turpentine and
fat oil, mat light yellow-green, mat dark-green, and mat blue
green. These colors can be used separately or any two mixed
if desired. Shade the leaves with mat yellow-brown mixed
with the different greens. Paint the body of the bird a flat tint
of mat gold-yellow and the top of its head and back green ;
the edges of wing and tail and eye must be of mat black.
When the bird is dry, shade its breast with broad sweeps of
mat gold-yellow, according to the copy ; then mix black with
yellow-brown for the other shading on the bird's breast, and
mix black with blue for painting and shading the wings and
tail.

While the paint is drying on the vase mix the mat relief for
the raised edges of bird, flowers, and stems. Mix the relief
with turpentine and fat oil, making it as stiff as it can be used.
With a very fine brush outline the bird, its wings, and tail ; also
a few strokes on its breast, tail, and back ; be sure the relief is

stiff enough to make a fine raised line ; then outline the flowers and the stems ; the leaves are not raised on the edges. When this is finished the vase is ready for its first firing. Allow the ware to become perfectly dry before sending it to the firers.

As great care should be taken with the firing of royal Worcester china, send your vase to the most reliable firers you know of, and when it is fired and returned, all that remains to be done is to carefully gild the vase. Mix pure gold with turpentine, but do not have it too thin, as the gold should be applied as thick as possible. For fine gilding use a fine small brush with long hairs ; this will make a distinct thread-like line ; first cover all the relief with the gold, next outline the leaves, veining them if necessary ; then with thick gold make your grasses according to the copy. When the gold becomes too stiff work in a little more turpentine. After you have finished this gilding, mix some mat gold with turpentine and gild the top rim of the vase ; use the small stipple brush cut off square at the end (Fig. 179), and bring the border down unevenly along its lower edge, making it the same way on the inside of the vase ; then with the fine long-haired gilder cover the upper edge of the vase thick with gold. This finished, gild the bottom of the vase in like manner and make the handle solid gilt ; after it is all dry the vase is ready for its second and last firing, and when it returns again from the firers you will have a piece of beautiful Royal Worcester ware similar to that seen at Tiffany's.

The mat colors used, remove all the gloss from the china, and when mat lemon-yellow forms the grounding, the china comes from the firing having the appearance of beautiful decorated ivory without any glaze.

This ware must be seen to be appreciated, and is suitable for vases and ornaments, but the Royal Worcester colors cannot be used on table china, for any grease coming in contact with the colors would spoil them.

Exquisite little vases of all shapes are decorated in this manner; the delicate gold tracery and outlining brings the designs out effectively. In this style of painting the decoration is more conventional, and does not require the same amount of working up and shading, but is as a rule, treated simply, flat tints with a little shading being all that is required. Almost any floral design can be used on royal Worcester, when outlined with relief and gold; there are, however, copies which come expressly for the purpose.

CHAPTER XXVII.

A CHAPTER ON FRAMES.

FTER the foregoing chapters on drawing and painting, it is surely our duty to provide the means
of framing the various pictures which we hope
will be the result of their teachings.   Un-
framed, a picture is apt to be tucked away out
of sight, or it becomes rumpled and spoiled
when left lying about, and a picture-frame, as a rule, is quite an
expensive article ; but with a little ingenuity and good taste
almost any girl may manufacture frames, if not of equal finish,
at least as durable and quite as artistic as any the dealer can
produce.

The cost ?   The cost is the price of a wooden stretcher and
a bottle of gold paint.

The first sketch shown here (Fig. 189) will give some idea
of the appearance of a frame decorated appropriately for a
marine picture.   The articles necessary for this frame are a
stretcher, some rope, a piece of fish-net, several dried starfish,
and gold paint.   The stretcher must first be gilded ; then the
rope, upon which the fish-net has been strung, should be fastened with small tacks around the outer edge, joining it at the
corner, where the starfish will hide the ends.   The net must
be large enough to drape gracefully across one corner, along
the top, and fall a short distance down the other side of the
frame.   When the starfish, graduating in size, are tacked

around the draped corner, and they, as well as the rope and net, are given a coat of gilt, a pretty, unique, and substantial frame is the result.

If starfish are not to be had, sea-shells may be used instead (these of course will have to be glued in place), and if fish-net

Original Design—Marine Picture Frame.

is also out of reach, a piece of fine netted hammock can be used as a substitute.

For the benefit of those who spend their summers at the sea-shore where such things are obtainable, I would advise that a small collection be made of the quaint and pretty products of the place, as they will be found useful in various ways for decorative purposes.

The next sketch (Fig. 190) shows a corner section of frame especially appropriate for a flower piece. The open lattice-like border is cut with a sharp penknife from stiff pasteboard and tacked along the edge of the frame.

Fig. 190.—Section of Decorated Frame.

The pattern shown in diagram (Fig. 191) is simple, quite easily made, and well suited for a border, though other and more elaborate ones may be used. This border must, of course, be made in sections. The edges to be connected should be cut to fit exactly, then after tacking them upon the frame the whole may be laid upon a table, face downward, and strips of paper pasted across the joints (see Fig. 192), which will hold them securely together. If the work is neatly done, when the gilt is applied all traces of the joints will disappear. The decorations of this frame consist of a spray of artificial rosebuds and leaves, gilded and tacked on the upper left-hand corner. A few scattered rosebuds look well upon the lower part of the frame near the right-hand side.

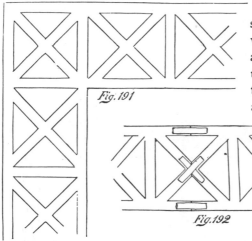

Fig. 191

Fig. 192

Section of Border for Decorated Frame.

Figure 193 is the section of a frame which will look well on almost any kind of picture. It is made by tacking a small rope around the inside edge and then covering it and the frame with crumpled tin-foil, which, after it is pressed to fit the rope, is brought around and tacked on the wrong side of the frame, joining that edge which is turned over the top. Care should be taken while handling the tin-foil not to flatten it, as its beauty depends upon its roughness. The pieces are joined by simply lapping one edge over the other, the uneven surface hiding all seams. This frame like the others must be gilded.

A very effective rough surface on a frame can be produced by dabbing on it with a palette-knife the scrapings of the palette. Of course this frame can-

Fig. 193.—Section of Frame covered with Tin-foil.

not be made in a day, but if every time the palette is cleaned the paint is used in this way it will not be long before the surface is covered and ready for gilding.

The cork paper used in packing bottles makes quite a handsome frame for black and white pictures or photographs (Fig. 194). This paper is sprinkled all over with small bits of cork, making a rough surface and one admirably suited to the purpose.

Fig. 194.
Cork Frame.

First the foundation of the frame is cut of stiff pasteboard exactly the size and shape desired ; then the cork paper is cut the width of the frame and glued securely to it, the corners being joined as in Fig. 195. The frame is very pretty when left its natural color, as it resembles carved wood at a little distance, but it can be gilded if preferred.

The inside mat is made of white or gray-tinted cardboard, cut with the open space for the picture, from half an inch to an inch smaller than the opening of the frame. The mat is pasted to the back of the frame and then the entire back is covered with strong paper pasted at the top and two side edges, and left open at the bottom until the picture is shoved in place, when the lower edge is fastened also. The mat will look well if the inside edge is gilded.

Another frame is made in the same manner as the one just

described, only instead of using cork paper a thick coating of glue is put all over the face of the foundation, and sand or small pebbles are sprinkled over the entire surface. This must be quickly done before the glue has time to harden.

The writer has in her possession a pretty little winter landscape done in water-colors. It is a snow scene, and its light effect is well set off by the frame, which is made simply of two pieces of heavy brown strawboard or pasteboard. The two pieces are cut exactly the same size ; then the centre is cut out of one, leaving a broad frame of equal width on all sides. The picture is placed between these two boards, which are then glued together. The cord for hanging it is fastened to two small brass rings which are attached to pieces of tape glued to the back of the frame, as in Fig. 196. Fig. 197 shows how a piece of paper is pasted over the tape to hold it more securely.

Fig. 195.

When making a frame of this kind the picture to be framed should first be measured and the width of the frame decided upon ; then cutting a piece of paper the size the open space is to be, or one-half inch smaller all round than the picture, it must be laid upon the pasteboard and a mark drawn around it showing its exact size and proportion (Fig. 198). The width of the frame can then be measured from these lines, which will place the opening exactly in the centre (Fig. 199). The lines must be perfectly straight and the measurements correct or a lop-sided frame will be the result.

Fig. 196   Fig. 197

In cutting out the frame a sharp knife should be used, and it will be a great help in keeping the lines straight if a ruler is

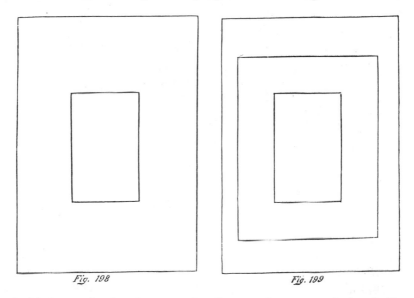

Fig. 198   *Fig. 199*

held down firmly close to the line to be cut, and the knife guided by that.

CHAPTER XXVIII.

THANKSGIVING.

 OT to Pagan ancestors in far-away countries, but to our own Pilgrim Fathers do we trace the origin of Thanksgiving Day—as purely American as our Independence Day. Instituted by William Bradford, the Governor of Plymouth, and first observed by the Puritans, who, suffering from hunger and privation, were truly thankful when the first harvest brought them the means of support for the approaching winter, it has come to us as "the religious and social festival that converts every family mansion into a family meeting-house." The pleasant New England custom of the gathering together of families to celebrate Thanksgiving is now observed in most of our States. From far and near they come, filling the cars with merry family parties, who chatter away of anticipated pleasures to be found in the old home. Little children taught to lisp grandma and grandpa are instructed by their mammas not to be afraid of the old gentleman who will meet them at the depot, nor the dear old lady who waits with open arms at the door of grandpa's house.

Children old enough to know what a Thanksgiving at grandpa's is like are wild with delight at the prospect before them.

Their eyes brighten at the thought of the great pantry where grandma keeps her doughnuts and cookies ; of the cellar with its bins of sweet and juicy apples ; of the nuts and popcorn, all of which taste so much nicer at grandma's than anywhere else.

And then what fun the games will be which they will play with cousins, who, though rather shy at first, will soon make friends. The lovely young aunties, too, who help grandma entertain all these guests, will join in the games and suggest and carry out schemes of amusements which the children would never think of.

What a happy holiday it is, how social and pleasant and comfortable and easy! How near and dear all the bright faces gathered around the long table at the

One Little Indian.

Thanksgiving-dinner, seem to be. Truly, we should all be thankful that we have a Thanksgiving.

However, this chapter is not written merely to generalize upon the pleasures of the day, but in order that we may offer something new, in the way of amusement, which will add to the fund of merriment on this occasion. The series of

Pilgrim's Spectacles.

Impromptu Burlesque Tableaux

illustrating some of the principal events in our history will be appropriate for this national holiday, and will prove a mirth-provoking entertainment.

When two rooms are connected by folding-doors, a whole room may be used for the stage. In this case no curtains are necessary, as the doors take their place, and, for impromptu tableaux, answer very well. When there are no such connecting rooms, one end of a large room can be curtained off with sheets, or any kind of drapery, suspended from a rope or wire stretched

Patterns of Pilgrim Father's Hat and Collar.

from one wall to the other. It is best to keep the audience as far away from this improvised stage as the room will admit of, for distance greatly assists the effect.

Landing of the Pilgrims.

TABLEAU I.—The good ship Mayflower has just touched Plymouth Rock. Pilgrim Father stands upon the rock, and reaches down to help Pilgrim Mother to land. A number of Indians sit upon the edge of the rock, fishing unconcernedly over the side, while the Pilgrims take possession. In the ship Pilgrim children are standing, with outstretched arms, waiting to be taken ashore.

COSTUMES.

PILGRIM FATHER. —Cape, a broad-brimmed, high-crowned hat and large, white collar, over ordinary boy's dress, spectacles—cut from black paper (Fig. 200). The cape may be of any material, so that it is of a dark color.

The hat can be made by cutting from stiff brown paper a crown (Fig. 201), fitting it around the crown of an ordinary flat-brimmed hat, bringing it

Costume of Pilgrim Father.

into a conical shape, and pinning it in place (Fig. 202). The brim should be cut from the same paper in a large circle (Fig. 203), the hole in the centre being just large enough to fit nicely around the crown, over which it is slipped, and pushed down until it rests upon the real hat-brim (Fig. 204). The paper brim should be about seven inches wide, and the crown nine inches high. Figure 205 is the pattern of collar, which can be made of white paper or muslin.

Manner of Making Pilgrim Mother's Cap.

PILGRIM MOTHER.— Full, plain skirt, white kerchief, small white cap, and large spectacles. A gentleman's linen handkerchief, put around the neck and crossed over the bosom, answers for a kerchief. The cap, too, can be made of a large handkerchief in this way.

Fold the handkerchief in the manner shown in Fig. 206 ; lay it flat upon a table, and turn the folded corners over as in Fig. 207 ; turn up the bottom edge over the other, and roll over about three times (Fig. 208) ; take the handkerchief up by the ends and the cap (Fig. 209) is made.

CHILDREN.—The young Pilgrims' costumes are like the others, on a smaller scale, but they wear no spectacles.

INDIANS. — Bright-colored shawls for blankets, and feather-

Costume of Pilgrim Mother.

dusters for head-dresses. The duster is tied on to the back of the Indian's neck with a ribbon which passes under the chin, and the shawl is placed over the handle, partially covering the head and enveloping the figure.

PROPERTIES.

The ship is a large wash-tub, which is placed in the centre of the stage; its sail is a towel, fastened with pins to a stick, the stick being tied to a broom, as shown in illustration. It is held aloft by one of the children in the tub.

Plymouth Rock is a table, occupying a position near the tub. On top of it is a chair, placed on its side to give an uneven surface, and over both chair and table is thrown a gray table-cover. The fishing-poles of the Indians are walking-canes with strings tied to the ends.

The Good Ship Mayflower.

First Harvest.

TABLEAU 2.—Pilgrim families, grouped in the centre of the stage, examining an ear of corn and rejoicing over their first harvest.

PROPERTIES.

A broom, upon which is tied one ear of dried corn, or popcorn, it doesn't matter which, and if neither is to be had, an imitation ear of corn can be made by rolling paper into the

Fig. 210.—Paper Ear of Corn.   Fig. 211.—Pattern for Outside   Fig. 212.—Ear o.
Husks of Corn.   Corn Finished.

The Corn-field.

shape of Fig. 210, cutting husks after the pattern Fig. 211, and putting them together like Fig. 212. The broom is held erect, with the handle resting on the floor, by Pilgrim Father.

Devastation by the Indians.

TABLEAU 3.—A long table reaches across centre of stage; upon it are empty dishes, and the remains of a feast.

At each end and at back of table are grouped the Indians, who are gnawing large turkey-bones and eating huge pieces of bread and pie. The Pilgrim family stand at each side, and view with horror the destruction of their dinner.

PROPERTIES.

The table is a board placed across the backs of two chairs. In the centre of the table is a large pie-plate, with only a very small piece of pie remaining in it; most of the other dishes are empty.

The Revolution.

TABLEAU 4.—This is represented by the revolution of a wheel. Pilgrim Mother stands in the centre of the stage, at a spinning-wheel, which is set in motion just as the curtain is parted.

PROPERTIES.

If a real spinning-wheel cannot be obtained, a velocipede, baby-carriage, or child's wagon, turned upside down, will answer

The Spinning-wheel.

the purpose. In the illustration the curtain has been made transparent, to show how the two back wheels of a velocipede are disposed of. A broom is fastened in an upright position to the velocipede, and on the handle is tied a piece of gray linen (a handkerchief will do), to represent flax. A string tied to the linen is held by Pilgrim Mother. The curtain must be dropped before the wheel ceases to revolve.

Slavery.

TABLEAU 5.—Pilgrim Mother is bending over a wash-tub, with sleeves rolled up to shoulders, washing ; a great pile of clothes lies on the floor at her side ; she looks angrily at the Pilgrim Father, who sits opposite to her with his legs crossed, calmly reading a newspaper.*

PROPERTIES.

The tub used for the ship, placed on two chairs ; a wash-board and a pile of clothes, white predominating. A rocking-chair for the Pilgrim Father.

Rebellion.

TABLEAU 6.—Pilgrim Mother stands in defiant attitude, facing Pilgrim Father, who has just arisen from his chair.

The tub and one of the chairs upon which it stands are tipped over, and the clothes are scattered about.

PROPERTIES.

Same as in preceding tableau.

Peace and Plenty.

TABLEAU 7.—Table extending across the centre of stage is heaped with all sorts of edibles—whole pumpkins, vegetables,

---

* Of course we all know that our Pilgrim fathers did not have the daily papers, but this fact makes it the more absurd.

fruit, and flowers. At one end of the festive board stands Pilgrim Father, at the other Pilgrim Mother, smiling at each other.

The Festive Board.

Pilgrim Father holds a long carving-knife, as though about to carve a large pumpkin in front of him. Pilgrim Mother is in the act of cutting a huge pie. At the back of the table are ranged the Pilgrim children, each holding outstretched an empty plate, waiting to be served, and all smiling. At each side of the stage, extending to the front, is a line of Indians

| Side View. | Back View. | Front View. |

Fig. 213.—Pumpkin Lantern.

sitting on the floor, smoking the pipes of peace. The Indians also are smiling.

PROPERTIES.

Table same as in Tableau 3 : Dishes, fruit, and vegetables. The Indians' pipes are canes with bent handles.

If, in arranging the stage, clothes-horses, with drapery thrown over them, are placed at the back, they will not only form a background for the pictures presented, but the space behind makes a nice dressing-room or retiring-place for those taking part.

Pumpkin lanterns, set in a row on the floor just inside the curtain, will be funny substitutes for footlights. They will decorate the stage appropriately, and at the same time be quite safe. Fig. 213 shows how they are made. The face is not cut through, but the features are scraped thin enough to allow the light inside to make them visible. If they were cut, as in ordinary pumpkin lanterns, the light would shine out from instead of on to the stage.

The Game of the Headless Turkey.

A large silhouette, representing a

Silhouette of the Headless Turkey.

headless turkey, is cut from black, or dark colored paper-muslin, and fastened upon a sheet stretched tightly across a door-way. To each member of the party is given a pin and a muslin head, which, if rightly placed, will fit the turkey. Then, one at a time, the players are blind-folded and placed at the end of the room opposite the sheet. After turning them around three times one way, then three times the other, they are started off to search for the turkey, that they may pin the head where they suppose it belongs. When the person going blindly about the room comes in contact with anything, no matter what, be it chair, table, wall, door, or another player, she must pin the turkey-head to the object touched. To the person who comes nearest to placing the head in its true place, a prize of a gilded wish-bone, tied to a card with a ribbon, is given. And she who makes the least successful effort is presented with a turkey-feather, which she must stick in her hair and wear for the remainder of the evening.

A Suggestion.

Amid all these bright and happy thoughts of feasting and merrymaking, comes an idea, so gently, yet persistently, forcing itself upon my notice, that it finally assumes the form of a definite plan which I will put to you in the form of a suggestion.

At this time, when, thinking over the numerous blessings, that most of you find to be thankful for, how would it do, girls, to form a society among yourselves, to be called the Thanksgiving Society, whose object will be to provide a real Thanksgiving for other and less fortunate girls, by giving them something to be thankful for before next year's Thanksgiving shall arrive?

There need be no formality about the society. The only necessary officer will be a secretary, to keep a record of what is done by the society, individually and collectively ; which report the secretary will read at the grand annual meeting on Thanksgiving Day.

Many girls, young, like yourselves, to whom it is just as natural to be glad and happy, have little to make them so, and to bring some brightness into their lives would indeed be worth forming a society for.

There are various ways in which kindness may be done these girls, and so many avenues will open to those seeking to benefit them, that it is needless to attempt any instruction as to what work may be performed by the society ; if this suggestion is adopted, I know it will be safe to leave it to the quick sympathy and warm hearts of the girls to do the right thing at the right moment. What think you, girls, would it not be worth while to make of this last Thursday of November a Thanksgiving for others as well as for yourselves ? and would not your own pleasures be doubly enhanced when sweetened with the thought of having done what you could to make someone else happy ?

CHAPTER XXIX.

CHRISTMAS FESTIVITIES AND HOME-MADE CHRISTMAS GIFTS.

MONG all the days we celebrate Christmas stands first and foremost in our thoughts, the holiday of holidays. Coming in the season of frost and snow it brings a cheering warmth to our hearts that defies the icy atmosphere, and the feeling of kindliness and good will toward everyone, which it awakens, seems in response to the words the angels sang on our first Christmas, " On earth peace, good will toward men."

Christmas is not merely a day set apart for feasting, giving and receiving presents, and for merrymaking. The day on which we celebrate the birth of our Lord is a time of rejoicing for rich and poor alike, and Christmas is Christmas still, although we may receive and can offer no presents and our feast is humble indeed.

Feeling this, let us keep the Christmas festival as it should be kept, right happily and merrily. Let us decorate our homes to the best of our ability in honor of the day, and supply all deficiencies with happy hearts and smiling faces.

A friend of the writer's once remarked, as she busied herself with some Christmas-cards she was preparing to send to the hospitals, " I always like to tie a sprig of evergreen on each card ; it looks and smells so Christmasy." And so it does. Even a few pieces of evergreen, tacked over doorways or branching out from behind picture-frames, give a room a festive, Christmas-like appearance that nothing else can, and as evergreens are so plentiful here in America there are few houses that need be without their Christmas decorations. Holly, too, with its brilliant red berries peeping cheerily forth from their shelter of prickly leaves, adds brightness to the other adornments, and when the white-berried mistletoe can also be obtained all the time-honored materials for the Christmas decorations are supplied.

Though we are Americans, our ancestors came from many nations, and we have therefore a right and claim to any custom we may admire in other countries. We may take our Christmas celebrations from any people who observe the day and combining many, evolve a celebration which in its variety will be truly American.

From Germany we have already taken our Christmas-tree ; from Belgium our Christmas-stocking ; Santa Claus hails from Holland, and old England sends us the cheery greeting, Merry Christmas !

The custom the French children have of ranging their shoes on the hearth-stone on Christmas-Eve for the Christ-child to fill with toys or sweetmeats, is too much like our own Christmas stocking to offer any novelty. The Presepio, or Holy Manger, of the Roman Catholic countries, which represents the Holy Family at Bethlehem, with small wooden or wax figures for the characters, is more suitable for the church celebration, but in Sweden and Denmark they have a peculiar method of delivering their Christmas-presents which we might adopt to our advantage, for it would be great fun to present some of our gifts in their novel manner.

Instead of describing this custom we will tell you just how to carry it out and will call it the

Julklapp,

which in Denmark and Sweden means Christmas-box or gift.

Before Christmas-Day arrives all the presents intended for the Julklapp delivery must be prepared by enclosing them in a great many wrappings of various kinds, none of which should in any way suggest their contents.

If one of the presents is a pretty trinket, wrap it up in a fringed tissue paper, such as is used for motto candy or sugar-kisses ; place it in a small box, and tie the box with narrow ribbon ; then do it up in common, rough brown paper, and wrap the package with strips of cloth until it is round like a ball ; cover the ball with a thin layer of dough, and brown in the oven. Pin it up in a napkin, wrap in white wrapping paper and tie with a pink string.

The more incongruous the coverings, the more suitable they are for the Julklapp. You may enclose others gifts in bundles of hay, rolls of cotton or wool, and use your own pleasure in choosing the inner wrappings. It will be the wisest plan to always use something soft for the outside covering, the reason of which you will understand when the manner of delivery is explained. Each package must be labelled with the name of the person for whom it is intended, and if an appropriate verse, epigram, or proverb be added it will be the cause of fresh mirth and laughter.

The Julklapp delivery may, and probably will commence very early Christmas morning, for the little folks, always early risers on this day, will no doubt be up betimes, and ready for the business of the day. The first intimation the less enterprising members of the family will have that Christmas has dawned, will be a loud bang at the chamber door, followed by a thump of something falling on the bed or the sleeper's chest. Then springing up and opening startled eyes, from which all sleep has been thus rudely banished, one will probably discover a large bundle of *something* on the bed or lying on the floor close beside it. It will be useless to rush to the door to find from whom or where this thing has come, for although a suppressed giggle may be heard outside the door just after feeling the thump, nothing will be met upon opening it, but dead silence, and nothing seen but the empty hall.

At any time during the day or evening the Julklapps may arrive and when all look toward the door, as a loud rap is heard, whizz ! something comes through the window and lands in the middle of the room. A sharp tap at the window is followed by the opening and closing of a door, and a bundle of straw, wool, paper, or cloth, as the case may be, lands in someone's lap. In short the Julklapps may come from any and every direction, and when one is least expecting them, and so the surprises and excitement are made to last until, weary with the fun and gayety of the day, the tired merrymakers seek their beds on Christmas-night.

If it has not been made plain enough who, or what causes the mysterious arrivals of the Julklapps we will say that the whole household join in the conspiracy, and the packages come from the hands of each of its members. The

Polish Custom

of searching for Christmas gifts, which have previously been hidden in all manner of places in the house, is one the children will delight in, and one that, introduced at a Christmas party, will provoke no end of merriment and fun.

The Bran Pie

is an English dish, but is quite as well suited to the American taste. It is an excellent means of distributing trifling gifts and may be new to some of you.

Use a large, deep brown dish for the pie. Put in it a gift for everyone who will be at the Christmas dinner, and cover them over thickly with bran, ornament the top by sticking a sprig of holly in the centre. After dinner have the bran pie put on the table with a spoon and plates beside it, and invite everyone to help her or himself, each spoonful bringing out whatever it touches. Comical little articles may be put in the pie, and the frequent inappropriateness of the gift to the receiver of it, helps to create laughter.

The Bran Pie should be the secret of not more than two persons, for, like all things pertaining to Christmas gifts, the greater the surprise, the more pleasure there will be in it.

The Blind Man's Stocking

may also be used for small gifts, or it may hold only candy and bonbons. Make the stocking of white or colored tissue-paper like the pattern given in Fig. 214.

First cut out one piece like the pattern, making the foot thirteen inches long and six inches from the sole to the top of the instep, and the leg of the stocking sixteen inches from the heel to the top ; then cut another, one inch larger all around than the first. Place the two together fold the edge of the larger over the smaller piece and paste it down all around except at the top

Fig. 214.—Paper Stocking.

(Fig. 214). Fill the stocking with small gifts or sweetmeats,

21

tie a string around the top to keep it fast, and suspend it from the centre of a doorway. Blindfold each player in turn, put a long, light stick in her hand, a bamboo cane will do, and lead her up within reach of the stocking and tell her to strike it. When anyone succeeds in striking the stocking and a hole is torn in it, the gifts or candy will scatter all over the floor to be scrambled for by all the players. Each player should be allowed three trials at striking the stocking.

Young children are always delighted with this Christmas custom, and the older ones by no means refuse to join in the sport.

Home-made Christmas Gifts.

That the children may do their share toward filling the Christmas stockings, adding to the fruit of the Christmas tree, helping with the Julklapps, contributing to the Bran Pie or Blind Man's Stocking, we give these hints on home-made Christmas gifts, all of which are inexpensive and easily constructed.

Fig. 215.—Chamois for Eye-glasses.

Chamois for Eye-glasses.

Cut out two circular pieces of chamois-skin about the size of a silver half-dollar, bind the edges with narrow ribbon, and fasten the two pieces together with a bow of the same. Print with a lead pencil on one piece of the chamois-skin, "I Make all Things Clear," and go over the lettering with a pen and India ink, or you may paint the letters in colors to match the ribbon. Fig. 215 shows how it should look when finished.

Glove Pen-wiper.

Cut four pieces from thin, soft chamois-skin, like the outline of Fig. 216. Stitch one with silk on the sewing-machine, according to the dotted lines. Cut two slits at the wrist through

Fig. 216.—Pattern of Pen-wiper.   Fig. 217.—Pen-wiper.

all the pieces as shown in Fig. 216, and join them together by a narrow ribbon passed through the openings, and tied in a pretty bow, Fig. 217.

Sachet.

Open out an envelope, and cover it with white or cream-colored silk, refold carefully, joining the edges with stiff mucilage, using as little as possible. In place of a letter enclose a layer of cotton sprinkled with sachet-powder, fasten the envelope with sealing-wax as in an ordinary letter. Address it with pen and ink, to the one for whom it is intended. Print on it,

Fig. 218.—Sachet.

like a stamp, " Christmas, December 25," and fasten a cancelled stamp, taken from an old letter, on one corner. The finished sachet is shown in Fig. 218.

Fig. 219.—Book-mark.

A Book-mark.

Cut out the corner of a full-sized, linen-lined envelope, making the piece four inches long, and one and a half inches wide. Write on one side with pen and ink, or paint the lettering in color, " A Fresh Mind Keeps the Body Fresh." The book-mark will fit over the book-leaf like a cap, and is excellent for keeping the place. Fig. 219.

A Scrap-bag.

Scrap-bags have been fashioned in many shapes and sizes, and of all sorts of material, still it remains to be shown in what manner Christmas

Fig. 220.—Pattern of Scrap-bag.

cards may add in decoration and beauty to these useful articles.

From your collection choose four cards of the same size, then on a piece of bright silk or cloth sew the cards at equal dis-ᵣ tances apart, as in Fig. 220, stitching them around the edges on the sewing-machine. At the dotted line fold over the top of the bag as if for a hem, making the narrow fold lap just cover the upper edge of the card; stitch this down to form a binding.

After joining the bag at the dotted lines on the sides, gather the bottom up tight and fasten to it a good-sized tassel; then sew on each side a heavy cord with tassels placed where the cord joins the bag, as seen in Fig. 221. The cord and tassels of the example were made of scarlet worsted.

Fig. 221.—Scrap-bag.

A Walnut-shell Turtle.

For an ornament to be used on a pen-wiper, or simply as a pretty toy,

Fig. 222.—Pattern of Turtle.

the little turtle is appropriate. It is made of half an English walnut, which forms the turtle's back or shell, glued on a piece of card-board cut after the diagram given in Fig. 222. Paint

Fig. 223.—Walnut-shell Turtle.

the card-board as nearly as possible the color of the shell, and the eyes black. When perfectly dry glue the shell securely to the card-board, bend down and out the feet a little, in order to make the turtle stand; bend the head up, and the tail down, as in Fig. 223.

Here are some home-made toys which the children can make to give to one another.

Miss Nancy.

Miss Nancy (Fig. 226) is fashioned from a piece of pith taken out of a dried cornstalk.　Cut away the stalk until the pith is reached ; then take a piece of the pith, about six inches

Fig. 224.　　　Fig. 225.
Manner of Making Miss Nancy.

Fig. 226.—Miss Nancy.

long and whittle out one end to resemble a head as in Fig. 224, draw a face on the head with pen and ink, and glue half of a lead bullet on the lower end of the pith (Fig. 225).　Make Miss Nancy's costume of a skirt, composed of some bright-colored Japanese paper, a shawl made of a piece of soft ribbon or silk, and a cap of white swiss.　The peculiarity of the little lady is that she insists upon always standing upright, no matter in what position she is placed.

A Soft Ball.

A very pretty and safe return ball for the little ones to play with may be made of paper (Fig. 227), which, being soft, precludes all danger of " thumps and bumps."

Take a piece of newspaper, and, using both hands, roll it and fold it into something of the required shape. Then place it in the centre of a square piece of bright-colored tissue paper ; take the four corners of the tissue-paper up to the centre of the top of the ball, fold them over, also fold and smooth down what fulness there may be ; next place a small round piece of gold, silver, or some contrasting colored paper on the top of the ball. Secure all by winding a string around the ball, making six or eight divisions ; tie a piece of elastic to the string where it crosses on the top of the ball, then paste over this a small artificial flower. In the other end of the elastic, make a loop to fit over the finger, or tie on it a small brass ring.

Fig. 227.—Paper Ball.

If a tiny sleigh-bell be placed in the centre when the ball is being made, it will give a cheerful little tinkling noise whenever the ball is thrown.

A Lively Rooster.

To make the rooster (Fig. 228), cut out of stiff cardboard Figs. 229, 230, 231, and 232. Tie on Figs. 229 and 230 each a piece of string seven and one-half inches long. Then attach

the head and tail to the body by running a string through holes
at A in Fig. 230 and A in Fig. 231, and another through B in
Fig. 229 and B in Fig. 231. Bring the head and tail up close
to the body and fasten the ends of the strings down securely

Fig. 233.—
The Weight.

Fig. 229

Fig. 230

Fig. 231

Fig. 232.

Fig. 228.—The Rooster.   Pattern of Rooster.

with court-plaster or pieces of paper pasted over them. Bend
Fig. 231 at dotted line C ; then on the space marked E, paste
the portion of Fig. 232 marked E after bending it at dotted line
O. Again bend Fig. 232 in the same direction at dotted line

P, and paste it across the space marked P, on Fig. 231. When all is fastened together, and the paste perfectly dry, paint the rooster to look as life-like as possible. Tie the strings of Figs. 229 and 230 together four inches from where they are fastened on, then again about three inches lower down, and attach a weight to the ends. A common wooden top, with a tack in the head (Fig. 233), will answer the purpose nicely. To bring

Fairy Dancers.

the rooster to life, place him on the mantel-piece, with a book serving as a weight on the projection of Fig. 232, swing the top and he will move his head and tail in the most amusing manner.

Fairy Dancers.

Among the gifts made by little hands, a box, containing a set of fairy dancers, will be a most novel and welcome addition. These little figures, when placed on the piano, will move as soon as the keys are touched, dancing fast or slow in perfect time to the music. They may all be made to resemble fairies as in Fig. 234, or a famous collection of figures in the costumes of different periods in history will be equally pretty and perhaps more interesting. Ladies in kirtles and tunics, gentlemen in slashed doublet and hose of the Tudor times, Queen Elizabeth's starched ruffs and farthingales, etc. All these dresses can be more easily copied from pictures of the period than from any written description of them. The materials used for the costume must be of the lightest kind, for a heavy dress will weigh down the dancer and hamper its movements. To

Fig. 234.—A Fairy Dancer.

Fig. 235.—Pattern of Fairy Dancer.

make the fairy (Fig. 234) trace Fig. 235 on cardboard and cut it out, sew a piece of bonnet-wire down the back, as shown in diagram. Mark the slippers on the feet with ink or black paint, select a Christmas or advertising card representing a child, with a head of a suitable size, cut the head out and paste it on the fairy.

Gather two short skirts of tarlatan, make a waist of the same, sew with a few stitches to the doll, and cover the stitches with a sash of bright colored tissue paper; add a strip of tarlatan for a floating scarf, gluing it to the uplifted

Fig. 236.—Pattern of Chinaman.

hands. Bend back the piece of cardboard projecting from the foot, and glue to it a small piece of bristle brush. The wire on the doll should be long enough to pass tightly around the brush, thus making it more secure.

Fig. 237. Fig. 238.
Chinaman's
Queue.

If you would like to have the Chinaman (Fig. 239) in your troupe of dancers, trace on cardboard Fig. 236,

Fig. 239 —The Chinaman.

draw a face with slanting eyes, or paint it; then take several strands of black thread and tie them together in the centre with another piece of thread (Fig. 237), bring the ends down together (Fig. 238), braid them and sew the braid to the back of the Chinaman's head (239). Cut a loose sacque from pattern Fig. 240, fold at the waved lines and sew together at the dotted lines ; cut an opening for the head as seen in pattern. Make the hat of dark green paper cut in the form of Fig. 241, and crimp it from the centre (Fig. 242). Sew the hat to the back of the Chinaman's head, bend the cardboard projection at the feet and glue it to a piece of brush.

Fig. 240.—Chinaman's Sacque.

Fig. 241. — Pattern of Chinaman's Hat.

Fig. 242. — Chinaman's Hat.

Butterflies of brilliant hues, all hovering and circling, may take the place of the fairies, or they may mingle with them in the dance, presenting a scene indeed fairy-like. To make a

Butterfly Pattern.

Butterfly.

butterfly, trace the pattern given in Fig. 243, on brilliantly colored paper. Form a body by rolling a small piece of beeswax between the fingers until it assumes the desired shape (Fig. 244) ; then attach the wings to the body by softening the wax and sticking them to it. Wax a piece of black thread to stiffen it, and make a knot in each end (Fig. 245), bend this in the middle and stick it on to the head to form the antennæ (Fig. 246). Fasten one end of a very fine wire securely in the middle of the wax body, and wrap the other end around a small piece of brush as seen in Fig. 247. A number of these butterflies placed on the pianoforte will move, bend and sway with the music as if endowed with life.

Toys, also, which are small and light enough, can be made to "trip the light fantastic" in time to the music.

Select those most suitable and glue them to pieces of brush in the way described for the other dancers.

The children, generous little souls, always long to do their part towards making Christmas presents, and we hope that the suggestion we have offered will help them to manufacture, without other aid, many little gifts which their friends will prize the more highly for having been made by the loving little hands.

CHAPTER XXX.

AMUSEMENTS AND GAMES FOR THE CHRISTMAS HOLIDAYS.

 WINTER passed in-doors would be irksome indeed for a healthy, hearty girl, and even the most delicate are the better for an outing now and then. The keen northwest wind, the biting frosts, the crisp atmosphere and the glistening ice and snow are not without their attractions, and we hope that no American girl will neglect the opportunities this time of the year affords for healthy, enjoyable out-door pastime. It is well to follow the example of our Canadian sisters, and, clad in garments warm and appropriate, indulge in coasting, tobogganing, skating, sleighing, and walking.

The country, wrapped in its winter mantle, is very attractive. Many of our small animals and birds that city people are apt to associate only with a summer landscape, are to be found abroad in mid-winter, and upon a bright sunny day the birds are not only to be seen, but heard twittering and even singing in the hedges ; they do not feel the cold and are enjoying themselves heartily. The reason the birds and wild creatures are so comfortably content, is because they are prepared for the weather, their clothing is not only soft and warm, but fits them perfectly, without interfering with their movements. Take a lesson from them, girls, dress as becomingly as you choose, the birds always do that, but do not wear thin-soled shoes or anything that is uncomfortable ; wrap up warm and you can enjoy yourself out of doors in the coldest weather just as well as the birds. The cold winds will only bring the roses to your cheeks, and the keen, invigorating air, health and suppleness to your body.

We do not think any person ever learned to skate, coast, or walk on snow-shoes from reading the directions that can be given in a book. It is for that reason we have no chapter devoted to these sports and not because we do not believe in, and enjoy them, too. Therefore we will direct our attention to indoor sports, for they can be learned in this way and are quite as important as the others in filling out the list of winter amusements.

There are a great many days in winter when it is so stormy and disagreeable out-doors, one is glad enough to have the shelter of a roof and the warmth of a fire ; these are the days and evenings when in-doors games are in demand, and during the holiday season, when work has been put aside, and you have nothing to do but enjoy yourself, any new diversion is always welcome. It is here then that we will insert the

New Game of Bubble Bowling.

When the game of Bubble Bowling was played for the first time, it furnished an evening's entertainment, not only for the children, but for grown people also ; even a well known general and his staff, who graced the occasion with their presence, joined in the sport, and seemed to enjoy it equally with their youthful competitors. Loud was the chorus of " Bravo ! " and merry the laugh of exultation when the pretty crystal ball passed safely through its goal; and sympathy was freely expressed in many an " Oh ! " and " Too bad ! " as the wayward bubble rolled gayly off toward the floor, or, reaching the goal, dashed itself against one of the stakes and instantly vanished into thin air.

The game should be played upon a long, narrow table, made simply of a board about five feet long and eighteen inches wide, resting upon high wooden " horses." On top of the table, and at a distance of twelve inches from one end, should be fastened in an upright position, two stakes, twelve inches high; the space between the stakes should be eight inches, which will make each stand four inches from the nearest edge of the table. When finished, the table must be covered with some sort

Bubble Bowling.

of woollen cloth ; an old shawl or a breadth of colored flannel will answer the purpose excellently. Small holes must be cut at the right distance for the stakes to pass through. The cloth should be allowed to fall over the edge of the table, and must not be fastened down, as it will sometimes be necessary to remove it in order to let it dry. It will be found more convenient, therefore, to use two covers, if they can be provided, as then there can always be a dry cloth ready to replace the one that has become too damp. The bubbles are apt to stick when they come upon wet spots, and the bowling can be carried on in a much more lively manner if the course is kept dry. Each of the stakes forming the goal should be wound with bright ribbons of contrasting colors, entwined from the bottom up, and ending in a bow at the top. This bow can be secured in place by driving a small brass-headed tack through the ribbon into the top of the stake. If the rough pine legs of the table seem too unsightly, they can easily be painted, or a curtain may be made of bright-colored cretonne—any other material will do as well, provided the colors are pleasing—and tacked around the edge of the table, so as to fall in folds to the floor. The illustration shows the top of the table, when ready for the game.

For an impromptu affair, a table can be made by placing a leaf of a dining-table across the backs of two chairs, and covering it with a shawl; lead pencils may be used for the stakes, and they can be held in an upright position by sticking them in the tubes of large spools. This sort of table the children can arrange themselves, and it answers the purpose very nicely. The other things to be provided for the game are a large bowl of strong soapsuds, made with hot water and common brown soap, and as many pipes as there are players.

The prizes for the winners of the game may consist of any trinkets or small articles that fancy or taste may suggest.

Bubble Bowling can be played in two ways. The first method requires an even number of players, and these must be divided into two equal parties. This is easily accomplished by selecting two children for captains, and allowing each captain to choose, alternately, a recruit for her party until the ranks are filled, or, in other words, until all the children have been chosen; then, ranked by age, or in any other manner preferred, they form in line on either side of the table. A pipe is given to each child, and they stand prepared for the contest. One of the captains first takes her place at the foot of the table, where she must remain while she is bowling, as a bubble pass-

22

ing between the stakes is not counted unless blown through the goal from the end of the table.

The bowl of soapsuds is placed upon a small stand by the side of the bowling-table, and the next in rank to the captain, belonging to same party, dips her pipe into the suds and blows a bubble, not too large, which she then tosses upon the table in front of the captain, who, as first bowler, stands ready to blow the bubble on its course down through the goal. Three successive trials are allowed each player ; the bubbles which break before the bowler has started them, are not counted.

The names of all the players, divided as they are into two parties, are written down on a slate or paper, and whenever a bubble is sent through the goal, a mark is set down opposite the name of the successful bowler.

When the captain has had her three trials, the captain on the other side becomes bowler, and the next in rank of her own party blows the bubbles for her. When this captain retires, the member of the opposite party, ranking next to the captain, takes the bowler's place and is assisted by the one whose name is next on the list of her own side ; after her the player next to the captain on the other side ; and so on until the last on the list has her turn, when the captain then becomes assistant and blows the bubbles.

The number of marks required for either side to win the game, must be decided by the number of players ; if there are twenty—ten players on each side—thirty marks would be a good limit for the winning score.

When the game has been decided, a prize is given to that member of the winning party who has the greatest number of marks attached to her name showing that she has sent the bubble through the goal a greater number of times than any player on the same side. Or, if preferred, prizes may be given to every child belonging to the winning party. The other way in which Bubble Bowling may be played is simpler, and does not require an even number of players as no sides are formed.

Each bowler plays for herself, and is allowed five successive trials ; if three bubbles out of the five be blown through the goal the player is entitled to a prize. The child acting as assistant becomes the next bowler, and so on until the last in turn becomes bowler, when the one who began the game takes the place of assistant.

When the evening lamps are lighted and the young folks, gathered cosily around the cheerful fire, begin to be at a loss how to amuse themselves, let them try the game of

Biographical Nonsense.

A paper must be written by one of the players which will read like the following :
The name of a noted man.
A date between the flood and the present year.
The name of a noted man.
A country.
The name of some body of water or river.
Some kind of a vessel.
A country.
A country.
The name of a school.
A city.
A city, town, or country.
A city, town, or country.
A number.
The names of two books.
The name of one book.
A wonderful performance.
The name of a well-known person.

A profession or trade.

A term expressing the feeling entertained for another person.

A term descriptive of someone's appearance.

A word denoting size.

A term describing form.

A color.

A word denoting size.

The name of an article of some decided color.

The name of any article.

The name of any article.

A number of years.

This paper is to be passed to each member of the party who in turn will fill up the blanks left, with the words, terms, and names indicated.

When the blanks have been filled, one player must read the following, and another supply the words, when she pauses, from the paper just prepared, being sure to read them in their true order.

A BIOGRAPHY.

———— was born in ———— the same year when ———— discovered ————, by sailing through the ———— in a ————. His father was a native of ————; his mother of ————. He was educated at ————, in the city of ————. His first voyage, which was a long one, was from ———— to ————. He wrote three books before he was ———— years of age. They are ————, and ————. He performed the miraculous feat of ———— with ————. He was a great ————, and one we shall ever ————. In appearance he was ———— being rather ———— of stature. His nose was ————, his eyes————, his mouth ————, and hair the color of ———— adorned his head. He invariably carried in his hand a ———— and a ————, by which he was always known, and with which he is represented to this day. He died at the advanced age of ———.

The ridiculous combinations found in this game make it very funny.

Comic Historical Tableaux

are very amusing, and being impromptu require no preparation beforehand.

As in charades, the company must divide into two parties. But instead of acting as in charades, one party decides what event in history they will represent, and then they form a tableau to illustrate the event, making it as ridiculous as possible. The other party must try and guess what the tableau is; if they are successful, it is their turn to produce a tableau, if not, the first party must try another subject, and continue to do so until the subject of their tableau is correctly guessed.

We will give a few suggestions for the tableaux.

BALBOA DISCOVERING THE PACIFIC OCEAN.

Place a pan of water on the floor in plain sight of the audience; then let someone dress up in a long cloak and high-crowned hat to personate Balboa, and stand on a table in the middle of the floor, while the rest of the performers, enveloped in shawls, crouch around. When the curtain is drawn aside, Balboa must be seen looking intently through one end of a tin horn, or one made of paper, at the pan of water.

NERO AT THE BURNING OF ROME.

Nero, in brilliant robes made of shawls, sits on a table, surrounded by his courtiers, who are also in fantastic costumes. Nero is in the act of fiddling, his fiddle being a small fire shovel, and the bow a poker. On the floor in front of the group is placed a large shallow pan or tray, in which is set a small house, which has been hastily cut from paper. A lighted match is put to the paper house just as the curtains are parted.

These two suggestions will no doubt be sufficient to show what the tableaux should be like and we need give no further illustrations.

Living Christmas Cards.

To impart seeming life to the little figures painted on the Christmas cards, is a performance intensely amusing to the little ones. A moving toy whose actions are life-like is always of great interest ; but when a little flesh-and-blood head is seen nodding and twisting upon the shoulders of a figure painted on a card, the children fairly shout with delight.

Fig. 248.—Manner of Holding Card.

Here is the method of bringing life into the bits of pasteboard.

Select cards with pretty or comical figures, whose faces are the size of the ends of your first or second finger. Carefully cut the face out of a card ; then with ink mark the features on your finger, and put it through the opening, as in Fig. 248. Place on this little live head a high peaked tissue-paper cap, and the effect will be exceedingly ludicrous (Fig. 249). A little Santa Claus who can really nod and bow to the children will be very amusing, and there are quite a number of Christmas cards which portray the funny, jolly little fellow.

Floral cards may have nodding fairies peeping out from among the petals of the flowers, whose heads are crowned with queer little fairy caps, as in Fig. 250. If among your collection you have a card with a picture of a house on it, it will be amusing to thrust a little head wearing a night-cap, out of one of the windows. Round holes will, of course, have to be cut in the cards wherever the heads arc to appear.

Still another way of managing these living puppets is to cut in a piece of cardboard, five inches long and two inches wide, three round holes a little more than half an inch apart. Sew around the edge of the card-

Fig. 249.—Live Head with Peaked Cap.

board a gathered curtain of any soft material six inches deep. Sketch faces on three of your fingers, pass them under the curtain and through the holes in the cardboard. The cur-

tain will fall around and conceal your hand, leaving the three
heads appearing above (Fig. 251). On these heads place any
kind of head-dress you choose, making them of paper; or

Fig. 250.—Nodding Fairies.

caps of white swiss look quaint, and wee doll hats may be
worn.

It is best to use a little mucilage or paste in fastening the hats on, that there may be no danger of their falling off with the movement of the fingers.

The hair may be inked, or little wigs made of cotton can be used.

Fig. 251.—Living Puppets.

If the little faces are painted with water colors, giving color to the cheeks and lips, the life-like appearance will be enhanced.

These little personages can be made to carry on absurd conversations, and a great deal of expression be given to the bobbing and turning of their heads. One person can easily manage the whole thing, and entertain a roomful with the performance of the living puppets.

Happy New Year

CHAPTER XXXI.

NEW YEAR'S AND A LEAP YEAR PARTY.

 Y earliest recollection of New Year's day is of being awakened at midnight by the clangor of the fire bells, and the ringing of the church bells, as they swung and rocked in their high steeples and cupolas, shouting, Happy New Year! from their brazen throats to all the sleeping town. Not being thoroughly conversant with bell language, I was very much alarmed because they seemed to say " Come, get up— Come, get up—House on fire—House on fire!" but, upon opening my eyes, I was assured that they were ringing in the New Year, and, as I again fell asleep, the bells were saying distinctly, "Wish you Happy New Year—Wish you Happy New Year."

Next day the table was decked with flowers, and was laden with roast turkey, fruits, salads, and mince-pies. Oh, my! what delicious mince-pies they were! None since have ever tasted as good as those made and baked by my grandmother.

I often wonder if the next generation of grandmammas will make such cookies, mince pies, and doughnuts as ours did; but this was in Kentucky, and you know that we still observed the old-fashioned customs, and all day long the gentlemen came dropping in by twos and fours, and such handshaking and laughing, and such courtly compliments, and such a bowing and a wishing of Many Happy New Years, it does me good to think of. Who knows but that so many kind wishes of a long and happy life, sincerely given, may really help to bring it to pass.

Small as I was at the time, and little as I understood the customs or conversation, the spirit of the whole day was intelligible and appealed to the little child, perhaps more forcibly than to the grown-up people.

It is really too bad that the crowded states of our large cities tend to lead to the gradual decline of the custom of New Year's calls, so that now many people confine themselves to sending and receiving cards, making the always stiff and formal bits of engraved pasteboard, do all the calling and receiving ; but

New Year's Parties

are not out of date, so we will have one on New Year's Eve, because then young and old are privileged to sit up all night, that is, until after twelve o'clock midnight, and have all the fun possible. Let us begin our frolic with a

Pantomime of an Enchanted Girl.

For this a damp sheet must be fastened up across the room or between the folding doors of the parlor. First, fasten the corners of the sheet, next, the centre of each of the four sides, in order that the cloth may be perfectly smooth ; then place a lighted candle on the floor, about four or five feet from the centre of the curtain. When the lights in the room occupied by the audience are turned out, leaving it in total darkness, so the shadows of the actors behind the curtain may be seen on the screen, someone, standing outside of the curtain and facing the audience, should explain or relate the story of the play : of how a young girl, while walking out on the last day in November, meets Halloween, who presents her with three gifts to try her fortune, and how, when she is about to do so, a witch enchants her, etc. After the story is finished, and a lively overture has been performed on some musical instrument, the pantomime is played as follows :

The young girl personating the enchanted one, comes gayly forward from the side, when almost across the curtain she meets Halloween, who approaches from the opposite side, arrayed in short dress, with wings made of newspaper folded fan fashion, and fastened on the shoulders ; in her hand she carries a cane with a silhouette of a cat, or two or three stars and a crescent cut of stiff, brown paper and pasted on the end ; the cane is so held that the profiles of the figures are kept toward the curtain. Seeing this queer being the young girl clearly demonstrates, by her actions, that she is alarmed. When Halloween quiets her fears, by surely and plainly indicating with slow movements of the head, and downward motions of the arms that no harm is intended, they shake hands ; then Halloween shows the maiden three gifts, an apple, a hand-mirror, and an unlighted candle. Before presenting them she illustrates by gestures, the use to be made of each. Holding the mirror in front of her face, she bites the apple, then looks quickly around, as if expecting to see someone, and, again holding up the mirror in one hand and the candle in the other, she takes a few steps backward, when a boy enters by jumping over the light, which gives the appearance of his having fallen down from the sky, Halloween looks around, and the boy quickly disappears in the same manner as he came.

All this time the girl stands transfixed, with her hands raised and all the fingers spread out in astonishment ; she receives the presents which are given with many nods and gestures. As Halloween walks away the fortune-seeker turns and watches her

with a telescope made of a roll of paper she finds at her feet on
the floor. The maiden then proceeds to examine the gifts ; as
she takes up the apple and mirror, her hand is stayed by a
witch with flowing hair, who has approached unperceived,
carrying under one arm a broom, and wearing on her head an
ordinary hat with a piece of newspaper rolled up and pinned on
to form a peaked crown. She motions to the girl to be seated ;
then stands over her and makes passes in the air, and taking up
her broom from the floor makes grand flourishes and departs
walking back towards the candle, which causes her shadow to
grow larger and larger. The poor girl looks anxiously around
and discovers she has been enchanted, for there are three girls
instead of one; this effect is produced by two more lighted
candles being placed on the floor on either side of the first candle, and every movement the girl makes is mimicked by her
other selves. The candles are removed and the Old Year instantly appears, his figure bent, a piece of fringed paper pasted
on his chin for a flowing beard, and carrying in his hand a cane
with a piece of stiff paper fastened on to represent a scythe.
Discovering him the girl runs forward to tell her sorrows, and
finds that it is only when alone that she is enchanted, for when
she attempts to point out her other selves they have disappeared ; making many gestures she looks here and there for
them, but in vain, then as the Old Year leaves she bids him a
sorrowful adieu. Again alone, the facsimiles reappear and she
grows desperate, so do the other two selves, she throws her arms
about, skips, jumps, and dances wildly around, the other selves
do likewise, and at the same time they are made to pass and
repass her, by two persons taking up the two extra lights, and,
keeping the lights facing the curtain, walking back and forth,
passing, and repassing each other but never stepping in front of
the candle on the floor. In the midst of the dancing the two
extra candles are taken away and immediately the little New

Year enters, crowned with a paper star and wearing wings of paper. The young girl rushes to meet the New Year with a hearty greeting, she then tells him of her enchantment, counting the three selves by holding up the first finger of the right hand three times in succession, and while the New Year makes gestures that indicate advice the maiden listens with her hand to her ear, and, promising by signs to be a good girl, she kneels down, and the little New Year raises both hands above her head, then, kissing her hand to the maiden, departs.

The glad New Year has disenchanted her, she carefully looks this way and that, but seeing all is well she tosses her head, dances around, makes a courtesy, kisses both hands to the audience and disappears.

When the play is over, and just as the clock strikes twelve, the party can instantly change its character if it is leap-year and become a

Leap-Year Party

for the remaining hour or so, thereby creating a great deal more merriment and sport; the novelty of the fact that the girls exchange places with the boys makes everything appear strange. And when the music commences for dancing the girls look from one to another, no one at first having the courage to invite a partner to dance, so unaccustomed are they to even the thought of such a thing. The boys of course laugh, and make no move to assist their timid, would-be partners in the part they must play, but quietly await the expected invitation. When, however, someone takes the initiative step, the others follow, and all goes merrily.

The supper presents a new phase, but here the girls do their part perfectly, providing all the boys with a plentiful repast, and each one is made to feel that his presence is necessary to the success of the party, thereby insuring a happy, pleasant time for all.

In giving a leap-year party it is very essential that all the guests understand perfectly that the idea of the entertainment is to have the girls take upon themselves all the duties and courtesies properly belonging to the boys, and that the boys shall wait for an invitation before dancing, promenading, or partaking of refreshments, and that a boy should not cross the floor unattended, but wait for some fair friend to escort him. The girls are at liberty to go and come as they like, though they must remember not to leave a partner standing after the dance is over, but politely conduct him to a seat, and the girls must also endeavor to make the party pleasant and agreeable to all. The chaperons, of course, should have charge of the boys during the entertainment.

The leap-year party need not necessarily be a dancing party, as any social gathering can take the form of a leap-year party.

When an entertainment is given on the eve of a new leap-year, with a view to dancing the old year out and the new year in, just as the clock strikes twelve the party can immediately change into a leap-year party as described, or should the New Year be a common year, then as the time flies and the hands of the clock approach the hour of twelve all are on the qui vive to be the first to have the pleasure of greeting their friends with a Happy New Year.

CHAPTER XXXII.

HOME GYMNASIUM.

VERYONE *must* exercise to keep healthy and strong, for life is motion and activity. It is natural to be well and happy, and to keep so we must exercise all our muscles, as well as our moral and intellectual faculties, or they will dwindle and wither. The arm of the Hindoo devotee, not being used, at length becomes completely paralyzed, and fish in the Mammoth Cave having no use for eyes pass their life without them ; so we find that *use* is the foundation of all things, otherwise they would cease to exist ; then, girls, it lies within your power to become stronger and more graceful each day by regular and graduated bodily exercise, which will bring life and energy to every part of your system by causing the blood to circulate freely through all the body.

There are some simple methods of carrying this into effect in the most agreeable and salutary manner, but the exercises must be very light at first, and as you advance they may be increased a little each time, but always stop before you feel fatigued, for when the calisthenics cease to give pleasure it is doubtful if they are beneficial.

The best time for exercising is in the morning after having partaken of some light refreshments, though any time will do

except directly after hearty meals. Try and have a regular time set apart each day for your physical culture. Commence by exercising five or ten minutes, then for a little longer period next time, and so on until you can exercise with case for half an hour or longer. You will feel refreshed, invigorated, and better prepared for the duties and pleasures which await you. Your clothing must not incommode the free action of the body, and it is essential that it be comfortable. What is suitable for lawn tennis is also well adapted for the gymnasium. An ordinary bathing-dress answers the purpose very well, as it is made for exercise.

The Egyptian water-carrier, with the jug of water poised so prettily on her head, and her figure so straight and beautiful, has always challenged admiration; her carriage is dignified, erect, and graceful, something worth striving for, especially when we have the certainty of success if we will only be faithful and persevering. The peasantry of foreign countries who carry all their burdens balanced on their heads have their reward in healthy, strong, straight figures, even in old age they do not stoop. Witness the emigrants landing at Castle Garden who carry their possessions done up in huge bundles on their heads with the utmost ease ; of this class, three generations—a grandmother, mother, and grown daughter—with baggage of the same weight on their heads, were lately seen at a New York ferry, each equally upright, strong, and vigorous.

A good straight back is an excellent thing ; and when the head is properly carried and all the movements are buoyant and elastic, then we may walk as it was intended we should, every step bringing a glow to the cheek and a sparkle to the eye. It requires only a few minutes' regular daily exercise for any girl to attain a carriage equal to that of the Egyptian water-carrier, and the only apparatus needed for

Exercise First

is a roll of paper. Now stand with your heels together, toes out, and shoulders well back ; then place on your head the roll of paper ; if your position is not perfectly erect the roll will fall off ; keep your chin straight and back against your neck, for it

is the *chin* which determines the poise of the body. You cannot stand straight unless the chin is straight ; throw out your chin and your shoulders will stoop forward, have your chin straight and your back will be straight ; bear this in mind in all your exercises. Now walk, keeping the roll balanced on your head (Fig. 252). Practice this walking back and forth until you can do so without the paper rolling off ; then try a tin cup full to the brim with water. Walk erect or the water will wash over, down on your head, and it will feel cold as it trickles through your hair ; soon, however, you will be able to carry the cup of water with ease and no danger of its spilling. But do not discontinue the practice on that account ; try something else in its place, until you are able to carry anything you wish on your head with no fear of it falling. The exercise affords amusement, and at the same time you will be acquiring a beautiful, dignified, and graceful carriage.

Fig. 252.—Balancing a Roll of Paper.

Exercise Second

is for gaining agility, suppleness, quickness of eye, hand, and foot. Standing as far from the wall as possible, take a common rubber hand-ball and toss it against the wall, catching it as it rebounds (see illustration), and again toss it against the wall. Vary this by allowing the ball to strike the floor, catching it on the rebound ; then try keeping the ball in constant motion by using first one hand and then the other as a bat for returning the ball to the wall. The exercise can also be changed by striking the ball against the floor, and on its return bound again striking it, thus keeping it in motion. You will find that activity is necessary, and the work so quick that it will keep you on the jump all through the exercise.

Exercise Third

is with a broom-handle. Saw or cut off the broom and smooth down the sharp ends of the handle, and it will be ready for use. Stand erect, heels together, toes out, chin well back and straight, so as to throw out and expand the chest. Now grasp firmly each end of the broomstick and bring it up over the head (Fig. 253); repeat this motion six or seven times ; then change by carrying the broomstick over back of the head down across and

Fig. 253.—Broom-handle Exercise.

back of the shoulders ; then up above the head again, repeating this, and all other motions in your calisthenics, half a dozen times. Another exercise is holding the stick down in front of you with both hands and bringing it up over the head and down back of the shoulders without stopping.

The side motion is made by grasping the broomstick at each end, holding it down in front of you, and swinging it sideways, thus bringing the right hand up when the left is down, and *vice versa.* Another way is to hold the stick by both ends above your head and swing it from one side to the other, which will cause the right arm to come in contact with the right side of the head, while the left arm is extended out horizontally to the left. Next carry the stick back of and against the shoulders ; then swing it from right to left, which gives another side movement. Vary all the movements in as many different ways as you can think of.

Exercise Fourth.

Stand erect always when in position for exercising, according to the directions given—heels together, toes out, etc. Now allow your arms to hang naturally down at your sides, raise your heels, and stand on your toes ; now lower the heels and repeat the motion ; then close your hands tightly and raise your arms out sideways at right angles with your body, next up straight above your head, and down again to the level of the shoulders, then back down to your sides as at first.

Again take position, close your hands tightly, and raise them up under the arms, bringing the elbows out to a level with the shoulders ; then bring your hands down at your sides again and repeat the movement vigorously ; resume position, firmly close your hands and carry them up to the shoulders, next extend them up straight above your head, down again to your shoulders, and back to the first position. A very good exercise is to extend both arms straight out in front of you, close your hands and bring them back to your chest, which will cause the bent elbows to project beyond your back.

Exercise Fifth.

Assume position, close your hands, and take one long step forward with your right foot, bend the right knee and stand with your weight resting on the right foot; then extend your arms out sideways straight from the shoulders, now bring your hands together in front of you, still keeping the arms on a level with the shoulders, and while doing so throw the body back, straightening the right knee and bending the left so the weight of the body will rest on the left foot; repeat this and vary it by taking one step forward with the left foot and going through with the same motions.

Resume position, and place your hands on your hips, with your thumbs turned forward and fingers backward. Now take a long step forward with your right foot, throwing the weight on that foot, then back again in position, and in the same manner step forward with your left foot and back again; next take a step backward with your right foot, resume position, and then with your left.

Again stand with your hands on your hips, thumbs turned forward, and without bending your knees move the body, first bending it forward, then backward, and resuming an upright position, bend over to the right and to the left.

Fig. 254.—Balancing Broom-handle.

Exercise Sixth.

In this the broomstick is used for balancing; hold it in an upright position, and first try balancing it on the palm of your hand; then on the back of your hand, next on each of the fingers in succession, commencing with the first finger (Fig. 254); be cautious, and when the stick wavers do not let it fall, but catch it with the other hand, and again balance it. This is an interesting, light, and diverting exercise, requiring all your attention, and, for the time being, your thoughts are concentrated on the effort to keep the broomstick properly balanced.

Exercise Seventh.

Pure blood means good health, and to purify the blood and keep the complexion clear it is essential that you breathe a sufficient quantity of *pure* air, and you cannot take in a proper amount of air unless your lungs are wholly extended. So take position with your hands correctly placed on your hips ; then very slowly draw in your breath until your chest and lungs are fully expanded ; next slowly exhale your breath, and repeat the exercise.

Exercise Eighth.

Screw in two large, *strong* hooks in the woodwork on each side of the doorway ; place the hooks as far above your head as you can conveniently reach ; slide the broomstick in so that it will extend across the doorway and be supported by the hooks ; have the apparatus on that side of the doorway where it will not interfere with the opening and closing of the door, and be sure that it is perfectly secure before attempting to exercise ; each time before commencing a new movement examine the stick, and be certain that it is not in any danger of slipping from the hooks. Unless you can be perfectly safe from liability to hurts or falls, do not include this in your list of exercises.

For the first movement grasp the bar firmly with both hands and swing the body forward and backward, standing first on the toes, then on the heels ; next, still grasping the bar, raise up on your toes, then back again. Change the movements in as many ways as you like, but do not try anything that may strain or hurt you. Now screw in two more hooks, on either side of the woodwork, below the first ones, placing them about two feet and eight inches from the floor ; take the stick from its elevated position and slide it across the doorway so it will rest securely on the two lower hooks. Standing in front of it, grasp the bar firmly with both hands and try to raise yourself up, feet and all, from the floor by bearing your weight down on the bar ; then let yourself gently back again. When you have finished exercising, re- move the stick and put it away.

Exercise Ninth.

In the top part of the framework of the doorway fasten a very strong hook by screw- ing it into the wood ; then take a broomstick and, after shortening it so that when held in a

Fig. 255.—The Swing.

horizontal position it will readily pass through the doorway, cut notches in each end and securely tie the two ends of a rope across the notches ; suspend this swing by slipping the centre of the rope over the hook in the doorway (Fig. 255); have the apparatus strong and firm, capable of any amount of wear and tear. Stand facing the stick, which should be at the height of the chest, and take hold of it with both hands ; now bend the knees until they are within a short distance of the floor,

then rise and repeat the exercise.   Next, with both hands on
the stick, take a long step forward with the right foot, throwing
the weight on that foot; return to your position and go through
the same exercise with your left foot.   Try different movements
which suggest themselves, and select those you like best.   When
not in use the swing can be slipped off the hook and put out of
the way.

Exercise Tenth.

To develop a weak voice and make it clear and sweet, and to
strengthen the lungs, reading aloud is an excellent exercise ; as
it requires both mental and muscular exertion and performs a
double duty, it should receive a full share of time and attention.   Begin with something you are interested in, then you
will find it much easier to read aloud than if you undertook a
book or an article which might be full of merit, but lack interest
for you.   When commencing this exercise read only ten minutes or less at a sitting, increasing the time as you practise and
the reading grows less difficult.   Do not be discouraged if your
voice sounds a little husky while reading ; stop a moment, and
then go on again.   After a few trials you will have no more
trouble in that way, for your voice will grow clear and distinct,
and the exercise will become a great pleasure as well as an attractive, useful accomplishment.

Let your reading matter be very choice and of the best ; do
not condescend to waste your time on other writings.

From the ten different exercises given, select those best
adapted to your size, age, and liking, and practise them for a
short time daily ; you can hardly realize the great advantage they
will prove to be.   In this way all parts of the system may be
strengthened and harmoniously developed.   But the constitu-
tion cannot be hurried : all must be accomplished little by little.
Allow yourselves to be happy and merry; be ready to enjoy

the little pleasures of life, and this, with kind and generous feelings for others, will do a great deal toward keeping you well and strong.

Out-of-door exercise is always to be preferred to in-door when one has a choice. Walking, tennis, archery, horseback, and swimming are some of the athletic sports for girls, and they all have their attractions. But there are times when we are denied the pleasure of these pastimes, and then we are glad of a little exercise in-doors, which also affords enjoyment and recreation.

CHAPTER XXXIII.

A DECORATIVE LANGUAGE.

 HEN in olden times the warriors went around the country dressed in suits of clothes made by a blacksmith instead of a tailor, their hats were manufactured at the forge also, and had *iron front doors* that moved upon hinges. When danger was nigh these doors were closed, locked, and barred over the poor men's heads, leaving only a loop-hole or two for them to peep through. At such times in meeting Mr. Brown it was impossible to distinguish him from Mr. Smith, who was arrayed in like manner, and it might happen that Mr. Smith was the last man in the world that one cared to meet, not being on speaking terms or some such reason. Well, as we were saying, there was no chance whatever of telling one man from another unless he wore a distinguishing mark of some kind.

So to prevent such uncomfortable mistakes and to distinguish friend from foe, every gentleman had to be marked and labelled, like an express package, so one might read as he ran, "I am Earl Jenkins, of Thunderland, who married a Rhazor, of. Stropshire." These names and addresses were not painted in words on their owners with a marking-brush, but worked and embroidered in translatable designs on cloaks, saddle-housings, and silken banners, or emblazoned on the shield they carried with which to meet the advances of their neighbors. Since that time our more recent ancestors in England have taken great pride in preserving and handing down from generation to generation these distinguishing marks, as a guarantee to their children that they came of gentle birth, which is very interesting and gratifying for European girls, but American girls need nothing of the kind ; it is sufficient that we are Americans.

Of course, some of us do take pleasure in knowing that our great-great-grandparents came over in the Mayflower, or that the name of an ancestor is among the signatures upon that Declaration of Independence which made such a stir a century ago, for that proves us to be Columbia's daughters.

When there was no other method of distinguishing a man his label became a very important item ; so these family devices were reduced to a science and protected by law.

The old countries' coats of arms may remain abroad, where they belong, but the ingenious scheme, that was gradually evolved, of picturing ideas, mottoes, and pretty sentiments we will adopt as our inheritance, with many thanks to our mediæval ancestors with the metallic clothes, who bequeathed them to us.

We propose to revive enough of this neglected knowledge of chivalry to serve our purpose in suggesting a method of designing devices which will not only be artistic decorations, but to the initiated can be made to portray almost any sentiment or set of principles the artist may choose.

The many uses to which these designs can be applied will, we hope, at once be seen by the quick-witted American girls, and we trust will interest the reader as much as they do the writer, who in this chapter can only give a few necessary, brief hints upon the subject, sufficient, however, to explain the application that can be made of this beautiful and perfect system of

Decorative Language.

In the following directions anyone can learn how to make a device which will not only be a decoration, artistic in form and color, but will at the same time express the peculiar traits, characteristics, and virtues of the friend for whom it is intended, or the precept, code, proverb, or creed of the designer. All technical terms, as far as practicable, are discarded, but the rules of heraldry strictly adhered to, with such simplifications as are necessary to render it intelligible.

Fig. 256.—The Field.

The Field.

The surface on which the design is portrayed is called the field. This may be of any shape ; originally it was supposed to represent a warrior's shield, but you may use a circle, oval, square, diamond, or any other form.

The Points

on the surface of the shield locate the exact spot where a design or object in heraldry may be placed. Refer by numbers to Fig. 257.

Fig. 257.—Points.

1. Fess point.
2. Honor point.
3. Nombril point.
4. Dexter chief point.
5. Middle or chief point.
6. Sinister chief point.
7. Dexter base point.
8. Middle base point.
9. Sinister base point.

If you desire to place a flower on the fess point, you find that it means the exact centre of the shield, and so on.

The devices take significance in accordance with the more or less importance of their position on the shield ; the honor point holds the highest grade, next to it the middle or chief point, and the right or dexter side is of more importance than the left or sinister.

The field may be divided, if desired, in any of the following

Divisions,

each of which has a significance, suggested generally by the form :

Fig. 258, the Chief, occupying the top or head of the

Fig. 258.—Chief.   Fig. 259.—Fess.   Fig. 260.—Parted per Fess.

shield, indicates pre-eminence, main object, intelligence, first principle.

Fig. 259, the Fess, denotes cause and effect, the central band containing the means by which the ends, in the other spaces, are accomplished.

Fig. 261.—Pale.   Fig. 262.—Parted per Pale.   Fig. 263.—Bend.

Fig. 260 is a partition, and partakes of the meaning of the division, it is denoted by the term, parted per fess.

Fig. 261, the Pale, represents rectitude, uprightness; also union, the object in the central division uniting whatever occupies the dexter and sinister sides.

Fig. 262 is parted per pale.

Fig. 264.—Parted per Bend.   Fig. 265.—Chevron.   Fig. 266.—Cross.

Fig. 263, the Bend, is auspicious, meaning prosperity, success.

Fig. 264 is parted per bend.

Fig. 265, the Chevron, is indicative of aid, assistance, support.

Fig. 266, the Cross, suggests humility, devotion, patience, perseverance.

Fig. 267.—Saltire.   Fig. 268.—Pile.   Fig. 269.—Canton.

Fig. 267, the Saltire, a variation of the cross, is recognized as order, discipline.

Fig. 268, the Pile, being in the form of a wedge, means penetration, incision, entering to divide or distribute.

Fig. 269, the Canton, denotes an additional, separate idea or principle; also some characteristic that is added to the original design.

Colors.

These also have symbolical meanings.

Fig. 270.—Gold or yellow is expressed in black and white by means of dots, and is used in the sense of wealth, ability, or knowledge.

Fig. 271.—Silver or white is represented by a plain white

Fig. 270.—Gold.   Fig. 271.—Silver.   Fig. 272.—Red.

surface, and being the color of light, signifies brightness, purity, virtue, innocence.

Fig. 272.—Red, represented by perpendicular lines, means ardent affection, love.

Fig. 273.—Blue is represented by horizontal lines; like the color in the heavens, it is truth, freedom, eternity.

Fig. 274.—Purple, represented by diagonal lines from sinister

Fig. 273.—Blue.   Fig. 274.—Purple.   Fig. 275.—Green.

chief to dexter base, being the royal color, is understood as authority, power, grandeur.

Fig. 275.—Green is represented by lines running diagonally across the shield from dexter chief to sinister base. Like spring foliage, it suggests hope, life, vitality, youth, freshness.

24

Fig. 276.—Orange is represented by horizontal lines crossed by diagonal lines from dexter base to sinister chief. It is the color of the king of beasts and signifies strength, honor, generosity.

Fig. 277.—Crimson, or blood-color, is represented by dia-

Fig. 276.—Orange.　　　Fig. 277.—Crimson.　　　Fig. 278.—Black.

gonal lines from dexter chief and sinister chief, crossing each other. It denotes boldness, enthusiasm, impetuosity.

Fig. 278.—Black is represented by horizontal and perpendicular lines crossed. It means darkness, doubt, ignorance, uncertainty.

To the principal design portrayed on the shield can be added such appendages as are appropriate—crest over the top and a scroll with a motto beneath the shield—but they are supplementary, and not of great importance ; their colors should be those of the shield.

Thus far our plans have followed the exact science of heraldry, but at this point comes a departure, for in the place of other armorial devices we shall place Dame Nature's sweetest thoughts—flowers.

If we now add to the significance of the forms and colors already given the accepted and authentic language of flowers, we shall have a possibility of combinations practically inexhaustible, and with such a dictionary of symbols to draw upon, we can successfully translate almost any terse sentiment into a unique decorative design.

In order to give all the assistance in our power we have culled from the most generally accepted authorities and authentic sources a short floral vocabulary, and now that we have the material at hand let us test the system and learn

How to Make a Design in Decorative Language.

Suppose our Natural History Society desires an appropriate pin or badge.

First we turn to the floral vocabulary and there find that the magnolia means love of nature. The flower has a good

decorative form, its sentiment is exactly appropri-
ate, and we unhesitatingly
adopt it.

After trying various
forms for the shield, we
select a very plain one that
the effect of the decorative
form of the magnolia may
not be lessened by too or-
nate surroundings, and to
show the large size of the
blossom we must have it
occupy the entire field
without any divisions.
Next, as to color ; let us
think. White, meaning
brightness, purity, etc. ?
No. Yellow or gold, sig-

Fig. 279.

nifying wealth, ability, or—ah ! here we have it—*knowledge?*
Yes, that will do nicely—a love of nature on a field of knowl-
ledge ; that certainly is appropriate. But the top of the shield

being so square and plain gives the device an unfinished appearance. Suppose we try a bar over it, and something not a flower.
As we wish this design to remain simple, a leaf of some kind
would be best; so we return to the floral vocabulary, and after
trying many and almost taking several, finally decide that the
oak leaf is just the form needed to give a finish to the top, and
its meaning, strength, will be an excellent element in the society.
There, our insignia is complete, good in form, attractive in color,
and appropriate in its meaning; but some of us prefer having
the motto written out in plain English, so we will add a decorative scroll, with the meaning of the design inscribed " True Love
of Nature." (See Fig. 279.)

To familiarize ourselves with the working of the method let
us try another experiment, and take the sentiment, " Wealth is
the Reward of Industry," to illustrate.

After deciding on the form of the shield, we turn to the divisions, and running them slowly over for something suitable, stop
at Fig. 259, the Fess, meaning cause and effect. That sounds
promising. Industry is the means by which the end, wealth,
is accomplished. Good so far. We can now see that a floral
emblem to represent industry should be placed in the central
division, and whatever signifies wealth on the other two spaces.
Among our legends of flowers we find industry portrayed by the
bee orchid, and wealth and prosperity are symbolized by wheat.
That is plain and easy. Now we have only to decide upon appropriate colors for the field to complete the design. Gold
would mean wealth, but that we have in the wheat; besides the
yellow of the wheat would not show well on the gold background,
while on white or silver the contrast is strong and the appearance agreeable. Silver denotes innocence and virtue, which
are so necessary that without them wealth would be undesirable.
Therefore silver or virtue shall be the groundwork for our wealth,
and for industry we will select purple as meaning power. In-

dustry possesses the power to acquire wealth. Thus we complete the emblematical design, as seen in Fig. 280.

The following is a problem given to us for solution : On a gold chevron in a black field is a scarlet lily, to which is added as a crest a sunflower, and under all a blank scroll. On this we must write a motto that will be appropriately symbolized by the design.

It would be excellent prac-

Fig. 280.

tice for the student in this new motif in decorative art to try, by application of the foregoing instructions, to decipher the meaning of this design before reading the analysis.

SOLUTION OF FIG. 281. —We do not think this is put together as scientifically as the system would admit of, but still it can be deciphered.

Fig. 281.

The scarlet lily (high-souled aspirations) on a gold (knowledge) chevron, which is aid, assistance, in a field of black (ignorance), surmounted by the sunflower (pure and lofty thoughts), freely translated, might be read : Aspirations after knowledge help to illumine the

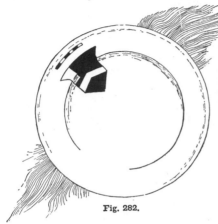

darkness of ignorance with p u r e and l o f t y thoughts. Aspirations (lily) after knowledge (gold) help (chevron) to illumine (the gold chevron and lily brighten up the dulness of the black field) the darkness of ignorance (black) with pure and lofty t h o u g h t s (sunflower).

For y o u n g e r girls the plain shield of one color with an appropriate flower had

Fig. 282.

best be used, which they may vary *ad infinitum.* A simple yet pretty shield can be made by placing a four-leaved clover, symbolical of good-luck, on a shield of one color, silver, meaning purity, innocence, showing that innocence, combined with the language of the clover, expresses good-fortune.

Fig. 283.   Fig. 284.

We might go on forming innumerable designs, each more beautiful than the last, but enough hints have been given to enable the young people to make any style of design in this decorative language which may best suit their purpose. Young

Fig. 285.

girls can decorate menu cards, having each motto exactly suited to every separate guest, the sentiment being indicative of some feeling or quality peculiar to each person. Invitations for parties, also orders of dances or games, may be designed in the same way.

Fig. 286.

This beautiful combination of flowers and heraldry is appropriate for ornamental needlework, to be embroidered on chairs, worked on screens, painted on velvet, wrought on scarfs, and adapted in innumerable ways to add to the refinement and attractiveness of home.

The idea can be utilized in stained-glass effects and in china-painting.

The chosen motto may be a decoration in marking personal

Fig. 287.   Fig. 288.

possessions, such as table china (Figs. 282, 283, 284), fan (Fig. 285), chair-back (Fig. 286), travelling satchel (Fig. 287), tidy (Fig. 288), handkerchief (Fig. 289), and sofa-cushion (Fig. 290).

Fig. 289.   Fig. 290.

These are only a few examples of the many articles which can be beautified and stamped with your individual márk. Portières offer a good ground for applique or embroidery in decorative language.

Book-Plates

seem to be regaining their popularity and usefulness. These book-plates are tablets in any style, which, when gummed inside on the front covers of books, have been used for many years to designate to whom the books belong.

There is a certain book-plate more interesting to us than all others. To the design on it we are indebted for our national shield and our Stars and Stripes. It was used by the Father of our Country, and we are glad to be able to give a print of the original in Fig. 291.

In the decorative language any style of book-plate can be designed, which, when pasted in a favorite book, will add to the value of the already treasured volume.

Fig. 291.

Floral Vocabulary.

Apple-blossom..............	Preference.
Almond...................	Hope.
Acanthus..................	Art.
Arbor vitæ...............	Unchanging friendship.
Bulrush..................	Docility.
Balm	Social intercourse.
Balsamine.................	Impatience.

Blue violet....	Faithfulness.
Bay wreath.................	Glory.
Box	Constancy.
Broom....................	Humility.
Buttercup.................	Riches.
Camellia japonica.......... ...	Unpretending excellence.
Cherry................. ...	A good education.
Canterbury-bell.............	Gratitude.
Chestnut...................	Do me justice.
China aster................	Love of variety.
Cabbage...................	Profit.
Coreopsis.................	Always cheerful.
Clover, red................	Industry
Cowslip...................	Winning grace.
Clover, white..............	I promise.
Daffodil	Uncertainty.
Dahlia.................. ...	Elegance and dignity.
Dandelion.................	Coquetry.
Fennèl....................	Strength.
Geranium	Gentility.
Grass.....................	Submission.
Heliotrope ,..............	Devotion.
House-leek................	Domestic economy.
Hollyhock	Ambition.
Ivy......................	Dependence.
Laurestine.................	A token
Lichen...............	Solitude.
Lettuce.................	Cold-hearted.
Lemon-blossom............	Discretion.
Lilac, purple...............	Fastidiousness.
Lily, white................	Purity.
Mullein	Good-nature.
Mignonette................	Worth.

May-flower	Welcome.
Nasturtium	Patriotism.
Oats	Music.
Olive	Peace.
Ox-eye	Patience.
Poppy, white	Dreams.
Snowdrop	Consolation.
Straw	United.
Sensitive-plant	Sensitiveness.
Star of Bethlehem	Reconciliation.
Sweetbrier	Simplicity.
Thyme	Thriftiness.
Thorn-apple	Disguise.
Tulip-tree	Fame.
Witch-hazel	A spell.
Winged seeds of all kinds	Messengers.
White violet	Modesty.
White rose	Silence.

CHAPTER XXXIV.

A FEW ITEMS ON OLD-FASHIONED NEEDLE-WORK, WITH SOME NEW AND ORIGINAL PATTERNS.

OME around early this afternoon and bring your fancy-work; we will have a nice, cosey time; all the girls will be there, and we can read that last new book." Such is the familiar and welcome invitation given and received, from time to time, by most young girls, and they find quiet but real recreation in these informal meetings, where, while listening to a friend read aloud, they believe it much easier to keep their minds on the subject if their hands are employed with dainty needle-work. Then, too, sewing is a real pleasure when one becomes interested in the work, and anyone who thoroughly understands plain sewing can with ease learn fancy stitches of all kinds, for good old-fashioned

Plain Sewing

is the foundation—the A B C—of all the more elaborate drawn work, embroideries, and some of the laces. As a rule we think

OVERHANDING.

comes first on the list of plain stitches; this is exactly the same as sewing over and over. Hold the two edges of the material firmly together between the first finger and thumb of the left hand, while with the right hand you take the stitches very close together and as near the edge as possible, sewing from right to left (Fig. 292). It is well to keep the edge nearest to you a little tighter than the outer edge, to prevent its puckering. Always baste the seam before sewing, and when the seam is finished open it and flatten out the stitches (Fig. 293), so that

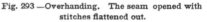

Fig. 292.—Overhanding ; or Sewing over and over.

Fig. 293 —Overhanding. The seam opened with stitches flattened out.

the edges of the material will not overlap, but just meet together and lie smooth and flat.

OVERCASTING

is the same as overhanding, except the stitches slant, are farther apart, taken down deeper in the material, and the seam is not opened.

HEMMING.

First turn in the raw edge four or five threads, according to the kind of goods to be hemmed, then turn it down again to the desired width ; this done, baste the hem down evenly and neatly—it must be of the same width throughout—hold the sewing over the first finger of your left hand, and have the

Fig. 294.—Hemming.

stitches small, even, and very near the edge of the hem (Fig. 294).

RUNNING.

Pass the needle in and out of the material in a straight line (Fig. 295), making all the stitches the same size. We believe the rule is to take up two threads and leave two; but the length of the stitch should be regulated by the kind of material used.

BASTING

is to take long stitches in the same manner as running.

GATHERING

does not differ much from running; the stitches are taken on the needle in the same manner, but in this case two threads are taken up and four left; the line should be kept perfectly straight.

If you wish to gather an apron or a skirt divide it into halves, then into quarters, in order to make the fulness even on each half of the band; mark the four places and gather on the right side; when finished draw the stitches

Fig. 295.—Running.

tightly together on the thread and stroke down evenly with a

needle. To sew in the
gathers, back-stitch each
one in separately.

STITCHING.

Take two threads
back of the needle and
two before, having each

Fig. 296.—Stitching.

stitch meet the last one, as in Fig. 296 ; keep the stitches even
and in a straight line.

BACK-STITCHING.

Proceed as in stitching, only make the stitches longer and
do not have them meet.

FELLING.

First baste up the seam, allowing the upper edge to extend
five threads beyond the lower edge (Fig. 296) ; then back-
stitch or stitch the two edges together ; next turn the upper
edge down over the lower one and lay open the seam so that
the fell will lie down flat
like a hem (Fig. 297) ;
then hem it down neatly.

Fig. 297.—Felling.

Button-holes.

Fig. 298 shows how
to take the proper stitch.
Be careful in cutting
button-holes to make the
slit even to a thread and cut the outer corner rounded ; bar
the inner corner by taking two stitches across it, and overcast

the button-hole around three or four threads deep from the edge, or if the material is not inclined to ravel run it with

thread, either double or single, drawing it a trifle tight ; then begin at the left-hand corner to work the button-hole, leaving one thread between

Fig. 298.—Button-hole Stitch.

each stitch ; keep the stitches exactly the same depth and the loop or pearl of the button-hole on the upper edge.

HERRING-BONE OR CAT'S-TOOTH STITCH

is used to keep the seams in flannel spread open and fastened neatly down. Fig. 299 shows how to take the stitch ; make the stitches all even and of the same size.

We have now given all the stitches which properly belong to plain sewing, and our next step will be

Darning and Mending.

" A stitch in time saves nine ; " this much most of us know from experience, and it is

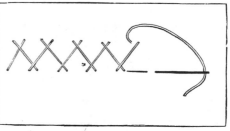

Fig. 299.—Herring-bone Stitch.

wise to devote a little time on a certain day each week to looking over the wardrobe and making any repairs that may be needed ; the little care and time thus bestowed will prove a true economy, and it is a real comfort to have all one's clothing in perfect order.

TO DARN A JERSEY OR A STOCKING.

With a needle and thread carefully draw out the uneven ravelled edges of the hole, in order to diminish its size as much as possible, and bring the loops and ends back in their proper places; then place under it a wooden egg or anything that will answer the purpose, and using thread of the same texture and shade of color as the garment to be mended, run back and forth across the hole as far as the material is worn thin, leaving a loop at the end of each turn. In crossing the threads, take up every other thread alternately each way (Fig. 300), and make the darn of an irregular shape, as one of an even outline does not wear well; when the weaving or darning is finished the loops can be cut off.

Fig. 300.—Jersey or Stocking Darn.

TO DARN A TEAR.

Carefully bring the ragged edges together and baste the tear as nearly as possible in its original position; then, if it is delicate muslin or dress material to be mended, use ravellings of the same instead of thread to darn with, and weave it in and out across the edges of the rent, as in Fig. 301; if the darn needs strengthening, baste a piece of the same material under the rent before darning, and catch down the edges of the piece on the under side of the goods. In mending broadcloth or like material, darn it on the wrong

Fig. 301.—Tear Darn.

side, and when the darn is finished, ruff up the nap with the point of the needle at the edges of the tear on the right side to cover the stitches; then dampen the darn, and after laying a thin clean cloth over it, press with a moderately hot flat-iron ; this should make the darn almost, if not quite, imperceptible.

How to Patch.

If possible cut the piece intended as a patch of the same goods as the garment to be mended, and if there is a pattern be careful to so cut and place the patch that it will match exactly ; baste and hem down the patch on the right side of the worn part of the garment ; then cut out the old material on the wrong side, leaving enough edge to form a firm hem ; sew this to the patch, taking care that the stitches do not show on the right side.

How to Sew on a Button.

Should much strain come on the button, as in little children's clothes, first hem down a small double piece of muslin, on the wrong side of the garment, at the exact spot where the button is to be placed, and with strong thread take a stitch on the right side ; then sew the button through about four times, being careful not to let the stitches spread on the wrong side ; wind the thread three times around the shank of the button formed by the stitches, drawing the thread a little tight, pass the needle through and fasten the thread neatly on the wrong side ; the extra piece of muslin can be omitted when not needed.

To Mend a Kid Glove.

If the glove is merely ripped, and there is no strain on the portion to be mended, sew the two edges together over and over on the right side with fine thread or sewing-silk matching in color the glove to be mended ; if, however, there *is* liability of its tearing out again, strengthen the edges by first working a button-hole stitch on each ; then sew them together over and over, passing the needle in and out of the loops of the button-hole stitch, so forming a narrow net-work of thread between the two pieces of kid. Should the glove need a patch, carefully cut a piece of kid out of the best part of an old kid glove corresponding in color to the one needing r e p a i r s ; make the patch exactly the shape and size of the hole, and b u t t o n-h o l e stitch all around the edge of the hole and the edge of the patch ; then sew in the patch over and over, c a t c h i n g together the loops of the button-hole stitches · this makes the mending firm, neat, and strong.

Fig. 302.—Feather Stitch.

Fancy Stitches.

These are in many varieties of style ; one of the most useful is known as the

FEATHER STITCH.

Fig. 302 gives the position of the needle and the manner of taking the stitch. Remember to make all the stitches of an exact length and the same distance apart, first one on this side and then one on that, keeping them in a straight, even line.

CHAIN STITCH

sometimes takes the place of braiding ; it is the same stitch as that used in the old-fashioned tambouring (Fig. 303) ;

many Persian embroideries are made in silk with the chain-stitch.

A NEW IDEA IN OUTLINE STITCH.

The stitch (Fig. 304) is used for outline embroidery, and when made with fine black sewing-silk resembles pen-and-ink

Fig. 303.—Chain Stitch.

work. We have seen figures outlined on linen with the drapery worked in colors, while the face, hands, and feet were simply in black and white ; being finely outlined, the effect was novel and artistic, for in this way the features were made as true as if drawn on paper with a pencil.

For filling in the solid colors take the common running stitch, but make the stitches long on the right side of the embroidery and very short on the wrong side, so as to give the appearance of the colored fabric copied.

Use filo-silk ; and English or French embroidery cottons, when

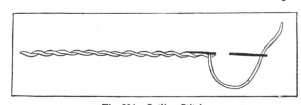
Fig. 304.—Outline Stitch.

colors are needed in the work. Always soak the silks and cottons in strong salt and water before using ; this sets the color and keeps it from running when washed.

HEM-STITCHING.

Decide upon the width of the hem and the width of the space for drawn threads ; carefully draw out the thread at one edge of the space, then the thread at the other edge ; next all the intervening threads ; this finished, fold and baste down the hem, allowing it to meet the edge of the drawn work, and taking five threads running lengthwise in the space, bind them together at the edge of the hem ; at the same time stitch them to the hem, as in Fig. 305.

Drawn Work

Fig. 305.—Hem-stitching.

always looks well and is very serviceable when made of linen. Scarfs for buffets, bureaus, or tables, and tea-cloths, tidies, or chair-backs, can be made of crash, butchers' linen, and linen sheeting ; it is better to have doylies of very fine linen.

In making drawn work, if the article is to be fringed, first draw out a few threads to measure the depth of the fringe, and at the opening thus made hem-stitch all around the edge of the material, leaving the ravelling out of the fringe until the drawn work is finished ; proceed to draw the threads wherever spaces are desired, and before working the pattern always hem-stitch both edges of the spaces. In Fig. 306 the pattern marked B shows the stitch called fagotting, made by crossing every other group of threads back over the one preceding and drawing the linen thread through in such a way as to keep the groups twisted ; the two lines marked A, in the Fig. 306, are intended

Fig. 306.—Fagotting Stitch.

more as a finish to some elaborate design than as a pattern in themselves ; these are made by hem-stitching down a number of threads to each group. Fig. 307 gives a favorite pattern ; for this count the threads, so that the spaces may be equal and regular ; draw the threads in all the spaces running one way first ; then draw the threads in the spaces crossing the first one and run linen threads diagonally across from the top of the

Fig. 307.—Drawn Work.

right-hand corner to the bottom of the left, dividing each linen square into two equal parts ; cross these by threads also running diagonally across from the top of the left-hand corner to the bottom of the right, again dividing the linen squares, making four equal parts ; then weave threads

Fig. 308.—First Knot.   Fig. 309.—Second Knot.

through all the spaces running both horizontally and perpendicularly, using the fagotting stitch (Fig. 306), and when crossing the threads in the open spaces tie the centres of each in turn, as in Figs. 308, 309; finish the pattern by running a thread in and out several times around the knots in the

Fig. 310·—Border in Drawn Work.

centres of the wheels and fasten the ends by tying neatly. Another pattern is given in Fig. 310.

Outline work is often combined with drawn work; fast colors, in either cotton, linen or silk, are used for the outline design. When the article worked is intended for daily use and must frequently be laundried, it is better to substitute in place of the fringe a wide hem-stitched hem edged with firm linen lace.

Very dainty fancy aprons are made of common scrim with spaces drawn and narrow ribbons of different colors simply woven in and out of the threads, running crosswise through the spaces.

Applique and Original Designs for Portières.

The pattern in this work is cut from one material and sewed on another.

Almost any kind of fabric can be used as either applique or foundation; velvet and plush are suitable for applique, but make poor groundwork, owing to the long nap; both materials in dark rich colors are handsome when used as a border on portières or table-covers. To applique a pattern of velvet or plush cut the design very exact and cover the wrong side with a slight coating of gum, being careful to have the gum thin on the edges so that it will not spread on the ground-work; then lay the velvet on the place it is to occupy, and after pressing it down very gently and lightly with your hand, allow it to dry; this accomplished, the edges of the pattern may be hemmed down neatly on the foundation. If a further finish is desired, outline the design by sewing all around the edge a small gold or silken cord.

Portières.

We give an original applique design for a portière in Fig. 311, representing Day. The foundation is of soft dark-blue momie-cloth, the sun a round piece of bright yellow or orange satin, and the rays are of gold or heavy yellow silk thread merely run in stitches of various lengths ; the cloud is of light blue crape or crazy cloth, and the bird is one of those which come prepared expressly for applique by the Japanese, and can be purchased at almost any Japanese or fancy store ; if possible a lark should be selected in preference to other birds. The border is a band of old gold velvet. Our other design (Fig.

Fig. 311.—Portière. Day.   Fig. 312.—Portière. Night.

312) represents Night ; the foundation and band are the same as those for the " Day " portière ; the star is of white silk, the moon of very pale Nile green silk, and the cloud of dark pearl gray crape or crazy cloth, much darker than the blue momie-cloth.

The applique work must be done very carefully. First cut out the designs, next turn in the raw edges evenly and smoothly, and with a very fine thread and needle baste the edges down ;

then baste the designs carefully on the foundations, and, with a fine needle and sewing-silk matching in color the piece to be appliqued, hem each one down neatly, making the stitches almost invisible. The band of velvet can be sewed on the bottom edge of the momie-cloth, then turned up like a hem and hemmed down.

Lace.

Very beautiful lace is made by cutting out the heavy patterns which are still perfect, from old and worn laces and embroideries, and transferring the designs to new fine wash-net. After first basting them on, hem them down to the netting with a fine needle and thread ; in this way the embroideries last as long again and look as well as when new.

Ribbon Embroideries.

We can give a clearer idea of this work by means of an example, and we will take the common white daisy as an illustration.

Thread a long-eyed coarse needle with very narrow white ribbon, and beginning at the centre of the flower, pass the needle from the wrong side up through your material, drawing the ribbon out nearly its full length and leaving only a short piece on the wrong side to be fastened down ; now take a stitch straight out the length of a daisy petal and pass the needle through to the wrong side ; then, taking a very short stitch, draw the needle out through on the right side ; next take another long stitch back to the centre of the daisy, thus forming the second petal ; continue in the same manner, making the petals radiate out in a circle from the centre of the flower. Work the centres of the daisies with yellow silk and the stems in dark-green silk ; the leaves can be either worked or appliqued.

For half-blown daisies make only about a quarter of a circle of petals, and in place of the yellow centre, work a green calyx. Ox-eyed daisies can be made in the same way with soft, thin yellow ribbon, a little broader than the ribbon used for white daisies. The work is rapid and pleasing, and almost any flower can be imitated very perfectly with ribbon embroidery.

CHAPTER XXXV.

SCRAP-BOOK AND HOME-MADE BOOK-COVERS.

HE fashion of collecting pictured advertising cards, so much in vogue among
the children a few years ago, seems to
have run its course, and dying out, it
has left on the young collectors' hands
more cards than they know well what
to do with. Many of the collections
have been pasted in scrap-books, of
which the children have long since tired. While examining
one of these volumes with its row after row of cards, it occurred to me that these advertisements might be utilized in a
new way by dividing and combining them. The experiment
proved a success, and I will now try to show you how, with
the aid of scissors and mucilage, the pictures which have become so familiar may be made to undergo changes that are
indeed wonderful, and how from them may be formed a

Mother Goose Scrap-book.

The nursery scrap-books made of linen or paper cambric
are, perhaps, familiar to most of our readers ; but for the benefit of those who may not yet have seen these durable little
books, we will give the following directions for making one :
Cut from a piece of strong linen, colored paper cambric, or

white muslin, four squares twenty-four inches long by twelve inches wide. Button-hole-stitch the edges all around with some bright-colored worsted, then place the squares neatly together and stitch them directly through the centre with strong thread (Fig. 313). Fold them over, stitch again, as in Fig. 314, and your book is finished and ready for the pictures.

It is in the preparation of these pictures that you will find the novelty of the plan we propose. Instead of pasting in those cards which have become too familiar to awaken much interest, let the young book-makers design and form their own pictures by cutting special figures, or parts of figures, from different

Fig. 313.—Scrap-book Opened and Stitched through the Centre.

Fig. 314.—Scrap-book Folded and again Stitched.

cards, and then pasting them together so as to form new combinations.

Any subject which pleases the fancy can be illustrated in this way, and you will soon be deeply interested in the work and delighted at the strange and striking pictorial characters that can be produced by ingenious combinations.

Stories and little poems may be very nicely and aptly illustrated ; but the " Mother Goose Melodies " are, perhaps, the most suitable subjects with which to interest younger children, as they will be easily recognized by the little folk. Take, for instance, the " Three Wise Men of Gotham," who went to sea in a bowl. Will not Fig. 315 serve very well as an illustration of the subject? Yet these figures are cut from advertising cards, and no two from the same card. Fig. 316 shows the materials, Fig. 315 the result of combining them.

Again, the little man dancing so gayly (Fig. 317) is turned

Fig. 315.—"Three Wise Men of Gotham." Fig. 318.—"Little Jack Horner."

Fig. 316.—Figures cut from Advertising Cards.

Fig. 317.—Figures cut from Christmas Cards.

into "Little Jack Horner" eating his Christmas pie (Fig. 318), by merely cutting off his legs and substituting a dress-skirt and pair of feet clipped from another card. The Christmas pie in his lap is from still another card.

In making pictures of this kind, figures that were originally standing may be forced to sit; babies may be placed in arms which, on the cards they were stolen from, held only cakes of soap, perhaps, or boxes of blacking; heads may be ruthlessly torn from bodies to which they belong, and as ruthlessly clapped upon strange shoulders; and you will be surprised to see what amusing, and often excellent, illustrations present themselves as the result of a little ingenuity in clipping and pasting. Another kind, which we shall call the

Transformation Scrap-Book,

will be found exceedingly amusing on account of the various and ever-changing pictures it presents.

Unlike any other, where the picture once pasted in must remain ever the same, the transformation scrap-book alters one picture many times. To work these transformations a blank book is the first article required ; one eight inches long by six and a half or seven wide is a good size.

Fig. 319.—Transformation Scrap-book with Pages cut.

Cut the pages of this book across, one-third of the way down. Fig. 319 shows how this should be done. The three-cornered piece cut out near the binding allows the pages to be turned without catching or tearing. Leave the first page uncut ; also the one in the middle of the book.

Cut from picture-cards, or old toy-books which have colored illustrations, the odd and funny figures of men and women, boys and girls, selecting those which will give a variety of costumes and attitudes.

Paste a figure of a woman or girl on the first page, placing it so that when the lower part of the next page is turned, the upper edge of it will come across the neck of the figure where it is joined on to the shoulders.

Cut the heads from the rest of the pictured women, and choosing a body as different as possible from the one just used,

Leaves from a Transformation Scrap-book.

paste it upon the lower part of the next page, directly under
the head belonging to the first body.   Upon the upper part of

the same page paste any one of the other heads, being careful to place it so that it will fit the body. Continue in this way, pasting the heads upon the upper, and the bodies on the lower, part of the page, until the space allowed for the women is filled up ; then, commencing at the page left in the middle of the book, paste upon it the figure of a man, and continue in the same manner as with the woman, until the spaces are all used and the book is complete.

The combinations formed in this way are very funny. Old heads with young bodies ; young heads with old bodies ; then one head with a great variety of bodies, and so on.

The first picture may represent a man, tall and thin, dressed in a rowing costume, as shown in the illustration. Turn the lower part of the next page, and no longer is he thin and tall, but short and stout, the position of this body giving the expression of amazement, even to the face. The next page turned shows him to be neither tall nor short, thick nor thin, but a soldier, well-proportioned, who is looking over his shoulder in the most natural manner possible.

The figures in the illustration were cut from advertising cards, and the head belongs to none of the bodies.

A curious fact in arranging the pictures in this way is that the heads all look as though they might really belong to any of the various bodies given them.

Instead of having but one figure on a page, groups may be formed of both men and women, and in the different arrangement of the figures they can be made very ludicrous indeed.

A scrap-book for older girls, which might be termed more fitly

An Album,

can be made by mounting engravings, wood-cuts, photographs, and water-colors on pieces of thin card-board all of the same size.

If any one subject be chosen, and such pictures selected as tend in some way to illustrate that subject, the book will prove more interesting in the making, and will be quite valuable when finished.

There will be no difficulty in mounting the pictures; simply paste them on the card-board with good flour-paste, and press under a heavy weight, keeping them perfectly neat and free from smears of paste on the edges. When two or more are mounted at the same time, place clean pieces of blotting-paper between, pile one upon another, and put the heavy weight on top.

Such a scrap-book should be bound in a

Home-made Book-cover,

which is made in this way:

Take two pieces of heavy card-board a trifle larger than the book you wish to cover, make three holes near the edge of each (Fig. 320) and corresponding holes in the edges of the

| Fig. 320.—One Side of Book-cover with Holes cut near the Edge. | Fig. 321.—Book-cover Tied with Ribbons. | Fig. 322.—Book-cover Laced together with Silk Cord. |

book, which must not be too thick—that is, contain too many leaves ; pass narrow ribbons through these holes and tie in bow-knots, as in Fig. 321. If the leaves of the book are thin,

26

more holes can be made in the back and the covers laced together with silk cord (Fig. 322).

These book-covers may be beautifully decorated by anyone
who can paint in water-colors, and tinted card-board can also
be used for them.   They are pretty, and suitable as covers for
manuscript poems or stories, or for a collection of autographs.

In making any kind of scrap-book it is very necessary that
the paste used should be good.   If the paste is poor, the pictures will peel off or the paste turn sour.   The recipe given
below we can recommend as an excellent one for

Flour-paste.

Mix one-half cup of flour with enough cold water to make a
very thin batter, which must be smooth and free from lumps ;
put the batter on top of the stove—not next to the fire—in a tin
sauce-pan, and stir continually until it boils ; then remove from
the stove, add three drops of oil of cloves, and pour the paste
into a cup or tumbler.   This will keep for à long time and will
not become sour.

CHAPTER XXXVI.

A HEAP OF RUBBISH, AND WHAT TO DO WITH IT.

N almost every house there is an attic, and in almost every attic may be found a room where trunks are stored, where broken toys and disabled furniture are put out of sight, and where all articles not worth selling or giving away gradually accumulate until this attic room contains, literally, a heap of rubbish. Entering one of these lumber-rooms not long ago, and glancing over the medley which comprised so much, from a tin can to a piece of broken bric-à-brac, the thought occurred to me that something might be done with it, some use be made of at least a few of the articles consigned to the place as utterly useless.

That was rather a thrifty thought. Do you not think so, girls ? Then let us make the most of it and together venture back into that mysterious and somewhat dusty chamber, and see if there really is anything there worth the making over.

In imagination we will stand in our attic lumber-room and begin to look about us with eyes and mind open to perceive possibilities.

On one side of the room, leaning against the wall, we see what was once a handsome old-fashioned mirror, quite large and of heavy plate-glass. It's poor dusty face, reflecting dimly its barren surroundings, is shattered in many pieces, and at first sight it seems hopeless to attempt to restore it to the plane of beauty or usefulness; but do not let us be hasty; we will examine it more closely. Yes, here is a piece of glass large enough to frame. Never mind its uneven shape and rough edges; we will work out that problem later. Now we must put it carefully aside and continue our investigations.

Here is a large tin can, which can be made into a lantern to hang in the hall, and this baking-powder can may be of some use, so we will take it also.

The tops of three cheese-boxes; something should be done with them. Perhaps they can be used for a table; put them with the other chosen things.

A croquet-ball! That will make a fine key-rack. This box of silks and ribbons we may need, and the large pasteboard-box will do for the foundation of our mirror frame.

We must have this piece of old brass chain this handful of large nails, the pasteboard roll which has been used for sending engravings through the mail, and that old broad-brimmed straw hat; also these three broomsticks and the piece of nice dark-gray hardware paper.

Now, seated in our own room, let us see what we can do with this rather unpromising array of objects spread around us. First we will try

The Mirror,

and must cast about us for the ways and means of framing it. The large pasteboard-box we have already decided will make a good foundation. After tearing off the sides, we will cut an even square from the bottom, which is smooth and unwarped.

Next laying the piece of mirror on the square of pasteboard we must cut, out of ordinary brown wrapping-paper, a square two inches larger all around than the pasteboard, make a hole in the centre as large as the shape of the mirror will allow, and

Fig. 323.—Brown Paper Pasted on Mirror and Pasteboard for Home-made Mirror-frame.

paste it down on the mirror and pasteboard (Fig. 323). Then, after clipping out the corners, we will turn the edges over on to the back of the pasteboard foundation and paste them down. Cutting four strips of the hardware paper, about two inches wide, we will fold them through the centre lengthwise and paste them around the glass, lapping them just a lit-

Fig. 324.—Bevel of Hardware Paper on Frame.

tle over the edge of the other paper, the folded side being next to the glass (Fig. 324). This will form a bevel for our frame. From the same paper we will now cut a square, three inches larger on all sides than the foundation; then, exactly in the centre, mark a square half an inch larger all around than the square of mirror showing. In the centre of the square marked out we must insert our scissors, cut it like Fig. 325, and after clipping off the points, as indicated by the dotted lines L, M, O, N, turn back the four

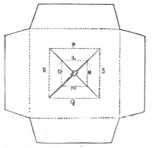

Fig. 325.—The Outside Covering for Mirror-frame.

pieces at the dotted lines, P, Q, R, S, leaving an open square. Then placing it over the mirror so that the same width of bevelled edge shows on all sides of the mirror, we must paste it down. Clipping out the corners, as shown in diagram, we will bring the edges over and paste them down securely to the back of the frame. A piece of hardware paper, cut in a

Fig. 326.—Back of Frame with Tape Attached.

square one inch smaller than the frame, we will paste on the back to finish it off and hide the edges of the paper where they have been turned over (Fig. 326).

Home-made Mirror-frame.

We must fasten on a piece of tape by which to hang the mirror, by pasting down the ends of the tape on the frame (letter T, Fig. 326), and pasting over each a strip of the hardware paper (letter U, Fig. 326). When the frame is quite dry we will paint a branch of dog-wood or some light-colored flower across it, and have as pretty a little mirror as anyone could wish for.

The next thing to commence will be

The Table,

which you can make yourselves by following these directions:

The three cheese-box lids will answer nicely as shelves for a work- or bric-à-brac table, and the broomsticks, which are all the same length, will do for the legs.

Upon each broomstick mark the distances for placing the shelves, allowing six inches from each end of the stick for the top and bottom, and the exact centre between these points for the middle shelf. With a pocket-knife cut narrow grooves around each stick, one-half inch on either side of the points marked on them (Fig. 327). This will make six grooves on each stick. Now measure the box-lids to find their circumferences, and divide them into thirds, marking the distances on the rim to obtain

Fig. 327.--Narrow Grooves Cut around Broomstick for Table-leg.

the true position for the legs. At these points bore four holes with a gimlet, one inch apart, two above and two below (Fig. 328). Through

Fig. 328.—Holes Bored in a Box-lid Used as a Table-shelf.

one of the top holes pass a piece of pliable wire, place one of the broomsticks against the rim of the lid, pass the wire back through the other upper hole (Fig. 329), fit it into the upper groove of the stick, and draw it tight.

Fig. 329.—Manner of Fastening a Shelf to Table-leg.

Twice the wire must be put through the upper holes and around the stick in the top groove; then, bringing it down

Bric-a-brac Table.

Fig. 330.—Table-shelf and Leg Fastened securely together by Wire.

on the inside of the lid, you must put it twice through the lower holes and around the stick in the lower groove; then twist the ends and tuck them under the wire on the inside of the lid (Fig. 330). In this way each leg will have to be fast-

ened to each shelf. When the table is all put together paint it
black, and, as soon as it is dry, tie a bright ribbon on one of the
sticks at the top, and a charming little bric-à-brac table will be
the result of your labor.

You can make a very pretty

Lantern

of the old tin can ; but first you must have some tools to work
with ; not many, only a piece of wood, rounded on one side to
fit into the can, a hatchet or heavy hammer, and a few wrought
iron nails. If the piece of wood is not large enough to fit the
can, another stick can be put in to hold the first one firmly
against the can. That being arranged, you must decide upon
some kind of a pattern to be made by the holes, and indicate
it on the can with a small paint-brush and paint or ink ; then,
laying the can on its side, the rounded piece of wood being at
the top, with one of the wrought iron nails puncture the holes
where you have indicated the pattern. With the hammer drive
the nail through the tin into the wood ; then draw it out, make
another hole, and so on until all the holes you wish are driven
through that part of the can held in place by the rounded
piece of wood.

This wood, you see, keeps the can from bending when the
nail is being driven through. In moving the wood as the work
progresses, you must always keep it under that part of the can
being punctured. To make the large hole, you will have to put a
number of the small holes close together, and then drive the nail
through the partitions, cutting them away. The pattern being
completed, puncture three holes, close to the top of the can, at
equal distances apart. These are for the chains to pass through,
by which to suspend the lantern. In the cover of the baking-
powder can make three holes at equal distances ; then divide

the chain, which is about one yard and a quarter long, into three equal lengths, separating the pieces by prying open the links. Put an end of each piece through the holes made for

them at the top of the can, and fasten them by hooking the open links through the links of the chain a little farther up, and hammering them together again.

Now pass the ends of the chains through the holes made in the lid of the baking-powder can, and, bringing the ends together, fasten them by joining the links.

Fig. 331.   Fig. 332.
—Stand in Lantern, with
Nails for Holding Can-
dle.

Paint the lantern, chain and all, black, and while it is drying make a stand for the candle which is to furnish the light. A square piece of thin board, just large enough to fit into the can without touching the sides will do for the stand. Drive four small nails in the centre to hold the candle (Fig. 331).

Lantern.

Make handles for lifting the stand in and out of the lantern, by bending two pieces of wire like Fig. 331, and fastening them to the board with staple tacks (Fig. 332).

When the paint on the lantern is dry, paste red tissue-paper all around the inside to give a cheerful red glow to the light, which will shine through it. If you would like it to resemble a jewelled lantern, paste different colored papers over the large holes and leave the small ones open. An S hook passed through the loop made by the three chains will serve to connect them to the chain which should suspend the lantern from the ceiling.

A Music-Roll

can be made of the pasteboard roll.

Cut a round piece of pasteboard just the size to fit into one end of the roll ; then cut out another round piece, this time of paper, one inch larger than that made of pasteboard. Clip the

edges (Fig. 333) and paste it over the end of the roll which is filled in with the round of pasteboard (Fig. 334).

Fig. 333.—Paper Covering for End of Music-roll.

Fig. 334.—Paper Pasted over End of Music-roll.

Among the scraps of silk and ribbons you will, perhaps, find a good-sized piece of dark-green or brown silk ; use this for the case, which must cover the roll neatly. To make the case fit the end of the roll you have just filled up, mark on a piece of the silk a circle the size of that end of the roll. This can be done by standing the roll on the silk, and running a pencil around the edge. When cutting out the silk leave a margin of a quarter of an inch on the outside of the pencil-mark for the seam. Cut the silk for cover-ing the roll three inches longer than the roll, and wide enough to allow for a quarter of an inch seam.

Music-roll.

Sew up the long seam, and then sew the round of silk into the end of the case. Hem the other end of the case, and run in a narrow ribbon about an inch from the edge. This is for a draw-string.

When the roll is fitted snugly in its case, tie a ribbon,

matching it in color, around the roll, making a loop to form the handle. Fasten the ribbon by taking a few stitches under the bows, catching them on to the silk.

The old straw hat can be transformed into a dainty

Work-Basket.

It is stiff and harsh at present, but pour boiling water over it and the straw will become soft and pliable, and can be bent into any shape you like. When dry, it will be again stiff, and will retain the form you have given it. After scalding the hat bend the brim in toward the centre, in four different places, at equal distances apart. This will make a fluted basket. You

Fig. 335.—Straw Hat Tied in Shape for a
Work-basket.

Work-basket.

must tie it in shape (Fig. 335) and leave until perfectly dry; then bronze the basket, line it with silesia, and sew silk or satin around the top to form a bag. Run a draw-string of narrow ribbon near the top of the bag, and the pretty little work-basket is finished.

The croquet ball you can make into a

Key and Button-Hook Rack.

First you must gild it, and then around the middle of the ball, at regular intervals, insert small brass hooks. A yellow ribbon and bow, tacked on the top with small tacks, will serve to suspend it by, and completes the rack.

With the gilt left from gilding the ball, and a piece of bright ribbon you can make a

Paper-Weight

of six of the large nails. Gild each nail separately, let them dry, and then tie them securely together with a piece of ribbon.

Key Rack.   Paper-weight.

All the articles brought from the attic have now been turned to some use, but there are many other things to be found there which we have not space to mention, and which with little trouble can be so transformed that no one would ever suppose they were taken originally from a heap of rubbish.

CHAPTER XXXVII.

HOW TO MAKE ATTRACTIVE BOOTHS AT A FAIR—A NEW KIND OF GRAB-BAG.

ECIDING to have our fair unlike those which have preceded it, we must do away with monotony and introduce not only variety, but originality as well. New ideas, something different from that which has served us heretofore, is what we strive for. Novelties are always attractive, let them be decorative also, and help to make the room or hall as inviting as possible.

The Tables

being the most important item, we will give them our first attention. Have each table or booth canopied in a style differing from all others, and make the canopy extend up as high as practicable, in order to avoid the flat, blank appearance so common in small fairs. If tables are arranged in this fashion, they will go far toward decorating the hall. Fig. 336 shows one style in which a framework for the roof or covering may be constructed. At the four corners of the table, where the top projects over the sides, fit in blocks of wood according to Fig. 337; the dotted lines represent the block. Nail the wood

The Fair.

fast to the table, so that the uprights may stand perfectly straight. Use laths or similar sticks for the four uprights, and screw or nail them at the corners of the table according to Fig. 336 ; then with small screws fasten a stick across the top of the laths at each side, and at the top of the sticks on the front of the table tie the two ends of a barrel-hoop to form the arch ; also attach another hoop at the back to the other two uprights, and connect the top centre of each by a wire running across. The hoops are fastened to the laths by binding the ends of the hoops to the ends of the laths with strong twine, or wire, wound around in notches which have previously been cut

Fig. 336.—Framework for the Canopy of a Booth at a Fair.

Fig. 337. — Block of Wood Fastened on the side of Table.

in the ends of both sticks and hoops. Should the barrel-hoops be too short for the arch, take children's large sized toy wooden hoops, and fasten them up in the same manner. Fig. 338 is another way to arrange the framework. The four upright sticks are attached to the table as described in Fig. 336 ; then in the top of each is driven a very large-sized tack, and a strong flexible wire is stretched from lath to lath and wound around each tack, thus connecting the four uprights together.* Flags, shawls, drapery curtains, sheets,

* If the uprights seem to need it, brace them with cross-sticks in place of wire.

and inexpensive cheese-cloth make good canopies ; undressed cambric and canton flannel in desirable colors drape nicely, and can also be used for the purpose.

Where you wish to produce light, airy effects, tarlatan, in one or more colors, will be found useful ; again, let some of the tables have only a suggestion of a roof, made by ornamenting the framework with flowers, or whatever is most suitable, according to the style of table and the place it is to occupy.

Try and have a variety of shapes and sizes in the booths, and avoid sombre dulness and monotony. Let the room fairly sparkle and shine with light and color.

Fig. 338.—Construction of Framework for the Canopy of a Table at a Fair.

To make a tent-like covering, firmly bind a large-sized Japanese umbrella to a pole, and fasten the pole in the centre of the table. To hold it securely, make a bench of two pieces of board, with a hole through the centre of each, and join them together by a block of wood nailed in each end (Fig. 339). The bench can be made fast to the table by screws put through from the under side of the top of the table.

Fig. 339.—Bench for Holding a Pole as a Support for a Canopy of a Booth.

In erecting the canopy place the end of the pole in the bench and it will be steady and firm. Attach pieces of string to several ribs on each side of the umbrella, stretch the strings down and fasten the ends securely to the table ; paste over the strings bright-colored tissue-paper fringe (Fig. 340). Cut the paper four or six thicknesses, and when pasted on turn the fringe part uppermost, so it will look fluffy and not hang down in a tame, fringe fashion. When a red umbrella is used, and the strings are covered with fringe of the same hue, it looks very pretty. Be extremely careful that no light comes dangerously near the tissue-paper, or any other inflammable material ; all the decorations must be arranged with a view to perfect safety from contact with gas, lamp, or candle.

In decorating the room remember to mass your color so the effect may be broad. If the colors are too much mingled the effect will be weakened, and in some cases lost entirely.

Paper-flowers and plants in great abundance will be needed, and if you can per-

Fig. 340.—Tissue-paper Fringe.

suade all your friends, as well as those actively interested in the fair, to make paper-flowers or plants, they will prove very acceptable, and after the fair is over the floral decorations can be safely stored away to do service again on like occasion. Large, showy flowers, like peonies, dog-wood, and magnolias, as well as large-leaved plants, are best to use, though the smaller ones look well in a few places.

In making

Flowers for Decorations

we aim at general effect, with less regard to detail than if the blossoms were to be used in other ways. Fig. 341 is a pat-

27

tern of the dog-wood. Cut the flowers of white writing paper and make them quite large.

Use wire to fasten them to a natural branch, and imitate nature as nearly as possible in the arrangement of the blossoms.

If you fold the paper a number of times and then place your pattern over it, you can cut out six or eight flowers at once, and save both time and labor.

Peonies are made of white, pink, or red tissue-paper, cut in squares of about eight inches each and pinked on the two

Fig. 341.—Dog-wood.

opposite edges. Twelve squares are needed for one flower. With your fingers gather the squares up in the centre (Fig. 342); then fold over the pieces, as in Fig. 343; when all are ready string them on a wire and shape the bunch to resemble a peony; twist the wire up tight and fasten the petals together, leaving a length of wire for a stem.

Make the cherry-blossoms (Fig. 344) in clusters of five or seven each, and attach green leaves (Fig. 345) cut in different sizes. Fig.

Fig. 342.—Peony Petal Gathered through the Centre.

Fig. 343.—Peony Petal Folded over.

346 shows the method of giving the leaf a pretty, crimped appearance. By holding the point of the leaf firmly under the head of the pin with your left hand, and with the right hand pushing the leaf up toward the head of the pin, you can crimp the leaves very rapidly, and they look much more natural than when left plain.

All the materials necessary for the manufacture of flowers for fair decorations will be paper, wire, and paste. The buds of different flowers can be imitated by pinching together the petals of open blossoms. Figs. 347, 348, 349 are the petals of the magnolia; the inside petals are five and one-half inches long, the others in proportion. Cut three of each size. No. 347 forms the innermost petals, No. 348 the next, and No. 349 the outer-most; these last should be double; make the outside of pink tissue-paper and the inside white, all the other petals are white; cut three, from Fig. 350, of green paper to form the calyx.

Fig. 344.— Cherry Blossom.

Fig. 345. — Green Leaf of Cherry Tree.

Other ornamental flowers may be manu-factured from these hints. Patterns can be cut from any natural flowers, and they may be made without the aid of fur-

Fig. 346.—Method of Crimping Leaf.

ther directions. When natural blossoms can be obtained, they are far preferable, though the paper plants make splen-did substitutes and at a little distance cannot be distin-guished from the natural ones.

If the fair comes off in the season when the trees are leafless, bare

Fig. 347.　　Fig. 348.　　Fig. 349.　Fig. 350.

branches with green paper leaves wired on will help very much where foliage is needed.

An excellent scheme in the arrangement of a fair is to divide the tables into twelve separate booths and let each one represent one month in the year. They should contain articles appropriate only to the month represented, and when planned in this way each month should be of appropriate color. For example :

December

can be all white, with tufts of cotton scattered about for snow, and mica or isinglass sprinkled around and over places to represent frost and ice. Icicles, varying in size, depending from the arch or canopy, add to the effect. The icicles are made of strips of paper first rolled up like paper-lighters, then completely covered with tallow from the dripping of a lighted candle ; the tallow being allowed to harden on in raised places makes the twisted paper resemble in form, a real icicle ; the tallow icicle is next covered with a wash of mucilage, and powdered mica or isinglass is sprinkled all over it, so that it sparkles and shines.

In place of the usual grab-bag at this booth, there should be a Christmas-tree without lights and burdened with little gifts tied up in colored tissue-paper. Santa Claus must have charge of the tree.

July

calls for flags and decorations of red, white, and blue, as well as flowers, fruits, and green foliage ; the table should be presided over by Columbia.

May.

Deck this table in spring blossoms and make the canopy of a slender May-pole. Pass the pole through the holes in the bench (Fig. 339) and screw the bench tight on the centre of the table ; fasten a wreath of flowers and the ends of a number of ribbons at the top of the pole ; bring the ribbons down and tack them to the sides of the table. Give the Queen of May care of the booth.

November

may be gay with late fall leaves and berries, and a very large pumpkin, which has been previously scraped out and lined with paper, can serve as a receptacle for odds and ends. A little Puritan maid should be in charge of the booth.

June

is all rose color, with the queen of flowers, the rose, holding the post of honor. This month is very suitable for the flower-table, and Flora, the Goddess of Flowers, may preside over it.

We have chosen these few months only as suggestions of the manner in which the idea can be carried out.

Those in charge of the different booths might wear as a badge a conspicuous sign of the zodiac appropriate to the month represented.

The Five Senses

can be illustrated by five booths, each one bearing its proper symbol as a sign. To represent

HEARING,

make a large pasteboard ear-trumpet and cover it with silver paper ; fasten this on the highest point of the booth and place the word Hearing in large letters under the trumpet; have these signs in plain sight, where none can fail to see and read. The articles on the table should consist of everything pertaining to the sense of hearing, such as sheet-music, musical instruments, telephones, and suitable toys.

It would be a great addition if a phonograph could be

rented or borrowed for the occasion, and a certain sum charged to each one speaking in the instrument and hearing the echo of his own words and tones ground out to him again.

An oracle would be a capital thing at this table, each person consulting it paying so much a question.

SEEING

likewise must be labelled with a sign in the shape of a very large pair of spectacles cut out of stiff pasteboard and placed over the lettering.

The goods offered here for sale should pertain to the sense of sight; and could be such articles as pictures, decorated candles, kaleidoscopes, and common blue glasses. All things pleasing to look upon may find place at the Seeing Table. Any kind of a peep-show can be used, five cents being required from every curious person wishing for a peep behind the curtain.

FEELING

is more difficult to portray. Perhaps an ordinary riding-whip will answer the purpose, with the word Feeling in large type under it.

Sofa-cushions, quilts, mittens, canes, muffs, fancy toilet articles, and almost anything adding to our personal comfort, or pleasant to handle, are suitable for the Feeling booth.

TASTING.

As an emblem for this booth make a huge cornucopia for candy, with the sign " Tasting " beneath, and the booth can be the candy-table.

SMELLING

naturally suggests perfumes and sweet-scented flowers. This sense will most fitly be represented by an immense bouquet fastened up over the table.   The booth, of course, must be the flower-table.

If you have only a few tables, make four booths of them, and let each booth represent a season.   They should be decorated in keeping with the time represented, and the idea fully carried out in all the details.

When the booths stand for different nations there is a great field for variety and beautiful decoration.   But in this, as in all cases where an attempt is made to carry out an idea, it must be faithfully adhered to, or the effect will not be that intended.

When it is necessary to decorate the

Walls

use flags, bright, soft draping cloth, and large palm leaves; also branches of leaves, showy flowers, and anything that can

be arranged to look well.   As rooms differ so much in size and style, it is impossible to give any but general directions, leaving it to the taste of the decorator to carry out the details.

Fig. 351.—Grab-bag of a Sheet with Holes Cut for Face and Arms.

Grab-Bags.

On a narrow sheet hung up in a door-way, and fastened securely at the sides, or attached to a frame, cut a hole large enough to allow of a false face being fitted in (Fig. 351 A).   The flaps of the cloth are left for pasting inside the face ; now cut two more holes for the arms to pass through

Fig. 352.—Apron Skirt Sewed on Sheet.

(Fig. 351 B).   In these holes sew sleeves of the same material as the skirt, which is made of bright-colored cambric in the

Fig. 353.—Grab-bag.

form of an apron, and sewed on the sheet (Fig. 352). The sides of the skirt are basted down on the sheet. When pasting in the false face, first cover the flaps, left at the opening for the face with stiff paste ; then paste these flaps down into the inside of the false face, which will bring it up close against the sheet. If small openings are left, or the sheet puckers a little after the face is fastened on, never mind, as all defects can be covered by sewing on a thin white frill all around the face, to form a cap, and making a collar of the same material (Fig. 353).

Leave an opening, or pocket-hole, through the sheet at one side of the dress, so that the hand can be slipped through to get the packages, which are placed within reach at the back of the curtain. Fig. 354 shows the inside of the sheet, and C the opening for the hand. Someone must

Fig.354.—Inside of Sheet for Grab-bag.

stand or be seated behind this curtain, and slip her arms into the sleeves, then she can look out through the mask and see with whom she is talking. In one hand she may hold a package, while she receives the money with the other.

On the sheet print these words : " Five cents for what is in my pocket."

The Lady of the Lake.

You will need a tin bath-tub for the lake, the longest one you can find, and a toy boat which will not easily tip or turn over. Place tiny flags in the bow and stern, and in one end of the boat glue a doll dressed like the "Lady of the Lake" in Scott's poem. Attach a pulley to each end of the tub, and fasten the string to the boat, as it must be run back and forth by means of the pulleys. Fill the tub nearly full of water, then cover the edges with moss and vines. The bath-tub must be completely disguised, and surrounded by plants and foliage, with an opening left at one end for purchasers, and another small one near the other end for the boat to pass through to those stationed behind the shrubbery, who have charge of the boat, and where the parcels are kept. At the store-room end the screen of vines or leaves should be so arranged that those in charge can see all that is going on outside without being seen themselves.

The boat should be stationed at the farther end of the lake, and whoever wishes to make a purchase must give the doll five cents ; then the boat may immediately leave, sail across the lake, and disappear behind the screen, only to emerge again laden with a parcel in place of the money, and lightly skimming over the water arrive at her destination, when the purchaser can relieve the " Lady of the Lake " of her package.

The Bubble Range described on page 335 can be used in a fair with advantage. Unless the fair is very small, it is better to have two Bubble Ranges, to prevent the tiresome waiting

for a turn, and give all who wish to try their skill the opportunity to enjoy the sport.

Fortune's Wheel.

Cut of stiff pasteboard a large circle (Fig. 355) with a point
on the edge at the end of one of the spokes, for the circle must
be painted to resemble a wheel. With a large
round nail fasten the wheel through the centre
to a board, which has previ-
ously had numbers painted
on in a circle somewhat
larger than the circumference of the wheel (Fig.
356); the wheel should
turn around easily on

Fig. 355.—Circle for
Fortune's Wheel.

the nail. Hang the board up flat
against the wall. The gypsy in
charge of the Fortune's Wheel
should be stationed by its side,
holding a basket filled with many
envelopes numbered to correspond
to the figures on the board, each
envelope containing some appropriate fortune-telling lines; and
when the people come to seek
their fortunes the gypsy must allow each in turn to give the wheel
a twirl, sending it around rapidly,
and then hand to the fortune-

Fig. 356.—Fortune's Wheel.

seeker an envelope whose number
corresponds with the figure at which the wheel pointed when it
stopped turning.

Rag-Balls.

Prepare a number of carpet-rag balls with a small gift in the centre of each one. These sell rapidly, and it is very amusing to see the buyers unwinding their balls to discover the contents, which may prove to be a thimble, a bundle of jackstraws, a grotesque Japanese toy, or any little comical conceit which can be hidden in the odd receptacle.

The same idea might be applied to the always pleasing pop-corn balls; then the knick-knacks must be first wrapped in soft paper to protect them from the candy used in making the balls.

Pleasant mysteries and surprises are always popular at fairs, and the more that can be invented the better.

Window Decorated with Imitation Stained Glass and Dutch Curtain.

CHAPTER XXXVIII.

WINDOW DECORATION.

OW, girls, we must have practicable ideas in regard to our decorations; they should consist of something which we *know* will be easy to make and at the same time look well ; the materials employed must be within possible reach of all, and nothing expensive or difficult to obtain allowed to enter into their manufacture. What are commonly called Dutch curtains are very popular ; they are short curtains of some thin, transparent fabric, fastened with rings to a slender rod of bamboo, and when drawn, cover the lower part of the window without intercepting the light. The curtains are very useful, but, while they do not obstruct the light, they do obstruct the vision.

We all know that the front window is just the place to sit when sewing or doing fancy-work, and although few ladies care to be seen by every passer-by, yet they all like to see what is going on outside, and while their deft fingers ply the needle their bright eyes take in the landscape out of doors and derive amusement and entertainment from the birds and flowers, if it be in the country, or the ever-moving throng, if in the city.

An ornamental screen, therefore, that will shield one and

yet not interfere with the view is desirable. What might be termed the

Oriental Window-Shade

not only comes up to the above requirements, but is inexpensive, and not difficult to construct.

Make a small lawn-tennis net, long enough to reach across the width of the window and about eight inches deep; make

loops of the rope on the ends for hanging the screen to knobs or hooks screwed in the framework of the window; spread the net out and fasten it up on a door, between two chairs, or any convenient place; then cut a number of pieces of fine twine, about four feet long, and attach them, a quarter of an inch apart, along the bottom rope

Fig. 357.—Manner of Making Fringe for Oriental Window-shade.

(Fig. 357); A shows a loosened loop and B the tightened ones. The ends of the twine hang free. On each double strand string glass beads and slender pieces of bamboo, reeds, painted clay pipe-stems, or macaroni broken in pieces of equal length and used in their natural color, or painted with oil-paints to any desired tint. Have the reeds four inches long, and thread them on alternately with the beads (Fig. 358); or you can form a design by cutting the reeds into different lengths; at the end of each strand fasten a large bead or glass button. A very simple

Ribbon-Curtain

is of red, blue, yellow, and black ribbons all cut the same length and sewed, a quarter of an inch

Fig. 358.—Fringe of Macaroni and Beads.

apart, on a narrow strip of black cloth long enough to reach across the window. The strip may be used as a band, or attached to a slender pole by means of small brass rings. The ribbons should be silk, and thin enough to admit of the light shining through ; they hang down fringe-like, with three glass beads fastened on the end of each ribbon (Fig. 359 or Fig. 360). If you prefer to have the shade all one color make it yellow, which gives a pleasant, mellow light. Any pattern you choose can be made by taking short pieces of ribbon and joining them together with glass beads. In this way bits of ribbon could be utilized, but those used must be semi-transparent, showing the color when held up to the light. Even smooth pieces of silk with their edges neatly hemmed might do service, only be very careful to join either ribbon or silk with the beads in such a manner as to prevent its twisting ; the beads must be heavy enough to keep the fringe straight.

Fig. 359.

Fig. 360.—
Beads on the
Ends of Rib-
bons.

Nearly all homes have their bags of silk and worsted pieces, and from these can be made a handsome

Drapery of Very Small Scraps.

Cut the pieces of silk or worsted into squares about an inch each way, using any and all colors ; then take a piece of twine of the length you desire your curtain, and with a large needle string the bright bits on the twine until the whole string is completely and closely covered ; next fasten the twine well to prevent its slipping, and with a large pair of scissors trim off the rough edges of the silken strand until the surface is rounded and even ; on one end attach a small brass curtain-ring, and on the other a heavy bead or button ; make as many strands as you will need to hang across the window and fasten them to a pole in which small hooks have been screwed.

This drapery resembles chenille ; it is rich in color, will wear well, and is best adapted for full-length curtains.

As a substitute for stained glass we give directions for

Painting Window-Panes.

These are very pretty and satisfactory. If good designs are chosen the window will surpass in beauty your expectations.

The materials necessary are : some of Winsor & Newton's transparent colors, such as rose-madder, Prussian blue, raw and burnt umber, burnt sienna, ultramarine, gamboge, ivory-black, viridian green, and orient yellow. Any transparent color can be used. For purple, mix rose-madder with Prussian blue.

Prepare the paints to be used by mixing each color separately with a little oil and siccatif Courtray. Almost any brush will do to paint with, but one of medium size made for oil-colors is the best, and another smaller one is necessary for the outlining, which takes the place of leading in stained glass. The dabber is a ball of raw cotton tied in a piece of fine cotton-cloth, and the manner of tinting or grounding is exactly the same as in china-painting; lac-varnish will be needed as a wash after the painting has dried.

When you have an opportunity, carefully examine real stained-glass windows, and you will see that each window is one complete design. The corners and borders are usually in rich, dark colors, while the central portion is of lighter tints or clear glass.

Always make your corners and borders first, and if you desire a centre-piece, it should be placed in position next, and the space between it and the border filled in afterward. A Gothic window may be imitated by painting the corners black, thus making it arched at the top. Very often good patterns can be

Fig. 361.—Border Pattern.

found in the many art and fashion papers. One copy may serve for an entire border, if it be pasted at the four corners to one pane of glass, and, when that is outlined, removed and gummed to the next, and so on until the border is finished. Fig. 361 is intended as a border. Fig. 362 is a very simple pattern of cracked glass, which you can readily make without any copy. Place a ruler across the woodwork of the window-pane, first one way, then another, and with its aid paint your straight lines, being careful not to have any two run parallel. A conventional design is always to be preferred. Should any mistakes occur during the

Fig. 362.—Cracked Glass.

28

progress of the work, remove the paint with a cloth dampened with turpentine and try again. The painting is not difficult, and the only delays are in waiting for the colors to dry.

First decide on your design, then trace it, making the outlines heavy and black; gum the pattern by the four corners to the outside of the window-pane, which it is essential to have perfectly clean and dry; close the window, and with a small brush dipped in black paint follow the outlines of your copy, keeping the lines of equal thickness throughout; when this is finished remove the pattern. In the same manner go over all the outlines you wish to make on the window, then leave the color to harden and dry, which will probably require hours. Begin again by laying on flat washes of paint to match the prevailing colors of the copy, and use the dabber in tinting each color as it is applied, so the surface may be even and uniform. While the decoration is drying it is best to protect it from dust by pinning up a newspaper or a large piece of cloth on the window-frame. When dry, the painting can be touched up if necessary.

After the last color has entirely dried apply a wash of white lac-varnish; when this is dry give the window another coat of lac-varnish and then it will be finished. Should your copies be in black and white, use your own taste in coloring the glass.

Another method of imitating stained glass is

Painting on Lawn,

batiste, or any kind of sheer white muslin. For this you will need the same paints that are used for painting on glass; these are mixed only with turpentine and the color put on as a stain.

Cut a piece of new thin white batiste large enough to cover a window-sash, with a margin left for turning in, and make an outline on it of the exact size of the sash; then select your pattern and place the lawn over it, when the outlines should show through ; trace these carefully with gum-arabic dissolved, but made *very* stiff, and when the entire design has been traced let the gum dry ; then go over it with ivory-black unmixed ; this latter makes the leading ; be careful to keep the lines even and of the same size. When the outlines have dried fill in the spaces with the stains made of paint and turpentine ; the gum prevents the colors from spreading. When the paint has dried you may add a few touches where they are needed, and the stained-glass design will be ready to place on the window. Use stiff mucilage or tiny tacks to keep it in place, having first turned in the margin left for the purpose.

An attractive window can be made with the upper sash of imitation stained glass, while the lower one is screened by a Dutch curtain, as in the illustration.

For the benefit of those who prefer sewing to painting we now tell how to

Imitate Stained Glass

with a piece of stiff white rice-net, such as is commonly used for bonnet-frames, and some pieces of thin batiste, or lawns, of the requisite colors. Cut the rice-net the proper size and lay it over your design ; then carefully trace off the pattern ; when all the outlines are finished cut the different-colored lawns of the shape and size to correspond to the different portions of the design ; paste these on in the places they must occupy ; then sew them on with the Automatic Sewing-machine, following with coarse black thread the outlines on the wrong side of the foundation, so that the chain-stitch will appear on the right side to form the leading ; or the stitching may be made by hand, or a very narrow black braid can be used as leading. When all the batiste is sewed on, cut out the net back of the design to allow the light to shine through.

We have seen such an imitation of stained glass, and when placed up against the window it was very good; but care must

be taken to have the colored lawns thin and of the right shades; if too heavy they obstruct the light and the colors do not look bright.

For full-length window-drapery of inexpensive material there may be had at any of the leading dry-goods stores beau-

Fig. 363.—Imitation of Ground Glass.

tiful soft fabrics, in yellows and different colors, the designs of which equal those of much higher-priced goods. These draperies hang in graceful folds and come as low as ten cents a yard; some of them are also well adapted for the useful Dutch curtains.

Windows of Imitation Ground Glass

can be made of white tissue-paper, cut in simple patterns and fastened on the inside of the glass with white lac-varnish. The window must be perfectly clean and dry. If possible have the pieces of tissue-paper exactly the same size as

Fig. 364.—Folded Paper with Diamond Pattern for Imitation of Ground Glass.

the window-panes, fold and refold the paper lengthwise until it

is an inch or so in width; then cut from stiff cardboard your pattern. If it

Fig. 365.—Paper Marked with Design for Imitation of Ground Glass.

be a diamond, as in Fig. 363, have it exact, and cut it in halves; use one-half as a pattern, place this on the edge of the paper, as in Fig. 364, and with a lead pencil draw a line around it; remove the pattern and place it lower down about a quarter of an inch from the first tracing, and again mark around the edge. Continue in the same way until you have the pattern marked on the entire length of the tissue-paper. Make the same pattern on the other edge of the paper (Fig 365). Cut out the pattern, then unfold the paper and smooth it free of wrinkles; give the window-pane a thin coating of white lac-varnish, and apply the paper, being very careful to have it *perfectly* smooth when on the glass. Sometimes it is necessary to join two or more pieces of paper, but if you are careful to make the edges come *exactly* together, the joins will not be noticeable.

Lac-varnish dries very quickly, and it takes only a short time to decorate a window in this manner.

When all the panes of glass are covered with tissue-paper, finish by varnishing each one with the white lac-varnish; at a little distance it is difficult to distinguish a window so covered from one really formed of ground glass.

For bath-rooms, or where the window is rather out of the way and the outlook not agreeable, the imitation of ground glass is suitable and useful.

CHAPTER XXXIX.

FURNITURE OLD AND NEW.

 NLY the other day we were appealed to by a friend for suggestions on how to furnish a room prettily, and at the same time inexpensively, and we know that there are many girls like this friend who, loving to surround themselves with beauty and comfort, have not the means of doing so in the ordinary way ; but must depend largely upon their own skill and ingenuity for the gratification of this taste. After all, there is more real pleasure in planning and contriving the furnishing of one's room, even with only a small sum for outlays, than there is in ordering a set from the furnishers which is exactly like a hundred others. In the former case we make our room expressive of our individuality ; in the latter we walk in the beaten track of those who have little or no individuality to express.

So much for the sentiment of the idea. Now let us turn to the practical side, and find the best way of carrying it out, and putting our theories into practice.

In mentioning old furniture in the heading of this chapter, we do not allude to the antiques in such high favor just now ; they are unique and handsome enough in themselves, requiring no contriving to beautify them ; but there are few families who do not possess furniture that is out of date, old-fashioned without being antique ; furniture that time and hard usage has reduced to a state of shabbiness anything but beautiful, yet not worth sending to the cabinet-makers to be furbished up. It is the renovation of such furniture that will help much toward making a room pretty and attractive.

We need not attempt to restore the furniture to its original state, that would be impracticable. But we can work wonders in transforming it ; in turning a homely article into one that will be an adornment instead of a blemish.

Bookcase.

Take, for instance, an old bureau belonging to a cottage set. The mirror, perhaps, is broken, or if it is not it can be used to better advantage elsewhere. Removing that, there is left merely a chest of drawers, which we will proceed to convert into a bookcase by the addition of shelves placed on top. If you have a brother who is handy with his tools the matter is simple enough ; without him a carpenter may have to be employed to make the shelves, or, by taking the plan and measurements

Fig. 366.—Diagram of Book-shelves.

to a carpenter-shop the materials can be obtained ready for use, and all you will have to do will be to put them together. Although there is a saying that "a girl can never drive a nail straight," we have reason to believe the contrary, and feel sure that a little practice will enable most girls to do many bits of light carpentry work as well as the boys. Three feet is the height of a bureau belonging to an ordinary set of cottage furniture, so we will take that as our standard for measurement, and make our shelves according to it.

Fig. 366 is the diagram for the frame of the shelves. The side pieces are made of boards three feet four inches long and nine inches wide ; the top of each of these boards is sawed into a point as shown in diagram. Four cleats made of sticks eight inches long and one inch thick are nailed to the side of each board, the distance between being nine inches.

The frame at the back is composed of two boards five and one half feet long and seven inches wide, and two, three feet three inches long (the width of the bureau) and seven inches wide. One of these short boards is nailed across the top ends of the long boards, and the other twenty-four inches below. The side pieces are nailed to the back as shown in diagram, the nails being driven through the back board into the edge of the side piece.

When the frame is made it is placed on the bureau, the sides resting on the top and the long back boards reaching down behind where they are nailed or screwed to the bureau. The shelves are thirty-seven inches long and nine inches wide. They rest on the cleats and are not nailed to the frame.

Screws may in some places, answer better than nails.

When the shelves have been adjusted, the whole is painted a dark olive green.

If the knobs are removed from the drawers before the bureau is painted, and brass handles substituted afterward, it will add materially to its appearance.

The bookcase shown in our illustration is finished off with curtains, which hang by brass rings from a slender bamboo pole. The pole is slipped through brass hooks screwed into the side pieces near the top.

Curtains of canton-flannel, or any soft material, are suitable for this bookcase. The colors may be a combination of olive green with old blue, yellow, cherry, copper color, dark red, or light brown.

The Chair

in the same illustration is an ordinary rocking-chair painted
olive green, with cushions at the back and in the seat stuffed

Bureau Transformed into a Bookcase.

with excelsior, covered with bright cretonne, and tied to the
chair with ribbons.

Chairs of this kind look well painted almost any color; one of yellow, with yellow cushions and ribbons, is exceedingly pretty.

If the chair to be remodelled is bottomless, reseat it in this way: Cut some strips of strong cotton cloth about one inch wide and sew them together, lapping one piece over another, as in Fig. 367; fasten an end on to the edge of the chair with a tack, and then pass the cloth back and forth across, each time putting it under and bringing it over the edge of the chair.

When the seat is filled up with the strips going one way, cut the cloth and tack the end to the chair; then,

Fig. 367.

commencing at the side, cross these strips, passing the cloth in and out as if darning. Fig. 368 shows just how it is done. Be sure to draw the strip as tightly as you can every time it crosses the chair, for if too loose it will sag as soon as the chair is used. The edge of the chair may be covered with the cretonne, or a ruffle which is sewed around the cushion.

Fig. 368.—How to Reseat a Chair.

Fig. 369 is an old settee fitted up with cushions, and a sociable, comfortable seat it is. It offers plenty of room for two, and ensconced thereon the girls may rock and talk to their hearts' content.

These settees are not often seen in the city, but are to be found in many a farm-house and country town. The one from which our sketch is taken is painted black, but, like the chair, it would look well any color.

Fresh, dainty prettiness should be the principal feature of a young girl's room, and this can be obtained at very little expense, much less than most persons suppose.

Fig. 370 shows what can be done with the commonest

Fig. 369.—Oome and Sit Here.

kind of furniture. This can be bought at the manufacturer's unpainted, and may be left its natural color and simply varnished, or, following the present fashion, it can be painted white, and decorated with slender bands or circles of gold.

As in the illustration,

The Bedstead

should have drapery suspended over it. This gives a soft, pretty effect, and takes away its stiffness. Dotted swiss or thin cottage drapery answers the purpose nicely.

Ten yards of material cut in two breadths of five yards each are required for these curtains. The breadths must be sewed together lengthwise and then passed through a small wooden hoop which has been gilded or painted white.

When the hoop is directly in the middle of the breadths, the material must be brought together close to the hoop and two of the edges sewed or basted together. This seam is to go at the back and keep the curtain from parting and hanging in two strips.

A ruffle of the same material, or lace, sewed on the edge and across the ends of the drapery gives it a soft, lacy effect. The ribbons which loop the curtains at either side should be of the prevailing colors of the room. If the furniture is white and gold, they should be yellow.

The hoop can hang from a brass chain fastened to a hook in the ceiling.

The bureau belonging to this style of furniture is too clumsy for our use, although without the mirror it will be convenient as a chest of drawers. Brass handles in place of knobs will improve it.

A Dressing-table

to take its place, like the one shown in Fig. 370, can be made of a small kitchen-table. The mirror suspended over it should have a broad flat frame of white pine, varnished or painted to match the furniture. Almost any cabinet-maker can frame a mirror in this way. Bracket candlesticks made of brass, which are very inexpensive, should be fastened to the frame on either side of the glass with brass nails or brass-headed tacks.

Fig. 370.—What can be done with Common Unpainted Furniture.

With a brass handle on the drawer, a pretty scarf of linen crash, ornamented with drawn work or outline, thrown over the table and hanging down at each end, and the addition of pin-cushion and toilet articles, this toilet-table looks very attractive and readily challenges admiration.

Washstand.

A piece of white matting bound at top and bottom, with yellow cotton cloth for a splasher, as in Fig. 371, and a pretty scarf and toilet-set, presents this most ordinary washstand in a new light.

Three common kitchen-chairs and one rocker, when painted white or varnished, as the case may be, and cushioned in pretty light-colored cretonne, completes this novel, pretty, and remarkably inexpensive set of furniture.

Fig. 371.—The Ordinary Unpainted Washstand in a New Light.

The curtains next to the windows should be of the same material as that used for the bed-drapery, with the inner one of cretonne like the chair-cushions.

White matting is suitable for the floor in summer, and during the cold weather it can be mostly covered with a pretty ingrain rug or art square, as it is called.

Instead of using gilt, the rings and bands on the furniture may be blue or red, in which case the trimmings of the room should correspond.

Fig. 372.—Hall Seat Made of a Common Wooden Bench.

A Hall Seat.

As another illustration of what can be done with the most ordinary piece of furniture, we have chosen a common wooden bench, and by painting it black and giving it a dark-red cushion with tassels at each corner, have transformed it into quite an elegant hall-seat. Fig. 372 gives the effect.

Fig. 373 – Window Seat and Book-shelves Combined, Made of Boxes.

Fig. 373 shows a

Window Seat and Book-shelves Combined,

made of boxes. Eight soap-boxes of the same size are required
for the shelves, and a packing-box about two feet high, two

feet in width, and as long as the window is wide, for the seat.

Remove the tops and two sides of the soap-boxes, and bore holes with a red-hot poker in one corner of the bottoms of six of the boxes, and in two of the tops which have been removed, making the holes one inch from either edge (Fig. 374). In the other two boxes bore in the same place, but not entirely through, making the holes about half an inch deep.

Place these last two on the floor and pile the others on top of them, three on each, nailing the bottom of each box to the top edge of the one beneath it. On the two upper boxes nail the tops in which the holes have been made.

Have ready two slender bamboo rods about four feet long. Insert a rod in the hole in the top of an upper box and let it pass down, slipping it through the holes in the

Fig. 374.—Hole in Corner of Box for Book-shelves.

bottoms of the other boxes and fitting it in the cavity in the lower box.

In like manner put the other rod in place through the other pile of boxes.

If the packing-box has a cover, it should be fastened on with hinges, so that it may be used for a shoe-box as well as a seat; if it has not, turn it upside down, place the soap-boxes at each end and nail them to it.

Paint the shelves black or the color of the wood-work in the room, and upholster the seat and the boxes on either side of it with cushions made of strong muslin stuffed with excelsior and covered with cretonne.

Fasten the edges of the side cushions to the boxes with gimp braid and tacks. Make a deep plaiting of the cretonne

29

and tack it across the front of the large box. When there is a lid a narrow plaiting must be tacked across its front edge, which will, when the box is closed, lap over the top of the deeper plaiting.

That this combination of window-seat and shelves is both comfortable and convenient, one may easily imagine, and that it adds not a little to the furnishing of a room, we leave to our illustration to show.

CHAPTER XL.

SOMETHING ABOUT MANTEL-PIECES AND FIRE-PLACES.

 HE spirit of hospitality and comfort presides over the ruddy blaze of an open fire ; yet, as we gather cosily around and bask in the delightful warmth and radiance, its cheerful influence is too often retarded by its very unattractive surroundings. This lovely household spirit should have a more fitting habitation than the one frequently accorded it. The fire-place should at least be pleasant to look upon, and not depend wholly upon the bright fire to make it inviting.

The ordinary marble and marbleized slate or iron mantel-pieces are the reverse of beautiful, but they may be very much improved at the expense of a small outlay of money, time, and trouble.

The examples we give here of the treatment of commonplace mantel-pieces are simple, and can easily be managed by the girls themselves, with but trifling aid from a carpenter.

In a room occupied at one time by a young friend of the writer, there was an old-fashioned white-pine mantel-piece. It was stiff and plain, with no attempt at ornamentation, and the border of white marble, about five inches wide around the fire-place, was apparently inserted to protect the wood from

Fig. 375.—Shelves over Mantel-Piece.

the heat of the fire, and not for beauty. A hint from the writer was sufficient to set this girl's brain and fingers to work. Soon the white-marble border was transformed into a row of blue and white tiles, which were not only pretty and appropriate, but were also the means of dispelling the impressions of coldness and hardness the marble gave.

The manner of effecting this transformation was simple enough. First the marble was divided into squares, the lines being painted black ; then conventional patterns were sketched with a pencil on the squares and painted in blue, oil-paints being used for the purpose.

How the mantel-piece was otherwise reformed, the writer never saw, but it might have been greatly improved and altered by the addition of shelves above, or a suitable lambrequin upon the mantel shelf. However that may or might have been, the tiles were a successful bit of work, and the painting of them within the capabilities of almost anyone. Then why should we long in vain for a tiled mantel-piece, when we have it in our power to gratify the wish ?

On a plain white-marble mantel a border around the fire-place may be marked out, and a set of tiles painted, which will look just as pretty as any that can be bought.

If the rest of the marble is painted black or brown, the tiles will look as though they were set in, and the contrast will make them more effective.

Fig. 375 illustrates our suggestion of putting shelves over the mantel-piece. The braces can be bought at any hardware-store, and the shelves may be of black-walnut or pine boards, stained or painted to match the mantel-piece.

Fig. 376 shows the effect of a mantel-shelf covered with enamel-cloth made in imitation of leather. The color of the material used for the one from which our sketch is taken is dark red, and has a dull, soft finish like Russian leather. It is ornamented with small brass curtain-rings sewed on in points or pyramids; a strip of enamel-cloth is also put behind the shelf, and at the top edge a piece of narrow gilt moulding is tacked.

Fig. 376.—Mantel-Shelf covered with Enamel-Cloth ornamented with Brass Curtain-Rings.

A mantel-board of pine, two inches longer and two inches wider than the shelf, is always necessary when there is to be a lambrequin, for upon this the lambrequin is tacked.

First, the board must be neatly covered with the material, enamel-cloth or whatever is used, the edges of the cloth being brought over and tacked under the edge of the shelf; then the strip composing the lambrequin must be turned in at the top edge and tacked across the front and two ends of the board with brass-headed tacks. It looks better if the corners of the board are rounded as shown in illustration.

The piece at the back of the shelf should be about eighteen inches deep and must be tacked at top and bottom• with small tacks, the edge at each end being turned in and tacked to the wall with brass-headed tacks.

Fig. 377.—Enamel-Cloth ornamented with Brass Rings.

Fig. 377 is the diagram of enamel-cloth ornamented with brass rings, and shows a section of the pattern. The bottom row of rings should be sewed on first, and the edge of the cloth turned up as the rings are fastened on. The stitches which hold the rings catch the hem also. This first row of rings should extend half way below the edge of the cloth, as shown in Fig. 377. Strong yellow embroidery-silk or saddlers' silk is the best to sew them on with.

The gilt moulding can be bought by the foot and small headless nails are furnished to tack it with.

Another mantel is treated in very much the same manner as Fig. 376, the difference being that, instead of enamel-cloth, the covering for the shelf and the piece at the back are dark-red canton-flannel, and around the edge of the shelf is tacked a worsted fringe, about six inches deep, matching the canton-flannel in color. This has a warm, comfortable look and is quite

Fig. 378.—Shelves around Projecting Chimney.

appropriate for a bedroom, while the other should be used only in a library or dining-room.

The writer was once invited into a young girl's room which was very attractive in its daintiness. It was not pretty in shape, and an uncompromising chimney, in which there was no fireplace, projected into the room ; but taste had overcome these difficulties, and the effect produced was decidedly pleasing.

Pretty wall-paper and the arrangement of the furniture helped very much, but the greatest triumph was in subduing the awkwardness of that chimney by surrounding it with a set of shelves for holding pretty bits of bric-à-brac.

In case another girl may have the same difficulty to surmount in decorating her room, we give an outline drawing of the shelves (Fig. 378) that she may see and profit thereby.

CHAPTER XLI.

HOME-MADE CANDY.

E have noticed that in none of the books we have seen, which were written especially for the amusement and entertainment of girls, has there been any directions or recipes for making candy. Knowing by experience that most girls consider candy-making one of their prime winter enjoyments, we consider the omission to be quite an important one, and we will in this chapter endeavor to supply the much-wished-for information.

Though cooking in general may not be regarded with much favor by the average school-girl, she is always anxious to learn how to make candy, and hails a new recipe as a boon.

The following recipes for peanut-candy, butter-scotch, and molasses-candy were obtained from a friend who makes the best home-made candy it has ever been our good-fortune to taste, and as she recommends them, we may rely upon their being excellent. We give them, with her comments, just as she wrote them.

Delicious Peanut-Candy.

Shell your peanuts and chop them fine ; measure them in a cup, and take just the same quantity of granulated sugar as you have peanuts. Put the sugar in a skillet, or spider, on the fire, and keep moving the skillet around until the sugar is dissolved ; then put in the peanuts and pour into buttered tins.

This is *delicious*, and *so* quickly made.

Butter-Scotch.

2 cups of brown sugar.
½ cup of butter.
4 tablespoonfuls of molasses.
2 tablespoonfuls of water.
2 tablespoonfuls of vinegar.
Boil until it hardens when dropped into cold water, then pour into buttered tins.

Molasses-Candy.

2 cups of brown sugar.
¼ cup of New Orleans molasses.
⅜ cup of vinegar and water mixed.
A piece of butter half the size of an egg.
When the candy hardens in cold water, pour into shallow buttered tins, and as soon as it is cool enough to handle, pull it until it is of a straw-color. *Splendid !*

Here are two recipes which another friend has kindly sent us :

Chocolate-Creams.

To the white of 1 egg add an equal quantity of cold water. Stir in 1 pound of confectioner's sugar. Flavor with vanilla. Stir until fine and smooth ; then mould into balls and drop into melted chocolate.

To melt the chocolate, scrape and put it in a tin-cup or small sauce-pan over a kettle where it will steam. Let the chocolate be melting while the cream is being prepared.

Walnut-Creams.

Make the cream as for chocolate-drops and mould into larger balls. Place the half of an English walnut on either side and press them into the cream.

The cream prepared in this way, we have found, can be used for various kinds of candy.

Small pieces of fruit of any kind and nuts can be enclosed in the cream, making a great variety. Chocolate may be mixed with it ; and if strong, clear coffee is used in place of the water, the candy will have the coffee flavor and color which some people like.

Walnut and Fruit Glacé.

Put 1 cup of sugar and ½ cup of water in a sauce-pan and stir until the sugar is all dissolved ; then place it over the fire and let it boil until it hardens and is quite crisp when dropped in cold water. Do not stir it after it is put on the fire.

When cooked sufficiently, dip out a spoonful at a time and drop in buttered tins, leaving a space of an inch or so between each spoonful. Place on each piece of candy the half of a walnut, or the fruit which has previously been prepared, and pour over them enough candy to cover them, always keeping each piece separate.

Any kind of fruit can be made into glacé. When using oranges, quarter them and remove the seeds. Strawberries, in their season, and peaches also make delicious glacé.

The remainder of our recipes have been taken from family recipe-books, and although we have not tested them ourselves, we think it may be safely said that they are good ones.

Marsh-mallow Paste.

Dissolve 1 pound of clean white gum-arabic in one quart of water ; strain, add 1 pound of refined sugar, and place over the fire. Stir continually until the syrup is dissolved and the mixture has become of the consistency of honey. Next add gradually the beaten whites of 8 eggs ; stir the mixture all the time until it loses its thickness and does not adhere to the finger. Flavor with vanilla or rose. Pour into a tin slightly dusted with powdered starch, and when cool divide into squares with a sharp knife.

Toasted Marsh-mallows.

Tie a string on the end of a cane or stick, fasten a bent pin on the end of the string, and stick the pin into a marsh-mallow-drop. Hold the marsh-mallow suspended over an open fire and let it gradually toast. When it begins to melt and run down it is done.

For a small party toasting marsh-mallows will be found quite a merry pastime, and a great many persons consider the candy much better for being thus cooked the second time.

Molasses Peanut-Candy.

2 cups of molasses.
1 cup of brown sugar.
1 tablespoonful of butter.
1 tablespoonful of vinegar.

While the candy is boiling remove the shells and brown skins from the peanuts, lay the nuts in buttered pans, and when the candy is done pour it over them. While it is still warm cut in blocks.

Chocolate-Caramels.

2 cups of sugar.
1 cup of molasses.
1 cup of milk.
1 tablespoonful of butter.
1 tablespoonful of flour.
½ pound of Baker's chocolate.

Grease your pot, put in sugar, molasses, and milk; boil fif-

teen minutes, and add butter and flour stirred to a cream.   Let
it boil five minutes, then add the chocolate, grated, and boil until quite thick.   Grease shallow pans and pour in the candy
half an inch thick, marking it in squares before it becomes
hard.

Pop-Corn Balls.

6 quarts of popped corn.

1 pint of molasses.

Boil the molasses about fifteen minutes ; then put the corn
into a large pan, pour the molasses over it, and stir briskly until thoroughly mixed.   Then, with clean hands, make into balls
of the desired size.

Saint Valentine.

CHAPTER XLII.

Saint Valentine's Day.

 ID it never occur to any of you to wonder who Saint Valentine was, and why we should commemorate his day by sending cards or letters containing all sorts of nonsense, like true-lovers' knots, hearts pierced with arrows, etc. ?

It is easy enough to tell you about the saint, but what he had to do with the popular observances of the day dedicated to him is a matter for conjecture.

Saint Valentine, they say, was a grave and earnest bishop, who was put to death in Rome on the fourteenth day of February, about the year 270 A.D., for his too zealous efforts in converting the heathen. When he was canonized, the day of the month on which he died was dedicated to him.

The customs of Saint Valentine's Day are, no doubt, derived from those practised at some of the Pagan festivals, for they are of very ancient origin. In olden times, in England, it was kept as a great gala day, and all the houses were decked with evergreen in honor of it. Ben Jonson says:

> " Get some fresh hay, then, to lay under foot,
> Some holly and ivy to make fine the posts ;
> Is't not Saint Valentine's Day ? "

The principal feature of the ceremonies was always the choice of a valentine for the ensuing year. The cavalier was expected to wait upon his lady, execute all of her commands, and act as her escort at all social gatherings.

The choice of a valentine was generally left to chance, one of the methods being that the first unmarried member of the opposite sex a person saw on Saint Valentine's morning should be his or her valentine.

Of course you have all had some experience in sending and receiving valentines, and perhaps consider that the only way of celebrating the day ; but don't you think it would be a good idea to invite some friends to your house and have a

Valentine-Party ?

We will give several suggestions upon what to do at a valentine-party, that you may have some idea how the affair should be conducted.

In the first place, let each guest, upon his or her arrival, deposit a valentine in a large bag placed in the hall for that purpose. The valentines must be addressed to no particular person, but the girls should write on theirs, " To my cavalier," and the boys address the ones they send, "To my lady." On one corner of each valentine (not the envelope) the sender's name must be written.

When all the guests have assembled, someone disguised as Saint Valentine, in a skull-cap, long white beard, made of cotton or wool, and long cloak, should enter the parlor, carrying on his back the sack of valentines. He must stand in the centre of the room and auction off each valentine as he takes it from his pack.

All sorts of bids can be made, such as the promise of a dance, a necktie, her share of ice-cream at supper, by a girl. A com-

30

pliment, the first favor asked of him, a paper of bonbons, by a boy. To make fun the bids should be as ridiculous as possible.

Saint Valentine is to be at liberty to accept whatever bid he chooses. The payment of the debt must be rigidly exacted by the sender of a valentine, whose identity is revealed when the valentine is opened.

Fig. 379.—Cupid's Bow and Arrow.

If unable to comply immediately with the demand, the debtor must give the creditor a card or slip of paper on which is written " I O U a favor," or whatever it may be that is owed. This I O U entitles the creditor to claim payment of the debt at any time during the year.

Another feature of the party should be Cupid's bow and arrow, which must be suspended from the chandelier or placed in some prominent position. The device is to be used for delivering such valentines as may be addressed to particular persons. The valentine must be stuck onto the point of the arrow, and no one may remove it save the person to whom it is addressed. At any time during the evening the arrow may be found to bear a missive, and we would advise the hostess to provide a valentine, to be delivered in this way, for each of her guests, that none may feel neglected. The rest of the party can, to be sure, send as many valentines as they like.

Make Cupid's bow and arrow of heavy pasteboard, like Fig. 379. Let the bow measure about

Fig. 380.—Notch in End of Feather. sixteen inches from tip to tip. Make the arrow twelve inches long, with a point or head three inches, and the feathers two inches, in length on the outside edge. Cut a notch in the feathered end, as shown in Fig. 380.

Strengthen the arrow by gluing a thin stick of wood along it to within one inch of the point. Gild both the bow and arrow, tie a silk cord to the tips of the bow, leaving it slack, and force the head of a worsted-needle into the point of the arrow (Fig. 381). Adjust the arrow by fitting the cord in the notch and pulling it back until the cord is taut; then fasten it to the bow by taking a few stitches with yellow silk through the bow and over the arrow. Fig. 382 shows how it should appear when in place.

To determine how the guests shall be paired off for supper, place the names of all the girls, written on slips of paper, in a bag; then let each boy in turn take out a slip, and the girl whose name it bears he shall escort to the supper-room and serve like a true cavalier.

Fig. 381.—Manner of fastening Needle in Arrow-head.

At a valentine-party the valentines should, if possible, all be original, or at least contain appropriate quotations. The more absurd the rhyme, the more fun it will create, and when one is unable to make a rhyme a bit of prose can be made to serve. As funny as you please let the valentines be, but remember to omit anything that is in the least rude, or calculated to hurt another's feelings.

With Saint Valentine's Day ends our vacation-calendar and with it we also bring this book to a close, for a whole year of

Fig. 382.—Cupid's Bow with Arrow in Position.

holidays, sports, and entertainments are now contained within its covers. If we may hope that our work has not been without profit, as well as entertainment, if we have been successful in opening any new avenues of enterprise and enjoyment for you, we are satisfied.   If we have done more, and with any of our suggestions have prompted the thought of adding to the comfort and happiness of others, we have achieved a success, and the mission of the AMERICAN GIRL'S HANDY BOOK is accomplished.

INDEX.

A FOREST IN THE CLOUDS

A FOREST IN THE CLOUDS

My Year Among the Mountain Gorillas
in the Remote Enclave of Dian Fossey

JOHN FOWLER

PEGASUS BOOKS
NEW YORK LONDON

A Forest in the Clouds

Pegasus Books Ltd.
148 W 37th Street, 13th Floor
New York, NY 10018

Copyright © 2018 by John Fowler

First Pegasus Books cloth edition February 2018

Interior design by Maria Fernandez

All photographs copyright © John Fowler unless otherwise noted

Library of Congress Cataloging-in-Publication Data is available.

ISBN: 978-1-68177-633-0

10 9 8 7 6 5 4 3 2 1

Printed in the United States of America
Distributed by W. W. Norton & Company

For Janet, Isabel and Ben

And for Mom and Dad

When I was about seven years old I knew I had to go to Africa,
and, I also knew that I would write a book someday.
—Dian Fossey

We live as we dream—alone.
While the dream disappears, the life continues painfully.
—Joseph Conrad, *Heart of Darkness*

CONTENTS

PREFACE

Dian Fossey was found murdered at Karisoke Research Center, in Rwanda, Africa, on December 27, 1985. At forty-eight years old, the once statuesque and commanding mountain gorilla behaviorist had become battle-weary, all but defeated in her long reign while struggling to hold on to her research camp, her mountain village, and the home she had created for herself through the years.

Along with chimpanzee research pioneer, Jane Goodall, in Tanzania's Gombe Reserve, and Biruté Galdikas, who launched an orangutan research project in Borneo, Fossey was one of the legendary trio of primatologists sent into the wilds under the mentorship of anthropologist Louis Leakey. At the time, being women made their bold pioneering efforts alone in the wilds even more newsworthy. But Dian Fossey had embraced the isolation a little too much, perhaps, and the autocracy that came with life in the remote enclave of her own making had not shaped her in a positive way, nor refined her best qualities and her social skills. She still had to contend with humans, if only because she needed them.

Ultimately, what had originally been seen as her courage and determination would be viewed by many as too much counterproductive behavior and an exhaustion of resourcefulness—in essence, a sort-of overstaying of her welcome. Relationships with former allies in research and conservation had soured, but the region's precious mountain gorillas were far too important, and endangered, for others to watch idly from a distance. Relocating Dian out of the Virungas and into a most worthy academic position at Cornell University in Ithaca, New York, had been a tenuous, and delicately executed maneuver. But for none that followed in taking her position at Karisoke Research Center did the cold and lonely camp become their home. They came and went. Meanwhile, the call of the wild—or the need to withdraw— never abated for Dian, and ultimately she made her way back.

On that morning, Dian's longtime house-servant, Kanyaragana, made his usual trek up the narrow path through the research camp as dawn began to light the sky. Hours would pass before the sun could burn even a peek through the pervasive mists. As on any other morning in the mountain forest at ten thousand feet, it was damp and chilly, and as usual, Kanyaragana was there to make Dian's coffee and reignite the fire in her woodstove that always burned out during the night.

Going to unlock Dian's cabin door, Kanyaragana found it already unsecured, and ajar, entirely out of character for the Research Center director who always made sure, with good reason, her doors were secure at night and who often slept late. Once inside, Kanyaragana walked across fragments of broken glass from camp lanterns littering the floor, past living room furniture that had been upended and knocked about.

Venturing toward Dian's bedroom, the faithful servant saw that this room, too, had been ransacked, with drawers and cupboards pulled open, books scattered across the floor. Dian's lifeless form lay face up on the dingy grass matting, a large gash gaping across her wan face. She had been hacked to death, disfigured by the sharp blade of a *panga*, Africa's two-foot long machete. It was kept saber-sharp for harvesting crops like sugar cane and bananas, or in these parts, by Rwandan camp staff, gorilla researchers, and animal poachers for cutting through the heavy green growth of the forests. Pangas also made handy weapons, and this savagery stood as a punctuation mark of hate and rage at the end of the famous primatologist's tumultuous life.

I hadn't seen Dian in over five years at the time of her death, which caused quite a stir internationally. My coworkers at the Audubon Zoo in New Orleans knew that I had spent a year as her research assistant, but it was not a subject I discussed much. There were no short answers, after all, to their questions: *What was it like? What was Dian like?* I had found it difficult to relate to others expecting a happy, inspirational story. There were so many who admired the noble *National Geographic* image of Fossey as intrepid scientist nestled among a peaceful family of mountain gorillas, *Gorilla beringei beringei*, against the lush green backdrop of equatorial Africa. To *not* know Dian, was to love her. Up close, however, her flaws cast a long terrible shadow, over even her most impressive accomplishments.

Details of the murder scene were released: A hole had been cut in the sheet metal exterior wall of her bedroom. The entry was just like one that had been cut soon after my departure from there five years earlier—to steal expensive sound recording equipment . . . by someone who knew it was there. I imagined the sound this must have made, the ripping and bending of sheet metal. It was preposterous that anyone could've done this with a pistol-packing Dian just inside, only a few feet away. *Impossible*, drunk or sober. And she was at her meanest when she was drunk. It had to have been done after the murder, a diversionary tactic to look like a break-in. And that could only mean that the killer was allowed inside. It was chilling to think beyond this.

The ensuing news reports of Dian's murder, combined with persistent questions of friends and acquaintances made me speculate. *Who did do the actual killing?* I soon learned that all staff that was present in camp at the time of the murder were arrested and thrown in jail. Over ensuing weeks, news trickled out that they were all released . . . all except Rwelekana. *Why was he detained?* I thought back to working side by side with this seasoned gorilla tracker . . . our conversations together, with the other staffers by the camp's fire. *Did Rwelekana differ from the others? Was he a little more independent than they? More aloof? Detached?* Dian had once referred to this valued gorilla tracker as an "ex-poacher." He denied it with a smile, but . . . *Was there something I didn't know?* I considered him one of the most intelligent of camp staff—clever too perhaps. But still he had been devoted to Dian for years. . . . *Why him? Why now?*

The only non-African in camp with Dian when she was murdered was an American named Wayne McGuire. His photo in a news story showed an odd and scruffy character behind the thick lenses of his horn-rimmed glasses. His overgrown beard and unkempt hair looked the picture of a man gone "bush"—like Dian, too long in the forest. I found myself thinking, saying even, "if anyone had even the smallest tendency to murder, Dian could sure bring it out of them." I didn't know McGuire, had never even met him, but it was natural to speculate any weird scenario, under the circumstances, upon seeing his solemn odd photo. He also looked exhausted.

Then, there was news that a poacher had killed Dian. Her own patrolmen had, in fact, captured and detained one not long before. She had taken away the man's amulet—the precious little sack of mostly dried herbs that these forest-dwellers hold so dear. It was a supreme insult, and Dian had long antagonized the poachers around her realm, waging war with them really.

Speculation didn't end there. I soon found myself whisked back to Rwanda by a TV film crew, and at one safari lodge, the wife of a Belgian park ranger told me, "Oh, everyone knows it was someone in the government." Rumor had formulated inside Rwanda's national park system that Dian had been boasting of having inside information about animal trafficking in the country. News had it that she was implicating government people, from local all the way up to Rwanda's president. Apparently, she had taken great delight in making it known that she would soon be blowing the whistle.

Earning a dollar a day from their boss for work shifts on the mountain, Karisoke staffers were paid less than two hundred dollars a year. A murder contract from someone who could pay any amount wouldn't cost much in Rwanda's economy, and if the murder was precipitated by corrupt politicians, they would certainly have arm-twisting power.

In retrospect, it seems fitting that things should have come to this end, Dian dying in battle. Knowing what I knew of her, it seemed preordained. She would have wanted it this way.

A young man of average achievements and yet-undefined goals, I was by all rights an unlikely candidate for one of only a handful of research positions at Karisoke. But for Dian, I was near perfect—what surer way for her to remain unchallenged in her position on the mountain. Unbeknownst to me, by that time she'd had enough of matching wits with the bright young postgraduates who came with clear agendas of their own. Such challenging interactions had taken a toll on her. Whereas I—enthusiastic and naïve—was ripe for the plucking.

A Forest in the Clouds is the story of my year living and working at Karisoke Research Center, Dian Fossey's mountain gorilla research camp. It is my careful, if belated, response to that inevitable question: *What was Dian Fossey like? Who was this woman who could leave behind so many murder suspects?* It is a question I've spent many years avoiding, ever since I left that place. For me, it is Dian's ghost.

A View from a Tree

We have arrived. The odor fills my nostrils, my mouth—heady, herbal, and animal, just a few chromosomes away from human body odor. I can taste it, pungent and salty, mingling with the smell of thistle and nettle, crushed and bruised under their bulk.

My heart pounds in my ears from the climb up Mount Visoke's steep muddy trail, just the end of the morning's hike from camp in Zaire, on the other side of the mountain, back into Rwanda. I have forty pounds of baby gorilla on my back. Three months ago this would have killed me. But I have lasted. Now my heart just pounds away in my ears as sweat steams inside my rain jacket, dampening the layers of clothes underneath. There is no comfort zone here, just overheat and sweat while moving, and cold wetness when we stop.

Nameye, our gorilla tracker, pops up from a stand of tall thistles, his skin lava-black against the bright green surroundings. His eyes, excited, gleam wide and white, in stark contrast to his careful silence. The stage has been set, and tension hangs in the air. Behind him, shreds of clouds drift down the volcano's steep sides, washing green to gray, swallowing us in a pervasive damp chill.

We balance on a thick mat of undergrowth slanting 45° uphill and down, that tiresome angle on which we must maneuver. Nameye gestures with the panga he clutches, it's long rusty blade pointed in the direction of gorilla Group 5, just downhill and to the left of where we stand. The others, too, are waiting, in position, for us to take our posts.

My place is high in a great hagenia tree. Maneuvering the baby to my front, I climb up the thick trunk, anchoring the arches of my boots onto a couple of branches, before squaring my back against the bark as I grab for another limb above me. My little gorilla obliges, adjusting her hairy grasp of hands and feet to my clothing. I am cold, but the baby is warm under my left arm, fuzzy black forearms clinging to my torso with leathery fingers. Her eyes, shining brown gems, stare into mine for reassurance. Then she belches into my face, and the weedy smell of digesting vines fills my nostrils.

The rain begins, light and misting, a cruel teaser of more serious rain to come, and with it drifts more cold. I maneuver the hood of my raincoat onto my head with my free hand, and pull the baby in closer to my side. My heart is still thumping away, though by now it has dropped back into place in my chest.

On the ground to the left, in a thicket just uphill, fellow student Peter is at the ready with a waterproof notepad to document what unfolds. Across-slope, to the right, the duo comprising the Japanese film crew, position themselves on a tangle of thick wet undergrowth, their vivid blue matching raingear glowing like neon against the shiny green landscape. Laden down with equipment, black hair sweat-plastered to their foreheads, they have lost their dapper neatness; clearly the climb has taken a toll on them as well.

Kaji sits cross-legged in front, nested in a tangle of undergrowth, wielding his bulky camera to his right eye while Taka stands upslope behind him, teetering, using both arms to steady the long tubular microphone out over his partner's head. Kaji trains the massive lens across the slope below him . . . toward our tree . . . up the base of the trunk . . . and *there*, he pauses.

The lens, a giant eyeball to the world, spins; the aperture tightens, twisting inward, focusing now on the woman directly below me. It is our leader, the famous Dian Fossey, who clings to the base of the hagenia tree, halfway between me and the ground. She, too, is focused, fixated on the other gorillas. From our vantage point, we can see the black hairy heads and shoulders of the gorillas of Group 5, shifting in the thickets across the mountainside on our left. Some forty feet away, barely visible through the green, they have not so much as glanced our way. But they know perfectly well that we're here.

The great apes continue feeding, despite the drizzle, pulling down stalks of thistles and nettles with crisp snaps of stems, their massive jaws producing muffled crunching, punctuated by an occasional low-rumbling belch vocalization, *ummwaah* . . . These are the sounds of contented gorillas minding their own business.

But we have made their business ours.

From underneath the hood of her drab green rain jacket, Dian's own dark hair pokes like disheveled ape fur, and I can't see her face until she turns to look up at the baby in my arms. *Her* baby. My leader's brow furrows above her puffy eyes, lips pursed in a look of worried concern. Dian knows the camera is trained on her. She is different today, poised and energized, and I am baffled by the transformation. Only days before she could hardly walk with me a hundred yards without doubling over in pain and retching, and yet today, somehow, she has climbed a mountain, and is perched halfway up a tree with me.

She knows important film footage is being made, that every gesture, every expression, is being recorded for the world outside of hers, the people she reaches only through film and the printed page. Only the camera, it seems, trained on her, brings real life to her, and meaning.

Sensing movement from the corner of my right eye, I glance over toward Group 5. Still forty feet away, one gorilla's upper torso is now in plain view. It's Beethoven, the family's four-hundred pound patriarch. He is seated, facing downhill—high, broad silver back and shoulders supporting an equally impressive head mounted on a thick neck, his cranium soaring to a high sagittal crest: his crown. Along with his silver back, this peaked cranium is the adult male gorilla's emblem of maturity, stature and might. Beethoven's powerful jaws crush the last morsel of nettle in his mouth, unfazed by stinging spines, the muscles in his head flexing underneath the gray hair at his temples. Defender of his group, now in repose, he sizes up where to lead his family next.

Suddenly, I am struck with the thought of how out of place I am. How far from home . . . in a tree . . . a baby gorilla in my arms! In a moment, Beethoven will see me, and *then* what? I find myself thinking, for the first time . . . I don't belong here.

Sure enough, the massive old gorilla shifts his head toward me now, suddenly taking in something that shouldn't be. He knows me, of course, by now, but not this peculiar scene—and worse yet, a baby gorilla in my arms! *Whose baby gorilla?* Instantly, his repose turns to alarm. I see it flicker across the eyes of this massive hominid as he fixes his glassy dark gaze on me, with my odd cargo. Baring his black teeth now, Beethoven releases a scream to end all screams—a primal sound, at once human and animal, screeching and voluminous, it rips across the mountain at me. This horrific noise that only a silverback gorilla can make. It peals through my body, rattling my inner core with a terror I have never known.

Now I *really* don't belong here! There is no reasoning my way out of this fear, which burns into me the most vivid memory of my time at Karisoke. And so we begin what my boss, Dian Fossey, will one day describe as the first time she had, ". . . ever been afraid of gorillas."

A FOREST IN THE CLOUDS

ONE

MY OWN VISION OF THE WILD

As the youngest of four boys in Fairfax, Virginia, a suburb of Washington, D.C., I'd had more than the usual exposure to the natural world. My mother loved the beach, and my father loved the mountains. Before I could remember, my dad had built a cottage for Mom on Chesapeake Bay, and like wild kids, my brothers, Paul, Steve, Dennis, and I spent weekends combing the beach for fossilized shark's teeth. Sometimes the bay would fill with stinging jellyfish we called sea nettles. Our desire to swim overcame our fear of these creatures, and eventually we learned to pick them up by their harmless pulsating caps. With stinging tentacles trailing on the sand we amazed passersby with our bravery. *Doesn't that hurt you? Nope.* We also mastered the ability to capture blue crabs

1

barehanded. With crab pinchers flailing madly before us, we chased after our innocent friends.

School field trips led to our nation's capital's great attractions. At the National Zoo, I reveled in the sights, sounds, and even the smells of living creatures from other worlds, marveling at the scale and scope of nature's diversity in form and function, from the smallest birds in the giant walk-through aviary, to the great apes, large cats, and super-sized mammals like rhinos, giraffes, and elephants. Even the beguiling, lifeless bronze of a giant anteater outside the Small Mammal House captivated me; so puzzled I was at first by which end was which. In the Smithsonian Institute's Museum of Natural History, I lingered far behind my schoolmates, spellbound in the intimate vision each specimen afforded with their lifelike glass eyes. I could almost see them breathing as they posed and I wished to drift away into their dioramas of exotic habitat and new horizons, where Tarzan and Mowgli lived in idyll.

Dad liked animals too, and we were the only home in our Fairfax neighborhood of Pine Ridge with, in addition to dogs and cats, chickens, pigeons, and peafowl. But it didn't stop there. Once, while Mom was out of the house, Dad was reading a *Field & Stream* magazine at the breakfast table, and in a near whisper, he called me into the kitchen. Pointing at an ad for mail-order squirrel monkeys, he said, "If you want to get one of these, go ahead and call this number." I was ecstatic. I had been admiring the pet monkey ad with its photo of a beguiling squirrel-sized simian staring from the page with a human-like expression, but I never thought I could have such a pet. Apparently my dad wanted one too, and the next day we sent our check for fifteen dollars.

I never knew how Dad broke the idea to Mom, but he deftly assembled a large cage from wood and chicken wire, and a week after our exotic cargo arrived, the basement rec room permanently reeked of overripe bananas and monkey poop.

Although Casper was never affectionate with me, we had a mutual respect, and I was able to carry him around attached to a harness and leash. That was the year of the emergence of the seventeen-year cicada in Virginia. My new monkey's favorite pastime was to perch on my hand as I ran through the front yard allowing him to grab cicadas out of the air and devour them, crunching and munching wings, legs and all like a handful of chips and creamy dip. That was the highlight of Casper's captivity. When he was back in his cage, he sat forlornly on his shelf and stared out the window toward the forest that flanked our backyard.

One day, while I was cleaning his cage outdoors, Casper made a break for it and escaped. None of us were able to grab him, and my brothers and I soon watched the agile monkey disappear into the woods behind our home, the same trees he had stared at through the window from his cage. In spectacular leaps and bounds, he traveled through the canopy of tall oaks and maples as if it was his native tropical American rainforest. Despite my loss, I felt Casper's exhilaration as he disappeared from view in the depth of what was, from my young perspective, an endless forest.

Dad also bought mail-order honeybees from Sears, Roebuck and set them up in a hive on the driveway behind our house. The bees were supposed to be docile. I had to find out for myself. Once as a young neighbor named Elisa looked on, I approached the hive to show her my bravery. Bees buzzed around me as Elisa gazed from a safe twenty feet away. The buzzing grew loud as they swarmed around my head next to the hive. One by one they began to light on me: arms, head, shoulders, and face. They began to accumulate around my eyes. Two, four, six, dozens—their mouth parts feeling for the edges of my eyelids then lingering, their tongue-like projections dabbling there.

"They're drinking from my eyes!" I said. Transfixed and horrified, Elisa just grimaced and stared, keeping her distance, but I was dazzled by this power that others feared. To be covered in bees is to be safe, because no one will come near you and I stood where others feared to.

Eventually, my dad, a carpenter and construction super-visor, indulged his yearning for the mountains and bought a one-hundred-year-old cabin in the Shenandoah Valley. As an escape from the city, it ultimately won out over the beach cottage, which was sold. Mom, outgoing and enterprising, decided it was Dad's turn and took willingly to renovating the old cabin and spending weekends gardening, canning, and stoking a coal-fired stove reminiscent of her childhood in the strip-mining region of Pennsylvania.

The Blue Ridge Mountains were beautiful but sterile, I thought, relative to the rich vitality of the shore. At the beach, we had been unfettered and free—in the mountains there were chores. My older brothers adapted quickly to skills like carpentry and driving tractors, but menial tasks like weeding the carrots and lettuce, or shoveling coal into buckets to haul to the house, became my domain. The mountains, great tidal waves frozen in time, loomed like walls around me.

As the youngest of four boys striving for an identity of my own, and unafraid of wild creatures, I found myself in my own vision of the wild. At age seven, I knew I wanted a career with animals. The creatures and fantastic tales of Dr. Seuss spellbound me, and I wanted to be Max in Maurice Sendak's *Where the Wild Things Are*. In later school years, I pored through the *World Book Encyclopedia* and *National Geographic* magazines, aching for wild places far away, but when I envisioned a career in the wilds of Africa, I rarely spoke of it. At the time, careers like that were rare and I believed that others, including my parents and brothers, would see my dream as a weird and frivolous notion, impractical and unobtainable.

By the time I was thirteen, Dad had grown increasingly tired with commuting and working in the ever-expanding and increasingly con-gested Washington, D.C. suburbs. My parents sold the house in Fairfax and bought an imposing white brick two-story farmhouse in Mount Jackson, Virginia. From its wide porches, we could see the Blue Ridge to the west and the Massanutten range to the east, and I often thought of the world that was beyond these mountains.

Dad became a full-time gentleman farmer. Too productive, really, we grew and dug enough potatoes to feed ten families and then watched them rot in a huge pile. In the chicken coop, two dozen brown hens cranked out two dozen brown eggs daily. The basement filled with jars of green beans, tomatoes, beets, and sauerkraut. Dad was a good provider.

Mom started cooking in the mornings: applesauce from the apples, eggs from the hen house, slab bacon from the pigs. Our large kitchen had a fireplace, a big oak table and a gas range but no automatic dishwasher. "You practically have to wash them before you put them in anyway," Mom always said. Instead, her prized possession was an enamel-coated, glossy, brown iron coal-fired stove, which vented through its own chimney. She cooked on its surface as adeptly as on gas or electricity. Breakfasts merged into lunches, which merged into suppers. "Do you want some applesauce?" she would ask each family member pausing at every chair. "No," we would answer in turn, before she placed a large dollop on each plate. Three humming refrigerators—one in the kitchen, one in the washroom, and one in the guest house—brimmed with leftovers among stacks of eggs in recycled cartons. Three dogs and three cats kept their noses in the air, hoping for scraps, and friends and neighbors strategically dropped in at meal times. They raved about Mom's fresh applesauce and often left with a bag of potatoes and a carton of eggs.

From that great old homestead, the only house I could see from my upstairs bedroom window was across a wide cow pasture. It was empty. Bored with the Virginia countryside, I matured and was consumed by a desire to travel. Africa fixed in my mind, the place where exotic animals roamed free and by the thousands. On television I saw a veterinarian who worked in the national parks of Africa. That seemed just right. Virginia did not have a veterinary school, but the University of Georgia annually admitted seven Virginia residents into its College of Veterinary Medicine.

After two years of core curriculum at Lord Fairfax Community College in Middletown, Virginia, I enrolled in UGA's pre-veterinary program and headed south. I had always had an aptitude for languages and art, but considered these frivolous and impractical pursuits, relegated to the realm of avocations and hobbies. But majoring in zoology, the discipline of real science caught me off guard. In my first quarter I dropped out of calculus, but lingered in physics beyond the deadline and flunked it. Determined, I linked up with other students having the same problem who convinced me to join them in taking physics the following summer at Gainesville Community College, forty miles away. The credits were transferable, and I scored an A!

From then on I strategized. I took remedial math and learned who the best teacher was in each subject before registering for a class. I also partnered with other students to discuss assignments and study collaboratively. This way I was able to tackle calculus, organic chemistry, and microbiology, and raise my grade point average to qualify for vet school.

Socially and intellectually, college was a great escape from rural Virginia and led to opportunities for exploration and discovery. In the spring quarter of 1979, a fellow pre-vet student, Leslie Smith, told me she was going to East Africa during the summer on a study program from Georgia Tech. Envious, I asked her for details. She had seen a flyer posted on the bulletin board in the biology building. She said the registration deadline had already passed, but the contact person was Dr. Terry Maple in the psychology department at Georgia Tech. I called him that day.

"Yes, we could fit one more in," Dr. Maple informed me on the phone. In his resonant baritone, he gave me the details. The trip would cost two thousand dollars and last fourteen days. In Kenya, we would be housed in a dormitory at the University of Nairobi. From there we would make trips to the country's national parks to observe animals in their natural habitat and learn about animal behavior research and conservation. This was too good to be true, but asking my parents to pay for a $2000 course made me feel terrible. I was nervous when Dad answered the phone.

"I guess we could if that's what you want to do," he said.

Yes! If he could go for it, Mom would be easy.

It was difficult to concentrate on spring finals with Africa waiting for me on the other side, but I got through them. I marveled at my first passport when it arrived and dreaded the series of shots I needed for entry into Kenya. The nurse said the gamma globulin shot for typhoid would hurt when she stuck the needle in my butt. It did. I was surprised by the malaria preventative—a big pink M&M-looking tablet disguised a bitter quinine derivative within. It had to be taken daily two weeks prior to departure, and for six weeks after returning. It is supposed to kill the malaria microorganisms that enter your body when a mosquito bites you, but it doesn't always work.

It was 3:30 A.M. on July nineteenth when our plane landed at the Nairobi airport. The cool air surprised me so near the equator, as did a pervasive smell of burning wood. No one offered an explanation for that. From the airport, our group of seven men and five women, led by Terry Maple and his student assistant Mike Hoff, shuttled to our dorm rooms. I strained to see through the darkness. In the headlights I could see abundant flowers in hedges of bright red, purple, and orange flanking the boulevard—bougainvillea. A quarter moon hung upside down, floating like a silver gondola transporting me to another world.

Our dorm rooms were on each side of a hallway at the top of a flight of concrete stairs. At each end of the hall, perforated concrete block walls let cool night air drift through. The rooms were simple, with twin beds and bookcases fixed to the walls. A vent at the top of each window was open to the outdoors. This room in the tropics was chilly.

Excited but exhausted, I slept soundly until dawn when I woke to a deep, reverberant noise repeated in a series of six booming notes—a natural sound, a creature! It was distant but loud and completely alien. I wondered what it could be—a baboon I imagined. I rose, pulled on my clothes and trotted down the dorm's cold staircase into the morning's chill. The smell of firewood was stronger than the night before. In time, I came to understand that the smoke was coming from the home fires in the communities of pale stucco houses that flanked the campus and mingled with other buildings of the city.

A large tree on the lawn outside the dormitory, with a trunk two feet thick, was covered in wide conical spines fading where the branches began ten feet above. Impossible to climb, I thought like a child. And as with a child, everything was foreign and new to me. I tapped on the trunk between the spines and it made a hollow drum-like sound, as if empty. A brown dove with a black mark at the nape of its neck fluttered down and landed on the grass twenty feet away. It bobbed its head as it walked, then stopped to cock one eye at me. The eye, brilliant red, gleamed like a polished ruby cabochon.

Before long, I heard the voices of fellow students, and dishes clanging in the dining hall adjoining our building. Breakfast was being served and our group was filing down the stairs to eat. Inside the cafeteria, a row of six smiling Kenyans served us food reminiscent of English colonialism—hard fried eggs on slices of toast that was also fried rock hard. An oddly tart-tasting fat round link sausage was added with a small plump tomato that had been pan-seared on its sliced top and bottom. I sampled everything with wonder. One attendant poured coffee, while another brought pitchers of hot milk and topaz-colored crystals of natural sugar. Yellow and reddish fruit juices were served in carafes. More sweet than tart, and tasting unfamiliar to us, we guessed what they might be. *Orange-mango? Pineapple-guava?* I reveled in the newness and difference of every detail of this new world, from the food, to the air I now breathed.

At the table, Dr. Maple chatted with a cheerful university representative and local Kenyan. They discussed details of our travels while in Kenya. *What days would we be at the University, and what days would we be away to other parts of the country? Would we need boxed lunches, or would we be out overnight?* This gentleman greeted our group in his crisp native accent, and asked us about our trip. I asked him about the sound I had heard at dawn. "That's a red-eyed dove," he replied, with a gleaming smile.

Our first field trip was to the Nairobi National Park. We loaded into two kombi minibuses and drove to the park's entry just outside of town. As we entered on a dusty dirt road through a thicket of acacia trees, Dr. Maple advised us not to shout nor shoot an entire roll of film when we saw our first animal. We laughed. We were much too sophisticated for that.

As we rounded a curve out of the trees into wide rolling grasslands, a towering giraffe stood thirty feet away grazing on the high branches of a tall acacia. "Giraffe!" we shouted clambering to our feet to poke our heads and cameras out of the kombi's open sunroof. "Shhhh . . ." we chided each other, each member of my group as giddily enthusiastic as I was. The kombis stopped and camera shutters clicked frantically at the giraffe who chewed a bolus of leaves while staring complacently at our ecstatic group.

As we traveled farther down the dirt road, we saw three more giraffes that moved along beside our vehicle thirty feet on our right. We stopped to admire them, our group drunken with awe, as these towering behemoths glided before us to cross the road. Their long necks undulated gracefully at a slight gallop, making them seem like a slow-motion optical illusion at fifteen feet tall, bedazzled with orange-brown puzzle-piece markings.

Ahead, a group of more than twenty zebras trotted along. We caught up with them and they veered away to the left. Fifty feet away, they slowed and paused. Fine-lined faces peered at us from beyond a jumble of bold black and white barred rumps. Tails swished, and skin quivered to shoo biting flies. We had to suppress the urge to shout and point, and temper the fingers on our camera shutters.

Terry Maple tried to channel our energy to the perspective of field research, instructing us to look for differences in each zebra's set of stripes. We began to notice the lines on their bodies, like fingerprints, were different on every individual. Terry informed us that field researchers keep photographic records to distinguish animals in a herd.

Our days in the field were followed by nights at an outpost camp or back at the University. We drank cold Tusker beer at the Serena Hotel near the campus or outdoors around a campfire. Terry Maple shared stories from a previous trip or talked about animal psychology. After a beer or two, he would often burst into one of his "psongs," as he called them—his own lyrics involving natural history or characters like Charles Darwin and Alfred Russel Wallace, cofounders of the Theory of Evolution, sung, or *psung* rather, to a popular tune. Among this group of people who shared my interest in the natural world, Africa strummed the chords of my emotional and intellectual core.

We had serious meetings too, when we would talk about our days in the field and how our observations related to our assigned texts on animal behavior and ethology. One of our reading assignments was *Portraits in the Wild* by Cynthia Moss, a comprehensive and monumental compilation of information on many East African mammals. From this we learned the social structure of animals like elephants, which live in groups of females and their young, led by a dominant matriarch. Male elephants travel alone or flank the herd seeking a receptive female for the opportunity to breed.

Moss's book also outlined the complex social system of many species of antelopes. A horned male impala or gazelle keeps watch over a group of hornless females with which he breeds—he must constantly defend his harem from the advances of other males in violent duels. During our travels, what at first seemed like animals randomly scattered across the savanna took on new meaning. We would notice the attentive male Thompson's gazelle near a group of thirty females, and we contemplated his struggles. We saw other males in the distance vying for the herd, and we knew what they wanted. We began to understand that grasslands had a structure and complex order to its robust vitality.

On our leg to Amboseli, Kenya, we visited Moss's camp of canvas tents and simple wooden tables tucked in a gallery of acacias. A notebook sat on a table next to odd-shaped bones, bleaching in the sun. Khaki clothing hung on a line stretched between two trees. Far from modern conveniences, the camp looked comfortable and idyllic. Moss's neighbors were elephants, rhinos, and lions from the surrounding grasslands, which were warm and dry, stretching farther than we could see. What else did anyone need?

Moss was away from camp that day, but at the end of our stay in Kenya, she came to visit us in Nairobi. She was laid-back and soft-spoken with medium-length wavy brown hair highlighted by the sun, which had given it the color of the dry savanna grasses. She began by thanking us for reading her book and told us she had come to Kenya from the United States years previously on a writing assignment for *Newsweek* magazine. After that, she didn't leave.

Her love for Africa was apparent in the tales she told us. Casual and relaxed amid our group of students, she patiently answered all of our questions about her life and work, unable to conceal a special admiration and fondness for elephants. This gracious behaviorist autographed each of our books before she left. I opened mine and read: *To John, With best wishes, Cynthia Moss, Nairobi, August 10, 1979.*

I marveled at her resolve, and understood her desire to live in Africa because I felt it myself.

Back at UGA that fall, I tried to knuckle under again for academic life. My pre-vet club needed speakers for future meetings and I thought of Terry Maple. He wasn't an authority on veterinary medicine, but he could talk to our group about his study-abroad program and provide an inspiring diversion to the sometimes uninspiring drudgery of undergraduate studies.

I called Terry at Georgia Tech, and he agreed to speak to our club. After setting a date for the next meeting, I told Terry yet again how much I enjoyed traveling in Kenya and seeing Africa's abundant wildlife firsthand, and learning so much while among them. In response, Terry surprised me with a request of his own.

"How would you like to go to Rwanda and study mountain gorillas with Dian Fossey?"

I was dumbstruck.

"Where? Who?" I stammered. Maple, an ambitious man with a profound interest in great apes, explained that he had learned of the opportunity from a fellow primate behaviorist, Dr. Ramon Rhine of the University of California at Riverside, who was on the research advisory board for Karisoke Research Center.

Dian Fossey was then little known outside the world of primate behaviorists, and I had to ask Terry more about her. As he explained that the National Geographic Society funded her and she had written articles in their magazine, I did recall seeing the stunning images of her sitting with wild gorillas. Rwanda, a tiny country in the center of Africa, was then little known to the rest of the world.

Terry explained that Fossey was looking for up to three students to staff her research camp because she was planning to leave for a year's teaching assignment at Cornell University. Terry's tone changed as he went on to say that through conversations with Dr. Rhine, he had learned that Fossey could be difficult to work with. Many students had clashed with her and left camp, ". . . and she hasn't been as productive with her research as expected." Apparently, Terry added, she felt men were more suited to the work and that women were not suited for mountain gorilla research and the Spartan living at Karisoke. This seemed bizarre to me because she was a woman, after all. I wondered what kind of a woman she was.

"She may just need a friend," Terry said.

This comment stuck in my mind. Although Maple and I briefly discussed research topics like mother-infant behavior in great apes, befriending Dian Fossey loomed as my primary objective. An easy task, I was sure. I saw myself as even-tempered and nonconfrontational. She wanted helpers, and I would be at her service. Someone doing such great work and not being appreciated for it, I thought, was sad and worthy of remediation. I honestly took the opportunity to assist her to be an honor and a privilege, not a problem. Without hesitating, I said, "Yes!"

Despite my obvious enthusiasm, Terry said, "Take the next twenty-four hours to think about it and call me back."

My roommates, Jeff and Kevin were stunned by my news, but not more so than my parents were. My mom's reaction was, "My God, a whole year in Africa?!" But after having raised four sons to adulthood with minds of their own, she didn't try to talk me out of it.

After twenty-four hours had elapsed, I called Terry and reconfirmed what I said before, "Yes, I want to go back to Africa." There was a thrill in the ensuing pause in our conversation. Terry seemed as excited as I was. "If I had an opportunity like this when I was your age, I'd go," he said. I knew then that he was living vicariously through this chance of mine.

Terry didn't know the exact time line for departure, but said that I might have to leave soon. I didn't care, and was foolishly willing to drop out of fall quarter if it was necessary.

From that point on, I struggled to remain focused on my studies while dreaming of mountain gorillas. Terry called me almost weekly to brief me on his progress with making things happen. "Dian is particularly interested in students who have their own source of funds," he said, "but I might be able to get a benefactor to pay your airfare over there." I told Terry that I had about five hundred dollars that I could live off of, and he put this all in a letter on my behalf to Dr. Rhine on the Karisoke Board. Dr. Rhine forwarded that on to Dian Fossey, and I wondered how many other students had been contacted and were being considered. We waited for an answer.

I sat through my microbiology course and remember nothing about it. My study sessions in the campus library turned into searches for the *National Geographic* magazines with articles by Dian Fossey about the mountain gorillas. Nights that I started working on my paper in

Principles of Human Ecology and Evolution turned into evenings reading George Schaller's book, *The Mountain Gorilla*.

"You're going to Rwanda young man," said Terry on the phone near the end of the quarter. "Dian has selected you and two other students to go to Karisoke. And I've found a woman named Betty Wisdom from New Orleans who will pay for your airfare." I was really going back to Africa. When I told my roommates and fellow pre-vet students around the UGA campus that I was going to Rwanda to work with mountain gorillas, I tried to be nonchalant instead of giddy. They were amazed. *Is she that woman who works with chimps? How did that happen? Why you?*

Why me? I wondered too. Just an undergraduate hoping to get into vet school, I had no research or field experience other than Terry Maple's course. I didn't dwell on my lack of qualifications, but struggled to remain focused on my studies while dreaming of mountain gorillas. I soon received the following letter from Dr. Rhine confirming my acceptance.

> *Dear John:*
>
> *I am very pleased to inform you that Dr. Fossey has wired acceptance of your application for research at her Karisoke Research Center in Rwanda. I had informed her that you are financially self-sufficient, will stay a minimum of 12 months, and can leave sometime around the first of the year . . .*
>
> *Remember, you may well hate Rwanda and Karisoke, especially during the first three months or so. After that, you may or may not learn to tolerate the place or even gradually fall in love with it. Be prepared for never-ending frustrations and loneliness.*
>
> *I'll be in touch again before long.*
>
> *Sincerely yours,*
> *Ramon J. Rhine*
> *Professor*
> *University of California, Riverside*

Getting this letter was like winning the lottery, and I shrugged off its foreboding undertone. How could I hate anything about this great opportunity?

Fall quarter ended and I went home to Virginia. Terry had forwarded a letter to me written by Peter Veit, the only student remaining at Karisoke. Veit recommended equipment and supplies that the new students should bring with them to Karisoke. My brother Steve, the forestry major, helped me shop for a pair of sturdy hiking boots, a backpack and a cheap set of plastic raingear. Veit had recommended bringing a compass and waterproof paper. Steve, who had spent past summers working as a land surveyor's assistant, also helped me find a good compass and the expensive waterproof paper at a surveyors' supply store.

A woman named Carolyn Phillips called me from Seattle, Washington. She was one of the other students who Dian had chosen to work at Karisoke. Until then, I assumed I would be traveling alone. Carolyn had learned from Dr. Rhine of the third student who had been selected, Stuart Perlmeter, living in Eugene, Oregon. She had called him and asked if they could travel from the West Coast together. Perlmeter told her he wanted to stick to his plan to leave around Christmas—being Jewish, the approaching holidays wouldn't slow him down. As that was too soon for Carolyn, he would travel alone. My new colleague was relieved when I agreed to coordinate my travel plans with hers after New Year's, telling me she had never been to Africa. I told her about my previous trip with Terry Maple, and she said she felt more comfortable knowing I had some experience traveling in Africa. From my adventurous but naïve young perspective, I didn't understand her cautiousness, but Carolyn seemed easygoing and friendly and I looked forward to meeting her.

Going through my belongings from my previous travels in East Africa, I marveled once again at my first passport I had used the previous summer and was thankful that the vaccines listed in my health certificate were still good for entry into Kenya. I wouldn't need another painful gamma globulin shot in my ass.

I was scheduled to leave for Rwanda on January 8. Terry called me a few days prior to departure to arrange a meeting somewhere between my home in Mount Jackson, Virginia and his in Atlanta, Georgia. He had a one-way airline ticket for me, some research-related reading material, a letter of recommendation to help me get an extended visa, and permission to conduct research in Rwanda.

"Did you hear what I said?" Terry asked. A one-way ticket?" I laughed at the implication, but remained undaunted. I could only think forward, about getting there, so excited was I about the opportunity.

We ate burgers and fries at an interstate fast food joint as Terry discussed the various research topics I could pursue with the mountain gorillas. Terry recommended a mother-infant study, or the role of adult males called silverbacks. He decided, of course, that whatever research topic Fossey wanted would be the way to go. Terry also told me that Dr. Rhine had said that Dian would be appointing one of the new students as acting director of the research center before she departed to begin teaching at Cornell. Terry paused for my reaction. I remained silent, but knew what he was thinking. This was too much. *How could I be acting director with such a limited background?* I barely understood the research topics and was overwhelmed by Terry's innuendo. Before we parted, Terry said, "I want you to know that January eighth is Alfred Russel Wallace's birthday."

"It is?"

"Do you know who Alfred Russel Wallace is?"

"Uh . . . no."

"He's the cofounder of the Theory of Evolution. Along with Charles Darwin, but Darwin publicized it first. Beat him to it. I have an Alfred Russel Wallace birthday party at my house every year. This year we'll be toasting you while you're in the air on your way to the mountain gorillas."

TWO

INTO RWANDA

On January 8, 1980, Carolyn and I traveled through waylays and delays for over five days via Nairobi, Kenya into Kigali, Rwanda. Along the way, we compared notes on how we fell into this opportunity. Carolyn had been a volunteer at Woodland Park Zoo in Seattle and knew the zoo's director, David Hancocks. Hancocks had learned of Dian's request for students from Dr. Rhine, the same as Terry. At thirty-four, she was eleven years my senior, and well read on Dian Fossey and her work. Petite and attractive with long dark hair, her qualifications consisted primarily of her zoo volunteer work; other than that, she had a BA in English, and a supportive attitude toward Fossey's work, with admiration bordering on reverence. By comparison, I felt ashamed to say how little I knew about Dian before this opportunity arose.

Upon arrival in Kigali, we were graciously taken in and hosted by US Embassy staffers stationed there. There was that much excitement and mystique about Karisoke and the people involved with it. The embassy's Communications Programs Officer, Judy Chidester, generously offered us her home, a spacious four-bedroom abode, which her coworkers had dubbed "Judy's Joint," with a sign proclaiming just that by the driveway. Judy was a full-figured gal in her early forties with a short crop of dark curls, dressed for the tropics in a sleeveless blouse and bright slacks. Robust and cheerful, she gave us a quick tour of her home and showed us our rooms. French doors in the large living area opened to a wide veranda facing eastward over Kigali's rolling hillsides. In the distance, we noticed an airplane taking off from the airport where we had just arrived.

I had read that Kigali was at 5,000 feet above sea level, and I commented about the temperature being just right at nearly 80 degrees.

"That's why I've put in for another three years here." Judy said, grinning. "But we're just at the end of the short dry season. It'll be clouding up here in the next few weeks."

Carolyn and I thanked Judy profusely for the luxurious accommodations, and joked about how the situation was not going to help prepare us for what we knew would be Spartan conditions ahead, among the mountain gorillas.

"I'll be heading up to Karisoke myself this week," Judy informed us, "To help take care of the baby."

At our surprised confusion, Judy went on to tell Carolyn and me that a baby gorilla had recently been confiscated from poachers and was now being cared for at Karisoke. In order for Dian to leave camp to retrieve us, Judy and her friend, Liza Escher, from the Swiss consulate would be traveling to Karisoke to babysit the little gorilla while Dian came to Kigali. This news just added another layer of excitement about what lay ahead.

"There's a box of chocolates on the end table there, help yourself to the top layer." Judy said, as she slipped out the doorway, on her way back to work. "The bottom layer's *mine!*" she added with a laugh.

Judy's friend Ann Yancey, the embassy's Economic/Commercial Officer and Vice Consul, invited Judy, Carolyn, and me over for dinner at her equally gracious home, to savor a repurposed pork loin, which they and others had already sampled in a meal at Judy's Joint. Ann, in her late twenties, was as cheerfully adapted to her Rwandan outpost as Judy.

"When we get a good cut of meat like that here," Ann said, a shock of blond curls bouncing around her fair-skinned face, "we've got to take advantage of it in more than one meal."

A few other embassy staffers joined the dinner party, as did Brooke Stallsmith, a tall, thin, bespectacled young man in his twenties. Brooke was stationed in Rwanda with USAID for agricultural development. It was obvious that Karisoke, the mountain gorillas, and particularly Dian Fossey were subjects of great curiosity, and Carolyn's and my presence provided a novel diversion and topic of interest. Our own curiosity at the table, about what lay ahead for the two of us at Karisoke Research Center, was met with cryptic responses from those who had already met the mysterious gorilla lady.

"Soon you'll know much more about her than we do," Brooke offered.

"Anyone who's had to live up at Karisoke as Dian has . . ." Judy offered, hesitating with a deep breath, "as remote as it is, and dealing with what she's had to deal with, fighting for the gorillas, like she has, and the poaching. Well, that's got to take a toll on you."

Just as I thought that Judy had answered this question before, Ann chimed in, "Well, you'll be able to form your own opinions after you've been up there a while."

To our excitement, Brooke also informed us that a volcano was erupting across the border in neighboring Zaire. Mount Nyamuragira, an active volcano in the Virunga mountain chain, had just recently blown its stack and was spewing molten lava down its slopes.

"Perhaps you'll be able to see it from where you'll be up there," our dinner group surmised.

We also learned from the group that our American ambassador, Harry Melone, Jr., along with family and friends, was currently visiting Karisoke. His considerable clout garnered him and his special guests the favor of accommodations, hosted by Dian Fossey herself, including exclusive access to her research gorillas. The presence of a baby mountain gorilla in camp made the timing all that more alluring and special.

By the time Judy left Carolyn and me in her home, and headed up to Karisoke with her friend Liza as planned, word was that Dian would arrive the next day. But even over the next couple of days, she had not yet arrived. Some speculated that the ambassador's visit to her camp, combined with the baby gorilla's arrival were the likely delays. Back then, Kigali was a small city of only 130,000 or so, and Carolyn and I passed the idle days walking its dusty dirt roads and intermittent pavement. To pass the time, we visited Kigali's central open market, and the shops around town featuring local crafts and souvenirs. The Hôtel des Mille Collines was the nicest venue in town, but too extravagant for us to even have lunch with our meager funds. English was rare, and everywhere we went, I found myself using animated hand signals to help communicate. I bought an assortment of vegetables at the market with a plan to make soup for lunch back at Judy's Joint. Tiny red peppers Rwandans call *pili-pili* had also caught my eye, and I added those into the mix as well. The result was too caustic to eat. I couldn't finish mine, and felt bad for Carolyn who somehow managed to eat all of hers.

"I'm just impressed that you can make soup," she said, as I wiped the perspiration from my forehead with my napkin.

I had been advised not to keep too much money at Karisoke, and at the suggestion of embassy staffers, I deposited my $500 cash into the Banque du Kigali for safekeeping, and in exchange received a small paper bankbook. I would make withdrawals as needed on my returns to Kigali to renew each three-month visa. The chaotic mass of people that formed at each bank window instead of the neat lines I was used to, and seeming lack of organization during the process, made me wonder if I'd ever see my cash again.

Judy had made us feel welcome at the American Embassy, and even got us clearance to enter and peruse their informal book exchange. We chose the books we wanted to take up to camp for reading. The embassy was an unassuming, single-story building with an entrance just a few steps from the street's sidewalk. In the vestibule, a plump Rwandan receptionist named Bernadette greeted us from behind a wooden desk. She wore the same close-cropped haircut typical of the locals.

"So you are the ones going up to Karisoke?" Bernadette asked in her clipped accent.

"Yes, we are," Carolyn and I answered in unison.

"Aha . . ." she said cryptically, returning her attention to papers on her desk.

After walking the hot dusty streets of Kigali, Carolyn and I were thankful to be given access to the embassy's lounge and pool, a short walk from the center of town. Comprised of a kitchenette with a couple of open rooms for card games, cookouts, and movie nights, the lounge area was beneath the residence of the Ambassador's secretary, Dorothy Eardley, and opened to the back lawn and pool. Upon our arrival there, we ran into Bill Weber, who had stopped in to use the pool and shower facilities. Bill had spent many months at Karisoke with his wife, Amy Vedder, who was studying gorilla feeding ecology. At that moment, Carolyn and I had no knowledge of the couple's considerable history with Dian, and upon introductions, Bill immediately became chilly and aloof, gathering his backpack and brushing past us out the door without the least bit of interest in answering questions, or knowing anything more about us.

On our fifth day in Kigali, still occupying Judy's well-appointed home without her, Carolyn and I relaxed on the wide veranda, discussing what lay ahead while admiring the view overlooking Kigali's eastern hills, and the airport on the horizon. A pair of speckled mousebirds flitted between shrubs across the lawn below, trailing their long thin tails like flying rodents.

"I see Dian as sort of a kindred spirit," Carolyn confided to me, "I've admired her for a long time."

In contrast to Carolyn's knowledge, I felt a little guilty, having not known so much about our soon-to-be mentor.

"I can't wait to see the gorillas," I mused, "and how they live, up there in the rain forest."

"I thought it was a rain forest too," Carolyn corrected me, "but our zoo director, David Hancocks, told me that at that altitude we'll be up in the clouds. It's actually called a 'cloud forest.'"

The mere concept of a cloud forest only made what lay ahead seem even more surreal. I gazed skyward at the clouds. Kigali was at five thousand feet above sea level; we'd be five thousand more feet above where we were at that moment, transported up into the very atmosphere to which I gazed.

Near the equator, the sun sets around six o'clock each day. As the light faded, a loud putter of an automobile broke the silence as it rounded the curve of Judy's driveway. I looked over the veranda railing and saw an old gray Volkswagen bus jostle to a stop below.

Dian Fossey had arrived!

Two car doors creaked and slammed in the cool air of twilight, followed by the shuffle of two pairs of feet trudging up the concrete steps. Carolyn and I rose to meet Dian and our other new fellow student Stuart as they walked in the open doorway. Expecting a warm greeting, I was immediately taken aback by Dian's cool detachment. I had read she was six feet tall, but here before me, she slouched just enough to bring her carriage a good inch or two below my own similar height. Her dark brown hair was mussed from travel, and wan, sallow cheeks only heightened her somewhat ascetic appearance. No warmth emanated from her in this moment of greeting, but rather a pall of preoccupation and weariness, as if uncomfortably out of her element. Stuart, twenty-six, stood a few inches shorter than me, with a lanky build like my own. He had a longish face and nose, and dark curly hair in the basic one-length rounded style of the late seventies. The two of them wore jeans and plain work shirts, dusty from the road.

Dian's reticent smile was noticeably labored as we introduced ourselves and shook hands. Her puffy eyes twitched with the effort to smile, as if our exuberance was a flash of painfully bright light. I thought of Terry Maple's advice to make a point of befriending her— Stuart certainly had, and by contrast, exuded charm and charisma— but I was struck dumb by her coldness, especially when she seemed to cringe while touching our hands, as if wincing at the pain of the encounter. The reaction was not one of engagement, but rather reluctance, even revulsion. She was not enjoying the moment, but rather restraining her contempt.

As we began idle chatter, Dian made eye contact with Stuart much more than with Carolyn or me, like a child among strange adults seeking refuge in a parent. It was obvious that Stuart had made good use of the lead time he had in getting to Karisoke ahead of Carolyn and me; it was obvious that he was already Dian's right-hand man. Reading our eagerness for information about what we were about to embark on, he broke the ice with easy chatter.

"Karisoke is beautiful," he said. "Surrounded by the volcanoes . . . and the gorillas are amazing!" He opened his eyes expressively when he spoke, rolling them slightly with a sideways tilt of his head.

I envied the knowledge he already had about the world of mountain gorillas, and the sights he had already seen. Stuart put his backpack down, and we moved to chairs in the living room. Dian sat herself down in a chair by the French doors to the veranda, leaning against the chair's arm, her legs crossed at the ankles. Her reticent movements suggested frailty, rather than the picture of strength I had imagined. She paused for a moment, blinking and twitching her eyes, as if adjusting her thoughts before speaking to us about the next few days: Stuart would be staying at Judy's with Carolyn and me, while Dian stayed at Ambassador Melone's house. Dian's monotone voice was low and soft, almost breathy, unemotional, and again incongruous with the image of strength and confidence I had envisioned.

Dian paused again and cleared her throat. "Uh, where's my valise?" she asked, reaching and looking by her feet.

"Oh . . . must be in the van," Stuart said, attentive.

"*Eht mwaaah* . . ." Dian growled, her face tightening in a scowl.

"I'll get it," Stuart chimed, leaping up and trotting toward the door. He must have noticed the looks on Carolyn's and my faces, because he smiled and stopped to explain the sound Dian had just made.

"That's a gorilla vocalization. We have to make that sound when we approach the gorillas, so they'll know we're near," Stuart said, authoritatively.

Clearly growing impatient, Dian began telling Carolyn and me that we had much to do the next day before going back to camp.

"Have you brought your letters of recommendation," she asked, "to get permission to work in the Parc des Volcans?"

"Yes," Carolyn and I spoke and nodded our affirmation in unison.

"*Mwah, mwah, mwah* . . ." Dian purred, in what we took to be approval.

Carolyn and I continued listening and nodding at Dian's instructions, already intimidated and obedient, as Stuart returned with a notebook-sized black leather case. Our new boss slowly unzipped her valise and riffled through some papers inside.

"Uh, okay, in the morning we have go to ORTPN and meet with, uh . . . Benda Lema," She said, then turned her head and spit toward the floor with a dour look of contempt. I glanced at Stuart, who smiled and maintained his composure.

"That's the parks department," Stuart explained.

"Shit *merde!*" Dian suddenly cursed, "*eht mwahh, mwahh* . . ." Fidgety, she shifted in her seat, pausing at various items in her valise.

I wondered what she might be searching for: *A to-do list, money, passport . . . ?* Suddenly, Dian lifted her head, a little more energetic now, and asked, "Is anyone getting hungry?"

All four of us piled into Dian's Volkswagen bus with Dian at the wheel and Stuart in the passenger seat beside her. The vehicle's vinyl seats had numerous tears at the seams and the metal floor was covered in dust from the roads. As we left Judy's driveway, I could see the dirt road passing underneath where bolts were missing, and with a raw, sore clatter, we rode into town to a small restaurant near the embassy.

"This is about the best place in Kigali," Dian said flatly as we entered the dimly lit café. A Rwandan man, recognizing Dian immediately, greeted her with an enthusiastic, "Bonsoir, Madame!" He led us to a table by the front window, and Dian ordered Primus for all four of us. Scanning the menu's French text, we struggled to decipher the offerings of beef, chicken, or fish.

"I made soup today," I volunteered, attempting some sort of interaction with Dian.

"*You* made soup?" she said, wrinkling her nose at me.

"Yeah, but, you know, I put those little peppers in it? And—"

"*Pili-pili?*" Dian said. "You don't put *that* in soup. *Eht mwaaah . . .*" She looked over to Stuart and smirked. Stuart smiled awkwardly, and I looked at Carolyn who shifted in her seat. Maybe I just need to be quiet, I began to think.

When the waiter returned with our beers, Dian watched as he opened hers. She immediately took a big swig as we all waited for her to take the lead in ordering food. She spoke laboriously in French, twitching and wrinkling her face at the waiter's responses to her questions before finally nodding and agreeing to something on the menu.

After we had all placed our orders, Carolyn asked about the baby gorilla at Karisoke. Dian said she estimated it to be about three years old and it was getting much more used to people now. It was a female, and Dian had named it Charlie.

"She screamed and hid under the bed at first," Stuart said, laughing. "We tried to coax her out with food."

The beer seemed to relax Dian, and she laughed easily with Stuart, while continuing on to describe the progress she had made by way of offering candy to the little gorilla. Dian's laugh was a low, quick series of "*huh, huh, huh, huh . . .*" which I would soon learn, like other of her idiosyncratic vocalizations, was reminiscent of a gorilla's chuckling. Our new boss finished her talk about the baby, telling Carolyn and me that we would have a lot of work to do with the new orphan when we got to camp. The very idea thrilled me.

"Dr. Maple suggested I do a mother-infant study," I said, looking for an enthusiastic response from my new boss. Instead, she looked at me and paused.

"What do you notice about him?" she asked Stuart, pointing at me with cold detachment, as if I couldn't hear or see from behind a glass window.

Stuart paused. "What do you mean?"

"Watch him; he does a lot of things with his hands."

I flushed and forced an awkward smile, too embarrassed to look over at Carolyn. Ever since our arrival in Nairobi, I had been relying more and more on my hands to communicate across Swahili, French, and Kinyarwanda. Now, apparently, I was even doing it in English. Ashamed, I lowered my hands to my lap and fell silent. The corners of Dian's mouth curled up in a derogatory smile as she looked at Stuart, who quickly stepped in. I really do need to just stop talking, I realized.

"You have to be observant like that when watching gorillas," Stuart said. Grateful for his intervention, I nodded apprehensively.

Our meals were served with a loaf of French-style bread. I ate silently, by now, loath to speak, listening, and observing. Dian picked at the food on her plate, before hacking a large slice of bread from the loaf and cutting hunks of butter to spread on top of it. On this she liberally sprinkled salt before eating it in large bites. Cutting another slice, she repeated the ritual. I tried not to stare.

Dian ended the evening by surprising me with an offering of one of her Impala cigarettes. Despite three and a half years having gone by since I quit my teenage smoking, I gladly accepted what appeared to be my only bonding moment with the great Dian Fossey. I took up smoking again.

While Dian stayed at Ambassador Melone's home, Stuart, Carolyn, and I stayed at Judy's Joint. Our hostess had graciously turned her house over to us while still up at Karisoke babysitting the orphan. With Dian absent, the three of us got to know each other a little better, and Stuart told Carolyn and I that his girlfriend from Oregon would be joining him soon at Karisoke.

The next morning at nine, Dian puttered down the driveway in her Volkswagen. A light shower had come and gone, but the sky remained overcast. This was just the onset of the long rainy season, and Dian wore an unbuttoned dark trench coat with the belt hanging open from its loops. Clutching her black leather valise, she might have been a correspondent for the nightly news, save for her dishevelment and irritability.

"Shit *merde, salber* and *shoissamakoff!*" Dian cursed in an international gibberish of her own, having just noticed that she'd driven across town with her coat's belt trailing from out of the closed car door. I tried to decipher the expletives, recognizing the French word for "shit," along with her own variant on the German for "shithead."

ORTPN—the Rwandan Office for Tourism and National Parks—occupied a long whitewashed building near the middle of town, and an African clerk escorted us down a long open-air gallery to the office of Monsieur François Benda Lema, who rose from behind his desk as we entered.

"Bonjour," said Dian, her demeanor suddenly changing to a forced congeniality. We all said "bonjour" to Monsieur Benda Lema, who smiled and shook each of our hands. The predominant tribe in Rwanda was the Hutu and Benda Lema was typical of the Rwandans we had met so far. He was just over five feet tall, with a rounded face and sturdy build. As was typical of Rwandan men and women, he had a plain close-cropped haircut.

Dian asked Carolyn and me for our letters of recommendation and our passports, which she handed to Benda Lema, speaking to him slowly in her laborious French. There were no other seats in the small office, so Stuart, Carolyn, and I moved just outside to a bench in the breezeway. I could not understand what was being said, but Dian's forced friendliness became increasingly strained.

Through the door, we could see Dian at the edge of her wooden chair with her back straight and tense. She shifted a little each time she struggled for a word. Benda Lema's impatience with her was as obvious as hers was with him, and he wasn't going to yield to her. After twenty minutes, Dian came out and asked Carolyn and me if we had letters from our local police departments, which stated that we did not have police records in our hometowns. Incredulous, we said no.

"Eht mwah, shit goddammit," Dian muttered in a low voice, acting as if we should have thought of this before. These sudden outbursts of vitriolic language brought we newcomers, Carolyn and me, to nervous silence, but Stuart maintained composure.

Dian returned to her debate with Benda Lema, and after another ten minutes of chilly, stilted dialogue, she emerged to tell us that our visas would be approved, but we would need to have letters from our home police departments before getting extended visas in three months.

Happy to have her dreaded encounter with Benda Lema over with, our new leader led us across the street into Kigali's commercial section.

"We've got to get some things for camp now, Stuart," Dian said, still shaking off her tension, as we made our way across downtown's busy avenue. "We *really* need parts for the pressure lanterns."

"Okay, Mom," Stuart said, facetiously, with a cheerful grin, drawing out the *o* in *Mom* like a winsome child. "Whatever you say." At this, Dian managed a smile.

"*Now* you've got it!" our boss replied, with a grin

"Whatever you need, I'll see if I can find it." Stuart added.

Then Dian was beaming at Stuart's enthusiastic spirit of helpfulness. I knew Carolyn was as relieved as I for the change of mood. Struck by Stuart's easy intimacy with Dian, not to mention her obvious delight at being called "Mom," I was by now a little envious of their genuine rapport, but already felt far too unsure of myself to approach this unpredictable woman.

The next few days were more of the same, driving around town in pursuit of Dian's supplies, visiting the American embassy and getting our letter home to police departments written and sent. "If I'm going back to the States, I'm going to need to take some gifts for people," Dian said to herself as we approached the gift shop near the embassy. She parked in front of the store and Carolyn and I followed her inside. Dian stopped at the glass case by the door and stared into it. On a previous visit to this shop with Carolyn, I had noticed a free-form gold nugget in the display case, fitted with a gold bail to wear as a pendant. My mom's birthday was coming up, and I thought how much she would enjoy such a souvenir from Africa.

Dian never let up on her cutting remarks to me, and I grew more and more silent within our Fossey entourage. But still I attempted conversation when an opportunity arose.

"I'd like to get that gold nugget in there for my mom's birthday," I said, pointing through the glass, "but I'm not sure how long my money will hold out." Dian turned a shoulder to me and shifted her view to the glass counter where I had pointed.

"*S'il vous plaît*," Dian said to the salesgirl, while pointing to the gold piece.

"*Oui, Madame.*" The cashier opened the case from the back and placed the pendant in Dian's hands. I moved away in the awkwardness of the moment while Dian handed the cashier a wad of francs in exchange for the piece, and stuffed it in her purse.

Rick Kramer, the American ambassador's assistant, was a big fan of Dian's and invited the four of us over for dinner. Rick and his wife, Theresa, had three young kids. Iambo, the eldest girl, and Stephan, the middle child, had been born in Madagascar to Theresa and her previous husband, a Madagascan. Sarah, a blonde little toddler, was Rick's and Theresa's together. While Theresa served coffee, Rick talked about his love of the hardship post, even the effects that a recent water shortage had had on them.

"I mean, where else would we get to drag a garbage can full of pool water into the house just to have clean water?" he said, with affection for his adventures in the third world.

As Rick talked, Dian's attention was directed at the children. Stuart and Carolyn joined in the conversation, while I, feeling by now permanently muzzled, became merely an observer of Dian. I watched as she sliced chunks from a wheel of Brie on the dinner table and sneaked them to the chubby little Stephan, who eyed his parents warily before taking them. I suspected that his parents didn't want him to eat so much, but the interaction was so satisfying to Dian that she didn't care.

After dinner, Iambo and Stephan placed a board game on the floor in front of Dian, who flung a tiny ball at a series of miniature bowling pins. Having witnessed her irascibility and foul mouth, I was struck by her calm demeanor as young Stephan scolded Dian for throwing too hard. Innocent and unthreatening, children and animals seemed immune to her wrath, I surmised as I tried to assess her complex personality.

On another night, we joined Dian at the home of her elder friend Dorothy Eardley, with whom she'd be staying for the next few nights. Dorothy was the ambassador's secretary, and was planning to retire after that year. The silver-haired simpatico of Dian's fixed a pitcher of martinis, and she and the gorilla lady had a real rapport as they drank and chatted about past embassy officials and Kigali social life.

"And you know, that's my avocado tree out back," Dorothy complained, "and I'm constantly having to chase people out of it before I can even get the first ripe one."

Dian sat on the floor, legs curled to one side, as she had at Rick Kramer's house and cleared her throat saying, "Ahem . . . ahem . . . really and truly Dorothy," the more she drank. The more Dian drank the more she cleared her throat. The telltale "ahem . . . ahem," would ultimately become all too familiar to me. Dorothy also offered martinis to Stuart, Carolyn, and me. So this is a martini, I thought, and my head swam as I tried to finish mine.

On our last day in Kigali, the four of us climbed back into the Volkswagen with Dian at the wheel. It was a quick ride to a group of shops near the open market. We entered one that looked like an old-fashioned general store, and the young Arab shop owner at the counter recognized Dian and greeted her heartily.

"Mademoiselle, bonjour!" he exclaimed.

Dian acted equally pleased to see him and assumed a coy girlishness as she asked for something in French. With a knowing chuckle, he immediately began removing bottles of Johnnie Walker Red Label Scotch from a shelf and placing them in a cardboard box: three . . . six . . . nine—twelve. Dian also asked for cigarettes, and her friendly salesman happily bagged several cartons for her. Then we were ready for Karisoke.

THREE

THROUGH THE MILLE COLLINES

O n January 19, Carolyn and I loaded our belongings into Dian
Fossey's Volkswagen bus. With Stuart in the passenger seat
next to Dian at the wheel, we drove away on the winding,
dusty dirt road leading to our ultimate destination in the Parc National
des Volcans.

The weather was warm and sunny, and driving out of Kigali on its
western side, we began to pass a long line of Rwandan soldiers dressed
in athletic shorts and T-shirts. They were jogging two by two toward us
up the hill that wound its way into town on the northwestern side. As
they passed, Dian hung her head out her window, and with her left arm
gesturing like a conductor, she started chanting in her deepest voice,
"hep, hep, hep, hep." At first stunned, the soldiers began to smile and

echo her with their own chorus of, *"hep, hep, hep, hep . . ."* until the entire unit was repeating her chant in loud unison. This sudden display of playfulness from Dian made us laugh and put our group at ease as Kigali disappeared behind a wide curve around a hill in the road behind us.

The stucco buildings on the outskirts of town soon gave way to the rich farmland of the Rwandan countryside, dotted with humble thatched mud-and-dung huts that marked individual family farm plots called *shambas*. Subdivision with each successive generation had parceled the land into infinite ever-shrinking, high-density homesteads. The road climbed and twisted through what European visitors had nicknamed the *Milles Collines*—Land of a Thousand Hills. Everywhere were people on the move. I recalled reading that Rwanda was one of the most densely populated countries in the world and had over four hundred people per square mile. Back home, the only house I could see from my bedroom window stood silent and vacant, a mile away across a wide cow pasture. Here, the scene in every direction was like a summer holiday weekend in a city park.

There was no point along the road from Kigali that we lost sight of people, men and women with close-cropped hair and round faces, ebony-black from life outdoors. They worked the fields digging potatoes from the black volcanic soil, or picking tea leaves from the flat groomed tops of bright green camellia shrubs. Children ran and played, or worked alongside adults. People stood on the sides of the road, watching us go by. They walked along the roads continuously, traveling toward the next small village or away from the last. They carried anything on the tops of their heads: clusters of bananas, bundles of sticks for fuel. Heavy-looking baskets were balanced with apparent ease. Rows of blue-uniformed schoolchildren carried their schoolbooks this way. I even saw a little girl walking from a small storefront with a single bar of gleaming white soap perched casually atop her head.

The farther we got from Kigali, the more hilly the landscape became. It was a little like driving from my home state of Virginia into the rugged mountains of neighboring West Virginia. In Rwanda, however, the hills were nearly treeless, with cultivation replacing the forests all the way to the tops of their rounded peaks. The road wound around the steep side of each hill, and the cone-shaped volcanic hills grew ever higher. As we got closer to the Virunga Volcano region, patches of blue sky became eclipsed by an endless gray cloud cover, and our conversation turned to questions about gorillas. Our ignorance was met with gruff condescension from Dian. In fact, the farther we drove along the twisting road through Rwanda's Land of a Thousand Hills, away from the warmth and sunshine of the lowlands, and into the gray, foreboding, overcast sky of the uplands surrounding the Virunga Volcanoes, the more stormy and irascible Dian became, as if reverting to a wildness within herself.

"What do gorillas do when it rains?" Carolyn asked, as a light shower spattered the windshield. "Do they put big leaves over their heads?"

"*Eht mwah, eht mwaaah*!" Dian growled with obvious disdain.

Carolyn blushed with a sheepish grin as Stuart turned around in his seat and chimed in diplomatically with an explanation.

"The gorillas just huddle together in a group," he said, "and wait for the rain to pass."

I felt Carolyn's embarrassment, but was a little relieved to have Dian's irritation not directed at me for a change. I felt a little less singled out in that moment. *Which way would Carolyn fall, I wondered? On the side of disfavor like myself . . . or would she remain in good standing?*

Here was Stuart, outspoken, confident and accepted by Dian. Here too was Carolyn, quiet, yielding, also seemingly accepted by Dian. *Where was I in this little array of personalities, and how did I need to behave?* None of my efforts to connect with her were working. A little while later we were out of the switchback roads and traveling along a stretch of road flanked by banana trees upslope and down.

"Where do banana trees come from?" Dian asked suddenly, with an unexpected upbeat tone, as if trying to break the iciness she had created. No one answered right away, surprised by the question.

"Where do they come from?" she asked again, looking at Stuart with a playful tilt to her head. I like trivia, so as our group pondered, I eventually mustered up some courage and offered my little-known fact hoping to make a favorable impression.

"Bananas do have seeds." I said, with conviction.

Stuart and Carolyn looked toward Dian.

"When you bite a banana you can see tiny dark specks in the cross section," I elaborated, recalling my own wonderment at having learned this myself.

"*Eht mwaaah . . .*" Dian growled in her gorilla vocalization of annoyance, while slumping back into her seat. My enthusiasm faltered, so I offered another explanation.

"Shoots also grow out from the base of big banana trees." I had witnessed this in my own observation of banana trees. "They probably just dig those up and transplant them to make more trees."

"Sheeeit," Dian muttered with a hint of a Southern drawl. This was not going over as expected for either of us, and I realized, Dian was not looking for some correct answer from a know-it-all, but rather just a means of stimulating puzzlement and amusing conversation. I had spoiled her fun, and we were back into our quiet, chilly drive through the Land of a Thousand Hills. It was clear that I annoyed Dian, and the silent contempt was embarrassing and painful.

In the silence, Dian steered the old VW bus onward, the road twisting and turning, sometimes up, sometimes down, wrapping around one hillside after another in a series of switchbacks. After rounding one of these tight downward curves, Dian slowed to a near halt before a throng of people. The milling group directed their attention at some commotion ahead. As Dian slowly advanced the automobile, she cursed under her breath.

"Shit *merde!*"

"What is it?" we asked, craning our necks to see out the windshield.

"*Sumu,*" Dian said.

"What's *sumu*?"

Dian did not offer an explanation, so Stuart chimed in.

"Black magic," he said, shifting in his seat to face Carolyn and me. "It's a common practice in Rwanda."

"What do you mean?" I asked.

Dian muttered more expletives, as she maneuvered the vehicle through the crowd, almost nudging people out of the way with the bumper, steering along the shoulder of the road by a steep drop-off, "Bloody mother-fucking wogs!"

As we lurched by, we could see a man sitting in the middle of the road with his legs splayed outward. He was behaving erratically. With his arms flailing and eyes rolled back in his head, he appeared as if in some sort of a trance. For all I knew, he could've been having a seizure. Although we were curious, Dian did not offer an explanation. I wanted to prod her for details, but knew better by then. I decided that she may not have known what was going on outside our vehicle and she chose silence and mystique over a confession of ignorance. In any case, Dian's heightened irritation at this cast an eerie pall over the rest of the trip.

The small town of Ruhengeri was the last outpost of Rwandan convenience before traveling on to Karisoke. There, we would stock up on supplies before continuing on the last leg of our journey to the base of Mount Visoke. This little village was not much different from Kigali in general appearance, except it was much smaller and all the roads were dirt or mud. There were the same pale, stuccoed concrete storefronts that might be in any poor country. The higher altitude at seven thousand feet was chilly and damp, and the gray sky hung low above our heads.

The center of town was dominated by a large open square of ground, containing the marketplace. Active and odorous, it rang with the clamor and chatter of hundreds of vendors and patrons. They came streaming in on the roads from north and south to buy and sell the goods stacked on their heads on what Dian told us was the town's big market day.

We climbed out of the VW to the amusement of the locals who gathered around eyeing us with curious interest. Although European expatriates lived in town, many of the market merchants and patrons came from far afield and rarely saw whites, or *wazungu* as we were locally called, with the singular form being *mzungu*. I saw the same bafflement on Carolyn's face that I felt, not knowing what we were supposed to take to camp. Neither of us dared to query Dian who led Stuart off in another direction to look for kerosene, or paraffin as the locals called it.

While Carolyn walked down one aisle of tables, I perused another. The smell of mud and rotten produce dominated while African hucksters beckoned me from right and left to their wares. As I worked my way into the market, and paused to look at a table covered with onions, potatoes, and cabbages, I heard a woman behind me say the words *"Yosu Kristo"* in her Kinyarwanda banter. I turned to see her in a group of women all staring at me. I realized with my new beard, and blond hair covering my ears, I must have looked like some missionary textbook Jesus to them.

At other tables, there were all sorts of basic foods and their accompanying unrefrigerated smells. There were tropical fruits and vegetables of many types: pineapples, avocados, oranges, tomatoes, yams . . . but I didn't know by what means I would be able to prepare meals. I had assumed dining would be a sort of communal effort at Karisoke, and without any information to the contrary I was clueless as to how to grocery shop for survival there, or for how long such supplies would need to last, or be stored. I bought a bunch of tiny five-inch bananas and a large loaf of bread, while no guidance came from our leader. As I was looking at a vendor's stand that included small brown chicken eggs bundled precariously in pieces of plastic bags, Dian passed by, and I sought some guidance.

"Should I get some eggs?" I asked my leader.

"Get eggs!" she barked.

"But, do you think they'll survive the climb up to . . . ?"

"Get eggs!" she repeated, with a little more annoyance in her voice, before moving on.

Dian was in an obvious hurry, so I rushed through this last errand before climbing back into the VW bus for our final leg to the Parc des Volcans. Several square five-gallon clear plastic jugs of paraffin sloshed amid the seats of the van, and I had bananas, bread, a half-dozen fragile eggs and the cheese I had bought in Kigali to live on until I could somehow buy groceries again.

As we drove west from Ruhengeri, I could see the ancient volcanoes that would soon be our home. A last bastion of the mountain gorilla's struggle to survive, they grew ever larger and dramatic as we approached. To the north, along the border of Uganda, stood a row of three of these extinct volcanoes. On the far left of this trio, westward, stood the one called Mount Sabinio with its top ridge of jagged teeth reaching for the sky. On the extreme right, eastward, stood the cone-shaped Mount Muhavura. Between these two, stood the smaller Gahinga, with a crater that gave it a flat-topped appearance. The country of Uganda rolled down the opposite far side of these mountains, out of view from where we traveled.

Directly ahead loomed the two volcanoes, Karisimbi and Visoke, that flanked the research center and from which Dian had derived the name "Kari-soke." Perching half in Rwanda and half in Zaire, Mount Visoke appeared to have a broad flat top, from our perspective below it. The large deep crater at its summit gave it this appearance when viewed from below. I longed to see the placid hidden lake at the top of this mountain that I had read about in George Schaller's book on mountain gorillas.

The tallest Virunga volcano, Mount Karisimbi, soars to nearly fifteen thousand feet, and is one of Africa's highest peaks. From our vantage point, its voluminous girth obscured a sixth volcano, Mount Mikeno, which lay just behind it in the country of Zaire. I would see it soon.

Plump Karisimbi has a beautiful smooth conical shape, and I noticed the striations of vegetation types and altitudinal zones as my eyes traveled up its slope. At the lower elevations, the greenery was lush and dense. This yielded to shorter vegetation and open meadow above the forest zone, before ending with an intriguing distinct black peak at the summit, its lava cone.

While I envisioned the world's last remaining mountain gorillas roaming through this lush landscape, gray clouds slowly enveloped the mountain peaks, obscuring our view. As we continued our ascending approach, the cultivated fields at the base of the mountains appeared dusted with snow, but approaching closer, we could see the farms were really covered with tiny daisy-like flowers.

"What's that flower they're growing?" Carolyn asked.

"That's pyrethrum," Stuart said, "a type of chrysanthemum they get the insecticide pyrethrin from." Again, he was well informed.

"They're pretty." Carolyn responded.

"*Eht mwah* . . ." Dian growled.

I later learned that in 1969, two years after Dian had set up her study site in Rwanda, nearly forty percent of the mountain gorillas' habitat in the Parc des Volcans was deforested for cultivation of this cash crop. Ironically, synthetic pyrethrins had largely replaced the need for the flower. They were still being grown, Stuart explained, because they were considered a prestigious export from this humble little country. President Habyarimana himself had reportedly decreed that people in that area must grow a certain percentage of the plant in order to occupy and cultivate the newly available precious land. It was said that over time the locals had come to resent this, because crops like beans and potatoes were more useful and profitable. But the farmers complied and the cool climate and rich volcanic soil provided ideal growing conditions for the tiny white flowers.

"What are the yellow flowers I've seen in the pictures of gorillas in *National Geographic*?" Carolyn asked.

Dian did not respond.

"Yellow flowers?" Stuart said, shifting around in his seat, to show interest.

"Yeah, they're in the background in the pictures."

"I don't know," Stuart said, looking toward Dian, "Do you know what they are, Dian?"

"There's different kinds of flowers," Dian said curtly as she focused her attention on the rough road ahead.

As we neared the base of Mount Visoke, the road grew rockier and more difficult to traverse. It took on more the look of a dry creek bed, rocks and all, than an actual road. The VW lurched on the uneven surface, and we jarred against the inside of the kombi and each other as it rocked in every direction over the bumps. Up ahead we could clearly see where the farmland ended and the Parc des Volcans began. Tilled soil abruptly gave way to thick wild forest in a line along the base of the volcanoes directly ahead. The once-even border of the park now had deep cuts where the farmlands were encroaching even deeper into the forest. The gorillas and their homeland were being traded for insecticide.

Our arrival had a distinct effect on the locals. In the last half-mile leading up to the park border, people dropped their hoes and shovels and ran from the fields toward the road on which we traveled. The Hutu families pointed at Dian and waved heartily, shouting *"Mademoiselli, Mademoiselli,"* followed by the typical Kinyarwanda greeting, *"Muraho!"* They shouted and began to follow us, in a friendly riot, as we bounced along. We could hear thumps as some boys daringly reached out and tapped the sides of the van. Dian's passing through was obviously an exciting novelty to the Rwandan country folk, and a cargo of new white people who would disappear into the forest with the gorillas must have fueled their imaginations. Dian smiled, then beamed and began waving enthusiastically in all directions like a homecoming queen on parade. I saw how her mood could shift without warning, and certainly felt more at ease with her upbeat demeanor.

The VW bounced to a halt as the road ended abruptly at the foot of Mount Visoke. A wall of cool green forest shot up toward the sky before us. Dian turned the engine off and became dour again as a swarm of locals crowded our vehicle in a babble of Kinyarwanda. She peered through her window into the cluster of ragged and barefoot men. "Shit *merde*! Goddammit!" Dian pushed her door open shouting, "*Oya! Oya! Oya!*" . . . the Rwandan word for *no*.

The mass retreated slightly and one man, wearing shoes and better dressed than the rest, emerged. He was also taller than most, and thinner without the robust rounded facial features typical of the rest in the throng. He wore a dark wool blazer. The others struggled to gain proximity to him, speaking and gesturing emphatically in a bustle of waving arms and chattering mouths. By comparison, they were dressed in tattered clothes and rags. Despite a certain frailty to the man at the center, and jaundice in his eyes, there was an air of arrogance and self-importance in his expression. Dian's tensions eased at the sight of him.

"That's Gwehandegaza," Stuart explained in a low voice to Carolyn and me. "He's the main porter." Dian struggled impatiently with a mixture of Swahili and French as she spoke to him. The group of men were fighting to be used as porters for our climb; for one hundred francs, or the equivalent of a dollar, each would carry as much as they could up the mountain for us. Gwehandegaza would cast their fates, sorting out those who would have this dubious privilege.

The mountain's swirling air engulfed us in a chilly dampness as we opened the door of the van and climbed out. I gazed up at the forest before us and saw heavy dark clouds rushing in overhead, churning around the top of Mount Visoke and engulfing it like a flood. Colder air poured down its slopes as Dian looked up at the volcano and cursed under her breath, "Shit motherfuckit!" The foreboding weather obviously heightened her irritability.

Gwehandegaza quickly chose several men to be our porters, grabbing them by sleeves and arms, and pushing them to the front of the mass. To my utter astonishment, they hoisted Dian's numerous sloshing five-gallon paraffin containers deftly onto their heads. Dian ordered us to put on our rain gear as we hurried to gather our things. I began to collect my belongings out of the back of the vehicle and searched for my parcel of eggs, but couldn't find it. Each of us donned our rain jackets, then stumbled to tug on our rain pants over our boots. In the chaos, it felt like it was everyone for themselves, and I decided the most efficient approach would be to carry my own weight, not expecting others to look after my things. Besides, turning my belongings over to these new strangers felt a little risky to me. I also thought it was more efficient to stay out of everyone's way, especially Dian's, but she chided me when she saw me pick up my bags.

"*Goddamn it*, get some of these things!" she barked, pointing to an assortment of groceries and supplies that she had purchased at the market in Ruhengeri. I donned my backpack, as a porter swept up my suitcase onto his head.

Stuart began pulling camp items onto his own personal load, and Carolyn followed suit. Soon the three of us were gathering anything and everything, stumbling over each other in an unorganized mass with the porters.

At the base of Mount Visoke, we were at eight thousand feet. Loaded down, we would be climbing to ten thousand, a total of two thousand feet up. The looming clouds appeared close enough to touch, and rapidly churning as if boiling downward. While Mount Visoke disappeared into the growing black cloudbank, I realized that our group, wearing rubber rain gear, would be walking up into this inverted cauldron of a sky in which the mountains were now immersed.

The stony road ended at the very base of the mountain slope where someone had erected a large steel rondavel by the forest's edge. It looked more like a temporary storage setup than a home. Just shy of this, Fossey's entourage of porters disappeared up a muddy trail through thick undergrowth beneath the canopy of trees. In a single file of skilled porters and naïve students, we left the heavily populated farmlands behind us, and, stepping into the realm of the mountain gorilla, we began our ascent into a forest in the clouds.

FOUR

KARISOKE WELCOME

*I saw the inconceivable mystery of a soul that knew no restraint,
no faith, and no fear, yet struggling blindly with itself.*
—Joseph Conrad, *Heart of Darkness*

It was the beginning of the long rainy season, and recent down-pours had made the Porter Trail thick with mud. The path quickly became steep as Dian, Stuart, Carolyn, and I mingled with the remaining porters and dispersed into single file, losing sight of each other. Dian trailed behind, along the narrow path that cut through the dense undergrowth. Eons of sporadic forest visitors, and erosion, had worn this trail to a sort of trench, here and there, deep and dark beneath the tangled canopy of green. Soon, we entered a sort-of tunnel, but open at the top, with walls of ancient lava covered in moss. As we emerged, I was awed by the porters upslope from me, deftly balancing Dian's large sloshing vessels of paraffin atop their heads while chattering away in Kinyarwanda. The image of their bare feet sucking out of the cold mud as they climbed burned into my mind's eye as I quickly became winded bearing my own cargo in the thin air.

Not far up the trail, I had to stop to catch my breath. To my left, I could see an endless row of tiny farm plots and mud huts stretching below and beyond, away from the parklands, where stands of bamboo, *Arundinaria alpina*, spread along the boundary, interspersed with tall vernonias, a tree form of *Vernonia calvoana*, where parkland gave way to cultivated soil. In contrast, through a clearing just beneath me, I noticed a tidy little camp harboring two dapper orange-red dome tents trimmed with bright blue pole sleeves, all glowing in sharp contrast to the neighboring tilled brown fields and thatched mud dwellings. A pair of folding director's chairs stood by an extinguished campfire in a ring of black stones. I paused for a moment, staring at this neat little camp, and wondered who the occupants could be.

A sudden downdraft of cold mist soon obscured the view and snapped my attention back to the trail ahead. I resumed my hike into the clouds in a gust of wind, and within a few more steps of climbing, the sky released its own burden, pelting our long caravan of travelers with a deafening rumble of rain. I paused to don my hood and button up, but the porters, exposed in only their cotton rags, didn't miss a beat. I struggled to keep up with them, as we emerged from the bamboo zone into an open forest of robust, spreading hagenia trees, *Hagenia abyssinica*, and wispy hypericums, *Hypericum lanceolatum*—a tree form of Saint John's wort.

In the torrents, rivulets of water began flowing down the trail, and we were soon trudging along in what became a steep creek bed of mud and tumbling water. And then the sound, already deafening, shifted to a roar, drowning out even the loudest of the men's voices ahead. White pebbles the size of marbles bounced and tumbled off of everything, settling into the lowest places at the center of our deep and narrow path. *Hail at the equator?!* My heart pounded as I let a couple more porters pass me, my legs slowing to a monotonous rhythmic pace, willing each step. The agile porters, with their burdens ably managed, moved rapidly upward and out of sight. Even those with the heavy, sloshing paraffin containers slipped deftly around me. I marveled at their bare feet tromping onward through the accumulating layer of ice pebbles in the cold sucking mud. Hail rattled against my plastic rain hood and the forest's thick leaf fronds. The icy pebbles quickly accumulated . . . two, three, four inches deep. I only had the energy to stare zombie-like at my feet while willing myself onward and upward through the storm, the noise and sensation too intense to feel the throb of my own heartbeat.

The downpour ended as suddenly as it had begun, and I was jarred out of my trance when almost stepping on what appeared to be a snake. The creature, fat and flesh-colored, lolled as if dazed by the storm, on a bare bump of the trail where the hailstones had rolled away. On closer examination, I recognized it as some type of earthworm—but over twelve inches long and an inch wide, more like a foot-long hot dog come to life! Several porters had stopped to watch when I reached a finger toward its long pink body. One of the men shouted at me. I drew back shrugging my shoulders at the startled men in an effort to show my confusion at their alarm. *Did they think this creature was dangerous?* In a moment, my curiosity regained its composure and I picked up a stick to poke the giant earthworm. At that, the worm writhed, squirting fine jets of milky fluid in all directions from the sides of its body. I jumped backward as my onlookers nearly toppled each other in their efforts to flee. I later learned that this critter was in fact one of the world's few species of giant earthworms. Neither toxic nor otherwise dangerous, the milky fluid is actually a lubricant that the animal uses to facilitate movement through its underground tunnels. Like earthworms and night crawlers in North America, this tropical counterpart surfaces when heavy precipitation floods its subterranean lairs.

Our climbing continued upward another half hour until the mucky trail became wider and grassy, leveling off and opening to a small meadow—the halfway mark, I would learn. Here the porters dropped their gear and sat on the ground, resting on clean patches of grass amid drifts of slushy hail already melting away around us. The men smiled as I dropped to my knees among them and gasped for the thin air in a disheveled heap of my own cargo.

The sky began to clear while I regained a more normal breathing pattern and heart rate. A couple of porters with the paraffin containers, in preparation to resume our hike, ripped up handfuls of long grass and rolled them into large, thick wreaths. These, they refined with careful winding of loose ends into neat, tight rings before placing them on their heads—cushions to stabilize their burdens. I watched their proficient skill with a little awe. Out of curiosity, and partially for their amusement, I grabbed some grass and tried to do the same. The porters laughed as my sloppy construction fell apart on my head and shoulders.

The second half of the climb felt as arduous as the first, as the trail resumed its slant, but the sun was out and hastened the melting of drifts of hail. My sweat, stranded inside my rubber rain gear, made me go from feeling sauna-hot one moment to being clammy-cold when I stopped to catch my breath. As the trail broadened into clearings and leveled off, I caught up with Carolyn, standing at rest near a small boggy clearing.

"Isn't it beautiful?" She asked, turning to face me, wet hair strands plastered to her flushed cheeks. Then I saw what she meant—behind her in the distance soared the towering steep rocky peak of Mount Mikeno, now visible in the clear rain-washed air. It stood entirely in Zaire, and I was dazzled by its sight. Its jagged monolith of bare dark gray volcanic rock jutted boldly upward over fourteen thousand feet, lit dramatically by the low-angled sun. Steam wafted from the stony pinnacles, tearing loose to drift away as small clouds. I knew from what I had read back home that Carl Akeley, the American naturalist, had his camp at the base of this mountain. I paused to take a picture of the dramatic volcano before continuing farther into camp.

A long green corrugated metal cabin on the right of the trail was the first building I passed coming into Dian Fossey's remote compound, Karisoke Research Center. A large glossy white-necked raven, *Corvus albicollis*, eyed my approach from the roof's apex, before emitting a deep throaty croak from its thick arched beak and flapping upward into the branches of a tall hagenia. Through the cabin's windows, I could see it was empty.

Traveling a hundred yards farther up the trail, I found a similar building on the left, just up from a gurgling streambed that cut through camp and was then engorged with water from the rain and melting hail. A square of the same green metal, supported by cut saplings, formed a crude entry portico to this cabin. Behind and beyond in the distance, cone-shaped Mount Karisimbi gleamed in the low-angled sunlight; higher even than Europe's Matterhorn, it is the tallest of the Virungas and one of Africa's tallest peaks. This mountain's pointed cap of volcanic cinders had been lava-black on our approach from below, but just then gleamed white with a crown of shining hailstones at its frosty summit. I would learn that *karisimbi* was a Rwandan word for the tiny cowry shells used for barter and adornment throughout Africa. Although these marine snail shells came from the coast, the lowlanders who rarely encountered hail created the myth that the white cap that appeared on Karisimbi after a storm was actually a layer of the cowry shells. The view was fleeting and Mount Karisimbi's gleaming white crown soon disappeared in a wash of mist.

"This one's ours," Stuart said to me as he emerged from the far end of the cabin, "Carolyn, yours is up ahead." Stuart showed me to the door of my half of our "duplex" and then accompanied Carolyn up the path. "Drop your things off and c'mon up this way to Dian's when you're done!" he shouted back to me.

Inside, I let my luggage slide to the floor and gazed around my new home. The air inside was colder than out, and it smelled like damp straw with the walls and floor covered with dun-colored woven grass matting. A large wooden office desk with chair and a cot-like narrow bed furnished the single room that measured about ten by twelve feet. A large pale green map of the Virungas, with odd place names labeled and the gorilla study range outlined in black, was pinned to the grass wall by the desk. A small, crude iron barrel stove stood by the door attached to a stovepipe that vented through the roof, and a long wood shelf ran under a window along the end wall, its right end serving as the bed's nightstand. A few wine bottles were grouped on this shelf, filled with a tea-colored liquid—water from the camp stream, boiled and delivered for drinking, I would soon learn. Outside the window, a pair of black-headed waxbills, *Estrilda atricapilla*, hopped in the thick grasses, plucking seeds here and there, before flitting upward with a flash of their bright red rumps.

My curiosity was next drawn back inside to a mysterious boarded-up section of the back wall under a row of cabinets. Here, someone had blocked a low two-by-two-foot opening to the outside, too small for practical human passage. Looking out a window on this wall, I could see a large cage made of wood and welded wire attached to the cabin where this opening had been. From the look of it, I was right to surmise that Dian's orphaned gorillas, made popular in a her previous *National Geographic* article, had once lived in this half of the cabin, granted indoor and outdoor access via the contrived pet portal. I was in Coco's and Pucker's house.

A rectangular gap in the wall's grass matting revealed the outline of a human-sized door in the cabin's shared inner dividing wall. Moved by my curiosity, I pulled at the wood toggle of a string pull, and opened the door into Stuart's half of our hut. The warm air inside this space felt welcoming after the ice storm. My new coworker's space matched mine in size and configuration, but was fully equipped with cooking utensils, a lantern, a small kerosene cookstove, and a typewriter. It was a home. Stuart's clothing and books, stacked along a shelf, with the fire flickering in his iron stove gave it a lived-in feel. Someone had even placed bright orange flowers in a jar on the shelf under his window, a gift from Dian, I surmised. In the scene of equipment and accoutrements, I saw the look of certain favor bestowed on Stuart.

My curiosity satisfied, I withdrew back into my own Spartan space. Outside my window, a final throng of porters accompanied Dian, bringing up the rear of our assemblage, and heading farther up the Porter Trail. I took a few moments to peel off my rain gear and organize my bags before heading out the door and up the path where Stuart, Carolyn, and Dian had already gone. The aromas of wood smoke and wet dirt permeated the damp, cool air, with another pungent smell— just beyond our cabin, a green metal outhouse stood, that would be Stuart's and my shared facility. Looking back to the left, toward the camp creek, I noticed four wood posts supporting a small metal roof over an eight-by-eight-foot dugout in the ground. Benches lined the excavation's interior around a smoldering fire pit in the center. A hand-hewn picnic table with its own benches stood nearby. All around this area, the grass was worn away to bare dirt by the foot traffic of many boot prints.

Turning right onto the camp's main trail I continued on past a large green metal shed, open at both ends. Inside, white enamel wash pans sat atop a workbench spanning the interior. Dingy dish towels and assorted rags hung from a clothesline strung over the dirt floor. A gray squirrel, looking similar to the common gray squirrels of home, but slightly smaller and flattened in appearance, bounded along the bare ground and scurried up the incline of a moss-covered hagenia. I would later learn this was the Ruwenzori sun squirrel, *Heliosciurus ruwenzorii*, endemic to these high montane forests.

Heading into the center of camp, the trail formed a narrow ribbon of wet black soil, worn down in the undergrowth, compressed by boot prints intermingling with the cloven hoofprints of forest buffaloes,

Syncerus caffer, who kept the path's edges mowed by their nocturnal grazing. Here and there, the moist air hinted of manure.

Not far up the trail, a sharp, raspy whistle shrieked from a stand of tall thistles on my right, and a small reddish-brown antelope sprang out and away from me, leaping and diving into a thicket toward the forest edge; this was the black-fronted duiker, *Cephalophus nigrifrons*, I'd read about. I only caught fleeting glimpses of the delicate creature's dark-tufted forehead and tiny black horns before it vanished. This disturbance, in turn, triggered another sound from farther beyond, the repeated single bark of dog, which struck me as so out of place here. From the direction of the noise, in a streak of golden brown, a bushbuck, *Tragelaphus scriptus*, bounded in repeated leaps and thuds over the undergrowth to just inside the forest tree line. As he fled, the large antelope raised its tail like a flag, flashing its snow-white rump just like the white-tailed deer I was so familiar with from home. Feeling safe among the trees, the bushbuck stared back at me, twitching his tail with agitation, and giving me a good look at his elegant horns, spiraling upward from his crown. His sides were patterned with an odd arrangement of white stripes and dots among the golden brown, as if designed with whimsy by a postmodernist painter. Witnessing these forest denizens firsthand only added to the enchantment of this equatorial montane habitat.

A hundred yards farther up the trail another metal cabin flanked the path. Situated on a slight rise, stone steps lead to its front door, giving it a quaint cottage appearance; its occupancy revealed by a waft of smoke from its stovepipe chimney.

I continued on through an open understory another hundred yards, where the last cabin stood. The largest of all, at thirty by fifty feet long, and made of the same green-painted corrugated metal, this one was a house compared to the others. Five times the size of the rest, it had been the last in the series of Dian's constructions, and was her current home.

Approaching it, I noticed the stony path split. A narrower path led up to what looked like a back door, while the other continued around the cabin to the left. Here a large bird flapped heavily upward into a small tree. It was a small red rooster, joining a couple of smaller red hens already perched there. The trio teetered a moment, balancing themselves to settle in for the night on a high branch. I followed the wider path around to a grassy clearing on the other side. There, I was greeted by Judy Chidester, the American Embassy's communications officer who had lent us her home back in Kigali. In a dark red jacket hanging open, cheerful Judy was obviously enjoying the brisk mountain air as she introduced me to her friend Liza, from the Swiss Embassy's Kigali office. Liza, petite, thin and waifish under a pageboy crop of strawberry blond, donned a thick, white wool cardigan against the chill. Her pallor contrasted sharply with Judy's florid cheeks, but she was equally jovial, and I noted her pleasant French-Swiss accent.

"And this is Cindy." Liza said, as a large golden-brown dog with a smooth coat approached us wagging her stumpy cropped tail. I reached to pet this friendly pooch while she sniffed my boot and legs.

"She's just the sweetest dog," Judy added. "And to think Dian confiscated her from poachers."

A bushel-sized black ball of fur sat a few feet away on the ground in the middle of a pile of greens that looked like they were plucked from the forest. The fur ball lifted its head, and the plaintive face of a baby gorilla stared into my eyes. Overwhelmed by its childlike expression, I moved closer, and hovered above the small round simian, staring back into her jewel-like dark brown eyes—my first mountain gorilla, *Gorilla berengei berengei*, in the flesh. Her bare face shone like polished leather, convoluted with folds and wrinkles radiating from the space between her eyes, along her broad flat nose, and beyond her flared nostrils. She turned away, and with her leathery fingers, picked up a handful of greens and brought it to her mouth. Then, as if in a greeting of her own, she ambled to my feet. *Hmm, hmmm . . .* a soft low purring voice rumbled from her.

"Can I pick her up?" I heard myself ask.

"Yeah, sure, she'd love it," Judy said, chuckling.

I leaned over, intuitively grabbing the baby by its underarms and lifting her like a child. She immediately wrapped her warm furry arms around my shoulders; her legs grasped around my waist. I could feel the solidness of her body in the heft of her weight, and as I put my arms around her for support, I was struck by the hard, broad bones of her hairy back; by contrast her belly was soft and pudgy. Again emitting the low purring rumble, she burped and her herbal breath filled my nostrils.

"We've been calling her Charlie," Judy said with a laugh. "Dian originally thought she was a boy."

As little Charlie resumed nibbling on her fistful of green leaves, completely at home in my arms, I noticed I was standing near the edge of a plot filled with little placards on wood posts. There were names printed on them: *Uncle Bert, Lee, Flossie, Kweli, Digit* . . . It was a gorilla graveyard outside the high narrow windows on this western side of Dian's cabin.

When little Charlie finished her handful of browse, she climbed from my arms to the ground to return to her mound of leafy gorilla foods. Loud coughing and shouting from Dian over the din of porter's chatter from the opposite side of the house sounded Dian's arrival up the mountain, and my gut tightened. With the sound of Dian's voice, a high tree branch shook from above and beyond the cabin, and a monkey appeared suddenly from the other side of the cabin's roof peak. It bounded noisily over the corrugated metal roof, chattering and muttering with abrupt clicks and chirps, its slender tail floating above and behind. It was a blue monkey, *Cercopithecus mitis*, named for its blue-gray coat. The quick-moving simian glared warily at each of us with glowing amber eyes as she scampered down onto the cabin's front door overhang.

"And *that* is Kima," Judy said, chuckling again. "She's Dian's pet." While Kima's gaze darted furtively from me to the cabin's entryway, Dian drew the door open from inside. As if this was their cue, Judy and Liza moved toward Dian's doorway too. From there, they coaxed the baby to enter the cabin. Dian crouched just inside, still coughing, and beckoned to the baby gorilla with a slice of fresh pineapple she had bought at the Ruhengeri market. Little Charlie followed her care-givers and snatched the fruit greedily from her surrogate mother's hand, before scrambling farther inside to more treats laid out on the grass mat floor. Dian pulled the door closed behind her, leaving me and Kima outside. The monkey leaned over the eave chirping franti-cally, glaring toward the door then at me as if in supreme indignation.

"Hey Kima . . . !" I called, approaching the expressive little being with my hand outstretched. At this, the monkey turned away, chirping sharply, long tail arched tersely above, before bounding back over the rooftop and leaping into a tree on the cabin's other side. Karisoke, at its high altitude, was not the normal habitat for a blue monkey; I would learn that Dian had brought this pet to camp.

Behind the gorilla graveyard, from where I stood facing northwest, the forested slope of Mount Visoke rose steeply upward from the level plain of the meadow area where I stood to its pinnacle at over twelve thousand feet. In the fading light, the volcano disappeared in the cloud cover that was again wafting in from the far side in Zaire. Massive and spreading hagenias dotted the level landscape of thick undergrowth and open grassy places in the flat saddle area between Visoke and Karisimbi. It looked like everything that grew on the ground also grew up the leaning trunks and heavy branches of these great trees. Thick cushions of green mosses and long dripping hanks of wispy gray *usnea* lichens hung from the limbs, making the trees resemble the live oaks of my American southland, draped in Spanish moss and ferns.

The sun had disappeared behind Mount Visoke, and cold drifts of mist began moving through this open forest like ghosts of giant gorillas, past the massive gnarled tree trunks and through the markers of the gorilla graveyard—cold billows of fog to those of us at Karisoke, but clouds to the people in the farmlands below looking up at these enigmatic sleeping volcanoes. Scarcely varying its schedule near the equator, the sun rises around six in the morning and sets around six each night. After twelve hours of day, twelve hours of equatorial night was settling in. My happiness about being in the forests of the mountain gorillas was tainted by the incomprehensible and irascible behavior of Dian that I had witnessed until this moment. I could not even imagine what was in store.

No one invited me inside from where the laughter and excited voices then drifted, but I shook off thoughts of the last few days and returned to the far side of Dian's cabin pondering what I should do next. Soon, two Rwandan teens appeared up the trail carrying heavy buckets of water. As they approached the back entrance I stepped in front of them to pull open the door. With heads down, the two young men lugged their burdens inside as a man's voice called out to me.

"Hey! C'mon in!"

I followed the young workers into a dark kitchen where a kerosene lantern's weak pulsing flare provided the only light. The smells of cooking permeated the small dark room. In the dimness, a young man my age extended a hand from the shadows, introducing himself as Peter Veit.

"Welcome to Deepest Darkest," he said, with a friendly handshake. "Great place, huh?"

"Yeah, it's beautiful."

Peter, twenty-three, was the student from California I'd heard about, who had been at camp for a year already. He had written a letter to Ray Rhine to be copied to us newcomers about what to bring: waterproof paper, warm clothes, boots, etc. . . . . I had followed his advice. With close-cropped dark blond hair, he wore a khaki work shirt and a pair of grass-stained blue jeans, with sturdy Vasque hiking boots. A third Rwandan man in a blue plaid flannel shirt, older than the boys, moved from the kitchen sink, smiling from under a blue-and-white New York Yankees hat, the teens joined him at the counter.

"This is Kanyaragana," Peter said, turning back around to introduce us.

"*Jambo*," Kanyaragana said, his smile drawing into a wide grin beneath his cap.

"*Jambo sana*," I replied. Kanyaragana perked up at my Swahili response.

"*Unajua Kiswahili?*"

"Oh . . . uh . . ." I stammered in response.

"He wants to know if you speak Swahili." Peter said, in helpful intervention.

"Oh . . . no, but I picked up a few phrases on a study-abroad program in Kenya last year."

Peter translated for me as Kanyaragana nodded and sat at a small table against the wall in the dim light. There, he pumped an old lantern that failed to ignite. Peter spoke to him again in Swahili.

"*Iko kufa,*" Kanyaragana replied.

I laughed, recognizing the word *kufa* for *dead*.

"*Ist kuput,*" said Peter with a one syllable laugh, "Hah!" Peter told me his parents were German immigrants and he and his younger sister grew up with some German spoken in the household. As a kid, he even went to a German school in California. He came to Karisoke as a graduate from the University of California in Santa Cruz.

"Is that a refrigerator?" I asked, noticing a small rectangular appliance in the corner. "I didn't think there was electricity . . ."

"Yeah, it runs on kerosene."

"You're kidding!"

"No, it even has a little freezer box. I keep gorilla urine in there."

"Really? What for?"

"I'm doing a study on female cyclicity. I hope to get the hormone levels analyzed eventually. If they last that long. The thing shuts down sometimes, but it stays cold here at least."

"How do you get gorilla urine?"

"It's from the females. Sometimes I just hold a vial right up under one. If not, I'll catch it dripping off the leaves when they move on."

My curiosity led me beyond the kitchen, and Peter soon guided me out of the dark work space into the brightly lit dining area. A doorway in the wall on the right led to a dormitory of four twin beds for Dian's overnight guests. To the left, the dining area stepped down into a large communal living space. All the walls and floors were covered in the same woven grass matting as mine and Stuart's duplex. The working pressure lanterns glowed brightly, hissing from nail hangers and side tables, illuminating the space. Judy and Liza waved at me from the couch against the far wall, beneath a long window, where they chatted amiably, sipping wine they had brought from Kigali.

A fire smoldered in a stone fireplace flanked by goatskin chairs, and faded African print curtains hung beside large windows over a desk and chair against one wall. Where Peter and I stood there was a long dining table with chairs, and a sideboard against the far wall. Dozens of black-and-white close-up pictures of gorilla faces stared from the walls in this area, pinned and taped here and there like a collage of makeshift wallpaper. I had read about these in one of Dian's *National Geographic* articles and knew she used them to identify individual gorillas she had documented in Karisoke's study range.

Dian emerged from her bedroom doorway by the fireplace and crossed the living area. We all watched as she reached up to a wood-and-wire conduit that ran the length of the room. Above the door to the outside, she pulled at a wooden panel, sliding it open. Kima the monkey bounded into the suspended caging from the chilly night air, chirping and whistling as Liza and Judy chuckled at the sight. Dian then slammed the exterior door shut, preventing Kima from retreating again to the outside. Above the middle of the room, Kima stopped to glare at what was surely an unusual number of visitors in the room for her nightly routine. It was clear she didn't like strangers, and only Dian could approach her.

"Poor Kima, come inside . . ." Dian beckoned. Kima's eyes darted nervously from Dian to each of us from her suspended caging. "I know, *Napati* . . . too many people." Our gathering watched in beguiled anticipation, but instead of scampering farther along, the nervous monkey froze, glaring at each of us, before releasing the contents of her bladder in a stream of golden urine. Down through the wire it trickled, splattering into a puddle on the grass matting, before soaking in. A wave of groans wafted from everyone in the room, followed by laughter—except from Dian.

"Uh, that's really good." Dian grumbled facetiously. "*Ehhht mwaaah . . .* c'mon Kima!" Dian tried to coax her frisky monkey farther along the conduit that led through the wall into her bedroom. At Dian's ire, everyone stifled themselves. "Stop being a little . . . bitch. . . . Get in the bedroom! You know the goddamn routine." As Kima scampered a few steps closer to a chute leading into Dian's bedroom, Liza followed Judy toward the outside door.

"We're going out to get the weather data." Liza said, raising her quiet voice above the din, waving a small notebook as she slipped out the door behind Judy.

The Rwandan boy named Toni peeked his head out of the kitchen to get a look at the commotion and the beguiling monkey at the center of it all. The young man was mesmerized by the furry creature suspended above the room, and stared, mouth open in a bemused half-smile. Upon seeing young Toni idle, Dian snapped.

"Get back in that goddamn kitchen!" she shouted, lunging toward him. "Shit, goddammit, motherFUCKIT!" The young man couldn't understand his boss's English words, but he got the universal message of her hostile glare and loud voice, and retreated. "Bloody *wogs*!" Dian grumbled, stomping back into her bedroom. Only then did Kima decide to follow her mistress from above and out of sight. With that, Dian slammed another sliding panel near the ceiling, successfully confining Kima to the caging within the bedroom.

"Dian's got a cage in there for the baby gorilla, too," Peter said. "You should see it . . . up on stilts." To my amazement at his seeming obliviousness to her volatility, he guided me over toward Dian's door. Unlike Kima, Peter was obviously energized by all the company of we new arrivals in camp. I was struck by his calm demeanor around what I found to be a very disturbing unpredictable environment. His jovial, relaxed banter made me uneasy in such close proximity to Dian's hair-triggered emotions. I thought he should tone it down, but still I craned my neck to peer through the half-open door into the room, and saw the foot of a king-sized bed mounted on a low platform. A half-empty bottle of Johnnie Walker Scotch stood next to a gray Olivetti field typewriter on a small desk against one wall. I could see one of the spindly tree trunks that supported the wood and wire cage suspended six feet off the floor near the ceiling. The baby gorilla, tucked in for the night, was obscured in her mound of leafy fronds of nest material cut from the surrounding forest. Suddenly Dian appeared from her room and stepped up into the raised dining area where Peter and I stood.

"Shit *merde* . . . get in there and help with dinner, goddammit!" she snapped at the sight of us.

"What do you want us to do?" Peter asked, with arms spread in bafflement.

"Do something *useful*, instead of acting like you know every fucking thing!"

I followed Peter as he skulked back into the dark kitchen.

"Everybody needs to pitch in around here!" Dian shouted after us, as she retreated to her bedroom, where the baby gorilla and her monkey were settling in.

"What does *wog* mean?" I asked Peter, the strange new word still resonating in my ears.

"It's a derogatory word for the Africans." Peter informed me. "More like something you'd hear from English colonials. Dian probably picked it up when she was in the UK. That's where she got her PhD, at Cambridge."

Stuart soon entered from outside, carrying the parts for the pressure lanterns he had purchased for Dian in Kigali. Hearing his voice, Dian called for him to join her as Judy and Liza returned with the weather data notebook. He quickly set his cargo on the kitchen table with Kanyaragana's *dead* lantern, and joined Dian and her guests in the living area. Peter, Kanyaragana, the two Rwandan teens, and I made a total of six men tripping and stumbling into each other in the dark little kitchen. In the Africans' banter I made out the recurring word, "Mademoiselli," their Africanized French title for Dian.

Peter invited me to help with the lantern repair and we took seats in the shadows at the table, while Kanyaragana sent his young helpers out for more water. Completely unfamiliar with the workings of the pressure lantern, I was still thankful for a project, and a seat, that would keep me out of Dian's way. In the darkness, I fumbled with the tiny brass tubes and rods, baffled by what went where.

Carolyn had taken her things down to a separate cabin where she would spend the night and, when she arrived, Peter sprang up to open the kitchen door.

"How do you like your cabin?" he asked her.

"Very nice, I can hear the stream running by it." Carolyn had toweled her hair dry from the rain, and had changed into a fresh dry shirt and jeans.

"Has Dian said anything about who will be going to what groups tomorrow?" Peter asked Carolyn and me. "I spend most of my time with Group 5."

"Oh, I've read about Group 5 in one of Dian's articles," Carolyn responded.

"Yeah, Group 5 is the most habituated group, great to work with. I'll show you their pictures on the wall out here." Carolyn followed Peter into the dining area. I wanted to go too, but stayed behind with my lantern project in the shadowy kitchen, which was beginning to feel like the only sanctuary from Dian's wrath. I continued to be amazed by Peter boldly venturing back out of the kitchen so soon after our scolding.

"*Ahem . . . shut the fuck up* Peter!" Dian hissed, as Peter began explaining the photos of Group 5's members to Carolyn, "You don't even know what the hell you're talking about . . . *ahem.*"

I peered out into the lighted dining room, while Carolyn edged away from the tension down to the living area where Stuart, Judy, and Liza greeted her. Peter pursued Dian to the other side of the table.

"Why are you treating me this way?" he asked, in a loud whisper.

"*Really and truly* Peter . . . You think you know every goddamned thing . . . *ahem.*" Dian cleared her throat in the telltale sign that she was well into her bottle of Scotch.

"Bullshit!" Peter exclaimed.

What balls, I thought. *Wish I could talk to her like that!*

After a brief exchange with Dian that was too hushed for me to hear, and interrupted by Dian's increasing throat-clearing and gorilla vocalizations, Peter came back into the kitchen clearly exasperated.

"What's she so mad about?" I whispered.

"She's drunk," he said, looking over his shoulder.

"She bought a case of Scotch in Kigali," I said.

"Yeah, good ol' Johnnie Walker Red Label." Peter leaned into Kanyaragana's ear. "*Shit . . . goddammit . . . motherfuckit!*" He said in a loud whisper, stomping his boots in a mockery of Dian.

Kanyaragana's shoulders bounced convulsively as he stifled his laughter, nearly spilling the potatoes he ladled out of a pot of boiling water.

"*Mademoiselli . . .*" he muttered, shaking his head, as he giddily tried to resume his task at the stove.

In a grand shift of demeanor, Mademoiselli summoned her guests to the dinner table.

"*Reeeally* and *truuuly* you *guuuys* . . ." she gushed with maudlin effect to Judy and Liza, characteristically drawing out her vowels for emphasis. "I *truuuly* can't thank you enough for coming all the way up here to take care of the baby for me while I was in Kigali."

I followed close behind Peter, as if he were my human shield, and joined the assembly at the long rectangular wooden table, strategically choosing a seat at the opposite end from our hostess. With everyone seated and scooted in, Kanyaragana brought plates, warmed in the oven, and set them on the table. He and the boys soon followed with larger platters of steaming potatoes, and roasted beef. Judy and Liza complimented Dian on her ability to find a decent cut of meat for us in the Ruhengeri market.

"Yeah, you have to find one without too much green on it," Dian joked as she picked at the food on her plate before hacking off chunks · of butter and working them into a slice of bread in a scene that had now become familiar to me. After a heavy shake of salt on these, she ate them with gusto, holding up her end of the conversation between bites and swigs of Primus. The small talk shifted to the latest news about expatriates in and around Kigali, and Judy asked Dian what she knew about the Japanese film crew that had been in Kigali requesting permission to camp in the Parc des Volcans and film gorillas.

"*Eht mwah*, did you see their goddamn tents down below?" Dian asked, referring to the tidy campsite I had noticed on the climb up from the base of the mountain. "Those Japs have been waiting down there for weeks now."

"What have they been doing?" Judy asked.

"The bastards want to come up and film the gorillas, but they can just stay the hell down there and do their thing with the V-Ws." Dian turned her head and mockingly spat at the floor, as if to get the bad taste of mentioning someone out of her mouth as I had seen her do in Kigali. I didn't yet know who she was talking about just then, but I would soon learn.

"Do you think they'll bother the gorillas?" Liza asked.

"*Eht mwah, mwaaah* . . . everybody wants to bother the goddamn gorillas."

To break the silence that followed, Dian quickly changed the subject to who would do what the next day. "Peter, in the morning, you and John will carry Judy's and Liza's luggage down the mountain when they leave."

"Uh . . . okay . . ." Peter replied, setting down his fork, his mouth open in a dazed look of mild surprise.

"After that, you can go to Group 5. And take John with you."

Peter closed his mouth without arguing. I thought about the arduous climb we made on the same route that afternoon; we would be making that same hike and much more, but the thrill of seeing the gorillas face to face outweighed my concerns.

"Carolyn . . . *ahem* . . . you'll move to the guest room up here, and help me with the baby." My heart sank for Carolyn. The idea of living under the same roof with Dian was unthinkable. But better *her* than me though, I thought. Carolyn had been a longtime admirer of Dian's, and Dian seemed to like her, but Carolyn, like myself, was just beginning to get to know our new boss.

Dian talked to Stuart about contacting Group 4 and Nunkie's Group. Named for its lead adult male or "silverback," Nunkie's Group had been missing for weeks.

"I just *know* they've been killed by poachers," Dian lamented loudly. "Really and truly somebody's just GOT to find them, Stuart." Stuart nodded emphatically while declaring his support to this cause, and everyone tried to offer possible alternative scenarios to placate Dian, each guessing and suggesting that Nunkie might be in safe territory on Mount Karisimbi, or high on the far side of Visoke. Dian shook her head bitterly at their words of comfort, shouting, *"Oya! Oya!"* the Kinyarwanda word for *"no."*

After dinner, we moved to the living area where Kanyaragana served coffee. While others occupied the available seating, Dian sat on the grass mat floor and offered a cigarette to me as she lit one for herself. Grateful for any friendly gesture from her, and to acknowledge the only bond we seemed to have, I accepted the cigarette and joined her as the only other smoker in the room.

The burning wood in the fireplace barely threw any heat, but the mood picked up a little and I started to relax and enjoy myself as we talked and joked about the rough road to Ruhengeri and the climb up the mountain in a hailstorm. The camp had a weather station outside of Dian's cabin that recorded temperature extremes, wind, and precipitation. Judy and Liza had been recording the data in a notebook while Dian was absent. Dian had an agreement to collect and send this information to Benda Lema's office at ORTPN, written in French.

"What's the French word for *hail*?" Judy asked, "I've got to write that in the weather log."

"It's *grêle*," French-speaking Liza said.

The women discussed the spelling with correct placement of the circumflex and wrote it in the logbook, while Carolyn excused herself.

"I am so tired, I think I'll head off to bed," she said. Amid a barrage of "good nights" she collected her lantern and headed out the door and back to her tent cabin. After Carolyn departed, the remaining women commented on how pretty she was.

"Does anyone know how old she is?" Peter asked.

"She's thirty-four," Judy said.

"She's the same age I was when I came here," Dian added.

"And, as I told her, she's a *young* thirty-four." Judy said.

"You should be happy," Dian said to Peter, as she pointed in the direction of the tent cabin. "You've got a Cheryl Tiegs up here now."

"Oh yeah?" Peter chimed, "Cheryl Tiegs, eh?"

"Yeah, but you leave her alone," Dian said, "She's here for the gorillas." Peter laughed. I laughed . . . and Dian then turned to me with a cold stare. I felt myself flush in anticipation with the awkwardness it brought.

"One thing I've noticed about *you* . . ." Dian said, pausing with an icy smirk. "You remind me of Peter when he first got here."

"Oh . . . ?" I muttered nervously in an effort to break the iciness.

"You are selfish, young, and stupid."

Speechless, I swallowed and tried to force a smile. *Was she being funny?* I feigned another, weaker laugh, but Dian locked her eyes on me. A cruel grin revealed her enjoyment of my discomfort as I glanced at the faces around the room. I was paying for something, but I didn't know what. My youth and enthusiasm simply annoyed her. Judy looked at me tilting her head sympathetically, but the room became tense and the conversation died. Even Stuart said nothing to intervene. I froze in the awkwardness, while the mood of the group became strained and uncomfortable.

"Well," Dian said, as if becoming aware again of the others in the room, "we're all tired and have a big day ahead of us tomorrow." With that, she rose to her feet, signaling the end of the evening. "I think everybody needs to get to bed."

Back in my half of the cabin I would share with Stuart, I lit a candle and brushed my teeth with the tea-colored creek water from one of the corked wine bottles. The porters had placed my items on the floor in the middle of my room. In the dim light, I sorted through the food I had bought in the Ruhengeri market. My eggs were scrambled, shell and all, and dripping from their tattered plastic bag. I found a piece of typing paper in one of the desk's drawers and slid it underneath the mess to catch the ooze. I wondered how long I could live off my loaf of bread, bananas and cheese.

Stuart opened his door and the light from his pressure lantern flooded into my room.

"Everything okay in here?" he asked.

Looking around for a pot or bowl to set the eggs in, I asked Stuart where he got his utensils.

"Dian had the men bring mine down. Don't you have any yet?"

"I don't think so," I said, pulling another desk drawer open, "I can't find anything like you've got."

"Ask Dian tomorrow . . . or I'll ask her."

"Okay."

"Dian's got a lot on her mind," Stuart said, "and she's really uptight about leaving to teach at Cornell."

"Yeah, I know," I said.

After Stuart closed the door, I set the scrambled egg mess outside into the darkness before unrolling my sleeping bag onto the blankets on my bed. Peeling off my muddy boots, I slid in, clothes and all, as yet too unsettled to fully settle in.

FIVE

A Cruel Climb

The next morning, when I arrived at Dian's cabin, Judy and Liza were finishing their breakfast. Kanyaragana was in the kitchen cleaning up. He offered me a cup of coffee when I entered.

"*Unataka kahawa?*" he asked, pointing to a coffee pot over a gas burner. I accepted and he poured a cup of hot, aromatic *kahawa* with milk. *Kahawa* is the Swahili word for coffee, and similarly *ikawa* is the Kinyarwanda word—we would use both interchangeably. Peter stood in the doorway to the dining area chatting with Judy and Liza.

"Dian and Carolyn are outside with Charlie," Judy said. I could see Carolyn through the window holding the baby, Charlie. Charlie had come a long way, I thought, from being terrified of humans upon her arrival in camp just a couple weeks earlier. Carolyn looked intently at Dian, who stood talking to her with the gorilla graveyard behind her.

Dian soon came inside to say goodbye to Judy and Liza as they gathered their things.

"I really appreciate you guys helping me," Dian said gushingly, "really and truly." Dian's face crinkled with lines as she strained to smile. Judy and Liza said they were happy to help. As they finished breakfast, Peter and I each picked up a large suitcase and headed back through the kitchen. As Judy and Liza gathered their other things and headed out the door, I noticed Kanyaragana washing pots and pans and it reminded me of my empty cabin.

"Dian, Stuart said to ask you about cooking utensils." I said.

"They're in your cabin," Dian said.

"I can't find any. I've looked everywhere."

"Stop worrying about your goddamn belly," Dian snapped. "We've got more important things to worry about around here. I'm sick of you people worrying about your fucking bellies." That shut me up. Grabbing a large suitcase, I headed out the door to catch up with Peter, Judy, and Liza. The air was cool and damp, but the sun was beginning to burn through the clouds that enshrouded camp. I was hungry, and as we passed by my cabin I wished I had eaten some of my bread when I got up. I also wondered what the daily routine would be in camp.

Peter, having already lived in camp for a year, led the way as we left the meadow, and entered the surrounding forest. He knew instinctively what grassy clearings to pass through among the trees before grass gave way to the well-trodden path of mud we had traversed the day before.

Judy was just behind Peter, and Liza followed her as I brought up the rear. Our group chatted amiably, and I asked Liza about Switzerland. She told me she was single and from the French-speaking region of her country.

"So you're a real Swiss miss," I said.

"I'm a real Swiss mess," she answered, and I laughed at her surprising American slang à la French accent.

Despite carrying my backpack and Judy's suitcase, traveling down-hill was much easier than the previous day's uphill climb. I shifted the luggage from left hand to right hand throughout the hike. We soon traversed the small meadow where I had rested with the porters the day before, and Peter told me it was called the "Tourist Spot." Over time, Dian had given names to many places on Mount Visoke and its surroundings for the purpose of notating gorilla locations. The occasional tourists that climbed the trail up Mount Visoke usually stopped to rest in this spot. Peter pointed to a muddy uphill trail on the left that tourists used, which was called, no big surprise, the "Tourist Trail."

"That's where we'll be going to find Group 5," Peter said. "I left them up there on the slopes of Visoke yesterday."

"Is it far?" I asked, suddenly aware that I would again be making yesterday's climb and then some.

"Yeah," Peter answered. "They were up high and pretty far off the trail."

No problem, I thought.

Eventually the tree line changed with the spreading hagenias, yielding to more upright vernonia trees and bamboo as we reached a lower altitude, passing above the tidy little Japanese camp below us on the right. No one was visible there, and we were soon down at the car park. Peter and I loaded the luggage into Judy's car parked near Dian's VW. I was a little out of breath as Peter and I waved goodbye while Judy maneuvered her small car onto the rock-strewn road that led away from the base of Mount Visoke.

As Peter and I walked back to the Porter Trail, we encountered a Rwandan in a tattered military-style uniform. He recognized Peter and they shook hands, speaking briefly in Swahili.

"This is Big Nameye," Peter said. "Nameye who works up at camp is Little Nameye." Big Nameye shook my hand, smiling broadly, and said *"Jambo, karibu,"* before heading down the road.

"Big Nameye used to work at Karisoke but Dian fired him," Peter said. "Now he's a park guard."

"Why'd she fire him?" I asked.

"I don't know," Peter said. "She's fired a lot of people, and rehired them too. When she gets mad, she fires them, and rehires them when she needs them again."

Before we headed up the trail, I asked Peter about the small gray building I had seen on arrival the day before, which stood about fifty yards upslope from the trail entrance. It was about twelve feet in diameter and round like an African hut, but made of galvanized sheet metal.

"That's Bill and Amy's *gîte*," Peter said. "They used to be up at Karisoke."

"Oh yeah, I saw Bill in Kigali. He didn't have much to say." I asked following Peter up the trail. "What are they doing down here?"

Peter explained that the couple was now working for The Mountain Gorilla Project, habituating gorillas for organized tourism, and educating the public. Amy did most of the gorilla contacts and Bill conducted programs in local communities teaching people about gorillas and conservation. Ecotourism had not yet become a buzzword, but the concept made sense to me, as did the idea of making the Rwandans aware of gorillas and dispelling the myths about them being dangerous and something to fear. I looked forward to meeting them and learning more about their work.

"Dian calls them the 'V-W couple'."

"V-W? Because they live near her Volkswagen?" I was beginning to get more winded as the trail become steeper.

"They're married, but her last name is Vedder and his is Weber. Dian doesn't like to mention their names and she usually spits on the ground if she has to, especially with Amy."

"Yeah, she did that last night talking about them, and when she mentioned Benda Lema, at Judy's house in Kigali."

"She refers to Amy as 'The Cunt.'" Peter laughed a little at the absurdity. I was stunned that even Dian would use that word.

"Really? Why, what happened?"

"Dian thinks people need to keep away from the gorillas. She doesn't like the tourism thing, and she had problems with Bill and Amy in camp."

I wanted to learn more, but with the uphill climb, I was soon getting too winded to talk. Peter climbed effortlessly, and I tried not to show my fatigue while trailing behind him.

Eventually, Peter and I arrived at the meadow, which marked the halfway point to camp. Peter again showed me the trail leading up Mount Visoke to Group 5, but seeing my condition of near exhaustion, suggested we rest briefly.

"Okay, you ready to climb?" Peter asked.

"Yep." My heart was still pounding, but my breathing was less obvious. We gathered our backpacks and clipboards and left the level ground of the meadow to climb the Tourist Trail up Mount Visoke. It started gradually, like the Porter Trail, but soon took on a 45° upward angle. Peter barely seemed to break a sweat, but I could feel myself dripping inside my heavy shirt and plastic rain pants. We traveled again without talking. I willed each step on the viscous volcanic mud, dropping back twenty feet behind Peter, who looked back periodically to make sure I was still following.

My head swam as I thought back to the previous summer with Terry Maple's group of students. One of our day trips was to Mount Longonot, an extinct volcano in Kenya's Rift Valley. Our group made the hot dusty climb up its arid slope. I secretly wanted to be the first to the top, to see the views in solitude, and surreptitiously passed everyone as we trod and panted our way up. I arrived at the rim of Mount Longonot a few minutes before the next person and privately admired the magnificent view alone in those moments. Before me was a steep wall that dropped hundreds of feet to a perfectly circular crater valley. Beyond the crater was the Rift Valley and shimmering Lake Naivasha. About fifty feet above where I stood a black-chested harrier eagle hovered stationary in midair, riding the hot dry wind blowing up from inside the crater.

As I struggled to keep up with Peter, I wondered why being the first one up Mount Longonot had been important to me. I'm sure no one else cared. It was just some personal little victory that meant nothing as I hiked the steep trail up Visoke.

Slowly I caught up with Peter standing slightly off the trail on the right.

"Are you all right?" he asked.

"Yeah, fine," I said, between gasps. "Whew, this is some climb." I dropped to the ground and sat, too winded to say much else.

"We're gonna cut across slope now," Peter said. He showed me where he had used his panga to slice through the trunk of a lobelia the day before to mark the spot where he had returned to the main trail. The lobelia, *Lobelia gibberoa*, is a soft-trunked plant with long blade-like leaves at the top, giving it the appearance of a miniature palm tree. I stared at the plant's stump, sliced cleanly by the panga the day before. Thick milky sap had oozed from the hollow trunk and turned brown overnight.

"Do the gorillas eat that plant?" I asked.

"No, that's low-altitude lobelia. They don't eat it, but they pull it over to make nests. They eat the high-altitude lobelia. You'll see that higher up, it looks different, with narrower leaves." The higher-altitudinal species Peter referred to was *Lobelia wollastonii*.

Peter asked if Dian had given me a panga yet and told me I needed to get one as well as an altimeter. There were extras in camp. We would need to note the altitude once we found the gorillas and their nests from the night before. Upon leaving the group, we would need to mark our trail with panga cuts as a reference to help locate them again. The pangas were also useful in getting through the dense vegetation of the forest.

I told Peter about asking Dian for pots and pans to cook with, and he said he would ask for those when he asked about a panga and altimeter for me. This simple task seemed like a brave effort, and I wondered about his complacency in light of his rough treatment from Dian at dinner the night before.

I stood up and Peter led our way off the trail across slope. Our footing went from mud to a substrate of thick weeds, and I noticed in most places we balanced on a matting of vegetation that kept us raised inches above the soil. As I balanced and stumbled to keep up with Peter I noticed the mountain slopes were covered in basic mountain gorilla foods: wild celery (*Peucedanum kerstenii*), thistle (*Carduus nyassanus*) and a tender creeping ground cover called gallium (*Galium spurium*) that has tiny Velcro-like leaves for gripping and climbing.

"Ouch, shit!" I exclaimed as I stumbled and swung my hand through a tall fuzzy plant.

"Those are the nettles," Peter informed me. "The gorillas eat that too."

I rubbed my hand and could see the redness forming on my skin from *Laportea alatipes*.

"What do you do for the sting?" I asked.

"I don't do anything. You just get used to it."

"That hurts! How do the gorillas eat that?"

"It doesn't seem to bother them, just like the thistle. They don't eat elephant nettle though. Watch out for those." Peter was referring to the much larger *Urtica massaica*, which I would encounter soon enough.

"Where is it?" I asked, looking around with my senses more acute.

A little farther on, Peter pointed to a stand of elephant nettle, a tall plant with large, heart-shaped leaves. On closer examination, I noticed the leaves and stems were covered in translucent spines. Some of these spines were larger, almost the gauge of a small hypodermic needle. I could see the clear fluid toxin through the rigid membrane that comprised the needles. This plant's evolution had put a lot of energy into a structure and function that would prevent it from being eaten by anything, including elephants.

As we traveled across the slope of Visoke, I swung one hand and then the other through stinging nettles as I tried to balance and watch out for the more distinctive and foreboding elephant nettle. My hands became tingly and numb as if they had just been electrocuted.

Despite an ambient temperature of about 65°F, my clothes were soaked with sweat and my heart pounded as I followed Peter in and out of one small ravine after another. I realized these formed the ruts and ridges typical of the sides of a volcano.

Eventually Peter stopped at a level area and looked at the ground around his feet. I dropped to my knees and sat panting.

"This is where I left the group yesterday," Peter said. I could see the weeds were trampled, as if they had been walked all over. He looked at me, and then his watch. It was getting late.

"I don't know why Dian wanted us to find Group 5 after taking the luggage down to the parking lot," he said. His calm demeanor was replaced with a look of frustration as he studied his altimeter and shook his head silently. We were near eleven thousand feet, a thousand feet higher than camp, and three thousand feet higher than the parking lot from where we had come.

"You can wait there while I look for the night nests," he said. I nodded as he walked upslope and down in big concentric circles until he was out of sight.

After about thirty minutes Peter returned and announced that it was too late in the afternoon to try and find Group 5 and be able to spend any time observing them. Peter usually spent four hours with the gorillas once he located them, and even if we found them and spent a short amount of time with them, it was a long way back to camp. It would be dark at six and Dian had established that time as camp curfew. She did not like having to worry about students who were not back in camp after dark. I was too tired to be disappointed at not seeing the gorillas and too tired to look forward to the hike back to camp, but we headed back across the deep vegetation to Mount Visoke's trail.

I remained exhausted cutting across the mountain's slope at a 45° angle. I was a little relieved to come out onto the open main trail downward, but when we reached the small meadow again, I wanted to drop and stay there. Peter waited politely, until I decided to get up and move on up the trail to camp. This time he followed me. As the trail resumed its incline, my ribs ached with each breath and I began to feel nauseated. I kept moving, and Peter stayed at my heels until we came to a small stream that crossed the path. I suddenly became aware of an overwhelming thirst and dropped to my knees by the edge of the water. As tempted as I was, I knew not to drink directly from this stream for fear of what tropical microbes might live in that water. I knew the men in camp boiled our drinking water from Camp Stream for good reason.

"Are you okay?" he asked.

"Yeah, fine," I said, picking my head up. "I just . . . wanna rest . . . a little longer."

"Are you sure you're okay?"

"Yeah . . . you go on." I preferred that he continue on rather than watch me gasping. Reluctantly, Peter headed up the trail and I sprawled on my back on a patch of cool grass by the stream, staring up at the clear blue sky. I remained there for a long time, with my ribs aching, before regaining the energy and composure to continue up the trail to camp.

SIX

Un-Settling In

The next morning, I walked up the path through thick cold mist, arriving at Dian's cabin promptly at eight o'clock, as my boss had mandated via Stuart. I was not going to be late, and quite frankly, thankful not to be doing another climb like the day before. Stuart and Peter had already headed in opposite directions in pursuit of gorillas, Peter went east to find Group 5, and Stuart headed west into Zaire, where Peanuts's Group ranged.

Upon my arrival, Dian's door was closed and the cabin was dark and quiet. I waited by a hagenia that dripped the mist it had captured in the moss and lichens draping its spreading limbs. I thought about Carolyn inside and wondered if she felt as uptight as I would, living under the same roof with Dian. For me, the simplest actions required the greatest of precaution to avoid triggering sudden anger from Dian. *Could Carolyn go in the kitchen and fix a cup of tea? Could she eat a piece of bread or sit in a chair? Did she keep the door to her room closed at all times?* I would.

At 8:20 I heard Dian coughing and the rattling of a lock from inside. Wearing Levi's that drooped from her hipless waistline and a long john top, Dian opened the door and invited me in with a tired monotone. She was puffy and pale and her disheveled hair covered her sunken cheeks. I knew Dian had moved Carolyn up to her cabin, and saw her seated at the couch with a steaming coffee cup in her hand.

"Good morning," Carolyn said. I was surprised to see that she looked relaxed, and I got the impression that she and Dian had been chatting idly. The little gorilla was on the floor and came to me immediately. I picked her up.

"She hasn't eaten yet," Dian said curtly, which I took as a hint to take the baby outside to forage. "She needs to be active so she won't retain gas."

Josephine clung very tightly to me as I walked outside with her. A thick mat of crisp stringy gallium covered the ground at one edge of the gorilla graveyard. Squatting down, I picked a strand of the trailing plant and placed it near Josephine's mouth. She looked disinterested, but slowly began to nibble on it, taking it between her own pudgy black thumb and forefinger. The hairless skin on her hands, feet and face was like supple polished black leather. I put her down in the thick growth of gallium and she quickly climbed back into my arms. I moved into the sunlight and sat with her on my lap. The warm sun felt good as it burned away the morning dampness. I noticed that Josephine was lethargic and didn't vocalize with her characteristic deep purrs that Dian called "belch vocalizations."

The baby wouldn't crawl off me and eat something, so I picked some gallium within arm's reach and dropped it on her distended belly. She ate a few bites when I placed it at her mouth, but then picked the rest off her stomach and dropped it on the ground. Knowing Dian wanted us to get the baby moving, I made Josephine get on the ground and tried to walk away from her. She clung tightly, desperately, I thought. Funny to think that just weeks earlier she had seen her first humans and was rightly scared to death of them.

After an hour, clouds wafted in from around Mount Visoke and obscured the sun. The air became chilly. Carolyn emerged from Dian's cabin and took Josephine in her arms. I noticed bruises on Carolyn's forearms and upper arms as she held the big black ball of fur at her chest.

"She seems lethargic," I said.

"Dian keeps telling me to make sure she stays active," Carolyn said, handing her back to me. "She thinks her stomach feels too tight, like she has gas. She was talking about Coco and Pucker again, saying that they had the same problem."

I felt Josephine's stomach. It was round and taut like a basketball, but I didn't know what a gorilla belly was supposed to feel like. I put the baby back on the ground and walked away so she would have to follow. She found a thistle and nibbled half-heartedly on a few leaves. I climbed the trunk of a fallen tree so Josephine could not cling to me and would have to move around on her own, but she pursued and tried to sit in my lap. As I jumped to the ground, she clung tightly, and giving in, I held her in my arms.

I thought about her insecurity and the conditions under which she must have been captured. You can't just walk up to a mother gorilla and take a baby from her arms. It must have been a traumatic scene with Josephine's mother being slaughtered. Others were surely killed as they tried to defend their group from a band of poachers. Josephine had been terrified of humans upon entering camp. Now, after three weeks of living in terror, she not only trusted them, but needed them to feel secure. Right then, she needed me, a human and recent alien to her world.

Dian came out of her cabin and offered a banana to Josephine, who tried to bite me before I loosened my grip and let her jump from my lap. At that, she grabbed the fruit and stuffed it into her mouth, peel and all. She emitted a soft, rumbling purr as she chewed, *hmm waaahhh.* Dian slyly stuck a second banana in my shirt pocket, which the baby didn't see.

"Thanks," I said.

"Eht mwah . . ." Dian growled. "That's not for you!" Carolyn politely moved toward the cabin and out of earshot as Dian continued. "You know, you really do remind me a lot of Peter when he first got here . . . selfish, young and stupid. Remember, we're here for the gorillas, not to feed our goddamn belly."

Ouch! As at the dinner with Judy and Liza, I was speechless. I stared at the ground. *Okay . . . what did she want from me?* I wanted to say something, but had really never been in a situation like that in my young life, and it left me utterly dumbstruck. I had come there planning to do as I was told, and I could do that, but I did not know how to respond to unprovoked and unexpected hostility and condemnation at a moment's notice. The best I could surmise is that she resented my naïve enthusiasm about being there. Peter must've been the same. He still had enthusiasm, when Dian wasn't looking, and he retained a respect for her, however tenuous it had become, which I hadn't even yet had the chance to develop. I was too new to realize that for Dian, Karisoke had become a maelstrom of turmoil and regret. Enjoyment and levity would neither be tolerated nor rewarded by her.

I had come there with enthusiasm and confidence, but soon felt that Dian despised confidence. It seemed to me she only liked the vulnerable, like children and animals, especially those disabled and endangered. Her first career had been working with disabled kids at a children's hospital in Kentucky; now she was saving the endangered mountain gorilla. She would have to break me in some way to find me tolerable, or punish me for being happy and pull me into her misery. Whatever her agenda was, she was good at humiliation and demoralization, and got satisfaction from it.

Carolyn had gone back inside, and Dian also headed toward the cabin. Josephine followed, but the door closed before she caught up to her mistress. Halfway down the forty feet between Dian's cabin and me, Josephine stopped and looked back. Those deep brown eyes stared widely at me from her solemn black face. Within a minute, she realized I was not going to follow her and she returned and clung to me.

I shook off the feelings from my interaction with Dian and focused my thoughts on the baby. I've got to get her to eat her normal gorilla food, I thought, and took her from thistle to gallium plant. Certainly, it didn't help that Dian plied her with sliced fruits, and even candy at bedtime. The baby would not eat on her own, and only nibbled reluctantly if I pushed a leaf or sprig to her mouth.

In an effort to initiate play, I took her by her arms and swung her outward. She turned upside down and hung with her feet upward. A playful sign, I thought, but in human terms her face was stoic and humorless. I placed her back on the ground.

Carolyn emerged from Dian's cabin.

"I don't know what Dian wants from me," I muttered. "It's like she just wants to break my spirit."

"I'll take her while you go in and have some breakfast," she said, reaching down to pick up the baby. I didn't expect this and speculated whether it was Carolyn's idea and if it was okay with Dian.

"Breakfast? Are you sure?" I asked, in a low voice. "How's it going in there?"

"It's okay, we're just talking. Dian's been telling me about what it was like for her when she first came here. She's had some tough times."

"I think she's just a miserable wretch," I said, passing the banana from my pocket to Josephine before nervously heading inside. A fire smoldered in the stone fireplace. I couldn't see Dian but heard the voices of several Africans on the other side of the house and moved toward the kitchen.

"*Jambo,*" Kanyaragana said, slicing bread by the sink.

"*Jambo,*" I replied. Kanyaragana uttered more Swahili that I did not understand. He was asking a question, but befuddled, I laughed and shrugged with my palms out to show confusion. Chuckling, he placed a plate with toasted bread and cheese on the dining table next to a jar of amber-colored jam, sliced pineapple, and a bunch of bananas.

"*Asante sana*," I said.

"*Ndio.*"

"*Ndio?*" I paused, recalling the Swahili word for "yes."

"Yesss . . . yore welkum," Kanyaragana added with a smile.

Chuckling at his blithe hospitality, I sat down and nibbled away at the delicacies on the table. Occasionally I could hear Dian's low, labored voice over the din of the Africans outside the kitchen door, who chattered and laughed loudly in unison. Dian's voice sounded strained and breathy, but not angry or annoyed. I grew uneasy that she might come back into the house. I didn't want her to see me eating, so confused was I by everything. When the voices stopped, I quickly finished my breakfast, thanked Kanyaragana again and headed back out to the opposite side of the cabin where Carolyn waited with the baby.

"Who's here with Dian?" I asked, taking Josephine from Carolyn's arms.

"Dian was waiting for the poacher patrol. It must be them." Carolyn said, and after watching me and the gorilla for a few moments, she went back into the cabin. It was a few minutes past ten and the temperature had dropped to what felt like the low fifties. Mist wafted down the slopes of Visoke and enshrouded the camp again in a damp, gray pall.

Josephine was still clingy, but I walked over to a fallen hagenia, and placed her on the ground before climbing onto its leaning trunk. Josephine followed and I squeezed around a branch that pointed into the air and blocked the baby's path. Puzzled, she stopped and stared forlornly at me before noticing a twig with leaves sprouting from the branch. She examined it closely with her eyes, smelled and tasted it, and finally ate a few of the leaves.

Suddenly a din of voices rose up from one end of Dian's cabin and six Africans in green plastic rain pants and matching jackets trod in our direction. The man in front held a small black handgun. Terrified, Josephine scrambled around the branch that separated us, and seeing her alarm, I bent down to pick her up. As the baby clung tightly with her eyes transfixed on the poacher patrolmen, I jumped down from the tree. Feeling her desperate grip, I walked away from the group as they passed, turning to block her view, but Josephine craned her neck to see around my shoulder. Dian's poacher patrol marched onward, under the spreading hagenias toward the large open meadow and the border of Zaire. Even after they faded out of sight, Josephine continued to hold tightly to me and stare wide-eyed in their direction.

I sat down next to a patch of gallium and thistle, hoping the gorilla food plants would entice the baby. Still shaken, Josephine kept her long furry arms wrapped tightly around my torso, and after a few minutes fell into a deep sleep. As I tried to remain motionless the baby's breathing changed to a faint gratifying snore. It was still cold and cloudy and I sat holding Karisoke's three-year-old gorilla as she slept.

I later learned that Dian's poacher patrol was another bone of contention between her and Benda Lema of the national parks office in Kigali. She had no official permission to send her own armed guards into the park, let alone across the border into Zaire, but she did it anyway. Feeling that there was insufficient protection from the park offices for gorillas and other wildlife in the Parc des Volcans, Dian put together her own band of men and paid them to go out and destroy traps set by poachers. Because she was planning on leaving Karisoke soon for an extended period, she was sending this group of men out twice a week on a blitz of the heavily poached areas just over the border in Zaire toward the Kabara meadow, where she once had her very first gorilla research startup camp. And from where she was captured and detained by the Zairois.

Our arrangement for the day was that I would babysit in the morning, and Carolyn would take the afternoon shift. It was a nearly an hour later when Josephine awoke and Carolyn returned to take over. I knew Dian wanted notes, so I headed off to begin typing. Back at my cabin, I stared at the wine bottles filled with the tea-colored creek water. A cup of hot tea would have been nice in my cold room, but I still didn't have a cookstove or any eating utensils. Not even a cup. After the day's comments from Dian, I certainly wasn't going to ask her about supplies.

A small portable Olivetti field-style typewriter and some typing paper had been placed in my cabin. Dian must have sent it via Kanyaragana, I thought. Peter, not Dian, had explained the rules to me: Dian supplied us with typing paper and carbons. We would use three sheets of paper with two carbons and type all notes in triplicate. One copy was for Dian, one was for camp records, and we could keep the originals. They had to be typed daily, and placed on our beds in the morning to be picked up by Kanyaragana when he came to pick up dirty dishes and make beds. Such service!

I pulled the remaining wedge of cheese out of my metal footlocker and used my pocket knife to carve away some green mold that was forming along its edges. When I got down to a clean portion, I peeled a slice and popped it in my mouth. Crumbly with a pungent moldy taste, it was a welcome treat. I ate another sliver and a couple bananas to take the edge off my hunger. I still had some vitamins from home and washed one down with the brown creek water in one of my old wine bottles, Virunga tea.

Mukera, the woodman, knocked on my door and came in to make a fire in my woodstove. Dian employed him to find and cut firewood daily and build a fire in each occupied cabin at night. Deftly, he stacked an armload of wood in the stove's tiny cylindrical chamber, and with a match and a scrap of torn cardboard, he brought a small fire to life. The damp wood mostly just smoldered, but made the cold cabin a little more comfortable.

I had taken a typing course in high school, but did not have much experience with a typewriter beyond that. I spent the rest of the afternoon pecking out my recollections of Josephine's behavior. I managed to fill a whole page, beginning with picking Josephine up at Dian's cabin at 8:20 A.M. and ending with our encounter with the poacher patrol:

> . . . *she watches until they are out of sight, but looks their way when*
> *patrol makes loud noise. 10:18 Cold and cloudy. I sit w J. next to*

gallium and thistle. Won't eat. Clings tight, shifts, sleeps. 10 min.
heavy breathing. This continues til 11:15. 11:20 I turn J. over to
Carolyn."

Not very scientific, but I didn't know how else to do it.

As I was finishing my typing late in the afternoon, Stuart returned from a visit to Group 5 with Peter. Still maintaining a positive relationship with Dian, he had visited her at her cabin. Stuart had become the only one that Dian talked to about her goals and objectives, and I came to rely on him for such information.

"Do you know what Dian wants in these notes?" I asked him.

"Not exactly, but she says Peter's notes are some of the best notes she's ever seen."

Hmm, she didn't show any liking for Peter, but she liked his notes. She must have really meant it if she made a point to tell that to Stuart. I would be going out to Group 5 with Peter in the morning and I made a mental note to talk to him about his note-taking techniques.

"Do you know when Dian is going to be leaving?" I asked.

"Well, she was supposed to have been gone by now, but first she was waiting for us to arrive and get settled in. When I got here, she told me she was going to leave on February 15, but now she's talking about leaving on February 26."

"Why the delay?"

"We've got to come up with a plan for the baby gorilla. Dian's not comfortable leaving until we know what we're going to do with her. She doesn't want to see her go to a zoo like Coco and Pucker did. They didn't live very long after that."

Stuart's positive relationship with Dian put him in a position of responsibility to her and he continued to describe Dian's concerns. Mountain gorillas were essentially absent in captivity and one would provide a significant attraction at any zoo. Although global concern for wildlife conservation had slowed the unchecked extraction of exotic animals from their native habitat, here was one that already had been taken from the wild and needed a new home. Most zoos would have an interest in her.

Although Dian felt that a zoo home for the baby was one possible option, she thought that one mountain gorilla would trigger interest in another for breeding. At the time many zoo collection managers poorly understood the methods by which poachers acquired wild animals, and simply seeing animals listed on an animal dealers price list, bought a specimen with little knowledge of the details of its acquisition.

Dian, however, was well acquainted with the blatant disregard poachers had for wildlife. She had seen firsthand how their wire snares fractured the legs of bushbucks and duikers and mercilessly held them until they died from shock, exhaustion, or starvation.

Animals couldn't speak for themselves and were helpless in the face of persecution by humans. As contemptuous as Dian seemed to be of humans, she could empathize with the suffering of a hyrax or duiker, and she could really relate to the persecution of gorillas, so much like humans without being human. For whatever reason from Dian's wounded past, or whatever, guarding the animals appealed to her psyche and made her worthy to go on living. Perhaps her suffering and sacrifice in the struggle was her punishment for being human and being the wretched Dian, from which she could not escape.

The poachers, from Rwanda or Zaire, came from a world that included a daily labor for the basic needs of food, shelter, and a feeling of safety for an entire family in a single-room hut made of dung and thatch. Education was scant and the world beyond the horizon was a great marvelous mystery. Animals were simply viewed as a local natural resource to the hunters that foraged with spears, arrows, and snare traps for bushmeat in the forests of the Virunga Volcanoes. Gorillas sometimes got caught in the snare too, and unable to remove the wire from their own arms or hands, they lost a limb or died from infection. With only about 250 mountain gorillas estimated remaining in the Virungas, population numbers couldn't afford losses.

Two worlds were colliding in the saddle area between Visoke and Karisimbi along the border of Zaire. Dian's contempt for poachers came to a head on New Year's Eve in 1977, when Digit, a young silverback in Group 4 was slaughtered by a group of men and their dogs. Dian had watched Digit grow up in his family group, and he was one of her favorites. Earlier, he had become immortalized in a *National Geographic* documentary, but poachers had hacked off his head and hands as items for sale in the souvenir trade.

Seven months later, poachers shot and killed three more members of Group 4: Uncle Bert, a female named Macho, and her offspring, Kweli—these were among the names I had seen in the gorilla graveyard by Dian's cabin. Dian had garnered fame through her study of these endangered apes; now, *what was this heroine to do in the face of full-blown onslaught?* I eventually learned that past students had suggested that these overt killings of gorillas were a revenge the poachers enacted on Dian. *What better way to get at Dian than to kill her beloved mountain gorillas? What better way to reverse her efforts at protecting them than to cause their demise?* The thought that she was somehow responsible for these overt gorilla deaths was too much for Dian, and I knew she would be hostile to anyone suggesting it. But I couldn't help but think that, deep down, she knew this could be true, and the shame of it only fueled her war and fed her wrath against poachers, with gorillas caught in the crossfire.

As Stuart and I discussed the dilemma of Josephine's future, he said that although Dian had not ruled out placing the baby gorilla with a zoo, she thought it might be worth the risk of trying to place her with Group 4, which had been decimated by poachers. If she was going to follow through with such an idea, she would have to do it before she left for her teaching assignment at Cornell. Dr. Glenn Hausfater, who had arranged her visiting professorship, was growing concerned about her continuing delays. Her teaching assignment was to begin in mid-March and her delays were allowing her less and less time to get settled in Ithaca and prepare for her series of public lectures.

It was clear Stuart was enjoying his stature as Dian's right-hand man. Dian had chosen him among the three of us as her confidant, a position I didn't envy at all. If he had any interest in becoming the acting director in Dian's absence, as I suspected he did, then he had reason to be happy about the way Dian had taken to him. He did a lot for her, agreeing with her when she ranted about poachers and reassuring her when she expressed her worst fears about the fate of Nunkie's Group. Dian communicated very little directly to me, instead letting Stuart relay information.

"Tomorrow's porter day," Stuart said, handing me a piece of paper. "Here's the list Dian gave me."

The three-by-five-inch note listed all the food we could order. On the right side of the paper, names of things were printed in English: onions, potatoes, rice . . . On the left side, their Swahili translations: *vitunguu, viazi, maziwa* . . . I tried to sound out the odd blendings of vowels and consonants: *"vitunguuu, mmmchele, maziiiwaaa . . ."*

The prices per kilogram, apiece, or other appropriate unit were also listed by each item. The porters, led by Gwehandegoza, whom we met upon our arrival in the Volkswagen three days earlier, delivered food and other items to camp twice a week. Dian and the students wrote their own orders from the list of available products and included the exact amount of Rwandan francs needed for Gwehandegoza to purchase everything at the marketplace in Ruhengeri. He picked up the next order each time he and a group of his handpicked porters delivered the previous requests. Gwehandegoza would also bring and deliver our mail to the post office in Ruhengeri.

In the fading light, I made my porter list and dreamed of food: potatoes, rice, pineapple, eggs, and yes, cabbage. I continued down the reference list. Cigarettes? They too were on the list. At one hundred francs, or a dollar per pack I decided to indulge myself in a pack of Impalas and added to my order. *What the heck.*

As the darkness settled in on camp, Stuart pumped up his lantern and began typing the notes he had taken with Group 4. We closed the door between our halves of the cabin and I lit a candle on the shelf by my bed before placing my large washpot filled with creek water on my tiny stove. The woodman, Mukera, had made a fire earlier, but the damp wood only smoldered and fizzled, despite my efforts to reignite it. Still the stove eventually produced enough heat to take the chill out of the water, and I bathed with an old washcloth that looked like it had been in camp for years. The smoldering fire didn't really warm the room much, and afterward I dressed in a sweatshirt and sweatpants for pajamas, with a fresh pair of wool socks to keep my feet warm. I crawled into my bed under damp blankets and a sleeping bag. In the dim candlelight, I began reading *A High Wind in Jamaica* that I had borrowed from the American Embassy in Kigali, until I was too tired to focus on a page.

In the darkness, with the acrid smell of a blown candlewick, I pondered conditions at Karisoke. I marveled at the positive relationship Stuart maintained with Dian. She was congenial to him, and he sought interactions with her while I met only with contempt and disapproval. After three nights in Karisoke, I could not imagine choosing to be around her. Dian talked to Stuart openly, using him as a sounding board for her ideas and confiding in him about her fears.

Peter also seemed to be an outcast, but had somehow managed to live in camp for a year already. Unlike me, he was not intimidated by her, because he had at one time had a positive relationship with her. I wondered if the arrival of Stuart in camp had allowed Dian to cast Peter aside for someone fresh and new and as yet oblivious to where that would lead.

Peter had been in camp long enough to know her better. He had also known other students who had come and gone, like the shunned V-W couple, and was privy to their tales of confrontation with Dian. I thought of Carolyn living under the same roof as Dian. She seemed to be handling it okay, and as I drifted off to sleep I was thankful to be in a separate cabin at the opposite end of camp.

Sometime in the cold predawn hours, I was awakened by the sound of a dull thud inside my cabin. This was followed by a dull but quick loping scuttle across the grass mat floor, *thump, thump, thump* . . . It continued from the base of my desk on the opposite side of the room to the foot of my bed. I sat upright and groped for the matches to light my candle, wishing I had set my flashlight at arm's length. A moonless night at Karisoke is pitch black. I couldn't find the matches. *Where was my flashlight?* Reaching farther for matches, I knocked the candle and its bottle-holder on the floor with a crash. At that, the creature on the floor scampered heavily but quickly away from my bed to the area under the cabinets against the wall. The sound of its footsteps ended with a brushing sound of something sliding through the grass mat that covered the wall.

I grasped my flashlight farther down the shelf by my bed and clicked it on. Slowly, cautiously, I stepped out of bed and shined the flashlight toward the corner where the noise had stopped. In the beam of light, I could see that the point where the grass mats met each other on the walls, and where the walls met the floors, were loosely secured. The cabin's simple construction of metal and wood allowed for gaps and holes throughout.

I shined my light where I first heard the noise and saw my remaining half-dozen bananas scattered and partially eaten on the floor. I gathered them up. Outside my cabin door was a small fruit cage made of hardware cloth stretched over a wooden frame about the size of a hatbox. Mounted atop four-foot stilts, I had thought it seemed a bit eccentric upon my arrival, but now it made sense. I went outside, triggering the bark of a bushbuck whose successive barks faded into the dark surrounding forest. I opened the door of the fruit cage and tossed my remaining bananas inside. Back in my cabin, I crawled under my mantle of damp covers, listening intently in the darkness for any other noises until sleep again overcame me.

SEVEN

GORILLA COMMUNION

As the cold morning light filled the room, I was still tired from my wakeful encounter with the creature that had invaded my cabin during the night. Hearing Stuart moving around on his side, I opened our adjoining door and told him about the nighttime escapades. He had already had a similar experience before I arrived, and told me that he had learned from Dian and Peter that the creature was a giant rat. Not just a big rat, the common name was "giant rat." Incredulous, I had remembered reading about these, and searched through my luggage to find my Larger Mammals of East Africa field guide. Flipping through the pages I found the color plate of the large rodent with a long naked tail. Its face was also longish with large naked ears. On the same page was a picture of a "brush-tailed porcupine," and the two appeared to be about the same size. A rat the size of a porcupine—I mulled the idea over in my mind.

The text identified the creature as *Cricetomys gambianus*, and described it as being up to eighteen inches long and weighing up to two pounds. The field guide provided other insight: "The Giant Rat often lives in cultivated areas and in gardens, though it rarely enters houses." Except mine, I thought. "Mostly nocturnal . . . Very docile and becoming tame in captivity, the Giant Rat makes a charming pet. It is much prized as food by Africans." *Ugh!* As a child, I had a rat as a pet, but just a fraction of the size, and they didn't repulse me, but I couldn't imagine eating one, even though this rat had finished off most of the little bit of food I had left to survive on.

It was porter day, and my first chance to order provisions. I counted out the correct amount of Rwandan francs to cover the cost of the items I had written on my shopping list, and stuffed them into an envelope. I also wanted to get a quick letter written to Terry Maple and one to my parents in Virginia. It was my first chance to let people back home know I had arrived at Karisoke.

At last, I had someone I could vent my frustrations to. I was uncertain about how much I should tell my parents for fear that my mom would worry about me, so I wrote to Terry first. On a piece of camp-issue typing paper I quickly wrote him a letter describing my relationship with Dian to date:

> *Dian is every bit the tough cookie people say she is. She's really miserable and likes to make those around her miserable also. Everyone seems to think she's particularly miserable because she has to leave. Dian just can't handle hectic situations no matter how minor. I really don't see how she's going to cope with teaching a class back in the states. She's really been pampered up here at the Research Centre and does things her way.*
>
> *We really have to humor her and pamper her, especially at night when we go to her cabin for meals. Everyone has to act busy or she*

gets really P-Oed. Peter and I in particular share the brunt of her wrath. I don't know what I did to make her feel this way, but she has told me that I am very selfish and care only about my belly! Just about everything I say is shot down by her and when she speaks to me she's very condescending. She also says I am young and stupid like Peter was when he came . . .

She hasn't said anything about your letter and [research] proposal, and one does not ask, especially me. But the mother-infant [study] opportunity is up for grabs and Dian has acquired a ~33-month-old infant from poachers. Carolyn will be studying the infant and I will probably be studying Nunkie's Group with about 6 infants, and we will compare data and alternate duties occasionally. I hope that sounds satisfactory. Well, I've got to go now. This morning I'm going to make a long hike with Peter to see Group 5.

Peter had stopped at my cabin and was waiting at my doorway as I stamped and addressed the envelope to Dr. Maple's office at Georgia Tech. I would have to write to my parents later and send it out on the next porter day. Peter handed me an altimeter and a panga he had managed to get from Dian, and gave me a crash course on using them. The altimeter was made of gray plastic and about the size of a cigarette pack with a dial and needle that pointed to numbered graduated lines: nine thousand, ten thousand, eleven thousand—standing in my cabin's doorway, the needle read ten thousand feet. Noticing the way Peter wore his, I hung my altimeter around my neck. I gathered my compass, clipboard, and waterproof paper and stuffed them in my backpack.

"Oh, should I bring my camera?" I asked.

"Uh, no . . . you won't need it," Peter responded. "Better just leave it here."

I had meant to put my camera in my backpack already, but at Peter's response I didn't retrieve it.

"Baraqueza!" Peter called out to one of the men sitting around their fire in front of Stuart's end of the cabin.

"Eh, *tugende*?" Baraqueza asked.

"*Ndio tugende.*" Peter said, and Baraqueza joined us with his characteristic goofy grin. It was 8:30, and with the swish-swish sound of our plastic rain pants, the three of us trod down the path away from camp to look for Group 5 on Mount Visoke. The chilly morning mists were lifting and the warm sun was beginning to shine through.

The climb up Visoke was as arduous as the day before, but not having to carry luggage to the bottom first, I had a little more energy to make the climb up Visoke from the small meadow on the tourist trail. Perhaps I was adjusting to the high altitude oxygen levels too. Although Baraqueza and Peter led the way, I used my new panga to cut through the dense vegetation on the mountain slope. Before long, I grew accustomed to the sting of nettles, that is until I had my first brush with the much more potent elephant nettle.

With one inattentive swing of my panga, I slammed my right hand straight into the needle-laden stem and leaves of one of the menacing plants.

"Owww . . . SHIT!" It felt like a cluster of bee stings. Small bumps instantly rose from the red rash forming on the back of my right hand. Instinctively, I sucked on the welts, but it made no difference. The tall elephant nettle toggled mockingly back and forth, a thousand fluid-filled spines on each large heart-shaped leaf. I hacked at it vengefully and it sliced in half. Its top portion fell against my other hand in one last attack. *Shit!* More stinging bumps and a red rash on my left hand too. I would later learn that these were the nettles Dian used to torture captured poachers in what she called her "nettle lashing routines," slapping their bare testicles with the needle-covered stalks. Peter and Baraqueza stopped and looked back to see if I was okay before we continued on. As they did so, I tried to stifle my gasping for air at such altitude.

Group 5 had moved a great distance from where Peter had left them the day before, so we had to trudge in a wide arc across the side of the mountain in our attempt to relocate the gorillas. I tripped and stumbled to keep up with my cohorts who moved nimbly over the undergrowth.

After traveling up and across slope for nearly three hours, Baraqueza spotted Group 5's trail. He and Peter studied the crushed vegetation and dry gorilla dung. Each lobe was desiccated but not too decomposed and the once white vernonia sap of the nesting material was brown, but not too dark. This was yesterday's trail. Peter noted the altitude at which we found it, and I did the same—10,600 feet above sea level. From this vantage point we could see east across Rwanda and the three volcanoes, Sabinio, Gahinga, and Muhavura, that ran along the border of Uganda. A series of small cone-shaped volcanoes linked these mountains to the base of Visoke. The velvety forest that covered the mountains shone emerald green in the bright clean sunlight and the clear high-altitude air.

The gorilla trail led us downslope into a ravine Dian had named "*Chimo ya Kukutana*," or "Meeting Ravine." Peter explained that over the years, Dian had named various landmarks like ravines, ridges and trails with a mixture of her best efforts at Swahili combined with English. "*Shimo*" is actually the Swahili word for "hole" but Dian's interpretations and spellings held as Karisoke vernacular, and in addition to *kukutana* (to meet) there was a *Chimo ya Chui* (leopard) and *Chimo ya Plastiki* (Swahili-English for "plastic raincoat") and there were many other named *shimos* scattered around the study range. I would later learn that *chimo* was actually the Swahili word for "sin."

Peter and I followed Baraqueza along the bottom of the ravine as its green walls rose up around us. Black volcanic boulders jutted from the crevasse at its upper edges. Willowy hypericum trees hung into the gorge, their airy limbs draped in gray moss drooping and swaying in an intermittent breeze. We traveled downward inside this ravine along its center and were heading up and out of its downslope end when we suddenly heard the deep rumbling vocalization of a silverback gorilla, "*huh-hmmm.*" It came from straight ahead south of the ravine, and sounded like Josephine only ten times bigger. More a loud purr than a growl, the deep rumbling sound moved through my body and made the hair stand up on the back of my neck.

"*Eht mwah*," Peter gave his own version of a Fossey-style belch vocalization, and crouching down he waved his hand toward the ground instructing me to do the same. I complied as the pungent herbal body-odor smell of gorillas filled my nostrils.

"That was Beethoven," Peter said, as he made a note of it and a similar sound came from off to the left. "That one's Icarus, the other silverback." Peter noted this on his clipboard, and I did the same, noting the time and altitude of contact. We were now at 10,480 feet and it was 11:38 A.M. Having taken three hours to get to Group 5, we were making contact relatively late.

Baraqueza had disappeared into the foliage behind us, crouching down and dropping back when Beethoven first made a sound. Peter explained that Dian did not allow the trackers to be seen by the gorillas for fear that the gentle apes would become habituated to people who resembled poachers. The poachers were African and she felt that the gorillas would be sitting ducks if they lost their fear of men with black skin.

From our vantage point at the edge of the ravine, Peter and I could see the tops of nettles and thistles jostling as the gorillas, still hidden from view, moved downhill. As we drew closer, I could hear the snapping and tearing of vegetation mixed with loud chewing noises, belches, and flatulence. Peter and I sat in the thick undergrowth that obscured our view of the gorillas. For over forty minutes I could only see an occasional patch of black fur as the group continued feeding noisily and slowly moving away from us downhill. My notepaper remained mostly blank as Peter periodically made notations on his. By listening to vocalizations and catching glimpses, he knew which gorilla was where at all times. I didn't know who was who.

"Stuart told me that Dian said you take some of the best notes of any student in camp." I said.

"Oh yeah . . . ?" Peter asked, beaming. "Fossey said that, huh?"

"That's what Stuart said."

"Ha! Way to go Fossey!"

"What does she like about your notes?"

"Basically she wants to know everything the gorillas do during the day. I'm doing a study on cyclicity, so I need to know what females are cycling and when they copulate and who copulates with them, but Dian wants to know that and everything else, like what they're eating, where they are, who's playing with who, who's sleeping with who."

I envisioned Dian back in her cabin, no longer making the daily treks to sit with gorillas. The students had to bring the gorillas to her, at least in words. Again, scientific data was the justification for a research camp, but what Dian really wanted was the ability to be, if only vicariously, with the gorillas. Also, *National Geographic* expected another article from her, and she was writing a book about her life among the gorillas all these years. No one really knew that she no longer went out in the field.

"*Ha!*" Peter laughed again as he recalled something. "One time I got really graphic about a copulation between Icarus and Puck. I wrote things like 'Puck waited with her hot thighs spread wide open and Icarus shoved it to her . . .' and Fossey loved it."

"What did she say?" I asked, a little stunned.

"The next morning, she told me how much she enjoyed reading those notes."

My understanding of Dian was becoming more complicated than I could have imagined. I was sure I would have been chewed up and spit out by Fossey for writing notes like that.

"She likes trashy novels," Peter continued. "One time I was up at her cabin and she said, 'Peter you've *got* to read this book,' and she handed me this paperback called *Something Nasty in the Woodshed*. She acted like it was some great piece of literature."

Laughing, I practically choked trying to repeat that title, "Something . . . Nasty . . . in the *Woodshed?* What's that about?"

"I don't know." Peter said, derisively. "Do you think I read it? It's still up on the bookcase in her cabin if you want to read it *yourself.*"

Peter's reaction just made me laugh even more. The silverback gorilla, Icarus, roused himself, hoisting his girth upright onto his rump. At that, I brought myself into check, and dutifully made a note of it.

While Group 5 dispersed and fed just downhill from where Peter and I sat and observed them, I queried my fellow student on his relationship with our mercurial leader.

"Believe it or not, Dian can sometimes be a lot of fun," Peter said.

"Really?" I was as intrigued as I was stunned.

"Yeah ... Ha!" I could see from Peter's amused open-mouthed grin, he was recalling something.

"How so?"

"When it was just me and her here for Halloween, she invited me for dinner," he reminisced. "I dressed as a pirate and she was a hooker."

I'm astonished to hear about this other Dian.

"Yeah, Mademoiselli can be a lot of fun," he added, "but watch out if she ever says your hands are cold, and then tries to shove them up the front of her sweater!" He paused for a second as I laughed, then added, "Her tits are real small."

I just couldn't envision any levity from Dian, and certainly not flirtatiousness based on the woman I knew so far.

"When the ABC film crew was here last month, it was just about the best time I've had here."

The actor, Earl Holliman, with a film entourage had been to Karisoke, just weeks earlier, to film a special on Dian and the gorillas for ABC Sports. Peter went on to explain how the attention Dian received during that time had buoyed her spirits, and she got on great with everyone. As the only student in camp at the time, she needed Peter to help with the event and treated him well. Of course, she couldn't portray negativity with her own student with cameras around. Peter had obviously reveled in the social atmosphere of the time, with camp filled with creative people, and Dian on her best behavior. She was at the center of attention, and in the lens of the camera, in all her glory among the mountain gorillas.

I found it all so confusing. Dian who at that time depended on Peter, had now suddenly cast him off as a mere stepping stone to the next fresh batch of students, with Stuart as her new golden boy.

While the gorillas roused from their rest to resume feeding, Peter and I shifted to a new spot to keep up with their activities. Peter scribbled busily on his notepad. When I realized he was noting the new locations and proximities of each gorilla, I tried to do the same.

Icarus looked at me.

I averted my eyes.

Hmwaaah . . . I uttered almost involuntarily, painfully aware of his intimidating mass. Still, I furtively stole glances at this behemoth. As he chewed, I could see his great teeth, were stained black from plant tars in the vegetation he ate, just as I had read about in Schaller's book. From his high pointed crest to the broad, white-draped shoulders and back, Icarus was superb, majestic. For some moments, he held his glance on me as if pondering who this new guy was, his jaw set, eyes dark and broody under the shadow of his thick brow—a no-nonsense kind of face. What a photo that would make, I thought, crouching lower, and edging a little closer to Peter. Then I recalled Peter's negative reaction to my wanting to bring a camera earlier.

"Do you have some good pictures of gorillas?" I asked, reintroducing the topic.

"Yeah, I've taken quite a few. . . ." Peter paused, "The reason I said not to bring your camera today, is because Dian gets really pissed when students take a lot of pictures right after getting here."

"Ah . . . thanks for the warning." I said, with a sense of relief. "I don't need to give her a reason to bitch at me."

"Just wait till you've been here a while, or . . . you know, after Dian leaves. Then you can start taking some pictures. In fact, you should write to *NG* for film. They send me all the 200 ASA I need, and you just send the exposed film back to them for processing at their expense."

"Really?"

"Who knows—you might even end up with one of your photos in a Dian Fossey article in *National Geographic*."

"That's awesome!"

"Just don't leave your exposed film sitting out in your cabin."

"Why?"

"Dian's stolen mine."

"*What?*"

"She just took it and sent it to *NG* as her own."

"You're kidding! She goes in your cabin while you're out with the gorillas?"

"Either that, or she has a houseboy do it when he goes in to clean the cabins. Mine was taken when Basili was in camp, and I've never trusted him since."

"I guess if she's not going out to the gorillas anymore, she's not getting any photos of her own."

"Nah, she's not very good with a camera. She asked me to take her to Group 5 one day to take some pictures of her with the gorillas. But they were pretty much ignoring her. *Ha!* Then she pulls out all this candy from her backpack. You know, those Crystal Bonbons she has at her cabin, the ones she gives the baby. And . . . well . . . as researchers, you know, we're not supposed to deliberately interact with the gorillas, let alone feed them, especially candy, but she wanted more of those photos of herself surrounded by them. When she pulled out the candy, they stopped ignoring her, and went for the bonbons. She got what she wanted." Peter smiled, staring into the distance in fond reminiscence. "I did get a bunch of great pictures of her, though, surrounded by gorillas." His amused smile faded. "After that, the roll of film disappeared from my cabin. A day when Basili was in camp."

"Kinda creepy, to think someone's going through our stuff while we're out here."

"Yeah . . . I confronted her about it, but of course, she denies it." Peter paused for a second before continuing. "Be careful what you write in your letters, too, because she goes through our mail."

"*What . . . ?* But the porters pick up the mail for us."

"Yeah and good ol' Gwehandegaza takes it right up to Fossey's cabin so she can go *through* it first."

"No way . . . !"

"He's her spy. If she wants to open it and read it, she does."

"How do you know that?" My stomach sank. I had just sent my candid letter to Terry out that morning. . . .

"She confronted Bill and Amy about some things that *they* said she could only have learned by reading their mail. They had a big fight about it. She'll read your *incoming* mail too if she thinks there might be anything in it about her."

I was even more astonished when Peter went on to describe how Bill had been attacked by the silverback, Brutus, of Group 6 while leading a group of French tourists to them. The silverback had sunk his teeth into Bill's neck in an unprecedented assault, which only cast doubt on the notion that mountain gorillas were peaceful and harmless, despite their "bluff" charges. The unfortunate incident also gave Dian the temerity to say that Bill was too nervous and awkward to work with wild gorillas. I felt a queasy sinking feeling pondering all this new inside information, but my thoughts of camp strife were soon averted when Icarus began to approach me. One meter downhill from where I sat he stopped and sat upright. Folding his arms across his chest, Icarus stared boldly at me. Having learned from Peter to lie down and make a whimpering sound when a gorilla approaches, I did just that. Knowing, too, that an ape may perceive direct eye contact as a threat, I averted my eyes, training them instead on Icarus's massive forearms directly before me. This was thus far the best view of a gorilla I had ever experienced, and, frankly, more than I wanted at that moment. Icarus was huge, and his close, unobstructed proximity was thoroughly chilling. For what would be the first of many times I ran through my mind the fact that gorillas were actually *docile* creatures, "*gentle* giants," *benign* vegetarians, just to assuage my second thoughts. Still this four-hundred-pound ape was intimidating as hell. Trying not to make any quick movements that he might perceive as aggressive, I slowly made a note about the approach of this great silverback before me. My hand trembled as I did so, and I hoped that Peter, only a meter away, didn't notice.

"*Uh-oh* . . . here comes Poppy," Peter said. "She's my favorite."

Looking up, I saw four-year-old Poppy, a round ball of black fluff about one-third the size of the adult females.

"Why's she your favorite?" I asked, as the youngster approached my feet with confidence.

"She's just nice," Peter said. "Gets along well with everyone."

As the big ball of fur examined my boots, her little cousin Cantsbee climbed boldly onto her back as if mounting a thoroughbred. Then to my amazement, Poppy and her fuzzy little jockey strolled right over my feet and onto my legs. Cantsbee stared me down with what I took to be an impish mocking grin, as if he knew how this was freaking me out and thoroughly enjoyed it.

As if not to be outdone, Tuck, a full-sized female, crawled past Poppy and . . . *this can't be happening!* . . . onto my chest! All under the watchful eye of giant Icarus. Peter wrote calmly onto his notepad as I was pressed into the ground by Tuck's weight. "Is this okay?" I asked, in a quavering voice.

"It's okay for them to touch you, but not for you to touch them." Peter answered.

"Huh?"

"If one of the silverbacks saw you reach out to touch one of them, he'd starting grunting to let you know."

"Oh God."

"And if you didn't stop, he'd probably charge you."

The shock of it all made me tremble like jelly, my nervous laughter stifled by my struggle to breathe.

"They do this to new people," Peter said, smiling nonchalantly as the rest of Group 5, in a promenade of dominion and fright, walked onto and over me, as if I was merely a carpet for them. I abandoned note-taking as I was pressed deeper into the undergrowth, too frozen in shock to even whimper. Peter remained composed and nonchalant, calling out their names as if announcing arrivals to a royal ball: "Pablo . . . Marchessa . . . Tuck . . . Muraha . . . Shinda . . ."

Excitement mixed with fear, and my trembling continued. I wanted to speak, to make a joke, make light of the situation, but I couldn't utter a sound. Each individual lingered a moment or two atop my quivering body, inspecting my clothing and gear, their weight holding me onto the substrate on which I lay. Their warm herbal breath filled my sinuses. I was covered in gorillas, literally being pressed *into* the ground!

Only when their curiosity of me, the new guy, was satisfied through ogling, smelling and touching in a baptism of fur, did they move on, one by one. Suddenly Cantsbee clambered off of Poppy in a wild dismount and, as if in a dare to walk over hot coals, he mockingly galloped across my chest before rejoining his mother, Puck, somewhere above my head.

Only Poppy, the first to have begun the siege, lingered upon me. Still sitting on my legs, and intrigued by my rubber rain pants, she began to mouth them. *Uh oh, what if she bites?* Aware that Mama Puck was still looming above me, just out of my range of vision, I watched in horror as Poppy's licking turned to nibbles and her teeth began to catch the hairs and skin on my thigh, through the rubber pants. With mighty Icarus still watching over us, I was afraid even to moan as the sixty-pound juvenile had her way with my clothing. When she caught another piece of my flesh between her teeth, I actually flinched. With that, Poppy stopped and drew back. I could see her pondering what she had done. She seemed to care about my reaction. Looking up, she scanned the rest of my outfit one more time before scampering over me to join the others just uphill, knocking my shoulder back to the ground in the process. I craned my neck to see that Puck was gone, and Icarus shifted to watch the others move on up the slope.

The old silverback, Beethoven, had traveled around us and upward from another direction, but Icarus decided to use the same path as the rest of the group and followed their trail over the crushed weeds along the length of my body. *Is he going to walk on me too?* Too cool to show any interactive interest in me, he strode quietly past, his girth brushing against me as he blocked out the sun like some great ocean liner. Soon, he and the rest of the group were out of sight, and I collapsed onto my back like a boneless chicken, while Peter simply penciled in his last notes, casually checking his altimeter. Just another day for Peter, this was the experience of a lifetime for me! We'd be heading back to camp soon, and facing Dian again, but just then I didn't care; I was riding the high of my gorilla communion.

EIGHT

GORILLA WITHOUT A NAME

Her father's drinking and run-ins with the law brought an end to Dian's parents' marriage when she was only six. A year later her mother remarried an ambitious building contractor. Despite financial success, her mother and stepfather refused to indulge little Dian, instead insisting she eat in the kitchen with the housekeeper at dinnertime. Pets were not allowed either—though the child was clearly fascinated by animals—save for a goldfish that soon died, causing their little girl to grieve for a week. She was not allowed to get another. Dian's mother never talked about her daughter's biological father, who drifted out of Dian's life early on. As an adult, she had sporadic reconnections with him via letters, until finally receiving news that he'd killed himself.

Dian's first career choice was veterinary medicine, but she lacked the academic aptitude to pass the necessary chemistry and physics courses, settling instead for a degree in occupational therapy and a budding career working with disabled children in Louisville, Kentucky, far from her mother and stepfather. There she rented a small cottage on a farm, surrounded by animals domestic and wild.

In 1963, Dian took out a loan to follow a dream of touring Africa. A fortuitous meeting with the famed archeologists Louis and Mary Leakey led to Louis encouraging this attractive young woman to follow up on George Schaller's landmark gorilla studies. Three years later, the determined would-be scientist set up camp at the former site of noted naturalist Carl Akeley's camp at the base of towering Mount Mikeno on the Zaire side of the Virunga Volcanoes, just a half day's hike through the forest and across the border from Karisoke's location.

Within a year, political strife in Zaire forced Dian to move her base into Rwanda. Despite an acute fear of heights, Dian persisted by sheer force of will at habituating several gorilla groups as they traveled through deep ravines and up steep volcanoes. Simply by enduring the bluff charges from the silverbacks long enough to wear them down to the point of blasé indifference to her persistent presence, she was eventually rewarded with the ability to sit among the giant apes and observe.

Dian had long since ended her regular treks to the gorillas, remaining instead in her cabin to peck away at her book manuscript on an old field Olivetti typewriter between drags from Impala cigarettes and swigs of Johnnie Walker. By the time I arrived, all of the gorilla research had long been carried out by students.

The three study groups lived within a practical morning's hike. At least, they started out that way. Peanuts's group consisted of the lead silverback and younger remnant males from Group 4, which had been tragically decimated by poachers just two years earlier, as reported by previous student Ian Redmond who returned to camp one day with the horrific news that the lead silverback, Digit, had been slaughtered by poachers. In the course of this struggle, other gorillas in the group had also been killed. The fracturing of these groups subsequently generated even further losses; for when a group loses its lead males, it's not long before other silverbacks draw these females away into their own groups. Tragically, after transfer, these new males kill any of the dependent youngsters that come with their new mates. This serves the selfish gene by getting the mothers cycling again so they can produce offspring with their new silverbacks.

Our gorilla orphan's rescue had been no small feat. When poachers had approached a local French doctor, Pierre Vimont, about purchasing a baby mountain gorilla, Dr. Vimont quietly alerted authorities. The good doctor then heroically agreed to participate in a sting operation to locate and confiscate the baby, even allowing himself to be arrested in the process so as not to blow his cover. Dr. Vimont was released immediately afterward, but the poachers stayed in jail, and the baby was brought to Dian.

The little one's care and well-being became a full-time job for Carolyn and me, sharing duties on alternate days. I was captivated by the baby gorilla and enjoyed spending time with her. Covered in lustrous black fur, save for her leathery black face, hands, and feet, the little ape was entirely childlike, playful and curious, with obvious emotions. At one point, as it started to rain, I took her into my cabin. When I tossed her onto the nylon sleeping bag on my bed, she slid across it on her own sleek fur. Excited by the sensation, she raised herself up and spun into another slide. Inspired by her play, I grabbed her arms and made her slide again. At that she chuckled happily—"*uh uh uh uh uh uh . . .*" like a child at a playground.

When that novelty subsided, her eyes were drawn to objects in the room, the water bottles, the typewriter, the papers, my notes . . . Nothing was out of reach for this long-armed little climber and she grabbed at everything, knocking over bottles, pulling papers to the floor. I whisked her back outside, but put her down too soon.

There she spied the fruit cage suspended just outside my door, containing my last few bananas. At the sight of the tempting fruit, she scrambled over to the spindly poles and attempting to climb, nearly pulled the whole thing down on top of her. I peeled her arms and legs from the dilapidated structure and carried her out of sight of any human temptations where she could instead resume feeding on her own natural bounty from the forest.

After realizing the baby was not a male as she had originally thought, Dian dropped the name "Charlie" and left her nameless. Needing a means to refer to the little orphan in my notes, I began using the name "Sophie" after a feisty, favorite aunt of mine.

"*Sophhhieee*," Dian said, crinkling her nose while drawing out the *ph* sound with a scowl. "What kind of a name is that?" The next day, Dian began calling the baby "Josephine."

Dian worried constantly about little Josephine's health, fearing the little thirty-pound gorilla was suffering from bloat, declaring that the baby's stomach was too tight because she wasn't passing gas.

"I want you to make a note of her bowel movements and urinating," Dian instructed. "If she stays bloated she'll die." Dian had a knack for emphasizing the dire in things. "Same for passing gas, and you and Caroline need to collect her dung so I can weigh it at the end of each day."

And so, by the end of each day, the pockets of my jeans bulged with gorilla dung that I had wrapped in leaves.

While I was still an undergraduate, Dr. Joshua Laerm, my zoology professor at the University of Georgia, had agreed to grant me credit toward my BS in zoology as an independent study in what he agreed was a rare and unique learning experience. Otherwise, I had little knowledge of research methods, but Terry Maple had suggested a couple topics and provided me with written research proposals prior to my arrival. Despite my ignorance, I finally made bold to present these to Dian. One idea proposed the study of adult males, or silverbacks, and the role they played with gorilla group dynamics, but the other was a focus on mother/infant behavior. Caring for our little orphan certainly seemed in line with such a study. I expected Dian to see these proposal efforts as a serious commitment to the mission of her research center. Her response, however, was no reaction at all. After I had handed her these in written form, she never mentioned them again.

"I'm going to have Carolyn take care of the baby gorilla full time." Dian wailed to Stuart soon after, with me within earshot. "John can just go out to Group 5 with Peter, or help you look for Nunkie."

Dian was frantic about her research gorilla Nunkie and his group of females who had moved out of the study range, and were last known to be in heavy poacher area far into Zaire.

"Nunkie's dead!" Dian shouted. "They're all dead! I know they are! And nobody gives a damn about it except me!" These outbursts served well to illicit a sympathetic response, and Dian calmed down when Stuart willingly agreed to make a series of arduous treks well into Zaire without visas or permits in search of this missing gorilla group. Dian directed me to accompany him, but on alternating days, she had me back in camp taking care of the baby while Carolyn went to Group 5 with Peter. She seemed unable to make any long-range plans, and decided our tasks each night for the next day. We dared not argue otherwise for fear of a hostile backlash. Our long, tiring hikes to find Nunkie were futile, even accompanied by the skilled trackers, but we made them dutifully, and hoped against hope to find him.

It became apparent to me that Dian had an acute need for people. In fact, she could only work through others to achieve her goals. There was so little she could do alone, and yet she held such contempt for everyone. I think this dilemma fueled her anger. The word she coined and accused others of was "me-itis" in reference to anyone thinking for themselves, but all our efforts were directed at her needs, as we could best interpret them.

On my second day of babysitting, I arrived at Dian's cabin at 8:00 A.M. sharp to pick up the baby, now dubbed Josephine. Stuart was outside with Dian when I arrived. The little ape clung to Stuart's arms playfully while he swung her by her long arms to me as I approached. As usual, Dian didn't acknowledge my presence, and feeling like an intruder, I carried Josephine away to a patch of tall thistles.

"I told the men to unlock the Empty Cabin this morning," Dian said to Stuart, "so John can take the baby in there if it rains." Dian gave Stuart instructions for me as if I wasn't standing there.

"You've got a place to get out of the rain," Stuart said to me, grinning.

"Oh . . .? Okay, great . . . which one is the Empty Cabin?"

"*Eht mwaah . . .*" Dian growled, showing her contempt of my mere presence.

"It's the first one coming into camp from the other end." Stuart said, softening the first blow of the day. I was increasingly thankful to have Stuart as a buffer between myself and Dian. His job as her right-hand man was no easy task, and I certainly didn't envy the demanding position he was now in.

"The *toto* is out cutting some food for her," Dian said, referring to her new young Rwandan camp staffer, Toni, with the Swahili word for *kid* or *child*. "That is if the little woggie-poo can ever figure out what the hell is what out there, and not just bring in more goddamn weeds."

Josephine crawled from me to Stuart's legs and reached upward to him. Stuart grabbed her arms and swung her back to me. I pulled the little ape upward and she latched her arms around my neck while I carried her the fifteen yards away from Dian's cabin to the edge of the forest. Upon reaching an area of tall thistles and mound of climbing gallium rising above my head, I placed Josephine on the ground. Out of sight of Dian and the cabin, the baby made no attempt to leave me.

After pondering her surroundings for a moment, Josephine immediately pulled down a tall thistle and walked to its distal end. One by one, she deftly broke off the crispy leaves. With each handful of food, she came back to me, sat on my lap like a child, and ate before going back to the thistle or nettle or gallium for another handful of leaves. I was impressed by her adeptness at feeding on the spiny thistle. Despite her leathery little face and fingers, I thought that Josephine's gums and tongue looked as tender as my own, and it amazed me to see her place the thistle's thorn-tipped leaves into her mouth and chew contentedly. But I noticed that she intuitively positioned each leaf with the spines facing outward, directed away from her teeth and gums, as she drew them into her mouth always backward, thereby avoiding spine trajectory from head on. With her small but powerful jaws, she ground each mouthful to a harmless pulp, spines included. While she ate, her deep brown eyes darted about, scanning the foliage in front of her to make each next selection before swallowing the last. I made a note on my paper of each plant species that she chose to eat from the abundant choices around us.

When she emitted a low belch vocalization, I decided to respond in her language with my own imitation, *hmmmwaaah* . . . As I did my rendition, the little ape responded with her own long series of contented belch vocalizations that became louder and more frequent with each of my like responses. I soon realized that if I was out of Josephine's sight, she would call to me for a response that assured her of my presence nearby. When I walked farther into the brush without responding, Josephine immediately came looking for me, emitting a loud whimper until I answered, *hmmmwaaah*, and allowed her to catch up. This way she made it clear that she didn't like for me to move too fast ahead of her, or get out of her line of sight. Our vocalizations served as a contact call by which my little sidekick could assure herself of my presence in the forest. She was teaching me to be a good gorilla parent.

My little charge was also teaching me her language. In addition to her whimpers of distress, and her purring sounds of contentment, her repertoire included the sharp staccato, *"eh, eh, eh!"* almost like coughs, to show annoyance and frustration such as when waiting for Dian to open her door at night and give her candy. When I tickled her she chuckled with a soft rolling guttural vocalization, which matched obvious contentment on her face—the gorilla smile, with squinted eyes and parted lips.

About mid-morning, Josephine stopped eating from a cluster of gallium about four meters up in a small tree. After a brief pause, a look of repose on her leathery face, she began pulling branches in toward her. These she tucked deftly under her seated rump and legs. I thought about Peter's description of a typical mountain gorilla's day while I realized that Josephine was building her mid-morning day nest. The sight made me imagine her family, the group she had been born into, which must have had this idyllic forest routine before the traumatic event of their baby's capture and abrupt extraction from the forest.

The rest of our day continued much the same, with Josephine feeding and resting intermittently. As required, I noted everything she did, including passing gas, urinating, and pooping. I dutifully collected Josephine's droppings at Dian's request, and, after wrapping them in paper or leaves, placed them in my backpack for the boss to weigh at the end of the day. This Dian did to "monitor the baby's health" as she put it, but I didn't know what she measured it against.

In an effort to encourage Josephine's independence, I walked through the dense vegetation ahead of her. Without whimpering, she followed, stopping to pull down a towering thistle stalk. A bushbuck suddenly barked from a short distance away in the forest and Josephine's eyes widened as she stopped chewing. I looked at the second hand on my watch—eight, nine, ten seconds—and made a note of her behavior and the length of time she took to resume feeding. A stalk of stinging nettles stood among the thistles, and Josephine nibbled a few of the buds, oblivious to the stinging hairs. Having been given no specific guidelines from Dian on what she wanted me to record, I tried to write down everything the baby did, noting exact times as I had observed Peter do. Reading these notes years later, I realized that Dian learned not only about gorillas, but also about each student when she reviewed these notes each day.

8:51   J eats a few nettle buds and climbs on my lap

8:52   She follows me farther into brush, whimpers as I am out of sight, BV (Belch Vocalization) as she finds gallium, eats few bites, and sits next to me

8:56   We move on, J whimpers while following, I stop, J climbs tree w gallium, eats
(Total Feeding Time: 8 minutes 10 seconds)

9:15   I walk farther into brush, she follows, I stop at fallen tree, J climbs for gallium and eats 4m up
(Total feeding time 18 minutes)

9:35   J begins building day nest by pulling branches in toward her

9:40   rests in nest, scratching and looking around

9:45   gas

9:57   climbs down on me, no dung in nest, J climbs for more gallium

10:03   branch breaks, J lands in nest, continues feeding (Total feeding time 5 minutes 40 seconds)

10:04   urinates through nest

10:06   climbs to me, I tickle, J playful, I tickle groin, much BV, I tickle, J BV with eyes closed, mouth open

10:12   gas, I tickle, BV eyes, eyes closed

10:15   approaches me (Total Play Time, TPT 9 minutes 10 seconds)

10:16   J eats more gallium, eats bark of thick gallium stem, approaches playfully, I tickle, BV, mouth open, eyes closed, I climb down, J follows, whimpering through tall grass, I slow down, we get on trail, J leads for 3 meters then follows

10:24   We come into clearing, J heads toward Dian's, I go other way, we are separated visually by brush, J whimpers, I BV, no answer

10:30   J heads into brush and climbs 4 meters for gallium

10:42   branch breaks, J 2.5 meters about ground, continues feeding, no BV

10:54   *climbs down and jumps from 1.5 meters, comes to me, I tickle and BV, J doesn't play*

10:56   *I roll over and run, J startled, runs after, looking behind her, she comes to me, I notice she is shaking (cold or fright?) I let her come to me, J clings, I BV, she is quiet*

11:00   *We go to empty cabin as it begins to rain*

NINE

THE EMPTY CABIN

The Empty Cabin's door was unlocked as Dian said it would be, as cold air and heavy mist blew down from Mount Visoke, foretelling rain. As I lifted the latch and pushed open the heavy hand-hewn door, Josephine followed me inside with a wide-eyed look of suspicion and curiosity on her shining black face. This cabin was twice the size of the one that Stuart and I occupied, and was split into two large front and back halves separated by a waist-high wood counter jutting across its center from one side, creating a defined kitchen area, but without electricity or appliances. It was as cold inside the cabin as it was outside, but I was thankful to be dry and out of the sudden wind. I peeled off my backpack and set it down on the grass-mat floor.

The baby soon spotted a pile of greens in the middle of the other room at the far end of the cabin, which Toni had cut from the forest and placed here for her. She scrambled over to it, selected a long strand of thistle, and dragged the morsel back to my feet to begin peeling off each leaf and slipping them into her mouth. As she chewed contentedly, I idly poked around, opening drawers and cabinets, thinking about the previous occupants and their lives at Karisoke. One drawer was filled with forks, spoons, kitchen knives, and other eating utensils. A cupboard held old gray pots and pans. It looked like Peter was right in thinking that the camp staff had taken my assigned kitchenware to the wrong cabin. I dreaded the thought of having to point this out to Dian.

I had already learned from Peter that the Empty Cabin had been home to past occupants of Karisoke whom Dian had initially embraced, but ultimately scorned. Kelly Stewart, daughter of the famous actor, Jimmy Stewart, had lived in this space. At the onset, Dian was very fond of the cheerful, even-tempered child of Hollywood, and smitten with her celebrity. One evening, when Kelly had hung some wet clothes to dry by the stove, she inadvertently burned the original cabin to the ground along with a month's worth of her own gorilla data. This she might have lived down, so star struck was Dian, but eventually even darling Kelly would be written off.

Kelly's downfall coincided with that of a young male fellow researcher in camp named Sandy Harcourt, a Cambridge University undergraduate. Originally, Dian adored and appreciated both of these students, but immediately grew contemptuous of them when their friendship intensified and evolved into romance. Insecure and paranoid, Dian simply could not tolerate camp fraternizing and socializing that did not include her, least of all romantic involvements. Perhaps they reminded her too much of her own, albeit self-inflicted, isolation and loneliness.

The most recent occupants, I had learned, were the archnemeses Amy Vedder and Bill Weber, the married couple who, during a growing feud with Dian, ultimately settled into this cabin, the farthest from hers. Amy had been doing a study of gorilla feeding ecology and habitat use with Group 5, while Bill was focusing on the social and economic factors of their work, which often took him off the mountain into communities below. Thinking their cabin had put them well out of earshot of Dian, the pair held court here with the camp's other disillusioned and alienated students, commiserating about the state of Karisoke. But desperately attempting to avert what she perceived as a mutinous conspiracy, Mademoiselli lurked in the darkness just outside with a tape recorder, feebly attempting to tape something to use against her foes. She later tried to intimidate them by saying she had an incriminating recording that proved they were scheming and plotting against her, but she was never able to produce such a tape. Instead, she read their incoming and outgoing mail in an effort to satisfy her suspicious mind.

When Dian found out about Bill and Amy's return to the base of Mount Visoke for the purpose of cultivating tourism, she was incredulous. Dian had fought for years against tourist visits to the mountain gorillas. Expecting the locals to learn and understand the importance of mountain gorillas and their habitat was unthinkable to her. Except for those who worked for Dian, Rwandans, for the most part, simply represented the threat of invasion on her gorillas' territory.

I was beginning to realize that Dian saw only an intrinsic value to the gorillas. More an animal activist than a scientist, she deemed the gorillas important because she liked them and they were victims of the outside world closing in. She must have felt the same about herself. Inviting the world in to share in the gorilla experience was inconceivable to Dian. She found them, named them, and they belonged to her. They were hers to share, or not share, with the visitors to camp, who may, or may not, have something to offer her in return, like the ambassador, or other embassy staffers, or photographers and filmmakers. Science and research were an inconvenient but necessary pretense under which she could be funded to operate and have permission to guard her forest. *How dare Bill and Amy make mountain gorillas available to everyone!*

Able and qualified graduate students, I was beginning to see, had proven to be the greatest threat to Dian's rule on the mountain, especially those that defended themselves. I began to realize that this explained her decision to bring in less accomplished, and less threatening, students like Stuart, Carolyn, and me, who lacked specific research agendas and defined ambitions of our own, but came simply to help.

In stark contrast to us new students, Amy had all of Dian's determination, backed up by a much stronger sense of scientific discernment. Strong independence, confidence, and ambitious ideas of her own eventually and inevitably made for a volatile clash with Dian. Word had it that in a pointed letter to the National Geographic Society's Research Committee, Bill dispelled images of Dian as an intrepid field scientist, revealing that Dian was no longer even collecting her own gorilla data, and was not only mismanaging the camp, but had also, through her antagonistic approach with poachers, brought on the deaths of several gorillas in acts of vengeance and retribution. This news only bolstered the facts and rumors already revealed to the conservation and scientific community that things were not as Dian, on the colorful pages of *National Geographic* magazine, would have people believe, but were in fact in need of drastic changes. The whistle had been blown.

The V-W couple had proved a force to be reckoned with. After leaving Karisoke Research Center in exasperation, the pair turned the tables on Dian by promptly setting up their own camp at the base of the mountain. Apparently, the entire Virungas did not belong to Dian after all. The two had since joined forces with other parties interested in the urgent need for gorilla preservation, and had gained the backing of an impressive consortium of several renowned conservation funding sources, including the New York Zoological Society, the UK's esteemed Fauna and Flora Preservation Society, as well as East Africa's African

Wildlife Leadership Foundation. Ushering in a new age of gorilla conservation, this formidable duo was working for the newly created Mountain Gorilla Project, organizing government-sanctioned gorilla tourism, and giving education programs around Rwanda on gorillas and the importance of the forested Virunga Volcanoes as a watershed. It was a grassroots approach that Dian had long disdained and resisted, if only because she wasn't doing it herself. Fossey had been decidedly trumped, and the rift set off a cold war between the two camps.

I had already seen her spit on the ground more than once when she had to reference this formidable husband-and-wife team, now entrenched so purposefully at the very trailhead to Karisoke. I soon learned that the ongoing conflict with the V-W couple only exacerbated Dian's erratic behavior and outrageous deeds over time, and had ignited a brewing revolution among the powers that be within East Africa's leaders in wildlife preservation and research. Dian's pending departure to teach at Cornell University, I soon realized, was not just an opportunity presented to her, but a carefully orchestrated plan to excise her from Karisoke, with dignity. I had merely landed in the middle of this storm.

While others were trying to unite forces in gorilla preservation to bring the mission to the masses and out of isolation, Dian tried her best to hold on to the reins; camp, after all, was her home, and the only one she had. She'd enjoyed many years of autonomy, determining who had access, when and how, to the small but special place she had built and the rare gorillas she had habituated. Dian Fossey had put mountain gorillas on the map . . . but *what next*? She hadn't built the place for others, nor habituated the gorillas for others than herself. And the gorillas she hoarded jealously as her own possessions. Like the person with too many cats to look after, or more dogs than they could feed, Dian was reluctant to surrender what she saw as hers, even if it meant they could fare better without her in the hands of a greater consortium. She held on as if her reputation and livelihood, indeed her very well-being, depended on it.

As I sat with the baby gorilla where she fed in the middle of the floor, images of the Empty Cabin's past occupants were vivid in my mind, and I could envision them finding camaraderie in here, seeking refuge at the very opposite end of camp, as far from Mademoiselli as possible. Plans for great changes in mountain gorilla conservation had taken place here, but I was thankful for my seemingly simple but important task of fostering this one orphaned baby, and hope for it returning to the wild.

The only furniture in the big empty dwelling was a large desk and a simple wooden chair placed against one wall under a wide window. One of the camp's portable Olivettis sat on the cold bare Formica desktop. While Josephine retrieved another stalk of thistle and dragged it to my feet to resume feeding, I sat at the desk and began poking through its drawers. The desk was empty except the top one, which held a stack of clean white typing paper and a pack of carbons. Realizing that I had already scrawled several pages of notes on my K & E field paper, I decided to get a head start typing them.

I counted three sheets of the paper and layered two pieces of carbon between them to create the triplicate copies Dian required, and rolled the bundle onto the typewriter's platen. I typed the date, January 25, 1980, and paused. I debated in my mind whether or not to write a letter home to my parents instead, and stopped to stare out the window in front of me. The camp trail led away from this side of the cabin toward the center of Karisoke across a small bog that had become choked with a reed-like flowering plant that I later learned was *crocosmia*, not native to the area, but a gift from Ros Carr, Dian's longtime friend who lived above Lake Kivu on the other side of Mount Karisimbi. As I gazed at them, they were blooming abundantly with stalks of tiny orange trumpet-shaped flowers like miniature gladioli. Their color glowed like flames in the swirling mist and light drizzle that fell. I hadn't noticed them before but realized that these were the flowers Dian had supplied Stuart's room with before I had arrived.

Again I thought of my parents back home. Mom had wanted a source of fresh cut flowers, and Dad had once bought her dozens of gladioli and dahlia bulbs. Together they planted them in long rows in the field in front of our cabin in Zepp, Virginia. During that summer they sprouted and sported an array of brilliant colors and exotic blossom shapes that I had never seen before. I was entranced by their tropical appearance bursting from the gray shale covering the ground along a dilapidated barbed wire fence row strewn with weedy locust trees and oak saplings.

As the rain picked up, and sounded on the metal roof of the cabin, it struck me in the moment that it would be an entire year before I would see Mom and Dad again. Suddenly it seemed like it would be an eternity. I missed them terribly. *What were they doing in their big old house without children? What were they thinking when they took me to the airport where I embarked on my trip to the middle of Africa?* I had teased Mom when she had worried about me, and was smug in my independence. At twenty-three, I had never been away from home that long. As a tight feeling in my throat welled up, I realized I had not felt homesickness since I was a child staying overnight with cousins in Pennsylvania. A whole year in this place, that had once seemed so exciting in anticipation, now loomed oppressive and eternal like the rainy season upon us.

Josephine grabbed the bottom of my shirt and I snapped back into the moment while she hoisted herself up the back of my chair. She adjusted her position, settling her fuzzy rump onto the top of the chair's back, right against the base of my neck. Once situated, she uttered a contented belch vocalization, *hm mmmmhh . . .* The pungent herbal smell of her digesting forage filled my nostrils.

Josephine began grooming the top of my head. I could feel her chubby fingers sifting gingerly through my hair and hoped she wouldn't find anything living there. The little gorilla's subtle touch sent a wave of relaxation across my scalp and down my neck and shoulders. I tried to resume typing, but stopped again to enjoy the sensation as if it was a scalp massage. Then I understood the mystique of primate grooming behavior.

When our traveling classroom had seen vervet monkeys or olive baboons in Kenya six months earlier, our leader Terry Maple had repeatedly emphasized the importance of grooming as a social activity within primate societies. "It strengthens the bond between individuals," he would say while we witnessed one monkey grooming another, its nimble simian fingers proficiently articulating the hairs of the other. Occasionally the groomer would pick some tiny particle out of its partner's fur and place it in its own mouth. Other times our group would see a mother baboon pull her baby out of play with another infant and draw it onto her lap. As the mother began grooming her offspring, the baby would stop resisting her and half-close its eyes in relaxed compliance.

Now I was enjoying the same luxury, and understanding its appeal, as Josephine worked her way down my left sideburn and into my beard. I tilted my head as if I was in a barber's chair. The beard grooming was even more relaxing than on my head. Suddenly a warm feeling started at the base of my neck and traveled down my spine accompanied by the smell of urine and the sound of liquid dripping on the floor. My little groomer was relieving her bladder down my back! In a reflex action, I intuitively pig-grunted . . . *eh eh eh* . . . and bolted to my feet. Josephine clung to the back of the chair, but without my weight as a counterbalance, gorilla and chair toppled to the floor!

"No, Josephine!" I exclaimed, but the little gorilla, righting herself, just stared blankly up at me as if asking, *what's your problem?*

Exasperated, I dropped to my knees in front of her and she crawled onto my lap, wrapping her furry arms around my neck. We sat quietly for a moment, and I shuddered as the urine on my back turned cold and clammy. I used the baby's body warmth to warm myself as I snuggled with her in apology for my allowing her to plummet to the floor. At least the rain outside had let up.

Minutes later, light shuffling footsteps approached on the muddy trail outside the Empty Cabin. I sighed in recognition of Dian's voice.

"Uh . . . John?"

"Yes? We're in here."

Dian lifted the latch and, easing the door open, stepped up into the cabin. I rose to my feet as the baby clambered to Dian, who crouched down and joined the little gorilla on the floor. I noticed Dian was feeling Josephine's stomach.

"She's had several lobes of poop today and she just peed down my back," I said, forcing a laugh.

"Did you make a note of it?"

"Yes, well I was just going to . . ."

"You know you've got to keep a record of her dung and urine, or we'll have no way of monitoring her health. No way *at all*." Dian had a distinct way of running the words *at all* together as if they were one *atall*.

"I know, I've saved the lobes right here." I retrieved the crumpled paper from my backpack with the seven clover-shaped segments of gorilla dung. Dian craned her neck and eyed the small turds dubiously.

As if embarrassed by the scene, but excited by our visitor, Josephine slapped at Dian. Dian was silent as Josephine climbed onto her lap. I turned sideways in my chair and began writing a note about Josephine urinating . . . on me.

"This . . . uh . . . Terry Maple . . ." Dian wrinkled her nose and scowled as she drew out the sentence, "Who is he again?" she asked, keeping her attention on the baby.

"He's a psychology professor at Georgia Tech." I answered optimistically, thinking that she must have finally read Terry's research proposals for a silverback study at Karisoke. "He's also worked at Emory and has a lot of experience with animal behavior, especially primate behavior."

Dian remained silent.

"He sponsored my coming here." I tried to temper the enthusiasm in my voice to prevent triggering her need to keep me suppressed.

"So far, I'm not very impressed with you . . ." Dian said, without looking up, "Or Carolyn either." My heart sank, and then my own feelings of disappointment were replaced by the angry feeling of being backed into a corner again, poked and prodded unrelentingly. As Josephine moved back to her pile of wild celery, Dian looked up at me. "You're not worth much to me." I was speechless, and thought to myself, *What the hell do you want from me?* I became aware that my lips had formed the tight-pursed posture assumed by an annoyed gorilla, and wondered if Dian could read my expression.

Dian shifted onto her left thigh with her legs tucked under her, and sat quiet and tense for a moment.

"Sometimes we have to make sacrifices . . ." she began. "We can't always have what we want." Dian fell silent again. My frustration turned to puzzlement as I waited for her to continue her speech. Slowly it began to come to me—Terry Maple . . . a silverback study . . . the baby gorilla . . . Dian must have read Terry's proposal, and was worried about who would take care of Josephine if I focused on a study of my own. *Why didn't Dian just come out and say what she needed? Why did she need to make me feel guilty and try to humiliate me into helping her?* I wished I simply could've confronted her on this, but I'd had no previous experience with someone like her, and lacked the skills and aptitude for the mind game that was playing out before me.

"Dr. Maple's proposals are just suggestions," I said. "Terry and I were just as interested in a mother-infant study even before we knew there was a baby in camp." I did not admit it to Dian, but I really didn't know how to approach a study of silverbacks and having had no real research experience, I thought a study of gorilla mothers and their infants would be simpler to conduct.

The lines in Dian's face softened as she looked at me. "It's important that someone is willing to devote themselves to the baby. Really and truly . . . she needs work."

"Well, I'll do it," I said, dumbfounded by the realization that Dian had been thinking I would not be interested.

Dian didn't smile, but her frown was gone as she looked at Josephine nibbling blissfully on a stalk of wild celery. I had hoped for Dian's approval from the moment I met her, but was just then strangely uncomfortable with the idea that we could have some sort of positive relationship. Although Dian's direct contempt was hard to take, I had grown comfortable with the distance it brought between me and this woman who I now found so unnerving.

Our silence was broken by the slow hiss of flatulence from Josephine.

"She's been eating a lot today," I said, "and farting a lot too." Dian cracked a smile.

"She needs to be active." Dian said, "You've got to play with her also."

"She's been active today. Haven't you Josephine?" I crouched down on the floor and swatted at the little gorilla who dropped her celery, raised her arms, and pounced on me. My furry friend and I tumbled across the grass mat floor into the other half of the cabin. Josephine chuckled as I tickled her ribs. Dian was smiling now as she crawled on her knees and followed the two of us on the floor. The little gorilla rose up on her legs and beat her chest like a miniature King Kong before pouncing on Dian who managed a restrained laugh while grabbing at her little foster ape.

"That's a 'two-hand slap,'" Dian said when the baby raised her arms and slapped both hands on my head. When Josephine banged her hand against her upper torso before falling onto Dian, my boss pointed out that maneuver too. "That's a 'one-hand chest beat.'"

Josephine let out a slow hisser, that filled the room with the essence of partially digested forest foliage, and I added a descriptor of my own. "That's a fart." Dian barely smiled at my joke, but I could see that the tension that was on her face when she arrived was mostly gone.

For the next ten minutes, Josephine played heartily with me as I chased and tickled her across the floor. The nimble gorilla farted repeatedly as she spun and rolled, her gas smelling like clean, fresh compost. Dian watched our antics until the baby at last collapsed in my lap to rest.

"That's good play," Dian said, with a relaxed smile on her face. The little gorilla sprawled languidly, face-up in my lap, allowing her heavy breathing to subside. Dian and I stared at the happy gorilla in repose on my legs as her deep breaths abated, and she closed her eyes in relaxed comfort. Soon, the baby was in the early stage of sleep, and Dian rose quietly to her feet and moved toward the door. Josephine roused and tried to follow her, but I picked her furry body up and turned her away to block her view of Dian's departure. As usual, there were no goodbye pleasantries from Dian while she made her exit, but I was relieved that her contempt and condescension upon arrival had abated and departed with her.

TEN

IT'S N'GEE!

After Dian had left the Empty Cabin, the clouds parted and sunshine swept over Karisoke, both figuratively and literally. I lifted Josephine into my arms and carried her out into the rain-washed air, down to the stream that ran through camp. At one place behind my own cabin there was a shallow ford with a broad flat lava flow to cross upon. The baby was attracted to this pretty crossing spot as much as I was and would linger on the stepping stones over the still pools, examining her reflection, staring as if in amazement at her own self.

When I crossed to the other side, Josephine followed. On the grassy bank, I found a black-and-yellow-striped caterpillar and picked it up to show my little friend. Obviously curious at first, she stared at it intently for a moment. Then, with a quick squeamish flick of her thick fingers, she tried to brush the insect larva from my hand. Her repugnance made me laugh. She was grossed out! Like a mischievous big brother, and still curious of her reaction, I moved the caterpillar closer to her. At this, Josephine scampered away from me.

Still holding the caterpillar, I sat back against a tree and waited to see what she would do next. Within a couple minutes, Josephine returned to me, pausing as if in thought about this dilemma—me with a caterpillar. Then with a succession of three squeamish swipes she knocked the larva to the ground and pounced onto me, grabbing me tightly like a child who thought there was a monster in the closet. Her little frame bounced with my convulsive laughter.

My curiosity piqued, I picked up the caterpillar again and held it out to Josephine. Showing her displeasure with a standard gorilla pig-grunt vocalization, *"eh, eh, EH!,"* she boldly smacked the bug from my hand. She'd had enough of my game. Her indignant disgust made me laugh some more until my eyes watered.

A few minutes later Josephine and I walked back up from the creek bank where I noticed a small frog tucked in the grass. Catching it as it leaped toward the water, I sat down and showed this new critter to Josephine. More tolerant of this greenish-gray amphibian than of the boldly striped caterpillar, the little gorilla examined it closely. Seated on my legs, she surprised me further by tasting the tiny creature with a lick of her tongue directly on its slippery back. With a blank expression of disinterest, and one brave swipe of her hand, she efficiently sent the tiny frog sailing back into the tussocks. Happy again, she drew herself in close to me, settling into my lap. Then, as if to thank me for annoying her, she urinated in a warm release of her bladder into my Levi's.

Just before 5:00 P.M. I started to lead Josephine up the camp trail for the night, but halfway up, Stuart approached from the direction of Dian's cabin with a folder jammed with black and white photographs of gorillas. He crouched in front of Josephine and began showing her the photos one by one.

"What are you doing?" I asked with a laugh.

"These are pictures of Nunkie's Group. Dian has a new theory . . ."

Stuart began showing each photo of a gorilla's face to Josephine who was mostly uninterested.

"And . . . ?" I asked.

When Stuart got to the photo of the silverback, Nunkie, the baby gazed at it with interest for a few seconds.

"Dian thinks the baby may be one from Nunkie's Group."

"Really?"

"Yeah, apparently one about this age has been missing."

Stuart gathered the photos back into the envelope, and as quickly as he had arrived, trotted back up the path toward Dian's cabin. Interested in learning more about this sudden turn of events, I soon followed. But not without the baby making a detour. Before I realized it, she had made a beeline for the fruit cage outside my cabin just as we passed it. Each cabin had a wire cage mounted on wood stilts outside the door. These permitted us to keep our fruits and other produce cool and safe outside away from the heat of the cabin stoves, protected from forest creatures like rodents and ravens. When Josephine made a quick reach for the caged fruit, again she knocked down one of the poles that supported the metal awning above my door. With the ensuing crash Josephine stopped in her tracks with a stunned look. After staring blankly for a few seconds at what she'd done, she opted to abandon her attempt at fruit theft and proceeded to a clump of thistles to dine, as if that was what she had really intended to do anyway.

When we finally reached Dian's cabin, Josephine took the lead, obviously anticipating the fruits and candies waiting for her inside. I was happy to see that the door was open, and I didn't have to restrain the baby while dodging her candy-crazed, gnashing teeth. Inside, Dian was sitting on her couch surrounded by pieces of paper and open ring binders. She was peering intently at a photo in her hands. Josephine just ambled past to the bedroom and climbed the ladder to her nest box where her treats awaited. Back on the couch, Mademoiselli burst forth with manic excitement at her revelation.

"It's Nnnn'gee! It's Nnnnnn'gee!" she exclaimed looking through me to Stuart standing behind me on the step up to the dining area. Dian stretched her neck and distorted her mouth as she tried to pronounce the combined "n" and "g" as one consonant in the Swahili-ized name she had created for a baby gorilla in Nunkie's group.

"NG" had become the nickname around camp for the National Geographic Society, and Dian had named one of Nunkie's babies "N'gee" after the organization that had backed her both financially and politically. Many Swahili words begin with an *n* or *m* and another consonant like *d* or *b* such as with *ndege* for *bird* and *mbogo* for *buffalo*. But most Swahili words also ended in a vowel that ran into the first consonant of the next word, thereby creating an easy flow as in "*iko ndege*" for "*it's a bird,*" or "*na mbogo*" for "*and a buffalo.*" These *n* and *m* words are difficult to pronounce in an English sentence with a preceding word that ends in a consonant. Having no gift for languages, Dian could barely say the Swahili-ized name she, herself, had invented.

"It's *Nnnn'gee!*" Dian repeated. She couldn't say it enough as she pointed to a page in the notebook balancing on her bouncing knees where she sat on the couch. Pages of photos of gorilla faces with sketches of nose prints lay strewn on the coffee table, floor and cushions surrounding her. Caught off guard, I looked blankly at Dian, who kept her focus on Stuart.

"You really think so, huh?" Stuart chimed.

"*Ehht mwaaah* . . . Look at this nose print drawing, Stuart. N'gee was born in '79. That makes her the same age. He's been missing since last November when Nunkie was in heavy poacher area in Zaire."

"Do you think N'gee could've been a female?" Stuart asked.

"Somebody might've got that wrong, Stuart . . ."

I later learned that N'gee was a male, but Dian did not express any concern that the missing infant from Nunkie's Group was the opposite sex of our little orphan.

"The motherfucking poachers could have had her all through December before we got her." Dian continued, as she closed her eyes and shook her head, emphatically lamenting, *"Oya, oya!* The goddamn poachers have killed the whole group by now!"

Stuart and I moved to the living area where Dian sat. The notebook on Dian's knees was a who's who of gorillas in the Karisoke study range, containing close-up photos of each gorilla with their estimated ages or birth dates, and their parentage. With each photo there was a corresponding hand-drawn sketch of a gorilla's nose. The faces of gorillas, and in particular their noses, have distinctive creases and folds that differentiate one from another. Most of the earlier sketches were drawn by Dian, but later sketches of new babies or gorillas that moved into the study range were drawn by some of the students. The nose prints and photos now served as a long-term record of Dian's gorillas.

"I need a nose print of the baby!" Dian surmised.

"I can do that." I offered, enthusiastic about being able to contribute in what seemed like a small but important assignment.

Dian scarcely heard me, instead lamenting that she couldn't find a close-up photo of N'gee in her folders. She went on to explain that there were better photos on file at the National Geographic Society's headquarters in Washington, D.C.

"Bob's coming from the States," she said suddenly, with the excitement of Nancy Drew on a case. "He should be able to pick up photos from NG." "Bob" McIlvaine, also known as "Rob" or Robinson McIlvaine, I soon learned, was a former US ambassador to Kenya, and current executive vice president of the African Wildlife Leadership Foundation in Washington, D.C. He was an old friend of Dian's, and some speculated that they had been more than just friends. After the brutal killing of the silverback named Digit from Group 4, he had helped her create and manage the Digit Fund. Dian used the money from the fund to equip and pay her poacher patrol.

Mr. McIlvaine, a staunch ally in the past, was on his way to visit Dian under the cloud of her continuing delays to leave camp and return to the States. I would eventually learn that an entire network of support that Dian had built up over the years, from the American Embassy in Kigali to the National Geographic Society in Washington, D.C., was eroding at an ever-increasing pace as Dian dragged her feet about leaving Karisoke. Rob McIlvaine was just one of the several individuals taking on the task of diplomatically encouraging Dian to move out of camp and on to Cornell.

That afternoon I sketched the baby's nose on a piece of paper from the art pad I had brought with me. I had always been good with pencil and paper, and so rendered a much more detailed drawing than the crude sketches on the walls of Dian's cabin.

"Oh John, you're an artist!" Dian exclaimed when I handed her the nose print that evening. "This is the best noseprint I've ever seen! *Eht mwah, hmm wah hmm waaah . . .*"

Score one for me!

ELEVEN

LOCKDOWN

It became more and more evident on my days with the baby, that our leader's indulgence of the little ape we were then calling N'gee had created nothing less than a simian Helen Keller, pre–Annie Sullivan. Under Dian's indifference, Carolyn's arms became covered in bite marks and bruises in her struggles to manage the small but sturdy thirty-pound gorilla. It was one thing to be the fruit and candy giver, but quite another to be the gorilla handler. Restraining N'gee became particularly difficult in the evening when it was time to return her to Dian's cabin. Candy was like a drug to her, and knowing it was waiting for her on the other side of the door, the mighty little ape, sweet and calm moments before, fought furiously, tooth and nail, for these seductive treats, grappling and biting with powerful arms and jaws.

Detached and unconcerned, Dian took her time. If we let the baby go, she would try to climb the flimsy poles supporting the entryway's sheet metal roof, dismantling it in the process. This, of course, annoyed Dian.

"You need to control her, goddammit!" Dian yelled when this happened. "Until her nest box is ready!"

The nest box could be fully ready, the *totos* having replaced the old nesting material with fresh new fronds, but if Dian wasn't ready with the treats, or otherwise distracted, it was a wrestling match with the baby just outside. Determined to master the situation, and drawing upon a childhood filled with animals of all types and sizes—from cats and dogs to cows and horses—I had to develop a means to hold the little ape that evaded her opposable thumbs. By grasping her from behind, high on both sides of her back, and extending her outward, I avoided not only her agile arms, hands, and feet, but her savage little bites too. When even this failed, and she managed a nip, I thought, *what would gorillas do . . . ?* Gorillas would bite back! Finally, I bit back, sinking my own dull teeth through a mouthful of her hair. The baby was stunned, but the tactic won respect. Her biting was instinctive, but just then she learned what it felt like to be on the receiving end of another's teeth. From that moment on, I developed a new sort of rapport with my surprised but much more compliant little charge. I became big brother gorilla.

Settling into my new roles, I began to understand that research itself was not Dian's priority for her "research center"; indeed it was in some ways by then a thorn in her side, necessary to justify Karisoke's existence and funding sources so that she could attend to her real interests, maintaining occupancy and control of her remote mountain home among her gorillas, and waging her ever-escalating war with poachers. Peter was the only one of us settled into a real research focus, and she allowed it to play out, if only because it added legitimacy to the camp's official research mission. There was no push for the rest of us to get started with projects of our own. Quite the contrary, we were there to take directives, serving her mission of keeping up with her gorillas, taking care of the baby, and battling the poachers.

And so my duties changed by the day. One day I accompanied Stuart on an arduous, but fruitless, climb to find lost gorillas, the next day I hiked with Peter to Group 5, and then the next I give Carolyn a break with baby gorilla duties. When I optimistically turned in my field notes at the end of the day, Dian informed me that they were *"reeeally bad."* She offered no specific guidelines by which to make them better, nor what she was looking for specifically, except to say that Peter's notes are some of the best she has ever seen. I thought she took some sort of satisfaction in letting me know this, as if bringing me down reaffirmed her authority. And so I tried to emulate Peter's method of simply writing down every possible action I observed among the gorilla subjects:

> *Beethoven moves away from Effie 5 m, sits, eats gallium. Puck rolls on back, closes eyes, naps 5 min, Cantsbee approaches from downhill, suckles from Puck's left nipple 10 sec, switches to R nipple 1 min. Cantsbee naps across Puck's belly . . .*

The long rainy season was full on, as I became painfully aware of during a subsequent outing to Group 5. As the first drops began to fall, members of the group began to huddle around the silverback Beethoven, while Peter and I donned our hoods. I assumed my raingear would keep me dry and warm, but as the deluge settled in on us, things began to leak like a bad roof. While the gorillas huddled motionless, and as unamused as we humans, I peered through the shower at Peter. Having been through this many times by then, he obviously knew his rain posture, cross-legged and hunched over, hooded well over his face.

I struggled to find a position that stemmed the leakage. When I thought the rain couldn't come any harder, it did. Rain hit my face, and drizzled down my cheeks, neck, and down into my shirt collar as if I was standing under a waterfall. If I moved my hand upward, water poured into my sleeves. Somehow, in my shifting, the rain even soaked past the elastic waistband of my rain pants, trickling into everywhere. My clothes were already sweat-soaked from the climb, and soon I was soaked to the skin as if I was naked. The cold air blew down from the mountain, taking the last remnant of my body heat with it, and I felt as cold as I'd ever been in my life. After days like that, my dry cabin and smoldering fire felt like a luxurious haven.

After returning to my cabin from another rain-soaked day in the field, I noticed that my porter list, and money envelope, had been picked up by Gwehandegaza, the head porter. I was disappointed that I had not received any mail from home, but I had my first delivery of food. The porters had placed the provisions I had ordered on my desk: fresh miniature bananas, a can of salmon, rice, eggs, sugar, onions, potatoes, bread, and a head of cabbage. I was beginning to see how the system worked, but alas, I still had no cooking or eating utensils.

I inspected my can of salmon suspiciously; its top and bottom were puffed out, instead of tightly drawn as they should be. Half-expecting an explosion, I punctured it carefully with my can opener. Inside, it looked normal, as far as canned fish goes, and although it had a strong smell of salmon, it seemed fine. The label said "Product of Peru" and I surmised that being canned on the South American coast, my altitude of ten thousand feet was responsible for the puffy can lids. Still, I couldn't bring myself to eat it, and I dumped the contents into the grass outside my cabin.

Back inside, I looked out my window to see a white-necked raven swoop down to inspect the salmon. Immediately, it gulped down several chunks, seemingly delighted by the find. I wondered if I had just killed the bird. Upon eating its fill, the raven couldn't simply leave the remains, instead it gathered another beak-full and hopped purposefully toward a tall, thick clump of grass. There it poked the mouthful deep into the base of the tussock until it was hidden. I watched, impressed by its intelligence, as it did this several more times, until all the salmon was cached. There went my dinner.

Stuart soon returned to his side of our cabin after his day in the field with Group 4 and he described this group of males—Peanuts, Tiger, and Beetsme—that was a remnant of their original large family group. Peanuts, who was a young male when Dian first encountered the group, was now a mature silverback. Beetsme was about fifteen years old and showing the first signs of becoming a silverback. Tiger was a twelve-year-old subadult, or "blackback."

Peter soon joined Stuart and me at our cabin and we talked idly for a while before Carolyn also wandered down the trail toward us. She had been living in the guest room at Dian's cabin and was somehow surviving there. The sun was drifting behind Mount Visoke, which cast its great shadow over camp, and the air rapidly cooled down to sweater weather. Moisture in the air began to condense, forming mist that drifted from the edges of the forest.

The cold sweat under my wool shirt made me shudder as I asked Carolyn how her day was with Josephine. Carolyn described a day very similar to the day before. Josephine had foraged in the undergrowth around camp, but wasn't too excited about her natural foods. Then, when Dian offered Josephine fruits and candy while letting her inside for the evening, the little gorilla became aggressively ravenous for the sugary treats.

"I hate the way Dian takes her sweet time doing that," I said, "while the baby's grunting and fighting to get out of your arms."

"How do you keep from being bitten?" Carolyn asked, rubbing her arms. I realized then where all the bruises on Carolyn's hands and arms had come from.

"I just grab her behind the arms," I said, gesturing the position with my hands, "on the upper back." I realized how difficult that must be without the necessary strength. Carolyn, unable to hold on to the gorilla, was relegated to being fiercely bitten. Dian had little sympathy as she dallied in her cabin each evening preparing the box of treats that made her the center of Josephine's attention. Meanwhile, the little gorilla attacked her handler in an effort to break free and approach the cabin door.

Carolyn listened intently as I described my gorilla-holding technique, but she maintained a solemn defeated expression. She had something else to tell us.

"I'm probably going to leave soon."

Stuart, Peter, and I were dumbstruck. Carolyn went on saying that she had been pondering her future at Karisoke while her boyfriend, Don, had been writing to her from back home, saying how much he missed her. That day she got another letter from Don again asking her to come home.

"At first Dian had been very supportive," Carolyn continued, "when I told her I was uncertain about how long I would stay. I told her about my letters from Don, and she spent a lot of time talking to me about her early days here. I really appreciated her being so open with me. She told me about the sacrifices she had made, and that I would need to do the same . . . to show a commitment to the gorillas." Carolyn paused and took a deep breath, water welling in her dark brown eyes. Stuart, Peter, and I listened silently, feeling the awkward tension and confusion in Carolyn's voice. "But this afternoon, I told Dian I was thinking of leaving and she just blew up. Her personality completely changed . . . she became really hostile."

I had already seen Dian hostile, so I could only imagine what *really* hostile meant.

Carolyn pulled her jacket close around her and stared toward the meadow behind us, adding, "She said a lot of cruel things to me tonight." She didn't elaborate on the painful details of Dian's cruelty, and Stuart, Peter and I didn't press her for any more that might be embarrassing. I imagined the worst.

Stuart broke the gloomy silence by suggesting we all have dinner together. Having not been invited to eat with Dian that evening, the four of us, happy to be among peers away from Dian, agreed to pool our resources and have a communal dinner at Stuart's and my shared cabin. Carolyn and I both had new provisions, but neither of us had the makings of a proper meal, since I had just fed my entrée to a raven. Of course, I knew where some of it still was, but bugs were probably already snacking on that. Peter had beans that he had soaked overnight, which the men had cooked for him during the day. Carolyn and I had offered anything from our new rations, and Stuart said he would cook rice to serve with the beans.

After gathering our meal components, the four of us reconvened in Stuart's half of our duplex and we settled in for a relaxing dinner. Over steaming plates of beans and rice, we joked about our culinary efforts and reminisced about the foods we missed back home. The lightness of the moment took our minds off the weighty responsibility of keeping Dian happy, and Carolyn's downheartedness had lifted.

The revelry of our evening, however, ended with an unexpected knock on the door. Each of us froze, forks in the air, silent.

"*Yeeesss . . .?*" Stuart said, eyes wide and unable to hide the baffled surprise in his voice at this unexpected visitor. A faint, breathy "ahem" we all then knew too well, revealed our visitor's identity, and her lack of sobriety.

"Ahem . . . Stuart?" Dian's voice was low and weak, and she followed this query with a choking cough.

As Stuart rose and opened the door, Dian squinted and stared into the glare of the pressure lantern. Her hair was disheveled and she swayed a little as she glanced at each of us.

"Ahem . . . has everyone typed up their notes from today?" Dian asked, blinking and squinting into the light of the small room. Stuart remained in the doorway and did the talking.

"Carolyn and John didn't have much to eat, so we got together for dinner."

"*Eht mwaaah* . . . Uh, that's really good," Dian muttered in a phrase I knew by then to mean not so good. "A fucking *dinner party*? We're here for gorillas, not to worry about our goddamned motherfucking bellies."

The four of us paused in dazed silence.

"We're about finished, Dian." Stuart responded. "I think we all still have plenty of time to type up our notes."

"Ahem . . . you guys have a lot of work to do here," Dian added, peering around Stuart to the rest of us, "and everyone needs to get their goddamn rest. Really and truly Stuart, we don't have time for little fucking *communal dinners*."

"Okay Dian . . ." Stuart lamented, "We're going to work on our notes next."

"Everyone needs to get the hell back to their own cabins NOW!" Dian shouted before finally turning to walk away. "I mean it! NO MORE COMMUNAL DINNERS!"

Stuart watched Dian shuffle back up the trail toward her own cabin before closing his door. The four of us sat in a moment of stunned silence before finishing our meal under an aura of tension, and retreating to our respective quarters, more with the intent to keep Dian unprovoked than to do our homework of typing gorilla notes.

The next morning, I walked with great effort up the camp trail to Dian's cabin. I really had just come to dread any encounter with her, and all the negative energy it brought. I didn't know I needed positive feedback to stay motivated, but I was learning that negative feedback without constructive criticism or direction was utterly de-motivating. I thought of Carolyn's words the night before and was beginning to doubt if even I could endure Dian and stick it out at Karisoke. *And where would I go?* I flew in on a one-way fare and didn't even have enough money for a return flight home.

As with my climbing efforts up Mount Visoke, I simply put one foot in front of the other and kept moving toward Fossey's cabin. I stopped wondering if I liked her, and told myself it was irrelevant whether she liked me or not. The important thing was the gorillas. That was why we were all there, I surmised.

Kima chirped and bounded across Dian's roof, disappearing into the upper branches of an adjacent hagenia as I walked around to the graveyard side of Dian's cabin where I had become accustomed to picking up Josephine in the morning. The front door was ajar, so with trepidation, I entered. In her living area, Dian was pacing in front of Stuart, waving her arms and again ranting about the need to find Nunkie's Group. Stuart was nodding understandingly and echoing her sentiments.

"Nobody gives a damn except me, and they want me to leave here?" Dian shrieked. "And what's going to happen to the baby gorilla?"

Carolyn sat on a chair in the living area, slumped as if in a trance, staring at the floor. Josephine sat at the doorjamb to Dian's bedroom, blissfully eating a piece of pineapple from an assortment of fruits on the floor in front of her. Like a zombie, I waited for Dian to exhaust her tirade and give me instructions to take Josephine outside.

"How can I *leave*?" Dian shrieked, "with things the way they are?" Suddenly she swung her arm in Carolyn's direction. "And that bitch over there can't take care of the goddamn gorilla!"

Shock snapped me from my apathy, and I flushed with contempt from feet to cheeks. Carolyn winced and shrank into a broken slump, ashen as she stared at the floor. As my heart sank, my mind raced. *Did I hear Dian right? How could she be saying such contemptuous words about Carolyn?* I had become accustomed to Dian's vitriol, having endured it from the start, but this was overt hostility beyond what even I had experienced.

"John's gonna have to take the baby all day," Dian said, "We'll just have to send Carolyn out to Group 5 with Peter."

I wished I could have said something, but as usual, I was struck mute. I wanted to confront Dian and defend Carolyn, but instinctively I remained silent. Josephine scampered to my feet and reached her arms up to me, oblivious to the human drama playing out in the room. I picked her up and headed out the door, glancing back at Carolyn, slouched in a heartbroken trance where she sat.

TWELVE

A SAD GOODBYE

The woman Carolyn had admired for so long in the pages of *National Geographic* magazine was not the woman she found herself working for, and the baby gorilla she adored had covered her arms in bites and bruises, under Dian's detached apathy. And with the onset of the rainy season, treks out to the wild gorillas were cold, wet, arduous undertakings. We all lived in one camp, but our interactions became only fleeting, so sensitized had we become of Dian's paranoia. Unless I was out to Group 5 with Peter, I saw little of him or Carolyn in camp. What was worse, I felt like none of us could let our ever-suspicious leader see us fraternizing without triggering her unbridled rage.

For me, life for the four of us took on the feel of being inside a sequestered cult in which, without question, we needed to carry out the impulsive directives of our mercurial leader in isolation from the rest of the world, as well as each other—"No communal dinners!" Dian reminded us at the end of each day.

At least by then, I had built up a store of basic foods from the porter list. I kept the dry goods in a metal footlocker on the floor, and the fresh fruits and veggies in the fruit cage on stilts outside my door. If we ordered dried beans, a camp staffer would cook them for us during the day on their campfire so they'd be ready to eat upon our return from the gorillas. After telling Stuart about the supplies I had found in the Empty Cabin, he was able to convince Dian to have them delivered to my space. I finally could have at least one square meal a day. It wasn't long, however, before my nocturnal visitor returned.

One night I awoke to the clang of my bean pot's lid being jostled aside on the shelf beside my bed. By this time, I had learned to keep my flashlight close at hand, and upon switching it on, I revealed the beady eyes of the giant rat staring into the light. Still chewing a mouthful of my beans, he poked his nose into the air in my direction, twitching his great whiskers as if trying to smell me beyond his own breath. He was the size of a cat! As I rose to grab for my panga, the thing flopped to the floor, dragging his thick naked tail like a snake behind him. There he held his ground, as if wanting to get past me to grab the pot of beans to take with him.

Blinded by the beam of light, the creature reared up into the air, sniffing and twitching his long whiskers, tail slung heavily across the flooring. Despite my fascination with animals of all types I found this creature disturbing in his scale and boldness. Giant rats, I soon learned, are not indigenous to the forest at this altitude, and had invaded only because of the food human presence brought. I reached for my panga by the wall, and swung. One broadside smack only sent him spinning around my feet, before he quickly regained his wits and slipped right back through the flap in the wall from which he'd entered.

As we were forced to withdraw into our own spaces, pet rat included, Dian became more withdrawn into her own. Except for sending us orders via camp staff, written on scraps of paper, our headmistress sequestered herself in her cabin for days. Even in her isolation, however, she ensured that no conviviality go on in camp beyond her walls. After dark, it seemed she could be lurking just outside, to intercept any attempt we might make at a social gathering. Like lockdown in a prison, each of us inmates were confined to our own cell; Dian, the warden, remained prepared to intervene at a moment's notice. One by one, I noticed Kanyaragana stockpiling a growing number of empty Johnnie Walker bottles he salvaged from her trash bin to store for use as valuable water vessels at his home off the mountain. These he asked to store in my cabin. Except for needing to use the kitchen, I imagined Carolyn must've withdrawn into her private end of Dian's cabin. At least she had a door to close and a wall between them.

Her hopes crushed by Dian's cruelty, Carolyn finally announced to Stuart, Peter, and me that she had made the decision to leave. After breaking this news to Dian, life under the same roof with the camp director went from awkward to unbearable, and though she was too reserved to provide details, Carolyn asked to move into Stuart's and my cabin the last couple of nights before her departure. She held on as long as she could. There, she insisted on sleeping on my floor, despite the giant rat's inevitable nocturnal visit, knowing that she would soon be whisked away forever by the camp's porters.

On February 1, less than two weeks after arriving hopeful and optimistic, Carolyn packed her few belongings for the last time and headed down the camp trail with the porters. That morning, as had become my full-time duty, I had picked up the baby gorilla then referred to as N'gee from Dian. As I watched N'gee forage on gallium cascading from a large fallen hagenia tree behind the Empty Cabin, I saw Carolyn approach with the group of porters who had finished delivering our supplies and were heading back down to the foot of Mount Visoke. Carolyn was dressed in the few clean clothes she had, but she wore a tranquil smile I hadn't seen since she sat on Judy Chidester's veranda overlooking a panoramic view of Kigali as we optimistically pondered what lay ahead. It was obvious that she felt good about her decision to leave Karisoke. I hugged her and she surprised me with a kiss on my cheek.

"You're right, Dian is a miserable wretch," Carolyn said, "and I agree with you that she's trying to break your spirit."

"Well, I don't know what else to think." I added.

"And she isn't worth my spit!" Carolyn added, alluding to Dian's displays of spitting on the ground in contempt of someone she hated mentioning.

Whoa! This was out of character for our own soft-spoken Carolyn, and I realized then that she had been internalizing all that she could and no longer needed to. I had never heard Carolyn utter anything disparaging, and still hadn't even heard her curse. Her experiences at Karisoke had somehow changed her. Obviously, she no longer clung to the hope of things working out, nor of giving Dian the benefit of a doubt. Her hope and optimism had buoyed me above the unrelenting ill-treatment Dian bestowed on me. At that moment I saw Carolyn as both defeated and stronger. She had become steeled in her decision to not keep trying to make this work and with that gained liberation in seeing Dian differently. Still, the hopes and dreams that she had arrived with had been shattered without mercy, and that had to hurt.

I knew that Carolyn's decision to leave was justified, considering the abuse she had endured from Dian. Still the reality of her departure was a blow to me because of its finality. Coming to Karisoke had been like a dream for both of us and Carolyn would never have this opportunity again. Still, as I watched her leave, part of me envied Carolyn's departure from Karisoke. I longed for home.

As the sound of the chattering porters disappeared with Carolyn among them, I was struck by the faint drone of an airplane. High above me in the equatorial jet stream, a distant passenger plane glinted silver as it flew westward. I watched wistfully, realizing how unusual it was to see any sign of the outside world from camp. My baby gorilla didn't take notice of the airplane, but stared toward the direction that Carolyn had departed.

Within moments my attention was brought back to the moment and my own reality. The baby and I could see through the trees that someone was entering camp from the trail on which Carolyn had disappeared. With a few porters ahead of him, a white man moved with the group quietly up the trail toward Dian's cabin.

Rob McIlvaine's timing could not have be worse for Dian. Her own appointee to head her foundation, the Digit Fund, arrived on the very day Carolyn left. A former US ambassador to Kenya, executive vice president of the African Wildlife Leadership Foundation, and longtime supporter and confidant of Dian, Rob was by then part of the cadre of professionals trying to finesse Dian's overdue departure out of Rwanda in the wake of her outrageous dealings with poachers, locals, tourists, and government park officials. The teaching position at Cornell University was a fine and dignified place for her to land on her feet while others took Karisoke in a positive new direction.

That night I dreamed that I was back in my home in Mount Jackson, Virginia. I was sitting on my dad's chair in front of the TV in the sunroom. Carolyn sat on my mom's old rattan couch. Refreshed and relaxed, we discussed having been at Karisoke. As we talked I became aware of a feeling of regret for having left Rwanda to return home. The feeling overwhelmed me as I realized that a lifetime opportunity had come and gone in a few short weeks, and I would never have such an opportunity again. I was missing the adventure that Africa offered me.

The sun was already coming up when I woke from this dream and maneuvered myself groggily into a sitting position against my pillows. My fire had gone out during the night as usual, and the clammy cold that had never fully been at bay had reestablished itself. Looking around my dingy, sparsely-equipped cabin I was relieved to be in camp.

Only in retrospect do I realize the effect this dream had on galvanizing my spirit subconsciously into sticking it out at Karisoke. It gave me the ability to fast-forward to my feelings if I had chosen to leave. I did not like what I saw in the choice to return home to the life I had outgrown in Virginia. Instead, with little motivation left in me I recommitted to spend a year in Fossey's camp, doing what I could do for mountain gorillas, and my little orphaned one. Dian might make me miserable, but she would not run me off.

I was only just beginning to understand the depth and complexity of the politics of gorilla field research and Dian's thorny stance at the center of it all. The morning after Carolyn's departure, in an uncharacteristic move, Dian graciously invited me into her cabin when I arrived to pick up the baby gorilla for that day's duty. Something I once would have treasured as a gesture of friendship, however, by then only made me wary and uneasy, and I soon realized that I was merely a prop, staged for Rob McIlvaine to witness some positive relationship Dian might have with her students. Naturally paranoid, Dian undoubtedly feared that Rob would have crossed paths with Carolyn, or at the very least would have heard controversial rumors of the sudden departure of yet another student. *And who knows what the Americans in Kigali were saying about Carolyn's unexpected exit?*

As the baby scampered to my feet, I was surprised to see Dian fully dressed so early, her hair nicely brushed. I was nearly speechless as she introduced me to Rob as if I was her treasured right-hand man.

"John's *reeeally* and *truuuly* been doing a wonderful job with the baby," Dian gushed to her authoritative visitor.

Head to toe in khaki, Rob was shorter than Dian; square, fit, and trim with close-cropped graying hair, he looked the part of a military sergeant. The photos he'd brought from *National Geographic* confirmed that our little gorilla was not N'gee, as Dian had been so convinced.

Kanyaragana brought Dian another steaming cup from the kitchen and she offered it to me instead, as if I was her dearest friend. Dumbfounded by this gesture, I awkwardly took the cup as Rob resumed his grilling of Dian.

"So, now tell me what the holdup is . . . ?" he pressed.

"I have a lot of things to get done before I go," Dian whined, "and the baby gorilla . . . !" The baby, I had realized by then of course, was Dian's ace in the hole for explaining her delay; it couldn't stay in camp indefinitely, and Dian needed to have a solution in place before leaving, "I'm still not sure what I'm going to do about her!"

Rob kept cool pressure on Dian until she mentioned wanting to take her head porter, Gwehandegoza, back to the States with her, at which point, grimacing in disbelief, he finally lost his patience.

"C'mon, Dian! You know you can't do that!" he blurted. "You'd never be able to get the paperwork done, for one thing!"

With the little gorilla under my left arm, I sipped my coffee, unable not to enjoy the scene before me—Dian made uncomfortable by someone more powerful than she, someone bigger than Karisoke in the broader world of wildlife conservation and foreign service. I allowed myself to envision a tolerable camp life with our leader gone.

The *National Geographic* photos Rob brought of N'gee, however, revealed that our gorilla orphan was not the missing baby from Nunkie's Group. Our baby, once again became nameless.

"Now that Carolyn is gone," Dian said tersely, as I followed with the baby on my back, "I need you to take full charge of the baby."

"That's fine. I'd like to do that."

"*Really* and *truuuly*, that cunt was not to be believed." I felt myself flush with anger at her choice of such a harsh derogatory word, but kept following silently like the dumb and diffident zombie I'd become. I couldn't even imagine where Dian drew her vitriol from.

"I'm sorry," Dian said dryly, in response to my silence, "I know how you feel about her, but I just don't need someone like THAT in camp." *Someone like WHAT I wondered . . . someone who admired you and came here with every intention of serving a woman who was to her a hero?*

THIRTEEN

THE POACHER PATROL

As an attempt to regroup after Rob McIlvaine's visit on the
heels of Carolyn's departure, and in defense of what talk
there may be in Kigali about yet another Karisoke exile, Dian
invited the three of us remaining males to her cabin for dinner, telling
us each to bring something. Apparently we could eat together as long
as it was under her roof, and her watchful eye. Suddenly, we were one
big happy bunch, or else . . . Dinner at Dian's came to be a familiar
tactic of her damage control.

Thankful to have regular supplies of food deliveries from the
porters, it was with great zeal that I prepared food of my own. I'd
learned a little Swahili and Kinyarwanda, reading a copy of the camp's
standard porter list—*vitunguru* for beans, *mchele* for rice, *viazi* for

potatoes—basic fare, but I got creative. A simple cabbage, or *amashoe*, became nirvana to me. Recalling my mother's skill at making paper-thin shredded coleslaw from Dad's homegrown cabbage, I did my best to re-create hers, making do with the juice of a lemon, vegetable oil, salt and pepper.

"*Tafhadahali*," Stuart said, as Dian's houseboy, Basili, offered him a cold primus.

"Ahem, *what* did you say?" Dian said, dryly, seated across from him. Peter and I poised in bemused anticipation.

"Isn't that the word for *please*?" Stuart asked.

"*Ahem* . . . We don't say that here," Dian replied brusquely, eyes red from another afternoon with Johnnie Walker.

We passed around our plates and bowls of rice, beans, and my Karisoke coleslaw as our conversation moved from the topic of Swahili to Dian's ideas about releasing the baby gorilla back into a wild group. As usual, Dian picked at her food as she talked, occasionally using her knife to slice and press thick chunks of margarine into her bread, before topping it off with a heavy shake of salt. This she ate heartily, sampling my slaw between bites.

"Who made this?" Dian asked, chewing on a mouthful of my shredded cabbage, like a gorilla finishing a bolus of gallium.

Sheepishly, I raised my hand.

"*You* made this?" She squinted her eyes at me warily, blinking several times. "I *like* it."

I had never known what it is like to have to bestow kindness upon someone who had been hostile to me, yet I discovered that I could muster up this kind of action. The next day when I broke for lunch from my baby gorilla care, I threw together a fresh batch of slaw, with a heavy shake of salt. As Basili passed by my cabin, I handed him a covered bowl of it to deliver to Dian, a sacrifice to the goddess.

That evening, after baby gorilla duty, I found something wrapped in paper on my desk. The paper was a note in response to the coleslaw: *I was just thinking of that this morning. Thank you. Dian.* Wrapped inside the note was a chunk of milk chocolate. Cabbage well invested! This simple gesture gave me the smallest glimmer of hope. Dian preferred those who had something to offer her.

From this point, Dian began to treat me with something akin to appreciation as she formulated her plan for the baby gorilla's release into gorilla Group 4.

With Carolyn gone, I became the full-time caregiver of our little orphan whose name had been changed from Charlie to Sophie to Josephine to N'gee. I thought Peter and Stuart felt bad for me being stuck in camp, unable to get out to see the wild groups, but I found a certain sense of comfort and satisfaction in this responsibility. It was certainly an important task, and it gave me my very own project, versus wondering where Dian would send me next, to tag along with whom, as if she didn't really know what to do with me anyway. Besides, I was good at it, able to get into the baby's gorilla mindset, meet her needs of feeling secure and give her the active play she needed without being spoiled. And because this caregiver task was so important to Dian, I knew it would curb my boss's antagonism toward me.

Dian's level demeanor may have been at least partly attributable to encouraging letters from Glen Hausfater, the man who arranged her teaching position at Cornell. Although I certainly didn't know the details, the arrangement also held the promise of male companionship stateside.

In preparation for her departure, she sent her poacher patrol out in a series of sweeps into Zaire to cut snares and confiscate dead animals. This makeshift army of Rwandans and Zairois was her pride and joy, in direct alignment with her own confrontational tendencies. She took particular delight in covering the bare feet of the towering and gangly Tutsi, Mutarutkwa, with new size-fourteen boots. These, she had special-ordered for him, and she laughed unabashedly as he ran in a comic and ungainly canter, in footwear for the first time.

The baby gorilla, nameless again, clung tightly to me, watching wide-eyed as this emboldened group of Africans marched past into the forest, and making me wonder about the day she was taken from her family. *Was it a band of men that looked and sounded like these? How many of her family of gorillas died in the course of her capture?*

Upon their return at the end of the day, the men of the poacher patrol proudly presented Dian with a bounty of poacher's traps in the form of rope and wire snares. Their booty also included purloined animals that had been caught in the traps. These they carried slung over shoulders, or carefully hog-tied in multiples onto wood poles carried between two men. Their victory put Dian in a victorious and maniacally upbeat mood. When her men returned with such loot, she made a party of it, replete with beer, and she swaggered at the center of it with great bravado. Vengeance against poachers clearly made her far happier than yet more gorilla data, and in light of the overt killings of Digit and other of her gorillas, it was obvious there was a very personal element to this war.

For the most part, these forays were conducted well across the border toward the direction of her original campsite, in the then-Congo, where she had once been captured and removed by Congolese soldiers; some accounts of this event include tales of rape and torture before Dian could outwit and escape her captors. How much of the pride she had for her own little band of soldiers heading back from whence she came to make their mark—her mark, actually—could be retaliation? Our research gorilla groups were not even frequenting the area where she sent her patrolmen; neither did she hold visa nor research permit for access there.

Dian played a dangerous game, but the game she played was more complicated than she appeared to imagine. I later learned, that unbeknownst to his trusting boss, her beloved Mutarutkwa, in his new Karisoke-sponsored supersized boots, was in fact, a poacher himself, spending his off days setting traps in the very region she paid him to patrol. So blindly gullible was Dian in her vengeance.

Dr. Pierre Vimont, the French physician in Ruhengeri who had rescued our orphaned gorilla from poachers, had asked Dian if a couple of his French countrymen could come to Karisoke for a visit with gorillas. In light of Dr. Vimont's heroics, and perhaps in thanks, Dian couldn't decline this request that she would otherwise be most unlikely to honor. Hosting these two men at her cabin and sending them off to Group 5 with Peter and me was a rare privilege reserved for only the most important people, or at least people who had something to offer.

On the morning of February 6, Dian had Peter and me wait for the two Frenchmen who had referred to themselves as *naturalistes*. While these gray-bearded gentlemen had a leisurely breakfast at her cabin, Mademoiselli came down to the campfire after sending Stuart to search for Group 4.

"John, would you come out and look at this . . . um . . . please?" Dian asked.

I followed Dian to the picnic table near the campfire. A dead black-fronted duiker, the species of small antelope that browsed each day in the meadows and forest edges around camp, lay dead and stiff on the ground by the table.

"What happened?" I blurted at the disturbing sight.

"The poacher patrol found it alive in a fucking snare two days ago." Dian lamented. "I was keeping it at my cabin, but it couldn't use its front legs and died."

I bent down and stroked the delicate creature's sleek russet fur. At such close range, I could see the beautiful details of the delicate animal, a female, her smooth fur, nearly orange, accented by a jet-black forehead. The tiny ebony horns were corrugated and tapered to a fierce point, and its nose was broad and black, resembling a dog's, I thought. Rwelekana stood nearby honing a large knife on a whetstone.

"I tried to feed her, but she never ate." Dian lifted one of the front legs. "Look at these legs and tell me what you think."

Feeling very self-conscious with Dian now soliciting my opinic
I took the dainty leg from her hand and articulated it back and forth
could hear and feel the crunching of a multitude of bone fragment
and shards; the leg had been destroyed beyond repair. Despite the stif
rigor mortis in the rest of the body, both front legs flopped in their
mangled sockets, limp like a rag doll's arms.

"You can feel the broken bones grinding in the legs when you move
it," I said, wondering if Dian understood that I wasn't actually in vet
school yet. At the time, I didn't know of Dian's aspirations to become
a veterinarian herself.

Dian summoned Rwelekana from the fire pit, speaking briefly to
him in Swahili. Placing his whetstone on the picnic table, the able
staffer rolled the dead duiker onto its back. One of Dian's most prized
longtime gorilla trackers, Rwelekana worked his knife with great
proficiency, slicing nimbly up the belly of the antelope in one stroke.
After cutting with the same dexterity up the center of each foreleg, he
deftly peeled back the hide.

"Wow, he knows what he's doing!" I said.

"That's because he used to be a poacher." Dian responded, dryly.

"*NOOO* . . ." Rwelekana blurted, surprising Dian and me with
both his apparent understanding of what she said, and his attempt
at English.

"*Ehht mwah* . . ." Dian muttered, looking at Rwelekana, who smiled
impishly before turning away furtively to sharpen his knife again on
the whetstone. Rwelekana gave me a side-glance and a furtive smile
me before resuming his task.

In no time, Dian's "ex-poacher" had the duiker's sinews cut away
revealing the tissues of its foreleg joints. The animal's muscles were
torn and near-black, clotted with blood from the hemorrhage that
had resulted during the animal's struggle, one foot having been
suspended in the air by a wire snare. The bones on the upper half of
each front leg were shattered into splinters. Dian and I stared down
at the dismembered carcass.

"You can see all the damage that was done," I said, bending down to move the leg again. "When she was stuck in the snare and fractured the trapped leg, she must've just struggled until he broke the other leg. These animals don't know when to stop in a situation like that and I'm sure this one thrashed around some more, grinding the leg bones to pieces."

"Do you think there was anything we could have done to save it?" Dian asked. This was the first time Dian had really asked my opinion on any-thing and I was taken aback by becoming more than just an outlet for her contempt. I really thought she wanted me to explain to her precisely what we could've done to save the animal, but actually I was surprised she had kept it in this condition for so long. I thought it should've been put out of its misery immediately, and hoped she would understand my response.

"We would've had to be able to put those bones back together . . . and then splint it. There's just too many fragments. All the bones and muscles would have to knit back together. She would've died in the process. These animals are so flighty in captivity, I don't see how we could've kept her alive even if we could put her back together. It would just be a longer, slower death."

"I know," Dian lamented with a sigh. "I just get so goddamned tired of not being able to do anything when these animals are brought in like this."

Dian spoke again to Rwelekana, and he resumed cutting up the duiker. I watched, surprised to see this man meticulously gutting and cleaning the animal, excavating its entrails before deftly removing the entire hide, like a deer being cleaned after the hunt.

"Do you just have them bury it?" I asked Dian, knowing that some-thing else was going on.

"I let the men eat them." Dian responded.

I was surprised by Dian's willingness to allow poacher contraband to become a feast, but accepted her ability to see the dead duiker as a food resource that her staff could utilize in the resource-poor environ-ment of our camp—and the poor country itself.

After Rwelekana carried the duiker away, Peter arrived, and Dian reminded us to wait for her two French guests who would join us on our visit to Group 5. Dian explained to us that they were acquaintances of Dr. Vimont, who had helped in the confiscation of our baby gorilla. Dian went on to explain that the older gentleman was interested in acquiring our little gorilla for his own animal collection.

"He's got *money!*" Dian exclaimed, in a hushed tone, leaning in close, "because he says he has a zoo in France. 'My zoo! MY zoo!'" Dian pointed emphatically at her own chest in her best mimic of the old guy. "He offered to take the baby . . ."

Knowing about Coco and Pucker, the two young confiscated gorillas she had nursed back to health years earlier before they were sent to Germany's Cologne Zoo, I was perplexed that Dian had not expressed complete contempt about this scenario of an individual wanting to acquire the baby for a private collection. Up until now, Dian had shown nothing but contempt for any outside parties interested in the affairs of her mountain gorillas. But these were special friends of Dr. Vimont and Dian was on her best behavior for her public persona and the stories told down below. And for what it might be worth, "He's got money!"

FOURTEEN

NYAMURAGIRA

That evening, Stuart returned to our cabin from Group 4, telling me that Dian was still frantic about Nunkie and this silverback's group of females. Because the photos that Bob McIlvaine had brought from *National Geographic* had confirmed our baby gorilla was not N'gee from Nunkie's Group, as she had been thinking, Dian gained a little optimism that Nunkie's Group was still out there, intact, somewhere beyond the research range.

"She wants you to come with me and Rwelekana tomorrow," he said, "to find Nunkie."

"Okay," I said, "sounds like an adventure."

"Yeah . . . you know, we're going to have to go way into Zaire," he added.

"Yeah . . . ?" We had already been out to visit Peanuts's group numerous times across the border.

"This time we'll be going all the way to the other side of Mount Visoke . . .

"And . . . ?"

"And we don't have visas for Zaire."

"I know, but, sounds like plenty of others have done it before us."

Stuart and I chatted about the risks of getting caught so far into Zaire without visas, shrugging off the danger as being negligible, considering that we'd be deep in the forest and high on Mount Visoke's slopes. I began to think that my willingness, or a possible lack thereof, was more a concern of Dian's than of Stuart's. I surmised that previous students had made a case of Dian putting them at risk, and she assumed I would be unwilling. Students unwilling to take the risks she required, or put themselves in danger, were of little use to her.

Nunkie had been a lone male who appeared on the scene within the Karisoke research range. Dian had learned a lot about how gorilla groups formed watching Nunkie draw females away from other groups. These were generally those who had been low ranking than others more senior, or otherwise dominant, within their groups. Low-ranking Papoose and Petula of Group 4 left their silverback, Uncle Bert, to move on with the bold new guy in town. These two females produced Nunkie's first known offspring, and from there on his new group continued to grow, with females lured away from other groups, and his subsequent breedings with them.

Nunkie's story would be a feature of Dian's next *National Geographic* article, and our finding him and bringing back the most recent field notes was essential to the story's outcome.

I went to bed early that night, and in the morning Rwelekana accompanied Stuart and me down the camp trail toward the border of Zaire. As the three of us passed the south end of Dian's cabin, we heard laughter and stumbled upon Dian with her two French guests. Dian stood just outside her door with the oldest gentleman, while the other man stood with his back toward us, aiming a camera at his *ami*, posing with the famous Dr. Fossey standing by his side. At the sound of our approaching footsteps, the cameraman turned his head to us exclaiming "bonjour!"

Dian was dressed in her typical work shirt and jeans, but they were clean and fresh looking; even her hair was brushed. This was the first and only time I saw her wearing makeup. She wore bright red lipstick that made her small mouth look large. The same color was rubbed onto her cheeks, exaggerating the whole effect of being *made up*. Dian's giggles became a taciturn smile at the sight of Stuart and me. As Stuart slowed, echoing their "bonjours," I almost ran into the back of him while staring at Dian. I caught myself ogling the sight despite fearing that she, out of embarrassment, wanted to curse at us. Instead, under the scrutiny of her visitors from the outside world, Dian forced another smile and an awkward, reticent, girlish wave to Stuart.

That day's trek to the other side of Mount Visoke seemed endless, and despite the distance we traveled into and across many ravines, we didn't find Nunkie's Group. Rwelekana spotted gorilla footprints in a trampled clearing, but eleven nearby night nests that the gorillas had made three days earlier did not fit the profile of Nunkie's clan. While Stuart and I measured and sketched the layout of the nesting area in our notepads, our skilled tracker lifted a single lobe of dung from each ring of bent and folded plant stalks. Each of these pieces, he wrapped meticulously in a broad lobelia leaf, before carefully placing them in his backpack.

It was 2:20 P.M. when Rwelekana, pointing his panga eastward, indicated that we should return. Dian's curfew was at 5:30 P.M., and Rwelekana began leading Stuart and me straight up the side of Mount Visoke from deep in Zaire. From the clearings, we could easily see the town of Rumangabo, Zaire to the northwest. Beyond, that in the far distance, green forest gave way to the golden plains of Zaire's Rwindi National Park glowing on the horizon, stretching to the southern shoreline of Lake Edward.

"*Tutarudi juaa*," our intrepid guide said, pointing toward the peak of the volcano. Stuart and I understood him to be saying that *we would return upward*—the shortest way home would be over the mountain's top.

Stuart and I huffed and puffed, but Rwelekana led the way effortlessly, hacking through thick undergrowth to cut a trail. The higher we climbed, the shorter and more open the vegetation became just beneath the alpine zone, until we hit stands of giant senecio, *Dendrosenecio adnivalis*, with twisting trunks. Their thick and large glossy, green leaves reminded me of the magnolias back home. Beneath these, Rwelekana paused, using his panga to break open a woody stem revealing a brittle white core.

"*Ngagi kula*," he said, breaking a piece of the crispy pith and holding it near his mouth, informing Stuart and me that this was another gorilla food. We each sampled a piece; the taste and texture reminding me of water chestnuts.

The three of us maneuvered through these tangled groves, upward, until the terrain changed to sloping meadows of grassy sedge, *Carex runsoroensis*, punctuated by expansive slabs of bare black volcanic rock. From an unobstructed vantage point on one of these exposed patches of ancient volcanic cone, we could see a great portion of Zaire that tumbled away from our feet. By contrast to tiny Rwanda, Zaire—later to be called Democratic Republic of the Congo, DRC for short—is one of Africa's largest and least populated countries. From where I stood, unbroken forest, in stark contrast to Rwanda's plowed farmlands, spilled downward to the lowlands westward. While rains on the Rwandan slopes fed the Nile, rains on this side fed the great Congo River basin all the way to the Atlantic Ocean. Although Rwanda was now obscured, we were so far around Mount Visoke that to the northeast, we could also just see into Uganda. I had to squint to see what I thought must be the dry grasslands where the dark green forest ended and golden yellow began. I later learned that this was Zaire's Rwindi Park that merges into Uganda's Queen Elizabeth National Park along the borders of great Lake Edward. As my sweat turned cold in the thin alpine air, I reminisced about the warm, dry savannas I traveled through in Kenya the previous summer.

"*Ehhh . . .*" Rwelekana said, pointing his panga directly south, "*iko Nyamuragira!*" Following his line of sight southward, Stuart and I looked to see a distant streak of brilliant crimson, a fountain of red light shooting into the air. It was Mount Nyamuragira, the active volcano that our new-found friends at the American Embassy had told us newcomers about when we first arrived in Kigali. Standing between the eruption and us, the jagged cone of Mount Mikeno obscured the eastern half of the more southerly low-lying volcano. I took my binoculars out of my backpack and viewed the sight. Glowing red-orange magma spewed from the western side of the volcano in a powerful arc, like the fire from a giant signal flare. Massive dollops broke away from the main jet and splattered on the slopes below. At the downhill edge of the resulting flow, smoke billowed from where the snaking mantle of molten rock set forest trees aflame with billowing smoke. We paused to behold the spectacle, passing binoculars around, uttering our *oohs* and *ahhs* of amazement. As Rwelekana viewed the scene through the lenses, he let out a descending staccato of whistles in the local's characteristic expression of surprise.

With our curiosity satisfied, our intrepid guide led us farther up Visoke. When we reached the summit at over twelve thousand feet, the cold bracing air offset the overheating of our bodies from the climb. Cool shards of sweeping mist, clouds actually, swept around and between us. The abating slope and leveling off of terrain made us feel lighter, and we picked up the pace, the hard climb becoming a brisk trot—that, with the bracing wind and a views of Africa in all directions, made me want to run. Whooping and hollering, I jogged past Stuart and Rwelekana, who laughed at my goofy enthusiasm. Just as I entered a swiftly moving cloud I had to bring myself to a sudden halt at the volcano's rim. Here, the ground sloped suddenly downward. Nestled one hundred feet below us at the bottom of the round crater lay a perfectly circular body of water, like the silent belly of a carnivorous pitcher plant waiting for me to drop in.

Protected all around from the high-altitude wind by the steeply sloping sides of the crater, scarcely a ripple disturbed the surface of the dark water. Plants that would have found the windy exposed top of the volcano inhospitable had refuge on the sloping walls inside this undisturbed basin. Dotted around the banks of the lake were more giant senecios and lobelias whose seeds had found refuge there beneath the volcano's wind-swept edge, in a sheltered microclimate. Stuart and Rwelekana joined me to view the lake in silent contemplation. As exhaustive as our trek had been that day, this rare place brought us rejuvenation. When a blanket of mist drifted in and obscured our scenery, we resumed travel.

The rim of Mount Visoke's crater is dotted with the tall rigid sedges. Over the eons, protected from regular overgrazing by buffaloes or other animals at such a high and out-of-the-way altitude, these spiny clumps have formed massive bases of thatch that buoy their crowns over five feet above the ground. Where these plants aggregate into thick patches, they create a catacomb of corridors. When the clouds settled in upon us, Stuart, Rwelekana, and I stayed close together to avoid getting separated and lost in this maze-like sedge forest.

The air cleared again as we walked out of the tussocks, and within minutes the three of us had traversed Visoke's volcanic rim from its western to eastern side; the reverse feat having taken us most of the day around the mountain's much wider base. Heading downslope, Rwelekana soon found a trail he knew. There he paused, aiming his panga downward, pointing out the view of Karisoke's meadow that the three of us had walked through from camp that morning. Through gaps in the swirling mists below, we could see the bright green clearing far beneath us, flanked by the darker green hagenias and other trees of our surrounding forest. Karisoke lay obscured among these beyond the meadow's northern edge.

Here, our tracker knew exactly where to begin our descent, and which pathways to take as we traveled back through the various plant zones of alpine grasses, giant senecios, and lobelias. With gravity in our favor, our descent was easy relative to our hike that morning. In no time, Rwelekana was leading Stuart and me down the Elephant Trail into the familiar hagenia and hypericum forest zone that surrounds camp. Viewing the Virunga mountains from a distance, it might seem incredible that one should use the summit of Mount Visoke as a shortcut at the end of a full day's hike, but we would climb over it and back again in a single day, time and again in pursuit of Nunkie's whereabouts. Dian's seasoned gorilla trackers had done this many times, and continued to do so in their hard task of monitoring far-ranging mountain gorillas.

It was getting dark as we trudged back into camp at curfew. I knew Dian would be pacing the floor of her cabin not only waiting for news of Nunkie, but any sign of the three of us. Behind us, the sky glowed red as if the sun was setting in the south. The jagged monolith of Mount Mikeno formed a dramatic silhouette against the backdrop of fire from its active erupting sister, Mount Nyamu-ragira, which kept the sunset alive with a fire of her own.

Back in camp, her French visitors having departed, Dian was alone again. Inside her cabin, Stuart and I sat on the step that separated Dian's raised dining area from the split-level sunken living room. Dian was disappointed that we had not found Nunkie's Group, but instead of launching into an emotional tirade, she thanked Stuart and me for making such a long trek.

"*Reeeally* and *truuuly*, I know you guys must be tired," Dian said, coming out of the kitchen and surprising us with bottles of cold Primus from her kerosene refrigerator—we had *done good*, and Dian was rewarding us. Next, Dian handed Stuart and me some tiny soup bouillon cubes wrapped in gold foil.

"Here, you can eat these cheeses," she said, "If you have the patience to unwrap them. I know I don't." In Dian's refrigerator, I had seen a small cardboard tray of foil-wrapped cheese cubes with a little laughing cow head on each. These were not those. Hungry as I was, instead of pointing out her mistake, I quietly ate one of the bouillon cubes she had just given us, grimacing and rinsing away the strong salty flavor with several swigs of beer.

By the light of the pressure lantern, Rwelekana unwrapped each lobe of gorilla dung and sorted them by size on the floor. Dian put her reading glasses on and examined each piece, poking and prodding with a pencil. After studying our sketches of the nest layout, she told us that she thought we had found the trail of Group 13, a fringe group that usually stayed out of Karisoke's research range. Dian informed us that Amy Vedder was now contacting this group regularly from the base of the mountain, to habituate it for tourist visits.

"*Eht mwaaah* . . . Group 13 is on the other side of Visoke trying to get away from that *cunt!*" Dian muttered. As if to get the bad taste from her mouth at mere mention of her archnemesis, Mademoiselli leaned sideways and spit on the floor with contempt.

Stuart and I had been back at our cabin for less than an hour before Dian knocked on Stuart's door. From my unlit room, I peeked through the open door into his side of our cabin.

"You *guuuuys*," Dian said, drawing out her words in the childlike whine she often used. "Come *onnn* . . . You've GOT to *see* this."

"See what?" Stuart asked.

"The sky is red! A volcano is erupting!"

"Oh yeah . . . it's Mount Nyamuragira," Stuart said. "We got a really good look at it today from the other side of Visoke."

I dropped back into the shadow of my room, surprised that she didn't know about the eruption.

"*Ehht mwaaah* . . . *hmmm whaaah* . . ." Dian grumbled, deflated and scowling. "You *knew* about this?"

"They told us in Kigali," Stuart said.

"*Eht mwaaaah!* How come everybody knew about this except me?"

"It's been erupting about a month now. I thought you knew!"

"Well this is too special to miss." Dian exclaimed, shaking off her disappointment. "You've got to come see it with me."

Thinking, hoping really, that she didn't mean me too, I tried to skulk back into the shadows of my room.

"*John . . . you need to come too.*"

Oh crap! I'm not getting outta this. Stuart and I put our jackets on and followed Dian into the night, trailing her and her bobbling flashlight up the path. Peter's light was on as we passed his cabin, but Dian didn't bother to rouse him. *Lucky bastard*, I thought. Still, it was an obvious slight to Peter from Dian, for her not to include him. Past her cabin, we followed Dian to the edge of the meadow and stared southwestward. Mount Nyamuragira's false sunset flared crimson from behind Mikeno's towering silhouette, as it had when Stuart and I returned with Rwelekana at dusk. Dian's cheerful mood was almost giddy while the three of us stood admiring the lighted sky. It was truly a beautiful scene, and I was buoyed by it, but by now well aware that Dian's moods were as changeable as Nyamuragira, and the climate we were in.

"Okay, I know you guys are tired from your hike today," Dian said after a few minutes. "I'll let you get back to your cabins. I just didn't want you to miss this."

The next night, still in manic celebration of Mount Nyamuragira's eruption, Dian invited us to dinner at her cabin, insisting that we bring our cameras. We were to make an evening of photographing the red night sky. This time, she even included Peter in our mix. Basili had come up to camp to begin his twenty-one day shift, replacing Kanyaragana as "house boy" while Kanyaragana returned to his twenty-one days at home with his family off the mountain. As Dian poured Primus into our glasses, Basili served us hot plates of spaghetti and sauce.

That morning, Dian had sent Rwelekana and Baraqueza out to look for Nunkie on the far side of Mount Visoke. By five-thirty, curfew time, they had not returned. Usually, Dian became very upset by this, ranting about every worst-case scenario when trackers or students failed to return on time, but this night Dian remained in a rare elevated mood, with nothing daunting her. While we dined, she occasionally looked over her shoulder at the window and commented about her trackers whereabouts, but she remained calm.

"They *did* have a long way to go," Dian said. "I gave them each a torch with fresh batteries."

Dian's rationale made Stuart and Peter comfortable and talkative. I was also more at ease than ever before, but in the shell that I had grown in Dian's presence, I remained a quiet observer enjoying the conversation around me.

Stuart talked excitedly about our trip over the top of Mount Visoke, and Peter reminisced about how beautiful the lake is at the volcano's summit

"Oh, it really is beautiful, isn't it? . . . ," Dian said, catching herself mid-sentence. "I mean, at least they tell me it is. I know *I've* never been up there."

"*Huh?*" I blurted. Dian had been in the Virungas thirteen years and she hadn't been to the top of the volcano in her backyard. Now I had to catch *my*-self. I shoved another forkful of spaghetti into my gaping mouth.

"I've tried, but . . ." Dian demurred, shaking her head, "but . . . *oya* . . . *oya* . . . I just can't do it." With some reluctance, Dian admitted that she had a keen fear of heights that prevented her from climbing above the tree line that blocked the view of the land far beneath her. Instead of the rare case of following gorillas beyond that point, she would have to leave them and clamber back down.

"I've seen it from an airplane," Dian said, before changing the subject to that of the erupting Mount Nyamuragira. She talked excitedly about past volcanic eruptions and mentioned the book that she was writing about her thirteen years in Africa.

"This is the reason I came to Africa," Dian said, ". . . the excitement and the beauty. *You guuuys*, I'm going to put this in my book!" At Dian's order, Basili brought us another round of Primus.

"I've heard some white women come to Africa to experience the black male," Stuart said with a laugh. Peter chuckled too, but I just about choked on a swig of my beer. *Where did that come from? Boy, is he pushing it!* I braced for an angry rebuttal, and an end to our happy evening.

"Not *this* white woman!" Dian said, with haughty defensiveness, but completely unperturbed.

Dian's spirits remained elevated throughout our meal, and she was even able to talk about the dilemma of what to do with the baby gorilla without falling apart. The idea of the infant being the missing baby from Nunkie's group made her think more about releasing the orphan back into the wild.

"Better for her to die a wild gorilla than end up in a zoo." Dian surmised. "If she goes to a zoo, and they can't get another mountain gorilla, and the motherfuckers will try, they'll just breed her with a lowland gorilla and make a bastard baby."

On this night, Dian seemed ambivalent about whether or not we helped with kitchen duties, but having been trained under fire by her in the past, Stuart, Peter, and I automatically began helping Basili clear the table. Before we could finish, Dian was beckoning us outside.

"C'mon you *guuuys*! Basili will get that. We've got to get some photos of this." The dark sky was starless and the clouds obscured all signs of the volcanic eruption we had witnessed the night before. "Shit *merde*!" Dian said, beginning to look dour before shaking off her disappointment. "Maybe it will clear up later."

Our party broke up at nine o'clock when weary Rwelekana and Baraqueza trudged back into camp with a backpack full of dung from Nunkie's Group, which they had found in a heavy poacher area far into Zaire. I watched as the expert trackers carefully unwrapped the thick lobelia leaf from each sticky lobe of gorilla dung, handing them to Dian as they did. She, in turn, examined them, matching each to the age and size of the members of Nunkie's Group. After examining Rwelekana's rough sketch of the nest site, showing in which nest each lobe of dung was retrieved, Dian was satisfied that Nunkie's Group had been found, though she was disturbed about the location, low and deep into Zaire. But knowing that Nunkie's Group was still intact, had obviously offset her worries.

Dian's mania over Mount Nyamuragira's eruption continued into the next night when Stuart and I were asleep in our beds. At half past midnight, Baraqueza knocked on the door to Stuart's side of the cabin. I listened to the murmuring through the wall, half-asleep and confused, before Stuart next opened my door and poked his head into my room.

"Baraqueza said Dian wants us to come up to her cabin," he said, with a weary chuckle, "and we're supposed to bring our cameras." I rolled over and groaned in disbelief before rousing myself from my warm bed. Having slept in my sweats, I grabbed some dry socks and pulled on my clammy sneakers.

"You *guuuys* . . ." Dian fawned, as she handed us each a cold Primus upon arrival at her cabin. Peter was already there sipping from a bottle, a little disheveled and bleary. Despite the odd hour, or because of it, the three of us students soon became giddy drinking beer. Dian was so upbeat, it seemed nothing could bring her down.

"The sky is perfect tonight," Dian said, lifting a tripod from her dining room table. Her Nikon camera was slung haphazardly by a strap around her neck. "It was cloudy earlier, but I had Baraqueza and Mulikasi sleep in the living room to watch for the sky to turn red."

These two men sat wearily together on a sleeping bag stretched out on Dian's couch. A second sleeping bag was laid out on the floor. Both men looked bedraggled and dumbfounded in the shadow of the unlit side of the living area. Caught like us in the wake of Dian's mania, these poor guys too weren't getting a restful night's sleep.

Balancing beers and camera equipment, Dian, Stuart, Peter, and I left the cabin and walked toward the open meadow. Hearing the snort and heavy hooves of a forest buffalo, *Syncerus caffer*, Dian shined her flashlight into the darkness.

"*Napati*," she called, in a soft voice as if the bovines were her pet poodles. "*Napati . . .*"

Stuart, Peter, and I chuckled nervously at Dian's odd pet name she used when greeting these nocturnal behemoths, and we dropped behind her as she approached each one. We could barely make out any image of the herd against the blackness of night, unless a flashlight caught their reflective eyes. Stuart chimed in with his own rhyming version of Dian's sing-song, "*Napatiii . . . get away from meee.*" Peter and I laughed, amid the irritated snorts of perturbed buffaloes.

As we continued through the herd, another sound arose from the forest. A low, guttural *hee-whahhh, hee-WHAH, HEE-WAAAAH . . .* rising in an eerie crescendo before ending in a descending series of whistles, *TSHIRRR, tshirrr, tshirr . . .* As soon as we heard the first one, we heard a dozen, then *dozens!* It sounded like hundreds of demented wails and whistles rising and blaring from all directions of the forest around us, *HEE-WAAAH, HEE-WAAAH . . . TSHIRRR, tshirrr . . .*

"What the hell is THAT?" I asked, stunned. The deafening croaks and screeches rattled from trees near and far, high and low, each vocalization joining in mad chorus rose to a reverberating crescendo before ending in the same raspy whistle.

"Tree hyraxes," Dian and Peter shouted in unison above the din.

I knew tree hyraxes were in this forest but had not yet seen these elusive nocturnal creatures. Now we seemed to be surrounded by them. A furry brown rabbit-sized mammal, the species *Dendrohyrax arboreus*, is surprisingly a relative of the elephant, as evidenced by obscure shared structural and physiological characteristics including bones and teeth. I had seen its similar-looking, diurnal lowland cousin, the rock hyrax, in Kenya.

"One girl left camp because she couldn't stand the noise they make," Dian said, with a laugh. "She was in your cabin, John. She left after two weeks." This, combined with Dian, I surmised.

The sound, almost deafening, was eerie but added even more surreal magic as we left camp's understory and stepped into the meadow against the backdrop of the glowing red midnight sky. It was as if the hyraxes had planned the moment at which they all, by the hundreds, climbed from their respective tree cavities and began calling like noisy katydids or frogs in a pond, enraptured in asynchronous cacophony. It was as if every tree hyrax in the entire Virunga mountain chain had joined in the moment, our moment. It was enchanting.

As the hyraxes exhausted themselves, with shrill voices waning to their last shrieks and whistles, the four of us stepped out onto the edge of the meadow, gazing southward at Mount Mikeno, outlined against the fire of Nyamuragira, the hyraxes silencing themselves as suddenly as they had begun. Stuart and Peter joked with Dian about getting us up in the middle of the night. The three of them laughed while I quietly observed the stunning view as silence reclaimed the surrounding forest.

"You *guuuys*," Dian whined, "this is what I came to Africa for . . . I'm going to put this in my book."

"Oh, yeah?" Peter said, adding his characteristic one-note guffaw. "Ha!"

"John, you're sure being quiet over there," Dian said, adding, "John's not happy." I should have been encouraged by Dian's concern, but even having her seemingly positive attention directed my way made me uncomfortable. I fumbled with my camera in the darkness, screwing the tripod's bolt into the base.

"John's not happy, and that's not fair," Dian added.

Poignantly aware of how cruel she could be, I couldn't utter a single response, but wanted her capricious attention directed away from me as I attended to my camera setup.

Dian placed her tripod on the ground and Stuart held the flashlight while she pulled at each metal leg.

"Shit *merde*, I always have trouble getting these fucking things to work," Dian grumbled, tugging at the bolts that held the telescopic legs nested inside each other. Stuart gave the flashlight to Dian and joined Peter, jumping in to release and extend the legs of Dian's tripod.

Next, Peter and I set up our own camera equipment while Stuart mounted Dian's camera onto her tripod before setting up his own. Dian seemed completely clueless as to what to do with her expensive camera equipment, while we guessed and debated how many seconds or minutes each timed exposure should be to capture the image of the night's red sky on film. If there were going to be any pictures of this event for Dian's book, or otherwise, they wouldn't be coming from *her* camera. She was hopeless with any type of equipment, from camp lanterns to her own camera. Perhaps her photos of this night would be coming from ours. I was reminded of Peter's story of stolen film. While we waited for our camera shutters to click off from their extended exposures, we finished our beers. Cold damp air crept across the meadow making us shiver and shift on our feet.

"Stuart, you're sleeping with me tonight," Dian said, giggling. That did make me laugh.

"Uh, no Dian . . . no I'm not!" Stuart said, laughing nervously.

"Yes you *are*." Dian persisted, as Stuart directed his attention to his camera.

"C'mon Dian, let's get some pictures here," Stuart said, in an effort to redirect her attention.

After taking several pictures, which seemed hopeless under the circumstances of dim light, we gathered our equipment and empty bottles and headed back into camp. Full of beer, we laughed and stumbled off the trail and through the mud. I was almost enjoying myself, despite Dian.

"What's that smell?" Stuart asked.

"Ha, Fossey laid one down!" Peter said.

"The term is 'put one out,' and *I* didn't do it." We were all laughing as we realized we had strode back into the herd of grazing buffaloes. Their indignant snorts surrounded us before they scattered, hooves thudding off and away from our sloppy, noisy entourage.

"*Mbogo*-poo, where are you?" Dian called out giddily into the darkness, using the Swahili word for buffalo, converting it to her own baby talk with "poo." As she wandered farther off trail toward one of the shadowy figures, Stuart tugged on her sleeve, drawing her back to the trail.

"Uh . . . c'mon Dian," he said, "I don't think you need to be petting an mbogo-poo right now . . . you'll get us all killed."

"*Stuaaart* . . . you *guuuys*," Dian said, "this has been really great. I'm going to write about this in my book . . . really and truly . . . all of you."

The prospect of appearing as a character in the published version of Dian's life story was exciting. I mulled this over as we walked toward the light of Dian's cabin, but couldn't help but surmise that with Dian's repeating this theme, that this had all been staged as a means of creating at least one positive Fossey-student interaction in her storytelling. After all, it hadn't been a week since Carolyn had made her escape from camp. And that same day, the visit from one of her bosses of sorts, Bob McIlvaine, who was checking up on things. Dian had much damage control to do. Plus, Stuart, Peter, and I would be going back into Kigali in only ten days to renew our visas and surely the American Embassy staffers would be curious about our impressions of Karisoke Research Center and Dian Fossey, especially with Carolyn, abused and spurned, having just blown back through. Better to send us off on a high note, I surmised.

I brought up the rear of our single file as Stuart and Peter followed Dian into her cabin, which felt warm relative to the damp night's early morning air.

Before we could leave, Dian insisted on making popcorn, clearly reluctant for the evening to end. The three of us couldn't resist an opportunity for food and despite the late hour we obliged, with Dian providing us with yet more beer to quench our salted popcorn–induced thirst. She was on a manic high, and we obliged, catching the fallout of free beer and food, so scarce under the circumstances.

It was after 2:00 A.M. when we pecked away at the last of the unpopped kernels at the bottom of their tin pan, and Dian's high abated enough for our little Saturday night/Sunday morning party to subside. Collectively, we headed for the door.

"Ohhh, Stuart, your hands are cold," Dian said, catching him just inside the doorway. "Let me warm them." She shoved Stuart's hands up the front of her sweater before he could pull them away.

"Wait a minute, Dian!" Stuart exclaimed, yanking his hands back with a nervous laugh. "No, thanks."

"You're sleeping with me tonight."

"Uh . . . no Dian, I'm not."

"Yes, you are," Dian repeated, wrapping one arm around his and drawing him back inside. Peter and I just reveled in the absurdity of the moment, and Stuart's dilemma, while maneuvering ourselves out the door.

"Oh, no I'm *not!*" Stuart blurted, sidestepping away from her to a spot between Peter and me. In a chortle of nervous laughter, we three students skedaddled out into the night and down the camp path through snorting buffaloes to the respite of our own cabins.

Back in my bed, I lay awake for a while, taking in the events of the night. *Would this evening really end up in Dian's book? A fond memory of Dian's wonderful interactions with students? Perhaps her editors were wondering too: Where is everyone in your life, Dian? All the camaraderie? The friendships?* And I thought about the former student who Dian had said couldn't tolerate the sound of the hyraxes. I doubted if that was really why she left. *What would Dian tell the next group about Carolyn's departure?*

I realized there had been many students through camp, none of whom Dian had maintained an ongoing positive relationship with. And Amy Vedder . . . Bill Weber, now entrenched in a cold war with Dian from their own home base at the foot of the mountain. There were other former students on the outs, like Sandy Harcourt, who, after helping create the Mountain Gorilla Preservation Fund in the UK, was now backing the Mountain Gorilla Project, with Amy and Bill, to organize and develop tourism to see gorillas. There was an irony to Dian's contempt of this, because she was once a tourist

ABOVE: Virunga Volcanoes on approach, immersed in clouds. Mounts Gahinga, Sabinio and Muhavura lie on the Rwanda-Uganda border. BELOW: In the chilly morning sunlight, mists of the cloud forest drift through branches of *Hagenia abyssinica*, a dominant tree species of the Virungas.

Dian Fossey with Bonne Année. The only picture I dared take of Dian in the moment, but I think she was actually posing and wanted me to take more of her that day.

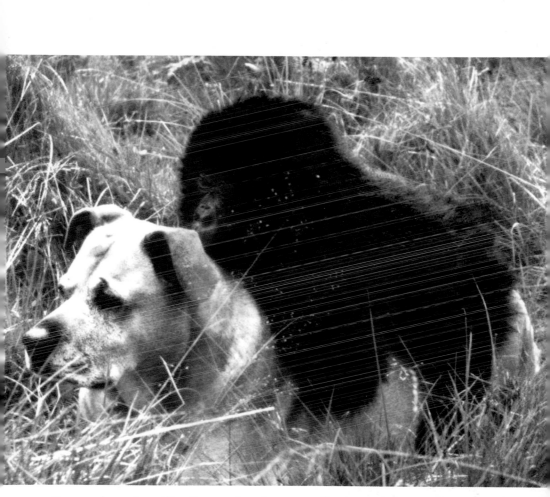

Our orphaned gorilla, Bonne Année, rests affectionately atop Dian Fossey's beloved dog Cindy. Both were confiscated from poachers, although under quite different circumstances.

ABOVE: Me, Bonne Année, Carolyn Phillips, and Peter Veit, sitting on the bank of Karisoke's Camp Creek, after a day of gorillas. BELOW: In search of Nunkie. Hiking across the boggy meadow from Rwanda into Zaire, just near the forest edge up ahead. Mount Mikeno looms in the background beyond, with clouds forming at its crown as the sun warms its dark stone monolith.

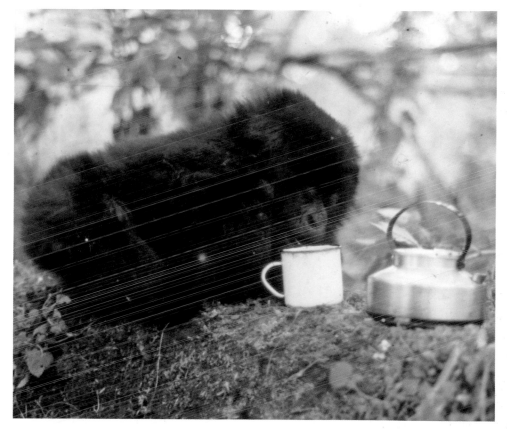

Bright, inquisitive orphan, Bonne Année, at our bivouac camp in Zaire, in preparation for her ill-fated release attempt. If it wasn't out of reach, she thought it was hers.

Dian at her desk in the bedroom of her large cabin, the same room in which she would one day be found murdered. Dian pecked away at writing much of *Gorillas in the Mist* here. The raised nest box, to which I returned baby Bonne Année each evening, is visible on stilts in the foreground.

ABOVE: Stuart Perlmeter, Dian Fossey, me and Bonne Année, in pensive pursuit of Group 4, to release the baby back into the wild. We would fail that day, but the outcome would not be as dire as what was yet to come. BELOW: Blackback Ziz, a subadult male, lounges in a tree on Mount Visoke while clouds drift through the forest. He would become the last silverback to lead Group 5 before it split into Pablo's and Shinda's Groups.

Family photo of members of Group 5: Pablo, Pantsy with newborn baby Jozi, silverback Beethoven and motherless Shinda. Here they have ended a rest period and look to be moving on again to resume feeding. A stalk of wild celery, a favorite gorilla food item, is in the right foreground.

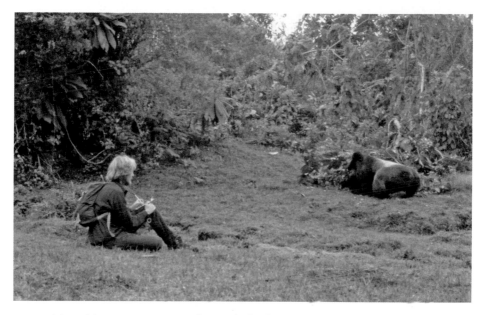

ABOVE: Me taking notes on Beethoven's feeding. He pulled down the vernonia tree, a relative of the sunflower, to get at the nutty-tasting fruits that form at the end of the long dry season. Beethoven, with second silverback Icarus, successfully defended a prime feeding area from other groups on Mount Visoke's southwestern slopes. BELOW: Beethoven feasts on vernonia bulbs, the seed pods that form after the flowers fade. He pulled the whole tree down for his convenience. Regrettably, I sampled these nutty, crunchy fruits, before realizing too late that each was riddled with tiny wriggling insect larvae.

ABOVE: I have often been asked about how close we got to the gorillas. A better question might be, how close did they get to us? Cheeky Pablo dropped onto my lap whenever he felt like it, as if that's what we researchers were there for. BELOW: Puck, an adult female in Group 5 rests next to Peter Veit, while he casually writes his famously good notes, preferred by Dian. She liked his photos too.

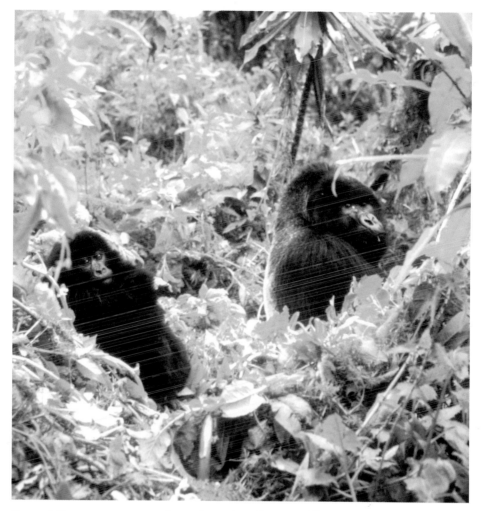

Pursed lips are an expression of tension for a gorilla, as seen here with little Bonne Année in her new home with the remnants of Group 4. The silverback Peanuts is keeping a wary eye on me. After spending her days with me for two months, the baby thought it was fine to come sit in my lap on our first reunion. Peanuts put a stop to that in a screaming rampage I wouldn't forget.

Half-sisters in Group 5, Poppy and Muraha, resting together affectionately. Gorilla's faces are very expressive; one can easily interpret the subtle looks of mirth and contentment here.

RIGHT: Little Cantsbee, son of Puck, was only two years old when I first saw him. Dian thought Puck was a male and exclaimed, "It can't be!" when she gave birth to her firstborn. Cantsbee would one day take over his brother Pablo's Group, which would grow into the largest group of mountain gorillas ever documented.

LEFT: Silverback Icarus, the secondary male of Group 5. He was believed to be the son of Beethoven, and was allowed females of his own within the group to which he sired his offspring.

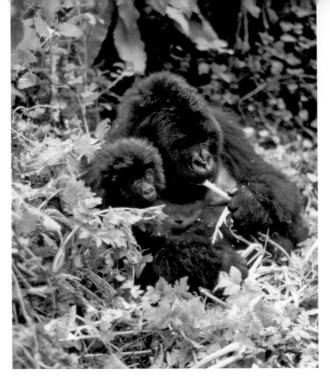

ABOVE: Maggie in her mother, Effie's, arms. I noticed that babies first learned about solid foods while watching their mothers feed and sampling what food items a mother selected from the many choices in their surroundings. BELOW: Tuck, a subadult female of Group 5, was captivated by her own reflection in my camera lens. She was also fascinated by the new babies in the group as she observed the parenting skills of the mature females. She would soon be having her own.

The bright and ever-curious female, Tuck, looking almost human. The distinctive noseprint of each gorilla serves as a means of identification for research. Tuck was fascinated by cameras and made for a willing photographic model. I think she was studying us humans, too.

Little Shinda of Group 5, became motherless after the silverback Icarus killed
Marchessa in an unprecedented event. As silverbacks themselves, Shinda and
Pablo would one day split Group 5 into two groups of their own, becoming
among the most long-range scientifically-observed animals on the planet.

ABOVE: Nude reclining. Group 5's adult female, Puck in repose, languorous in the fleeting sunlight after a rain. Dian thought both Puck and Tuck were males, hence the names. Here, Puck is obviously feminine, and producing milk for her baby Canstbec. BELOW: Silverback Icarus of Group 5 sauntering across the grassy clearing called the Tourist Spot halfway up the Porter Trail. He served peacefully as Beethoven's secondary silverback within the group, assisting nightily to defend territory during interactions with other groups.

ABOVE: Peter Veit, me, and Stuart Perlmeter in a bivouac camp on the cloud-covered rim of Mount Visoke. From there, we hiked down to the placid Lake Ngezi on the Rwanda-Zaire border, ever in search of Nunkie's missing gorilla group. My parents gave me that sweater for Christmas, okay? BELOW: Me and the intrepid gorilla tracker, Rwelekana, up in the clouds atop a misty Mount Visoke. His long association with Dian Fossey would ultimately lead to a tragic end.

ABOVE: Karisoke gorilla trackers, Nameye, Baraqueza, and woodman Bernardi join porters to strip saplings and deftly assemble a gurney, on the spot, to transport Marchessa's body out of the forest. The locals had intimate familiarity with forest resources and surprised us with their skills. BELOW: Stranded at the Nairobi airport, I am rescued and swept up into the luxurious estate of Karl and Anna Merz in Karen, Kenya. Anna's passion for wildlife conservation simmered just beneath this facade and she would one-day trade horses for black rhinos, giving all this up to help launch the Lewa Wildlife Conservancy.

ABOVE: Kanyaragana, Dian Fossey's long-time housekeeper, cook, and launderer, asked me to escort him to the top of Mount Visoke to see its hidden crater lake. He took it all in quietly for a long time. I was surprised that he had never been before, but neither had Dian. BELOW: Here, I am perched on a giant hagenia tree on the southern slopes of Mount Visoke while visiting Peanuts's Group 4. Days like these were idyllic in the long dry season of the Virunga Volcanoes. The sleepy town of Rumangabo, Zaire was visible below in the distance. It would become a hotbed of political strife and military logistics in troubled times to come.

LEFT: Young tracker in training, Toni, just returning from a trip with Dian's poacher patrol, a dead duiker slung over his shoulders. Dian would let the men keep and eat the fresh meat that they salvaged from the poachers' snares.

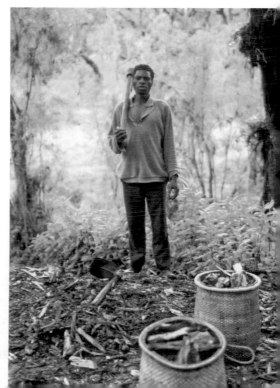

RIGHT: Camp domesticity. Old hagenia trees fell with some regularity in and around camp. Mukera the woodman would chop these into suitable pieces to stock our cabins. He built a fire in each of our stoves each night, and in Dian's large fireplace. He also had a bawdy sense of humor and could play the inanga, a traditional stringed instrument.

ABOVE: Karisoke staffers: Mukera, the woodman who chopped wood and made our nightly fires, me, gorilla trackers, Toni and Nameye, Peter Veit, and Dian's housekeeper, Kanyaragana who cooked, cleaned and did our laundry. After each twenty-one days in camp, they swapped out with an alternate crew. BELOW: Teamwork in the midst of gorillas: Me, Rwelekana, Jean-Pierre von der Beck, Rosalind Aveling, Sam Koechlin, and Peter Veit. Making hard work the best of times. Important conservation benefactor, Sam Koechlin was a Swiss business magnate, and along with his wife, the renowned Olympic equestrienne Pat Koechlin-Smyth, joined us on a trek to see Group 5. *Image courtesy of Rosalind Aveling.*

ABOVE: A birth near the end of my stay. Pantsy of Group 5, tends to her newborn we named Jozi. A baby will have pink skin for the first 20 days, before turning black and moving from hanging ventrally, to riding on the mother's back. BELOW: Pablo, proving that he's big enough to knock me over. It's just as well that I'll be gone before he becomes a silverback. He would one day go on to form Pablo's group, a large family group that would break all records in size at 65 members.

ABOVE: Conrad Aveling, Peter Veit, and me on the summit of Mount Karisimbi, the tallest of the Virunga Volcanoes and one of Africa's highest peaks. Mount Mikeno looms in the clouds behind us in Zaire. BELOW: Beethoven, lead silverback of Group 5, looks out over the farmlands where forest once was.

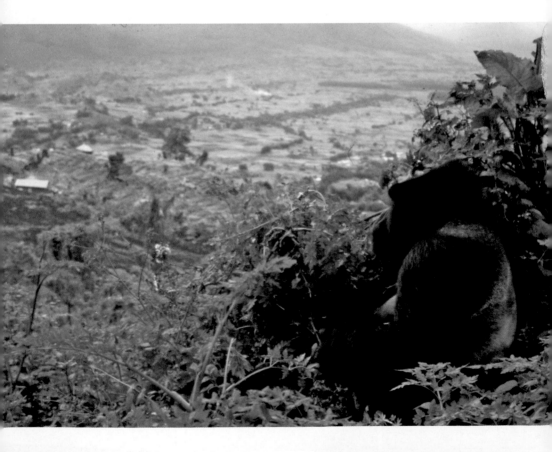

herself—the one that didn't leave. The experience had changed her life, but after that, it was as if gorillas were hers alone.

Sandy and his wife Kelly Stewart were once-beloved supporters of Dian, now ostracized. Kelly had been a student in camp, like ourselves. As for Peter, having been more a part of her life, these former students were all more worthy of inclusion in Dian's life story than we newcomers, and yet time made them more the unmentionable outcasts. For Dian, familiarity *really and truly* bred contempt.

Even a favorite among Dian's former students, Ian Redmond, was on her latest shit list because he had assisted with the operation of the Mountain Gorilla Project, training new park guards in collaboration with the V-W couple and making him a traitor in Dian's mind. I was young, but I knew there was something wrong with Dian's inability to maintain relationships. *What was next for us? For me? What would bring about my end?* My head swam thinking about all the former camp residents that had come and gone, only to become more of the ever-growing list of those estranged from Dian Fossey.

FIFTEEN

A Man a Plan a Gorilla Dian

What to do about the baby gorilla, who would run the poacher patrols in her absence, and Nunkie's unknown whereabouts remained at the top of Dian's list of complaints as she dragged her feet about leaving Karisoke. Stuart reassured her as best he could that we would continue to run the poacher patrols, despite the risks and legal ramifications of sending armed men into a neighboring country. In another ambitious effort to finally find Nunkie, Stuart and I travelled farther into Zaire, even camping overnight high on the far side of Mount Visoke to extend our search. Rwelekana never shied away from these most-arduous forays, and led us to a beautiful grove of giant heath under which we pitched our tents. Despite the valiant effort, we couldn't provide Dian with evidence of Nunkie's existence.

Dian discarded all the names she had ascribed to our gorilla baby after photos confirmed that the little one was not the missing N'gee from Nunkie's Group. After that, she neglected to give her any name at all. I needed something to refer to her as in my notes, and after looking up the word for *who* in my little green *Up Country Swahili* book; I started using *Nani* for the former Charlie, Josephine, N'gee, Sophie . . .

With Nani's origins once again a mystery, Dian had to quickly change her plans of putting her in Nunkie's Group, but the idea of releasing the baby into a wild group persisted. Instead, she decided Group 4 would have to suffice as the little gorilla's new family. This had only been tried once before, with eastern lowland gorillas in Zaire's Kahuzi-Biéga National Park, and with a much younger baby. The results were tragic. That infant was never seen again.

I was more than a little surprised that Dian decided that if the baby died in the wild, it would be better than if she had gone to a zoo. Dian said that Coco and Pucker, the young gorillas she had rehabilitated in 1969, barely tolerated life in Germany's Cologne Zoo. Dian also thought that because there were no mountain gorillas in captivity, bringing an individual female into the zoo world would trigger a market for a male to pair her with. She feared this would result in yet more poaching as others scrambled to get mountain gorillas out of the wilds and into their zoos.

As the full-time caretaker of our little nameless orphan, I continued to learn much about gorilla infant behavior, including what and how gorillas eat, the importance of play and affection to a nonhuman primate, and perfecting my technique to hold an ape—so spoiled by Dian—without getting teeth imbedded in my skin. Impressed by the way I cared for the baby, Dian continued to bestow a certain respect for me as she formulated her plan for the little one.

In a complete about-face, Dian decided to invite the Japanese film crew that had been camped at the base of the mountain up to Kari-soke. Disappointed by having gotten minimal gorilla footage with the V-W couple, these documentary filmmakers had been desperately wanting footage of the internationally-known Dian, who until now had remained standoffish, perhaps because she had nothing new to say or show about her work.

Energized by her new plans, Dian continued to treat me as a team member. Then again, as Nani's primary caregiver, I had become an important player in this grand scheme. With uncharacteristic trepidation, she asked me if I would agree to camp out with the baby for several nights in the forest across the border in Zaire. Actually, she did this through Stuart, and I was surprised that she didn't just make this an order, or else . . . Of course, I well knew by then the consequences of declining, the verbal abuse and condemnation it would trigger. I had witnessed it with Carolyn. You're either with Dian or you're not, and if you're not, you are an outcast, shunned by the leader of this remote cult.

Dian of all people knew the consequences would be dire if I were to be caught in Zaire without a visa. She had been held hostage there. But with my willing participation, she would have the men set up a bivouac campsite, within the natural range of Group 4, where I would help prepare the little gorilla for transition back to the wild. I accepted the mission eagerly as an honorable role in the little one's hope for a proper life as a gorilla, and, yes, as a way to remain in good standing with our headmistress. Dian seemed truly grateful when I agreed, which surprised me. But perhaps that was just her way of showing relief that things would be progressing as planned.

With Group 5's curiosity of me apparently satisfied, its members wouldn't feel the need to examine and crawl upon me en masse again. But six-year-old Pablo remained a very forward and charismatic youngster, who would often rush up to me with a slap, or even plop himself right down in my lap before trying to nudge me over. Perhaps his attraction to us humans was a consequence of his earlier life and abandonment. Before he was four years old, his mother Liza transferred into the rival Group 6 to become the consort of the silverback, Brutus, leaving her son behind. It was documented by Dian that silverbacks will kill the offspring of rival males after winning over their females. This harsh strategy causes the new female to come into estrous sooner, thereby allowing the new male to sire his own offspring with her. Whatever the intuition was for Pablo, he chose wisely to remain behind with his biological father, Beethoven. But as a consequence, he was denied an ongoing motherly connection. This he made up for by being everyone's playful, comedic friend, including us humans.

Out with Group 5, as the days drew on, Peter and I often talked of home, and of food, and of favorite foods from home.

"Boy, I could really get into some pierogis right now," I mused, while Group 5 napped in the warm sun, after a rain. "That's my favorite thing that my mom makes. With the cheese and potatoes inside."

"That would be *käse-piroggen* in German," Peter said. "I like my mom's *spaetzle*. I wish I could make that here."

"What's that?" I asked, with Peter trying to correct my attempt at pronouncing the German dish.

Peter went on to describe what seemed to me like a dumpling-meets-noodle kinda thing, made from flour and eggs. I had seen my mother make noodles from scratch, and the process sounded similar to me.

"My mom cut the dough really fast from a board into boiling water." Peter responded to my queries about the process, as I pondered trying to make them that evening. It would certainly be a nice diversion from our regular rations. We were forbidden to eat together, but I offered to give some to Peter later if they were a success.

Back in camp, I described my culinary plan to Stuart, but I didn't have much flour or eggs.

"I've got some spaghetti noodles," Stuart said. "Maybe we could throw those in with them."

"You know, I've actually got a can of spaghetti sauce I've been hanging onto," Peter revealed. "You wanna get together?"

At that point, the dinner plan had taken on a life of its own. My stomach knotted up at the very thought.

"Hey guys," I said, "I don't know about this."

"C'mon," Stuart said, "we'll just try to keep it quiet. Dian won't even know."

Peter and Stuart were much more eager than I, but I relented. They laughed at me as I went to each window, drawing the curtains closed tightly.

Soon, I was scrubbing out my wash pot, in which to prepare the salted boiling water. Peter watched as I cracked the eggs into a bowl of flour and kneaded the dough with a wooden spoon.

"That kinda looks about right," he said, when the mixture gained a smooth workable texture. When the water came to a rapid boil, I took a knife and cut a few as quick and best I could into the pot. They sunk, then floated up with the bubbling water, and within minutes looked done enough for our taste test.

Although they weren't quite like Mrs. Veit's, a little too thick and clunky, we agreed they were good enough for Karisoke fare at the end of another long day of gorilla trekking. I chopped the rest of the batter into the pot, before Stuart broke and dropped his spaghetti noodles in after them. At that moment I realized, while the pasta might take ten minutes or more, the spaetzle would get overcooked. Sure enough, we watched as the water turned milky and the delicate German dumplings sank and vanished. By the time the spaghetti was done, not a spaetzle remained. At least the spaghetti had swelled enough to feed the three of us, and with the sauce, made for a pretty decent meal by Karisoke standards.

The camaraderie and banter made me forget about Dian. Our laughter occasionally became too loud, but surely our mistress didn't keep constant vigil enough to know everything going on at the far end of camp, and there was quite a bit of scattered forest between us.

How wrong I was.

"Ahem . . . Stuart . . . ?" Dian queried, with a knock at the door. "What the fuck is going on in there?"

The three of us stared at each other, deflating at the sound of Dian's telltale breathy *ahems*. When Stuart opened the door, Dian squinted into our lantern light.

"Shit goddamn motherfuckit, Stuart!" Dian muttered with contempt. "I meant what I said! NO goddamn communal dinners!"

"Dian . . ." Stuart stammered, unable to hide the exasperation in his voice, "Dian, why . . . ?"

"We've got work to do here!" Dian answered. "And we're here for the gorillas, not to feed our goddamn bellies!"

"Okay, Dian . . ." Stuart relented. "We've finished eating anyway."

"I said no communal dinners, and I meant it!" Dian yelled again, "Peter, get back to your own goddamn cabin." We stood dumbfounded once again as our boss turned away into the darkness.

Stuart let the door swing shut, and Peter and I started gathering the dishes into a stack on the desk. Stuart grabbed the pot of pasta water, thick with dissolved spaetzle, and Peter opened the door for him. In one bold swoop, he flung the contents out into the darkness.

"Oops! Sorry, Dian!" Stuart said, laughing cathartically.

Peter laughed with him. I cringed.

"It's too late for Dian to get mad at me." Stuart declared. "She needs me now."

When the door flung closed again, I saw the beam of a flashlight shine through the gap at the top from outside, sweeping across the ceiling. I knew Dian must still be out there somewhere. Neither Stuart nor Peter seemed to care, but I was ready to wrap it up and turn out the lights. That party was over for me.

With characteristic crassness, Dian insisted on referring to the film crew from Japan's Nippon AV Productions as "the Japs." I asked the camp staffers for the Swahili word for Japanese and they said it was *Abashinwa*, which I later deduced must simply be the Franc-ified

Kinyarwanda word for *Chinese*, placing the French *Chine* between the Kinyarwanda prefix *Aba* and suffix *wa* for *people*. With the camp's crew knowing little about individual Asian countries, this word must have served as their name for all Asians.

To my utter surprise, Dian invited me up to her cabin where she had planned a meeting with the two Japanese cinematographers. I was being rewarded for good behavior, plus I made a good prop for appearances to the outside world. As she offered me a cold beer, I realized I still didn't know how to act when she showed me friendliness, so cautious had I become under her volatility, but I thanked her, and with every sip, I found myself relaxing. Dian had brushed her hair and wore a fresh pair of jeans with a clean blue cotton turtleneck. On this day her cabin was not only freshly cleaned and tidy, but uncharacteristically bedecked with tiny arrangements of orange and yellow flowers gathered from around camp.

While I waited with her for the Japanese film crew to arrive, Dian pulled out some photocopied documents from the bookshelf on her wall.

"John . . . uh . . . here's something I did on the vocalizations of the gorillas . . ." She said, flipping through the pages, pausing at the complex images of sonograms. She slid her hand across the zigzags of vertical black lines on the page, as if trying to read braille. I recognized the papers as part of her doctoral thesis on gorilla vocalizations; Terry Maple had given me a copy.

"You can take this," she said, passing it into my hands. "Try and understand it if *you* can. I know *I* sure don't."

This only corroborated what I'd heard about her difficulty in getting her PhD at Cambridge; apparently her mentors had to do much of the work in order for her to graduate.

Dian had a PhD in Zoology, but to me, she didn't seem to have a broad understanding of science, biology, or wildlife, beyond her beloved gorillas. These beloved consisted primarily of gorillas in her research groups, the ones she had met and named, giving them human names, even family names, like Uncle Bert and Aunt Flossie. She was desperately concerned about Nunkie and his welfare, but when a research group had a confrontation with a fringe group, that fringe group was just an interloper, an unknown with which she had neither connected emotionally nor developed a bond. It was as if her groups were her pets, like Cindy and Kima, part of her family, versus the neighbor's pets, or the neighbors themselves. All else were outsiders to her cloistered world. What belonged to her, what she had staked her claim upon, became an extension of her, and any assault upon it, she took personally with a deep lament and vengeful wrath. Karisoke and its surroundings had become her turf, her gorilla territory, and she was there to defend it . . . to the end.

Soon the film duo of Haruhiko Takenaka and Jinzaburo Kajiura arrived, smiling and bowing repeatedly as Dian welcomed them into her home and beckoned them to take seats on her couch. The contempt she had previously shown about them being parked at the base of the mountain while wanting access to Karisoke had dissolved into a gracious pandering welcome from her.

Haruhiko, looked to be in his late thirties and was obviously more comfortable with English. He introduced himself and Kajiura, explaining that they go by the nicknames Taka and Kaji. Reading the gestures, Kaji, the elder at around fifty, nodded affirmatively.

"Did you notice the flowers?" Dian asked the befuddled pair who glanced around the room and nodded emphatically.

"Yes, very nice. Very nice!" Taka responded.

"I once took a course on Japanese flower arranging, back in the States." Dian said with a proud smile.

More polite smiles and nods.

"I've always been interested in Japan and would love to visit your country."

While Kanyaragana served us cheese sandwiches in the living area, Dian cut a deal.

"I've decided that I'm going to release the baby into a wild group of gorillas."

The two listened and nodded, wide-eyed and attentive, as if straining to understand across the language barrier.

"And I'd like you both to film this."

At this, Taka's mouth dropped open, and he turned to repeat the news in Japanese to Kaji. Soon, both were nodding with wide-eyed excitement at this prospect. It became apparent that Taka spoke more English than Kaji.

"And I'd like you to relocate your camp up here," Dian stated, pointing to the floor. "Up here to Karisoke. You. Come. Bring your camp."

Taka again turned to chatter to his sidekick, the word "Karisoke" blending in perfectly with their Japanese. More excited nodding. Then Dian came to the terms.

"You know, I have many expenses to run this camp."

"Yes . . . I see." Taka said.

"For this, I will need ten thousand dollars."

Both continued nodding, but their smiles were gone. Taka, the film director, more fully understanding what was just said, reiterated what he understood the deal to be.

"Our company pay you . . . ten sousand dollar? Yes?"

"Yes. And you will get your film."

"Okay. I see . . . I contact my company, Nippon AV Productions," he said slowly, finding his words, "and see . . . if they will agree."

"Let them know I have a lot of expenses, to run this camp."

"Yes . . . yes, okay . . . we will see."

"Okay . . . and there *is* one more thing."

"Ohhh . . ." Taka spoke, like air leaking from a tire. Next to him, Kaji remained deadpan, only his eyes moved, blinking and darting from his partner's face to Dian's.

"I've always wanted to visit your country. Perhaps your company would send me there."

"Ohhh . . . yes, okay!" Taka maintained his composure, while Kaji furtively studied his partner's demeanor and emulated it. "I will have to see . . . yes . . . you know, talk to my company . . . but yes, okay."

This settled, Dian leaned back in her chair and summoned Kanyaragana for more beer. Belly full, and enjoying the effects of a midday beer buzz, I was sublimely content, even seated next to Dian, excited even, about the prospects ahead.

"But I've got to warn you . . ." Dian said, followed by a foreboding pause, "I can be difficult to work with sometimes."

"Ohhh . . . ?" Taka said softly, with a confused tilt of his head. "Yes . . . okay . . . no problem."

"No, I mean *really* . . . sometimes I can be a real *bitch*." Dian looked at me. "Right?"

"Oh, *YEAHHH!*" I said, with perhaps a little too much conviction, instantly regretting my cheekiness.

"*Ehht mwaah,*" Dian growled, scolding me back into silence, staring at me to remind me I was just a prop.

Against the exotic backdrop of the Virunga Volcanoes, my life had become routine. Each day, at 8:00 A.M. I trudged up the trail to Dian's cabin at the opposite end of camp and waited to pick up the baby gorilla. Never knowing what time Dian would actually arise, I waited by the gorilla graveyard for fifteen to thirty minutes before our mercurial headmistress would finally emerge. Often the first sign of life I heard coming from inside was the shaking of a giant bottle of Darvon she kept in her bedside table. Having stayed up until the wee hours drinking and typing her book manuscript, Mademoiselli was usually hung over, hair lopsided from bed, and undressed but for dingy long johns bagging at the knees. She was extra gruff and short-tempered at this hour of the day, and I would beat a hasty retreat as soon as I had the baby, carrying my little charge off into the forest edge to forage and feed on her natural fare.

The Japanese film crew duo of Taka, the director and sound man, and Kaji, the cameraman, wasted no time packing up their dapper tented camp from the base of the mountain and moving up to Karisoke. Dian must've taken more than a little satisfaction knowing they had dropped their filming with Bill and Amy for the one and only Gorilla Lady and the dramatic footage she promised. In camp, Dian moved them into the Tent Cabin at Karisoke's eastern side—a large military-style tent with a proper metal roof mounted above it. But after that, Dian was hardly the hostess. Like us, they were left to fend for themselves.

Her already poor health then took a turn for the worse, deteriorating more each day. In addition to her deep chronic cough, sciatica sent sharp pains from her sore hip down her leg with every heave from her lungs. She also complained of a festering spider bite on her arm, and lamented constantly of mysterious brown spiders in her cabin that no one else saw. I began to wonder if she was imagining them.

One morning, Dian asked me to accompany her to select a site where I would camp outdoors with the baby in an effort to re-acclimate it to life in the wild. As I picked up little Nani, Dian leaned on a walking stick, pale and sickly. Dressed in jeans and a thin turtleneck shirt, she slowly tied the arms of an old green rain jacket around her gaunt waist. We slowly moved from the cabin down the trail out of camp, Dian wobbling precariously with each step, frequently stopping to wince from pain.

"I just can't make these hikes anymore, *goddammit*," Dian gasped, stopping to lean on her walking stick. A light drizzle began and, even with the cold, Dian left her raincoat off. The baby clung under my arm to support herself, looking baffled by our slow progress, as the Rwandan teen Toni trotted up to join us, likewise decked in rain gear.

We were still within view of Dian's cabin, when she just gave out, saying, "Maybe this will do. Let's sit down." I lowered Nani to the ground and Dian dropped onto one thigh, holding her torso up with one hand on the ground beside her. Her legs, like a newborn foal's, were crumpled and frail in contrast to the heavy Vasque hiking boots weighing her feet down. Dian was dressed for a real hike, but we weren't even beyond the bounds of camp. *This could hardly be what Dian had in mind for a bivouac camp,* I thought—not yet away from the smell of humans, of smoke, nor the din of camp activities.

When we rose to our feet again Dian coughed uncontrollably. "I'll send the men out to look for a suitable bivouac," she said, coughing again and doubling over unabashedly. She grabbed her stomach until her coughing subsided. Toni and I stood by awkwardly, uncertain what to do. "I know I can't do it," she muttered, before resuming an upright stance.

At that, we turned around and headed back into camp. Before reaching her cabin, Dian doubled over again with a deep heaving sound. I thought she was trying to make herself vomit, and Toni and I stood by with the baby, both disturbed and a little embarrassed for Dian. Finally, she stood upright, and slinging little Nani onto my shoulders, I followed her and Toni back to her cabin, where our boss shut herself in for the rest of the day.

While Dian's health waxed and waned, she communicated with Stuart daily, running ideas by him, sharing her plans. Peter and I knew only the bits and pieces we could glean from Stuart. This served Dian as an effective means of keeping Stuart in her pocket, while also preparing him for her departure by elevating his rank within the camp hierarchy. For my own part, I was happier to continue having Stuart as a buffer between Dian and me.

Under Dian's edict, we still had to abide by her rule of "No Communal Dinners!" Clearly, any gathering beyond her watchful eye continued to strike at some acute, deep-set paranoia, which triggered compulsive rage. I felt self-conscious if she even saw the three of us standing together chatting. But Taka and Kaji were exceedingly friendly and congenial in camp, bowing, nodding, and inviting us to dinner each time one of us ran into them.

"We really want make special dinner for you," Taka would remind us when any of us would run into them. "Kaji very good cook!"

Under the mounting pressure and awkwardness of evading our exceedingly friendly would-be hosts, Stuart asked Dian if we might accept their offer just once. In no uncertain terms, Dian forbade it, saying that we were not to bother them. But they were just biding their time, waiting for Dian to be ready for filming, and wanting to interact with us in the meantime. Under Dian's strict rule, their repeated offers became increasingly awkward for us to dodge.

"When can join us?" They asked at each opportunity. With blank stares, they were visibly disappointed and perplexed by our steadfast refusals. None of us were successful at explaining why.

In their blissful ignorance, Taka temped us further, reminding us of Kaji's camp culinary skills and that they had a delicious menu planned, with food a young production assistant had just brought in from Japan just for this occasion, a temporary third man to their party. From the perspective of our own meager and monotonous rations, the offer was, of course, extremely appealing.

In temptation and exasperation, Stuart eventually announced to Peter and me that, despite Dian's warnings, he accepted an invitation for the three of us.

"What's she gonna do," he said, "Embarrass herself in front of them?"

I was scared to death, but the next evening I relented and joined in the wonderful spread, which included teriyaki beef, Japanese-style egg foo yong, and dried squid with mayonnaise dip—a fascinating and wonderful repast. This we washed down with all the Primus beer we wanted, numbing my fears of Mademoiselli emerging from the darkness fit to kill. Communicating across the English-Japanese language gap just added to the drunken fun around a blazing fire. Drinking, swapping stories, and laughing into the night in a cloud of Impala cigarette smoke under the stars gave us a well-needed respite from the camp's oppressive atmosphere. And we were quite noisy.

Despite the distance from her cabin, or because of her unrelenting paranoia, Dian was entirely aware of our merriment. Stuart avoided her the next day, but that night, drunken and enraged, she staggered down to our cabin and confronted him.

"Stuart, you *reeeally* fucked up!" she yelled, leaning in Stuart's doorway, absolutely livid. "We don't need all this me-itis around here, with everyone worrying about themselves and feeding their goddamn bellies all the time!"

Uncharacteristically, Stuart stood his ground.

"C'mon Dian, what was I supposed to do?" he protested. "They kept asking us." Dian cursed and berated him unrelentingly before staggering back into the darkness up the trail toward her cabin.

After she was gone, Stuart cut the tension, declaring with a laugh as he slammed the door, "I still LOVE the bitch!"

SIXTEEN

THE BIVOUAC

Y ou *reeeally* fucked up, Stuart," Peter and I would chide our
fellow sufferer at every opportunity, out of earshot of Dian.
"*Reeeally* and *truuully* . . ." Stuart would accept our ribbing with
a cathartic laugh, before heading back up to Dian's cabin to assist with
whatever task was at hand in her preparations for departure.

Dian had coined the term "me-itis" in reference to one thinking only
of themselves, but I was beginning to realize it meant, not directing our
efforts at her needs. Our dinners without her sorely represented a lack
of devotion to her, triggering a blind rage. She would also remind us
"We're here for the gorillas," which really meant we were there for her.

Under the crunch of ever-shrinking time before Dian would have to
leave Rwanda, she scheduled Nani and me to start our bivouac camp

on February 26. Filming of the baby gorilla's release process began that afternoon. With Taka holding a long foam-covered microphone and directing in Japanese, Kaji deftly aimed his camera at Nani and me as we walked from my cabin down the camp trail toward our new temporary home in Zaire. I felt awkward and a little embarrassed in front of the camera. My spare clothes were jammed into my small, bulging backpack and I had strapped a flashlight and boots onto the outside of it. As I walked, these boots, hanging from their laces, began flailing wildly back and forth, pulling at my pack and gear, to and fro, until the rhythmic sway almost made me lose my footing. Feeling self-conscious, all I could think about was how dumb the scene must have looked as Kaji filmed me from behind.

I would come to understand that Dian had become a brand of sorts, an admirable one—the woman who gave up everything to live with gorillas in the forest to protect and save them. It had brought meaning and importance to her life since photographer Bob Campbell had first rocketed Dian to fame with his photos for *National Geographic* magazine. Cameramen and film crews were how she established and cultivated the brand, conveying it to the world. This phenomenon, I would realize, afforded her the ability to both remain withdrawn from society, and yet connected to the world, detached and yet fulfilled in the knowledge that she was admired by so many. She may have struggled with friendships and intimate relationships, ending them with irrevocable finality, but she had found a way to be adored by the masses. She guarded her brand jealously, as if her life depended on it.

Dian came alive in the presence of the film crew and stepped ahead of me on the trail. Moments earlier, she had been her dour self, irritably barking orders to all of us. In front of the camera, she became the doe-eyed gorilla martyr she wanted the world to see. When Kaji aimed his lens at her, Dian widened her eyes in a dramatic expression of compassionate concern. She did this frequently as we walked down the trail past her cabin, letting her gaze linger with emotion for the baby, knitting her brow, well aware of the camera trained on her.

Dian had told the Japanese crew that she wanted Nani to begin her readjustment to the wild the moment I carried the baby out of camp. The smiles had dropped from Taka's and Kaji's faces as Dian had explained that they could not follow me and Nani to the bivouac camp. By design, there would be no cameras rolling without Dian in the scene. This was not going to be a film about her students. Obediently, the film duo halted and stood with Dian as Nani and I walked on into the meadow. Oblivious to the load I already had on my back, Nani grabbed at my legs. I hoisted her into my arms and kept walking. Under the weight of gorilla plus backpack, my boots sank deep into the soggy meadow and I struggled to balance my load.

Where the tussocks grew thick at the western side of the marshy plain we crossed a cool clear bog and trespassed into Zaire. At that spot, I recalled Peter having told me that Jacques Cousteau had traveled there to identify the headwaters of the Nile. Cousteau believed that the mighty river may, in fact, start at that very spot where the Virunga Volcanoes, like the Mountains of the Moon in Uganda to the north, divided West Africa from East. The idea captivated me as I trudged across the wetland leaving one country for another in one step. Nani stared blankly from my arms when I paused in this wide-open space to muse over the idea that the water in front of me trickled down westward into the Congo River basin, while the water behind me flowed northward to the Nile. Despite the load of baby and backpack, I took it all in. At that place, I felt like I was at the top of the world and pondered the irony of having one foot in one of the smallest, most densely-populated countries in the world, and the other foot in one of Africa's largest and least-populated provinces.

As Nani and I reached the southwestern edge of the meadow, and the open forest of airy hypericum trees and mighty hagenias converged around us, I set Nani down and encouraged her to walk on her own. Wide-eyed and pensive, she stared in all directions, scrambling after me. With a whimper, she grasped my leg, insisting I carry her again into this new region unknown to her. I stayed on the narrow trail kept worn by forest buffaloes, and forays by us few humans out of Karisoke. The trees grew thicker as I hauled my gear and baby gorilla farther along the trail, another ten minutes, until the level ground began to slope gently downward. Here Stuart's bivouac had been set up by camp staff under a spreading hagenia, beside an opening in the forest. The site was well equipped with a tent, a sleeping bag, a stove, and cooking utensils. Stuart was out with Rwelekana keeping tabs on the location of Group 4. Dian had dubbed this site the "Midway Camp," because it was between my bivouac and Karisoke. The game plan was for me to eat meals here. Toni would be spending each night with Nani and me, and I would come here to eat while he looked after the baby.

To keep Nani out of the campsite gear, I carried her farther along the trail and set her down to forage in a thick stand of vegetation. She stayed close to me, and fed contentedly, purring over mouthfuls of her familiar foods, *hmwaaah* . . . The land dropped gently from that point on in terrace-like gradations, downward and westward into Zaire. Here, I felt aware of Africa falling away from the upland Virungas, down into warm lush forests and into the deepest darkest basins of the Congo River, which snaked like a fat python to the Atlantic Ocean far beyond the horizon.

Without a visa for Zaire I speculated as to what the consequences would be if Zairean park officials or soldiers were to find me, camped out in their country as an illegal alien. Dian hadn't talked about this, and I shrugged off the notion that anyone would encounter us during our three-day campout. But I knew Dian had been abruptly extricated from her Zairean camp, a three-hour walk from here; after which, she was held hostage until she pulled off an escape in Uganda.

When Nani had fed for a while and began crawling back to me, I kept a few steps ahead of her, allowing her to travel on her own. This gave me a lesser burden on the rest of my trek, and conditioned her to some independent walking that I knew she would need back in the wild. My little gorilla scampered along on all fours, but whimpered loudly about every fifty feet. I relented intermittently, and carried my furry bundle another fifty feet before setting her down again. We continued with this alternating travel plan for nearly an hour, before we reached our own camp, a large gray canvas military tent under a spreading hagenia. From Karisoke, we had walked about four kilometers, nearly a quarter of the distance around Mount Visoke to the base of its western slope. From here, we stared directly into Mount Mikeno's eastern face and its rocky tower, jutting starkly into the clouds to an altitude of 14,460 feet.

Our bivouac made a serene setting where the forest opened into a green glade. Around the edges of this clearing, Nani's favored foods, gallium, thistle celery, and nettle, grew abundantly. When I stopped to peel the backpack from my shoulders, Nani crawled to the ground and sat on a comfortable moss-covered log. Because Dian had wanted Nani's hair and body to lose the camp's pervasive smell of wood smoke, I didn't have a supply of firewood here. Dian believed the wild gorillas would associate a smoke smell with poachers, who typically had campfires in the woods. The rising smoke from a fire would also draw attention to our location from all around. Instead, camp staffers had provided me with a small kerosene stove to heat water for coffee or tea stored in a metal canister.

Nani crawled across the fallen log, examining the lantern and mouthing a sleeping bag. When she pulled at the tent's support cords, I pig-grunted, *"eh . . . eh . . . eh . . ."* She well knew what this gorilla word meant and stopped her exploration, peering up at me with her innocent dark brown eyes. To divert her attention, I carried her to a stand of thistles and gallium. With Nani feeding one minute and sitting on my lap the next, we made our way around the little glade under a cold gray sky. By the time Toni arrived in late afternoon, we knew every inch of the half-acre clearing that was our camp.

At 5:00 P.M., I left Toni watching the baby, and walked back up the trail toward Stuart's bivouac. I realized that the distance that had taken me nearly an hour with Nani foraging along the way was only a ten-minute walk alone. When I arrived, Stuart offered me an enameled bowl of steaming beans and rice. It was the best indulgence I could have imagined since my last bit of cooked beans had been finished off by the giant rat in my cabin.

"Dian also sent us some Primus," Stuart said, grinning as he pulled two of the large half-liter beer bottles out of a box—a sure sign of our leader's approval for our efforts. It was clear by now that when we did good, we got beer. As the minutes of my precious dinner hour ticked away, Stuart and I chatted about our arrangements for the next few days. Always upbeat and talkative, Stuart also talked a lot about his girlfriend and how he was looking forward to her coming to camp to begin a research project of her own.

"She's going to do a project on gorilla anatomy and locomotion," he mentioned. "That's kind of her area." He had spoken of her often, but seemed vague about when she might actually arrive.

I enjoyed the beer and conversation, but as it grew dark within the hour, I headed back to my campsite. Glancing back, I thought Stuart looked more out of place than me, camping completely alone in the forest. Stuart was a people person, and the social skills and congeniality that helped him win over Dian at Karisoke seemed moot in his isolation here.

Back at my campsite, Toni and I readied ourselves for the first night of our assignment. Dian had provided the tent for Nani and me but I decided that if the baby gorilla was supposed to readjust to the outdoors, we should sleep outside. Besides, Nani would urinate whenever she wanted to, and I could envision the pee seeping across the tent's canvas bottom only to be blotted up by me and my sleeping bag.

As the light faded, heavy mists rolled down Visoke and wafted into our tiny meadow, enveloping us in a bank of cold cloud. Knowing it was as likely to rain as not, I unfurled a blue plastic tarp, compliments of the Japanese film team, and stretched its corners to tree branches in opposing directions. When he saw what I was doing, Toni jumped up from the entrance of his tent and helped me secure the bits of twine to the grommets of my makeshift shelter. In the remaining light I unrolled my sleeping bag on a plush salad of weeds beneath the hagenia.

In the darkness, Toni held the flashlight while I lit the wick of our lantern. When it glowed to life at the touch of a match, I hung it on a tree branch out of Nani's curious reach. The lantern illuminated our immediate area, but the night loomed black, cold, and mysterious beyond the short radius of its glow.

I had looked forward to Toni's company as an opportunity to practice my Swahili, but soon learned that this youth, who spoke Kinyarwanda, still knew less Swahili than me. When I tried a few words on him, he nodded saying "eh . . ." the Rwandan version of "yeah," or "huh?" depending on intonation. I was never quite sure if he understood or misunderstood any word I was saying.

To get Nani back on a normal gorilla day cycle, of dusk to dawn, I decided to put out the lantern and get to bed. Toni crawled into his tent, and I took off my shoes and slid, clothes and all, into my sleeping bag. Nani, keeping her hand on me during the process, snuggled close. Instinctively, she knew what time it was and pulled a couple of nearby senecio stalks over, tucking the leafy ends under her to make a proper gorilla nest. Settled in and satisfied, my bed buddy made a contented belch vocalization, *hmwaaahh* . . . obviously happy to know we'd be sharing a nest, her breath suffused with the pungent smell of digesting herbs.

Out from under the edge of the tarp, I could see the night sky clearing. Like stage curtains, the clouds parted and in the high thin air, brilliant stars sparkled in countless numbers, like the whole of the sky was the Milky Way. The monolithic silhouette of Mikeno was visible against their luminosity. Northern stars were always bright back home in the mountains of Virginia, but never had I seen so many. I was far from home.

Cold air drifted down from Visoke's slopes, but I felt the warmth of my little gorilla. Warmth flowed from her body through my sleeping bag, through my clothing to my skin. And with it, wetness . . . Gorilla pee! I bounced and wiggled like a caterpillar trapped in a cocoon, in my effort to roll away from my little bedmate. But she was on me, clinging. My sudden actions startled Nani, making her draw even closer for security while she emptied her bladder. I maneuvered off the wetness, and she maneuvered too, staying close. My T-shirt was soaked, but I'm sure she wondered what the heck was wrong with me.

I shifted onto my side so at least her rump wouldn't be on top of me. Realizing she wasn't going to tolerate any distance from me, I pulled more vegetation under her nest and my sleeping bag until we were both buoyed at least six inches above the ground, for drainage. With this arrangement, urine-soaked, and tired, I finally fell asleep.

At first, I didn't know why I had woken. Curious about the time, I tried to read my watch face, but the little glow-in-the-dark dots were never bright enough. Nani was sleeping soundly with slow rhythmic breathing, and I found myself listening for other sounds. *Did I just hear something?* I shifted to listen. The silence was disrupted by the rustling and cracking of something moving through the brush on the edges of our little meadow. I froze. There it was again, only louder. *Footsteps?* Nani lifted her head, awake now. As I reached without success for the flashlight, Toni shifted in his tent. The strange sounds, like heavy boots, closed in on all sides, and I wriggled free of my sleeping bag. Nani grasped at my legs as I bolted upright. It sounded like an army shuffling their feet slowly through the brush. We were surrounded!

Toni popped his head out of the tent, clicking on the flashlight as he stood to join me, but we couldn't see a thing in the weak beam. As we strained to see, the sounds grew louder, enveloping us in the darkness. Nani climbed into my arms with a silent wide stare. The noise continued, accompanied by a loud crunching and munching. Then I heard the familiar snort, *whoosh*—buffaloes!

Mbogo, I said to Toni.

Eh . . . mbogo, Toni echoed with affirmation. Nani clambered onto my shoulders. Our idyllic little meadow by day was obviously a favored buffalo feeding ground by night. Nani's hands clasped around my forehead from her perch on my shoulders made me realize that we would not be getting much sleep in the middle of this herd.

"Hey!" I shouted, in an effort to scare our visitors. I was answered with indignant snorts from the darkness and a tighter grip from Nani around my face. As hard as I tried, I could not see a single animal, black on black as they were, and the dim flashlight was of little use. Shifting the baby to my back, I grabbed two metal coffee cups, and clanged them together. The snorts grew louder, and the heavy hoof sounds moved around and past us as if the giant bovines didn't know which way to go. I had only succeeded in irritating them. From the sounds, I could tell this was a big herd. Toni moved in closer to me while Nani nearly choked me with her arms around my neck. I could see in the flashlight beam, her eyes stared as widely into the darkness as Toni's and mine. I found myself wishing I had one of Dian's pistols, just to make some noise.

Balancing Nani, I bent over to pick up a large plastic trash bag on the ground next to my sleeping bag, Nani's restless, shifting weight at my shoulders almost pulled me to the ground. I cupped my hands around a portion of the bag and blew into it to make a crude plastic balloon of sorts. Twisting the end closed, I torqued the plastic bag progressively tighter until, with a sharp slap from my left hand, it ruptured in a loud *bang*. At that, the unwitting denizens of the darkness lurched in unison before crashing around and past us where we huddled amid their throng. These great bovines were barely visible in the shadows that matched their black hides, but I could smell their steaming breath as they huffed and snorted their displeasure at us. Toni grabbed another plastic bag and we repeated our little explosions, over and over, until the buffalo stampede we had started abated into the forest.

Although completely exhausted, Toni and I sat up with Nani for a while afterward before retiring again. With our language barrier, Toni and I made no conversation in the darkness except to say "*mbogo*" every few minutes and laugh, as we struggled to get back to sleep. In the absurdness of our circumstances, we had at least one word in common.

The morning came cold and damp, with a light misting rain. We were in the clouds. After coffee and toast at Stuart's camp, I went back to my own. Dian had instructed Toni to return to Karisoke to do chores during part of the day, and Nani followed him to the edge of the clearing before scampering back to me when he disappeared into the forest toward home camp. In this new place away from Karisoke, Nani reached up for me repeatedly when I set her down to forage. Intermittently, when the drizzle turned to downpour, we took refuge under the tarp, huddling together like two gorillas in the rain. When Toni returned at noon, the rain had stopped, and I trekked back to the midway camp for lunch. Stuart, still out with Group 4, wasn't there, but I knew to look for my lunch, a cheese sandwich and bananas, in a metal locker in the tent. After I ate, I didn't go immediately back to my bivouac, but lingered around Stuart's empty camp to enjoy a full hour of solitude. As much as I cared for Nani, it was a relief to be temporarily free from the grasp of a clinging toddler. The sound of water drew me to a gushing stream that had become swollen in the day's rain. It flowed in a series of pretty waterfalls through a sequence of terraced pools. By the stream, I sat on a large moss-covered rock until it was time to return to my duties.

When I got back to our bivouac, Nani scrambled from Toni's feet over to me, and hoisted herself up my leg into my arms. The rain had ended, and surprisingly the clouds parted allowing us a view of Mount Mikeno shining in the brilliant afternoon sun.

In 1926, the famed naturalist Carl Akeley died beneath Mount Mikeno while on a collecting expedition for the new Africa Hall of New York City's American Museum of Natural History. He was buried according to his wishes at the edge of the serene Kabara meadow, just under this mountain. Akeley had described the spot as one of the loveliest places on earth. From the same meadow, in 1959, American scientist George Schaller launched his landmark study of mountain gorillas. His research culminated in the 431-page comprehensive treatise, *The Mountain Gorilla*, and a popularized account of his experiences titled *The Year of the Gorilla*. When I thought of Schaller's work, I realized how scant Dian's productivity seemed in her thirteen years compared to Schaller's single year of studying gorillas. It was obvious Dian had achieved greater fame despite George Schaller already having produced the definitive books on mountain gorillas.

In January 1967, like Schaller, Dian also launched her career as a primatologist from the meadow at Mikeno's base. I would later learn that
after six months, she was removed from the Kabara meadow by Zairean
soldiers. For two weeks, she was abused and molested before fleeing into
Uganda. (Some of her closest friends reported that Dian had confided
that she was raped repeatedly during that detainment.) What she lacked
in scientific productivity, she made up for in determined tenacity. Five
weeks later, she climbed back into the Virungas on the Rwandan side
and founded the Karisoke Research Center. I couldn't help but think
that her desire for isolation, even after her horrible experiences in Zaire,
outweighed her willingness to return to society.

As I mused at Mikeno's history to the sound of Nani's contented
munching, I noticed a wispy cloud was always perched above its summit
like a white beret. I was transfixed by the way the cloud was always
moving eastward, yet never leaving the volcano. Only after a long period
of pondering did I realize that Mikeno was making the cloud cap it wore.
The warm sunlight accelerated the evaporation on its black peak, and
as the vapor rose, it quickly condensed in the cold air at its 14,553-foot
summit. As the mist moved away, it dispersed and dissipated into thin
air like the steam from a whistling teapot on an enormous scale.

To pass the time, I tried to converse in Swahili again with Toni,
pointing at items and trying to recall the Swahili words for tree, rock,
cup, gorilla . . . Toni would just cock his head and knit his brow saying,
"Eh?" I'd laugh. He'd laugh. We'd both laugh. I wondered what his
sense of duty was in an occupation as rare to him as mine was to me,
far above the rest of Rwanda, Zaire, and the worlds beyond. He had
a steadfast understanding of his role in assisting me with the bivouac
camp and taking care of the baby. *But what did he think of all this gorilla
business and camping with a baby ape and a white guy in the cloud forest?*
I was curious to ask him, but our language barrier stood between us.

As the afternoon drew on, the low-angled sun cast a bright golden
light through the rain-washed air. Having brought my camera, I decided
to take some photos in the rare lighting. Noticing Toni's apparent interest

in what I was doing, I showed him how to aim and focus and click the shutter. I posed with Nani in my lap and Toni took a picture of the two of us as a memento of what were to be our last few days together.

After dinner with Stuart, I rejoined Toni and Nani, settling in for our second night in the bush. With Nani huddled next to me on a fresh bed of greens, I listened and waited for the buffaloes to return to our meadow, but they didn't. Apparently last night was as unsettling to them as it was to us.

Late in the night, I woke to the sound of pelting rain on the tarp suspended above me. It was sagging on one corner and water was dripping onto the foot of my sleeping bag. With my feet, I drew my bedding inward out of the rain and sat up to pull my backpack farther under the tarp. I checked the contents to make sure that my camera and spare clothes were still dry. Nani shifted in from the drips and snuggled closer to my shoulder.

Suddenly the tarp's right hand corner near my feet snapped loose with a splash. Water, which had pooled on the tarp, gushed into my backpack. Springing upright, I grabbed the pack in an effort to save the contents. *Shit! Shit! Shit!* All I could do was to invert it and dump the water out as quickly as possible, hoping my camera stayed dry on the inside. To make matters worse, our makeshift roof was reduced by half and water seeped across the ground into my sleeping bag. What was once a fluffy grass bed became a muddy mess beneath us, before the downpour abated just before dawn.

In the growing light, I examined the contents of my backpack, really feeling the stress of the bivouac experience. My spare clothes were soaked, but my greatest disappointment was lifting my treasured Pentax camera, and watching the water pour out of it. It had cost me $250, a fortune at the time. Looking through the viewfinder, I tried to get the light meter to respond. The needle didn't bounce to life and my camera's shutter wouldn't click. It, and my last pictures of Nani, were ruined.

Three days of the bivouac camp with my simian dependent was taking its toll on me. For the last seventy-two hours, the two of us had been in near complete physical contact with my baby gorilla clinging to my legs, waist, and neck during the day, and wanting to be picked up after every few minutes of feeding on her own. With the long hike ahead, I reasoned that if she was going to be thrust into a new group of wild gorillas, she could afford to be a little more independent.

This third day of this round-the-clock parenting made me feel the strains of having a baby gorilla attached to me night and day. That, combined with a growing sleep deficit, had begun to put cracks in my emotional state. During the night, she had shifted and wriggled and urinated on me whenever she felt like it. I was experiencing the kind of battle fatigue that only a parent understands after spending too much time with a needy child; Toni's mealtime relief was no longer enough. I was weary from not being able to take a few steps without having what was beginning to feel like a furry ball and chain around my leg. Despite my affection for her, I reasoned that Nani needed to develop some self-sufficiency; no silverback, or other wild group member, was going to indulge her like I had been doing. And so, while Nani was feeding at my feet, I walked away from her.

As usual, she grabbed for my leg, but this time I sidestepped her grasp. Perplexed, she stared blankly up at me, as if sizing up this sudden change in my behavior. I walked farther away. She pursued. I trotted farther ahead, repeatedly just out of reach. I wanted her to just stop and feed again on her own, but Nani scrambled to keep up, grabbing at me. I kept one step ahead of her. In the middle of this crazy game of tag, my little orphan finally had enough. She let out a long scream I hadn't heard before. The sound welled from a deep emotional place that I had not yet witnessed in her, sounding as if she was being eaten alive by some unseen carnivore within. Her hands formed small fists, and slammed the ground angrily at her sides while she wailed. Screaming again, she spun around in a blind rampage of bewildered frustration. She was having a tantrum . . . a *meltdown!*

I stared in astonishment as Nani continued her wailing, her fit stunning me into a state of sympathy, and making me realize that she was capable of a much deeper range of emotions than I understood. Despite my own exhaustion and frustration, I was reminded of the trauma she must have had in the course of her extraction from her family, in the certain witness of her mother's death, and spending weeks of her young life confined in a box, the victim of violence and kidnapping. Then we frightful humans insisted that she accept us, and now my insistence that she stand alone, entirely unaware of what awaits her with a new group of wild gorillas. I rushed to calm her, gathering her in my arms from the wet grass. She had won the argument.

On our fourth and last morning of February 29, Nani started her usual stirring at dawn, shifting and adjusting positions, nuzzled against me as forest birds began their morning chorus. I waited for a light shower of rain to move over us before crawling from the warmth of my sleeping bag. Toni didn't stir from his tent until I started pumping the kerosene stove to make coffee. It was the day of Nani's release.

Just as Toni crawled through his tent flaps, the sound of loud gorilla screams rang from the base of Mount Visoke, just above us. The roaring voices, combined with the characteristic *pokka-pok* of leathery hands beating a bare chest, went on intermittently for several minutes. The screaming sounded like mayhem. By the time Dian had arrived with Taka and Kaji, lugging their camera and sound equipment, the rain was pouring. I told Dian about the gorilla screams, and she peered into the forest squinting and blinking from under her rain hood in silent contemplation for a few minutes. Then, with Nani on my back, I joined Dian and the film team, following Rwelekana up the slope of Mount Visoke.

In the three months she had been with us in camp, our little ape had gained good weight, and with the steep angle of the mountainside, I could well feel her forty pounds. In the same time, I had gained the physical strength and endurance to navigate this volcanic terrain, and surprised myself with the ability to keep pace with Rwelekana at the head of the pack. The rain didn't let up as we continued onward on what appeared to be Group 4's trail. I was surprised by Dian's ability to keep up with the rest of us considering her feebleness and coughing bout just weeks earlier, when she first tried to show me a site for a bivouac. Now, she showed little of the infirmity I had seen before, and although she brought up the rear, she kept up in the arduous climb. Kaji too, impressed me as he lugged his massive movie camera over the tricky slanted footing of Visoke's weedy slopes.

Just a short distance away from the bivouac camp, our tracker picked up a fresh gorilla trail leading out of a large area of crushed vegetation. The ground here was covered in loose gorilla feces that Dian called "fear dung." She explained to us that when gorillas are stressed from fear they excrete this loose, formless stool. When one group of gorillas interacts with another, the silverbacks usually lead the onslaughts, emitting their strong body odor in the process. Here, this odor hung thick in the air, a pungent, near-human, sweaty smell. Rwelekana chattered to Dian in Swahili, pointing his panga across the broad expanse of cleared ground and toward what looked like the various points of entry and exit of gorillas in frantic action.

"Group 4 has had an interaction with one of the fringe groups," Dian surmised, after Rwelekana finished his discourse.

Rwelekana chose one fresh trail that led in a long straight line toward Visoke's western side, opposite of Karisoke and farther into Zaire. We trudged along, slipping and sliding on the wet undergrowth, and somehow, even with forty pounds of baby gorilla on my back, I ended up just behind Rwelekana, who was blazing the trail with his panga. I had developed much endurance since my first weeks at Karisoke. The film crew kept pace as best they could with all their heavy equipment, and miraculously, Dian brought up the rear. What a contrast, I thought, to the month before when we made the short hike to look for a bivouac site, never even making it beyond the fringes of camp before she was too pained and agonized to continue. It was as if she was now willing herself to keep up with us.

When we came to the first ravine, I didn't think Dian would be able to follow. But taking her time, she carefully slid and sidestepped down one side before groping her way up the steep embankment on the other. While our group paused to rest afterward, Rwelekana forged ahead to scout out directions of gorilla trails. The apes had dispersed while crossing the ravine, and each had reached the other side at various points, leaving no one clear path as to where they headed next. Our able tracker would be checking for where they had regrouped into a single trail. As we waited, the rain picked up in a stronger downpour, and the cold damp set in under our rain gear as steamy sweat turned to cold dampness against skin. Nani used the downtime to eat some gallium and thistles that grew on the ravine's upper edge. By the time Rwelekana again picked up the gorilla group's collective trail, the heavy rain had made the soft ground worse, deep and slick with mud.

Exhausted, but with our mission still ahead of us, our group collected our things while Nani scrambled onto my back as I rose. Rwelekana led us onward to where the gorillas' trails regrouped as one, and we headed yet again into another ravine. While the rain pelted us unrelentingly, so too, the terrain was unforgiving; as soon as the ground leveled off from one ravine, another crevasse fell away before us in a brutal trek on the 45° angle of Mikeno's pitch. Despite my heavy living cargo, I kept up with Rwelekana and we drew well ahead of the others, who followed with their own burdens as best they could.

As we struggled along in the worst conditions imaginable, with mud, rain, ravines, and Visoke's steep angle, it began to seem we would never catch up with these gorillas, who had obviously made a mad dash far and away after the morning's clash with another group. The task of releasing the baby into Group 4 at the end of our trail seemed increasing dubious and daunting on this day.

Then we were upon them.

Before realizing we were even closing in on our quarry, the deafening roar hit my eardrums: *AAARRRGH!* The undergrowth just in front of Rwelekana exploded and slammed to the ground under the swing of a massive forearm, and the silverback screamed again in his charge at Rwelekana and me. But we were already flat on the ground, eyes averted. The deafening voice sent chills through my body as we braced for impact, we were so close. Intuitively, we two humans voiced our gorilla whimpers in pathetic unison, *hmm, hmm, hmm, hmmm* . . . while Nani clung tightly to me, her eyes wide in startled awe. It had been months since she had been among gorillas and she was as stunned as we were when only eerie silence followed. As quickly as he had appeared, the silverback vanished. His thick angry odor hung in the air.

Raising our heads, Rwelekana and I listened in the silence for several minutes, trying to hear above the steady rain, staring into the green maze beyond. Dian and the film crew had not yet caught up with us. Surely, they heard the charge and halted. After several minutes on the ground, waiting and listening, Rwelekana rose cautiously. I swung Nani around to my back and followed back down the trail we came in on, to where Dian waited with the Japanese. Rwelekana and Dian conversed briefly in Swahili about what just happened, before Dian surmised that we had been following the trail of the interloping rival group instead of Group 4. This fringe group of gorillas had not been habituated by camp researchers, and in this area rife with poachers, had every reason to fear being pursued by a band of humans.

"Shit *merde* . . . we're not going to be able to do this today," Dian muttered, "In this *motherfucking* rain! And Group 4 is going be too goddamned agitated after interacting with this fringe group." She was flustered, for sure, but her discontent wasn't directed at anyone then, least of all me. I admired her diligence and fortitude in the moment, but was soon to see much more of what she was capable of.

Knowing that this was also a heavy poacher area, Dian called off the plans to release Nani that day. Seemingly resigned to getting Nani's release over with, she changed plans entirely.

"John, you need to spend one more night in the bivouac," Dian informed me. "Tomorrow, we'll release her into Group 5 instead." Discouraged and exhausted, we made the long trek back in a frigid downpour.

SEVENTEEN

A NEAR-DEATH EXPERIENCE

On the morning of March 1, the birds began their usual chorus as the predawn sky lightened. My baby gorilla remained fast asleep, huddled in our nest next to me, out of character at this hour. I took advantage of her stillness and languished in the accumulated warmth of my sleeping bag. We were in the clouds again, and the dew lay thick and cold on the crumpled weeds around our campsite. It wasn't until 7:30 and full daylight that the little ball of fur roused her head. After looking around briefly, she crawled to the base of a hypericum and climbed four meters up to begin her breakfast of gallium that she pulled toward her strand after strand.

I watched the little gorilla feeding, lingering in my sleeping bag for a precious fifteen minutes longer before crawling out into the damp cold mountain air. I struggled to keep my socks off the wet ground while maneuvering my feet into cold boots. Toni soon crawled from his tent to help me pack up camp and fold the plastic tarp that had been my feckless shelter.

Nani continued to feed for nearly half an hour before climbing down from her tree and trying to cling to me. When Toni finally emerged, we began disassembling his tent, struggling to fold the bulky canvas into any sensible form, while Nani grabbed at my legs whenever I passed near her. I dodged her clingy fingers at every turn.

At 8:30, Kanyaragana arrived with Mukera the woodman, and the two joined Toni in gathering the bundles and utensils that had been our camp. I still wanted Nani to do some walking on her own, but finally just relented to her grasping and let her climb onto my backpack as we began the hike back into Rwanda. We passed by the site of Stuart's midway camp, now cleared and vacant. The long, boggy meadow leading to Karisoke was draped in curtains of mist when we reached it, the far end invisible in the cloud cover. The volcanoes above us were obscured by the very clouds through which we hiked. To avoid getting the smell of smoke on the baby, Dian had requested I walk around camp instead of through it, so I stayed to the right of the meadow until it narrowed into a thin clearing to the south of camp and just behind my cabin that on this day seemed like my cozy home.

When we passed the research center, we crossed the camp creek on the lichen-covered stones that Nani had perched on many times before to stare at her reflection in the water, and touch that enigmatic mirror of its surface that had intrigued her so. I wanted to let her linger there with me one last time, but Dian was waiting for me down the Porter Trail.

As I carried Nani along the path, I thought about the amount of time we had been together, and what we had become. My mom had once taken in two foster girls who had been removed from an abusive, neglectful home by the local social services in a town near where we lived. The girls, aged seven and eleven, were very withdrawn their first day in our home. Like Nani, they were wild too, with bangs growing over their eyes, their growing feet busting through their worn-out shoes. To coax them from their shyness, I joked with them and teased them as much for my amusement as theirs. Within a few days, they were following me everywhere in and around the house, amusing me one minute, annoying me the next.

One day, while I was reading a children's book to the youngest girl, she asked me, "Can I call you 'Dad'?" In my mid-teens, I didn't feel like a dad. I told her just to think of me as a brother instead. Social services doesn't let foster children stay in one home too long because the interpersonal bonds grow so strong over time, it becomes increasingly difficult emotionally to separate the child from the fosterers.

Nani was becoming this to me. We had spent most of our waking hours of the last five weeks together and I had become a family member to her. At twenty-three, I saw myself as somewhere between a foster parent and a sibling to her, and now I was taking her to a new permanent adopted family of gorillas. Instead of allowing myself to think too much about her being in any danger, I focused on the idea that I would still get to see her regularly, and looked forward to monitoring her progress as she grew up—a normal nonhuman in her new ape family.

Dian was standing alone by the first little stream that crossed the Porter Trail when I arrived with Nani on my back. I expected annoyance from Dian in some form, about my being either late or early, or thought she would otherwise just be in a foul mood about having to do this all over again, but she was even tempered and focused on our task at hand. I appreciated her calm demeanor and again felt honored to play such a key role in our orphaned gorilla's rehabilitation and release.

"The rest have gone on ahead to find Group 5," she said. "They'll be waiting for us up the Tourist Trail."

Nani clung tightly to my shoulders as I followed Dian down the Porter Trail. Downhill was easier, but I again marveled at Dian's ability to hike after her failed attempt at walking a short distance from her cabin just weeks earlier. We continued at a steady pace, and I realized how my physical stamina had changed since the day Peter and I carried Judy's and Liza's luggage down the mountain soon after I arrived in camp. Like the day before, I was now carrying a forty-pound gorilla. It was hard, but the strain of the effort became a sort of monotonous mantra for me as I placed one heavy boot–clad foot before the other.

In ten minutes, Dian, Nani, and I met Nameye and Baraqueza waiting for us at the grassy clearing called the Tourist Spot. Nameye spoke in Swahili to Dian and pointed to the Tourist Trail, which led from this meadow at a 45° angle up Mount Visoke. After a brief rest, I hoisted Nani onto my back again and followed Nameye and Baraqueza up the Tourist Trail. Dian followed at her own pace.

Up until then, this hike, like the one the day before, had been on gently sloping or level ground. On the steep angle of this trail, Nani now felt like herself, plus all the gorillas she had been: Charlie, Sophie, Josephine, and N'gee. With every step, I found myself hoping Group 5 was low on the mountain and just a few steps off the Tourist Trail.

I rested and caught my breath while Dian and Baraqueza caught up. With my heart pounding from the climb and my live cargo, I let the two move ahead of me to follow our tracker's lead. Nameye guided us through the thick nettles and thistles of Visoke's northeast slopes for another fifteen minutes, and I struggled to balance myself with Nani over the dense tangle of thick and slippery weed stems, wet from cloud mist. Finally, Nameye stopped and pointed downslope. About thirty-five meters below, Dian and I could see Peter pointing across to our lower left, indicating the location of Group 5. The dark tops of Taka's and Kaji's heads were visible above the thistles across from where Peter stood. For Dian and me, the gorillas were still out of view, but we could see the vegetation moving where they fed. Dian scanned the scene below us, her eyes twitching and squinting in silent concentration. She was well winded, but had an energized vitality I had never seen before.

"There's a tree we could get up into." Dian whispered, pointing to a large hagenia, downhill on our lower right about twenty meters from Group 5. This tree, leaning downslope at a 45° angle, looked easy to climb and would provide a good vantage point from which Nani could be seen by the gorillas below.

Nani clung tightly to my shoulders while I followed Dian downhill, and Nameye and Baraqueza promptly vanished into nearby thickets. With Nani still clinging securely, I climbed up the sloping tree, three meters up until I had a foothold onto a side branch. At that point I could turn around, and half-sit, leaning against the hypericum's main trunk with Nani holding onto my torso under my left arm. Dian climbed up and positioned herself two meters below me. From our vantage point we could see the heads and shoulders of a few of the gorillas of Group 5, but they did not yet notice us.

Peter, now in plain view, scrawled notes on his waterproof pad of paper, as cold air drifted down from the mountaintop, ushering in a light drizzle. While I held the baby tightly under my left arm, I used my free hand to pull on the hood of my raincoat in a careful balancing act.

Below us to the right, Kaji and Taka had settled into place in the thick wet undergrowth, readying their bulky film equipment. They looked weary and disheveled from the haul, but energized nonetheless by responsibility and anticipation, their vivid blue raingear glowing absurdly in the descending gloom of mist. As Dian clung to the base of our tree, halfway between me and the ground, Kaji focused the giant lens of his camera like the eyeball of a cyclops on her. She too was poised, her eyes trained on the unwitting gorillas, just visible off to our right, from where we faced uphill. We could just see the tops of their heads and shoulders, as they quietly foraged just forty feet away, snapping crisp wild celery and emitting their tranquil rumbling vocalizations.

With the camera rolling, Dian adopted the same dramatic expression I had seen days earlier. She slowly turned to look up at the baby in my arms. Her baby. Dian's brow furrowed above her puffy eyes, her lips pursed in a dramatic look of worried concern. She knew the camera was trained on her, and she was poised and energized in the moment. She knew important film footage was being made—ten thousand dollars' worth—and that every motion, every nuance, was being recorded for the world beyond the forest, those she reached only through her deeds on film and in print. As withdrawn as she had become in these mountains, the camera connected her to the world and gave meaning to her life.

Within five minutes, Nani, having not yet noticed the family of wild gorillas nearby, crawled free of me and climbed slowly, purposefully down the tree trunk, arm over leg, over foot, over hand. Dian let her pass. Remembering that my boss wanted notes, I fumbled to get my pencil and begin writing on my now damp paper. Just past Dian's feet, Nani reached for a handful of gallium near the ground. As she chewed and grabbed for more, Dian leaned over and stripped several handfuls of the stringy gorilla food from the base of our tree and passed them up to me. Understanding Dian's intent to keep Nani visible to Group 5 from the tree, I draped the sticky vines on the trunk and branches around me. We didn't want Group 5 to move on without having noticed our orphan.

Nani fed for ten minutes before deciding to climb back up to Dian. We all watched and waited in silence. Then seeing the gallium Dian had given me, our little gorilla crawled back up onto me and resumed feeding from the comfort of my arms.

Sensing movement from the corner of my right eye, I glanced over toward Group 5. Still forty feet away, one gorilla's upper torso moved into plain view. It was Beethoven, the family's four-hundred pound patriarch, leader of the group. The giant was seated, facing downhill. A broad silver back and shoulders supported an equally impressive head mounted on a thick neck. His cranium soared to a high sagittal crest:

his crown—along with the silver back, these are the adult male gorilla's emblems of maturity, stature, and might. Beethoven's powerful jaws idly crushed the last morsel of nettle in his mouth; unfazed by the stinging spines, the muscles in his head flexed underneath the gray hair at his temples. Alpha male, defender of his group, at the moment in repose, he sized up where to lead his family next.

Watching Beethoven, I was struck with the thought of how out of place I was. In a moment, Beethoven would see me, and *then* what? I found myself thinking, for the first time, that I didn't belong there.

Sure enough, the massive old gorilla shifted his head toward me, suddenly taking in something that shouldn't be. He knew me, of course, by now, but not this peculiar scene—a baby gorilla in my arms! *Whose baby gorilla?* Instantly, his repose turned to alarm. I saw it flicker across this massive hominid's eyes as he fixed his glassy dark gaze on me. Baring his black-stained teeth in a shining flash, Beethoven released a scream to end all screams, *AAARRRGH* . . . a primal sound, at once human and animal, screeching and voluminous—the horrific noise that only a silverback gorilla can make. It pealed through my body, rattling my inner core with a terror I had never known.

Now I really don't belong here. There was no reasoning my way out of this fear, which burned into me the most vivid memory of my time at Karisoke. And so we began what my boss, Dian Fossey, would one day describe as the first time she had "ever been afraid of gorillas."

I whispered loudly down to Dian, "Beethoven just saw us," my throat constricting on the words.

During the next two minutes in which Beethoven and Nani stared at each other, I saw myself as having made a terrible irreversible mistake. *What am I doing here? Up a tree on a mountain in Africa with a baby gorilla in my arms? Thousands of miles and days away from home?* The feeling of being completely out of place, and way out of line, overrode any romantic, adventurous spirit I might have had up until that point. I wanted to be gone. Dian remained installed on the sloping tree trunk beneath me, blocking my descent to the ground. Besides, the gorillas were on the ground. I had visions of silverbacks climbing up the tree after the baby . . . and me! Selfishly, I surmised that they would get to Dian first.

Nani, having not seen other gorillas for over two months, surprised me by breaking free of Beethoven's stare and, still in my arms, nonchalantly resumed her feeding as if it was going to be just another day. Beethoven stared for a minute longer before Tuck, a young adult female, came strutting out of the brush uphill from him to have look at what caused the commotion. At the sight of Nani, she held her lips tightly pursed, and boldly slapped down a palm-like lobelia before beating her chest in the typical two-hand whack of a cocky gorilla—she was piqued.

Nani watched intently as Tuck approached the base of our tree and knocked down another lobelia before assuming the stiff four-legged stance of an agitated and indignant gorilla wanting to be noticed. In this posture with her neck held out stiffly, Tuck kept her lips tightly pursed while twitching her head sideways, stealing furtive glances up at Nani in my arms. Her face asked, *what is this outrage?*

I thought Nani didn't read the tension at all. Instead, she loosened her little arms from my torso and began climbing downward. The adult female, Effie, mother of four-year-old Poppy, joined her grown daughter, Tuck, at the base of the tree while our baby climbed down past Dian. In the middle of the action, Kaji kept the camera pointed at our baby when she reached the ground to meet her new acquaintances. Immediately Tuck and Nani touched noses and mouths. As they did this, I could see soft dung come out of Nani, typical of what wild gorillas excrete when they are afraid. Her calm demeanor belied some inner tension in the moment. Effie instantly took an interest in this and began sniffing the little one's anus and rump area. I was encouraged by the gentle approach these two grown females were showing our little gorilla, and thought Dian must have felt the same optimism then. For a few more minutes, Tuck and Effie inspected the new small stranger among them, sniffing and delicately touching her with their noses and puckered lips. I was struck by how small Nani really was, towered-over by these full-grown gorillas. She was a mere fraction of their bulk, but a sense of relief washed over me with the gentle delicacy of the scene. The fear that Beethoven's scream had raised in me was fading while I watched what I thought was the first successful reintroduction of a baby gorilla back into a wild group, feeling so proud to be a part of it.

I was jarred from my optimism when, without warning, as if jealous of her mother's interest in this newcomer baby, Tuck grabbed Nani by a handful of hair. Clutching the baby, Tuck galloped downhill, deliberately dragging the little one away from Effie in a rough tumble. Nani pig-grunted in helpless protest of the upset and pain this inflicted. My boss crouched in a tense posture, leaning over to observe the scene below, and now behind, us.

Not to be outdone, Effie pursued the tumbling baby, grabbing her by the hair on her tiny back. Tuck grabbed another hank of Nani's hair from the opposite side and mother/daughter began a vicious tug-of-war with the baby as rope. Nani screamed and grunted in desperation, but the larger females pulled at her like a mere object, dragging our orphan farther downslope. I feared they would drag her into the thickets beyond our view, leaving only the horrific sounds of this cruel game. *What would we do then?* While Nani excreted more fear dung, Tuck sniffed at it as before. But the larger gorilla's investigation returned to overt aggression and she brutally bit into Nani's backside. By a mouthful of Nani's rump hair, Tuck viciously dragged her backward, farther across the slope in the direction of the other members of Group 5, who still remained mostly out of view.

Despite Nani's plaintive screams, Effie grabbed the helpless infant by her hair again, pulling against the grip of Tuck's teeth. For us humans, the scene had become a vivid nightmare. It looked like Tuck and Effie were fighting to be the one who dragged Nani, by any means, toward the other members of Group 5—to show them this intruder. The other gorillas were still dispersed widely through the undergrowth, and mostly unaware of what was taking place.

Kaji kept one eye pressed against his camera's viewfinder and moved downhill into the very middle of the scene. Taka followed dutifully, hauling the bulky sound equipment. Kaji didn't flinch, even with these angry gorillas just inches away from the camera's lens. At one point, Tuck *was nearly in his lap.* Peter, shifting for a better view, remained calm in the fray, dutifully observing and making notes for Dian on his clipboard. Finally, in a break in the melee, Nani tried to crawl away from her assailants. As the little gorilla neared the base of our tree, Dian eased down its trunk and grabbed her furry arms. But Tuck would not be outdone, and just as Dian tried to hoist our orphan back, the grown female grabbed Nani's leg. A new tug-of-war ensued, this one between human and ape. *My God, Dian's having a tug-of-war with a gorilla!* Both primatologist and primate pulled aggressively at our foster baby who grunted and screamed helplessly. In one direction, lay rescue, in the other, who knew what.

I feared the worst for Dian, now in a brawl with these gorillas. *Would Tuck and Effie pounce on Dian? What if one of the silverbacks comes charging in?* I looked around for Beethoven, but could no longer see him. *And where was mighty Icarus?* In the moment, I had nothing but respect for Dian. Up until this day, I had not seen my boss interact with the very gorillas that had brought her international recognition. Now she was in their midst, in what seemed a battle of life and death. In my turmoil of fear and confusion, I then saw what must have been the original courage and tenacity of this woman, and was grateful for it.

Dian maneuvered baby—*with Tuck still attached*—closer to the base of our tree, and . . . in a final *yank*, little Nani broke free from the bigger gorilla's clutches. I slid myself lower as Dian stumbled and slipped in the wet undergrowth to hoist Nani up to me. Her strength nearly spent, my boss struggled to hand the baby up to me as I reached downward to grasp Nani's outstretched arms, and draw her up to my chest. Nani clung tightly to me as I repositioned myself, while an exhausted Dian maneuvered herself back to her position on the tree trunk below me.

I hoped that was the end, but we were still up a tree. Tuck planted herself with vigilance at the base looking up at the baby in my arms. I envisioned Tuck clambering up the tree to snatch Nani from me, and again was relieved that Dian was between me and the ground. I wondered what Dian wanted to do next, but she didn't speak. In the cold, soaking rain, she stared at Tuck who remained fixated on the baby in my arms. I suppose Dian was wondering, just like me, what we would do next.

Within minutes of this standoff, Nani surprised us by releasing her grip on me, fixated again on the gorillas below. I allowed her to climb down to Dian, but was baffled when Dian didn't stop the baby from climbing past her. Onward, the little one ambled, hand over foot to the ground.

"She wants to be a gorilla . . ." Dian whispered.

We all watched in renewed anxiety as our brave and determined little baby rejoined her fellow species on the ground. To welcome her back, Tuck grabbed Nani by the hair and once again dragged her brutally downhill as if she were nothing more than a sack of stones. And as before, Effie joined in another cruel tug-of-war with her daughter, while our baby screamed helplessly in the middle. Hope for the little one only came in the form of Beethoven who burst from the foliage with another horrific scream, *AAARGH* . . . At that, Effie and Tuck released Nani in startled retreat, lurching backward and averting their eyes from their alpha male's steely glare. I looked at Kaji seated in the middle of the ensuing standoff, baffled by his courage and worried for his safety as he sat glued to his camera's viewfinder. Nani squatted, dazed and forlorn in the middle of the trio of towering adult apes, her dark eyes wide and glassy in a blank catatonic stare. The cold drizzle turned to a hard pelting rain that rattled on our rain gear and the leaves around us, drowning out all other sound, numbing the aftermath of our trauma. Beethoven, riled and disgruntled, turned his back on Effie, Tuck, and the baby to assume the Buddha-like huddle of a gorilla in the rain. Nani, as if insisting on acceptance in the group, roused herself and shifted close to the alpha male's broad backside, adopting his same position as if to say *I'm yours now, just another gorilla in the group.*

When the downpour let up, Effie's four-year-old daughter Poppy ambled into the clearing that had been beaten down during the struggle. The adult female Pantsy soon followed with her three-year-old daughter, Muraha. I then noticed that the young male Pablo had arrived directly beneath me, and was swinging on a vine hanging from where I sat. He directed his attention at Nani and beat his chest repeatedly as if trying to elicit a reaction. The young females, Poppy and Muraha, approached to within one meter of Nani, staring down at her with curiosity, while Pablo continued taunting with alternate chest-beating and strutting on all fours. Even these youngsters of Group 5 were two and three times the size of Nani.

Five minutes later, as the rain slackened, Beethoven rose and moved downhill. Nani started to follow him, but stopped as he disappeared ahead of her into a thicket of undergrowth. Nani looked small and lonely in the center of the four-meter clearing. Pablo, Poppy, and Muraha immediately closed in on Nani, sniffing and peering at her impishly. As the three larger youngsters crowded around her, Nani picked a spindly nettle stalk and began to nibble at its crumpled leaves that had been trampled and bruised under the feet of the other gorillas.

"She's eating!" I whispered to Dian, leaning over so she could hear me.

"That's displacement behavior," Dian whispered back, without taking her eyes off the scene below. "They do that when they want to avert attention away from themselves."

Nani was trying to fit in, acting like she was intent on feeding while the three gorilla juveniles beat their leathery chests with small fists and strutted around the newcomer among them. This sight was the saddest moment for me. Nani had been brutally traumatized by Tuck and Effie before Dian rescued her from Tuck's clutches, and yet she climbed back down the tree to join this family of her own kind. Then, being taunted by the *kids* of the group in the cold rain, Nani sat chewing on a nettle as if she was home at last—as if to say: *See? I'm one of you.*

With their smaller size and childlike antics, the juveniles looked much less menacing than the adult females had become. Pablo, Poppy, and Muraha were trying to get a play response from Nani, and I thought that if she had it in her to reciprocate, this might help integrate her into the group and make her acceptable to the adults.

Tuck and Effie had moved away several meters to the periphery of the clearing that they had beaten down in their skirmish. They were no longer focusing on Nani as the three youngsters now vied for her attention. The minutes passed as Dian and I watched expectantly from our perches, trying to be optimistic about Nani's desire to integrate herself with her fellow apes despite what had just transpired.

"She wants to be a gorilla," Dian repeated under her breath.

After five minutes, the younger silverback Icarus bolted through the undergrowth into the clearing. Equally the size of his father, Beethoven, the giant moved his legs in the characteristically stiff, mechanical strut of a piqued silverback, chin held high and hairs erect, flashing the bright gleam of his white mantle with every jarring step. The posture made the ape appear even larger than his four-hundred-pound frame. In a showy gallop, Icarus bolted without warning past Nani, snatching her up like a football with a sideways sweep of his massive arm. He dragged the tiny newcomer downhill by a hank of her hair, and flung her with another violent swing of his arm, as if tossing out a tub of dishwater. In a rough tumble over trampled weeds, the baby landed in a heap near Effie, who immediately approached the little one. Nani righted herself and moved forward to meet Effie halfway. But the adult female greeted the baby with a hard swing of her arm, knocking the little one onto her back again.

I wanted to ask Dian what we should do, but knew she must have felt as baffled and helpless as me. We were stymied by Nani's apparent will to integrate herself into this group after her first encounter, and paralyzed by these group members' resultant aggression. Our orphan, bedraggled and wan of energy, pulled herself up to a seated position, and I wanted her back with me. She sat quietly as Puck entered the clearing with her two-year-old, Cantsbee, riding on her back. Cantsbee was the only one smaller than Nani. Both mother and son peered down quizzically at the newcomer while circling in a loop around her. Nani just hung her head pathetically and huddled in the drizzle, staring blankly at the wet ground.

Taka and Kaji dutifully loaded another roll of film into their camera. Each reel was the size of a pizza and had to be pried out of a wide silver canister while dodging the rain. Taka carefully held a plastic tarp over the opened film to keep it dry while Kaji deftly maneuvered it into the camera. Once the new roll was installed, Kaji quickly resumed filming. An hour had elapsed since Dian and I, with Nani, had taken our positions in our tree.

A loud shrill scream pealed from below us, and I jolted around to see Icarus running downhill in a bold dash. Nani was gone from her spot. The scream was hers. She was in the silverback's mouth! Like a dog with a rabbit, Icarus carried the baby as if he was going to eat her alive! Beethoven protested the disruption with pig grunts from down-hill, *eh . . . eh . . . EH . . .* his massive shoulders bouncing in disdain with each grunt. Poppy, Muraha, and Pablo grunted too, and chased after Icarus. As if Nani were a trophy of conquest in his mouth, Icarus rushed back uphill with her before dropping the baby just downhill from the base of our tree.

"We've got to get her back," Dian said, craning her neck to see the baby beneath us. My heart pounded thinking about what this meant now that a silverback was involved. *Could we even save her now?*

We watched in torment as Nani used her remaining energy to crawl toward our tree. Pablo resumed his display of chest beats at Nani as Poppy and Muraha followed suit, strutting behind him. Nani struggled uphill, and I could see her eyes were wide and glassy, her hair wet and matted from the rain . . . *and was there blood?*

When she reached the base of our tree, our tiny orphan sat huddled and unmoving. With her arms folded in close to her body, so tiny compared to the others looming around her. Pablo, Poppy, and Muraha continued their jeering displays, but retreated and paused when Icarus began a series of foreboding hoot vocalizations. These hoots, typical of an agitated silverback, are usually followed by a rapid-fire chest-beat, but Icarus rose to his feet and swept past Nani, knocking her over while he tried to grab her. This time Nani just remained on her side, huddled and spent in a catatonic ball of matted fur.

Then Tuck showed renewed interest and moved in on Nani. As she did, Dian slid down the tree and grabbed a woody stem of senecio. When Tuck grabbed for Nani, Dian swung the leafy stalk with a loud *swish*, causing Tuck to flinch and miss. Tuck tried again, and Dian followed suit with another swipe of her switch. While Dian continued to thwart Tuck's ongoing attempts to grab the baby, Icarus rose up repeatedly just one meter away, hooting and beating his chest in a manner more tense and strained than I had seen before. I worried for Dian now, as much as for our baby. Then Icarus paused his brash displays. And, in a move that defies easy explanation, Nani roused herself, and instead of crawling to human safety in our tree, she hobbled over to Icarus and huddled against his back.

Pablo and Poppy pursued with antics of chest beats and strutting, still trying to initiate a response from this gorilla they had never seen before. As if Nani's bizarre strategy worked, Icarus surprised us all by moving away downhill. Pablo and Poppy closed in where she sat alone, but never reached out to touch the little stranger, despite their obvious curiosity. Two minutes later, Icarus hooted and beat his chest, rushing back uphill to grab Nani again. Nani grunted and screamed while the silverback dragged her brutally back downhill and away from Dian and me.

From where I clung, I could no longer see her. Instead, I tried to read Dian's face as she craned her neck to view below and behind us. Dian's gaze was transfixed and tense. The film crew shifted position and aimed their equipment somewhere beyond my view. I watched the movement of Kaji's camera as it panned in a slow arc back uphill. Finally, Nani reappeared at the base of our tree, and Dian, still near the ground, bent over and grabbed her. I slid down the tree trunk to take Nani back in my arms. Hoisting her to one side, I climbed back up to my original spot.

Nani's hair was soaked in dense mats. While she clung to me more feebly than before, I needed to support more of her weight. She looked miserable against my cold wet rubber raincoat. Remembering how she liked to put her hands inside my rain gear against the warm cotton of my clothing, I unsnapped my buttons and drew her to my chest. She pig-grunted in discomfort when I moved her, and I saw the injury—a quarter-inch deep laceration stretching from the outer edge of her left hand to the center of her palm. She cradled this hand feebly against her chest, and I adjusted her to accommodate her weakened ability to cling to me. Icarus and Tuck approached the base of our tree and stared upward, as if sizing up their next assault. Dian remained midway down the tree between me and them. The faces of the two gorillas below were ominous.

My coat was large enough to draw around Nani's back, and I closed her in against the cold and drizzle. One by one I snapped each button, being careful not to jar her hand. Inside my rain gear, Nani was completely concealed from anyone's view, especially that of Icarus and Tuck. The two assailants still flanked the base of our tree, and peered upward, only now they wore looks of perplexity. *Where had the little gorilla gone?*

"We've got to talk about what we're going to do," Dian said, summoning Peter to approach closer. Supporting Nani, I climbed down to Dian's level on the tree.

"They don't know where she is now," I said, feeling the first sense of hope since the onslaught began. "If we can keep her hidden, maybe the others will go away." Dian, Peter, and I discussed a plan, speculating that if Nani remained quiet and out of sight, perhaps I could eventually just walk out of the area to safe haven. With all in agreement to give this a try, I maneuvered back up to my previous spot in the tree. Tuck and Icarus kept ominous vigil below. I was ready to get Nani and myself out of there, but with the baby now hidden from view, had a renewed sense of composure in my secure position up the tree.

For twenty minutes, Icarus and Tuck peered suspiciously up at me. Although their presence remained ominous in light of what had taken place, their baffled expressions almost gave them a comical air, shifting positions and craning their necks to look for the little gorilla that had disappeared as mysteriously as it had first materialized. To my relief, Nani remained motionless inside my rain gear. Utterly exhausted, she occasionally raised her small leathery face to breathe fresh air through the opening of my collar.

With time, Icarus's interest began to wane. He began to look up at us less and less, and even ambled away from the base of the tree. Tuck kept her vigil, but I held my breath as the silverback disappeared into the undergrowth in the same direction the other members of Group 5 had moved on to.

"Oh good," Dian said, in a hushed tone, looking down at Tuck. "We can get rid of *her* easy." I laughed for the first time that day, thinking how Dian sounded like a kid up a tree who had just ended a battle with neighborhood bullies.

While I pondered what Dian might be thinking of doing to "get rid" of Tuck, this gorilla finally followed Icarus down the mountainside. This was the break we needed. When Dian climbed down the tree, I followed, supporting Nani, still tucked securely under my raincoat. I didn't look back as Dian and Peter formed a human screen to block the view of any gorillas that remained within sight of us.

Methodically, I walked past Kaji and Taka . . . and kept going. Up Mount Visoke's steep embankment, step by step I plodded, not knowing who or what was behind me. As I trudged along the path we had made coming downhill two hours earlier, I envisioned Icarus grabbing my ankles and dragging me backward in search of the phantom gorilla baby that he had last seen climbing back into *my* arms.

At last, forty meters uphill, I was overjoyed to find Nameye and Baraqueza in the thick weeds where they had waited out the bedlam. Having been well within earshot of all the turmoil and gorilla screams, they looked unsettled and perplexed by the bulge at my belly under my raincoat. The two gorilla trackers relaxed and chuckled when I unsnapped a couple buttons to reveal Nani's wide-eyed face. Dian and Peter soon joined us, followed by Kaji and Taka, and all their film equipment.

Group 5 had been moving toward the Tourist Trail that we would need to traverse to get off Visoke. Dian sent Nameye ahead of us to make sure that our group did not stumble into the middle of the gorillas again.

By three o'clock, we were back at Dian's Cabin. Dian, Peter, and I examined the gash on Nani's left palm. It was obvious to us that Icarus must have done it with one of his massive canines when he grabbed the baby in his mouth. Dian was worried that bones might be broken and articulated Nani's hand. To this, the baby grunted in pained protest. Satisfied that Nani's hand was intact, Dian rubbed the little gorilla's wet fur with a dry towel. To our relief, Nani used her left hand as well as her right as she climbed with renewed vigor back into her old nest box in our boss's bedroom. Dian had placed extra pieces of pineapple and banana, sprinkled with a few hard candies, on top of the soft bed of leaves that Toni had made for the baby. Nani made soft contented belch vocalizations, *hmm waaah, hmm waaah* . . . as she snacked blissfully in her cozy bed.

That evening, after Stuart had returned from Group 4, Dian called Stuart, Peter, and me to a meeting about the day's events. At her cabin, Dian asked Peter and me to reiterate from our notes the sequence of events that had transpired in our attempted release of the baby. Stuart listened, incredulous, hearing horrific details for the first time. After recounting our observations, we discussed the possible reasons that this attempted introduction failed. Dian surmised that unlike Group 4, which was made up of males in the process of rebuilding after the decimation of their group by poachers, Group 5 was stable, content in their makeup, and not seeking new members. As such, Group 5 saw even our benign orphan as an intruder, not needed in their composition. At only three years old, she was far from reproductively viable for the group's adult males, and to the adult females, she was an unrelated interloping female.

Dian ended the day by retelling the story of the only other known attempt at releasing a baby gorilla back into the wild. This event had taken place in a nearby part of Zaire called Kahuzi-Biéga, where the eastern lowland mountain gorillas live. Like Nani, a baby had been confiscated from poachers, but was a much smaller and younger infant, only a year old, Dian surmised. Dian had seen the film footage of this attempt and described it to us.

"They just flung the baby at the charging silverback and ran," she said, disdainfully. "They never saw that baby again."

EIGHTEEN

Siku ya Uhuru!

The filming of the baby's release attempt behind her, Dian finally focused on her pending departure, which she knew she needed to make soon lest she lose her opportunity to teach at Cornell University. This didn't stop her from agonizing about leaving. With the fate of the baby still unresolved, Taka and Kaji remained camped at Karisoke, if only in hopes that the story of the little orphan would continue. Dian had gotten their promise of ten thousand dollars, and a trip to Japan in the works, so she couldn't just run them off.

As Dian moved forward with departure preparations, the floor of her living and dining areas became strewn with the items she wanted to take home. With so many boxes being filled, it really looked like she was moving permanently. Among the books, notebooks, and suitcases partially filled with clothing, there was an odd assortment of old stuffed animals scattered about. I hadn't realized she had so many.

"Dian asked me to try to find her gun in the things she's taking home," Stuart told me back at our cabin. "She's leaving two of her guns in camp for the poacher patrol, but smuggling one back to the States with her."

"Did you find it?" I asked.

"No, but I think she's taken it apart and sewn the pieces into her collection of stuffed animals."

As Dian's departure date drew closer, Stuart bore the brunt of Dian's vacillating insecurities about leaving. One day she accepted it, the next she wailed in resistance.

"How can I leave here, the way things are?" Dian shouted as Stuart reassured her. "Nobody's going to run the poacher patrols when I'm gone!"

Stuart tended to her constantly, hearing her out, reassuring her, and assuaging her fears—and there were many. In addition to the plight of the baby, and Nunkie's group either missing or far into Zaire where poaching was rampant, Dian fretted about leaving her dog Cindy and monkey, Kima. She was embarking on a new career path, and without any real teaching experience would soon be facing so many expectant young students—a daunting task for anyone who hadn't taught formally before. I wondered too, how much the fear of entering society again played into her worries. The Dian I had met in Kigali, and had come to know on the mountain, would not be an easy fit for a return to civilization. There was also a new worry brewing, a big one for Dian. Her former student, Sandy Harcourt, was successfully jockeying for permission—via the Rwandan park officials, outside of Dian's authority—to return to Karisoke. This time, to take charge of the place with Dian gone. Originally Dian had, albeit grudgingly, sanctioned this change of command as the only option, but as Sandy's influence grew and the time drew nearer, she back-pedaled and resisted.

"He is NOT to be believed," she protested ambiguously, with a phrase she used to complain about those she didn't like, such as Bill and Amy, or Benda Lema. "Really and truly, they are ALL not to be believed!"

We were caught up in this dramatic turmoil. Throwing us new-comers into the mix while grooming Stuart as her Acting Director only confounded the plans she had been instrumental in creating. Dian latched onto this turn of events as well as all her other fears. In this case, her lack of cooperation put her at a loss of control of the fate of Karisoke, and lack of control and sharing the stage were among her worst fears.

Stuart's careful doting gave Dian just enough reassurance to stay on track, comforted in the knowledge that he will remain as her hand-picked agent in camp, carrying out her directives and enforcing her mandates from stateside, diluting Sandy Harcourt's position of power. Stuart and Dian had long heart-to-heart conversations, during which Dian increasingly opened up and confided in Stuart.

"Dian's father committed suicide," Stuart explained to me back at our cabin. "Dian says she's even had suicidal thoughts of her own." Stuart showed a genuine sympathy for Dian at this hectic crossroads in her life, but this knowledge only unsettled me more, with wild imaginings of what drastic measures Dian might consider under duress.

As a condition of her departure and extended absence, Dian stipu-lated that Stuart take occupancy of her cabin. She did not want it left vacant at any time. In his new role Stuart would also be in charge of camp finances, meager as they were, and the camp's guns, which she feared would be a target for theft. In addition to overseeing Karisoke's Rwandan staff and their pay, our director instructed Stuart on the care and feeding of her pets, Cindy, Kima, and the chickens.

Although we were well aware of her plans, Dian took me and Peter aside at the fire pit, just before she left, to officially inform us she had appointed Stuart "acting director," in her absence.

"He's a really, *reeaally* good guy," she said, beaming and holding her thumb up with a self-assured smile.

A few days before Dian's departure, I mustered the courage to carry my camera and take some photos of little Nani in the meadow just before rain forced us into the Empty Cabin. When the sky cleared, Dian paid a rare visit to our end of camp. Recalling what Peter told me about Dian being annoyed when students would take pictures in camp or of the gorillas, I was certainly self-conscious about having my camera with me, but then I notice Dian had her camera too.

"The sky is clear again," Dian said, eyeing my camera. "Why don't you bring the baby out and we can get some pictures of her?" Outside, I soon realized Dian was posing for photos as she cuddled the baby and swung her around playfully *Is she mugging for me to take photos?* Despite my confusion, or because of it, I snapped the only photo I would take of Dian.

"I can take your film back for you and have it developed," Dian offered afterward.

"Oh . . . okay, thanks," I said, thinking fast. "I still have a few more to use up on this roll." That evening in my cabin, recalling Peter's warnings and woes of stolen photographs, I buried my canister of undeveloped film deep inside a sock-stuffed shoe shoved to the far corner under my bed.

Dian left Karisoke early on the morning of March 3, among a throng of porters bearing her belongings in their hands and atop their heads. I watched quietly from my window as the noisy band passed, with Dian near the rear. When their voices had finally faded, I emerged from my door and approached the camp staff at their fire pit, trying to feign a solemn look to suppress my shameless grin. Once among them, I threw my arms up, panga raised in my right hand, shouting *"Siku ya Uhuru!"*— Independence Day! The men burst into laughter, and I broke into my own imitation of their Rwandan dance.

Not only did Stuart, Peter, and I soon enjoy another dinner with the Japanese, we did so that very night, and unabashedly at Dian's cabin. *Siku Ya Uhuru*, indeed!

In the wake of Dian's departure, Peter soon realized that yet more of his photographic slides were missing from his cabin. This time he'd had it, and not only dashed off a letter to *National Geographic*, warning them that Dian would be presenting these photos to them as her own, but he threatened legal action as a consequence.

As soon as Stuart moved into Dian's cabin, I moved into what had been his side of our duplex. It had more windows, shelving, and a better stove. With Dian conveniently out of the way, the V-W couple boldly wasted no time trying to get a foothold back at Karisoke. Amy sent a note to Stuart requesting permission to spend more time with Group 5, so that she could follow up on some research for her doctoral thesis.

Stuart didn't want to create ill will with our well-intended collegiate neighbors; still, he felt the pinch of his obligation to Dian, and well knew how much she would disapprove. Via worried letters and telegrams, Dian confirmed what Stuart already knew: Under no circumstances should Amy or Bill be allowed access to Karisoke research gorillas. Attempting to alleviate the tension and extend an olive branch, Stuart diplomatically made plans to invite the couple up to camp for dinner.

While our nearest American neighbors made no effort to reach out socially, nor communicate outside of Amy's request for access to Group 5, Jean-Pierre von der Beck, who had been working in the region for many years, certainly did. Dian had helped to secure this elder Belgian's job as the local project manager for the Mountain Gorilla Project, only to regret it as that project took on a life of its own without and despite her. He had become part of the larger collaborative team effort that included Amy, Bill, and Sandy Harcourt.

Despite Dian's determination to keep Karisoke separate from the rival gorilla project, Stuart found himself unable to resist Jean-Pierre's quirky brand of charisma and charm, so informal and friendly. He was the charming uncle to Karisoke. The two became fast friends.

"He used to walk in from Zaire to spend the night with Dian," Stuart told me, laughing. "Now she hates him!"

With Dian gone, this eccentric elder Belgian hippie gentleman began making regular visits to camp. With the void left by Dian, Stuart welcomed the input of this fatherly, French-speaking expat, whose lanky frame and gray beard lent him an almost wizardly appearance. With this new mentor's encouragement, Stuart soon collaborated on a new plan for the baby gorilla's release into Group 4. Stuart was obviously appreciative of the benevolent guidance and input.

"After what you went through with the first attempt," Stuart told me, "We're not expecting you to come to this release." Despite the importance of the project, I was relieved. Not seeking recognition, and wanting to keep this task as calm as possible, he and Jean-Pierre also barred the Nippon AV duo from filming the event, much to the film crew's disappointment; and they were already out ten thousand dollars.

Stuart and Jean-Pierre simply hung a burlap bag of sliced fruits in a tree near Peanuts's Group, and left the baby there to feed. Her having to work at getting the fruit out of the bag gave them enough time to make a getaway before she could realize it. Less than an hour later, by the time the two returned to see what had happened, she had already begun playing with the other youngsters in her new family. Mission accomplished! To commemorate the success, Jean-Pierre gave the baby a new and permanent name.

"I always zought she should be called *Bonne Année* . . . French for 'New Year,'" he said with grand purpose, "because we confiscated her on zat day."

The Nippon AV pair left camp soon after Bonne Année's release, graciously donating their tents, raingear, and camping equipment to Karisoke. Jinzaburo and I had become good friends, and he offered to take my rain-damaged camera back to Japan for repairs. He would return it to me via a traveling reporter, Yuki Sato, who came to Rwanda several weeks later. The repaired camera also came with a surprise gift, I would see to my utter delight when the bubbly young woman handed her cargo to me outside the American Embassy.

"Jinzaburo said you die for this," she said cheerfully, pulling a big jar of peanut butter out of her knapsack.

The success of Bonne Année's release further cemented Stuart's and Jean-Pierre's relationship, and soon Stuart was even visiting with his new father-figure at the elder Belgian's home, a rented stone castle on a eucalyptus farm called *Plantation de Gasiza*.

"You gotta see Jean-Pierre's place!" Stuart said enthusiastically to me after a visit there. His descriptions of the old gray stone building was so intriguing, I soon joined him on a short trip.

"Stuart?" Amy called out, appearing up the hill with a big grin, near their rondavel as we exited the trail at the base of Mount Visoke. "Did you get my note?"

Stuart was caught off guard by Amy as he and I headed toward the Volkswagen for our trip to Jean-Pierre's. Stuart let out a deep sigh, slumping his shoulders while bracing for what he knew would be an awkward encounter.

"I can't accommodate," Stuart said bluntly as Amy trotted up.

"What?" Amy stopped in her tracks in front of Stuart, her boots sliding to a stop in the dust and pebbles of the road.

"I can't accommodate." Stuart repeated, shaking his head with an apologetic tilt.

Amy's cheeks flushed red. I could see she was choking back an immediate upwelling of both anger and tears.

"I'm really sorry, but—" Before Stuart could finish his sentence, Amy spun her heels on the gravel beneath them, and with arms swinging, stomped back up the hill where Bill appeared. Bill, in turn, came storming down the hill in bold strides from their metal hut like an angry dad, with Amy trailing behind.

"I'm really sorry. I was going to invite you both up for dinner to talk about—"

"We don't want *dinner!*" Bill said, cutting him off with obvious disdain. "We want access to Group 5!"

This was a request, which, under the directives of Dian, Stuart could neither easily nor immediately honor. Just then, Stuart had to stand his ground, but with a little patience and open communication, perhaps things would have changed.

Although presented with a crack in Dian's defense, and a perfect opportunity to get a foot in the door, as Jean-Pierre certainly had, the duo preferred to eschew diplomacy and Stuart's opportunity for dialogue with their deliberate snub, making it clear that Stuart, Peter, and I were of little interest to them and hardly their peers. The very idea that any of us could stand in their way must have been a supreme insult. I would like to have gotten to know them, and learn more about the work they were doing, but fraternizing with us was well beneath them. And so with brusque disdain, they perpetuated the cold war between their camp and Karisoke, undermining even their own agenda.

Aside from the long road to Kigali, traveling up the rocky road to Jean-Pierre's castle with Stuart was my first foray off the mountain in a while. Stuart had invited me to join him overnight at the old Belgian's bachelor pad, at the base of Mount Muhavura, near the border of Uganda. On a whim, Stuart stopped the car for a hitchhiker, only to eject him a few kilometers up the road when he realized the young man was just taking a joy ride, standing the entire time, looking out the windshield, grinning at the view zipping by, and never revealing a destination. We could've driven him all the way into Kigali and I don't think he would've complained.

As we rounded the end of a grove of tall eucalyptus, Jean-Pierre's rented Belgian plantation house came suddenly into view—a gray stone castle, complete with crenellated turret. I enjoyed the respite from Karisoke at the beguiling, if Spartan, bachelor pad this turned out to be, and the hospitality of our eccentric gray-bearded host who slept in his round turret up a spiral staircase, like a genie in a bottle. The evening in front of the castle-worthy great fireplace and its roaring fire made for a relaxing interlude. I envied Stuart's camaraderie with Jean-Pierre, as the two chatted and joked with each other. I had become increasingly self-conscious, and felt mute by comparison. *Was it the isolation at Karisoke? Had holding my tongue with Dian cost me the ability to converse and socialize normally?* I was beginning to wonder . . .

In the morning, Bill Weber dropped by with a European colleague, snubbing Stuart and me with scarcely a glance our way. He pointedly excluded us by speaking only in French, for which our lack of comprehension forbade participation. Watching them, I could only surmise that Bill reveled in his acquired fluency of French, especially with the audience of Stuart and me, relegated to the sidelines of incomprehension. Upon his departure though, diplomatic Jean-Pierre gave Stuart and me a full rundown of the conversation of Bill's updates on his and Amy's progress with tourists visiting the newly habituated gorilla groups.

Days later, Stuart suggested I visit my former foster baby, warning me, however, about the silverback's reaction to her acquired fondness for humans.

"He got really upset that Bonne Année wanted to come near me," he advised, with a nervous laugh, "But it's great to see her. You need to pay her a visit."

I would soon learn that Stuart's account failed to prepare me for what was in store for me as we hiked to Peanuts's Group, down the trail across the boggy meadow into Zaire. We passed near the sites where Stuart and I had the bivouac camps in preparation for the baby's ill-fated release attempt. Things would have been so different if we had simply found Peanuts's Group as planned. The Nippon AV footage would have shown our baby gorilla integrating seamlessly into a wild group—the first reintroduction of a gorilla into the wild. I saw then that Dian should've waited, and stuck to her original plans instead of the attempt with Group 5. Plan B had seemed rushed, something to check off her list before departure under the pressures of deadlines passed. The blunder had nearly cost Bonne Année her life. Perhaps it had put us all in danger, in a situation that had never been tested.

After climbing into and out of several deep ravines, Stuart and I found Group 4 low on the slopes of Mount Visoke's northwestern side, well into Zaire.

"*Hmwah, Hmwaaah,*" Stuart and I vocalized in unison with our approach, a response that had become so automatic to us over our many days approaching gorillas. Excited to see Bonne Année for the first time as a wild gorilla, I moved ahead of Stuart, peering over the undergrowth. Spotting Peanuts's high sagittal crest, where he sat feeding next to our baby, I squatted down respectfully, as had become my custom. Stuart followed suite behind me.

Bonne Année's shining eyes stared into mine. I could see the recognition on her face. Immediately she stopped chewing, dropped her handful of gallium, and scrambled straight for me. Peanuts, by contrast, glared at the scene unfolding before him as she plopped herself half on my lap.

"*Eh, eh, eh . . .*" the old silverback grunted loudly in disapproval. But our little baby just settled right in on me. At that Peanuts rose up, and with a swipe of his powerful arm through stinging nettles beside, me he screamed his loudest roar.

"*Aaargh!*"

All four hundred pounds of him rushed me with his scream, and he landed nearly upon me, slamming his fists on the ground. It's moments like these, you feel the size of a silverback with a shake of the earth beneath them. I could feel the heat of his breath, smell the crushed nettles in his black teeth. I cowered as required, flopped over to one side, and whimpered. Bonne Année be damned. At that moment, I wanted her off me! And away from me! Instead, she stayed seated, oblivious to what Peanuts's problem was . . . what MY problem was, in fact—I should be as happy to see her as she was to see me. At his little female's lack of response, and my mere proximity to her, Peanuts rose up again, beating his chest directly over me with his high-pitched hoot.

"Hoo woo woowoowoowooWOOT!"

He slammed the ground again, sending a shudder through me. I made my required whimpering sound involuntarily. Bonne Année was settled in, half on my lap, pressed against me. I thought she must be confused as to why I must ignore her. Trembling now, in a crumpled heap, I peer under my arm toward Stuart, sitting nonchalantly just a meter and a half away. His stoic demeanor only annoyed me as he calmly took notes of my misfortune, with Peanuts's ire directed at me. *The bastard set me up!* He had roused a similar response from Peanuts just days earlier, and he had left out the key details of Peanuts's rage.

During our ill-fated release attempt with Group 5, I had feared for Bonne Année's life in the mayhem that resulted in her injury, then I feared for Dian's, as she yanked the baby directly from the clutches of the marauders. This, to me was more frightening than those moments. All four hundred pounds of a silverback was directly over me, nearly on me. I could feel the hot breath, smell every fleck of vegetation in his teeth. All of that gorilla's anger was directed at me, the intruder, in contact with his newest member. I was a threat to his authority, but no match for him.

In the worst moments of being charged by a wild gorilla, I would remind myself that no one's really been harmed by these research groups. I had nothing else to do but run these thoughts through my mind again. And Bill Weber *was* attacked. *Was this circumstance different? Was it worse? Anyway, there's always a first time. Bill's attack was a first. Could I be a first?* As I trembled and shook under Peanuts assault, Stuart sat nonchalantly by, scribbling notes. *He knew this would happen!*

I needed Bonne Année to get off me! My left hand was out of sight from Peanuts, and I slid it under my right forearm, trying to push the baby away. I couldn't get enough leverage without Peanuts knowing I was deliberately touching the baby. I decided to make the experience uncomfortable for her. Feeling her hair against my right arm, I maneuvered my left hand toward her, underneath me. Gathering a cluster of the hair of her butt between my thumb and index finger, I yanked. Peanuts kept up his angry vigil, and loud complaint, beating his chest and slamming the ground. Stuart sat idly by, taking notes, as helpless to intervene as I. The little gorilla didn't budge. I yanked harder. She shifted, pulling the hair from my clutches. I reached again, this time grabbing more hair, and yanked. Finally, a few hairs came loose in my hand. The baby shifted again. Out of reach! Peanuts beat his chest, and slammed the ground again. I felt the baby let out a deep breath, as if in a sigh, then, miraculously, she moved away. Peanuts was quiet. I dared to look from my flattened position. Bonne Année was moving up hill, Peanuts's eyes on her intently. I too breathed a sigh. As the baby moved uphill, Peanuts turned and followed. I held my submissive position until Peanuts followed Bonne Année out of view uphill, into the undergrowth. Finally, I felt I could sit up.

"Ohhh, you bastard, Stuart!"

"I told you she'd be happy to see you."

"You knew this was gonna happen."

"Well, it may have been a little more intense with you. She stayed with you quite a while."

"Thanks a lot!"

I didn't bear any grudge to Stuart. In the wake of the horror, I felt such relief. That was enough for the both of us, and as Peanuts led his group onward up Mount Visoke, we headed back. I felt as if the very weight of a silverback had lifted from me, and the hike seemed effortless, even as we climbed back down into the biggest ravine we had crossed.

"I feel so alive!" I caught myself saying, realizing there was a true high from such adversity and feeling of danger, as if I had died and was reborn. "I've never felt so ALIVE!"

Still, I didn't want to go through that again. Despite my worry, subsequent visits to Peanuts's Group were peaceful. It was as if Bonne Année had gotten the message too, and kept a respectable distance from me, much to my relief.

Over time, Stuart's interest in camp waned. From the onset, he had planned for his girlfriend back home in the States to join him, but that no longer seemed to be in the offing. He didn't talk much about the reasons why, but he let me know that Dian had informed him in a recent letter that she had taken it upon herself to intervene. In an effort to keep Stuart in place, Dian had the nerve to call his girlfriend in the States to encourage her to join Stuart in Rwanda, Dian was put off by the young lady's having made up her mind to do otherwise. After that, Dian decided she didn't like her. Instead, she thought one of her female students would make for a better fit for Stuart and camp. The student had no doubt appealed to her professor's ego.

In response to Peter's complaint to *National Geographic* about Dian's having stolen his photographs, she simply wrote to Stuart that Peter was clearly going crazy and should leave Karisoke.

Eventually Stuart simply stopped mentioning his girlfriend. In time, he began complaining of having injured his knee in a ravine, before spending longer periods away from camp, at Jean-Pierre's rented *Plantation de Gasiza*. Soon, Stuart talked about leaving camp.

"I'm getting more interested in gorilla conservation, actually, than research," he surmised.

During his absences, he asked me to stay at Dian's cabin, because she had requested that it always be occupied. Also, the two wooden lockboxes, one containing the camp finances and another containing Dian's precious handguns, were kept in her room—one .32 caliber Walther PPK, and one .25 caliber Beretta 950B Jetfire. Uncomfortable sleeping in Dian's king-size bed, and never feeling quite as safe in her large multi-room cabin, the closest to the open meadow and the border with Zaire, I complied nonetheless. Each time, though, I longed only to get back to my own small cabin tucked in the middle of camp.

Away from camp, however, Stuart seemed to have found an ever-sympathetic and supportive ear in Jean-Pierre, and spent more and more time with him off the mountain. And in return, Stuart opened up a dialogue between the Mountain Gorilla Project and Karisoke. For my sake, he stopped requesting I stay in Dian's cabin, instead, moving the money and gun boxes down to my own place during his absence. In an effort to keep the diplomatic Stuart happy in Rwanda, Jean-Pierre introduced him to a young French girl who was visiting friends in Rwanda.

"The funny thing is, she looks kind of like a young version of Dian," Stuart finally confessed after a visit with her at Jean-Pierre's.

A Dutch film crew with an American writer-producer, Barbara Jampel, arrived to gather wild gorilla footage for a *National Geographic* documentary about the mountain gorillas. They brought food and beer, and we put them up in the Big Cabin. Knowing Dian had already returned stateside, Barbara had met with her before coming to Africa. Dian had been hospitalized with emphysema soon after returning, and that's where the interviews took place.

Over dinner and beers, the funny and feisty documentarian entertained us with tales of trying to get a story out of an irritable and distracted Dian in the hospital. Despite being kept under an oxygen tent with pneumonia, Dian remained unfocused and fidgety during the interview, repeatedly interrupting to plead for a cigarette.

"You could sneak some into the hospital in your purse," Dian finally suggested to the incredulous Barbara.

Satisfied with her camp visit, Barbara left filming in the hands of her crew: director André Gunn, cameraman Jan de Ruiter, and sound man, Dick Rector. The team had already been filming with Amy and Bill down below, but weren't satisfied with the fleeting shots of their less-habituated gorilla groups.

"Amy said we could get good footage of her with your Group 5," André told Stuart. "Would that be possible?"

Once again, Stuart was back in the awkward position of keeping Amy at bay under Dian's directive. We all thought Amy had to know how Dian would feel about her appearing in the documentary back among Karisoke's gorillas instead of Dian. But we had a valid reason to keep even the film crew away from Group 5 for the time being. Per Peter's ongoing observations of Effie's estrus and copulations, this gorilla matriarch was due to give birth in early June. At that, we decided to minimize disturbance of the group during this period.

This time, we let André break the news to Amy. Upon his return to camp, he told us that Bill and Amy scoffed at the idea that Peter could predict an impending birth with any degree of accuracy, let alone time of cycling, ovulation, and impregnation. Peter just hung his head, shaking it in bemused exasperation. Effie gave birth on June 10, giving great credence to Peter's growing understanding of gorilla behavior and female cyclicity.

Peter had planned the name Maggie for a long time, simply because he liked it.

"Maggie, Magpie, Maggie-May . . ." Peter said, "Don't you just love that name?"

I didn't love it. All I could think of was Stephen Crane's novella, *Maggie: a Girl of the Streets*, which a high school English teacher had assigned our class to read, so I wasn't as enamored of the moniker. But Peter had certainly earned the right to name the new baby of Group 5, so I didn't argue.

It was amazing to see a baby mountain gorilla within the first hours of her life, after a trail of blood spotting had led us from a steep ravine to Effie that morning on Mount Karisimbi. Little Maggie still appeared to be damp, her hair slick to her head, as if we'd just missed the event. She looked to be about four pounds, and a six-inch portion of the umbilicus still clung to her navel. Her eyes remained closed. Although her hair was dark, her skin was pink with grayish shading, lacking the full melanin that would eventually color it. Effie tended to her like the skilled mother that she was, cradling her newborn gently in one arm, and nudging her onto her nipple to suckle. The fascination by other group members was obvious, as each approached to stare at the baby, but none was more fascinated than Tuck, who was nearly old enough for a baby of her own. This oldest daughter of Effie stayed close, obviously captivated by her new little sister.

Although male gorilla genitalia are remarkably small, Peter and I could visibly confirm that Maggie was a girl within days of her birth, and so I found it surprising that so many of the research gorillas had erroneously been given male names like Puck, Tuck and Augustus, and even Bonne Année, who had first been called "Charlie" in camp.

In three days, Maggie's eyes were open, and she began clinging to her mother's body hair. Over the next twenty days, Maggie clung only ventrally on her mother's chest and abdomen, with frequent support from Effie's hand. Over the days, her pink skin became splotched with black, and almost overnight on day twenty she was black, and moved dorsally, riding on Effie's back with her fuzzy bobbling head held high, eyes wide in observance and wonderment.

The timing worked out because after the film crew's return up to camp from final filming below, André had become ill with a bad cold, and was laid up at the Big Cabin for a couple days with his teammates, Jan and Dick, who relaxed during the downtime, and tended to their boss. They took advantage of this down time to interview Jean-Pierre, visiting the camp. Stuart, Peter, and I could only laugh at the jovial old *parc conservateur* who was completely uncomfortable in front of a camera and fumbled his words comically in response. Jean-Pierre laughed with us, from where he sat casually on the trunk of a large fallen hagenia, until André made the three of us go inside the Big

Cabin to stop being a distraction. Jean-Pierre had a habit of crossing his legs when he sat, and in his awkwardness with the film crew he crossed his arms nervously over his lap. Stuart, Peter, and I could only laugh all the more from a distance, watching André repeatedly pulling Jean-Pierre's arms apart, and untying the jumbled knot of his body language. Finally, Jean-Pierre came through, and was glad it was over.

Peter and I observed Maggie's successful first few days and Effie's good health, before the film crew came with us to Group 5. They were happy with the up-close-and-personal footage they were able to get in the midst of the world's most habituated mountain gorillas, being themselves as they filmed.

In the days following the film crew's departure, Stuart confided in me and Peter that recent letters and telegrams from Dian had begun to take on a more defensive, threatening tone. Stuart then let us in on the news that Dian was planning a return trip before June was over. Our leader, I could only surmise, must've been having some trouble coping with her new role at Cornell, and life back among the civilized. We were all concerned that she might be going go so far as to give up her new job in order to reclaim her throne at Karisoke, holding down the fort in the face of what she saw as a hostile takeover.

Her former student Sandy Harcourt, now well-regarded as a field scientist in his own right, had gained growing support from funding sources and decision-makers including the Rwandan park service's director, Monsieur Benda Lema, no fan of Fossey. Indeed, Sandy had even colluded with Benda Lema to block Dian's reentry into Rwanda. Perhaps Dian's biggest flaw was her idea that everyone needed her approval and support to do their own gorilla research and conservation. To her indignation, Bill and Amy had already proven that wrong. In light of these growing pressures, and what looked like a maelstrom, Stuart announced that he planned to leave Karisoke by the end of June.

NINETEEN

KIMA KUFA

The routine of my evenings alone in my cabin rarely varied, and I fell into a gratifyingly monotonous rhythm upon returning home from my routine visits with gorillas: eat, type, read, sleep. I savored this routine, becoming inventive with my simple kerosene stove as I concocted camp cuisine ranging from crude pizzas to oddly satisfying "Karisoke soufflés" made from sautéed onions, peppers, tomatoes, flour, and eggs.

One night, within a week of Dian's departure, someone knocked on my door.

"*Ndio?*" I said, now automatic with my knowledge of the Swahili word for *yes*.

No response. I rose from my chair, unlatched and opened the door.

"*Jambo*," Dian's houseboy Kanyaragana said, standing in the failing light, smiling pleasantly from beneath the bill of his navy-and-white New York Yankees cap.

"Uh . . . *jambo*," I replied, baffled by this unexpected visitor. After an awkward standoff in the doorway during which Kanyaragana uttered a few phrases of Swahili well beyond my dozen words, I spoke and gestured to him that I needed to fetch my Swahili book on the desk.

Next, he was inside. He spoke again, more Swahili. Exasperated, I dropped into my desk chair, feeling a little annoyed. He didn't need anything, and there was obviously no urgent Karisoke business afoot. I shuffled my notes, placed paper into my typewriter—anything to look busy. Too busy for idleness. Installing himself on the only other seat, the edge of my bed, Kanyaragana sat silently. For lack of any other explanation in the moment, I could only surmise, Kanyaragana was paying me a visit. I decided I had to respond somehow, but first I had to understand what he was saying.

Soon I was thumbing through my little green Swahili book as my guest uttered simple phrases one at a time: *Where are you from? Do you have a family at home?* My frustration soon turned to a sort of appreciation as I began to communicate in a simple conversational Swahili.

After that, Kanyaragana became a regular visitor, showing up after we had both eaten dinner. Jarred out of my hermitic routine of gorillas, dinner, and typing notes, I remained a little inconvenienced at first, but I welcomed him inside, nonetheless, taking advantage of the opportunity to learn Swahili. He was always polite, never staying longer than fifteen or twenty minutes. Slowly, with my little green book in hand, I built my Swahili vocabulary into fluency word by word.

Soon I was speaking with the others, joining them at the fire pit. With this newfound communication they became different people. They had stories and backgrounds and histories. Young Toni was just learning Swahili too. He was a newlywed; though happy to be working, he missed his bride while up with us at Karisoke. "*Bernadetta iko mzuri sana*," he told me wistfully. I learned that Toni's father lived in Uganda, and couldn't return to Rwanda, something to do with the ethnic violence that took place between 1959 and 1962. On this topic, they became quiet. Like the horrid genocide that was yet to come, there had already been ethnic violence between Hutu and Tutsi while the country transitioned from a Belgian colony to an independent nation. This earlier genocide, in the dearth of telecommunication, was little-known to the world relative to what would follow in 1994.

In our camp pidgin Swahili, I pointed out stars and planets to Nameye and explained that these are suns like our own, and the planets are other worlds. I was surprised that he wasn't so surprised, and instead shared my belief that there could be other life out there in other worlds. I was impressed too, that gorilla tracking wasn't just a job for him, he expressed a true devotion to the mountain gorillas he had come to know so well, and a real dedication to preserving them. He nodded with understanding as I explained that our studies of mountain gorillas could give us insight into our own human behaviors and the common ancestry we share with great apes. Mukera the woodman was a funny guy, and told me the Kinyarwanda words for male and female genitalia. They all laughed when I pronounce these, and then made up funny sentences with them. Boys behaving badly.

I asked what *napati* meant, the pet name Dian used for Kima, or when she was trying to speak to a forest buffalo, as if to tame it. "*Iko bure*," they all agreed, a phrase they use to say *it's nothing*, something she made up, or a mispronunciation of something else. None could say how Dian came up with that. I ask about *Nyiramachabelli*, the name Dian said the locals gave her. "*Iko bure*," they all agreed. None knew of its meaning. They shared the opinion it was only something Dian had contrived or misconstrued. Perhaps it was her misunderstanding of some other word or words she had heard, but none of the men could come up with any actual local word it resembled. As with our tracker, Baraqueza, whose name in camp was Dian's best guess at his actual name, Werebguereza. And Dian's head porter, whom we knew as Gwehandegoza, was actually Gwahamogozi. I also asked about family names. Rwelekana spelled his out for me on a piece of cardboard as Banyangandora, but they didn't use these. Instead, each had a western name too, usually French. Rwelekana was also Emmanuel. Dian had documented and described gorilla language, but after thirteen years in the Virungas, had little knowledge of, or interest in, the region's native tongue.

Kitchwa mgonjwa, the men would say about Dian's irrational behaviors, meaning *sick in the head*. In reference to Dian, the men would also use their own Kinyarwanda word, *umusazi*, meaning *crazy*.

Treks to gorillas, too, became filled with chatter. Learning about these men—their lives, backgrounds, the culture of Rwanda—I was, for the first time, discovering who they were. They all wanted to come to America.

I enjoyed a little renaissance of sorts during this time, finally unpacking the charcoal, watercolor paints, brushes, and paper I had brought from home. I sketched a charcoal of Bonne Année to give to the Vimonts, who rescued the little orphan, who held special interest for them. I painted a similar watercolor and pinned it to my grass-mat wall. With pen and ink, I practiced a technique I learned in high school art class of drawing a picture with a single line, without looking at my sketch paper. As a subject, I choose a photo of a beautiful girl in the pages of a *National Geographic* about Dutch colonials in Indonesia. At the end of my line, when I finally lifted the pen and looked down at the paper, I was stunned to see that it was not the beautiful Dutch-Indonesian girl at all, but an *umusazi* image of Dian Fossey staring back at me. As if the paper was the Ouija board and my pen the gliding planchette, Mademoiselli emerged telepathically, as if to scold me for talking about her with the men. Recovering from my shock, I resigned myself to continue the piece, applying watercolors, thereby only enhancing it as an eerie abstraction of Dr. Fossey.

For the Africans, Kima the monkey had always been the terror of camp, chasing and lunging at them from above like some angry arboreal watchdog. Neither is it all bluff. Once when Dian invited her employees' families to a staff Christmas party in camp, Karisoke staffers recalled that Kima bit the Achilles tendon of one of the tracker's wives so severely that the woman had to be taken to the hospital in Ruhengeri.

With Dian long gone, however, Kima had no one to align herself with.

"Kima's getting a lot nicer to me since Dian's been gone." Stuart told me one day, "She even lets me pet her sometimes."

The next morning, I emerged from my cabin to see Kima sitting by the fire pit with the Africans, nearly on Nameye's lap. Nameye looked every bit as baffled as I did. I approached with cautious disbelief as the monkey merely looked up at me, uttering a few soft chirping sounds. Soon we were all taking turns stroking her soft fur as she warmed herself in the glow of the fire like one of the gang.

Stuart had been away again visiting Jean-Pierre at *Plantation de Gasiza*, but the morning of June 4, after his return, he banged loudly on my door.

"John! John! Open up!" Stuart's voice was frantic. "Something's wrong with Kima, she won't move."

I followed Stuart quickly up the path to Dian's cabin. Inside, Stuart had Kima in a cardboard Johnnie Walker box in front of the fireplace with its usual smoldering, soggy fire. Kanyaragana stoked the wood, blowing on the sparse embers in a futile attempt to rouse the flames. Dian's pet monkey lay huddled in the box on a crumpled towel.

"I've got to do something," Stuart said, "I've gotta get her to a vet!" I agree to drive into Ruhengeri with him, but neither of us had any idea where to find a veterinarian.

In desperation, Stuart and I raced down the mountain on foot with a blanket draped over Kima's box. Later, on the long bumpy van ride into Ruhengeri, I peered into the box repeatedly checking on the sickly monkey. Her eyes remained listless and half-closed.

In a desperate dash through town, we sought directions to the nearest vet just outside the south end, on the road to Gisenyi. I cringed as the livestock vet injected a cow-sized hypodermic filled with a thick white liquid I could only surmise was an antibiotic of some sort under the skin between Kima's shoulders. At this, Kima rose up weakly, and, grabbing the edge of her box in a silent pantomime, rolled her head back, mouthing the air as if there was a bad taste on her tongue. Then with a long, slow shudder, Kima's body tensed and fell limp. Dian's pet monkey of eleven years was dead—*kufa*, as they said in camp.

Stuart was beside himself.

"We've got to have an autopsy done," he said, "Dian's gotta know that Kima died of natural causes."

Back into town in a cloud of dust, we raced around the Ruhengeri hospital grounds on foot, lifeless blue monkey in tow, looking for any physician we could find. In a worst-case scenario, the first physician we encountered was Dr. Peter Weiss, a fit, trim and distinguished white-haired gentleman, and one of the hospital's top administrators. Unbeknownst to us, he was also Dian's infamously scorned ex-paramour-cum-fiancé. The two, we later learned, once enjoyed a famously passionate romance before a bitter, volatile breakup during which, as word had it, Dian stormed down the mountain and smashed the French doctor's windshield. In the moment, he well knew Kima, but we didn't know him.

"I am very zorry," Dr. Weiss said, without a trace of emotion in his distinct French accent, "I have very important things to do here with PEOPLE and can NOT take zee time to perform an autopsy on a MONKEY."

Back in camp, I carved a plaque for Kima, and we buried her by the gorilla graveyard. In a sympathetic letter, Stuart informed Dian of the tragic news.

TWENTY

A Break in the Clouds

T he best weather in the Virunga Volcanoes comes during the long dry season between June and September. Our anticipation of the rains ending was compromised by word from Dian that she would indeed visit camp in June, but after receiving the news of Kima's death, she informed Stuart in another letter that she would not actually be coming due to her conflicting trip to Japan, where she would be attending the premiere of the Nippon AV film of Bonne Année's attempted release.

Sandy Harcourt continued to make strides in his efforts to return to Karisoke and take charge, garnering major grant monies from the Guggenheim Foundation and even *National Geographic*, Dian's own funding source. He continued to win favor with the Rwandan park service, ORTPN, whose director, Benda Lema, wrote to the African Wildlife Leadership Foundation's office saying that Dian was "psychologically sick."

Stuart, Peter, and I, along with our intrepid tracker Rwelekana, took advantage of the good weather to make an overnight trek up Mount Visoke, hoping to spot signs of Nunkie's Group along the way. It gave us a nice break from the routine and mounting drama of Karisoke. We used the lightweight tent left by the Japanese and camped in the thin could air above Visoke's placid lake, marveling at the starry skies from our twelve-thousand-foot vantage point.

The next morning we woke in frost before hiking down its northern slope to the tranquil Lake Ngezi just on the border with Zaire. There, we were on the direct opposite side of the mountain from Karisoke. Along the way, we found no sign of Nunkie. The lake lay beside a trail that snaked up from low in Zaire, reputed to be long used for smuggling coffee into Rwanda, where the market was better. Rumor was that Rwanda exported more coffee than it actually grew because of this trail and its secret traffic when coffee was harvested.

A pair of plump red-knobbed coots, *Fulica cristata*, made their home on the small scenic lake. I watched as these dark, buoyant waterbirds diligently built a floating nest from the stems of soggy plants they plucked from the marshy edges. Their red knobs shone like bright berries atop their heads as they floated and bobbed along on their busy task. A lone little grebe, *Tachybaptus ruficollis*, or "dabchick" was the only other bird who joined them on the water. With its ruddy cheeks and stark white patches at the base of its beak, it disappeared intermittently as it dove for what small aquatic prey it might find beneath the mirror-like surface, only to pop up unexpectedly in another spot on the small quiet lake.

We camped in the vacant green cabin, originally built to accommodate the occasional tourist, but by then mostly forgotten. In the thick forest behind the small structure, Rwelekana showed us a deep narrow pit once used by Twa hunters to capture forest elephants. The hole was about eight feet long, and only a couple feet wide. Its depth, at nearly seven or eight feet, would have been over my head. When covered by leaves and branches, an elephant might unwittingly step in it, Rwelekana explained. As the big animal struggled to free itself, its other legs would slip in, thereby wedging the animal tightly into the gap. The weight and bulky structure of an elephant prevented its escape before hunters would be upon it with sharp spears.

Back in camp, in addition to dispatching Dian's poacher patrols, Stuart continued his daily treks to Peanuts's Group while continuously sending out trackers in search of Nunkie. The groups that Dian had habituated were of most importance to her. Fringe groups were fringe groups, gorillas she hadn't met, and therefore had no emotional connection to. While a conservationist might be as concerned about the total population of mountain gorillas, even those yet unidentified, Dian was most protective of her own gorillas, like one's indifference to a neighbor's pet dog versus one's own beloved pet. The gorilla graveyard stood as testimony to her emotional connection to her named gorillas and surrogate family: Uncle Bert, Flossie, Old Goat, Digit . . .

We went out every day, seven days a week, averaging a one- or two-hour hike to gorillas; uphill, downhill, or at a 45° angle across ravines, four hours with them, then one or two hours back, followed by an hour or two of typing notes. I soon learned that mountain gorillas do have a sort of average day, like humans in the home and workplace.

In the Virungas, near the equator, the sun comes up around six o'clock every morning, year round. The gorillas rise with the sun and begin foraging for breakfast, an easy task where they live, within the salad bowl upon which they feed. As they feed, they move into fresh stands of thistles, nettles, wild celery, and creeping gallium, so abundant on the volcanic slopes. By midmorning, they slow their movement and become sedentary for a short while, picking their teeth, burping, and farting while they digest their breakfast. Some may groom one another, especially mothers to their infants. Some may sprawl out to rest, especially in sunshine, while others may make day nests to lay in by snapping and pulling in nearby plants to tuck around themselves in a loose, low circular support mat. The leafy fronds of low-altitude lobelia are a favorite for these nests. A mother's inactivity during rest makes a perfect opportunity for an infant to nurse, and they suckle contentedly during these rest periods. Like human children though, gorilla kids may not sleep much at nap time, instead wrestling or playing a game of chase and tackle in and among the sleeping grownups.

Feeding resumes in the second half of the morning, with the group moving on again to fresh foods not flattened by gorilla rest and play. Like the human lunchtime, or siesta, midday marks the mountain gorilla's long rest period. As for the morning rest, the group becomes idle again, either sprawling out, particularly if there's sunshine, or huddling into day nests. Again, the youngsters may rest or play, with long periods of nursing for the infants, and grooming of each other and the silverback. After as much as an hour or more of snoozing farts and burps and picking teeth, appetite spurs them on again to forage as before.

While males become silverbacks at around fifteen years old, they become sexually interested before that, and potentially reproductive. These subadult blackbacks, like Ziz of Group 5, don't have the social rank within a group to breed with mature females. Females mature earlier, at about eight years old, and if a female is cycling, copulation may occur at any time of the day. Sex is a largely public affair for gorillas, with only a modicum of privacy vegetation might provide. If the relationship is sanctioned by the alpha silverback, in non-competition for his select females, privacy is less of an issue for other sexually mature males in the group. If the affair is clandestine, and adulterous by gorilla standards, privacy is a must, but difficult to achieve. Although a couple might linger behind, or move off peripherally from the group into a thicket, their staccato copulation vocalizations, emitted in a series of *eh eh eh eh eh* . . . rises in vigor and volume until revealing the tryst to all and giving away its location. Then, the cuckolded male intervenes and disrupts with his best display of screams and chest beats.

I did witness another clandestine copulation in an isolated instance of lesbian sex between Effie and Pantsy. The two adult females lingered away from the others as they solicited each other. Their playful advances culminated in the two hanging frontally by their arms from a leaning sapling while rubbing their genitals together. Their pursed lips and swaying heads revealed their gratification at this brief secret tryst before each dropped to the ground and moved on to rejoin the group.

As with humans, gorilla youngsters are curious about sex, and seem to find humor in the conjugal antics of the adults, impishly gathering near the scene of a copulation, or dashing through daringly in play, as if taking advantage of the conjoined pair's distraction, baffled and bemused. Despite a silverback's massive body size, his penis is remarkably small; even when erect it is only about half the size of a man's pinkie. Neither does the scrotum, covered in fur, protrude enough to be obvious. Although one eventually learns what to look for on either sex, Dian never seemed to master the ability to determine gorilla gender, which resulted in a number of females given male names.

I once watched Beethoven sprawl on his back after a cold rain. His tiny penis became erect in the warm sun. Young Poppy was passing by, and stopped to stare at it as if to say, *"What IS that? I never knew THAT was there . . ."* When little Cantsbee wandered into the same scene, Beethoven, still on his back, idly dragged the youngster back and forth over his rigid member a few times before releasing the befuddled tyke. Afterward, Cantsbee simply scampered off to play with the other youngsters. The scene would have earned the silverback prison time had they been human. Onward movement to forage and feed is usually determined by the lead silverback, but the group will also follow an alpha female who, done with waiting around, might also initiate the direction of the next feed. Vulnerability and risk of danger ahead will limit the distance an assertive female will move from her protective male, and a silverback will usually resume the lead again. After the first afternoon foray, the group has another short rest, similar to that of the morning, before once again moving on to feed. A group may traverse a relatively short distance where food is abundant, or may cover a great distance in search of seasonal plants, like coveted blackberries or bamboo sprouts. Sometimes they may climb high on the volcanoes to eat high-altitude lobelia or favored senecio, cracking the thick stems with their mighty teeth and arms to extract the tender crunchy white pith inside. Nights are cold in such places, and the group usually moves lower before the day ends. Near sundown, as the day darkens and cools, the group stops for the day, and each builds its own night nest, a more substantial version of their day nest, and settles in for the long sleep of the night. Infants sleep in one nest with their mothers. Sometimes younger adolescents will too. I could soon see how gorillas represent humans at their most basic primal state in their daily endeavors to meet the fundamental basic primate needs for food, security, sex, and possession—possession being in the context of the feeding grounds they occupy, much in the sense of human property. The silverbacks defend this real estate in uproarious fervor, with loud hoots, chest beats, and even violent maulings, when another group ventures into their stomping grounds. It is easy for me to understand humans as primates, not so far removed from our great ape cousins.

In the tradition of American labor, each day worked out to at least an eight-hour day. It was funny that an approaching holiday would mean anything at ten thousand feet up in the remote Virunga Volcanoes of Rwanda, but I found myself thinking about the approaching Easter Sunday, as if I should take a day off. Peter recalled that Kelly Stewart had dressed up like a bunny one Easter and went around camp, distributing Easter eggs. Dian had loved it at the time, but that was before she had written Kelly off like everyone else.

Peter had been wanting to take a trip to the town of Gisenyi, on Lake Kivu, one of the Rift Valley's great lakes. It lay below five thousand feet on the far side of Mount Karisimbi, and was within a morning's drive from the base of Visoke, via Ruhengeri. I was intrigued by the lake's reputation as being safe for swimming due to its high methane gas content, which while safe for humans, rendered it mostly free of the aquatic snail that served as the vector of Africa's nasty bilharzia parasite. This flatworm used a snail as its host, and infected the urinary and gastrointestinal tracts of unwitting swimmers in tropical and subtropical lakes, rivers, and waterways. The disease, also known as schistosomiasis, infects its victims with bloody diarrhea and anemia. It was rare to be able to swim in a tropical African freshwater lake, and Lake Kivu even lacked dangerous crocodiles and hippos. I was in for a Spring Break at the beach, of sorts. We packed up Karisoke's green military tent for the trip. Although we didn't know where we'd camp exactly, we felt sure we'd be able to find a spot. It was a resort town, of sorts, after all.

"We'll have to stop at a friend's of mine in Ruhengeri," Peter said, "I met him a while back, and he's been wanting me to come down and have lunch."

When we got to André Servais's house, his girlfriend, Mary, greeted us at the door. André wasn't home yet, and it was a little awkward, because we spoke neither French nor Kinyarwanda, and she spoke neither English nor Swahili. Still, through gestures, and a few common words of the aforementioned languages, she invited us inside and had us seated in the living area of their simple, comfortable white stucco home.

Mary was a beautiful girl, tall, graceful, and elegant, with delicate features. She wore her hair close-cropped like most Rwandans, and was dressed *très Americaine* in a trendy denim dress, which clung perfectly to her lithe body. A row of buttons up the back accentuated the graceful arching bow of her spine from hem to neckline. Her youth and femininity made me realize how long it had been since I'd seen a pretty young lady.

But what kind of a lady was she, I wondered, when André arrived. Mary excused herself to check on things in the kitchen as the Belgian expat greeted us heartily, especially Peter, whom he obviously adored. He was much older than Mary, and not so handsome, with thinning hair, spindly salt- and-pepper moustache, pot belly, and scrawny appendages, I could only surmise that Mary had taken up with him for all the wrong reasons. Especially when Peter told me that André had a wife back home in Belgium. Things just got weirder when our host took Peter aside in another room to show him a collection of nude photos of his live-in concubine. I could see Peter's bewilderment, when he told me about this later.

Soon Mary served us lunch at a long dining table next to the kitchen. After setting the table, she sat at the head. I was struck by the dish she served with our roasted chicken, a mixture of beans and plantains. It had been stewed with dried beans until everything had become tender in a rich sauce, like American chili, and just as satisfying.

"*Igitoki*," Mary said, when I asked her about it; the Rwandan word for plantain.

It was good, very different for us Americans, and uniquely African.

André poured white wine, making small talk with Peter and me as we ate, asking about Karisoke and the gorillas. He seemed genuinely interested, especially about the birth of little Maggie, which he translated for Mary to her delight. It was nearly two hours before André needed to get back to work, the nature of which I don't recall. We said our farewells to our host on his fenced front lawn, as a friend of Mary's arrived on foot.

"That's Dr. Weiss's wife," André said with a grin, before leaving us. "She started out as his housekeeper." André didn't need to fill Peter and me in on the back story of Dian's victorious rival and her ill-fated romance with the Frenchman. Dr. Peter Weiss was the same gent Stuart and I stumbled upon with Kima's lifeless body at the hospital. Despite the doctor being in his seventies, this young wife of his appeared to be only in her twenties.

Compared to Mary, Faina was a sturdy gal, thick-set, loud, and boisterous in her mannerisms. Unlike the très chic denim dress that Mary wore with hip elegance, Faina had on the common French-cut T-shirt, a wrapped kanga for a skirt, and simple Rwandan factory flip-flops. Still, Mary obviously took comfort in her friend's self-assuredness, letting her take over the entertaining.

"*Iko lugha yangu!*" Faina said boisterously with a husky laugh, as Peter and I tried our Swahili on her. *That's my language!* Her voice was loud and confident, compared with her friend Mary's soft-spoken demeanor.

"Oh, *where are you from?*" I asked in Swahili.

"Tanzania!" she said, again laughing.

I noticed she wore a fine gold chain necklace with her name, "*FAINA,*" spelled out in a pendant. The whole scene of Dian coming down the mountain and smashing Dr. Wiess's windshield in a blind rage over this rival lover flashed through my mind. Faina looked like she could kick Dian's ass back up the mountain with one blow, and I guess in a way she had.

Lake Kivu shimmered beautifully on descent from the volcanic uplands into the small city of Gisenyi, extending far southward along the border between Rwanda and Zaire. Looking down the shoreline, this city on the lake merged into the adjoining city of Goma, Zaire, just across the border, where Rwanda's sandy beach ended. Upon arrival, I felt the warmth of the lower altitude and sunshine, and quickly changed into swim trunks in the van. The golden sand felt good under my bare feet. The lake's waters were warm and inviting, and as I waded in up to my neck, I took comfort in knowing its volcanic methane gas ruled out the risk of tropical disease. Fishermen in carved dugout canoes drifted on the horizon, casting nets for the tiny sardine-like *samaki* so abundant at the marketplace. I allowed myself to soak blissfully in the warm water and idyllic views of the Kivu District in all directions.

After our relaxing swim, we set out to find our home base for the next two nights, but soon realized there were no proper campgrounds.

Our search led us to a large green expanse of picturesque shoreline just to the southeast of town, along the lake. The manicured lawns turned out to be owned by a Catholic convent, and an elder nun met us upon arrival.

"I'm sorry, that would not be possible," the Belgian sister in a gray-and-white habit informed us when Peter asked if we could pitch our tent on the beautiful lakeside spot.

Back in town, our luck, and hunger, landed us at the small but chic Palm Beach Hotel, a relic from the art deco era, and an earlier period of colonialism. A block in from the lake, the hotel's raised patio with a bustling clientele was, as far as we could tell, Gisenyi's center of activity after dark. Peter and I, on our shoestring budget, were satisfied that a room was available for just ten dollars. Tired from the day's travels, we took seats at a dining table al fresco, and enjoyed a couple bottles of Primus in the balmy night air before dinner.

As we finished our meal, and ordered more Primus, a couple of men in a small pickup truck drove up to the wall of the raised terrace. Upon their arrival, women came trotting out of the hotel, adjusting their simple kangas and T-shirts. Each wore their hair in a short Afro, and looked like typical Rwandan farm wives. Except for their common attire, it was obvious they were prostitutes, finished with their tour of duty for the day. Our table was just above where the women boarded the bed of the truck en masse. One of them, looking no different from the rest, but more brazen, caught me staring.

"*Bon soir, Monsieur!*" she exclaimed. "*Je t'aime!*"

I looked away, but couldn't contain my nervous laughter.

She said something again in French, before trying English.

"*Hallooo!*" she said, drawing out her vowels as if she couldn't stop them, "how *aaare youuu?*"

"Fine!" I said, giving away my language.

"*I looove youuu!*" she responded, obviously up for one more. "Do *youuu looove* me?"

Peter just laughed silently into his beer, so as not to direct attention to himself, leaving me on my own—the bastard.

"Do *youuu* . . . ?" she said again, still working it. "Do you love me, *toooo*?"

"I don't even know you!" I responded at last, laughing at the absurdity of my cliché.

"Hallo Mister!" she persisted, having no inkling of what I'd said in response. "Hallo, I love *youuu*. Why don't *youuuu looove* me?"

By then, I could only squirm in my seat, wondering what the other diners and drinkers must've been thinking, but they acted as if they'd seen it all before. As the last of the women emerged from the hotel and entered the back of the truck, the driver's assistant closed the door to the bed and hopped back to the passenger side. To my discomfort, the driver gave the assertive hooker one last chance. She was only a few feet away from me, just off the terrace, making the moment that much more awkward. I wanted to get up and go.

"I love you Mister!" my new would-be friend persisted, even as the truck finally drove away. "Why don't you looove meee . . . ?"

That was enough romance. When Peter and I finally ascended the hotel's tiled stairs, our room key unlocked a tiny square space with one full and one twin bed, taking up nearly all of the small floor. A communal bathroom was down the hall. Too tired and tipsy to care, we carefully secured the row of door locks before flopping onto the beds and laughing about the absurdity of the day's events.

The next day was Easter Sunday, and we visited the Gisenyi Market, at the top of the hill above town center. There, we could easily see Mount Karisimbi in the clear morning air. I thought about how Karisoke lay in the saddle area just beyond it. Peter mentioned that Dian's friend, Ros Carr, had a home somewhere up in the direction of this familiar volcano, and on Sundays she had African dancers and a picnic lunch open to all visitors. Ultimately realizing we didn't really know which road would get us there, we opted to stay in Gisenyi and peruse the market.

"*Iko mzungu,*" one local said to his friend, grabbing his shoulders and turning him toward me as I ventured into the center of the marketplace.

When I turned away in the awkwardness of the moment, the friend plucked a fallen hair from my shoulder and carried it through the crowd, showing others. I could only surmise that they didn't get many whites up there, but I also thought of Dian's tradition of throwing her own brushed hairs and nail clippings into the fire so they couldn't be used against her in black magic. I found myself wondering where that hair would end up.

A woman soon approached with a large handwoven basket atop her head. Struck by the bright magenta geometric pattern intricately woven into its base and matching lid, she zeroed in on my interest. She declined my offer of ten dollars, but her friends urged her on when I brought a pair of my mom's mod-era dangly earrings out of my backpack to sweeten the pot. I had prepared for this based on my experience from the year before in Kenya. The women's friends, more dazzled by the earrings than the seller was, urged her on, and the basket was mine.

The owner of a small restaurant flanking the market showed a similar excitement when Peter and I decided to eat there.

"Come, come, sit down!" he said, grabbing my shoulders, and guiding me to a seat in a booth. "We have rice and chicken meat!"

The sound of "chicken meat" was a little sketchy, but we were hungry, so *what the heck*. The chicken was as tough as the old rooster it must have been, but flavorful, and right within our budget at three dollars a serving. After that, we took a couple of cold Primus back down to the beach for a final swim.

Not wanting to spend another ten dollars on a cramped room at the Palm Beach Hotel, Peter and I drove the length of Gisenyi before dinnertime. Finally, just shy of the checkpoint into Goma, at the border of Zaire, we spotted a small guest house with a restaurant, and stopped in for dinner. Fortunately, the kindly white-haired Belgian proprietor spoke some English.

"Would you mind . . ." Peter asked, pointing to the lawn as we paid for dinner, "If we put our tent out here for one night?"

"Of course," he responded. "No problem." That could at least ensure we'd be eating again in his restaurant for breakfast.

That night I slept well, but Peter said he woke in the middle of the night half-dreaming that the hookers and their drivers were breaking into our van as burglars. After coffee and breakfast on the guest house terrace over the beautiful Lake Kivu, our spring break was over, and we headed back to the gorillas and our chilly mountain home in the Virunga Volcanoes.

During the long dry season, Stuart began to come back from Peanuts's Group with reports of hearing the rumbles and loud trumpets of forest elephants on his gorilla visits. Camp staff were as surprised as the rest of us, saying that elephants hadn't been around for a long time. They surmised that persecution by *bawendagi*, their word for *poachers*, must have driven them up from the lowlands into the mountains with us. These were the true forest elephants, the subspecies, *Loxodonta cyclotis*, which were slightly smaller than the more familiar savanna species, *Loxodonta africana*, with smaller rounded ears and downward pointing tusks, versus the larger splayed tusk of their cousins. They had adaptations like the forest buffalo, which had equipped them for a life in the forest. Knowing that the taxonomy as a distinct species was still under scrutiny for these pachyderms greatly intrigued the young zoologist in me. I had to see them.

"They're known to be really dangerous." Peter advised me, when I confessed my desire to go look for them, "But the trackers have seen them. You could ask Nameye or Rwelekana to take you."

"*Iko kali sana. Hatari kabisa,*" Fierce and dangerous, Nameye replied, politely declining my request to take me into Zaire in pursuit of the forest elephants. Rwelekana echoed the same sentiments that these elephants were not worth the risk. These guys were brave, willing to track down poachers, and had seen it all, so their reluctance to encounter these denizens of the forest was worthy of heeding. The elephants' nervousness at being driven into the mountains only added to their already aggressive nature. In the end, I had to heed our intrepid tracker's advice, as they knew much from their years in the forest. Still, I secretly longed to encounter them somehow.

As the weather dried and warmed, pink orchid spires of *Disa stairsii* bloomed in sunny spots through camp and surrounding the forest, their roots anchored among the other epiphytes growing on live or dead and fallen trees. One orchid, *Polystachya kermesina*, small and unassuming before, sprouted tiny bright waxy red-orange flowers on the sides of trees where they clung as playful sparks from out of the gloom.

With dry weather, flocks of brown-necked parrots, *Poicephalus fuscicollis*, flew up from Zaire in the mornings to feed on something budding or fruiting in the forest canopy across the meadow behind my cabin. Their screeching alerted me to their presence, where they bounced and flitted among the higher branches in joyful raucous discord throughout the day, before flitting westward back into the warmer Congo Basin each evening.

On a couple of rare occasions, during clear skies, a helicopter appeared over Mount Visoke—Rwandan President Habyarimana flying a few VIP guests over the Parc des Volcans for a bird's-eye view of the beauty of the Virungas, the crowning glory of his homeland's thousand hills. Rarely even seeing an airplane overhead in our remote corner of Africa, I wondered what the gorillas must've thought of that great mechanical bird circling above Mount Visoke's hidden lake before veering off and away.

On May 14, Stuart and I went out with the poacher patrol. Our trek led us on their usual path well into Zaire and far across the saddle area into heavy poacher territory. I thought the area was closer to Dian's original camp near the Kabara Meadow than it was to Karisoke. There, in the level terrain, we collected 118 wire and rope snares, cutting their bamboo tension poles and freeing four live duikers. An additional six duikers weren't so lucky, and lay stranded in various states of death and decomposition. We also destroyed smaller hyrax traps, three of which contained decaying corpses of these unique small mammals. It all seemed so wasteful, but in line with Dian's edict, the men lashed the freshest duikers onto a pole, and brought them back to camp to feast upon that evening.

Before each sundown, as the dry air cooled, shy bushbucks would saunter cautiously into the camp's clearing to nibble on grasses and other tender plants that grew in sunnier spots. They munched warily, lifting their heads between bites, their russet brown fur glowing in the low-angled sunlight. The smaller females, lacking horns, were doe-like and delicate while males were crowned with a pair of spiraling horns, forming the graceful shape of a lyre.

Always guarded, these ungulates stared at our comings and goings, prepared at any moment to bound away with an upright flash of their white tails and sound their warning call, a bark similar to a dog's. Often their alerts would trigger the much smaller black-fronted dui-kers, feeding unseen among them in the tall weeds. These tiny red-and-black antelopes, when startled, snorted an airy whistle alert as they leapt and vanished into thickets.

After dark, the camp was stunningly silent with the creek having dried and retracted to a series of small, still pools in its deepest places. Too chilly at night for noisy insects or tree frogs, the occasional voices of tree hyraxes sometimes broke the stillness with their vocal madness. Only the evasive forest elephants provided a show of sound to rival their cousins the hyraxes when they rolled through one night. Their mass and voices shook the ground as they traveled through where the big meadow narrowed across the creek just behind my cabin. With trumpets, deep roars, and rolling rumbles from all directions they bar-reled through to their next new feeding grounds. Bravely, I opened my door, shining my flashlight, feeble as it was, into the darkness toward their sounds. But they were moving swiftly, beyond my weak beam of light, as if made nervous by the smell of us humans and the smoke from our chimney pipes.

The next morning I walked into the meadow and found their footprints sunk deep into the mud of recent rains. Flattened weeds and broken saplings indicated they had headed east, farther into Rwanda, and toward the lower portion of Group 5's range, not far from the shambas and human habitation. From then on, our treks to Group 5 were comingled with these deep and treacherous holes. Baraqueza quietly complied with my request for him to pose in one, and I snapped a photo of him up to his knees.

On May 25, Baraqueza served once again as Peter's and my tracker to Group 5. Forty five minutes down the trail that ran along Camp Creek, we wandered into old and new elephant paths. Then, we saw them, two of the great gray behemoths feeding calmly, accompanied by a younger one half their size. None had visible tusks. Although we stood in plain sight, just thirty meters away, they appeared not to see, nor hear, nor even smell us, and fed idly, wrapping their trunks around myriad vegetation, stripping the leaves and placing it into their mouths oblivious to our presence. Although we couldn't see the others, we could hear at least two more, tearing away at the abundant forage the forest provided them there. Perhaps lacking the coveted ivory tusks had saved them from poaching thus far.

"*Iko mingi*," Baraqueza said, surmising that there were *many* more dispersed in the forest beyond. Silently, we marveled at the sight of the trio for a half an hour, before slipping away to a visit with Group 5.

Twelve days later, on June 6, we encountered more, with young Toni as our guide, just north of a small side volcano called First Hill toward the base of Mount Karisimbi. We perched on a small knoll to observe. Eight were clearly visible, gathered around a mud hole, where they drank from deep puddles, slurping up the water with their trunks and squirting it contentedly into their mouths. Three of the adults, about seven feet tall at the shoulder, had tusks, as did one juvenile about two-thirds grown. Three other adults lacked tusks, although they were as big as the other full-growns. A tusk-less baby, only four feet tall, mingled among them. Two more adults fed nearby, partially obscured by the undergrowth upon which they fed, and we could hear countless others feeding in the forest ahead of them. Although we were in plain view of those at the watering hole, and within twenty meters uphill, they seemed completely unaware of us. These were the true forest species, *Loxodonta cyclotis*, and I marveled at their differences from their savannah cousins, *Loxodonta africana*. Their tusks pointed downward and close in to the line of the trunk when relaxed, compared to splaying widely outward as for *L. africana*. Their heads looked smaller too, in proportion to their bodies, and lacked their lump on the forehead, and their ears were more rounded.

We observed them quietly for over half an hour before they began to move away from the mud hole. As soon as they did, it was as if they had moved into our line of scent. Clearly startled, they suddenly packed together in a group to move quickly on ahead of us, and disappeared amid their weighty cracklings and thrashings into the forest.

If Stuart's commitment to the camp had been faltering before, it had spun into a sort of free-fall. He was caught between Dian's wishes and the pending change of hands ushered in with Sandy Harcourt's inevitable arrival. He spent more time away from camp, traveling with Jean-Pierre to Akagera, Rwanda's beautiful plains park. He also accompanied his elder pal to Lake Kivu, and even made a clandestine crossing over the border into Goma, Zaire, during which he had to lay low in the vehicle so as not to be seen without an entry visa. But with the state of Karisoke so tenuous under the pending return of Dr. Harcourt, and Dian's return visit canceled for the moment, he hung on in a kind of limbo, even as Jean-Pierre did his best to keep his morale up.

"You worry too much, Stuart," he told his young pal. "How doez zat song go? *'Every day'z a 'oliday, zee skies are baby BLEUUU . . .'*" he sang, comically on his visits to the camp, swinging his arms around in a wide waltzing swath. "Don't worry about Dian *Fussy!*"

We all laughed, enjoying Jean-Pierre's supportive spirit, and he often wrapped up a conversation saying, "Let's get cracking!" As he'd say this, he exaggerated the staccato of his guttural French 'r' for added effect, rolling and snapping the final word like a whip crack. But despite his elder friend's pep talks, Stuart remained doubtful of his fate with the unease created by Karisoke being pulled in two directions, and the eerie pall caused by Dian's letters with strange claims and accusations.

Cindy the dog was always slightly overweight in a fat-and-happy sort of way, but now she had started looking thin. I also noticed she had developed a rash at the base of her tail. Typical of what I knew as "flea allergy" in my own childhood dog, the hair on her lower back had become sparse, and the skin was red and irritated. Also, I hadn't ever noticed fleas at the high altitude of the camp. Thinking it may be a fungal infection of some sort, I treated the irritated area daily with iodine solution. Cindy certainly didn't mind the massage that came with that, the rubbing application doubling as a good scratch of her itch. She stood cooperatively with her best dog-smile as I scrubbed the solution into the skin. Within days, the skin started looking normal again, and the hair began growing back.

With Stuart away again in late June, Ann Yancey took a few days off from the US Embassy to visit Karisoke. Peter and I hosted her on a visit to Group 5, during which she got to experience an immersive gorilla baptism of her own, with members of the group crawling over her and checking her out, with the same fascination they had shown me months before. Ann reveled in the experience as the "new girl," with smiles and giggles, and was so appreciative of our hospitality she insisted Peter and I stay with her on our next visit to Kigali.

Like Easter, the Fourth of July became a vacation target date from which to break from our duties, especially after we received an invitation from the American Embassy to attend their annual Independence Day party; we knew Judy and Ann were responsible for this honor. Stuart, perhaps by then feeling guilty about his wavering commitments and time away from camp, passed the privilege on to Peter and me, insisting on staying in to run things while Peter and I attended the festivities. By then, through our embassy connections, we had met Susan Poats, a visiting scientist who was studying the lowly, but important, *pomme de terre à Rwanda*—otherwise known as Rwanda's potato—and its value in agriculture and the local diet. Susan knew a few US Peace Corps workers, and soon we had a group of young peers with which to make a tour of Rwanda's plains park of Akagera on the border with Tanzania. Someone even came up with a roadworthy vehicle for our safari.

Because the park's wildlife hadn't been adequately protected over the years, there wasn't the diversity and abundance of animals like in Kenya or neighboring Tanzania. But there were the basic herds of zebras, Cape buffaloes, and clusters of giraffes gracing the wide open spaces. And it was dry, sunny, and warm, a welcome change from the cloud forest. The one thing the park did have over many places, perhaps because of the lack of predators, were vast herds of the unique topi antelope, *Damaliscus lunatus*. With their odd blue-gray rumps, these cousins to hartebeest welcomed us in great numbers soon after our entry into the park. Hundreds of them leaped before our vehicle, crossing the road en masse, merging into other hundreds in the open plain, bounding in great balletic leaps, as if pursued by predators, and yet there were none. At the time, Akagera had been under-served with protection against poaching, and was all but devoid of predators like lions, leopards and hyenas. Elephants too had been obliterated by the hand of man. Those w that had been reintroduced by relocation were so traumatized by violent culling from which they'd come that they remained hidden skulking in the gallery forests which ran through the park.

did pass through these scattered forests, in hopes of catching se of the hidden elephants, but our search didn't last long. ve found something much smaller and potentially dan- ere the brush grew thickest, we were assailed by a barrage etse flies. These drab brown insects descended upon us f hungry little zombies, and we sped up immediately ught. But despite our speed, they dropped in from all directions, riding the draft at the back of our vehicle in a swarm, before deftly swooping inside the open back to land on us. Just knowing they could carry the blood-borne parasite for sleeping sickness, or trypanosomiasis, put us in panic mode, brushing them off in horror and nervous laughter as they landed upon our bare arms, legs, and faces. Fortunately, upon landing, they were rather sluggish, and none of us were bitten before dispatching each little assailant with a quick slap.

Out in the open again, we passed by one of the park's freshwater lakes, wherein dwelled the dreaded bilharzia-laden snails we had been warned about. With its idyllic beauty and wonder, Africa can be a savage paradise.

Throughout our day, we scarcely saw another vehicle, and at sundown we were alone. We parked in the middle of the dusty road, and laid our sleeping bags around to make camp before cracking open our lukewarm bottles of Primus and quenching our thirst. I had enjoyed Judy Chidester's recipe for spaghetti carbonara, and loosely planned a remote replica of that for our dinner. To eat, we had a package of spaghetti, eggs, a tin of margarine, Spam, and a can of ubiquitous Lindsay brand black olives we had bought at the grocery store in Kigali. We cooked the mess on a small camp stove in the center of the road, and despite its dubious culinary appeal, ate it with gusto and laughter.

"Spam carbonara!" someone would shout above the clink of an empty beer bottle, as we lay exhausted and giddy in our sleeping bags strewn upon the open road. This was followed by laughter and another shouting, "With Lindsay Olives!" so well aware we were of the divine absurdity of our meal and open-road accommodations. Still, Akagera's endless sky, fading from twilight to a spectacle of twinkling stars and glowing planets, provided a dreamlike setting, and we each drifted off to sleep knowing, or at least hoping, that the park was really devoid of large predators such as lions, leopards, and hyenas.

TWENTY-ONE

DIAN RETURNS

*Even extreme grief may ultimately vent itself in violence—but
more generally takes the form of apathy.*
—Joseph Conrad, *Heart of Darkness*

I had felt a tremendous sense of relief when Stuart told Peter and
me that Dian said in a letter that she had canceled her plans to
visit Karisoke in June. Nippon AV Productions had completed
their documentary on her and the gorillas, and offered to fly Dian to
Japan so she could introduce the film's premiere showings and give
a series of lectures. Dian accepted the invitation, and in a letter told
Stuart that because of her tight schedule she would not be able to
travel to Africa after all.

While he was on a trip to Kigali in late July, Stuart learned from others that Dian had developed a different set of plans unbeknownst to us. Still thinking that Stuart was expecting a visit from her, and unaware of anything to the contrary, American Embassy staff told him that Dian's plane had been grounded in the Seychelles Islands for repairs and that she would be in Kigali in a few days. Stuart was stunned. This information, in light of the ever-increasing reports of Dian's false accusations and other bizarre behaviors stateside, made this news even more ominous.

Well on her way back without letting us know, Dian had clearly planned some sort of ambush of her own team. Adding to the alarming news, Stuart received a shocking letter from his father in the States saying that Dian had telephoned him.

"She told my father I've taken five thousand dollars from camp funds!" Stuart lamented to me, incredulous, "and that I've stolen her guns!"

"What? You gotta be kidding!"

"She even told him I've been going out on strange ventures with Jean-Pierre . . . and get this, she told my dad she currently has lawyers looking into this.'" Stuart raised his fingers in quotation marks at the end of his sentence to highlight Dian's words.

"Who knows what Gwehandegoza has been telling her?"

I felt my skin crawl at what I could only surmise was a pending cataclysm. As a precaution, I hid my eerie portrait of Dian in the footlocker in my cabin for fear that she would see it.

In mid-July, Dr. Ramon Rhine, the University of California at Riverside professor, who served as a member of Karisoke's research advisory board, paid us a visit. He brought with him a student named Guy Norton, who had been managing the professor's baboon research center at Mikumi National Park in Tanzania.

Professor Rhine had helped place we students at Karisoke, and duly took a professional interest in our well-being and dedication to the research center's functions. By then, of course, he already knew of Carolyn's untimely departure, and had arrived under the threat of

what appeared to be Dian's ambush amid accusations against Stuart. We were happy at least for him to witness firsthand the uneasy circumstances this created. It was the dry season, but Dian was brewing up a storm of her own for us.

Neither we nor our trackers had found missing Nunkie, but when Guy Norton decided to take a hike up the Elephant Trail alone right behind camp he walked into the middle of this lost silverback's group practically right in our back yard. We were at least able to get updates on these wanderers before they drifted out of range again.

In a letter home to my parents on Wednesday, July 23, I summarized recent events:

> *Presently, we are anticipating Dian's return. She was supposed to have climbed two days ago, but has yet to materialize. She sent a telegram to the American embassy in Kigali saying that she would fly in on Monday for a brief visit, although she was at the time on tour in Japan. It seems it must be something rather urgent to have interrupted her Japanese tour to come here. Furthermore, it seems that she did not intend for us to know of her return Stuart just happened to be in Kigali at the time and heard from the embassy.*
>
> *Stuart has decided to return to the states at the end of this month. After a long period of indecision, he has decided that the gorilla business is not for him, and for that, I'm sure Dian will not forgive him. Also, Peter has been denied renewal of his authorization to work here in the park. This is the most likely reason for Dian's abrupt return visit since Peter sent her a letter in Japan concerning this problem. She may have returned to try and renew his authorization for him, but who knows?*
>
> *Speaking of surprises, Stuart just got back from Kigali and boy is he fit to be tied! He got a letter yesterday from his father whom Dian called, and claimed that Stuart has stolen $5,000 from camp along with 2 handguns and is going out on strange ventures with Jean-Pierre . . . She says she currently has lawyers looking into this.*

Needless to say, none of it is true, but it's this type of thing that makes Dian more than just a little bit irritating. I am certainly glad that Dr. Rhine was here to see this. Since Dian clearly has a split personality, it is rather difficult to try and explain her dark side to someone who has only seen her charming side.

At the time of Dian's expected arrival, Stuart and Peter went to Kigali to meet her. Peter needed to renew his visitor's permit to stay at Karisoke, and he thought that only Dian might be able to convince Benda Lema to authorize it. In Kigali, Stuart would also be able to talk with Dian in a forum outside of her domain at Karisoke. He was more than just a little concerned about where their relationship stood and decided to intercept her there to hash out any arguments in neutral territory. The three of us would soon learn that Dian had a different plan.

With Stuart and Peter away in Kigali on July 29, I spent the morning with Group 5, thinking back on how I danced for the camp staff the day Dian left, expecting never to see her again. With a sense of guilt, I reminisced about joking with the men and referring to Dian's departure day as the camp's *Siku ya Uhuru*, or Independence Day. Knowing that Stuart would be her liaison and correspondent as Karisoke's acting director, I had expected never again to communicate with Dian Fossey. The thought of her unexpected return was chilling, in light of all that had transpired. It occupied my mind all that morning, despite my attempts to lose myself in observations of the gorillas.

Group 5 was on the slopes of Mount Visoke, very near the Porter Trail when I found them at 10:00 A.M. It was the middle of the long dry season and the group was finishing a midmorning rest period under a rare cloudless sky. Effie cradled Maggie loosely in her arms, dozing at the center of the group in the warm sun. A breeze stirred the vernonia branches and whipped down into the lobelia fronds where the young ones chased each other in a game of gorilla slap-tag, grunting and chuckling in their guttural staccatos, *eh-eh-eh-eh-eh-eh-eh* . . .

The warmth made me lazy too, and I sprawled on my back across a hummock of soft gallium in the midst of the group, half closing my eyes and listening idly to the drone of insects interspersed with the soft belches and farts of a resting family of gorillas.

During the dry season, the Parc des Volcans is a beautiful and hospitable place. Rain is absent, and daytime temperatures climb into the seventies. From my vantage point that day, the verdant northerly peaks of Gahinga, Sabinio, and Muhavura looked like they were covered with green velvet spilling down their slopes into Rwanda on one side, and Uganda on the other. As the gorillas began to resume feeding, their dull munching sounds and placid belch vocalizations added to the serenity of a dry Virunga day.

When Group 5 began to move, I roused myself, noticing that they were edgy, scrambling in a silent jerky pace upslope as they looked backward toward the Porter Trail. When Icarus screamed, I jolted upright and heard the voices too.

Jonas, a self-employed tourist guide froze in his tracks behind a thicket. As I approached him, I could make out the figures of two khaki-clad white tourists cowering just off the Porter Trail twenty feet behind their guide. Jonas knew he wasn't supposed to disturb the research gorillas, but with a fat tip likely for the encounter, he couldn't resist bending the rules a little, so close to the trail he had to use anyway. Upon seeing me, Jonas slunk back to his patrons without a word and the trio of interlopers disappeared obediently up the trail.

I made a note of the intrusion and resumed my observations of Group 5, but just as the gorillas relaxed and resumed their feeding, an odd sound punctuated the drone of normal gorilla noises: *Ehht mwaaah . . .* It came again through the dull munching sounds of gorillas stripping and chewing wild celery: *"Ehht mwaaah . . . um waaah . . ."* Not a gorilla sound, but the sound of someone poorly trying to imitate a gorilla. A sound I'd heard before.

A chill ran up my spine. *How could Dian be here?* Stuart and Peter were not due back until much later, *if not tomorrow.* I looked toward the Porter Trail and saw the top of Dian Fossey's dark hair, turning right then stumbling left while she struggled to find a path through the thick weedy substrate. She approached slowly, awkwardly tripping over the undergrowth, *"Eht mwaah . . ."* When she came into the area of trampled vegetation where the gorillas rested, Dian paused and stared silently at the members of Group 5. Although I was in plain view of her, and we hadn't seen each other in five months, Dian didn't speak to me.

"Hello," I said, trying to hide my shock.

"As I was coming up the trail, I saw Ziz," Dian said, pointing to the female named Puck. "He's really getting big."

"Uh . . . that's Puck," I informed her, bracing myself for castigation. Puck had, in fact, been erroneously given her mythological male name by Dian when she originally mistook this gorilla's gender.

"I'm so out of touch with them." Dian said. "Really and truly. *Eht mwaaah . . ."*

I was surprised to see that my boss looked invigorated and refreshed. As the *National Geographic* producer Barbara Jampel had informed us, Dian had ended up in a hospital oxygen tent with pneumonia and bursitis after leaving camp in March. Now she was tan from her stranding in the Seychelles. *Did she actually relax there?* She had also put on a few pounds and was less sallow in the cheeks. I thought about her love for Pringles potato chips; her propensity for grease and salt in the junk food she loved must have been indulged with unlimited access stateside in Ithaca.

Dian's hair was different too. It had been neatly trimmed and now hung down in an even length to her shoulders. Even its color had changed. Instead of the dull dark ash brown with gray roots that I remembered, her hair was an even, henna-like auburn. A little playful, I thought. *Was she enjoying stateside? Was there a gentleman friend on the Cornell campus to inspire her whimsy?*

"Gorillas are the best. I'm so glad I chose them." Dian said. I remained silent, still wanting to enjoy a one-on-one conversation with Dian, but overwhelmed by the tense circumstances. "I visited Jane's chimps at Gombe when I first started out." She added, scowling with disapproval. "They're nothing like gorillas."

We talked awkwardly about gorillas versus chimps, and I wondered what Jane Goodall would have to say about Dian's gorilla elitism. I thought Dian was as uncomfortable near me as I was with her and our conversation soon dwindled to an uneasy silence while we both stared at the gorillas.

"How did you get here?" I asked. "Stuart and Peter went to Kigali to get you."

"I flew to Ruhengeri," Dian said, dryly. "I wanted to get to camp as quickly as possible and didn't want to wait around for anyone."

More silence.

"I found out what really happened to Kima," Dian muttered cryptically.

I knew Dian was waiting for my reaction, but I had learned my first week in camp that silence was often my best response to her. Instead, I pondered the meaning of her words; we all knew Dian's head porter, Gwehandegaza, had been keeping his boss informed in his own way via letters, but I wondered what this reference to her dead pet monkey meant. Gwehandegaza was essentially her paid informant, and the other camp staffers believed he would tell Dian anything just to be rewarded. Whether true or false, the man needed to maintain Dian's illusion that he had inside information, and because of this he was viewed with suspicion as untrustworthy by camp staff. This negative perspective of him inevitably spread to Karisoke students as well.

At last Group 5 began moving uphill and away from us. Thankful that I might have to leave Dian and the awkwardness behind, I feigned concentration on my note-taking and followed the gorillas onto a steeper upward slope. Without saying anything more, Dian moved back toward the Porter Trail, and I watched her back as she faded into the foliage to join her patient band of porters.

With the thought of Dian back at Karisoke, I wanted to stay with the gorillas and out of camp as long as possible that day, but by the time my boss moved on, I had already spent the typical four-hour time period with Group 5. It was really time for me to head up to camp too. I waited for the voices of Dian's entourage of porters to fade into the distance before leaving the gorillas and walking slowly back toward camp. I lingered, straining to hear Peter's and Stuart's voices, hoping they too, were returning now, up the Porter Trail somewhere behind me. Under the auspices of Dian's return, I did not want to be alone with her in camp.

The warm day cooled and the long shadow of Mount Visoke had crept over camp by the time I returned to my cabin. I felt the renewed aura of oppression at Karisoke with Dian's return. Camp staff sat with Dian's porters around the edge of the fire pit chattering and gesturing animatedly in Kinyarwanda. There was a lot of buzz in their voices, and tension hung with it in the air like the damp mist of the rainy season. I knew it was gossip about Dian, and the circumstances of her visit.

As I sorted through the day's notes and drew the paper with carbons through my Olivetti, Kanyaragana knocked on my door. His face was grave and I invited him in.

"*Iko lewa*," he said: *She's drunk.*

"What has she been doing?" I asked him, in Swahili. Kanyaragana sat down on the edge of my bed with his usual pleasant half-smile. He never really showed signs of anxiety, even in the most stressful situations. I asked him about Dian, and he told me that she immediately went to Kima's grave upon arriving in camp. There, she dropped to her knees and cried over her dead monkey for a long time. Afterward, she went into her cabin and began drinking . . . Johnnie Walker, Red Label. She'd had her porters carry a case of her favorite Scotch up when she climbed to camp.

"*Iko umusazi sasa?*" I asked about Dian's behavior using the Kinyarwanda word for "crazy" because my Swahili book omitted any such word. Kanyaragana said Mademoiselli was acting *umusazi*, and described how she later took a bottle of Primus out to the graveyard. As she trickled the beer on Kima's grave, Dian kept repeating, "Drink Kima . . . Drink."

I felt the hairs stand up on the back of my neck thinking of what we were in for with this visit from our boss, but Kanyaragana remained stoic as he relayed to me these details about her. He had worked for her most of the thirteen years since she'd founded the research center, and he had seen her at her worst. He had been fired by her and rehired more than once, and weathered every storm because jobs were almost nonexistent in Rwanda. Kanyaragana was a Fossey expert of sorts, and I sought some comfort in the fact that he had survived so many years with Dian, and remained calm even now.

Still, I anxiously waited for Stuart and Peter to return. Kanyaragana left my cabin and rejoined the other men all atwitter under the pall of Dian's return. When they soon left the campfire and disbanded, an eerie silence hung in the air in the growing shadows. While the light outside faded, I feared that my fellow students would not be returning at all that day. Without fond memories of interactions with Dian to reassure myself, and never having really developed any kind of rapport with her, I loathed being the only student in camp with her for the evening, especially under the current circumstances of her surprise return and present drunken status.

Thinking about what Kanyaragana had told me, I pondered what Dian might be doing in her cabin at the other end of camp. I locked my door. I felt exposed and began drawing the curtains of each window. As I did so, the dull thuds of hurried footsteps came up the trail. I froze to listen as voices joined the sound . . . right up to my door, followed by frantic knocking.

Despite their barrage of anxious questions, seeing Stuart and Peter again brought me a tremendous sense of relief.

"Where's Dian? What's she doing?" they asked, talking over each other.

The three of us moved to the campfire, which was still burning brightly although the porters had gone, and camp staff had returned to their cabin for the night. Huddled by the glowing flames, I told Stuart and Peter about my surprise encounter with Dian while I was with Group 5, and her cryptic remark about "knowing what really happened to Kima." Like children hearing ghost stories, they both listened intently as I recounted Kanyaragana's report of Dian drinking and mourning over her pet monkey's grave.

From the darkness at the other end of camp a light flashed and flickered. I had almost forgotten the telltale "ahem" that disclosed Dian's drunken state until I heard it again that night coming down the camp trail. The beam of Dian's flashlight bounced and jostled as it slowly drew closer, and we braced for confrontation.

The three of us stared quietly, as the figure of Dian staggered into the faint light of the campfire. The rested look I had seen earlier on Dian's face was gone. She had taken on more the look I remembered from my early days at Karisoke. Her hair was tousled and her puffy eyes twitched and squinted as she squared her shoulders to stand erect.

"Stuart . . . ahem . . . where are the guns?" she asked. I felt my skin crawl. After these five months, and all that had transpired, including the accusations she'd been making about Stuart, these were her first words to him. Stuart paused before responding.

"They're up at your cabin, Dian."

"Where are the fucking guns? I can't find them," Dian said dryly. Despite the silent standoff that followed, there was only one thing for Stuart to do. Still, I was amazed that he was bold enough to accompany Dian back to her cabin to find her pistols. Drunk or sober, she just plain scared me. Peter and I watched Stuart follow Dian back up the camp trail, and remained by the campfire a little longer, lamenting Dian's demeanor and the oppressive pall it cast over Karisoke again. Dian's contempt for us was truly in stark contrast to her need for us. What madness I thought it was when one's wants are diametrically opposed to one's needs, as I could see was the case with Dian and us. This lack of reasoning only added to my anxiety.

Eventually, Peter and I retreated to our own cabins. I pumped up my pressure lantern and ignited it. The bright glare made me feel exposed and I resumed my task from window to window, drawing the curtains tight. Having anticipated Dian resuming occupancy of the big cabin during her return visit, Stuart had planned to stay in the other half of my cabin. He had moved his things into the vacant side, and our living arrangement was much the same as it had been when Stuart and I shared this duplex during our first three months at camp, except he was now relegated to my old room.

As had become my habit, and in an effort to resume some normalcy, I rolled the triplicate typing papers and carbons into the Olivetti on my desk and sat to begin typing up the notes from that day's visit with Group 5. I knew that if we got through the night, Dian would want to be reading the latest gorilla notes over the next few days. That is, if we got through the night.

Normalcy wouldn't last long. My apprehensions were soon justified by the sound of a pair of boots frantically pounding down the trail. Without knocking, Stuart flung my door open, and I flushed at the sight of the look on his face.

"She's crucifying me!" he exclaimed. Stuart's eyes were wild and glazed. He had always been up for the task of anything Dian could deliver, but now, without even looking at me, he grabbed his backpack from the floor and began gathering his other things from around the room.

"What do you mean?" I asked.

"She wants to know where the guns are!"

"Why?"

"She's drunk and all she can say is, 'Where are the guns? Where are the fucking guns?' She's accusing me of stealing!" Without breaking stride, Stuart frantically scoured the cabin for his belongings and stuffed them, one after another, into his backpack.

"She's crucifying me!" he lamented, completely lost in his rant. "She's crucifying *all of us.*"

"Why does she want the guns?" I asked.

"I know what she's going to do. She's going to count the bullets . . . find one missing . . . and accuse me of shooting Kima." Stuart scarcely listened to me in the state he was in, and appeared more to be talking to himself as if thinking out loud.

"Is that what you think?"

"I don't know what she's going to do once she's convinced herself that I killed Kima." Stuart heaved his bulging backpack onto his shoulders and stood upright. He took a deep breath. "I tried to talk to her rationally, about camp, and what's been going on . . ." His eyes were wide and fixed staring into space. "And she just kept saying, *'Stuart, where are the goddamn guns? Give me the fucking guns!'*"

"Why? What's she gonna do with the guns?"

"Then I see a half-empty bottle of Johnnie Walker on the table." With a labored shrug, Stuart squared his loaded backpack, and grabbed the door latch. "I'm not gonna stay around here and find out."

At that, he disappeared into the darkness, the cabin's door slamming behind him. His quick heavy boot steps trudged around the cabin and faded down the trail into the forest. Stuart was gone.

At the edge of camp, the trail leading into the forest and down the mountain was poorly defined and intermingled with a cross-hatching of trails made by the buffaloes that foraged in the camp at night. There was no well-worn footpath in the series of small grassy meadows that led away from Karisoke to the narrow path down the mountain. During the daylight we used visual cues to find where the path picked up on the other side of each clearing. Certain trees or fallen logs served as indicators to guide the way to the next section of trail. As many times as I had been down the trail, there were points at which I sometimes strayed a little off the path and had to retrace my steps.

Field guides and tourist brochures report that Cape buffaloes are one of the most dangerous animals in Africa with numerous human deaths caused by them each year. Their forest cousins that grazed at night in the meadows in and around Karisoke have the reputation of being even more aggressive. Stuart was motivated with enough fear to flee down the mountainside in pitch darkness where pugnacious forest buffaloes filled the grassy clearings and flanked the trails like Cerberus at the gates of hell.

Stuart, the human buffer zone between me and Dian, was suddenly gone—the guy who had dealt with Dian so masterfully it seemed, and who had, with ease, achieved what I could not—Dian's acceptance, friendship, and support. I had originally wanted and expected that kind of friendly relationship with Dian, but after enduring her ceaseless hostility toward me, I found comfort in Stuart taking all of her attention, and marveled at their unflinching relationship. Stuart had not only won Dian over from the onset, he actually enjoyed his relationship with her, "But I still love the bitch," he had once said to me after an argument with Dian. Now Stuart was gone. Dian's brazen confidant, in a matter of moments, had been reduced to a frightened exile.

Feeling anxious and paranoid— and remembering Dian's nocturnal ambushing of our dinner gatherings—I secured the deadbolt on my door and went to each window checking again for gaps, making sure that not even the tiniest space remained to allow someone outside to see me. In the quiet that followed, I thought about what might be next for Peter and me. Dian had demanded her guns. *What would I do if I heard a gunshot in the dark?* I found myself listening keenly for any sounds. The bushbucks had long since ceased their dusk-time barking, and I could imagine the sounds of snorting forest buffaloes along the mountain trail as Stuart crashed down through the dark forest, looking for the bottom, and the solid ground of anywhere but Karisoke Research Center.

Selfishly, I was relieved that Peter's cabin was between Dian's and mine. *Wasn't she more likely to go to Peter next with any questions she might have?* Dian had known him much longer than me. Or maybe she'll just slip into a drunken slumber and by morning be hung over and less volatile. We could speak to her then, in the daylight. *But would she survive this night? Would any of us?*

Many times in the past Dian had simply ostracized her students, not speaking to them at all, but instead communicating by notes that

Kanyaragana or Basili delivered as if everyone at Karisoke lived miles apart. I found myself hoping for this and wishing Dian would slip quietly back to Cornell University to resume her attempt at an academic career, with only a note left behind.

I hadn't heard any footsteps approach, but my heart sank at the sudden sound of knocking on my door. A silent being waited there for my response. At first I remained quiet, pulse pounding in my ears. Terrible moments with gorillas had not been more frightful: neither Nunkie charging down the mountain screaming his deafening primal scream, nor Beetsme standing over me beating his chest in fury had been more disturbing.

"*Yesss?*" I said, trying to steady the tremor in my voice.

"*Mademoiselli anataka wewe.*" I recognized Kanyaragana's voice saying *Dian wanted to see me.* My heart sank, and a knot formed in my stomach. I had to pause for a few seconds letting my gut wrench and settle before opening the door.

"Why?" I asked in Swahili, slowly opening the door and looking for clues on Kanyaragana's face.

"*Sijui.*" Kanyaragana did *not know why.* His face was calm and his voice was normal, but just then he might as well have been Igor to Dr. Frankenstein. *Didn't Kanyaragana witness what had just happened between Dian and Stuart?* He doesn't speak English, *would he understand the context of their argument? Did he know Stuart had fled?* I tried to surmise all possible scenarios in my mind at once.

"*Stuart teremuka,*" I said, telling Kanyaragana that Stuart had *gone down the mountain.*

Kanyaragana stood waiting patiently for me in my doorway, but I hesitated to leave my cabin. *Would it be worse if I didn't go to her now? Would she just come down here?* I also didn't like the thought of sitting there, not knowing exactly where Dian was, or what she was up to. *Had she found a gun? Would she sober up and walk down later? Should I wait outside my cabin and ambush her?* My mind was racing.

"Where's Peter?" I asked Kanyaragana.

I felt a small sense of relief when Kanyaragana said Peter was with Dian, knowing that I wouldn't be dealing with her alone. I asked Kanyaragana what Peter and Dian were doing, but he said he didn't know.

With my thoughts jumbled, I followed Kanyaragana out into the darkness. His flashlight faintly illuminated the trail. As we neared Peter's cabin, buffalo snorted and trotted in different directions, their black hides camouflaging them against the night as always. At that moment, they seemed like a harmless sideshow compared to what I imagined lay ahead.

Kanyaragana and I passed Peter's cabin and it was dark. Up ahead, a light from Dian's house glowed ominously, and as we approached I stopped, straining to hear any sound. Kanyaragana slowed and turned to look back at me. His calm demeanor encouraged me onward. When we reached the steps to the cabin's back door, I paused again and listened, faintly hearing Peter's voice coming from Dian's bedroom, straining to hear any sign of conflict. Dian's weakened voice, barely audible, debilitated by alcohol and emotional exhaustion, emanated from within. Kanyaragana opened the door to the kitchen and I followed him inside. A glow from a Coleman pressure lantern in Dian's bedroom spilled out into the living and dining areas, washing the straw-colored floor in a fan of pale light. The rest of the large room was hidden in giant shadows.

Kanyaragana stayed in the kitchen while I moved from dining to living area, running a plan through my head of how to grab a gun from Dian's hand. Approaching the doorway to the bedroom, I could see the profiles of Peter and Dian, both seated on the floor. Their voices were quiet and calm. Dian's voice was weepy and she cleared her throat repeatedly with the faint "ahem" that confirmed she was still quite drunk.

I stepped into the light of the bedroom.

"Stuart's gone," Dian said, closing her eyes and shaking her head as if she was hearing voices and trying to ward them off.

"I know," I admitted, squatting on the floor next to Peter. "He came by and got his things." Dian opened her eyes wide. They were red and watery.

"He said I was *crucifying* him," Dian said, looking aghast at the very thought while staring beyond Peter and me. "Crucifying him! *Oya! Oya!*" Our boss squared herself a little and flushed with anger. "And he's taken things from camp. The binoculars are missing, and I can't find one of the Olivettis."

"He loaned one to Jean-Pierre," I said. "Jean-Pierre needed to type some letters and asked Stuart if he could borrow it."

"Do you know where the guns are?" Peter asked me, "Dian's been looking for them, and I don't know where they are." Because Stuart had been away so much lately, he had put me in charge of the guns and money, and I was quite familiar with what went where. Both guns and cash had always been as safe and secure as Dian had kept them, but she then sure seemed convinced otherwise.

"They're in their box," I said.

"We looked, and couldn't find them," said Peter, pointing to an open wooden box on the floor beside Dian. It was the cash box. I looked just past Dian into the shadows of the room, directly at the small wooden container tucked under the bedside table, against one wall within arm's reach behind Dian. Either in the emotionally charged chaos of the evening, or because Stuart didn't want guns added to the equation, the box remained closed and locked.

Quickly, I assessed the situation: Peter is here, Kanyaragana is in the other room, Dian is weak and intoxicated. I took the plunge.

"It's right there," I said, pointing just behind her.

Peter moved the lantern to illuminate the area by the bed as I crawled behind Dian and retrieved the box. Dian dragged the container in front of her and with the camp's ring of keys opened the small lock. As she lifted the hinged lid, I thought about what I would do if she picked up one of the guns. Instead, Dian only stared down at her pistols, one Walther and one Beretta. The bullets were there too, but Dian didn't count them.

Dian closed the lid of the box and stared at it. Peter and I watched awkwardly as Dian closed her eyes and shook her head slightly as if adjusting her thoughts.

"I'm going to have two of the men sleep here in the cabin tonight," she said, "so that I don't do anything crazy." Dian lifted her head and looked at Peter and me through red watering eyes. "So that I have *witnesses* that I don't do anything crazy."

Peter and I nodded and sat on the floor with Dian, trying to recall where items were that Dian had thought were stolen. Stuart may have left a pair of boots at Jean-Pierre's that he had forgotten to bring back on his last trip. He had also loaned a pair of binoculars to Jean-Pierre, but we hadn't considered them stolen.

Dian had gone "bonkers" as she called it, and now sat in the aftermath, near catatonic in her over-expenditure of emotions. Late into the night, Peter and I sat with Dian, reassuring her that things were okay, until the pressure lantern, on its last fumes, hissed and sputtered and dimmed.

TWENTY-TWO

DIAN'S FRIEND

The morning after Stuart's exile, I longed to climb down the mountain too, and wander off into the lowlands away from Karisoke, to the respite of Kigali and gracious embassy hosts. I wanted to *teremuka* as we learned to say, the Swahili word meaning literally "go downhill" and figuratively "get off the mountain." Stuart had gone *teremuka*. Part of me envied his escape. I had gone to sleep pondering how far our colleague had gotten in the darkness. No one set out from camp at night. It was crazy, but that's what he'd been driven to. I believed he must've eventually made it down the trail, *but where to then? And in the dark no less!* Bill and Amy were gone, and no one had yet taken occupancy of their metal hut, locked, secured, and guarded at the base of Mount Visoke. I surmised he was headed for

Jean-Pierre's *Plantation de Gasiza*, a long and tortuous hike across the lowlands, through the shambas, to the base of Mount Muhavura not far from the Ugandan border.

I wanted to linger in bed, dreaming of being *teremuka* with the rest of the world, but knew I needed to make an attempt to find Nunkie's Group before Dian asked me to. I had to pull myself together. That would be Dian's next big issue: *Where's Nunkie?* Despite being seen again in July, after his longtime status as missing, the silverback had continued to make himself scarce, skirting the higher elevations of Mount Visoke to avoid poachers and competition with other gorillas. With Stuart gone, I would have to be the one trying to keep up with this evasive silverback. His travails had kept him nervous and difficult to approach.

Dian had learned much about the formation of gorilla family groups from the irascible Nunkie. This silverback had first appeared in the Karisoke study range in 1972 as a lone male who didn't match any of the existing noseprints Dian had thus far collected. Until then, Dian had not known of a gorilla traveling by itself in the forest, and she was at first in disbelief when a student reported the interloper in the proximity of Group 5. Nunkie was alone, but not to be lonely for long. He had come a-courtin'.

While mighty Beethoven's females proved to be a challenge, Nunkie managed to lure away two consorts from the less-experienced Uncle Bert of Group 4. Within a year, two of Group 4's lower-ranking females, Papoose and Petula, jumped ship to run off with this bold new rogue. Within another year, Petula gave birth to a female, and Papoose next gave birth to a male. While Nunkie went on to take females from other groups, a new gorilla family had formed right in the Karisoke research range. Sort of . . .

Nunkie traversed in and out of our study range, an area of about twenty-five square kilometers. He had taken females, but he hadn't taken the choice feeding areas of the mountain's lower altitudes and saddle area surrounding camp, still held jealously by the other established silverbacks and their groups. Nunkie's struggles had left him protective and defensive, even to us well-intended researchers. Visiting him meant finding him, and finding him meant a hard climb up Mount Visoke, or well into Zaire, rewarded by repeated charges and spine-chilling screams. He stayed between me and his females, scarcely allowing me to see any other behaviors, or even glimpse and count his harem and offspring when I wasn't laid out on the ground whimpering respectfully.

But Dian would be featuring Nunkie in her next *National Geographic* article, and she needed someone to keep up with him for the most up-to-date data and his current story. Of course, Nunkie's travels into poacher area only fueled her fear that they would again make more casualties of her gorillas. With Dian back in camp, I knew best to make yet another foray out to Nunkie a top priority.

Young Toni would be my tracker that morning, and I joined him by the fire pit outside my cabin. In single file, we trudged along the trail toward the western end of camp, and Dian's cabin. I wondered what he had learned of the night before. Although my Karisoke Swahili had blossomed into a fluency, this young tracker still hadn't yet learned much of it to communicate in camp. The two of us walked in silence.

As we approached Dian's cabin, I scanned through the trees for any sign of her. I recalled her late mornings after a bender, when I waited outside to pick up the baby gorilla, until she unapologetically appeared at the door in her dingy men's long johns, bagging at the knees. Surely she had slept in late the day after last night's traumatic events. Aware of Toni's heavy footsteps, I tried to quiet mine, nearing the house to round the corner and slip away quietly toward the meadow beyond.

Tap. Tap. TAP!

Did I hear something? Keep moving Toni . . .

I tried to keep up the pace as we passed by the cabin, hoping I hadn't really heard the rapping, which shifted to the next window on the south end, where the trail ran right beside the house. *Tap tap tap!* A muffled voice followed, sounding through the glass. "John! John!"

There she was, reaching for the window latch and loosening it. I stopped, stifling a deep sigh. With a creaking sound, the frame opened on its hinges and Dian's head was in plain view.

"Uh . . . John . . . Are you heading out?" Dian asked in a soft, plaintive voice.

"Yes, Toni and I are on our way out to Nunkie's Group."

"Oh, good." A sunbeam through the hagenias shone directly on Dian's face and hair, and I was surprised to see she had regained the rested look I had seen when she first appeared on the trail the day before. She looked composed. Despite the late, anguish-filled night before, she had been up a while, and was already dressed in a clean flannel shirt. In the low-angled morning sun, her new hair color glowed, showing its reddish tint. From her open, white window frame, she looked like a quaint, and very tall, English country lady.

"I don't want to keep you, but . . . uh . . . could you come inside?"

"Um . . . yeah . . . sure." *What else could I say?*

Toni nodded and wandered ahead to the picnic table by the gorilla graveyard. I continued on around to the same side of the cabin, and Dian greeted me at her door, beckoning me inside.

I felt the same nervous tension around her I always had, since meeting her for the first time in Kigali—on guard and cautious of what was next. Dian offered me a seat in her living area, leaving the door open to the warming outside air.

"Kanyaragana," she summoned, in her emotionless breathy voice, "bring John some coffee." Her devoted houseboy, back in his old routine, peeked his head around the kitchen doorframe with an amused and knowing smile; he had seen and heard so much drama unfold from his view from that kitchen. I sat, leaning my panga on the goatskin chair and sliding my backpack to the floor, while Dian remained standing.

"I'm just getting some things together before I leave again." A few boxes were in the middle of the floor, papers stacked here and there. "You know that gold piece I bought at the craft shop in Kigali?"

"Oh, yeah." I sure remembered because I had pointed it out to her.

"Well, I had that wrapped in a tissue, you know, for safe-keeping in my purse, and, well, I ended up losing it."

"Oh no, I'm sorry to hear that." Funny she should bring that up just then, but I legitimately felt bad for her, knowing it had been a gift for someone.

"I know I must've just thrown it out somewhere on my trip back home, thinking it was just trash." Perhaps she was thinking one of us had found it there in the cabin after she left.

Kanyaragana handed me a steaming cup of coffee with milk, and I accepted a cigarette from Dian as she stretched her pack of Impalas and matches out toward me. She remained standing and turned away to stare out the window as I lit up.

"I know I was making false accusations against Stuart," she said.

I guessed she wanted a reaction from me, but as usual, I kept my poker face.

"I just wanted to pin something on him because I know he killed Kima."

I was surprised and a little impressed by her admission of guilt, but remained dumbfounded by her lingering accusation.

"I saw Kima when she got sick, and I went with Stuart to take her to the vet," I said, surprised she didn't have direct questions for me about the details of that event—I could tell her the whole damn story.

"I know he killed her through neglect."

Dian was calm and collected, but I dreaded where she was headed with this. *Was she waiting for me to agree? To incriminate Stuart somehow? Spill my guts with some revelatory news she hadn't yet heard?* I sipped my coffee as Dian moved toward the window, staring out to where Toni waited at a table near the gorilla graveyard.

"I can't stand walking around camp because of all the memories," she said. I felt more awkwardness with these words. "Without Kima, there's nothing here for me anymore. She was *everything* to me." There was strong emotion rising in her voice, but she tempered it.

I didn't facilitate a dialogue with her on this, instead, just listening to her as she seemed to be justifying her reasons to no longer be at Karisoke. Finally she changed direction, and focused on a piece of paper on a desk beneath the window.

"I know you tried to help Cindy and I am really and truly grateful for that. I typed up instructions for feeding her and the chickens." She handed me the paper. As she paraphrased the instructions, I read along, guessing what the camp staff must have thought of Cindy's dietary rations, indulgent relative to their own meager fare. The men were paid half the cost of Cindy's daily meat, powdered milk, margarine, and eggs.

Cindy:
200 RWF [Rwandan francs] of meat twice a week
About 400 RWF of rice once a week
One tin of Nido [powdered milk] once a week
One tin of Blue Brand Margarine once a week
Seven eggs a week

If Cindy is going to pull through this condition, her diet is going to have to be improved over what she's been getting in the past 4 months.

In the morning the man fixes her food, and now with margarine.

In the afternoon I give her a light meal with some glucose in it (bottle is in kitchen) and in the evening before I go to bed another bowl of milk mixed up with an egg and some bread.

She is eating 4 times a day now, and acts as though she really wants the food.

I am putting a combination of medicine (in dining room) on her back and Especially Spectrocin M. Same combination of medicines on her legs.

Please don't leave her out in the rain, and if you have any extra time, she loves to play and chase sticks, etc.

Chickens:
50 RWF of corn twice a week usually
20 RWF of mtama [sorghum]
I mix rice in their corn box.

One glance at these instructions and I guessed at why Cindy's weight had diminished. The men in camp were paid one hundred francs a day. Cindy, just a dog to them, was eating twice that amount in her food bowl. The meat, powdered milk, margarine, and eggs were luxury items to the locals. In a country where beans, rice, and potatoes were the mainstay most could afford, the men must have been hard-pressed to place delicacies into a dog's dish rather than their own.

To oversee this food and medicine regime, I would have to be vigilant or do it myself. I would apply the medicine, but I couldn't feed Cindy four times a day when I was out in the field with gorillas. Cindy's daily diet, like Kima's routine of feeding and brushing must have evolved as part of Dian's raison d'être while her number of regular visits to the gorillas dwindled down to nothing. In depending on her, Dian's pets made her feel good about herself. I was surprised to learn years later than Dian always wanted to have children, that she always envisioned getting married and having a family. Somehow, despite her parents' divorce, her father's suicide, and her unhappy childhood, Dian thought she would be part of a family of her own.

Now in her forties, as despair must have replaced hope, pets like Cindy and Kima had become her family. The gorillas too, had become her extended family, but Dian no longer made the trek to see them, instead living with them vicariously through the notes of the interloping, but necessary, students she allowed into her sanctum.

As I read over these instructions, the sound of brisk boot steps rounded the corner of the cabin, approaching at a fast clip along the outside wall. Dian turned to see. The top of a white man's light brown hair bounced past the high bay of windows along Dian's living room. I couldn't see well, from my seated position, but Dian did from where she stood. Her reaction was sudden and violent.

"*OYA! OYA! OYA!*" Dian wailed, the Rwandan word for "No!"

As the figure rounded the next corner and approached the open door, Dian rushed to slam it shut. "*OYA!*" She wasn't fast enough.

"Whaaa . . . ?" Ian Redmond couldn't finish his words as his big grin turned to a look of shocked puzzlement when the door slammed his shoulder. Dian turned her face and backed away, holding her hand out as if the young man was a flame too hot to approach.

Ian stepped farther inside, cheeks flushed from the hike, mouth open in bewildered astonishment at Dian's behavior. Recently in from England for a brief stint training park guards at the base of the mountain, he had obviously planned a happy surprise reunion with Dian. But she was hardly receptive. Standing there, he looked like an English schoolboy that just got busted for troublemaking.

"*Ian, you know how I feel!*"

"What did I do?"

"You joined THEM!" Dian turned to spit on the floor.

"Them?"

"*OYA!*" Dian turned away again, wincing as if in pain.

"I didn't *join* anybody." Ian stood half inside as Dian laid into him about working with her archnemeses Amy Vedder and Bill Weber after they had set up their own camp at the base of the mountain for gorilla tourism, in direct conflict with Dian.

"Dian . . . c'mon . . ." Ian attempted a smile. "I was just trying to help our furry friends."

In the silent awkward standoff that followed, Dian kept her face turned away from Ian, who stood frozen in the doorway. I wished I were out the door and off to Nunkie's Group with Toni.

Finally Ian spoke.

"I knew you were back, and I just came up to see if there was anything I could do to help you."

Dian turned to look at his face.

"*Eht mwah, humwaaah . . .*" Dian chided in her gorilla language, "I was *sooo* disappointed in you, Ian. *Really and truly.*"

"But if you want me to go, I will."

Dian slumped into the chair behind her, keeping her eyes on Ian, sizing him up.

Slowly, Ian walked farther into the house, as if the wild animal in the room had been tamed, his eyes beginning to wander around the living area, a look of nostalgia on his face.

"I see you still have my mobile," he said, pointing to a cluster of tin can lids hanging from a stick suspended from the ceiling.

Dian's face softened. "You gave that to me for Christmas."

Ian smiled.

Dian turned and pointed to a small framed card on the wall with a picture of mountains and a short saying. "I still have that too."

Ian recited it for her: "*When one is in the mountains, one forgets to count the days.*"

"I've always found that to be true," Dian said, managing a smile. Ian's foot was more than just in the door, it was right back into Dian's heart.

"Oh Ian . . . how's your hand?"

"It's alright, I suppose." Ian raised his left arm so Dian could better see his hand.

"Let me look at it." Dian reached out, and Ian moved into the living area to sit down across from her and me. I had heard about this injury, and watched as Dian examined it. His wrist had been mangled, and a heavy scar ran from it up into his palm. Dian ran her fingers over the scar, examining it thoughtfully, flexing his hand to judge the movement. Two years earlier, while out cutting traps for Dian, Ian had run into poachers. One had punctured his wrist with a spear before fleeing, badly severing tendons and nerves. I knew Dian saw Ian's wound as the ultimate symbol of devotion and dedication to her cause.

"We captured some poachers after that." Dian said, grinning eerily.

"Yes . . ." Ian replied.

"I wasn't holding the pliers . . ." Dian continued grinning, partially crossing her eyes with a sinister demented look. Ian grew quiet and I joined him in his uneasiness. Dian was telling something I thought I wasn't supposed to know. But by then I'd heard the stories of Dian with the local *Chef des Brigades*, Paulin Nkubili, a sort-of sheriff from Ruhengeri, torturing poachers. Someone had reputedly used pliers to squeeze fingertips to get these men to give names of their accomplices.

"Remember Munyarukiko?"

Ian stayed quiet, letting Dian do the talking.

Dian sneered, with a sinister grin. "He died." She held the demented look, giving me flashbacks of the night before. Ian remained awkwardly quiet and stared at the floor.

By that time, I had heard the hearsay of Dian asking her head porter Gwehandegaza to use *sumu* on her most reviled enemy poacher, Munyarukiko. Now the evidence was before me. The camp staff told me that when this poacher died of natural causes, Gwehandegaza quickly accepted full credit for his death, telling Dian that he took care of Munyarukiko, as she had requested. No wonder she was devoted to this head porter of hers whom the rest of us, including camp staff, mistrusted. The men said Gwehandegaza was then paid his ill-gotten gains for this perceived service. He well knew how to maneuver and extract from his boss. She had even bought him the moped he used to travel into Kigali for us on market days.

And so it came to be that Dian, in her own mind, had taken a contract out on a Rwandan enemy. And she was proud of it. Her happiness to be a hit-woman troubled me further. Our camp director, in effect, showed she was capable of contract murder, and thought that she, in fact, had carried one out.

Now Ian, shifting in his seat, seemed as uncomfortable as me. In the awkward silence that followed, Dian changed the subject to current affairs, bringing her long-lost friend up to date on her plans to return to the States, opinions on the present state of Karisoke, and her resentment of the neighboring Mountain Gorilla Project. Intermittently she playfully chided Ian with gorilla sounds: *eht mwah . . . huummwah . . .* just to remind him of how disappointed she had been in him.

While the two were catching up, Dian let me rejoin Toni, still waiting patiently outside, and the two of us headed into Zaire and the upper slopes of Mount Visoke to search for Nunkie's Group again. I knew I was in for another long day in the field, with a hard climb ahead, and an irascible silverback screaming and charging at me if I found him, but I felt relief walking out of Karisoke for the day, thankful that Ian provided some new distraction for Dian.

Toni and I failed to find Nunkie on our hike, instead running into the silverback Peanuts and his Group 4 high on Mount Visoke. With our delayed start and long climb, we didn't return to camp until nearly sundown. I expected Dian to be frantic at our late return, but instead she was in high spirits. In the aftermath of Mademoiselli's volatile return to camp, combined with Stuart's unexpected flight, she must have felt like she did after Carolyn left, worried about what was being said about her in the civilized world below. *Who has Stuart spoken to by now? What has he told them?* Same as then, she hosted a damage-control dinner for Peter and me—with her newly redeemed Ian included in the feast. I surmised this was *her* displacement behavior, her way to make things feel better in camp, as if nothing was wrong and all was jolly-good, even rapport with us students. Dian's life and work had become a cycle of angry outbursts and emotional breakdowns, fueled by intolerance and paranoia, followed by damage control to the best of her ability. Like faithful dogs, we students were at least in it for the food. And the beer!

Kanyaragana brought Peter, Ian, and me cold Primus, while Dian emerged from her bedroom where she'd downed another shot of Johnnie Walker Red Label from the bottle on her desk. Her characteristic throat-clearing, "ahem" gained frequency with every return visit to the bedroom and in direct proportion to her increasing inebriation.

"You *guuuys* . . . Ian . . . it's so good to see you again! Ahem. *Reeeally* and *truuuly!*" she exulted. While we chowed down on hot plates of spaghetti, Dian began telling us about her trip to Japan, where she had been treated like a celebrity.

"Before they showed the film, I gave a short talk at the podium, and . . . you guys, they were so nice to me . . . everyone clapping and cheering, and the Japanese are so polite. *Reeeally* and *truuuly!* Bowing and nodding to everything."

I wanted to ask if Peter and I were shown in the film, but she never mentioned this. Her effusive soliloquy soon took on a somber tone, as she described the footage.

"When they showed the baby, after Icarus nearly killed her . . ." Dian adopted a dramatic expression looking toward the ceiling, pausing until water welled up in her eyes—*willing* it, I thought. Peter, Ian, and I grew quiet until Dian finished describing the film, and I flashed back to those nightmarish moments in the hagenia tree when Dian literally pulled the baby from the clutches of the other gorillas.

"*Ahem* . . . I *know* she wanted to be a gorilla again," Dian surmised with a swallow of beer at the end of her story.

When Kanyaragana asked in Swahili if I'd like some more food, Dian began to translate for me.

"John speaks Swahili now." Peter interjected.

"*Eht mmmwaaahhh* . . ." Dian growled, scowling at me. I knew she had struggled with learning to communicate with her staff for years, so I didn't show her my new skills. Instead, she changed the subject.

"You guys, because word is spreading from the base of the mountain . . ." Dian took a deep breath, and continued in a normal tone, "that I tried to kill Stuart, I'm going to have to be on my best behavior during the rest of my stay."

None of us knew quite how to respond to this, and we remained silent in the awkwardness, knowing her man Gwehandegaza must have already gotten word to her with something to this effect, whether factual or fabricated.

"Now, you guys, back in the States, I've had someone helping me," she continued, "and they tell me that sometimes, sometimes you have to step outside yourself." She gestured her right hand out to her side, "and look back at yourself to see how you're acting." *Was she referring to the advice of a psychotherapist? It's about time*, I thought, seeing the blatant irony in Dian giving *us* advice on how to keep one's bad behavior in check.

Ian stayed overnight in my cabin, and made the hike down the mountain the next morning, to resume his temporary stint training new park guards. During her remaining days in camp, Dian busied herself in her cabin, placated by my daily attempts to locate Nunkie, and my observations of Group 4. Each night after my long hikes with one of the camp's gorilla trackers, she beckoned me into her cabin for news, handing me a tall cold Primus. The alcohol did help dull the angst in the room, but there was a lot of angst to dull. Usually, I only had news of old gorilla trails and maps of former nest sites. Peter continued his daily visits to Group 5, and Dian interacted very little with him. I had obviously been moved up the ranks in favor, but felt very uncomfortable in that spot, knowing how quickly her favor could turn, and how vehement it could become. I was well aware by then that those closest to her were the biggest targets.

The day before she departed, Dian was happy when I brought back news of a long encounter with Nunkie's Group, and a report of all of those gorillas being in good health, despite being deep into Zaire where they were vulnerable to poachers. That same night, Mademoiselli took a break from packing to visit me in my cabin. Her all too familiar and distinct, *"ahem"* gave away her drunken state before she even knocked on my door. Seeing she was tipsy but composed, I let her inside. Cracking a smile, she stood in front of my desk where I resumed a seat at my typewriter.

"Ahem . . . I've decided to take Cindy back with me," she said. "I don't know why I didn't think of it before!"

"Well, I guess that *is* a good idea . . ." I wanted to say more, to converse with her, but the fear of castigation I developed from my first days with her remained.

"There's nothing left here for me now." Dian's tone turned somber. "And, I want you to know, I really appreciate all you've done." Again, I didn't know what to say. As hard as it had been to take all her berating, it felt just as hard to deal with this semblance of appreciation, especially on the heels of her going "bonkers" just days before. I knew better than to trust her.

Dian held out her left hand, stretching it toward me. The awkwardness for me was overwhelming, but I had to act. Sheepishly, I took her hand in mine. What I thought would be a handshake became a handhold . . . as she lingered, locking eyes on mine. I wanted to look away.

"I want you to know that I am your friend," Dian said. Continuing her stare, water began welling in her eyes. She was waiting for my response. The woman who stole film, read our mail, tortured poachers, and took out contracts on enemies was asking me to be her friend. Does she really mean *friend*? I needed to respond in some positive way, if only as displacement behavior. I had half planned this upon her departure, and now needed to follow through to ease the awkwardness.

"I have something for you," I said, rising to release her hand. "It's my watercolor painting of Bonne Année." Like that bowl of coleslaw months before, it was a sacrificial appeasement to the ruling goddess. I had rolled it into a paper tube for transport and handed it to her.

"Ohhh . . . John, thank you so much!" Her ensuing glee only made things tougher for me. "Really and truly, I want you to know that I

believe you tried to help Cindy. And I also want you to know that you can come back to Karisoke anytime you want."

She paused. I froze. This was her ultimate gift, permission to come to Karisoke. Really, it was all she had to give—the rare gift of Karisoke, the Virungas, and mountain gorillas. The mountain gorillas were *hers* to give.

"I'm going to leave my address with you." She lifted a pen from my desk and began writing on a piece of my field note paper. I watched as she scrawled her name and the address of Langmuir Lab at Cornell University.

"Shit *merde!*" Dian muttered, crossing out some letters before finishing.

When she handed the paper back to me, I saw she had automatically started to write her Karisoke address, B.P. 105, Ruhengeri, as she must have done for the last thirteen years.

With that, she seemed satisfied of her visit. We said our goodbyes while she fumbled to click on her old duct-taped flashlight, and headed out into the darkness. Her faint *"ahems"* became fainter as the wobbling beam of her flashlight moved up the trail like a fallen star bouncing through the forest.

TWENTY-THREE

GORILLA MURDER

The next morning, Dian departed with her usual band of porters, this time with the faithful Cindy at her side. As I was pulling on my rubber rain pants for a visit with Group 4, I heard the chattering throng trudge by my cabin. I peeked out one window, just to verify that Dian was really leaving. As the porters' voices finally faded, Kanyaragana appeared at my doorway, lowering a cardboard box from his head to my floor with a loud clink of glass cargo inside—the eight empty Johnnie Walker bottles Dian consumed during her five-day visit. He wanted to store them with me, to later take for water vessels at his home off the mountain. Stunned by the quantity, I had to know.

"Did she drink all of these while she was here this time?" I asked in Swahili.

"*Ndio!*" Kanyaragana replied, with the affirmative.

I let him in and helped him maneuver the box onto a high shelf.

Outside, we heard Peter shouting something from his cabin. In no time, he was striding briskly down the camp trail, arms flailing in exasperation.

"Fuck it!" he shouted, loud and clear.

"What?" I asked. "What happened?"

"She did it again! She did it again!"

"Did what?"

"She stole my goddamn film!"

Peter clenched his jaw in frustration, tempering the anger. Dian's departure, just moments before, had made him think to check that his most recent exposed film rolls were still in his cabin. They were gone. After venting his anger at this new turn of events, Peter stormed off to Group 5. Stunned by the news, but relieved to have Dian gone again, I decided to take the day off—another little *Siku ya Uhuru* for me.

The next day, I got back early from a brief visit to Nunkie's Group, although tired from the hike up Mount Visoke, and an afternoon of Nunkie's nervous screams and charges. I sought refuge in the camp's tranquility in the wake of Dian's departure, enjoying the warm cloudless weather of the long dry season. My reverie was short-lived, when by 5:30 P.M., camp curfew, Peter had still not returned. Group 5 hadn't been far from camp as of late, and that made the circumstances even more odd. As it began to grow dark, I really began to get worried, and pondered getting trackers together for a search party. Finally I heard Peter's footsteps outside my door. They were rapid and uncharacteristic, with a sense of keen urgency.

"Everybody down by the fire!" he shouted in Swahili, "*Tugende! Sasa!*"

I immediately stepped out of my cabin as Peter waved his arms for us to assemble.

"Marchessa's dead!" he told us, still out of breath from his return hike. "Marchessa *kufa!*" he repeated for the men.

My first thought was poachers, but I waited to hear him describe how he hadn't seen the old female Marchessa in the course of his four-hour visit. Then, just before he departed, aggressive vocalizations from the young silverback Icarus led him to a grisly scene—Icarus beating his chest, hooting and pouncing on Marchessa's nearly lifeless form. All this while her mate, the lead silverback Beethoven, sat idly feeding nearby. The old matriarch soon took her last breath and was dead. We ended the night sending a messenger down the mountain to summon porters for the old gorilla's body the next morning. I volunteered to take it into Ruhengeri for a necropsy.

Peter said that upon arrival that morning, the group was feeding quietly near the night nests they had slept in the night before. As usual, Peter noted each member as he encountered them over his usual visit.

"A couple of hours in, I knew I hadn't seen Marchessa yet, but I didn't think too much about it until it got later," Peter said.

As the hours passed, and it grew closer to the end of his typical four-hour visit, he became concerned that he still hadn't seen the old female.

"I wanted to at least make a note of her being there, you know. I couldn't just leave without having seen her."

By mid-afternoon, Peter heard Icarus emit an unexpected sequence of hoots with chest-beats, typical of an encounter with another silverback or group. Drawn to the ruckus, he found Marchessa immobile, splayed on her back under a vernonia tree, Icarus standing in a domineering strut-position next to her. Stunned by the scene, Peter had to move in close to see if the old female was alive. He could see that her eyes were glazed and unfocused, but she was breathing in labored gasps. As Peter pondered the macabre sight, Icarus suddenly grabbed the old female with one mighty hand, and dragged her fiercely from under the tree, out into the trampled clearing. Astonished, Peter couldn't discern what was happening.

"Then Icarus just rushed in again and pounded his fists on Marchessa's chest."

"What did Beethoven do?" I asked about Marchessa's mate, in disbelief of what I was hearing.

"Only when he saw Icarus try to drag Marchessa again did he rush in on Icarus and stop him," Peter explained, "but when Icarus beat her with his fists, he didn't react at all." Icarus, Peter explained, vocalized his onslaughts with train-grunting, the sound usually made in association with sexual interest and intercourse by gorillas.

During the mayhem, Marchessa's infant son, Shinda, moved in to nurse on his dying mother, rushing away between Icarus's repeated onslaughts.

The men and I were chilled by Peter's story, and sat listening in the growing darkness by the campfire with mouths and eyes agape.

"I basically saw her take her last breath." Peter added, describing it as one big congested exhale. "After that, I could see she wasn't breathing anymore."

Peter had continued to observe the raw scene, while Shinda continued his sad efforts to nurse from his dead mother between Icarus's beatings. Marchessa's mate Beethoven permitted the younger silverback's onslaught, only intervening when Icarus made repeated attempts to move the body. Only when darkness was imminent did Peter finally break away from the bizarre, tragic scene to return to camp.

The shocking story left us all stunned where we sat around the fire. Peter and I discussed the meaning of what happened, and what needed to be done next. *Had Marchessa been sick?* She was fine the day before. *What brought this all about?* We decided a necropsy would be needed to determine the real cause of death. Perhaps she was sick, and Icarus finished her off. Perhaps not. Before turning in, we made arrangements with the men to summon porters the next morning to carry Marchessa's body off the mountain. I volunteered to drive the corpse into Ruhengeri in the camp's Volkswagen bus. Dr. Vimont had already shown so much interest and support of Karisoke and the mountain gorillas with his rescue of Bonne Année, we hoped he would be willing to perform the postmortem.

The next morning Peter and I hiked to where he left Group 5 the day before. Marchessa's lifeless body lay in the middle of a clearing trampled by the group's extended presence in one place around her lifeless form. Mountain gorillas always move on to a fresh feeding site daily, but not this time, their cohesive bond being so strong. Remains of their night nests revealed that they had even nested around Marchessa's body, confounded and stalled by her immobility in death.

The old female had been dead for nearly eighteen hours, but within minutes, Icarus resumed the onslaught Peter had described from the day before. The young silverback began his emotional series of hoots, rising in crescendo. While beating his chest and thumping his voice into a sharp staccato, he rushed in and pounced on Marchessa's flaccid belly. He then simply sat at her left side, staring blankly down at her body as if looking for a sign of life, utterly perplexed by her unresponsiveness.

Moments later, Marchessa's three-and-a-half-year-old son Shinda strutted downslope, approaching his dead mother to within inches and joined Icarus in staring at the cadaver's sunken face. Shinda then moved to Marchessa's right breast, whimpered lightly and began suckling. His older half-sister Poppy approached, and began peeling back Marchessa's lips, examining the inside of her mouth. I thought this was a rare opportunity for the curious Poppy, because no living gorilla would allow such invasiveness. Poppy, being shy but curious, began probing gingerly, as if Marchessa could wake up at any moment, but eventually became bold enough to use her finger to pick and eat pieces of vegetation from Marchessa's teeth, as if grooming.

Shinda continued to suckle for over three minutes, until interrupted by little Canstbee, who scampered over to initiate play. Shinda shrugged him off and stared into Marchessa's face, with Poppy still picking her teeth. They were like unsupervised children at an aunt's funeral. Beethoven and the other members of the group continued to feed, occasionally pausing to rest, or look downslope toward Marchessa's body.

Icarus, still staring at the body he had assaulted, resumed the same train-grunting, or copulation vocalization, which Peter had witnessed the day before. Within minutes, the young female Tuck strutted downslope and solicited Icarus with a sexual posture. Icarus obliged, with a brief copulation before resuming his fixation on Marchessa, at one point train-grunting again, and laying his chin on her motionless chest.

A few minutes later, Icarus again began his hoots, beating his chest and pouncing on Marchessa, scaring Shinda away. He repeated this onslaught four more times within the next thirty minutes, only to return to the body as if dumbfounded. Most of the group was far less interested, and continued feeding on vegetation beyond that which had been trampled. Even Shinda fed nearby, but soon resumed suckling from his mother, switching frequently from breast to breast as he was apparently no longer getting milk. Cantsbee made several more attempts to play with Shinda as he suckled, but his playmate only ignored him. At one point, Shinda tried to force his head under his mother's left arm as it lay across her neck, as if he wanted to be held. The arm, by then stiff with rigor mortis, did not yield, and Shinda resigned to himself laying his head on her chest.

It was 10:00 A.M. when our group of porters arrived up on the Porter Trail about twenty meters away. Beethoven screamed and rushed down toward them as the rest of the group fled upslope, except for Icarus and Shinda, the two most interested in the cadaver, but alerted by Beethoven's alarm. During such alarms, an infant would naturally go to its mother, but Marchessa was of no more use to her Shinda. When the porters hid themselves and remained quiet, Group 5 soon returned. They would not be able to move in until the group moved on. Icarus once again hooted and pounced on Marchessa. Poppy resume her exploration of Marchessa's mouth and was joined by Cantsbee and his mother, Puck, and another juvenile female, Muraha. Minutes later, Poppy, who had been so cautious at first, seemed finally to realize just how inanimate Marchessa was and slapped the body's chest before boldly walking across her body. She then, like Icarus, beat her chest with her small fists and pounced on Marchessa before laying herself across the belly, something she would never have dared do when Marchessa was alive.

By then, Peter and I were waiting for the group to move on. They couldn't remain there indefinitely. We wanted to see if the group would soon move off and allow us to move in and retrieve the body, but they had settled in for their midmorning rest period, and we would have to wait them out. Meanwhile, Muraha started grooming Marchessa's belly, now beginning to bloat in the warm air. Shinda made another attempt to suckle before trying again to squeeze under his mother's stiff arm. Icarus stayed near the body, frequently exchanging belch-vocalizations with Beethoven, still settled into the midmorning rest with the others.

Finally, just before noon, the group grew hungry again and began to move away into fresh forage. Shinda stared into Marchessa's face one last time, made one more vain attempt to nurse, before scampering on to join the group, moving out of view. Tuck and little Cantsbee were the last to remain behind with Icarus as he charged roughshod one more time over Marchessa's distended belly, as if he could do more harm. Only after Tuck and Cantsbee moved on toward the others, did the young silverback leave the scene of the crime.

When the group was out of sight, Peter and I quickly ushered the porters in, covered Marchessa's body with a blanket and carried her out to the Porter Trail. Our efforts did not go unnoticed. Beethoven and Icarus both caught site of the porters, and let out their terrifying screams, accompanied by several bluff charges in the thick vegetation just uphill from us. The porters quickly carried Marchessa's body out to the Porter Trail.

In the clearing, a couple of porters began whacking at the bases of young saplings, felling them easily, deftly trimming away the tops and branches, to create the sturdy poles and cross-pieces for the stretcher. Other porters identified sturdy vines nearby, and yanked them from the shrubs, quickly stripping them of their leaves in one swoop of their toughened hands. These they wrapped around the poles, lashing cross-bars to the makeshift stretcher with great dexterity, forming supports for the heavy gorilla body. I had seen the locals below carrying their injured, sick, and dead this way, and was amazed by these men's skill.

Before laying Marchessa onto the contraption, Nameye surprised me with an earnest plea. He said the men had asked that a photo be taken with them and Marchessa. Struck by Nameye's pleadings, I complied with the strange request. As I pulled the camera out of my backpack, the men propped Marchessa up in a seated pose and gathered around her as if she was some dearly departed family member. The macabre scene was also reminiscent of colonial safari photos of wild game trophies.

Although the men would never see this photo, they were satisfied, and lashed Marchessa's wrists and ankles securely to their stretcher before hefting her above their heads like pallbearers. Peter moved on to Group 5 to continue his observations as I followed behind the porters, once again awed by their strength and nimbleness despite their heavy burden on the tortuous trail.

The day's task would take too long for me to return to Karisoke before dark, so my plan was to drive to Jean-Pierre's castle after the postmortem procedure. I knew I'd be welcome there for at least a cold Primus and a place to sleep.

Word had already spread of the day's event, and as soon as our entourage emerged from the forest at Dian's parking spot, locals moved in for a look at a dead gorilla, pointing and chattering. The porters slashed the ties holding the corpse's wrists and ankles, and lifted it into the side door of the bus, sliding it onto the floorboards. As I could see others trotting in from the surrounding shambas I jumped into the driver's side and cranked the engine. I grew irritated as men, women, and children already crowded the way in front of me, slowing me as I lurched down the stony road. Everyone wanted a look, and many tapped on the sides of the vehicle as I slid through the throng, trying to pick up speed.

My irritation turned to exasperation as two men insisted on blocking my way, one waving frantically at me as he held the other's arm. His partner appeared solemn, by contrast, staring glumly, as the animated one swung him around to my window, shouting in Swahili.

"Hospitali! Daktari! Iko mgonjwa!"

"Oya!" I shouted back, the Kinyarwanda word for *no*. It was almost noon, and I just wanted to get moving out of that crowd and down the road.

"Iko zamu! Zamu kwa motokari!"

Ugh! It was Dian's *zamu*. Our *zamu*. The local man Dian paid a stipend to for guarding Karisoke's VW bus.

"What's wrong with him?" I asked, forced into stopping the car, suspicious that they were just taking advantage of me for a ride into town. I was not putting them in the back with a dead gorilla. I didn't even want to open the door again with so many people around.

In broken Swahili, the two men explained that an argument had turned into a fight the night before, while drinking pombe at a local hut. In the melee, the antagonist speared our zamu in the back. Spears were common weapons in the shambas of rural Rwanda, with each household having one or more on hand for defense, just in case. Like guns and knives back home, they could do lethal damage in a drunken brawl. Unconvinced of the severity of the injury, I hesitated. Locals might say anything for the rare ride into Ruhengeri. Seeing the doubt on my face, the flustered attendant spun our zamu around and lifted up his shirt, revealing a long deep gash in his right erector spinae muscle, the large loin along the right side of his vertebra. Shocked silent, I could only stare, the gaping wound was the width of a two-and-a-half-inch spearhead, sliced deep into the dark red muscle, like a slab of meat in a butcher's cooler. It was unquestionably severe and in need of sutures and medication.

"Okay," I relented, and they rushed around to the side door. As the zamu's helper slid the door open, Marchessa's body was exposed again to the onlookers. This new group gasped at the sight, stumbling backward in shock. I urged the men into the car quickly, the friend helping the zamu over the body and onto the back seat. I was relieved once again when the zamu's friend closed the door and we could get moving.

"I can drop you off at the hospital," I informed them in Swahili, as we bounced along the stony road, "but I won't be able to bring you back." Relieved to have transportation, they were fine with that. And so I drove down and away from the base of Mount Visoke with a dead gorilla and a skewered zamu.

I didn't even know when I was coming back, or exactly where I was going, for that matter. I knew where Dr. Vimont lived, but he would probably be at work at the hospital. *How long would I have dead Marchessa in the van? What if Dr. Vimont was out of town?* Peter and I had decided, if he wasn't available, or couldn't do the post-mortem, I'd head to Jean-Pierre's home before dark. After that, I'd simply return and get Marchessa's body up to camp for burial. Either way, we would bury the remains in the gorilla graveyard.

Forty-five minutes later, my cargo and I rolled into town. I headed straight for the hospital, a pale stucco compound near the center of town, and dropped off my forlorn passengers at the entrance.

"*Murakoze cyane*," each thanked me sincerely in their native tongue, while the zamu's friend helped his charge along the walkway toward the hospital entrance. I felt for them under the circumstances, and was happy they had flagged me down. I didn't know how they'd get back home, but as resourceful Rwandans, I knew they'd find a way.

I sat for a moment, pondering how I might find Dr. Vimont there on the sprawling hospital grounds. I dared not even open the side door for the crowd it would draw. These thoughts gave me flashbacks to Stuart's and my travails with dead Kima in tow months earlier, and our terse encounter with Dian's scorned ex-fiancé, Dr. Weiss, right near this same spot. I didn't want to run into him again, knowing the disdain he'd already showed us. With those memories fresh in my mind, I headed for Pierre Vimont's home. If I was lucky, at least his wife Claude would be there. By then, I had been to their house at least once, and remembered it to be on a side road along the way out of town toward Gisenyi.

Claude didn't speak much English, nor I much French, but she greeted me at her back door, where I had parked the VW.

"*Gorille . . . morte . . .*" I muttered, pointing to the van with emphasis. Claude, attractive, coiffed, and always neatly dressed, tilted her head in perplexed attention.

"*Hein?*" she responded quizzically.

"Is Doctor Vimont . . . uh," I persevered, "Doctor Vimont . . . here?" I continued, pointing at the ground to represent "here."

"Pierre? Oh, no . . . *à l'hôpital.*"

At least he wasn't out of town. Relieved, I coaxed Claude over to the van.

"*Gorille . . . morte . . . autopsie?*"

"*Gorille?*" she muttered quizzically. Perhaps she thought I had another orphaned baby inside.

"Oh!" she gasped, as I slid the van's door open. I wanted to tell her the whole story, but that was way too complex and elaborate for our sign language. Claude simply held her hands up in astonishment, mouth open, staring at Marchessa's lifeless form. At that, she seemed to know exactly why I was there. With our best efforts in our own languages and hand signals, I understood that Dr. Vimont would be returning later.

"Pierre . . ." Claude said, pointing at her wristwatch, then at the ground, "*Quatre ou cinq heures.*"

Thanks to Madame Slack's *Parlons Français* program on our elementary school televisions in the Washington, D.C. area, I at least knew how to count in French—Pierre would be back at four or five o'clock.

I didn't want to take any more of Claude's time, and with the awkwardness of our language barrier, I decided to run an errand, and pick up the Karisoke mail at the post office. I explained as best I could, and saw that Claude understood that I'd return. I killed more time by taking the opportunity to write a letter home, describing to my parents, in the least alarming way, what I'd been up to lately.

It was after four when I headed back to the Vimonts' home. I pushed back thoughts of how I'd find the road to Jean-Pierre's after dark. Dr. Vimont and a friend were standing in the backyard when I returned to his house, and both greeted me heartily. I was lucky that the English word for "autopsy" is similar to the French *"autopsie,"* so I didn't have to say much before both men helped me hoist Marchessa out of the car, and onto her back on a concrete slab under an outdoor covered storage area.

Pierre's friend was Giles, who had lived off and on in Africa for some time. He didn't speak English either, but he did speak Swahili. At that revelation, Dr. Vimont's enthusiastic friend became our interpreter. I couldn't help seeing the irony of two mzungus having to communicate via an African language. But with that we were off and running. I spoke to Giles in Swahili, Giles spoke to Pierre in French, Pierre spoke back to Giles in French, who spoke to me again in Swahili. And so I described the macabre story of Marchessa's death to these men, who responded with wide-eyed bewilderment.

I emphasized to Pierre that we wanted to know if Marchessa may have been sick prior to Icarus's beating. The good doctor then armed himself with a scalpel from his medical bag, and expertly made an incision down Marchessa's midline from just under her sternum, down to the vagina. I marveled at his skill, with the blade cutting so cleanly even through the tough gorilla hide.

Giles served as willing surgical assistant, helping peel back the skin and viscera to reveal the organs beneath.

At first glance the severe hemorrhaging from Icarus's repeated pouncing was apparent on the soft tissues beneath the skin of her stomach and chest. Even the bases of both lungs had hemorrhaged, explaining Marchessa's labored and gurgling final breaths. Results of the beating extended internally to what Pierre described as *la grande courbe* of the stomach, comprising a good third of that organ's outer surface. I was most shocked to see that the trauma by the repeated pouncing of a four-hundred-pound silverback had also caused a one-inch slice-like puncture through the old female's stomach wall. It was very telling to see that the stomach itself was full of undigested vegetation, indicating that Marchessa had been feeding normally just prior to her death. This made the killing all the more perplexing.

Pierre gave it his all with an enthusiastic curiosity of his own. This was his first gorilla autopsy, and for him a chance to see how similar an ape was to humans internally. He located and identified each organ deftly. Fortunately I'd already studied vertebrate anatomy, because both Giles's and my Swahili did not extend to internal organs. As he probed, prodded, and sliced, Dr. Vimont could see that Marchessa was indeed an old female, with some atrophy of the leg muscles. Other organs looked normal and healthy, except the spleen, which had a large golf ball–size hydatid cyst, filled with fluid. There were numerous other pea-size cysts of the same type throughout her spleen, but Pierre emphasized that the biggest one was unusually large. Hydatid cysts contain the larvae of tapeworms, which gorillas and other wild animals are naturally exposed to, and are part of the parasite's life cycle.

As Giles and I looked on with interest, Pierre moved on to the reproductive organs. Marchessa was neither in estrus, nor pregnant at time of death, although these organs appeared normal and healthy. He did note some atrophy of the uterus. A mountain gorilla's gestation is eight and a half months. With mountain gorillas typically giving birth every four years, and with her offspring, Shinda, at three and a half years old, she was just beyond the point where she would be expected to be pregnant again, if she was even going to reproduce. Her death guaranteed no further reproduction.

When Dr. Vimont was finished with his careful assessment of Marchessa's cadaver, we loaded the body back into the VW for transport back up to Karisoke and the gorilla graveyard. As I described details of Icarus's unexplained beating of Marchessa, our conversation turned to a fatal incident Giles had witnessed at Akagera, Rwanda's plains park near the border with Tanzania.

Peter had told me a story of Dian's fear of *sumu*, or black magic, the stuff of African lore in which someone might put a curse on you. This usually requires the services of a witch doctor, and a piece of the intended victim's hair or fingernails. Because of this, Dian always pulled the hair from her hairbrush and tossed it in the fire. Her fears were exacerbated by the death of someone she had known. In 1975, a twenty-nine-year-old female photographer friend of Dian's, named Lee Lyon, had visited her at Karisoke in 1975. She had asked Dian what she knew of *sumu*. She had explained to Dian that someone had gotten some of her hair and used it to put a curse on her. Lee was deeply disturbed by this. A week later she was dead, killed by an elephant.

Giles had been present at the time, and witnessed Lee's death. By 1975 all of Akagera's elephants had been eliminated by poaching. A group of young elephants had been orphaned by culling of adult elephants in Rwanda's heavily human-populated Bugesera District. Lee was there to photograph the event. During the unloading and release, one of these young elephants came after her, knocking her to the ground.

"Alipiga, na piga, na PIGA!" Giles explained, punching his fists downward, describing how the elephant repeatedly struck the ill-fated photographer into the ground. Although the elephant was young, it was still huge relative to the young woman. Giles and the others tried their best to distract the elephant and ward it off, but Lee was injured beyond hope with just the first couple of blows.

Before I had to worry too much about how I would make it on to Jean-Pierre's before dark, dead Marchessa in tow, Claude graciously invited me to join them for dinner and to spend the night, offering me a clean, comfortable bed, and the first shower I'd had in months.

Back at Karisoke, we buried Marchessa in the gorilla graveyard and I made a plaque for her to match the others. Group 5 continued on as normal, but for the next three days, Beethoven would whimper spontaneously with a mournful high pitched moan as he led the group through their usual feeding grounds. I hadn't heard him make that sound before, nor again after those few days.

TWENTY-FOUR

NAIROBI

Terry Maple came through on his promise of flying me to Nairobi on September 19 for a bit of reprieve. Seeing the riot of bougainvillea colors down the grass median of Uhuru Highway felt like a homecoming of sorts, as Terry drove me from the Nairobi airport to the Jacaranda Hotel, where his academic entourage had their base camp. The hotel was an upgrade from the University of Nairobi's Spartan dorm rooms from which we had based our forays the summer before, but I wouldn't have traded the immersive experience the dorms had provided us into Kenyan academic life.

My fellow UGA student and roommate from the previous year, Jim Weed, was serving as Terry's assistant with a group of ten other students. It was great to see Jim again, who had been truly excited for me being at Karisoke, but knew little of the details of my experience so far. The students' makeup of nine females to one guy showed the impact that the celebrated women in field biology were having on the rising student population.

The lone male student, Dan Reed, was a wiry little guy apparently overwhelmed among so many bright young females. He seemed to invite the teasing and taunting the girls bestowed upon him as we got acquainted at the hotel's bar. While I enjoyed the change of scenery among rounds of Tusker beer with these coeds, Dan sipped on soft drinks or water, while some of the girls threatened to buy him a beer. It was clear to me that he had landed on the bottom of the pecking order, as their tour was drawing to a close. Among these students, I began to feel again like the undergrad I really was, away from the responsibilities of Karisoke, and the dependency of Dian.

Soon we were on the streets of Nairobi as the group made their final forays for souvenirs among the shops and marketplaces to take home to friends and family. The shopping safari ended at the Stanley Hotel's iconic Thorn Tree Café, where Terry pulled me aside to a streetside table for a pep talk. My letters to him had been quite honest about my experience at Karisoke so far, and the experiences of those who had arrived when I did, now gone. Jim Weed was interested in taking my place after I left, and Terry hoped for Karisoke to remain a unique and important opportunity for other students. I knew he wanted my experience to be one of the successful ones, and I reassured him that I would persevere. Besides, I had already survived Dian's vengeful return to camp, and somehow came out on a high note, and she was back in the States.

Our reverie ended with Terry informing his students that I'd be speaking to them at a gathering the next day. He had blocked out a full hour for the presentation. This caught me off guard. I had never been comfortable speaking in front of a group, and hadn't prepared myself for that. Still, I didn't let it show, and lay awake, pondering what I might talk about. So many things ran through my mind, I fell asleep knowing there was indeed much to tell.

I began by describing the average day of the mountain gorilla, and the group listened politely as I went on to describe the different habitat zones of the Virungas, and the gorillas' food sources. When I began talking about taking care of the baby gorilla, the group seemed quite captivated, and as my story evolved into Bonne Année's harrowing, ill-fated release attempt into Group 5, my listeners were riveted with mouths agape. I, myself, nearly choked as I recalled zipping her exhausted body up under my raincoat to make our escape.

After I answered questions about gorillas, the questions about Dian began to emerge. It was only natural that so many young women would want to know about her.

"What is Dian like?"

"What's it like to work with her?"

"Actually . . ." I heard myself say finally, followed by a deep breath, "She's very difficult to work with."

I don't know who was more disappointed, me or them. But my little presentation ended among blank stares that I could only interpret as disappointment and bewilderment.

I was relieved when attention on me and Dian Fossey was redirected to primatologist Dr. Shirley Strum, whom Terry had arranged to meet with us on the lawn of Nairobi's Central Park. We sat in an informal circle in the middle of the wide green expanse surrounded by the bustling tropical city as Dr. Strum told us about the extensive work she'd been doing with a group of olive baboons, *Papio Anubis*, on the Kikopey Ranch in Gilgil, north of Nairobi near Lake Elementaita. Petite beneath dark curls, and tan from the bright sun of the arid uplands, she smiled easily as she greeted us. She had already popularized her work in *National Geographic* magazine, so it was exciting for us to be hearing her stories firsthand. If Dian Fossey was the Jane Goodall of gorillas, Shirley Strum was the Jane Goodall of baboons. In any case, she certainly wasn't the Dian Fossey of anything: unabashedly friendly, obviously bright, and enthusiastic in her teaching. Clearly, she enjoyed spending time with people.

This showed through her research efforts as well, working in a very public forum on the Kikopey Ranch where the world of baboons collided with the world of humans. She worked to alleviate the strife brought upon struggling farmers by marauding baboons, in an effort to meet the needs of both in an arid land where food was all too scarce.

After her talk, Dr. Strum patiently answered questions before we thanked her and wished her continued success.

Back at the Jacaranda on their last night, Terry had booked a large meeting room for his traditional awards ceremony, recognizing students for specific achievements during the trip, reminiscing and laughing about high and low points. At one point on their safari, their kombi had become bogged down in mud. The students had to get out of the vehicle and pitch in, wallowing in the muck to push the vehicle out.

"That's when you all became men." Terry informed them, among a collective groan from the women. I remembered from the previous summer, after particularly trying days when things didn't go as planned, Terry would say to us all, male and female, "Today, you became men."

Obviously, this new group had been hearing this remark as well, but with ninety percent females, they turned the tables on him. At the end of their banquet, the women surprised Terry with a tribute of their own, cleverly written in verse. The contents, which one student read aloud, summarized various points in which Terry impressed them, throughout their travel. The piece ended with the female students uttering collectively, "Terry . . . today you become a woman."

At that, a smart, tall blonde named Beth Stevens rose from her chair with a wry smile and approached Terry at the head of the table. In her outstretched hand, she carried the trophy, a small white cylinder the size of a tube of lipstick. But it wasn't a lipstick Beth handed her professor, it was a wrapped tampon, lovingly adorned with a ribbon. Terry's face went bright red as he accepted the token, grinning and convulsing in his stifled mirth as the group burst into laughter and applause.

My return flight to Rwanda left a day later than the group's, so it was me waving from the sidewalk as they drove off to the airport and back to the USA. Terry had kept a room at the Jacaranda for me for one more night and I was careful not to oversleep. A hotel staffer called a cab for me the next morning, and I waited at the front of the hotel, for what seemed too long. By the time my cab driver was nudging us through the early traffic onto the Uhuru Highway roundabout, I was getting worried about the time. With the long highway stretch ahead of us, my morning plan soon became one of those cutting-it-too-close trips to the airport. My worry was founded when I arrived out of breath at the Sabena Airlines departure gate just twenty minutes before takeoff.

"I'm sorry," the agent said in his Belgian-French accent, when I told him my flight number, "it's too late for you to get on the plane."

I was dumbstruck. This was Nairobi. People weren't that strict about timeframes. My cab driver certainly hadn't been. Close connections happened all the time. I was sure I'd been in closer calls than this before and still been able to board. I just stared in disbelief with these thoughts running through my mind.

"Well, what do I do?" I asked the agent, finally snapping out of my stupor.

"You can go to our office," the man responded, as he pointed down the concourse to my left.

The door to the small Sabena office was open when I arrived, and I stood in the doorway trying to look pleasant.

"Hello," I said, "I need help."

This agent didn't even look up at me as he shuffled through some papers on his desk. When I knocked on the door frame, he turned away from me and loaded a piece of paper into his typewriter. I knocked again, and entered the room, to where I stood over him at his desk.

"They wouldn't let me on my plane," I said, loud and clear.

"Which flight?" he mumbled.

"To Kigali, Rwanda."

Finally he looked up at me.

"The next one leaves on Monday. Same time," he said curtly, "come back then."

With that, he turned abruptly away, and I exited. Outside, the doorway, I had one more question.

"Can I use this same ticket?"

"Yes, be sure to bring it," he snapped.

Before turning to leave, I noticed that someone had written the letters for *S A B E N A* with a black marker down the right side of the door frame. Next to each letter, they spelled out a mantra of the time for this airline with a sullied reputation.

Such
A
Bloody
Experience
Never
Again

My problems had just begun. As with everything in my Spartan college life, I had budgeted down to the wire, and barely had money for a cab back into town, let alone a hotel room. Even if I could stay at the YMCA, or a youth hostel, I didn't have money for food for two full days. I had never been one to panic, so I just stood, calm but dumbfounded, in the center of the concourse, running the reality of my situation through my mind, watching the travelers coming and going. *What was I going to do?*

Professor Cunningham von Sommerin was an unmistakable man, and it was my good fortune that Terry had introduced him to our study-abroad group the previous summer outside the Nairobi Museum. One of Africa's most renowned ornithologists, he had even posed for a picture with us, standing out from us American students as if from another era: tall, thin, and bespectacled; with his long wispy beard, he looked like a professorial wizard from another era. I had admired our group photo often enough that I knew just then who I was seeing across the throng, standing near the airport's row of ticketing counters, among a group of other silver-haired men and one woman.

"Well, I'm afraid we're just on our way to Malawi for a bird census," Dr. von Sommerin said, upon hearing about my dilemma. "What will you be doing in Rwanda?"

After telling them I had been working with the mountain gorillas at Karisoke, they took great interest. One man, Karl Merz, an elder Swiss with a long shock of white hair over his ears, had been their driver, and was heading back to town.

"You must come vith me!" Karl declared decisively, in his German-Swiss accent. "I must take you home to meet my vife."

"Oh . . . um . . . okay." I stammered, while no alternatives ran through my mind.

I picked up my bags and was soon swept away back into Nairobi, where Karl stopped in at the historic Norfolk Hotel, saying he had to meet briefly with someone in the hotel's offices. As he disappeared, I wondered if he had stopped to call his house to let his wife know he was bringing home a foundling. As I waited, I perused the garden and aviaries filled with native birds. A bright green Fischer's turaco swooped down in a flash of red flight feathers to a perch and cocked his red-and-white-trimmed eye suspiciously at me through the wire. I remembered the brilliant bird from my visit there the year before.

Back in the car, Karl and I continued westward, out of the city on Ngong Road, and upward. I could see the Ngong Hills ahead of us, and the Aberdare mountain range beyond to the north. I didn't really know where I was going to end up.

"Vee live in Karen," Karl said. "You know of Karen?"

"Um, well, no . . ." I stammered. "I don't think so."

"The writer, Karen von Blixen? She wrote as Isaak Dineson. *Out of Africa*, ja?"

"Oh, *ja* . . . I mean, yeah . . . yes." Karl said *ja* so commandingly with his clipped German accent, I felt I had to respond in kind, before catching myself. The book he mentioned hadn't yet gained much attention in the United States, but I remembered the title from its mention in J. D. Salinger's *The Catcher in the Rye*. I had always longed to read it, but had never found it.

Before long, we were up in the cooler air of the Ngong hills, Nairobi's skyline forming the backdrop to our commute. Karl veered his car left into the center of the little town of Karen. There, in a grassy, park-like setting stood a sturdy old wooden wagon with a bench seat.

"Dat vas Karen Blixen's vagon," Karl explained. "She used to drive it all der vay into Nairobi from her coffee plantation here."

Satisfied at the sight, my gracious new host made a U-turn, and soon we were into forested suburb just off Ngong Road on Mwitu Drive. Rounding the tree-lined street, scattered woodlands gave way to a neighborhood of expansive lawns, tucked among surrounding acacia forest, dotted with grand homes of stone or stucco, some Tudor, some Italianate, but none more beautiful and captivating than what came into view as we turned into Karl's circular driveway. There before me was my new, if only temporary, digs—a white stucco manse of colonial grandeur, adorned with flaming pink bougainvillea and surrounding gardens. I didn't mind a bit.

Karl's wife Anna emerged from the house as we arrived, and Karl introduced me. In her late forties, she was tall and robust with a short crop of dark hair. At the mere mention of my thwarted attempt to get back to Rwanda and the mountain gorillas, Anna greeted me heartily with her quite proper English accent.

"Well, by all means, get your things!" my new hostess exclaimed. "Do come inside!"

Soon I was plunged into an overstuffed chair with an ice cold Tusker in hand, although it was not yet noon. Three well-mannered German shorthaired pointers rounded out the welcoming, while Anna wanted to know all about me and what I'd been up to. Having done his job of delivering me so courteously, Karl relaxed, letting Anna take over. The view through a wide bay of windows in their large living area at the back of their home revealed the full graciousness of their estate, surrounded by spreading acacias.

"This was actually the home of the Leslie-Melvilles," Anna said, "before they got so involved with giraffes and buying the other place not far from here."

"The giraffes?" I asked, before making the connection, "You mean Daisy Rothschild?" I well knew this story, from magazine and film, and couldn't believe I had landed in the middle of so much history.

"Yes, indeed," Anna said. "We had just moved here from West Africa. Karl was retiring from his construction business in Ghana and we got really lucky finding this place when we did. We bought it at just the right time, at a good price."

After our chat, their gentlemanly Kenyan home cook, Joseph, announced that lunch was ready, and we adjourned to the dining room where the table was set. Anna and Karl chatted away, seemingly energized by having a visitor.

"I did visit the Virungas once," Anna said, with a laugh, "and ended up having to sit on a poacher!" She went on to explain how she and a group of friends went on a guided hike into the park from the Uganda side. Park guides ended up running into illegal hunters, immediately capturing one and asking Anna's group to detain him while they pursued another.

"Our guide laid the poor little man on the ground in front of us," Anna said, laughing, "and, all I could think to do was sit on the poor bugger with my big rump, so I did just that!"

After a lunch of roasted chicken and a mountain of salad from their vegetable garden, the chef poured us a round of shots, brandy for Karl and me, while Anna requested her usual: a shot of half-vodka and half-port.

"Well, I guess I'll get back to my writing," Karl said, after dumping the generous remains of the salad onto his plate and devouring it.

As Karl headed upstairs, Anna led me through the dining room's glass doors, followed by her dogs, to her aviaries just beyond the patio. There amid stands of giant red salvias, towering orange crossandras, and stands of golden cannas, under a canopy of tall crepe myrtles covered in mauve blooms, she kept an eclectic mix of Australian and African finches and small parrots. Some flew into shrub plantings at our approach, while others bounced from perch to perch expectantly, as their mistress opened a small feed bin.

"In addition to everything else," I said, marveling at her collection, "I'm fascinated by birds."

"Oh, so am I!" Anna responded, as she entered the first aviary to pour a scoop of seed mix into a hanging feed dish.

"And Africa certainly has some great ones."

"Indeed, as does Australia."

I fed the water hose through the caging as Anna flushed and refilled each water bowl.

"Believe it or not, I once saw a wild kiwi in New Zealand." Anna said, to my great surprise, knowing how rare these flightless birds were.

Anna went on to describe the experience as I followed her with the water hose to the next aviary.

"Friends I was staying with said that if I was willing to get up before dawn and walk to a specific spot at the edge of the forest, I'd be guaranteed to see one just before sunrise."

Dragging the hose, I followed Anna to the next aviary, as she continued her story.

"So of course, I was certainly willing, and the next morning, just like they had said, at that exact spot, in the dim light, a real live kiwi came scampering out of the forest."

"Really? That's amazing!"

"Indeed, it was! At first, it was so dark, I wasn't sure what I was seeing. They had warned me to be very still, so I didn't move, and before I knew it, it was at my feet. Then I could see it clearly, probing its long beak into the leaf litter, scampering here and there. It nearly went right between my feet!"

"I'd love to see that myself, someday."

"Yes, it's a shame what's happened to so many of New Zealand's birds that once were all over those islands. The rats and cats and so many things brought in by settlers have just nearly wiped them out."

Anna exited and secured the last aviary, and I rolled up the water hose. In a side paddock, beyond the aviaries, a pair of thoroughbreds, one bay, one chestnut, grazed lazily, tails swishing at occasional flies. They lifted their heads and sauntered toward us as we approached. Anna entered their stalls from a side door.

"I'm involved with a few local conservation groups," she told me, as she reappeared from inside the paddock and greeted her horses with hearty pats, "but I want to do so much more. It all makes me so angry, really, especially what's happening to the black rhinos. They'll all be gone soon! And nobody's really doing enough about it."

As Anna tethered and groomed each of her steeds, we chatted, comparing the plights of gorillas and rhinos. As a conservationist, Anna's respect for Dian Fossey's achievements was obvious. I was just learning how to skirt the details of life at Karisoke and the particulars about Dian, focusing instead on the gorillas and Karisoke's well-intended mission of research and conservation.

When we returned inside, Karl was banging away raucously on an upright grand piano against the far wall of the large living area, his hands and arms bounced boisterously to the rhythm of something akin to a German folk tune.

"*Ja*, she takes care of dogs, birds, horses undt a husband," he shouted above his own clamor.

Anna smiled, unfazed by the din until the dogs began to bark. At that, she peered out the bay of windows toward the back of the lawn, and her smile became a scowl.

"Oh John, the monkeys are playing bloody buggers in my garden!" she exclaimed. "Would you mind taking the dogs and running them out of there?"

At that, the three big dogs skittered and slid to the door, nearly tripping me as I opened it. In the maelstrom of their bravado, I trailed the pack across the wide green lawn to the farthest corner of the grounds. A large troupe of Sykes monkeys, *Cercopithecus albogularis*, adults and juveniles, momentarily stared wide-eyed at our approach before bounding away in a flourish of soft grays, ambers, and white hair, to the fence line and upward into the trees. The acacias' branches and ferny fronds bounced wildly under the springing leaps of each as they fled in chaotic dispersal, their long tails trailing behind. I watched with the barking dogs from below, as the monkeys settled down among the treetops, one magnificent male who remained closer than the others, daringly glared at me with glowing amber eyes, and shook his branch at me as I admired his bold white collar of fur, and finely speckled gray mantle.

"We're very near Nairobi Park here, so, of course we get all sorts of animals." Anna informed me back inside. "Even the occasional leopard, I dare say."

Karl and Anna made for gracious hosts, bestowing upon me a lavish respite in stark contrast to my Spartan existence at Karisoke. That evening, Joseph served me another Tusker before beckoning us to a delicious dinner of Nile perch, followed by the same garden fresh salad that had survived the monkeys. Same as for lunch, Karl enthusiastically finished off the remaining mound of salad greens.

Afterward, Karl opened a bottle of wine and poured us each a glass back in the great room, while Anna bid good night to Joseph, who lived somewhere nearby.

"Tomorrow's Sunday," Anna said, "and Karl and I will be going for our ride. I'm sorry we only have two horses."

"Oh, that's okay," I interjected, "Is it okay if I go for a walk?"

"Oh, but of course." Anna said, "It's a lovely area for walking."

I retreated to my spacious sleeping quarters off the upstairs living area, as my hosts bid me good night. My hot soak in the footed tub felt great, and when I emerged just after ten, the house was dark and quiet. Settled into bed, I drifted out of my dream and fell into a deep, restful sleep.

Hearing the morning stirrings, at 7:30 I rolled out of bed, dressed, and was greeted with the offering of coffee in the kitchen, where Joseph was busily preparing eggs, toast, and sausage. After breakfast, Anna and Karl mounted their thoroughbreds and headed across the back lawn trailed by one of their pointers, the scene so idyllic I snapped a picture of them. After they rounded the house and disappeared, I followed on foot down tree-lined Mwitu Drive. The morning air was cool, but not cold, and dry, perfect for walking, and I moved in great strides across the level ground. The stroll felt effortless, conditioned as I was from the daily hikes up and down volcanic slopes.

The few neighbors' grand homes, mostly obscured by groves of acacias and scarlet flame trees, stood down long lanes on large properties. I strode along, scanning the trees for birds and hoping to catch sight of hornbills, turacos, or parrots. Eventually, I came to a curve in the road, rounding to the left, where trees opened up to patchy clearings. There before me to the right, a pair of Masai giraffes, *Giraffa tippelskirchi*, towered above, feeding languidly among the highest branches of acacias. Their orange-and-white reticulations glowed boldly in the morning sunlight as they gazed at me indifferently with their shining dark eyes under long lashes. I marveled like I had as a child at the National Zoo, while their long dark tongues wormed out in spirals to ring the tender leaves and draw them back into their mouths. There I lingered with these tallest creatures on the planet, until their foraging took them out of sight into thicker groves beyond.

Back at the house with Karl and Anna, the day took the same course as before, remarkably so, in fact, with beer before lunch, and shots of liquor. This time I tried Anna's drink of half-port and half-vodka. Not bad at all.

Neither were surprised by my giraffe sighting in the neighborhood.

"Reminds me of the time I was out riding my horse as a young girl in Cornwall," Anna said, with fond reminiscence, "As I rounded the curve of a hillside, there was an elephant!"

"*Ja, ja!*" Karl muttered, as he polished off the remainder of the garden salad like the day before.

"My father didn't believe me that night at dinner," Anna continued, "until, of course, he read next morning that the circus was in town. They had let the elephants out to graze." Anna laughed heartily at the fond remembrance.

After lunch, Karl went upstairs to peck noisily on his typewriter, before abandoning that for the piano again. Like clockwork, Anna gazed out the window amid the din.

"Oh, John! The monkeys are playing bloody buggers again in my garden!" Anna exclaimed. "Would you please . . . ?"

At that, the dogs and I were unleashed again in our counter-raid, as the brazen Syke's monkeys retreated once again into the forest's canopy. As before, the alpha male lingered behind to join in our staring match—me, marveling at his beautiful coat and markings, and he, glaring at me for my bold intrusion.

That evening, a friend of Anna's was flying in from Perth, Australia for a visit, and Anna asked if I'd go with her to pick the woman up.

"I von't need to go vis you to zee airport," Karl said, "as long as dis young man can accompany you, *ja?*"

I was only too happy to oblige, especially considering all the hospitality they were bestowing upon me.

"Vis John here, you von't need me," Karl exclaimed with a sense of drama, as I sat in the passenger seat with Anna at the wheel, "undt John can carry the Morgenstern!"

"The . . . the what?" I stammered.

"The morning star," Anna interceded. "It's under your seat there. Go ahead, make sure you can reach it."

I reached under my seat, and retrieved what at first felt like a hammer, lifting it to reveal a small club. At the end of a short wooden handle was a ball of steel, covered in flattened spikes, like the rays of a three-dimensional Moravian star, but with many more spiky points, otherwise known as a mace.

"Anyone give you trouble, you hit dem mit dat!" Karl proclaimed with a dramatic sweep of his hand in demonstration. "Right on der noggin!"

I could only laugh at the absurdity of the situation, but agreed to use it if necessary, so beguiled was I by the very eccentricity of the situation I was in.

I had already told Anna of my interest in attending vet school, and as we traveled down Ngong Road back into Nairobi, I told her I had considered going to the University of Nairobi's School of Veterinary Medicine, thinking it would be a great way to become a wildlife vet in Africa.

"Well, I hope you do," Anna said with enthusiasm. "That would be wonderful for us." Her unabashed kindness left me nearly speechless for the rest of the way to the airport. It was like I suddenly had an aunt and uncle in Africa.

Anna's friend was tired from her long trip across the Indian Ocean, but back at the grand home, the two ladies of similar age chatted energetically, catching up with each other after many years. Anna ended the evening returning to the plight of the black rhino, informing her friend how the species is being wiped out in pursuit of its horn, and so very little is being done.

The next morning brought my hiatus to an end, and I slipped back into the car with Karl at the wheel. Anna waved heartily from the doorway of her beautiful home, surrounded by her dogs. A passionate fire for conservation burned within her more than I knew. We would become lifelong pen pals. The next time I would see her, two decades later, all this would be long gone from her life, her vibrant and eccentric Karl deceased, her grand estate sold, her finances redirected, the routine of her domesticity undone both willingly and willfully. In its stead would be the world-renowned Lewa Wildlife Conservancy to the north, with her as a founder at the center of its exemplary mission to save the black rhino from extinction.

TWENTY-FIVE

DIAN'S FOE

I returned to Karisoke, expecting the return of Dian's nemesis, Sandy Harcourt. He was coming on reconnaissance to visit Karisoke and to check in on the Mountain Gorilla Project that he had helped launch and fund. Despite Dian's reluctance to accept it, she had to concede that Sandy was the most qualified choice as Karisoke's new overseer in her absence. Indeed, he had been her protégé as one of her earliest students. Anyone else would have been proud, but not Dian. For her, familiarity only bred contempt, and she couldn't let the transition happen without kicking and screaming and dragging her feet. As the plan came closer to reality for Karisoke to change hands, it was obvious that Dian's fears grew. Like Bill and Amy, Sandy had become a free-thinking scientist in his own right, beyond the control and influence of Dian. It became increasingly apparent that Dian feared nothing more than losing control of Karisoke, and ultimately being upstaged in the science and salvation of the mountain gorilla. Dian couldn't share the stage, let alone relinquish it.

While I was away in Nairobi, Peter fired our camp housekeeper, Basili, when he failed to return to camp as scheduled. He had long suspected Basili of being an accomplice to Dian in the theft of his film, and seemed relieved about his decision. Basili, like others, had already been fired by Dian, only to be rehired in time of need. Unlike other camp staffers, he had always been a little aloof and detached from the others, and the rest of the staff seemed fine with replacing him with the friendly part-time staffer, Nshogoza.

With his quirky cone-shaped felt hat, and intelligent, soft-spoken demeanor, Nshogoza was well liked and respected by the others, as he was to Peter and me. On occasion, he stopped by my cabin to visit, much as Kanyaragana had, but he knew little Swahili, and no English. This time, it was me teaching a new-comer, and a local, the language of Karisoke. He marveled at my typewriter, and enjoyed watching me type, uttering, *intelligence* with a French pronunciation while watching the process. His humble praise just embarrassed me, but his wide-eyed curiosity and dignified manner made me think he would have thrived in an opportunity for higher education in an academic setting.

Bill and Amy had returned to the U.S. for a spell, and the friendly English couple who had replaced them, Conrad and Rosalind Aveling, had taken occupancy of the Mountain Gorilla Project's humble metal hut at the base of the mountain. The couple came from working at Biruté Galdikas's orangutan research station in Borneo, and unlike the V-W couple, these two had neither history with, nor personal interest in, Karisoke or Dian Fossey.

They knew Sandy Harcourt, and diplomatically tried to prepare me for his arrival. "He's all science," Conrad explained after I told them about Dian's fears. "Some people think he's kind of stuffy . . ." Rosalind assured me not to worry and all would be fine.

Just about everyone else who knew him, including Peter and Jean-Pierre, echoed the sentiments about his dry formality. But all I could think was: *hallelujah!* The idea of an organized, science-minded researcher taking the reins at Karisoke seemed like nothing short of salvation, and I happily volunteered to time my next trip to Kigali with his arrival, and give him a lift back to camp.

Peter had good reason to be a little uneasy about the prospect of Harcourt's arrival, considering the research value of Group 5, Karisoke's most habituated and stable gorilla family group, the best resource for studying natural gorillas in the wild. No matter how difficult Fossey had been, she had become to him at least, a known quantity. And setting aside her stealing his film and treating him badly, she did let him get on with his research with unlimited access to Group 5. She owed him that. Besides, he must have taken great pride knowing that she thought his notes were the best ever, at least in describing the day-to-day lives of the gorillas Dian needed to keep up with. Peter had no way of knowing how Harcourt might intend to run things. And with past students who had claim on Group 5 long since out of the way, Peter had grown accustomed to the autonomy he had gained.

I, on the other hand, was intrigued by the notion of there being an archnemesis for Fossey. *The anti-Dian? Hmm . . . is this a bad thing?* I had to go back into Kigali anyway, to renew my three-month visa for the last time, and staying at Judy's Joint was always a nice break, with our unofficial official hostess being ever generous and hospitable on our forays into Rwanda's capital.

On this trip, too, I was happy to finally meet Rosamund Carr, an old friend of Dian's and others in Kigali who had emigrated from the U.S. and up the Congo River decades earlier in a steamer. She had come by Judy's to enjoy lunch with her and Ann Yancey. People had always remarked about how the elder Mrs. Carr, despite making the dusty trek into the city from her remote flower farm above Gisenyi, was always elegantly attired and perfectly coiffed, with nary a silver hair out of place. She had become the stuff of legend, and as I shook her hand I could see they were right. This elegant lady in a seemingly fresh-pressed floral sheath dress looked as if she had just stepped out of a limousine in Manhattan, from whence she'd come so long ago. She would go on to survive Rwanda's genocide with the same grace she approached everything, only to start an orphanage for the children left in the wake. With her niece Ann Howard Halsey, she would go on to write her loving memoir, *Land of a Thousand Hills: My Life in Rwanda*.

When Harcourt arrived at last, Rosalind was in Kigali as well, and introduced us. Of a medium build and stature, with neatly trimmed dark blond hair, he was a rather dapper guy, his English accent was clipped with an almost Gaelic brogue to my ear. But despite his disciplined and orderly appearance, in his green military surplus sweater, replete with gun patch at the shoulder, I didn't find him intimidating at all. If anything, I was rather amused by what I saw as the archetypal British explorer-adventurer. This ought to be fun, I thought. As for gorilla research and conservation, having some order brought into the wildly dysfunctional workplace that was Karisoke could only be a good thing.

In camp, Sandy maintained the staid demeanor others predicted—his greeting with Peter was short and businesslike—but most of this I passed off as simply cultural differences. Besides, he had to be at least a little uptight, given the auspices of his visit, here among Dian's handpicked students. While Peter made his usual hike to Group 5, I guided Sandy to Group 4 and Nunkie's Group in order to reacquaint him with new individuals and youngsters who had been born since his time here years ago. He expressed his amazement at how big some had grown.

Unable to contain my curiosity, I ventured a pointed question as we hiked. "When you were here before . . . was Dian . . . uh, in any way . . . like she is now?"

"Well," he said, very much the *behaviourist* making a careful assessment. "There were signs of it." He didn't crack a smile, but I burst out laughing at this tactful yet telling response—signs of it! It, indeed! I could certainly imagine.

After four hours of contact with Nunkie's elusive group on the far side of Mount Visoke, Sandy understood the quickest route back to camp would be over the top. Watching Sandy trudge ahead of me, huffing and puffing as he climbed Visoke for the first time in years, I was reminded of my first climb. When we paused to rest, I saw that his face was as flushed as mine must have been on that first hike nine months earlier, and I paused to rest with him. I found it reassuring that he was as human as the rest of us.

"Wouldn't it . . . be great . . ." he muttered between breaths, "if there were a table and chairs at the top . . . with a white tablecloth . . . and two cold Primus set out for us."

"That's Sandy for you," Conrad Aveling responded later, when I mentioned this to him. "Anyone else would have just been happy with a cold beer, but Sandy wanted the white tablecloth."

The trip down Visoke's other side was much easier, but on the far side of the camp's meadow, smoke was billowing from inside a large hollow hagenia tree. While we were out, the Rwandan military had been here on a drill and clearly set the hollow tree on fire with their campfire at the base of the trunk.

By then the fire was simply smoldering in the damp live wood, and I thought we could just let it die out, but Sandy sounded the alarm, rushing into camp to get buckets. Together we scooped water from the bogs and doused the cinders until they were thoroughly soaked.

"I'm going to write a letter to the army's office in Kigali," Sandy snapped as we trudged wearily back to camp.

Sandy, having taken residence in the camp's Guest Cabin, invited me to dinner. I was surprised that Peter hadn't been included. Still I enjoyed myself, joking around with this very proper fellow.

"If you're from Georgia," Sandy ventured at one point, "and that's in the South, why don't you talk . . ." He paused to phrase the rest of his question. "I mean, in the southern U.S., don't they . . . ?"

"You mean *'Waah down't Ah tawk lack thiyas?'*" I said, in the most exaggerated hillbilly drawl I had in my repertoire. Breaking from his rigid posture, Sandy busted out laughing, nearly spitting out his food. I enjoyed seeing this formal Brit crack his crusty exterior. I could work with this guy, I thought.

"Yes. Precisely," Sandy replied after regaining composure. "I thought that's how they talk."

He listened with the interest of an anthropologist as I went on to explain the subtle differences in accents found throughout the Southeast, explaining to him that I'm originally from Northern Virginia, where the speech patterns represent more of a national norm. He listened patiently while I described the clipped country twang of the Virginia mountains with the slower drawl of the Deep South. Sandy busted out laughing again at each of the examples I dredged up.

"I see," he said finally. "Still, some of it can sound a bit . . ."

"Lower class?"

"Uh . . . well, yes."

Watching Sandy shift uneasily, and knowing he didn't mean any harm, I laughed at his crusty perspective and candor. His wife, Kelly, is American after all, the daughter of the actor Jimmy Stewart. I enjoyed Sandy's funny perspective of my homeland, and his curiosity about it. What exposure could he have had to the southern U.S. other than stereotypes generated by Hollywood? I chalked it all up to different customs from different worlds, and in part because I clearly wasn't put off by Sandy's mien, we enjoyed a good rapport and I would even say mutual respect.

Conrad and Rosalind were working diligently to keep the tourist groups habituated, as well as hosting the sporadic groups of visitors arriving to see wild gorillas, in line with the plan of the Mountain

Gorilla Project, and the initial efforts of Bill and Amy. Group 11, one of these groups, had a juvenile male named Nshuti who recently had gotten trapped in a snare. Although he had broken free, the wire was still cinched tightly around his wrist, cutting off nerve impulse and circulation to his hand.

It was almost as painful for them to watch the suffering this brought to Nshuti himself, and they wanted to do something other than watch irreversible damage to this youngster's hand. Peter knew of a blow dart kit Dian had stored in her cabin, which looked like it had never been used. To retrieve it, we entered the locked storage room of Dian's large cabin. It was the first time I had entered that room, and I was astonished to see the mountain of students' notes that had accumulated over the years. One quarter of the twelve-by-fourteen-foot room had paper stacks and boxes up to my chest. I thought about these rotting away in the dark and musty dampness there.

The Avelings came up to camp to look over the equipment. The kit had an air pistol, and a few unused CO_2 cartridges. It also had a few expired vials of ketamine, a potent tranquilizer that produced agitation and hallucinations as side effects.

Together, we pondered the risk—outdated tranquilizer or permanently disabled hand and arm, possibly leading to infection and death. No mountain gorilla had ever been darted and tranquilized. This would be a first. We all agreed the risk was worth taking, over watching Nshuti continue to suffer or die from infection. They estimated Nshuti to be about sixty pounds and Rosalind determined the appropriate dosage of ketamine.

Excited by the break from my own routine work, I joined Conrad, Rosalind, with Sandy at their request to help them with what would be the first darting of a mountain gorilla. The tourist groups had been habituated relatively recently compared to Karisoke's research groups, and proved to be a bit of a challenge to our efforts. Our first day's attempt was thwarted by the group's evasiveness, preventing us a clear view, and shot at Nshuti. The second day, to our disappointment, was the same. It was during this time that I realized how fast I could clamber back up to camp on the Porter Trail from its base. That grueling first climb that had taken me nearly two hours nine months earlier, I had become able to hike at a near-jog in almost fifteen minutes.

On the third day, we were able to get close enough to Group 11 on Visoke's northern slopes, not far from tranquil Lake Ngezi. Nshuti provided a perfect opportunity as he moved into a small clearing. The moment was tense as Conrad readied the pistol.

"You want to have the honor?" he asked, offering the pistol to me.

Knowing this could be a one-shot deal, with the group fleeing from us at the first failed shot, I politely declined. After waiting days for this moment, I was happy to leave that moment of truth to someone else.

With the group foraging in blissful ignorance of what was about to take place, Nshuti lingered a little behind in the center of their trampled clearing, doing his best to feed himself with one hand. He held the injured right hand awkwardly inward to his torso, clearly disabled. Conrad raised and fired. *Pshewt!* It was a great shot, right into Nshuti's thigh. He screamed, sprang, and ran. The rest of the group hoot-barked their alarms at the upset and scattered in all directions away from us. This presented our first not-fully-anticipated hurdle, finding our drugged gorilla.

None of us were experts at this, nor was anyone in this first darting of a gorilla. Conrad found the steel dart not far uphill from where Nshuti had been shot. It was a good sign that the ketamine had been expelled as hoped, but we could not be certain of it fully injecting, nor the dosage, especially considering it was well expired.

We had to spread out, following the scattered trails of individuals in all directions up Visoke. Scattered gorilla trails are much harder to follow than the large trail of a group moving in unison. We had to consider every broken plant stalk and the direction in which it was bent for clues as to who had gone where. Ten minutes of frantic searching had passed, then twenty, as our worry grew. *What if we didn't find him?*

A long and worrisome half hour after Conrad had made his heroic shot, I stumbled upon our quarry, lying motionless in a crumpled heap. I could see the wire snare, bound tightly around his right wrist, surrounded by swelling. The hand was gnarled in a loose fist.

"Over here!" I shouted, and Conrad, Rosalind, and Sandy came rushing in to join me.

I lifted the arm, showing the snare. The poor young gorilla had pulled it tight in his efforts to escape the trap, pulling hard enough to break the strong wire. The skin, inflamed and swollen, had torn and begun to grow into the ligature.

"Go ahead," Conrad said, and I pushed at the wire's broken end, jiggling it through the loop that kept it snug. The wire was imbedded deeply into the skin, but gave way with my maneuvering. It was with a feeling of great honor that I drew the loosened snare over and off his hand. The moment symbolized effective collaboration among the camps of Karisoke and the Mountain Gorilla Project, sharing the resources of staff, equipment, and skills. And I couldn't tell Dian about it.

The tight snare had imbedded a deep pit around Nshuti's wrist, but then at least it was free to resolve and heal properly. Rosalind examined the hand, flexing the black leathery fingers, which all seemed to have a blood supply.

"Time will tell," she surmised, "if he'll have use of that hand again."

It was only then that we realized our project was far from over. In a way, it had just begun. We had a knocked out gorilla member of Group 11, but the group was nowhere in sight or sound. They couldn't have understood that one of their own would not have been able to flee with them, and they had vanished, leaving us with their sixty-pound male.

With Rosalind gathering up as much equipment as she could carry, Conrad, Sandy, and I tried carrying Nshuti's limp form, lifting arms and legs. The three of us were too awkward to move in unison. We switched to pairs, one taking gorilla arms, and one taking legs. Even then, the steep slope and convoluted terrain made it cumbersome. By the time we returned to the main trail, it was obvious the only way to make any kind of progress was for each of us males to take shifts, carrying the full sixty pounds of gorilla as far as we could before exhaustion. Then each of us would rest while another carted our drugged gorilla as far as they could.

We were lucky that Group 11 had at least fled in a general line along the open trail from the lake, and in the direction homeward. Still, this was an arduous task, and the going was painfully slow. Even after the first hour of transporting our living cargo, we seemed no closer to finding the group. None of us was certain of how long the effects of the ketamine would last. The thought of Nshuti recovering from anesthesia during transport added another dimension of concern to our travail. *What would we do with a fully recovered gorilla on our hands?* As a juvenile, we couldn't just abandon him alone in the forest, and he damn sure wouldn't let us carry him anymore.

As another hour passed, Nshuti remained immobilized, while our level of exhaustion increased. Rosalind looked for vital signs, checking for breathing and heartbeat during each stop. Realizing we just weren't covering distance fast enough, Conrad ran ahead to see if he could catch up with Group 11 and at least get an idea of how much farther we needed to go.

Sandy and I continued as best we could, swapping off with our sixty pounds of gorilla as we stumbled up and down the trail in shifts. It was a long time before Conrad returned with at least the good news of having located Nshuti's family. Still far ahead, but at least they seemed to have stopped fleeing, and had settled down enough to feed. But the other twist had begun, Nshuti was beginning to recover from the effects of the drug. Instead of being the dead weight we had been dealing with for the last four hours, he had begun flopping his arms and legs in a determined but haphazard way. One of the side-effects of ketamine is hallucinations, and we could see the fear in the young gorilla's eyes. For him, he was waking into the nightmare of being captured by humans.

It was nearly another hour before we caught up with Group 11, which had finally slowed their momentum. By this time, Nshuti was soon going to be too much to handle. Rosalind gave him one last examination before Conrad, Sandy, and I, holding whichever appendage we could manage, lugged him as close to Group 11 as we could without startling them further. As we released our hold, I remember Nshuti staring into my eyes, and managing a terrified grunting, *eh, eh, EH*, at the horror that was no hallucination.

Immediately, we all retreated back onto the main trail, but still within sight of Nshuti, who then flailed sloppily, unable to crawl away. Then, the most touching event occurred. A female emerged from the group, mostly still hidden. It was Nshuti's mother! With a caustic glare at us humans, she approached her son, and put her arms around him. Clearly confused by his inebriation, she tried pulling him up on her back, as if he were still her infant. When he failed to hold on, she grabbed her boy by the arm and dragged him back to the group.

Only then could we breathe a sigh of relief that our work was over. The four of us, exhausted from the longest day, were happy to rest a while longer as Group 11 moved onward and upward out of sight onto Visoke's forested slopes.

TWENTY-SIX

GOING BUSH

Only with Dian's absence did Karisoke become a tranquil place, temperate and wonderfully livable in what remained of the long dry season. I had been warned about feelings of lonely isolation there, but settled back into my daily routine of a two-hour trek to gorillas, observing for four hours, and then the two-hour trek back home, to change into dry warm clothes, light my fire, and prepare my one meal of the day, as had become my custom. I looked forward to this mealtime with great hunger and anticipation. And if the rare surprise visitor wandered into camp at my feeding time, I felt as raw and territorial as a dog at his bowl—not really interested in seeing anyone.

It was with no small irony that in the end Dian could only rely on we whom she had dubbed the "selfish, young, and stupid." To compensate for Peter's and my dual role in running the camp, its staff, the poacher patrol, wages, finances, and monitoring of the research gorilla groups, we split what had been Stuart's one-hundred-dollar monthly allowance for food evenly. Peter suggested we also salvage perishables from Dian's pantry, and so we raided it like starving rebels that had just overthrown an oppressive despot. While Peter seemed to survive on bananas and rice for breakfast, and beans and rice for dinner, I had long grown weary of this readily available but monotonous fare, even developing severe stomach cramps from repeated bean dinners, although I'd learned to pick the rat turds and broken glass out of the beans before cooking them. The pain, which ebbed and flowed, had become so bad that on one hike to Nunkie, I doubled over just as I reached the group. With Nunkie rushing down upon me and screaming, the agony was more than I could bear, and I ended my contact, making the return hike between doubling over in pain and resuming only when it intermittently subsided.

After that, I was done with beans for a while. Instead, I got creative with flour, eggs, canned margarine, and such meager supplies as I had at my disposal. When avocados were available, I added tomatoes and onions to make guacamole. This I ate slathered on stovetop-toasted bread slices. From raw flour, I made pizza dough covered with tomatoes, peppers, onions, and cheese, baked in a makeshift oven made from my wash pot and stove. When forest blackberries came into season, I baked them in crude cakes, or made syrup with them to pour on pancakes. Peanuts, sugar and margarine yielded peanut brittle, and seeing a recipe in one of Dian's cookbooks, I even made a crude candy nougat from powdered milk. But my absolute favorite dish—which soon became my staple—was sautéed onions and peppers topped with a flour, egg and baking powder batter, all baked inside my wash pot to a fluffy mound. This I called my Karisoke Soufflé.

Despite the difficult climbs and wild-goose chases, finding Nunkie led me on some of the most beautiful treks high on Mount Visoke. I can't say how many times I've summited that mountain. Returning from one exhaustive hike, I stumbled upon an immense side crater of the mountain before joining up again with Nameye, who waited somewhere downslope toward camp. I had taken a wrong turn, and came to a halt above the chasm. It was a rare clear day, and the view was breathtaking. I later learned this landmark was known in camp simply as the Big Hole, or *Chimo Mkubwa* in Karisoke Swahili. The name didn't do it justice.

I sat to rest above its stunning sheer volcanic cliffs, which plummeted to a lush green meadow at the bottom, a hidden valley, invisible from below. Little yellow white-eyes, *Zosterops senegalensis*, which favored these altitudes, flitted among the low shrubs in the thin air, searching the leaves for bugs with their bright white-rimmed eyes. Mounts Mikeno and Karisimbi served as splendid backdrops with this special place at center stage, and I felt as if I were the first human to ever sit at that exact spot, and one of the rare few to witness that hidden world below me. Much of the time the Virungas, with their mercurial climate and exhaustive climbs, could take everything you had. Other times, they only gave back to you, surrendering their dazzling beauty.

On another trip, Nameye and I trekked up into an odd precipitation akin to some form of snow not far below the volcano's rim. Different from the familiar hail, the tiny swirling crystals were barely visible in the hand, and melted instantly, as if frozen mist. I could only surmise we had walked up into a frozen cloud. The fine flurries scarcely accumulated on the ground, instead swirling off and away like dust. In the middle of this, we stumbled upon a handsome francolin hen, *Pternistis nobilis*, in a grassy lava clearing, frantically trying to lure her chicks out of our path and into a thicket of giant senecios. I was surprised to see this partridge-like bird up so high, especially with her hatchlings. The frightened peeps hid among the grasses at our approach, and Nameye and I were able to pick them up. We marveled at each tiny speckled ball of fluff while carrying them to the forest edge and releasing them to their frantic, squawking mother.

The Elephant Trail was our usual path down Mount Visoke, because it routed us quickly downward right into camp. Halfway down, the trail took me under a grove of tall pygeum trees, *Prunus africana*. There I'd sometimes spot a pair of Ruwenzori turacos, *Gallirex johnstoni*, feeding on the cherry-like fruits. They'd cock their eyes at me warily as I admired their gaudy green, red, blue, and violet plumage. They hopped and bounced among the branches while foraging, before flapping away in a flash of crimson flight feathers.

Near there, I'd once stumbled upon a patch of white bird droppings. Looking upward, I saw a pair of long-eared owls, *Asio abyssinicus*, staring silently back at me from their roost like two mottled brown moths, their long ear tufts resembling tufted antennas. Despite glowing golden eyes, they wore blank and stoic expressions, blending in with the tree's bark and limbs.

On one visit to Nunkie's Group, low on Visoke's western slopes, I finally heard the startling roars and rumbles of forest elephants myself. Sublimely excited, I moved to a clear vantage point from which I could see through the trees of the saddle area below me. They sounded as if they were just right there, and should be in view, but try as I may, I couldn't catch even a glimpse. Certainly they were large enough. Obviously on the move, their sounds faded away before it was time to leave. So close I felt I had come to their rare sighting.

Kanyaragana, Dian's longtime servant and my friend, came to my cabin door one afternoon after I returned to camp.

"Ninataka kupanda Visoke," he said. He wanted to climb Mount Visoke.

"Visoke? Kwa nini?" I asked why, baffled by this idea. He was a Rwandan who had worked at Karisoke, in the Virungas, much of his life, who lived in the very shadow of this volcano. *Why would he want to climb Mount Visoke?* Surely he'd done this before. The trackers and I surely had . . . on a long, hard day.

"Bado kupanda. Ninataka kuona ngezi huko."

Much to my surprise, like Dian, he had never been to the top of Visoke. This caught me off guard. His life had been devoted to Mademoiselli, and Karisoke, and we students. He wanted to see the volcano's lake, which he had heard about for so many years. With Dian gone, he knew things were changing; perhaps he thought his one chance was with me. Throughout his many years at Karisoke, anyone could've taken him, or he could've simply gone by himself. But just then he was asking me. He wanted me, his *msungu* pal, to be his guide. When I asked him when he wanted to do this, he suggested the very next day, as if it was a now-or-never option. So moved was I by his unexpected and sincere request, I simply agreed.

And so we climbed the very next day, on the most direct route up the Elephant Trail behind Dian's cabin. It was a warm day, but with swaths of chilly clouds sweeping around us, Kanyaragana was surprisingly quiet throughout our hike, as if in deep thought about many things. When we reached the top, he became even more introspective. He had brought Dian's big military binoculars, and quietly glanced through them between gaps in the clouds that swept through us. There were no gasps of awe as he studied the views at his disposal, no looks of astonishment at the quiet lake he had longed to see. Just quiet reflection.

I asked him if he wanted to climb down to the lake.

"Hapana," he said, decisively.

Standing behind him, I gave him a little nudge toward the lake, just to get a reaction. He jumped back and laughed quietly. I knew the Rwandans had a myth about the lake, that to touch its waters would bring bad luck. Despite my suggestion to venture farther, Kanyaragana had no interest in entering the caldera where the tranquil water lay. Instead, he stood silently, taking in the vast world of Rwanda, Zaire, and Uganda below and around him as if lost in some silent and profound prayer.

After a while, he was ready to go. I had brought my camera, and he let me take his picture before we left.

The giant rat continued to plague me with his nocturnal raids, leaping onto my counters, nudging pot lids off my leftovers to get at the contents, and rousing me from sleep. He had even eaten a small lobelia plant I had brought down from the upper slopes of Mount Visoke and potted in a coffee can, leaving the gnawed stump and soil scattered across my floor. Seeing our tracker Bernardi kill one of these varmints with a single swipe of his panga one night made me realize I didn't have to put up with it. But, with stealth and agility, the big rodent evaded each swipe of my panga, slipping right back out through the same seam in the wall's grass matting as lithely as he had entered. Over time I saw his potential weakness—greed, combined with an ever-increasing brazenness as I repeatedly failed to kill him. One night, he mockingly stood his ground, knowing he could outrun my attack. Instead, I opened the pot of beans for him. The smell of food drew him in, and I tilted the pot his way. With my right hand, I reached for my panga, slowly, silently . . . My meager rations were as precious to me as to him, but I saw him as my competitor, each out of place here on the mountain. One of us had to go. Finally, with one fatal crack I rid myself of him.

After that, it was only the tiny groove-toothed rats, *Otomys denti*, and the pretty little woodland dormice with furry tails, *Graphiurus murinus*, that shared my cabin with me. The mice were too small to get into my food, but did chew holes in a sweater to make a nest. The tiny rats were mostly uninterested in my supplies and belongings, and only seemed to be using the space below my cabin floor as a warm, dry home. They were usually quiet, but one morning I awoke to a squealing skirmish under the floor. Moments later, a groove-toothed rat emerged from out of where the wall met the floor, staggered onto the grass mats, and fell over dead. A pool of blood flowed from a slit in his throat. I could only surmise that a territorial dispute had led to the tiny rodent's violent murder.

Bonne Année appeared to be thriving in Group 4, enjoying a close alliance with the silverback Peanuts. I continued my regular forays into

Zaire to keep track of her progress with her adopted family. Nunkie still drifted in and out of our study range, even for our intrepid trackers, and so I resumed my monitoring the whereabouts of this irascible renegade gorilla and his band of consorts. I never got quite used to his greetings of repeated screams and charges, followed by a standoff of knocking down vegetation as I lay before him in whimpering repose. It was only against this unwelcoming onslaught that I was able to learn that two of his females, Augustus and Papoose, had given birth. I at least had the honor of naming the new babies, Ginseng and Shangaza.

As Fossey would have it, I developed no specific research project of my own, instead simply writing down everything the gorillas did and their whereabouts, so our director could read it later. I surmised that perhaps someday, some way, I could at least extract some useful data out of the narrative. On other days I accompanied Peter to Group 5. We'd become great comrades in the field, later retreating to our own solitudes back in camp. Sometimes the camp staff asked if we could spend a little more on their rations and they invited us to *supe na umbati* at their cabin—a pot of hearty vegetable soup with a side of manioc paste that we ate with our fingers around a camp fire until our stomachs were bulging painfully.

We were a tiny remote village of six men at any given time, four of whom rotated out every twenty-one days of work shifts to return to their farm plots below. Each made one hundred Rwandan francs per day, the equivalent of a U.S. dollar, and I paid each twenty-one dollars at the end of their shifts from the few hundred dollars in Dian's wooden money lockbox.

For fear of theft, Dian had never kept too large an amount in the box at any one time, but I noticed the box was so loose at its joints, that I could simply pull it slowly apart at the bottom. The nails slipped back into their holes as easily as they had slid out. I imagined someone had done this many times, but on my watch, with the box in my cabin, the money count stayed mostly accurate, but for five or ten dollars on occasion, which I attributed to my own accounting errors. Still, I wondered.

I kept the guns, too, still in their own now-infamous wooden box. These I handed over to the poacher patrol when they came up, and they took them out with them into Zaire to cut traps. Dian's camp funds had dwindled, and we didn't have the money to send them out as much as she had before her departure. After Peter and I had cut a cluster of snares we had stumbled into with Group 5 at the base of Mount Karisimbi, Nameye and I went back out farther into the area to cut and confiscate some more. It was eerie with just the two of us, in this distant, unfamiliar territory, especially when Nameye got a whiff of *hashishi* on the air, always associated with a Twa campsite. Watching Nameye stop and raise the pistol, with eyes wide, silently sniffing the air, gave me chills, as if danger was imminent. I didn't want to get into a shootout.

On another occasion, while out with Group 5 on the western slopes of Mount Visoke, I spied a pair of poachers in the saddle area below me. As I watched silently from above, I could clearly see a man carrying a dead duiker across his shoulders. The young boy who accompanied him carried a bow and arrow. Except for the fate of the duiker, the scene looked harmless, almost idyllic—a father and son hunting together to provide food for their family as these Twa people had been doing for centuries in these forests. But for the greedy poachers who set dozens of traps in a single area, endangering mountain gorillas and leaving their glut of quarry to die and rot on the pole, subsistence hunting for common duikers and bushbucks may have had little impact.

I received an appreciative letter from Dian, profusely thanking me for writing to her about Marchessa's death. I saw she was a different person on paper, focused and without angry outbursts, having chosen her words thoughtfully. She recounted in droll detail her trip back to Ithaca with Cindy in tow. I would again read this humorous account as a fond reminiscence in her book, *Gorillas in the Mist*.

Peter and I developed a good rapport, the kind that single young men in their twenties develop—plenty of mutual respect and camaraderie, with insults and ribbing.

"Shit goddammit motherfuckit!" we'd shout at each other just for fun, quoting our fearless leader in remembrance of volatile and oppressive times with her among us. The other might answer with, "Shit *merde salber* and *sheisamakopft!*" as an appropriate response, or simply, "You *reeeally* fucked up. *Reeeally* and *truuuly*. You are NOT to be believed!"

In conversation and reminiscence of home, we talked a lot about food, family, and our different upbringings on opposite coasts. I swapped my Van Morrison and Jesse Colin Young cassettes for Peter's Blondie and Patti Smith, left with him by an ABC film crew member.

On rare occasions, we combined resources of simple fare and ate dinner at one another's cabin. On one of these nights, I noticed a clump of dried herbs in a cup on Peter's desk.

"That's pot," Peter said. "You want some?"

Hearing that the ABC film crew liked to smoke it, Dian had made her head porter, Gwehandegoza, buy the "hashish" at the market, despite his protests, and threatening to fire him as an ultimatum. If he could put a contract on a poacher for her, after all, he certainly could score a little dope. When the film crew arrived for a dinner at her cabin, Dian had the dried bundle of weed in a vase as a table centerpiece. The film crew loved the gesture and gave the remnants to Peter when they left.

Not a big fan of pot, but in the absence of beer or other libations, I gave it a try anyway, listening to Debbie Harry and Patti Smith belt it out on my dragging cassette player, its precious batteries dying an ever-slowing death. *What the hell else did I have to do on Saturday night in Karisoke, anyway, fergawdsakes?* Camp was not a good place to get the munchies. I ended the evening nibbling on unrefined sugar, savoring the crunch of each large brown crystal between my teeth, and keying in on nuances in the music. *Eat to the Beat!*

My Swahili fluency grew as I studied past and future tenses, later trying them out on the men at the campfire near my cabin, discussing with them everything from their own family lives to the possibility of life on other planets. I showed them pictures and articles in magazines cast off by visitors from Kigali. They were smitten with Linda Ronstadt's face on the cover of Time—*iko mzuri sana!*—and bowled over by Ola Ray's centerfold in *Playboy*, although baffled that she had pubic hair—*so bad for lice!* Some of the men, I learned, had relatives who fled into Uganda after Rwanda's civil war of the fifties, but the men grew quiet on this topic.

With Dian gone, I began to feel I needed to get serious about some sort of research direction of my own. Dian had never returned to me the research proposals Terry Maple had written, and by then, it felt too late to get started. Still, I tried. The longhand notes Dian wanted seemed superfluous to me and cumbersome to write. *Peter be damned, with his detailed narratives Dian favored!* I thought scientific check sheets would be more efficient to both produce and analyze, versus weeding through long narratives for data. I ran ideas by Peter, who simply warned me I could unleash the wrath of Fossey if I didn't give her what she wanted. How well I knew. And how well I knew she could come blowing back in at moment's notice, as she'd done already, with a vengeance. And so I continued the longhand notes, recording everything and anything in a shorthand of abbreviations, Fossey-style, in hopes that I could still extract something useful in the end.

At the end of the long dry season, Juichi Yamagiwa, a student from Kyoto University, was granted permission by Dian to visit Karisoke for a couple weeks, and Peter and I hosted him on visits to the research groups. Studious and quiet, he didn't speak much English but was appreciative of our welcome, and uncomplaining about accommodations. He had already been to see the eastern lowland gorillas, *Gorilla beringei graueri*, at Kahuizi-Biéga National Park in Zaire and showed particular interest in the differences between those eastern lowland gorillas versus the mountain gorillas. I was baffled when he told us that gorillas in Kahuizi Biéga didn't eat wild celery, although it grew there. It was a daily staple for gorillas in the Virungas.

The announcement of Juichi's arrival had come from Kigali, and the letter included Dian's commendation. Her words described Juichi as "tractable" among his qualifications for Karisoke. Neither Peter nor I were familiar with this word, and I looked it up in a dictionary in Dian's cabin. I had to laugh when I read the definition to Peter: "capable of being easily led, taught, or controlled." I could only surmise our headmistress was scouting new recruits to be her next "students" at Karisoke. I would gladly pass the torch to Juichi, who unbeknownst to us at the time, would one day lead the International Primatological Society and become the 26th president of Japan's prestigious Kyoto University.

My hair and beard grew long, and I spent most of my time inside my head, either reading or thinking about what I'd read. Whatever old magazines had been brought in by the rare visitor, or left over from the US Embassy staffers, I read cover to cover. I finally read J.R.R. Tolkien's epic *Lord of the Rings* trilogy, and imagined the Virungas as Middle Earth, seeing Frodo's trek to Mount Doom as like my own hikes through the volcanoes.

Judy Chidester commented, "You seem even more quiet than usual," on my last trip to Kigali to renew my work visa. Then again, knowing little of current world news events or politics, and nothing of the latest movies or music, I had little to contribute to the conversations of her worldly set. I was a nearly wild and isolated creature out from the forest. The true tales of Dian I kept to myself; everyone wanted to admire her so.

Karisoke felt mostly safe, high above the world, but one night, I had a disturbing dream in which my body was an abstract *Makonde* carving, stuck in the chimney of my childhood home. I had seen these bizarre tribal carvings in a market on the border of Kenya and Tanzania the previous summer and their bizarre forms had left an impact. The Makonde people who create them from their native ebony seem to have no rules about where disproportionate heads, hands, feet, or teeth belong on the body. Their work is reputed to have inspired Picasso's cubism. In my dream, I was trapped in this grotesque form with my distorted body rising from the hearth up through the flue. My malformed mouth gaped in the wind above the chimney like a frozen scream.

I woke with a feeling of paranoia. *How safe was Karisoke? What if bandits were to come in from Zaire to raid our camp, to take what little we had . . . the money, guns? Or try to take what they thought we might have? Or kidnap us in hopes of ransom? Were bandits in camp now? Is this a premonition?* With my mind racing, it took a long while for me to drift back to sleep. By dawn these feelings were gone with the morning light and the familiar comforting sounds of the men readying camp for another day.

On another night, I awoke to a clamor of strange yips, chortles, and cackles amid the sounds of swift feet dashing through the grass and undergrowth of camp in all directions. Startled, I lay in bed, wide-eyed and wary as I recognized the calls as those of spotted hyenas, *Crocuta crocuta*, similar to what I'd heard and seen in Kenya the year before. Their voices rang from all directions, as if communicating among group members on reconnaissance as they moved. A few dashed close by both sides of my cabin, making hurried calls before their sounds faded away toward the west end of camp and the large meadow beyond. I could only imagine that the forest buffaloes had already retreated from the clearings back into thicker forest, to avoid harassment and predation in the open spaces, but who knew what would take place beyond my earshot?

Otherwise, Karisoke was mostly a quiet place at night, but for the infrequent chorus of the tree hyraxes, who nearly drowned out one's own thoughts before fading to silence as unexpectedly as they had begun. They served as a nocturnal version of the occasional hailstorm in sound, and rivaled its rancor. Forest buffaloes were so regular that I expected their occasional hoof-thud or snort while tossing my tooth-brushing water outside the door into the darkness, or during that final pee of the night before bedtime. Their dark hides kept them invisible in the darkness, like benign phantoms. Knowingly, we always kept our respectful distance from them, and they left us alone in exchange for camp's rich grassy patches.

Throughout the remaining dry weather of August, our paths out with gorillas would cross those of these forest buffaloes who often rested during the day after a nighttime of traveling and foraging. While most of the group moved away, the silverbacks might put on a little display of hoots and chest beats, just to run them off and keep them at bay. To this the bovines snorted their indignation and crashed away. Often Beethoven would let his younger silverback Icarus carry out this task, and the young blackback Ziz watched as a gorilla-in-training. It wouldn't be long before this esquire of Group 5 would be a silverback too.

Perhaps my closest brush with danger was with a buffalo. I had already heard the story of Sandy Harcourt's goring by an angry female. Regardless of how much time one of us students might have in the field, our skills never achieved the level of Karisoke's longtime trackers, who could discern the slightest spoor when finding gorillas each day. The dryness of dung, or the color of sap on broken plant stalks determined the ages of overlapping paths, while a partial hoofprint, versus a partial handprint, needed to be observed and discerned. The direction in which twigs and stalks were broken, and snagged hairs on tree bark provided clues to who, what, when, and where. I sometimes ventured out alone to find gorillas, on days when trackers were spread thin to keep up with other groups.

One frustrating day of having searched on my own for Group 5 amid a tangle of buffalo trails, I began my return up the Porter Trail toward camp. By then, I was conditioned enough to do this hike at a fast pace, and was ready to get this last uphill portion of my day done with. At one spot, a thick hagenia's trunk had grown into the trail, creating a curve in the path around it. Rounding this tree, I nearly ran smack into a foraging female buffalo. Instantly, we were together, and in the moment, she lowered her horns with a snort. All I could do was bring in my arms and brace for impact. I even closed my eyes in preparation. Then, to my own disbelief, I opened my eyes to see this cow just staring at me, as stunned as I was. I could've reached out to pet her on the forehead. For a moment, it was if she was in disbelief of a human appearing before her so suddenly. I remained frozen, and within seconds she shook her head and horns, as if to shake us both out of a nightmare, then turned and crashed away through the underbrush.

Her departure gave me short-lived relief, as others of the large heard caught wind of me, and began a stampede, galloping across the Porter Trail before and behind me. I could neither progress toward camp, nor flee downhill, as more buffaloes closed directly in on me. The big hagenia leaned enough that I could crawl up its thick, gnarled trunk. As I did, I reached for a lower branch and hoisted myself onto it. From that vantage point I became clearly visible to others of the herd, who stopped in their tracks from a distance and stared up at me.

Great! I thought, *now how long will this day last?* With a man in a tree above them, the herd of cows and their young seemed paralyzed to move on, wanting instead to keep their suspicious eyes trained on me. There I clung, tired and hungry, in the late afternoon. The minutes passed, five, ten, fifteen . . . We were at a stalemate, and I wanted to speed things up. The long, late shadow of Mount Visoke was upon us.

"Hey!" I shouted.

This only made them huff and stare all the more.

"Get out of here!" I shouted. They looked dumbfounded, and I felt stupid talking to them. *What else could I do?* A song came to mind.

"Buffalo gals won't you come out tonight, come out tonight, come out tonight . . ." My shouted song sounded so pathetic to my own ears, but

it must've been even more horrid to these buffalo gals. At last, one by one, each shook her head and trundled off, as if disgusted and tired enough of the sight and sound of me.

When I was sure the herd had moved on, I clambered down the tree and resumed my ascent to camp, "Buffalo Gals" still stuck in my head. I belted out a few lines along the way home, to clear a path and keep the herd at bay.

"And we'll dance by the light of the moon . . . !"

At least I hadn't stumbled into a herd of elephants. I wouldn't have known what song to sing.

On August 30, Peter and I found Group 5 low on Mount Visoke, not far from where the Camp Stream neared the shambas. The group was dispersed widely among the vernonia trees, as young Poppy lingered in the rear long enough to break a fresh sprig with the favored flowers and bulbs and scamper off behind Pablo to join the group somewhere ahead. Here, the vernonias, the tree-form cousin of sunflowers and asters, had become full of mature fruits, crisp white bulbs that the gorillas coveted. Gorillas made their crunching sound so good that Peter and I decided to sample them ourselves. We were impressed with their water-chestnut like texture, and nutty flavor, similar to the pith of the giant senecio at higher altitudes. Hungry as usual, we sampled several before I took the time to really scrutinize what I was eating. Looking closer, I saw the extra protein hidden within. Each nutty fruit was studded with tiny insect larvae, white worms with dark heads wriggling in the path of our teeth. *Ugh! The gorillas could have them!*

Elephants obviously liked them too, as their trails were marked by many of them, felled and stripped of bulbs, flowers, and leaves. We began seeing elephant footprints combined with felled vernonia trees well into August on our treks to Group 5. We had to watch our step as we traveled to avoid these unintended booby traps, and a broken leg. Over the next few days, it became apparent that forest elephants and Group 5 were sharing the same feeding spaces, yet the great pachyderms remained unseen by us as if invisible, vanishing to parts unknown by the time we would arrive at their feeding grounds.

As Peter and I followed Group 5's path, I suddenly felt a strange sensation run through me. It made me pause, unsure if I was imagining a deep vibration move through my torso.

"What is that?" I asked Peter, stopping in my tracks.

"I don't know," Peter said, sensing it too.

"Is it a sound?" I found myself asking, one hand on my chest and surprised by my own question. The sensation then morphed into a reverberating noise, finally audible as a low rumble as if from all directions.

"Is that a helicopter?" I asked, as we both glanced skyward. When we heard the loud crack of a vernonia tree, and a rumbling roar, we knew the gorillas were between us and forest elephants beyond. With our senses piqued, Peter and I moved swiftly and quietly toward Group 5, which had suddenly vanished. This brought us closer to the elephants. Seeing a cluster of three large steep volcanic rocks, we climbed atop the nearest one for safety, about twenty feet high. By the time we reached the top of the knoll, the elephants, just on the other side, were somehow alerted to our presence. Obviously confused about our location, they let their alarm be known, choosing their flight path in a stampede directly toward us, trumpeting, rumbling, and roaring. Only the steep face of our rocky knoll diverted their course off to the left below us. More dazzled than terrified, I counted eighteen before averting my eyes from them to set my camera. As at least as many more stampeded in and around, following the others in a bouncing canter, I realized it was a herd of fifty or more, careering before us, back into the forest in a crashing column.

As the swerving rank and file disappeared over a rise to our left, remaining stragglers moved in slower, too late to feel the security of the herd. They approached Peter and me, then stalled twenty meters before us, trunks raised, sniffing the air cautiously for the clues to our whereabouts. Their ears were folded back, pressed against the sides of their necks making them look attentive and guarded. Our vantage point and close proximity to this pair really gave us a good opportunity to better observe their unique adaptations, than for previous encounters. Each of these two was about the same size, six to seven feet at the shoulder, small, relative to their savannah cousins, but huge relative to us. Oddly, the slightly larger one lacked visible tusks. The smaller one had tusks about one meter long, tucked in and pointing downward. This characteristic, along with the smaller, rounded ears, was their adaptation for a life in the forest, where greater protuberances, like the large splayed tusks of savannah elephants, would only snag in the undergrowth and slow their movement. I could see another difference which I hadn't noticed during previous sightings: these forest-dwellers were covered in an even distribution of short dark hairs over back and sides, lending a dark hazy shadow on their wrinkled gray hides, a sort-of sparse, wiry fur. Peter and I kept silent, well aware that they were searching for us, side by side, trunks raised like olfactory telescopes taking in the surrounding smells. So conditioned were we by then at taking notes, we scribbled away on our paper pads as we observed.

Soon, another large one with tusks moved in from beyond. Directly behind her was an infant, only four feet tall. The little one stayed in close to its mother as one more adult brought up the rear close behind. Peter and I watched in awe as these five elephants lingered silently, senses alerted to the sounds and smells of the forest, wary of any possible danger, keeping their baby in close. With their size, forest elephants are no match for the other forest animals. Only man is their real natural enemy, sadly in pursuit of their ivory, if only for adornment. They have good reason to fear us.

Within twenty minutes, the two with the baby moved on down the slope in the direction of the group that had circled back around, but had since moved on. At this, the two sentries dropped their tusks and brought up the rear, disappearing with the rest of their group.

By then, it had been nearly an hour since Peter and I'd lost contact with Group 5. We followed the curve that the stampede had taken, moving up the same gentle ridge. The elephants hadn't gone far, and we encountered some again just downhill on the other side, relaxed and feeding quietly on the abundant undergrowth. Without the rocky outcrop to protect us, Peter and I froze as one approached idly, ripping up trunkfuls of stalks and leaves to place in its mouth, oblivious to our presence. Then on the ground at their level, with an even playing field, we didn't want to make even the sound of a footstep to reveal our presence. But this oblivious elephant moved in closer . . . twenty feet . . . fifteen feet . . . At that proximity, the big gray pachyderm raised it trunk and clearly took in a big whiff of Peter and me. At that, it lurched and turned, barreling noisily through the herd ahead. This triggered another stampede of these nervous denizens, causing them to disperse widely, rushing east and west in chaotic rampage.

Peter and I needed to get out of there, but we were then in the middle of the herd. We wanted to rejoin Group 5, but there were elephants between us and them. Within moments, a gorilla screamed. An elephant answered with an angry roar, and it sounded like a gorilla-elephant interaction was taking place ahead of us near the Porter Trail. Icarus hooted and beat his chest, *pokka pokka POK!* Elephants charged through the forest, the rancor punctuated with more of their loud roars. Seeing a large hagenia tree, Peter and I climbed its wide trunk to get above the fray. Icarus sounded again, his chest beats answered with more elephant trumpet blasts. The two of us remained treed, out of harm's way, as we saw and heard that the herd was moving collectively again, rushing to regroup in a southeasterly direction.

Only when the last trumpets and roars faded far enough away to our southeast did Peter and I feel it was safe enough for us to leave the security of our tree. On the ground again, we soon picked up the trail of Group 5, which led us uphill to them near the Porter Trail. There they fed again in more vernonia trees, as if all was well, except Icarus, who was gallantly bringing up the rear, like a soldier coming home from battle. Eyeing a tree, Icarus climbed its trunk and snapped it down effortlessly to reward himself with a cluster of the favored bulbs. We saw elephant footprints scattered all about as we reached the Porter Trail, but not without flushing a buffalo from a thicket, just to add one more rush of excitement. After Icarus depleted the last of his vernonia bulbs and moved across the trail to join his group, Peter and I called it a day. I call it a most memorable one.

As our days at Karisoke drew to a close, Peter and I talked about leaving. Peter, who had been there a year longer than me, felt saddened by the very thought, but I looked forward to it with longing, and Christmas at home.

"I hope it fucking rains like hell the day I leave," Peter said. "That would at least make me feel better about it."

"Really? Not me," I said. "I want it to be a beautiful, clear, warm, sunny day, so I can remember this place at its best."

There had been too many mixed emotions for me, starting with Dian. I wanted the experience to end the way I had dreamed it would, wonderful, exciting, and beautiful. It had been all that, but in a much more complex way than I could've ever imagined. I had become, in many ways, a different person. Not jaded, but aware and wiser in the ways of the world.

Out with gorillas, we had many hours staring at the scenic vistas before us. I never tired of the views, always taking delight when the clouds cleared. Once, as Rwanda's short rainy season began, the young tracker Toni and I could see fourteen waterfalls cascading from the slopes of Karisimbi after we sat through a downpour with Group 5. I was mesmerized by the stark white cascades, falling from the velvety green, lit by the bright sunlight in the rain-washed air.

Each Virunga volcano was beautiful in its own way, but Karisimbi dominated the others in sheer height of its symmetrical cone as one of Africa's tallest. Its visage was a textbook illustration of altitudinal zones, and volcanic geology up its slope, from the hagenia-hypericum tree zone below, all the way up to its alpine region and barren cinder cone. As our departure dates neared, Peter and I vowed to climb to its summit. Our new friend and neighbor, Conrad Aveling shared our enthusiasm, and opted to join in.

"If nothing else, I'm up for the camaraderie," Conrad said, joining in our plans.

Karisoke's peak was a place even few Rwandans had ever been, but when we told our accomplished tracker Nameye of our plan, we were a party of four. Enthusiastic Nameye knew of a route, and would be our guide. When the rains of the little rainy season had abated, and we were into the short dry season, we would climb. That way, we would ensure not only better weather for climbing and camping, but a good view from the summit. Once again, Peter, through his study of Group 5, had forecast another baby. There was a good chance Pantsy would give birth while we were up on Karisimbi, but Peter doubted his own predictive skills just enough. Although he had a one hundred percent accuracy rate so far, Maggie's birth had been his sole sample size of one. The doubt was just enough to go through with our plan. Besides, we would only be gone one night.

The climb took us two days. One long day's hike marked the first leg of our journey through thick Virunga forest—not steep, but ever an upward climb. Nameye led our way, hacking through the undergrowth with his knowledge of the region. We traversed a long expanse of rising land to Karisimbi's foothills, just to get to the base of its steep slopes, and there were no tourist trails. Finally, where thick brush gave way to a high plateau of boggy alpine meadow, we set up camp. With my small camp stove, I treated everyone to my Karisoke Soufflé. Each ate it with gusto. Under the circumstances, who among us could complain? There the air was cold and damp, but the little dry season held for us, keeping the rain and hail at bay. The night was clear, and the stars, already dazzling from Karisoke, seemed that much closer on the base of Karisimbi.

In the morning, thick frost lay all around us. We warmed ourselves with fresh coffee in the thin chilly air, and scrambled up some eggs against the backdrop of what struck me as a surreal wet desert. The tussock grasses and high altitude lobelia dominated the landscape much like the few specialized plants of America's Mojave Desert. From there it wasn't much more than just another climb up Mount Visoke, for which we seasoned gorilla trackers had developed the wherewithal. Still, the air was yet thinner, but by then, rich red blood cells pumped through our veins. We traversed a great expanse of giant senecios and towering high-altitude lobelia, before we were where only thick grasses grew, then the barren rock and ash of our final ascent.

Reaching the dark, stony summit, Rwanda and Zaire fell at our feet in a tumble of grays and saturated greens. Mount Visoke took on a new look from our perspective, no longer towering above us, it stood slightly below us, more stunning than ever, with its side crater clearly visible. I could see that spot where I had sat months before above the Big Hole, charmed as I was upon finding it myself Looking southeast of where we had camped on the climb up, we could see that our flat, expansive meadow fell into a large side crater of Karisimbi that rivaled Mount Visoke's caldera. Likewise, at the bottom lay a serene hidden lake. From the lands below, you wouldn't know it was there.

Vast Lake Kivu, where Peter and I had done our "Spring Break" shimmered and vanished into distant haze, and we looked for Ros Carr's flower plantation between us and Gisenyi, only guessing at which farm it might be. Most moving to me, on Karisimbi's opposite side to the southwest, and at the base of striking Mount Mikeno, I could finally see a clear view of the famed Kabara Meadow from above. There Dian had first begun her studies, and Carl Akeley's love for the beauty of the Virungas had taken hold of his heart. A green cabin, much like Karisoke's, was visible from where we stood, the prototype for Karisoke. Jean-Pierre had told us that Akeley's grave had been recently disturbed by grave robbers looking for valuables, and his remains had been dug up and secured in the cabin. Through my binoculars, I could clearly see the raw exposed dirt of the disturbed grave.

We debated about heading down to Kabara—it had been a tentative plan—but with our climb up, and our lingering on Karisimbi's summit, such a trip would have made a timely return to Karisoke before dark unlikely. And so we began our descent with gravity in our favor, running down the western side of Karisimbi in a wild, unfettered release of energy, hooting and hollering, the descent always so much easier than the climb. Just below the summit on the western side lay a deep field of volcanic ash we traversed. Dashing downward, our legs sunk up to our ankles, then our knees, and all we could do was stumble and fall as if in deep powder snow, rolling and laughing in the soft gray depth of volcanic particles that slid and gave way beneath our weight.

Reaching solid ground, Nameye took the lead again, guiding us downward, back into thick forest where we hacked and whacked our best possible route through the rich undergrowth of the saddle area back to camp.

When Peter and I visited Group 5 the next day, Pantsy had given birth, as he had predicted, while we were on Mount Karisimbi. Only a bit of uncertainty had afforded him the leeway to climb the great volcano when we did. Hoping we had a shot at witnessing a gorilla birth, we were both disappointed to have missed the exact day of the blessed event. In his nearly two years at Karisoke, observing the females of Group 5 almost daily, he had gone two for two at predicting births. This time Peter wanted to choose the name again. He liked the name "Josie." I liked the sound of it, but wanted to give it at least an African spelling, and advocated that we spell it "Jozi," the Swahili word for "pair." With Maggie, little Jozi would be the other half of the newest pair of infants in Group 5. The name and its spelling stuck.

Little Jozi and her mother Pantsy fared as well as Maggie and Effie had, adding another novelty to the group for the adoration of Group 5. Observing these new babies with their mothers, I could see how baby gorillas learn what foods to eat by the time they're weaned off mother's milk. Even while still on breast milk, they had a front row seat to their mother's feeding, eventually mouthing and nibbling on the bits and pieces of plant material that fell onto them or their mothers' arms. They were naturally curious, and as they got a little older, they would reach out and grab a piece of what their mothers were eating, and place it their mouths, thereby sampling their parents' foods, and developing a taste for them.

TWENTY-SEVEN

GRAY WINTER HOME

I remained at Karisoke for my full commitment of one year. In my final week, Judy Chidester came to camp, and Peter and I took her out to Group 5, low on the slopes of Mount Karisimbi, where the gorillas gave her a deservedly warm welcome. It was fair trade for all she had done for us, and I made my last trip back into Kigali with her. Peter, the only other student still remaining at the time, would leave as planned a few weeks later.

Peter and I had talked at length about our pending departures. Mine would come in the short dry season. I wanted my last day with gorillas to be sunny and warm, with clear views of the surrounding volcanoes, reminding me of all the best days I had spent there. It was. Peter, by contrast, wanted his last day to be cold, wet, and miserable, to dampen his inevitable feelings of loss at leaving what he described as the best thing that had ever happened to him. I envied his appreciation of the place. For me, the experience had been a dream fulfilled, but far too complicated by Dian and her personal struggles—much more than I bargained for. With the Mountain Gorilla Project in full swing, and Sandy Harcourt's pending return to manage Karisoke, there was much happening in support of the gorillas. It felt like a good time to go.

Banking to the left as the pilot circled Atlanta's airport on our descent, I was struck by the gray winter landscape below. Already I was longing for Rwanda's endless green. Taking in the bleak view out my window, I was chilled too, by the notion that I was once again in the same country as Dian, that somehow the U.S. was not big enough for both of us.

Back home in Virginia, that nagging fear would prove justified as I settled into the mundane routine of being a college kid home on break.

"John!" my mom called to me from downstairs, "Someone's on the phone for you. I think it's Dian Fossey." My stomach sank. I knew intuitively that there was no interaction for me with Dian that would not be on her terms, and with her goals in mind.

Her voice was as flat and charmless as I remembered when she was holding back her irritation. There were no pleasantries.

"Uh, John, I need to get some information on camp," she began, "and the gorillas."

"Okay, is there something in particular?"

"I heard from Peter, and you know, the Nagra was stolen."

Dian was referring to her sound recording equipment, and no, I didn't know it had been stolen.

"Do you remember me asking you to take that with you down to the embassy when you left?"

"Uh, no . . . the Nagra?"

"Ugh . . . you forgot!" Dian sighed, with exasperation.

"I'm sorry, Dian, I really don't remember that."

"Well, it's gone now. Peter said someone cut a hole in my bedroom wall to get inside and take it."

The idea that someone would do that gave me chills, especially considering how remote camp was. The rest of the conversation was about the gorillas. I knew she was working on her book, and another *National Geographic* article, and she wanted updates on Peanuts and Bonne Année, and the births of babies in Nunkie's Group, so I filled her in on everything as it was when I left. I had never expected her to track me down at home, so I was anxious to end the conversation, which felt more like an inquiry with one terse question after another from her.

"I need your notes." Dian said finally.

I had dutifully left copies of my notes in camp as was her rule, so I really wasn't feeling obligated to make additional copies to ship to her.

After a standoff of chilly evasiveness and long silent gaps, Dian finally said goodbye.

"Send me your notes." Dian said, as we ended the conversation.

Over the next few weeks, Dian made repeated calls to me, her voice always without emotion, flat and dry. Under pressure to finish her book, *Gorillas in the Mist*, she needed more details, like what were the new gorilla baby's names, why were they named that. I had named Nunkie's newest baby Shangaza, which means *surprising* in Swahili, because while being out of the study range for so long, none of us knew that her mother, Papoose, was pregnant. Another of Nunkie's females, Augustus, gave birth to another female I named Ginseng, simply because I was intrigued by the plant of the same name, due to its scarcity and mystique, and its reputed health benefits. Mostly, I just liked the sound of the word. I had to give Dian some other relatable reason, so I reminded her that as the Japanese film crew had informed us it was because 1980 was the Year of the Ape and Monkey in Asia, and ginseng was a popular health tonic there. Dian was unimpressed, but didn't argue.

"Send me your notes," she'd demand at the end of each inquisition. Her serious tone and commanding demeanor still held sway over me, and I had to shake it off after each call. I was not at Karisoke anymore.

In later phone calls, she got to her other questions: *What was Sandy Harcourt's visit like? What did he do there? What did he say?* Unhappy with my uneventful story, she soon abandoned any semblance of tact, "I know that bastard's got a conspiracy going against me!"

She strategically left a pause after statements like these, putting me in a position to show her which side of the fence I was on—to defend or not to defend. Finally, I felt squeezed into a corner.

"Dian, I just can't be a part in your battles with people," I said as nonconfrontationally as I could. With that, Dian grew silent, and we ended the call.

Soon after my return, Terry Maple had taken the position of deputy director of New Orleans's Audubon Zoo, and with his wife Addie, and baby daughter Molly, had moved to New Orleans. After settling in, he gave me yet another opportunity, this time to begin a career at the Audubon Zoo. Establishing a new address in New Orleans, and setting up my home phone, I intentionally listed my number under "JDFowler" among the few Johns and other J-named Fowlers, in my surname's column. I was hiding from Dian.

A little put off by all the ego, territoriality, and competition I had so far observed among primatologists, I choose to work in the bird department. Besides, having spent so much time with gorillas in the wild, working with them as captives, even in a vastly improved modern zoo, felt pale by comparison.

I was completely caught up in my new career direction among these like-minded animal enthusiasts of the zoo world. And zoos were changing dramatically: the bars were coming down, and soft naturalistic spaces were being created for zoo animals as ambassadors to their species. Education was moving ahead of entertainment as a mission, in a subtle but determined way, and science was moving in. Terry Maple linked academia and science to the zoo. It was a creative movement, and I enthusiastically became a part of it. There was a great movement afoot! The experience supplanted my aspirations for vet school, which I had once seen as the only career with animals.

Dian's article appeared in the April 1981 issue of *National Geographic*. In a box story within Dian's, I was surprised and impressed to see that Peter was duly given his own full spread of photos amid his own written account of Marchessa's death. I have to laugh when I see the latest iconic photo of Dian sitting among her gorillas of Group 5, the young female, Tuck, mouths an orange Crystal Bon Bon—payment from Dian for posing with her as if in splendid adoration. I know enough about gorillas by then to see that the others are waiting expectantly for their next surreptitious candy treat.

"You didn't tell me you worked with Dian Fossey," people exclaimed as if I should announce this as soon as I enter a room. And despite my college major in general zoology, most coworkers remained baffled by my new job choice. Except for the bird people, of course.

"So why are you working with birds?" many asked, as if I'd had some fall from grace. I was typecast. Everyone was equally baffled, if not disappointed, that I had so little to say about Karisoke Research Center.

"Wow, that must have been wonderful!" They prodded. "Working with Dian Fossey!"

Where do I even begin?

The story is such a long and convoluted one. My longest statement becomes my old standard—"Dian was kind of difficult to work with."

I soon learned that women in particular identified with Dian, full of praise for what they saw as groundbreaking—not only in terms of the fieldwork, but in challenging the sexism of the scientific establishment. Recalling the arc of Carolyn's experience, I thought how Dian would have treated these starry-eyed fans. No one lasted, or remained in Dian's favor long—least of all, these *kindred spirits*. Such notions were only fantasy; there certainly wasn't room for two Dians on the mountain.

Dian never reached me again, but a letter from Sandy Harcourt did manage to find me. I was surprised, and in fact quite honored, to read his offer for me to return to Rwanda for a two-year stint, this time with expenses covered and even a paycheck, of all things. In the letter, he explained that the student doing the gorilla census work wasn't faring too well, and they wanted me to replace her. It was with a little shame that I wrote back to him declining this offer. It all just seemed too soon, and I was quite enjoying my new zoo career, among the many coworkers who had become my like-minded friends. Rosalind Aveling wrote me too, in a kind and flattering effort to recruit and lure me back to the Virungas to work with Conrad on the gorilla census. With her letter also came bitter news as she wrote:

> Bonne Année died of double pneumonia at the end of a long rainy season. The group had been ranging very high and far, and we think she just got exhausted trying to keep up, and succumbed to the pneumonia while weak.

Here, I had to pause and take a deep breath before continuing. Life as an independent member had been too much for our little one at such a young age within this group of older members. My hopes of returning to the Virungas one day had been most inspired by seeing my little one as a grown-up gorilla, perhaps with a baby of her own. Alas, she had to grow up too fast under the circumstances, and that had taken her life. I take solace knowing she had died a wild gorilla, free in her homeland, in a group of her own who cherished her.

Houghton Mifflin published *Gorillas in the Mist* in 1983. It was with some pride I found my name in the index, and flipped to the pages on which Dian recalled our horrific attempt at releasing Bonne Année into Group 5. But that's the extent of it, all the credit for caring for our little orphaned gorilla she gave to her dog Cindy. My cohorts—Peter, Stuart, Carolyn—are absent, as if they never existed. But Peter's photos appeared, the ones Dian had to have, and Peter was given full credit.

Otherwise gone was everyone who spurned her, and that list was a long one. I tried to read the book from page one, but soon realized the story was sanitized to the point of sterility. The writer bore little resemblance to the woman I knew. Nearly all those who bolstered Dian's efforts were missing from the pages. With little intrigue, Dian attempted to divert the reader with meandering stories of the gorillas. In print, as in life, she was withdrawn from people, hiding among gorillas in a fantasy world of her own design.

I could see why she insisted we write as complete a narrative as we could in our gorilla notes, as these are what she drew from to create her embellished interpretations, such as the following:

> After her mother's emigration from Group 4 Augustus seldom hand-clapped; however, she resumed the activity when Titus started chin-slapping. Together the two sounded like a mini-minstrel band. On sunny, relaxing days, their claps and slaps could prompt playful spinning pirouettes from Simba, Cleo, and little Kweli. After several months of closely scrutinizing Titus's attention-getting feat, Kweli began chin-slapping whenever he was without play partners.

What I was reading, in essence, was that gorillas make music, have little bands, and dance parties to celebrate good weather and times of peace. This passage, like so many, gives good insight into Dian's anthropomorphic mind, and flights of fancy.

The battle over camp continued for Dian among African wildlife leaders and the world of primatology. Although news from there, and my knowledge of goings-on back at Karisoke, diminished and faded, mention in the book only bolstered my being typecast as "the gorilla guy" among peers, but in the zoo, I immersed myself in a broad world of myriad species. I had neither transitioned into primatologist, anthropologist, nor behaviorist, but remained a student of zoology. With so much attention on the charismatic mountain gorillas by competent -*ologists*, there was little need, or room, for me.

Dian Fossey was found murdered at Karisoke Research Center on December 27, 1985. Wayne McGuire, the only student in camp, and Kanyaragana stumbled upon her lifeless body, hacked to death, her face disfigured by the gash of a panga blade. She had found her way back to her mountain home, but this brutal flourish served as a punctuation mark of hate and rage at the end of the famous primatologist's tumultuous life.

By this time I hadn't seen Dian in over five years. My fellow zookeepers knew her from the *National Geographic* articles showing her as an intrepid scientist nestled among a peaceful family of mountain gorillas against the lush green backdrop of equatorial Africa, and wanted to know my reaction to her shocking death. They seemed a little stunned when I simply replied, "I'm not surprised."

Terry Maple had since returned to Atlanta, and had taken the helm for Zoo Atlanta's new direction as a respectable modern zoo. Two months after Dian's death, he invited me to accompany a television film crew to Rwanda to produce a documentary on East Africa, culminating in a story about the famous gorilla researcher Dian Fossey. My role, he said, was to help serve as a tour leader and Swahili interpreter, but after learning that I worked with Dian Fossey, the crew turned their cameras on me.

In the course of interviews with the film's director/producer, Bert Rudman, I mentioned briefly that Dian believed in *sumu* or local "black magic." Bert fixated on this to sensationalize his story, urging me to speculate on the relationship of black magic to Dian's death. But I remained unwilling to conjure up some fictionalized account of Dian's life and death in this manner. More and more, I found myself avoiding Bert's persistent questioning on the topic.

During a break in filming at Rwanda's plains park, I spoke with the wife of a Belgian park ranger at the Hotel Akagera bar. She told me something I hadn't yet heard, that the real reason Dian was killed was because of her knowledge of the poacher trade.

"Everyone in the park system here knows this!" she proclaimed, in her Belgian-French accent.

She then continued on with her story that Dian had openly boasted of having enough information to link high-profile figures, like Rwanda's President Habyarimana, to poaching and international trade in wildlife, including endangered mountain gorillas. Apparently she had been threatening to bring everyone down in a spectacular exposé. This plausible conjecture, at the time, was obscured by an official accusation against Dian's longtime tracker Rwelekana, and Wayne McGuire—convenient patsies at the scene. Rwelekana died in prison, leaving none more haunted by Dian Fossey than Wayne McGuire.

When we reached the base of the trail up to Karisoke, I was thrilled to see familiar gorilla trackers for the Mountain Gorilla Project. The tourist program had taken hold, and it was obvious from the sturdier mud huts with fresh thatching, and the better clothing worn by the locals, that it had positively affected the local economy.

I was ashamed as Bert, arriving unannounced with the TV crew, got pushy with the park authorities about letting them film.

"John, can't you do something?" Bert asked me.

But I remembered being on the receiving end of pushy interlopers wanting special access to gorillas. When I politely asked one of the original tourist gorilla trackers, Zumalinda, about getting back up to Karisoke, his answer was enough for me and the film crew.

"If you try, you may become a suspect in Dian's murder," Zumalinda politely warned me. Karisoke was still a crime scene.

After Dian's death, her Digit Fund survived through changing leaderships, eventually changing its name to the Dian Fossey Gorilla Fund International. So many still love her name, especially the women who see themselves as "kindred spirits" as Carolyn once had. In 2007 they celebrated Karisoke's fortieth year, and I was invited by the fund's director, Clare Richardson, to accompany a tour of their patrons. The trip included a special visit to the former site of Karisoke Research Center and a hike to see gorillas.

Standing once again among the towering Virunga Volcanoes, I was dazzled by the scope and scale of Rwanda's gorilla tourism. Daily throngs were organized into small groups to visit the gentle giants. Signs read: "Welcome Dear Tourist" and "Given Peace, Gorillas Bring Currency." Gorillas are featured everywhere on billboards, signs, and logos throughout the country. They are a true symbol of pride for the small nation.

Today's organized tourism of gorillas, and the resultant boost to the economy of the region, and all of Rwanda, grew out of the Mountain Gorilla Project. The little seed planted by Amy Vedder and Bill Weber, with Jean-Pierre von der Beck, Sandy Harcourt, and nurtured and cultivated further by Rosalind and Conrad Aveling, and those that followed. That seed had taken root and held fast among the rich volcanic soil to become a model for neighboring countries. The program has grown and flourished into a tree of life—establishing the mountain gorillas' value as an economic resource, more valuable alive than dead. Protection of this precious resource has led to a growth of the Virunga mountain gorillas' vulnerable population. It's no small irony that most people still associate today's gorilla ecotourism with Fossey, who, of course, always fought against tourism, although she had started as one herself.

From below, on this rare clear day, I see all the towering volcanoes around me, and I well know each by name: Muhavura, Sabinio, Gahinga, Mikeno, Visoke, Karisimbi . . . My eyes stop at the low-slung curve of the saddle region, and Karisoke, where I lived such a formative year, so privileged to live among the rumbling elephants and the snorting buffaloes and the barking bushbucks and the whistling duikers and the screeching hyraxes. And privileged to have known Bonne Année, and to have cared for her, among those imperiled great apes, the mountain gorillas, a purer version of ourselves.

What was it like? I am asked. *What was* Dian *like?* The answer is a long one. Karisoke was the answer to my dreams of life and work in Africa. It was also a brutal dose of disenchantment amid the harsh reality of that deceptively beautiful place—its frigid rains and bone-chilling mist, its rugged tangled terrain, with gorillas on the brink of extinction and its impossible headmistress at the center of it all. My responses have always been short, vague, and inexplicit because the answer is a long one and counter to expectations. And so I tell my story.

EPILOGUE

THE RUINS

*It is like a running blaze on a plain, like a flash of lightning
in the clouds. We live in the flicker—may it last as long as
the old earth keeps rolling! But darkness was here yesterday.*

—Joseph Conrad, *Heart of Darkness*

The herbal smell of undergrowth, wet from recent rains, triggers memories with every step. The mountain's morning air is cool, as always. Deep hoofprints still puncture the black volcanic mud, as they have done for eons in these scattered clearings, evidence of where the forest buffaloes foraged the night before.

I have returned for the first time in twenty-six years, on the trail I knew, now overgrown. I linger behind the others, stalling, searching my memory bank and looking for visible landmarks. My cabin is gone, but at the site of its faded outline by the familiar flowing streambed I am overwhelmed by a rush of memories so jumbled and bittersweet, they choke me. A powerful gravity brings me to my knees on the grass where my doorway used to be. I am thankful that the others follow some newer pathway, their voices fading somewhere ahead where the forest gives way to open meadow. I gather my emotions. A weathered sign above the sun-bleached skull of a buffalo reads, "Dian Fossey's Original Cabin." It had been my cabin.

All the cabins are gone, even Dian's large one at the far end of camp, and the paths between them in our little village, once so well worn and defined by our boots and the hooves of buffaloes. Karisoke has been reclaimed by the forest from which it had emerged decades ago, and I see it as Dian must have seen it upon arrival. A brutal civil war that swept the country has erased all but the gorilla graveyard. There among the markers for Dian's beloved apes, is her own stone tomb.

Today is the fortieth anniversary of Dian Fossey's founding of Karisoke Research Center. The program has grown to a scale and scope none of us could have foreseen, relocated to a town below. So many Africans now are a part of this; Rwanda's own now carry the torch. I am stunned to see Baraqueza, now fifty-six years old, still a gorilla tracker, and a former anti-poacher patrolman, Sekalyongo, now a tracker, too, at sixty-four! We greet each other heartily. They are true survivors. Both have lived through Rwanda's horrific genocide, remaining hale and fit enough to hike these mountains daily, even in the harshest weather. We chatter away in Swahili, rusty from the passing years, pausing to recall words and the names of others now dead. Of the dozens in the throng, the three of us are the only ones present who knew Dian Fossey. Our history bonds us, and separates us from the others.

The congregation gathers around her gravesite—a massive slab of stones and concrete, as if a fortress against desecration. I cringe at the thought of this becoming a Fossey worship scene with maudlin displays and tears from those who never knew this troubled woman. Mercifully it doesn't. Baraqueza and Sekalyongo stoically place flowers on the cold stony slab. None in the throng cries, and I wonder what they think and know, murmured into ears via second hand, second generation, faded and filtered over time, becoming lore, distilling into legend. The research center's new director, Katie Fawcett, remains professional, somber but steadfast, emotionally sound in stark contrast to her long-gone predecessor, Karisoke's troubled founding mother.

Dian's grave is surrounded by the wooden placards marking the burial grounds of her research gorillas: Uncle Bert, Flossie, Puck, Digit . . . Fittingly, Dian lays among them now. I recognize so many of the names, and am saddened by the monikers of those I knew. Marchessa's name brings back vivid memories of taking her body into Ruhengeri for necropsy and returning her here for burial. One marker is missing, the one I had made . . . not that of a gorilla, but of Dian's beloved monkey, Kima. I deliberate with Baraqueza and Sekalyongo about its location. We three agree on a spot where the monkey's remains lie hidden and I am again thrust back in time to her ill-fated return to camp. I also don't see a marker for Bonne Année, our little orphan, with whom I'd spent so many days. I realize I don't know the story of our little orphan's remains, only of her passing. Perhaps she was left on the slopes where she died. For me, Mount Visoke serves well as her shrine.

On Dian's tomb there is that strange word again, "Nyiramachabelli," which she cultivated for herself, with its *ch* and *ll* spellings not characteristic of Kinyarwanda words. She didn't need a label to become a legend. Fittingly, the plaque says, NO ONE LOVED GORILLAS MORE. She is given great honor in return for bringing the plight of an endangered species to so many, to have sparked global interest with those pictures of her among gentle mountain gorillas, and her stories of them. While Dian ended her close personal relationships spectacularly and abysmally, the admirers she couldn't spurn remained undaunted. To not know her is to love her.

Dian inspired the world, but despite the dire situation of the Virunga's last gorillas, she couldn't work collaboratively and cooperatively. Any disagreement set her off, triggering her contempt and withdrawal. Her isolation was self-inflicted. But since her death, people have rallied and the mountain gorilla did not die with her, although her resistance did. Her wall crumbled and fell, like the cabins of her long-gone camp. Karisoke, and its mission, has grown and flourished, like the remaining gorillas of these mountains—not because Dian made the world love her, but because she made them love gorillas more.

Off the mountain and down below, I am dazzled by the new Karisoke, now part of the Dian Fossey Gorilla Fund International. Relocated to the town I knew as Ruhengeri, which changed its name to Musanze after the genocide. The mission has broadened too, by adding education and community development to the original goals of research and conservation. It is even a major employer for the town. Katie Fawcett was lighthearted on this occasion, even joyful. After the merriment of uplifting speeches, acrobatics, and dance performances, one of her senior Rwandan staffers dutifully advised his team not to overindulge, reminding them that they must be back at work the very next day.

"Oh, tomorrow's tomorrow," Katie interjected with a wave of her hand, and the festivities continued. Moved by the real joy expressed on the faces of so many now employed by the new Karisoke to serve a burgeoning population of mountain gorillas and a new generation of Rwandans, I joined Baraqueza and Sekalyongo in the dancing.

ACKNOWLEDGMENTS

Before this story was a book, it was an experience, and for that, I must first acknowledge Terry Maple. He has given countless opportunities to so many people. If you wanted, he could drop you into the middle of a zoo or the middle of Africa. It was up to you to find your way out, and you might have quite a story to tell. Thanks for the memories, Terry.

After I began putting my memories into words, it was my good fortune to have the late author Rod Thorp take interest in my work and teach me how best to write prose worthy of a book. He was gone too soon, but did get "the boat out of the harbor," as he promised. For that, I will always be grateful.

I must also express due gratitude for my publisher, Claiborne Hancock, who said yes to my manuscript and made this book happen. Many thanks also to Jessica Case and the creative team at Pegasus Books, including Sabrina Plomitallo-González, Bowen Dunnon, and Katie McGuire. I give special thanks to Maria Fernandez for her patience and letting me have some fun in the layout process.

Andrew Plumptre of Cambridge University's Conservation Research Institute and Julian Kerbis Peterhans of Chicago's Field Museum of Natural History helped provide taxonomical names of the lesser-known flora and fauna mentioned in this book, information which I could not find elsewhere. I am grateful to them for their expertise and taking the time to respond to my queries.

I must also express my gratitude to Judy Chidester from the American Embassy in Kigali, Rwanda who so generously took us gorilla students in, providing a home away from home during our forays off the mountain. I don't think she realized how much that meant to so many. I also thank her for helping me recall the names of those we knew along the way, and for her enduring friendship through the years.

I have not forgotten my writer pals, Paul Abercrombie, Norman "Buddy" Chastain, and Bill Chastain, for their supportive camaraderie throughout our adventures and misadventures as aspiring authors in the jungles of the book biz. Thanks for making it interesting and hilarious.

My wife Janet Fowler, daughter Isabel Fowler, and son Ben Fowler have also shared in my hopes and aspirations for writing this book, and I thank them for their loving support and enthusiasm along the way. At the end of the day, this book is for them.

I also want to acknowledge my brothers—Paul Fowler, Steve Fowler, and Dennis Fowler—for the enriching childhood adventures that older brothers bring. I give special thanks to Steve for his helpful and technical advice on waterproof paper, sturdy boots, and pistols.

ACKNOWLEDGMENTS

My parents are gone, but not forgotten. I thank them for their supportive tolerance of my insatiable fascination with all things wild, as well as putting up with the likes of tarantulas, monkeys, cockatoos, and other living things I brought into the house, at least until they finally sent me off to where the wild things are.

INDEX